ChemCom

Chemistry in the Community

ChemCom
Chemistry in the Community

American Chemical Society

Kendall/Hunt
Publishing Company
Dubuque, Iowa

ChemCom Personnel

Principal Investigator:
W. T. Lippincott
Project Manager:
Sylvia Ware
Chief Editor:
Henry Heikkinen
Contributing Editor:
Mary Castellion
Assistant to Contributing Editor:
Arnold Diamond
Editor of Teacher's Guide:
Thomas O'Brien
Revision Team:
Diane Bunce, Gregory Crosby, David Holzman, Thomas O'Brien, Joan Senyk, Thomas Wysocki
Editorial Advisory Board:
Glenn Crosby, James DeRose, Dwaine Eubanks, W. T. Lippincott (ex officio), Lucy McCorkle, Jeanne Vaughn, Sylvia Ware (ex officio)
Writing Team:
Rosa Balaco, James Banks, Joan Beardsley, William Bleam, Kenneth Brody, Ronald Brown, Diane Bunce, Becky Chambers, Alan DeGennaro, Patricia Eckfeldt, Dwaine Eubanks (dir.), Henry Heikkinen (dir.), Bruce Jarvis (dir.), Dan Kallus, Jerry Kent, Grace McGuffie, David Newton (dir.), Thomas O'Brien, Andrew Pogan, David Robson, Amado Sandoval, Joseph Schmuckler (dir.), Richard Shelly, Patricia Smith, Tamar Susskind, Joseph Travello, Thomas Warren, Robert Wistort, Thomas Wysocki
Steering Committee:
Alan Cairncross, William Cook, Derek Davenport, James DeRose, Anna Harrison (ch.), W. T. Lippincott (ex officio), Lucy McCorkle, Donald McCurdy, William Mooney, Moses Passer, Martha Sager, Glenn Seaborg, John Truxall, Jeanne Vaughn
Evaluation Team:
Ronald Anderson, Matthew Bruce, Frank Sutman (dir.)
Field Test Coordinator:
Sylvia Ware
Field Test Workshops:
Dwaine Eubanks
Field Test Directors:
Keith Berry, Fitzgerald Bramwell, Mamie Moy, William Nevill, Michael Pavelich, Lucy Pryde, Conrad Stanitski
Social Science Consultants:
Ross Eshelman, Judith Gillespie
Safety Consultant:
Stanley Pine
Art:
Rabina Fisher, Pat Hoetmer, Alan Kahan (dir.), Kelly Richard, Sharon Wolfgang
Copy Editor:
Martha Polkey
Administrative Assistant:
Carolyn Avery

This material is based upon work supported by the National Science Foundation under Grant No. SED-88115424 and Grant No. MDR-8470104. Any opinions, findings, and conclusions or recommendations expressed in this publication are those of the authors and do not necessarily reflect the views of the National Science Foundation. Any mention of trade names does not imply endorsement by the National Science Foundation.

Cover photos: Eye dropper, Comstock; kids on beach, Image Bank; San Francisco streets, FPG International; beach, Comstock

Copyright © 1988 by American Chemical Society

Library of Congress Catalog Card Number: 87–81710

ISBN 0–8403–4423–6

Printed in the United States of America
10 9 8 7 6 5 4 3 2 1

CONTENTS

PREFACE

The United States is a world leader in science, technology, and the education of scientists and engineers. Yet, overall, U.S. citizens are barely literate in science. In responding to this situation, our government and many professional groups have assigned high priority to improving the nation's science literacy.

Chemistry in the Community (*ChemCom*) is a major attempt to enhance science literacy through a high school curriculum that emphasizes the impact of chemistry on society. Developed by the American Chemical Society (ACS) with financial support from the National Science Foundation and several ACS funding sources, *ChemCom* has been written by teams of high school, college, and university teachers, assisted by chemists from industry and government.

This year-long course is designed primarily to help students:

- Realize the important role that chemistry will play in their personal and professional lives
- Use principles of chemistry to think more intelligently about current issues they will encounter that involve science and technology
- Develop a lifelong awareness of the potential and limitations of science and technology

Each of *ChemCom's* eight units centers on a chemistry-related technological issue now confronting our society and the world. The topic serves as a basis for introducing the chemistry needed to understand and analyze it. The setting for each unit is a community. This may be the school community, the town or region in which the students live, or the world community—Spaceship Earth.

The major *ChemCom* topics are: "Supplying Our Water Needs"; "Conserving Chemical Resources"; "Petroleum: To Build or to Burn?"; "Understanding Food"; "Nuclear Chemistry in Our World"; "Chemistry, Air, and Climate"; "Chemistry and Health"; and "The Chemical Industry: Promise and Challenge."

The eight units include the major concepts, basic vocabulary, and intellectual and laboratory skills expected in any introductory chemistry course. The program contains a greater number and variety of student-oriented activities than is customary. In addition to numerous laboratory exercises, including many developed especially for *ChemCom,* each unit contains three levels of decision-making activities, and several types of problem-solving exercises.

Dozens of professionals from all segments of the chemistry community have given their talents and energies to create *ChemCom*. Their hope is that its impact will be substantial and lasting, and that those who study *ChemCom* will find chemistry interesting, captivating, and useful.

CREDITS

ChemCom is the product of teamwork involving individuals from all over the United States. The American Chemical Society is pleased to recognize all who contributed to *ChemCom*.

We also want to take this opportunity to thank the National Science Foundation for its support for this program, and our project officers, Mary Ann Ryan and John Thorpe, for their comments, suggestions, and unfailing support.

Consultants:
Alan Cairncross, Michael Doyle, Donald Fenton, Conard Fernelius, Victor Fratalli, Peter Girardot, Glen Gordon, Dudley Herron, John Hill, Chester Holmlund, John Holman, Kenneth Kolb, E. N. Kresge, David Lavallee, Charles Lewis, Wayne Marchant, Joseph Moore, Richard Millis, Kenneth Mossman, Herschel Porter, Glenn Seaborg, Victor Viola, William West, John Whitaker

Synthesis Committee:
Diane Bunce, Dwaine Eubanks, Anna Harrison, Henry Heikkinen, John Hill, Stanley Kirschner, W. T. Lippincott (ex officio), Lucy McCorkle, Thomas O'Brien, Ronald Perkins, Sylvia Ware (ex officio), Thomas Wysocki

Pilot Test Teachers:
Food—Howard Baldwin, Donald Fritz, Grace McGuffie, Gloria Mumford, Ellen Pitts, George Smeller, Thomas Wysocki

Health—Virginia Denney, Elaine Kilbourne, Nancy Miller, Dicie Petree, Charles Ross, Jr., Susan Rutherland, Samuel Taylor, Gabrielle Vereecke

Industry—Diane Doepken, Mary Gromko, Polly Parent, Steven Rischling, David Roudebush, Thomas Van Egeren

Nuclear—Karen Cotter, Allen Hummel, Kathy Nirei, Kathy Ravano

Petroleum—Joseph Deangelis, Andrew Gettes, Joseph Linker, Larry Lipton, Beverly Nelson, Cheryl Snyder, Jade Snyder, Joseph Zisk

Resources—Ellen Byrne, Beverly Nelson, Elliott Nires, Ruth Rand, Joseph Rozaik, Cheryl Snyder, Jade Snyder, Ronald Tempest, Joseph Zisk

Water—Donald Belanger, Charlotte Hutton, Navarro Bharat, Eugene Cashour, Donald Fritz, Robert Haigler, Anna Helms, Grace McGuffie, Mary Parker, Gabrielle Vereecke, Howard White, Thomas Wysocki

Field Test Teachers:
California—Leanne Kogler, Jay Maness, Jay Rubin, Paul Shank, Mitzi Swift, Bob Van Zant

Colorado—Bobbie Craven, Jim Davis, Lu Hensen, Gary Hurst, Don Holderread, Dave Kolquist, Bob Volzer, Terri Wahlberg, Tammy Weatherly

Hawaii—John Southworth

Illinois—Daniel Vandercar

Iowa—Nancy Dickman

Louisiana—Allison Booth, Theodis Gorre, Margaret Guess, Yvette Hayes, Michael Ironsmith, Robert Kennedy, Willie Reed, Dawn Smith, Belinda Wolfe

Maryland—Naomi Brodsky, Gene Cashour, Frank Cox, Anne Kenney, Sherman Kopelson, Patricia Martin

New Jersey—Lydia Brown, Grace Giglio

New York—Vincent Bono

Texas—Pat Criswell, Kenn Heydrick

Virginia—Mary D. Brower, Dave W. Gammon, Frank Gibson, Joyce Knox, Mary Monroe, Mike Morris, Phyllis Murray, Bill Rademaker, David Ruscus, Richard Scheele, Joyce Willis

Wisconsin—George Bulovsky, Lucy Jache

Washington—Kay Burrough, Larry Jerdal, Ed Johnson, Grant Johnson, Jon Malmin, Douglas Mandt, Silas Nelsen, Larry Nelson, Bill Rudd, Steve Ufer, Lee Weaver

Field Test Schools:

California—Chula Vista High, Chula Vista; Gompers Secondary School, San Diego; Montgomery High, San Diego; Point Loma High, San Diego; Serra Junior–Senior High, San Diego; Southwest High, San Diego

Colorado—Bear Creek Senior High, Lakewood; Evergreen Senior High, Evergreen; Green Mountain Senior High, Lakewood; Golden Senior High, Golden; Lakewood Senior High, Lakewood; Wheat Ridge Senior High, Wheat Ridge

Hawaii—University of Hawaii Laboratory School, Honolulu

Illinois—Project Individual Education High, Oak Lawn

Iowa—Linn-Mar High, Marion

Louisiana—Booker T. Washington High, Shreveport; Byrd High, Shreveport; Caddo Magnet High, Shreveport; Captain Shreve High, Shreveport; Fair Park High, Shreveport; Green Oaks High, Shreveport; Huntington High, Shreveport; North Caddo High, Vivian; Northwood High, Shreveport

Maryland—Charles Smith Jewish Day School, Rockville; Owings Mills Junior–Senior High, Owings Mills; Parkville High, Baltimore; Sparrows Point Middle–Senior High, Baltimore; Woodlawn High, Baltimore

New Jersey—School No. 10, Patterson

New York—New Dorp High, Staten Island

Texas—Clements High, Sugar Land; Cy-Fair High, Houston

Virginia—Armstrong High, Richmond; Freeman High, Richmond; Henrico High, Richmond; Highland Springs High, Highland Springs; Marymount School, Richmond; Midlothian High, Midlothian; St. Gertrude's High, Richmond; Thomas Dale High, Chester; Thomas Jefferson High, Richmond; Tucker High, Richmond; Varina High, Richmond.

Wisconsin—James Madison High, Madison; Thomas More High, Milwaukee

Washington—Bethel High, Spanaway; Chief Sealth High, Seattle; Clover Park High, Tacoma; Foss Senior High, Tacoma; Hazen High, Renton; Lakes High, Tacoma; Peninsula High, Gig Harbor; Rogers High, Puyallup; Sumner Senior High, Sumner; Washington High, Tacoma; Wilson High, Tacoma

Student Aides:

Paul Drago, Stephanie French, Patricia Teleska

A SPECIAL NOTE TO STUDENTS

Chemistry is an intimate part of everyone's life. As we increase our use of and dependence on technology (the application of science), more and more of the decisions made by individuals, communities, and countries will involve scientific concepts and consequences. Everyone—not just scientists and science educators—should know about scientific concepts and the vital contributions of science to society. As a future voter, you will help make decisions on issues involving chemical knowledge.

Chemistry is the study of the substances in our world—from sugar and baking soda to propane and water. What are substances made of? How do they act and interact with each other and in the presence of various forms of energy, such as heat or electricity? What is their role in living things? Thus, chemistry focuses on food, photographic film, moon rocks, fabrics, medicines, life processes—in fact, chemistry is concerned with all materials.

In response to a growing recognition of the need for scientific awareness and good decision-making skills, the Education Division of the American Chemical Society has developed this high school chemistry course. *Chemistry in the Community* (*ChemCom*) uses chemical concepts to help you understand the chemistry behind some important societal issues.

ChemCom contains eight units. Within each you will find topics affecting your life and your community. A range of activities will help you understand how chemistry relates to the topics introduced. Each unit concludes with a special activity that allows you to apply your chemical knowledge to a specific problem; to describe or propose solutions to the problem; and to evaluate the impact of your solutions.

We hope *ChemCom* will help you view the world with greater understanding and appreciation. Some of you may even decide to study more chemistry! But whether you do or not, we hope you will experience some of the challenge and excitement felt by those of us involved in chemistry and chemical education.

Water is our first major topic. You will now enter the fictional town of Riverwood as a student at Riverwood High School. We begin with a newspaper article about a water-related emergency in Riverwood. The story surrounding this problem will serve as the theme of the first unit. Welcome to Riverwood and to *ChemCom!*

SAFETY IN THE LABORATORY

In *ChemCom* you frequently will perform laboratory activities. While no human activity is completely risk free, if you use common sense and a bit of chemical sense, you will encounter no problems. Chemical sense is an extension of common sense. Sensible laboratory conduct won't happen by memorizing a list of rules, any more than a perfect score on a written driver's test ensures an excellent driving record. The true driver's test of chemical sense is your actual conduct in the laboratory.

The following safety pointers apply to all laboratory activities. For your personal safety and that of your classmates, make following these guidelines second nature in the laboratory. Your teacher will point out any special safety guidelines that apply to each activity.

If you understand the reasons behind them, these safety rules will be easy to remember and to follow. So, for each listed safety guideline:

- Identify a similar rule or precaution that applies in everyday life—for example in cooking, repairing or driving a car, or playing a sport.
- Briefly describe possible harmful results if the rule is not followed.

Rules of Laboratory Conduct

1. Perform laboratory work only when your teacher is present. Unauthorized or unsupervised laboratory experimenting is not allowed.
2. Your concern for safety should begin even before the first activity. Always read and think about each laboratory assignment before starting.
3. Know the location and use of all safety equipment in your laboratory. These should include the safety shower, eye wash, first-aid kit, fire extinguisher, and blanket.
4. Wear a laboratory coat or apron and protective glasses or goggles for all laboratory work. Wear shoes (rather than sandals) and tie back loose hair.
5. Clear your benchtop of all unnecessary material such as books and clothing before starting your work.
6. Check chemical labels twice to make sure you have the correct substance. Some chemical formulas and names may differ by only a letter or a number.

7. You may be asked to transfer some laboratory chemicals from a common bottle or jar to your own test tube or beaker. Do not return any excess material to its original container unless authorized by your teacher.

8. Avoid unnecessary movement and talk in the laboratory.

9. Never taste laboratory materials. Gum, food, or drinks should not be brought into the laboratory. If you are instructed to smell something, do so by fanning some of the vapor toward your nose. Do not place your nose near the opening of the container. Your teacher will show you the correct technique.

10. Never look directly down into a test tube; view the contents from the side. Never point the open end of a test tube toward yourself or your neighbor.

11. Any laboratory accident, however small, should be reported immediately to your teacher.

12. In case of a chemical spill on your skin or clothing rinse the affected area with plenty of water. If the eyes are affected water-washing must begin immediately and continue for 10 to 15 minutes or until professional assistance is obtained.

13. Minor skin burns should be placed under cold, running water.

14. When discarding used chemicals, carefully follow the instructions provided.

15. Return equipment, chemicals, aprons, and protective glasses to their designated locations.

16. Before leaving the laboratory, ensure that gas lines and water faucets are shut off.

17. If in doubt, ask!

UNIT *ONE*

Supplying Our Water Needs

CONTENTS

Water Emergency in Riverwood

Severe Water Rationing in Effect

Mayor Edward Cisko, citing possible health hazards, today announced the shutdown of the Riverwood public water pumping station and cancellation of the "Fall Fish-In" that was to begin Friday. River water will not be pumped into the water treatment plant for a minimum of three days, starting at 6 P.M. tonight. No plans have been made yet for rescheduling the annual fishing tournament.

During the pumping station shutdown, water engineers and chemists from the County Sanitation Commission and the Environmental Protection Agency (EPA) will search for the cause of a fish kill discovered yesterday at the base of Snake River Dam, five miles upstream from the Riverwood water intake point.

Jon Jacobson

"While there is no immediate cause for alarm, as preliminary tests show no immediate danger to townspeople, the consensus of last night's emergency meeting of the Town Council was to undertake a thorough investigation of the situation immediately," said Mayor Cisko.

The alarm was sounded when dead trout were found floating in a favorite fishing spot by Jane Abelson, 15, and Rob Steiner, 16, both students at Riverwood High School. "We thought maybe someone had poured poison in the reservoir or dam," explained Rob.

Mary Steiner, biology teacher at Riverwood High School, accompanied the students back to the river. "We hiked downstream for almost a mile. Dead fish of all kinds were washed up on the banks and caught in the rocks as far as we could see," Abelson reported.

Mrs. Steiner contacted the County Sanitation Commission and preliminary tests were made for substances that might have killed the fish. Chief Engineer Hal Cooper reported at last night's emergency meeting that the water samples looked completely clear and that no toxic sub-

stances were found. But he said he was concerned. "We can't say for sure that our present supply is safe until the reason for the fish kill is known. It's far better that we take no chances until we know the water is safe," Cooper advised.

Arrangements are being made for drinking water to be trucked from Mapleton, with the first shipments arriving in Riverwood at 10 A.M. tomorrow. Distribution points are listed in the accompanying story which also gives details on saving water in your bathtub and using it for activities other than drinking or cooking during the water emergency.

The mayor gave assurances that essential municipal services would not be affected by the water crisis. Specifically, he stated that the fire department would have access to adequate supplies of water to meet any fire-fighting needs.

Riverwood schools will be closed Monday, Tuesday, and Wednesday. No other closings or cancellations are known at this time. Local TV and radio stations will announce any later information.

A meeting will be held at 8 P.M. at Town Hall tonight. Dr. Margaret Brooke, ex-

pert on water systems at State University, will answer questions concerning water safety and use. Dr. Brooke has agreed to aid the County Sanitation Commission in explaining the situation to the town.

The Town Council agreed to close the pumping station after five hours of heated debate. Councilman Henry McLatchen, also a member of the Chamber of Commerce, described the decision as a highly emotional and unnecessary reaction. He cited the great financial loss that town motel and restaurant owners will suffer from the fish-in cancellation as well as the potential loss of future tourism revenue due to adverse publicity. He and others sharing his view were outvoted by the majority, who expressed concern that whatever had caused the fish kill might have public health implications.

Asked how long the water emergency would last, Dr. Brooke refused to speculate until she had talked with chemists who were conducting the investigation. Scientists from the EPA, in addition to collecting and analyzing water samples, will examine dead fish to determine if a disease caused their deaths.

Townspeople React to Water Crisis

In a series of person-on-the-street interviews, Riverwood citizens expressed their feelings to the *Herald*. "It doesn't bother me," said 9-year-old Jimmy Hendricks. "I'm just going to drink milk and soda."

"I knew it was just a matter of time before they killed the fish," complained Harmon Lewis, a lifelong resident of the Fieldstone Acres area. Lewis, who traces his ancestry back to original county settlers, still gets his water from a well and will be unaffected by the water crisis. Until 1967, Lewis's well was hand operated, but development of the area brought electricity and he installed his present system. "I wouldn't have even done that except for the arthritis in my shoulders," said Lewis. He plans to pump enough well water to supply the children's ward at Community Hospital if the emergency continues more than a few days.

Bob and Ruth Hardy of Hardy's Ice Cream Parlor expressed annoyance at the inconvenience but felt relieved at the Council's actions. They were anxious to know the reason for the fish kill and what possible effects there might be on the future water supply.

Hardy's son, David, said he was worried that the late summer fishing season would be ruined. An avid fisherman, he and his father won first prize last year in the Chamber of Commerce's angling competition.

Don Harris, owner of the Uptown Motel, expressed concern over the health of the town residents, but was equally concerned over the loss of business due to the tournament cancellation. "I always earn a reasonable amount of money from this event and will most likely have to get a loan to pay my bills in the spring."

The unexpected school vacation was seen as "great" by 12-year-old Toni Price. Asked why she thought schools had to close because of the water shortage, Price said all she could think of was that "the drinking fountains won't work."

Elmo Turner, whose yard and flower beds have won Garden Club recognition for the last five years, allayed one concern. Since it has been such a wet summer, lawn-watering has been unnecessary; thus yards are not in danger of drying out due to water rationing.

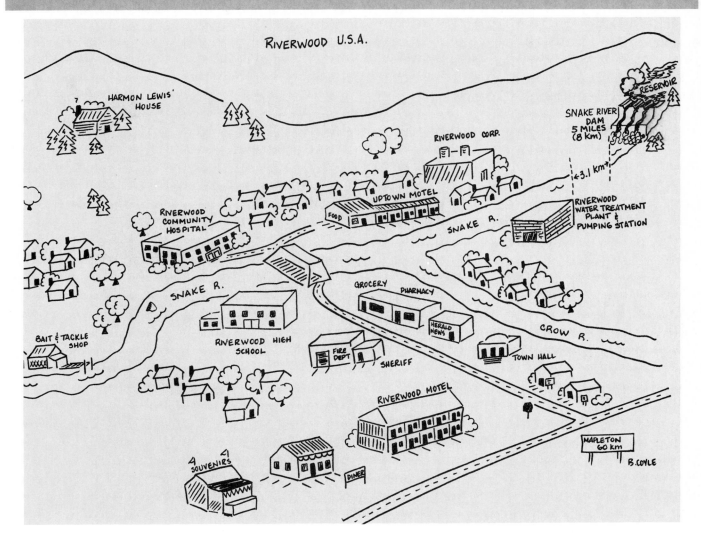

Riverwood will be without adequate water for three days. As the newspaper articles you have just read indicate, the water emergency has created understandable concern among the citizens, town officials, and business owners of Riverwood. What caused the fish kill? Does the fish kill mean that the community's water supply poses hazards to humans? We will follow the town's progress in answering these questions as we learn about the properties of water.

Even though our Riverwood setting is imaginary, its problem is one a real community might face. Two major challenges confront us daily. Can we continue to obtain *enough* water to supply our needs and can we get sufficiently *pure* water? These two questions are co-themes of this unit.

To meet these challenges requires understanding the chemistry of water through investigating the properties of water. Some properties can be observed by the unaided senses while other properties must be measured. Scientists choose to report measurements in the units of the metric system.

A.1 Measurement and the Metric System

Metric units were first introduced in France more than 100 years ago. In 1960, a modernized form of the metric system was internationally adopted. It is called "SI," from the official name, Le Système International d'Unites (International System of Units). SI units are now used by scientists in every nation, including the United States. All SI units are derived from seven base quantities and their units. Some SI units (such as the gram, degree Celsius, and second) you may have already heard about and used. Other SI units that you will encounter in your study of chemistry (such as the pascal, joule, and mole) may be new to you. We will explain each unit when it is first used.

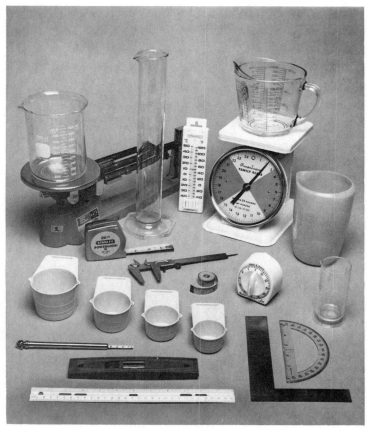

Jon Jacobson

Can you think of a use for each of these measuring devices?

In the following laboratory activity, you will make measurements of length and volume. The SI unit of length is the **meter** (symbolized by m). Most doorways are about two meters high. Many lengths we wish to measure are either much larger or much smaller than a meter. SI prefixes have been defined to indicate different fractions and multiples of all SI units, including the meter. The important prefixes for our use now are deci-, meaning one-tenth (1/10); centi-, meaning one one-hundredth (1/100) (recall that a cent is one one-hundredth of a dollar); and milli-, meaning one one-thousandth (1/1000).

The width of an audiocassette cartridge is one decimeter (dm) and its thickness is about one centimeter (cm). A millimeter (mm) is approximately the width of the wire in a paper clip.

The derived SI unit for volume is the cubic meter (m^3). You can visualize one cubic meter as the space occupied by a box one meter on each edge. (The volume of a cube is calculated as length $\times$ width $\times$ height.) This cubic meter box would be big enough to hold a very large dog comfortably. This is too large a volume unit for our use in chemistry!

Consider a smaller cube, one decimeter (dm) on each edge. The volume of this cube is one cubic decimeter (dm^3). Although a cubic decimeter may not be familiar to you, you probably know it by another name—a **liter** (L). For example, the volume of a large bottle of cola can be given as 2 L or 2 dm^3.

One cubic decimeter (or liter) of volume is exactly equal to 1000 cm^3 (cubic centimeters). A full-scale drawing of one cubic centimeter is shown in Figure I.1. You may know the cubic centimeter by another name—the **milliliter** (mL). Because the liter and the milliliter are more familiar and more common, we will use these units for volume.

Let's summarize the metric units for volume by considering a can of soft drink labeled 12 fluid ounces. If we "think metric," this is 355 cm^3 or 355 mL of beverage. Using larger units, we have 0.355 dm^3 or 0.355 L of drink. Notice that this metric unit conversion just involves a change in decimal point location. This is one advantage of metric units.

The following exercises will help you become more familiar with the metric units for length and volume.

The meter (m) is the SI unit for length.

1 dm = 0.1 m
1 cm = 0.01 m
1 mm = 0.001 m

1 mL = 1 cm^3

1000 cm^3 = 1 dm^3
1000 mL = 1 L

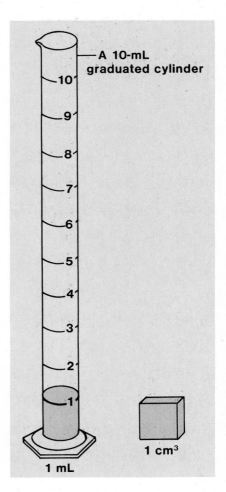

Figure I.1 One cubic centimeter equals one milliliter.

Arrange units and cancel them like numbers. This is a great help in solving problems of many kinds.

YOUR*TURN*

I.1 Meters and Liters

Examine a ruler graduated in millimeters. Note that there are 10 markings between each centimeter (cm) mark. These smaller markings represent millimeter (mm) divisions where 10 mm = 1 cm, or 1 mm = 0.1 cm. A small paperclip is 8 mm wide. To convert this to centimeters move the decimal point one place to the left. Thus, 8 mm = 0.8 cm because 1 mm = 0.1 cm (from 10 mm = 1 cm). Since there is 1 cm for every 10 mm then the unit can also be converted like this:

$$8 \text{ mm} \times \frac{1 \text{ cm}}{10 \text{ mm}} = 0.8 \text{ cm}$$

The same paperclip is 3.2 cm long. This can be converted to millimeters:

$$3.2 \text{ cm} \times \frac{10 \text{ mm}}{1 \text{ cm}} = 32 \text{ mm}$$

1. Measure the diameter of a penny, a nickel, a dime, and a quarter. Report each diameter in millimeters and centimeters.

2. Sketch a 10 cm-by-10 cm square. Now imagine a three-dimensional box made up of six of these 10 cm-square sides. What would be the total volume of this cube in cubic centimeters (cm^3)? In milliliters (mL)? In liters (L)? (You can calculate the volume of a cube by multiplying its length $\times$ width $\times$ height.) Grocery-store sugar cubes are approximately 1 cm^3 in volume. How many of these cubes would fit into the cube with 10-cm sides?

3. Read the labels on some common beverage containers, such as a carton of milk or a can of soft drink, to see how volume is indicated. Can you find any beverage containers that list only U.S. customary units of volume such as the quart, pint, or fluid ounce?

4. State at least one advantage of SI units over U.S. customary units. (*Hint:* How are the basic units subdivided in each system? How are the units of volume related to length?) Can you think of any disadvantages to using SI units?

A.2 Laboratory Activity: Foul Water

Getting Ready

If you haven't done so already, read carefully Safety in the Laboratory, which is found at the beginning of this book. The purpose of this activity is to purify a sample of "foul" water, producing as much "clean" water as possible. DO NOT TEST THE PURITY OF THE WATER BY DRINKING IT. Three water purification procedures will be used: (1) oil-water separation, (2) sand filtration, and (3) charcoal adsorption/filtration.

Filtration is a general term for separating solid particles from a liquid by passing the mixture through a material that retains the particles. The liquid collected after filtration is called the **filtrate.**

In your laboratory notebook prepare a table similar to the one below (but with more space for the entries).

Procedure

1. Obtain a sample of foul water from your teacher. Measure its volume using a graduated cylinder; record the value in your data table.

2. Carefully examine the properties of your sample: color, odor, clarity, presence of solids or oily regions. Record all observations on the top of your data table.

Data table

	Color	Clarity	Odor	Presence of oil	Presence of solids	Volume
Before treatment						
After oil-water separation						
After sand filtration						
After charcoal adsorption/filtration						

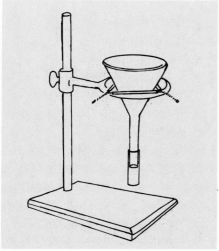

Figure I.2 Funnel in clay triangle.

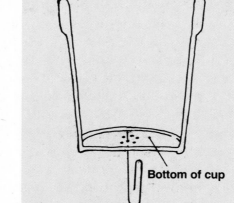

Figure I.3 Preparing Styrofoam cup.

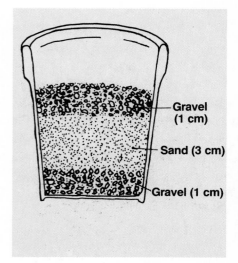

Figure I.4 Sand filtration.

Oil-Water Separation

Oil and water do not appreciably dissolve in each other. If a mixture of the two is left undisturbed, two layers form with the oil layer on top.

1. Place a funnel in a clay triangle supported by a ring clamp and ring stand. Attach a rubber hose to the funnel tip as shown in Figure I.2.
2. Close the rubber tube with a pinch clamp (or nip it with your fingers). Pour about half of your foul-water sample into the funnel. Let it stand undisturbed until the liquid layers separate.
3. Carefully open the pinch clamp to release the lower layer into a 150-mL beaker. When this layer has drained, close the clamp.
4. Drain the remaining layer into a second 150-mL beaker.
5. Repeat steps 2–4 using the remainder of your sample, adding each liquid to the correct beaker.
6. Dispose of the top, oily layer as instructed by your teacher. Observe the properties and measure the volume of the remaining layer (containing the water). Save it for the next procedure.

Sand Filtration

A sand filter traps solid impurities that are too large to fit between sand grains.

1. Using a straightened paper clip wire, poke small holes in the bottom of a Styrofoam cup (Figure I.3).
2. Add gravel and sand layers to the cup as shown in Figure I.4. (The bottom gravel prevents the sand from washing through the holes. The top gravel keeps the sand from being churned up when the sample is poured in.)
3. Pour the sample to be filtered *gently* into the cup. Catch the filtered water in a beaker as it drains through.
4. Dispose of the used sand and gravel according to your teacher's instructions. Do *not* pour the sand or gravel into the sink!
5. Observe the properties and measure the volume of the water. Save it for the next procedure.

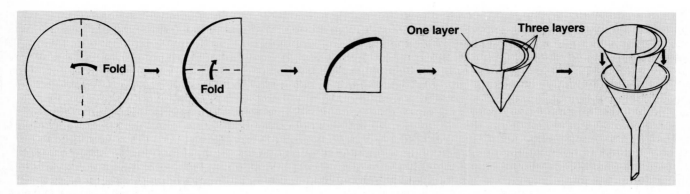

Figure I.5   Folding filter paper.

Charcoal Adsorption/Filtration

Charcoal adsorbs (attracts and holds on its surface) many substances that could give a bad taste, odor, or cloudy appearance to water. Fish tanks include charcoal filters that serve the same purpose.

1. Fold a piece of filter paper as shown in Figure I.5.
2. Place the folded filter paper in a funnel. Wet the paper slightly so it adheres to the funnel cone.
3. Place the funnel in a clay triangle supported by a ring clamp (see Figure I.2) and lower the ring clamp so the funnel stem is 2–3 cm inside a 150-mL beaker.
4. Place charcoal in a 150-mL beaker to a depth of 2 cm.
5. Add the water sample to the charcoal in the beaker, stir the mixture, and gently pour it through the filter paper. Do not let any liquid flow between the filter paper and the funnel. Keep the liquid below the top of the filter paper.
6. If the filtrate is darkened by small charcoal particles, refilter the liquid. Use a clean piece of moistened filter paper.
7. When you are satisfied with the appearance and odor of your purified sample, pour it into a graduated cylinder. Observe the properties and record the final volume of the purified sample.

Calculations

Complete the following calculations. Record the answers in your notebook.

1. What percent of the original foul-water sample was recovered as "pure" water?

$$\text{Percent of water purified} = \frac{\text{Vol. of water purified}}{\text{Vol. of foul-water sample}} \times 100$$

2. What volume of liquid was lost during purification?
3. What percent of your foul-water sample was lost during purification?

Post-Lab Activities

1. Your teacher will demonstrate another water purification technique called **distillation.** Write a complete description of this process.
   a. Why did your teacher discard the first portion of recovered liquid?
   b. Why did your teacher leave some liquid in the distilling flask at the close of the demonstration?

2. Your teacher will test the electrical conductivity of the purified water samples. This test checks for the presence of dissolved, electrically charged particles in the water (discussed in Part B.6). A sample of distilled water and one of tap water will also be tested. What do these tests suggest about the purity of your water sample?

Questions

1. Compare your water purification experiences with those of other lab teams. How should the success of various teams be judged? Why?
2. Distillation is not used by municipal water treatment plants. Why?

A.3 *You Decide:* Information Gathering

Keep a diary of water use in your home for three days. Make a chart similar to the one below and record how many times various water-use activities occur. Have each family member help you.

Notice the activities listed on the chart. If any of the ways your family uses water are missing, add them to your diary. In completing your water-use diary, estimate the amounts of water used where possible.

This activity is an important first step in understanding water use. We will now examine why water is so important.

Data table	Days		
	1	2	3
Number of persons in family			
Number of baths			
Number of showers			
Length of each in minutes			
Number of washing machine loads			
Low setting			
High setting			
Dish washing			
Number of times by hand			
Number of times by dishwasher			
Number of toilet flushes			
Other uses and number of each			

A.4 Water and Health

Living organisms need a constant supply of water because body water is constantly being lost. Each of us must drink about two liters (roughly two quarts) of liquids containing water each day to replace water losses through bodily excretions and evaporation from skin and lungs. You can live 50 to 60 days without food but only 5 to 10 days without water.

For thousands of years people simply drank water from the nearest river or stream with few harmful effects. However, as cities grew larger, this practice became risky. Wastes were dumped, or washed by rain, into the same streams from which people drank. Soon, there were mysterious outbreaks of disease. Such an outbreak took place in London in the 1850s when the River Thames became infected with the bacteria responsible for the often-fatal disease cholera.

A water treatment plant.

In modern times, water quality has become everyone's concern. We can no longer rely on nature to provide pure water. It is necessary to purify water ourselves and to maintain adequate water supplies. These supplies are necessary because we use large quantities of water. We will now examine our nation's overall use of water and some of the ways in which our communities and industries use this resource.

A.5 Water Uses

Do we use so much water that we are in danger of running out? The answer to this question is both no and yes. The total amount of water available to us is far more than enough. Each day, some 15 trillion liters of rain or snow fall in the United States (equal to four trillion gallons). Only 10% is used by humans. The rest flows back into large bodies of water, evaporates, and falls again as part of a perpetual water cycle. However, the distribution of rain and snowfall does not necessarily correspond to the locations of high water use.

There are regional differences in the way we use water in the United States (see Figure I.6). In the East, 88% of used water is returned to natural waterways. However, only 48% is returned in the West. Why should there be such a great difference?

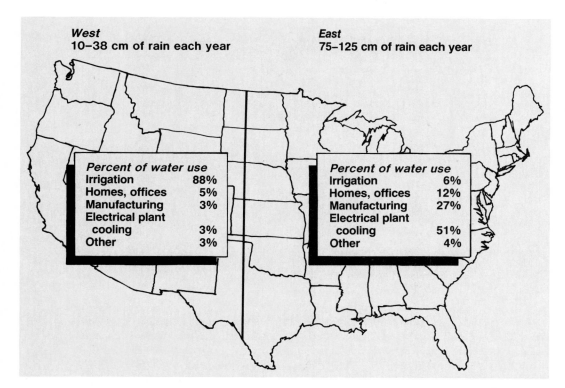

West
10–38 cm of rain each year

East
75–125 cm of rain each year

Percent of water use
Irrigation	88%
Homes, offices	5%
Manufacturing	3%
Electrical plant cooling	3%
Other	3%

Percent of water use
Irrigation	6%
Homes, offices	12%
Manufacturing	27%
Electrical plant cooling	51%
Other	4%

Figure I.6   Water usage in the continental United States.

In the East, rain and water soaking into the ground provide much of the moisture needed by crops. However, much less rain falls in the West, so irrigation water must be obtained from streams or wells. Most irrigation water evaporates from the leaves of growing plants. The rest evaporates directly from the moist soil. This evaporated moisture is driven away by the prevailing winds to fall, days later, on crops in the East.

YOUR*TURN*

I.2 U.S. Water Use

Refer to Figure I.6 in answering these questions.

1. What is the greatest single water use in the eastern part of the United States? In the West?

2. Using your answers to Question 1, account for the difference in the amount of water returned to rivers and streams in the East and West.

3. Explain the differences in water use in the East and West in terms of other factors such as where most people live and the location of most of the country's factories and farms. What other regional differences help explain these patterns of water use?

According to authorities, a family of four (living in any part of the United States) uses about 1300 liters of water *daily*. This value represents direct, measurable use. Beyond direct uses of water are many hidden or indirect uses that you may have never thought about. Each time you eat a hamburger, a slice of bread, or an egg, you are indirectly using water! Why? Because water was needed to grow and process the food.

Ponder the following Chem Quandary.

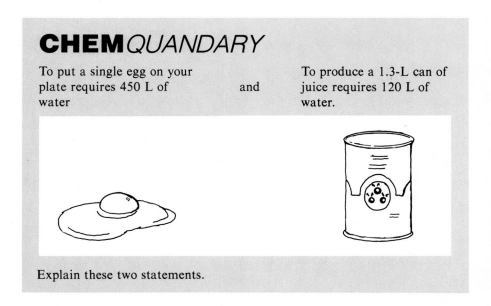

CHEM*QUANDARY*

To put a single egg on your plate requires 450 L of water   and   To produce a 1.3-L can of juice requires 120 L of water.

Explain these two statements.

Average daily indirect and direct water use per person is 20 times direct use alone.

At first glance this Chem Quandary seems absurd. How could so much water be involved with one egg or one can of fruit juice? These quantities represent two typical hidden (indirect) uses of water.

The chicken that laid the egg needed drinking water. Water was used to grow the chicken's feed. Even the small quantity of water used for other purposes in processing adds up, when eggs sold number in the billions.

In a Riverwood newspaper article you read earlier, one youth said he'd just drink milk and soda until the water was turned back on. However, drinking a glass of water consumes much less water than does drinking the same amount of canned fruit juice. Why should that be so? Because the liquid *in* the can is insignificant when compared to the water used to make the metal can itself. That's where the mysterious 120 L of water mentioned in the Chem Quandary comes from!

In normal times, when faucet taps are turned on in Riverwood or in your own community, water flows freely. How does this happen? What is the source of this plentiful supply? Let's take an imaginary journey back through the water pipes to find out where the water comes from.

A.6   Back through the Water Pipes

If you live in a city or town, your home water pipes are linked to underground water pipes. These pipes carry water from a reservoir or a water tower usually located at the highest point in town. (This ensures that water will flow downhill to your faucets.) Before water is pumped into the water tower, it is cleaned and purified at a water treatment plant.

Water may enter the water treatment plant from a reservoir, a lake, a river, a stream, or a well. If your city gets its water from a river or stream, it is using **surface water,** which flows on top of the ground. If the water comes from a well, it is **groundwater,** which collects underground and must be pumped to the surface.

Immense supplies of groundwater are under your feet. Even when surface soil appears dry and dusty, millions of liters of fresh water are stored below in regions called **aquifers.** These porous rock structures act like sponges, holding water sometimes for thousands of years.

Neither groundwater nor surface water is pure. As water flows over the ground to join a stream, or seeps deep into the soil to become groundwater, it dissolves small amounts of soil and rock. These dissolved substances are usually

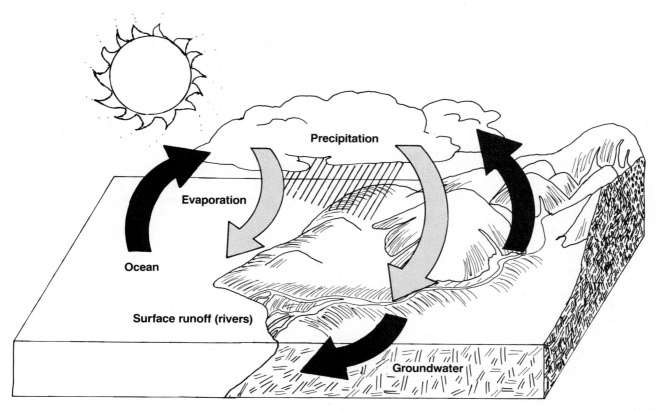

Figure I.7   The hydrologic cycle.

not removed at the water treatment plant because they are harmless in the amounts normally found. In fact, some mineral components (such as iron, zinc, and calcium) are essential to your health in small quantities.

If you live in a rural area, your home probably has its own water supply system. A well has been driven deep into the aquifer and water is brought to the surface by an electric pump. A small pressurized tank holds the water before it enters the pipes in your home. About half the people in this country use drinking water drawn from their own wells.

Let's continue tracing water to its origins. Most water falls to Earth as rain (and, if it's cold enough, as snow). When rain falls on flat ground, much of it soaks directly into the soil, seeping downward to join the groundwater. Rain falling on sloping terrain runs downhill before it has a chance to soak into the soil. Starting as tiny rills and brooks, it flows into lakes, streams, and rivers. Much of this water eventually finds its way to the ocean.

Where does rainwater come from? Rain falls as tiny water droplets from clouds formed when heat energy from the sun causes surface water to evaporate. Upon cooling at higher elevations, the evaporated water forms droplets that, in large quantities, become clouds. This endless sequence of events is called the **hydrologic cycle** (Figure I.7).

But we can go back even further—to where water came from in the first place. Geologists tell us the world's total supply of water has been the same for billions of years. Most scientists believe our world's water supply originally formed from hydrogen and oxygen gas when the young Earth was covered with molten rock. This same total water supply continues to cycle throughout the environment.

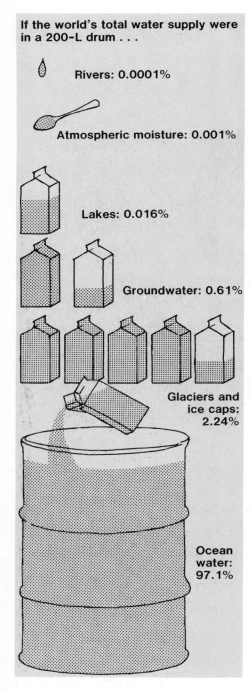

If the world's total water supply were in a 200-L drum . . .

Rivers: 0.0001%

Atmospheric moisture: 0.001%

Lakes: 0.016%

Groundwater: 0.61%

Glaciers and ice caps: 2.24%

Ocean water: 97.1%

Figure I.8 Distribution of the world's water supply.

A.7 Where Is the Earth's Water?

Scientists tell us that about 97% of the Earth's total water is stored in the oceans. The next largest storage place is not as obvious. A common incorrect guess is in rivers and lakes. Actually, the second largest source is in the Earth's ice caps and glaciers! Figure I.8 shows how the world's supply of water is distributed.

As water proceeds through its cycle, it is found in three different forms or states. Water vapor in the air is in the **gaseous state.** At high humidity in summer months, this gaseous water often contributes to human discomfort. Water in the **liquid state** is obviously found in lakes, rivers, oceans, clouds, and rain. Water in the **solid state** may occur as ice, snowflakes, frost, and even hail.

Water vapor will fill any size container since, as a gas, it has no fixed volume. It also has no fixed shape, since it assumes the shape of the container in which it is held.

A liquid water sample has a definite volume. But liquid water has no shape of its own; it takes on the shape of the container into which it is placed. Other liquids have similar characteristics. In the solid state, a water (ice) sample has both a fixed volume and a shape of its own.

We are very fortunate to have an abundant water supply in the United States. We turn on the tap, use what we need and go on about our business, not thinking about how much water we use. When the water supply is shut off, as in Riverwood, it's usually for a short time.

Suppose the shortage were a permanent one, as it is in many countries. Priority would go to "survival" uses of the available water. In fact, some water uses would probably stop.

Refer to your water-use diary. How much water did *you* use in your home during the three-day period? For what purposes? Let's turn to the data you've collected for a close look at these questions.

A.8 *You Decide:* Water Use Analysis

Table I.1 lists typical quantities of water used in various home activities. Use the table to answer the following questions.

Questions
1. Estimate the total amount of water your family used in the three days. Give your answer in liters.
2. On average, how much water did each family member use during the three days? Give your answer in liters per person per three days.
3. On average, how much water was used per family member each day? Give your answer in liters per person per day.
4. Compare the daily volume of water used per person in your household (Answer 3) to the average daily water volume used per person in the United States (325 L per person per day). What reasons can you offer to explain any differences?

You are now much more aware of the amount of water you use daily. Suppose you had to live with much less. This is exactly the situation facing the residents of Riverwood.

A.9 *You Decide:* Riverwood Water Use

Riverwood authorities have severely rationed your home water supply for three days while the cause of the fish kill is investigated. The County Sanitation Commission recommends cleaning your bathtub and filling it with water for all uses except drinking and cooking during the three-day period. (Water trucked from Mapleton will meet these important needs.) Assume, then, that your family has one tub of water, 375 L (100 gal), to use during this period.

Use this list of water uses to answer the following questions.

- washing car, floors, windows, pets
- bathing, showering, washing hair, washing hands
- washing clothes, dishes
- watering indoor plants, outdoor plants, lawn
- flushing toilet

Table I.1 *Average water volumes required for typical activities*

Use	Volume of water (in liters and gallons)
Tub bath	130 L (35 gal)
Shower (per min)	19 L (5 gal)
Washing machine	
Low setting	72 L (19 gal)
High setting	170 L (45 gal)
Dish washing	
By hand	40 L (10 gal)
By machine	46 L (12 gal)
Toilet flushing	11 L (3 gal)

Questions

1. How could you reduce the total water use in your household for these three days?

2. Which water uses could be eliminated? What would be the consequences?

3. Suggest ways to reduce the water needed for essential tasks.

4. Which uses would allow you to recover most of the used water, even if it were not as clean as it was before?

5. Impurities added through some water uses may not interfere with its use for some other purpose. Some water uses may add impurities to the water, limiting future use. For instance, laundry water probably should not be used to water plants because the residual detergent or bleach might harm them. List a series of water uses where the impurities added by one use would not interfere with the next. Use this type of diagram for your examples:

   Hand washing $\longrightarrow$ Dog washing

To get started, complete the following:

   Hand washing $\longrightarrow$ Dog washing $\longrightarrow$?
   Washing clothes $\longrightarrow$? $\longrightarrow$ Washing the car

Now create additional sequences of repeated water uses. Try to include some water uses not listed above.

Clearly, pure water is a resource no one should take for granted. Unfortunately, water is easily contaminated. In the next section we will examine why.

PART A
SUMMARY *QUESTIONS*

1. For each item, select the better answer:
   a. Is the thickness of a dime closer to 1 mm or to 1 cm?
   b. Is the volume of a glass of water closer to 250 dm^3 or to 250 cm^3?
   c. Is the diameter of a pencil closer to 7 mm or to 7 cm?
   d. Is a gallon of gasoline closer to 38 mL or to 3.8 L?

2. Complete the following conversions:
   a. 735 cm^3 = ? mL = ? L
   b. 10.7 mm = ? cm

3. Give reasons why you think it is or is not necessary to conserve water (a) within your family; (b) in your town; (c) in your region of the country; (d) in the United States as a whole; (e) on the planet.

4. What is meant by the term "indirect water use"?

5. The total supply of water in the world has been the same for billions of years. Explain why.

6. Name a serious epidemic that can be caused by the drinking of polluted water.

7. Consider the large volume of ocean water in the world and also your experience with the foul-water laboratory activity. Why is there concern about the availability and purity of water? What could be done to permit use of more of the world's water? How could we use more ocean water?

EXTENDING *YOUR KNOWLEDGE (OPTIONAL)*

- One of water's unique characteristics is that it occurs in all three states (solid, liquid, and gas) at normal temperatures found on our planet. Why is this characteristic important to the hydrologic cycle?

- Use an encyclopedia or other reference to compare the maximum and minimum temperatures naturally found on the surface of Earth, the moon, and Venus. The large amount of water on Earth serves to limit the natural temperature range found on this planet. Suggest ways that water does this. As a start, find out what the terms *heat of fusion, heat capacity,* and *heat of vaporization* mean.

- Look up the normal freezing point, boiling point, heat of fusion, and heat of vaporization of ammonia (NH_3). If an unknown planet's life forms were based on ammonia rather than water, what special survival problems might they face? What temperature range might be reasonable so this planet could support life?

- Write a historical report on the development and spread of SI metrics and its precursor, the metric system.

A vital resource not to be taken for granted.

B A LOOK AT WATER AND ITS CONTAMINANTS

Meeting Raises Fish Kill Concerns

Dr. Harold Schmidt, a scientist from the Environmental Protection Agency (EPA), reported to concerned citizens at a Town Hall public meeting last night that no evidence has been found at this time indicating any danger, past or future, to Riverwood water users.

Dr. Margaret Brooke, water-systems expert from State University, was also present to help interpret information regarding the mysterious fish kill in the Snake River. About two-thirds of Riverwood's citizens attended.

Local physician Dr. Jason Martingdale and Riverwood High School home economics teacher Alicia Green joined the speakers during the question-and-answer session that followed the reports.

Dr. Brooke confirmed that preliminary water-sample analyses revealed nothing that could have caused the fish kill. She reported that an EPA chemist will collect water samples at hourly intervals today to look for any unusual fluctuations in the levels of dissolved oxygen. She explained that, although fish don't breathe as we do, they must take in an adequate amount of oxygen gas through their gills.

Dr. Schmidt expressed regret that the fishing tournament had to be cancelled but strongly supported the Town Council action, saying that it was the safest course in the long run. He reported that "nothing has yet been found to determine the cause of the fish kill," but that "all of the examined fish, including ones found since the initial discovery of the kill, show unexpected and puzzling signs of biological trauma. These signs include hemorrhaging, and small bubbles under the skin along the lateral line." His laboratory is presently looking into the implications of these findings.

In response to questions, Dr. Schmidt indicated that he would not yet recommend rescheduling the fishing tournament.

Concerning possible causes of the fish kill, Dr. Brooke reported that "it must be something dissolved in the water, since suspended materials filtered from the water show nothing unusual."

She explained further that water is a unique substance and that the nature of water itself makes the question of the fish kill quite complicated. Important factors to consider include the relative amounts of various substances that water will dissolve and the effect of water temperature on solubility. She felt certain, however, that further studies would shed light on the situation.

Dr. Martingdale reassured citizens that "thus far, there has been no illness reported either by private physicians or the hospital that can be linked to drinking water."

Green offered water-conservation tips for housekeeping and cooking that could make life easier for inconvenienced citizens. She distributed an information sheet that will also be available at the Town Hall office.

Mayor Edward Cisko announced that water will be trucked in again today from Mapleton and expressed hope that the crisis will last no longer than three days. Those attending the meeting appeared to be dealing with the emergency in good spirits. Citizens leaving Town Hall expressed a variety of opinions.

"I never will take my tap water for granted again," said Trudy Anderson, a resident of southern Riverwood. "I thought scientists had all the answers," puzzled Robert Morgan of Morgan Enterprises. "They don't know either! What's going on here? There's certainly more than I ever imagined involved in all of this."

B.1 Physical Properties of Water

To understand the issues involved in the fish kill, it is clear that we need to know more about water. First, we will take a look at water's **physical properties**—those characteristics shared by all water samples that can be determined without changing water into something else.

Water is a familiar substance. We drink it, wash with it, swim in it, and sometimes grumble when it falls from the sky. We are so accustomed to water that most of us are unaware that it is among the rarest and most unusual substances in the universe.

Kilo is the prefix meaning 1000.
1 km = 1000 m

The space probes that explored the moon, Mars, Jupiter and its moons, and other planets of our solar system sent back pictures showing an almost total absence of water. Earth, on the other hand, is half-covered by water-laden clouds. More than 70% of the Earth's surface is covered by oceans to an average depth of more than three kilometers (two miles).

Water is the only common liquid found naturally in our environment. Many other liquids are actually solutions of substances in water. Water is never entirely pure. Surface water contains dissolved minerals as well as other substances. Even the distilled water used in steam irons and car batteries contains dissolved gases from the atmosphere. So does rainwater.

Pure water is clear, colorless, odorless, and tasteless. Some tap water samples have a characteristic taste and even a slight odor, due to other substances in the water. (Boil, then refrigerate some distilled water. Also chill a glass of tap water. Compare the taste of the two. The "pure" distilled water tastes flat.)

Density is an important physical property that can help identify a substance. It is determined by taking two measurements on a sample of matter—volume and mass. You have already been introduced to a commonly used unit of volume, the milliliter (mL). The SI unit of mass used most often in chemistry is the **gram** (g). A nickel has a mass of about 5 g. Density is mass per unit volume.

At 4 °C, the mass of 1.0 mL of liquid water is 1.0 g, so the density of water is about one gram per milliliter (1.0 g/mL). It is interesting to compare the density of water with that of other familiar liquids. Corn oil has a density of 0.92 g/mL. A given volume of corn oil has less mass than the same volume of water. Pure automotive permanent antifreeze has a density of 1.11 g/mL. Therefore, a given volume of antifreeze is more massive than the same volume of water. Liquid mercury, with a density of 13.6 g/mL, is one of the highest density substances. Table I.2 shows some characteristic densities of other materials.

Gases are much less dense than liquids. The solid form of a substance is usually more dense than its liquid form. However, ice is an important exception. As water freezes, it expands to occupy a larger volume. One milliliter of ice has a mass of about 0.92 g. Thus the density of ice is 0.92 g/mL, which is less than the density of liquid water. As a result, ice cubes float on water. If ice had a greater density than liquid water, and sank to the bottom as it froze, aquatic life in rivers and lakes could not survive freezing temperatures.

Table I.2 *Densities of some common materials (g/cm³)*

Solids

Cork	0.24
Ice	0.92
Aluminum	2.70
Iron	7.86

Liquids

Gasoline	0.67
Water	1.00
Glycerin	1.27

Gases (at 25 °C, 1 atm pressure)

Hydrogen	0.00008
Oxygen	0.0013
Carbon dioxide	0.0018

© Nancy Simmerman/AlaskaPhoto

How many states of water are shown in this photograph?

This property of water causes erosion in nature. Rainwater seeps into tiny cracks. As it freezes, it expands and cracks the rock further. After many seasons, and with other contributing factors, rocks become soil. Highways are destroyed in a similar fashion, but more rapidly due to the effect of traffic on the cracked pavement. Potholes are particularly bad following a winter of many freezes and thaws.

The boiling point and freezing point of water are important physical properties. The Celsius temperature scale, used commonly in most of the world, divides the interval between the freezing point of water and its boiling point into 100 divisions. Water's freezing point is defined as 0 °C, and its normal boiling point as 100 °C.

The Fahrenheit temperature scale is still used in the United States. Water boils at 212 °F and freezes at 32 °F on this scale; there are 180 divisions between these freezing and boiling temperatures (Figure I.9).

Evaporation and boiling are related physical properties of liquids. In both processes, liquid is changed to gas. However, evaporation occurs at all temperatures but only at the surface of the liquid. At higher temperatures, evaporation occurs more rapidly. During boiling, by contrast, gaseous water (water vapor) forms *under the surface* of the liquid. Because the vapor is less dense than the liquid, it rises to the surface and escapes as steam. We cannot see steam, but it condenses into visible clouds of tiny droplets as it contacts cooler air.

Water has an unusually high boiling point. The life-supporting form of water is its liquid state; water's high boiling point is responsible for its presence as a liquid at normal temperatures.

Another very important and unusual physical property of water is its high surface tension. This property causes water to form spherical drops and to form a curved surface in a small container. Surface tension enables a water bug to dart across the surface of a quiet pool and makes it possible to float a dry needle on the surface of a dish of water (Figure I.10).

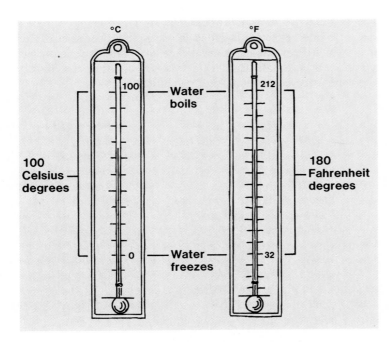

Figure I.9   Celsius and Fahrenheit temperature scales.

Figure I.10   Water has a high surface tension, allowing a needle to float on its surface, and causing it to form beads as on a newly polished car surface.

B.2 Mixtures and Solutions

If two or more substances are combined and retain their individual properties, a **mixture** has been produced. A mixture of salt and pepper is described as **heterogeneous** because it is not completely uniform throughout. A pepper and water mixture is also heterogeneous.

Mixing salt and water has a very different result—a **solution** is formed. In water, the salt crystals dissolve by separating into particles so small that they cannot be seen even at high magnification. These particles become uniformly mingled with the particles of water, producing a **homogeneous** mixture, one that is uniform throughout. All solutions are homogeneous mixtures. In the salt solution, the salt (the dissolved substance) is the **solute** and the water is the **solvent.**

Water mixtures are classified according to the size of the particles dispersed in the water. **Suspensions** are mixtures containing relatively large, easily seen particles. The particles remain suspended for a while after stirring, but then settle out or form layers within the liquid. Suspensions are classified as heterogeneous mixtures because they are not uniform throughout.

Muddy water includes suspended particles of soil and other matter. A solid layer forms when this water is left undisturbed. Even after several days, the liquid will still appear somewhat cloudy. Some very small particles remain distributed throughout the water. These tiny particles, still large enough to produce the cloudy appearance, are called colloidal particles. This is a type of mixture called a **colloid.**

Milk is a colloid with water as the dispersant (solvent). The colloidal butterfat particles are not visible to the naked eye. Milk can be classified as homogeneous (thus the term *homogenized milk*). Under high magnification, however, individual butterfat globules can be seen floating in the water. Milk no longer appears homogeneous (Figure I.11).

There is a simple way to decide if the particles in a mixture are large enough to consider the liquid a colloid rather than a solution. When a beam of light shines through a colloidal liquid, the beam's path can be clearly seen in the liquid. The particles are too small to see, but are large enough to reflect light off their surfaces. This reflection is called the **Tyndall effect,** named after the Irish physicist who first explained the phenomenon. Solutions are mixtures in which the particles are so small that they do not settle out, do not show a Tyndall effect, and cannot be seen even at high magnification.

Solutions in which water is the solvent are called aqueous solutions.

suspension
(largest particles)
↓
colloid
(intermediate-sized particles)
↓
solution
(smallest particles)

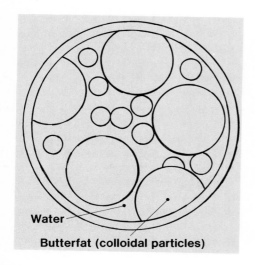

Water

Butterfat (colloidal particles)

Figure I.11   Milk under magnification no longer appears homogeneous.

Debi Stambaugh

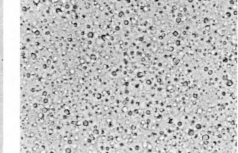

Debi Stambaugh

On the left is skimmed milk, on the right whole milk, both under 640✕ magnification. The particles are fat globules in a water solution.

The foul-water sample you purified earlier illustrates all three types of mixtures. It certainly contained some particles large enough to form a suspension. Its persistent cloudiness suggests that suspended colloidal particles were also present. Even your final clear, purified sample had atmospheric gases and electrically charged particles dissolved in it. Thus your "purified" water was actually a solution.

Now let's put your knowledge of water mixtures to work. The following laboratory activity will give you firsthand experience in distinguishing among these types of mixtures.

B.3 Laboratory Activity: Classification of Mixtures

Getting Ready

In this laboratory activity, you will examine four different mixtures containing water and classify each as a suspension, a colloid, a solution, or a combination of these. You will filter each sample and look for the Tyndall effect in both the filtered and unfiltered samples. Particles in a suspension can be separated by filtration, while those in a colloid or a solution are too small to be retained by the filter paper. The occurrence of the Tyndall effect shows the presence of colloidal particles.

In your laboratory notebook, prepare data tables for your observations on the original samples and the filtrates, and for your conclusions about each mixture.

Data table—Original sample

Beaker	Color	Clarity (clear or cloudy?)	Settle out?	Tyndall effect	Mixture classification		
					Suspension	Colloid	Solution
1.							
2.							
3.							
4.							

Data table—Filtrate

Beaker	Color	Clarity	Settle out?	Tyndall effect	Filter paper	Mixture classification		
						Suspension	Colloid	Solution
1.								
2.								
3.								
4.								

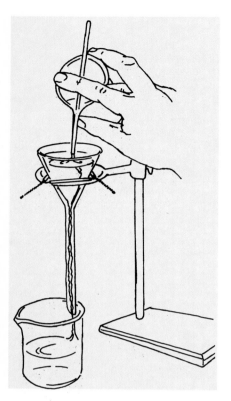

Figure I.12   Filtration setup: Filter paper, funnel, clay triangle, ring clamp, ring stand, beaker.

Procedure

1. Obtain eight 250-mL beakers and number them in two sets of 1 to 4.
2. Add unknown mixtures provided by your teacher to one set of four beakers. Half-fill each beaker.
3. Examine each mixture and record your observations on its appearance:
   a. Is the sample colored?
   b. Is the sample clear or cloudy?
   c. Do any particles settle out after you shake the mixture?
4. Perform a Tyndall effect test on each mixture as demonstrated by your teacher. If the liquid is relatively clear, shine a light beam through the side of the beaker and observe the liquid from the top. If the liquid is very cloudy, shine the beam across the liquid surface and observe the beaker from the side. Can you see the light beam as it passes through the sample? Record your observations.
5. Filter each numbered sample using the apparatus shown in Figure I.12. (If you have forgotten how to fold a filter paper, look back at Figure I.5.) Use a fresh filter paper for each sample. Collect enough filtrate in a clean, numbered beaker to allow you to repeat steps 3 and 4.
6. Examine each filter paper. Were any particles removed from the liquid? Record your observations.
7. Repeat step 3 on each filtrate and record your observations. Compare the properties of the filtrates with those of the original liquid samples. Record any differences.
8. Repeat step 4 on each filtrate, and record your observations.
9. Based on your observations, decide whether each unknown mixture was a solution, a colloid, a suspension, or some combination. Record your classifications.
10. Compare your observations and conclusions with those of other laboratory teams.

B.4   Molecular View of Water

So far in our investigation of water, we have focused on properties that are observable with our unaided senses. To understand why water has such special properties, we look at it from a different point of view—from the perspective of **atoms.**

A simplified picture of an atomic view of matter can be easily described. All samples of matter are composed of atoms of different types. Oxygen is considered an **element** because it is composed of only oxygen atoms. Likewise, the element hydrogen contains only hydrogen atoms. Approximately 90 elements are found in nature. Each element has unique identifying properties.

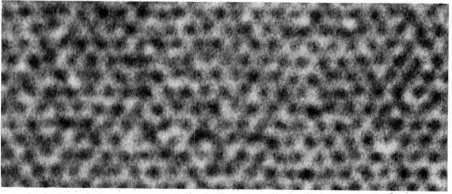

An electron micrograph of a thin crystal of a low-temperature form of niobium pentoxide (Nb_2O_5). The image reveals individual atoms.

Water is not classified as an element because its atoms are of two types—oxygen and hydrogen. Nor is it classified as a mixture because its properties differ from those of its component elements. Also, water cannot be separated into oxygen and hydrogen by simple physical means. Water is an example of a type of matter called a **chemical compound.** Over eight million compounds have been identified by chemists.

Every compound is composed of atoms of two or more different elements linked together through **chemical bonds.** Two hydrogen atoms and one oxygen atom are bonded together in water to form a unit called a water **molecule.** Even a drop of water contains an unimaginably large number of water molecules.

Chemical reactions involve the breaking and forming of chemical bonds, causing atoms to become rearranged into new substances. These new substances have different properties than the original material. Not only are their physical properties different, but the chemical reactions they can take part in are also different. In other words, these new substances have different **chemical properties** than those of the starting materials.

The following Your Turn will help you see how an atomic and molecular view is used to explain a variety of common observations.

YOUR*TURN*

I.3 Matter at the Microlevel

If you add a few drops of food coloring to a glass of water, you will see the color slowly spread out. If you stir this mixture, the color will become lighter and evenly distributed. How can this be explained in terms of molecules?

The food coloring contains molecules that appear colored. After the drop enters the water, these molecules begin to spread throughout the colorless water. Eventually a solution forms with uniform distribution of color. Explain the following observations from an atomic or molecular perspective.

1. The solid form of a substance is usually more dense than the liquid form, which is, in turn, much more dense than the gas.
2. When 50 mL of water is mixed with 50 mL of methanol, the total volume of the liquid mixture is less than 100 mL.
3. Inflated balloons gradually decrease in volume as time passes. Helium-filled balloons shrink particularly rapidly. Metal-foil balloons shrink much more slowly than do plastic ones.
4. When a chemical reaction occurs in a closed container, the total mass remains constant, despite changes observed as the original substances are converted to different substances.

B.5 Symbols and Formulas

To represent elements and compounds on paper, an international language has been developed. The "letters" in this language are **chemical symbols.** Each element is assigned a chemical symbol of one or two letters. Only the first letter of the symbol is capitalized. For example, C is the symbol for carbon and Ca is the symbol for calcium. The symbols for some common elements are listed in Table I.3. The "words" or **chemical formulas** of this chemical language each represent a known chemical substance. In a chemical formula, symbols represent each element present.

Table I.3 *Common elements and symbols*

Element name	Symbol
Aluminum	Al
Bromine	Br
Calcium	Ca
Carbon	C
Chlorine	Cl
Cobalt	Co
Gold	Au
Hydrogen	H
Iodine	I
Iron	Fe
Lead	Pb
Magnesium	Mg
Mercury	Hg
Nickel	Ni
Nitrogen	N
Oxygen	O
Phosphorus	P
Potassium	K
Silver	Ag
Sodium	Na
Sulfur	S
Tin	Sn

Subscripts (numbers written below the normal line of letters) indicate how many atoms of each element are present in one unit of the substance. For example, in the chemical formula for water, H_2O, the subscript 2 shows that, in a water molecule, two hydrogen atoms are present. Note that although there is one oxygen atom present the subscript 1 is not written.

Finally, the "sentences" in the language of chemistry are **chemical equations**. Chemical reactions are represented on paper by chemical equations. The chemical equation for the formation of water

$$2\,H_2 + O_2 \quad \longrightarrow \quad 2\,H_2O$$
$$\text{reactants} \qquad\qquad \text{product}$$

shows that two hydrogen molecules and one oxygen molecule react to produce two molecules of water. The substances that are changed in a chemical reaction are called the **reactants** and their formulas are always written on the left. The new substance or substances formed are called the **products** and their formulas are always written on the right. Note that this equation, like all chemical equations, is balanced—the total number of atoms (four H atoms and two O atoms) is the same for both reactants and products.

Household ammonia is made by mixing ammonia (a gas) and water.

YOUR*TURN*

I.4 Symbols, Formulas, and Equations

Let's look at the kind of information available from a simple chemical equation and the formulas included in it:

$$N_2 + 3\,H_2 \longrightarrow 2\,NH_3$$

One molecule of N_2, the element nitrogen, will react with three molecules of H_2, the element hydrogen, to give two molecules of the compound ammonia (NH_3). Each molecule of ammonia is composed of one nitrogen atom and three hydrogen atoms. There are two nitrogen atoms and six hydrogen atoms in the reactants and in the products.

1. Name the elements represented by the following symbols: P, Ni, N, Co, Br, K, Na, Fe.
2. For each formula below, name the elements present and give the number of atoms of each element shown in the formula.
   a. Sulfuric acid (battery acid) H_2SO_4
   b. Sodium hydrogen carbonate (baking soda) $NaHCO_3$
   c. Calcium chloride (deicing salt for roads) $CaCl_2$
   d. Hydrogen peroxide (antiseptic) H_2O_2
3. Interpret the following chemical equation, which shows the formation of the air pollutant, nitric oxide, NO.

$$N_2 + O_2 \longrightarrow 2\,NO$$

We must consider another question before we return to our discussion of "foul water" and the problems in Riverwood: Why is the water molecule in Figure I.13 drawn in that particular shape, rather than in some other shape? That is, do the order and arrangement of atoms in a molecule (called **molecular structure**) make any difference in its properties?

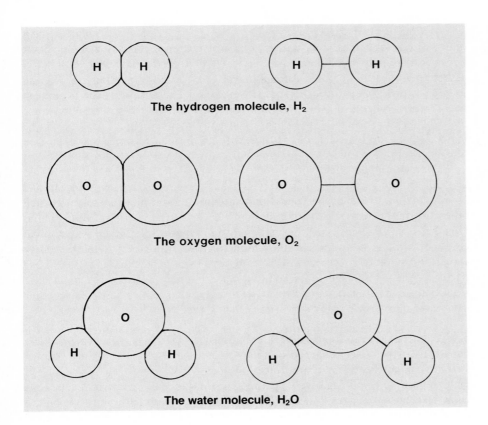

The hydrogen molecule, H₂

The oxygen molecule, O₂

The water molecule, H₂O

Figure I.13 Hydrogen, oxygen, and water molecules. Atoms in molecules are held together by chemical bonds, represented by the lines on the right.

B.6 The Electrical Nature of Matter

You have already experienced matter's electrical nature although you may not have realized it. Clothes often display "static cling" as they exit the dryer. The pieces of apparel stick firmly together, and can be separated only with some effort. The shock you sometimes receive after walking across a rug and touching a metal doorknob is another reminder of matter's electrical nature. If two inflated balloons are rubbed against your hair, they will both be attracted to your hair, but will be repelled by each other. (This experiment is best conducted in air having low humidity.) The electrical properties of matter can be summarized as follows:

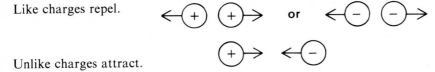

Like charges repel.

Unlike charges attract.

What are these positive and negative charges? How do they relate to the idea of atoms and molecules? For now, you need to know only a few major points:

- Neutral (uncharged) atoms contain equal numbers of positively charged particles (called **protons**) and negatively charged particles (called **electrons**). In addition, most atoms contain a number of neutral particles (called **neutrons**).
- The attraction between protons of one atom and electrons of another atom provides the "glue" that holds different atoms together. This "glue" helps explain chemical **bonding.**

A number of observations suggest that a hydrogen atom can bond to only one other atom at a time. By contrast, an oxygen atom can form two bonds, and thus be joined to two hydrogen atoms. The result: H₂O!

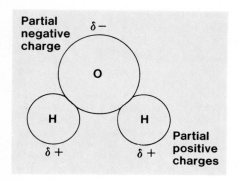

Figure I.14 Polarity of the water molecule. The δ+ and δ− are tiny charges. They balance so the molecule as a whole is neutral.

Na   sodium atom
Na⁺   sodium ion
Cl   chlorine atom
Cl⁻   chloride ion
Na⁺Cl⁻   sodium chloride (table salt)

Evidence also suggests that water molecules are electrically **polar.** A polar molecule has an uneven distribution of electrical charge. That is, each molecule has a positive pole on one end and a negative pole on the other end. Instead of assuming a linear or sticklike shape as in (H-O-H), water molecules are believed to be bent or V-shaped (see Figures I.13 and 14). The "oxygen end" is an electrically negative pole (having a *greater* concentration of electrons) compared to the two "hydrogen ends" which form electrically positive poles. Even though the molecule as a unit is electrically neutral, within the molecule there is a separation of charge.

The combined effects of its molecular shape and electrical polarity help account for many properties of water described earlier. For instance, since unlike charges attract, the opposite "ends" of neighboring water molecules attract each other, causing them to stick to one another. This gives water its high boiling point. (It takes a large quantity of thermal energy to separate the liquid water molecules to form water vapor.) Water's high surface tension and reduced density when it crystallizes as ice can also be explained by its molecular shape and electrical polarity. Also, due to its polarity, water is attracted to other polar substances or to substances composed of electrically charged particles. Thus water is capable of dissolving a great variety of substances.

In certain substances, such as common table salt, the smallest particles are neither uncharged atoms nor molecules. Atoms can gain or lose electrons to form negatively or positively charged particles called **ions.** Some compounds, known as **ionic compounds** or ionic substances, are composed of ions. There are always enough positively and negatively charged ions so that the total positive charge is equal to the total negative charge. The ions are held together in clusters by the attraction between the negative and positive charges. The resulting compound has no overall electric charge. When an ionic compound dissolves in water, individual ions become separated from each other and disperse in the water. The designation (*aq*) following the symbol for an ion, as in $Na^+(aq)$, means that the ion is present in water (aqueous) solution.

B.7 Pure and Impure Water

We are now ready to return to the Riverwood fish kill. You will recall that various individuals in Riverwood had different ideas about the cause of the problem. For example, longtime resident Harmon Lewis was sure the cause was pollution of the river water. Let's examine water pollution in greater detail.

Most communities in this country receive clean, but not pure, water at an extremely low cost per liter. Check your family's monthly water bill to see the rate you pay per gallon. Divide that number by 3.8 to find what you pay per liter of water.

It is useless to insist on *pure* water. The cost of processing water to make it completely pure would be prohibitively high. Even if costs were not a problem it would still be impossible to have pure water. The atmospheric gases, nitrogen (N_2), oxygen (O_2), and carbon dioxide (CO_2) will always be dissolved in the water to some extent.

In fact, it's unnecessary and even undesirable to remove all substances from the water we use. Some dissolved gases and minerals give water a pleasing taste. Fish and other water-dwelling creatures need oxygen gas dissolved in the water to survive. Some dissolved substances also promote human health. For example, a small amount of certain chlorine-containing compounds ensures that harmful bacteria are not present.

Unfortunately, not all substances that become suspended or dissolved in water are helpful or even desired. High concentrations of substances containing iron (Fe) give water a bad taste and cause unwanted deposits in pipes and fixtures. Compounds containing sulfur (S) give water a bad odor. Compounds containing elements such as mercury (Hg), lead (Pb), cadmium (Cd), and arsenic (As) can dissolve in water, and even at low concentrations all can be harmful to human health.

Many manufactured substances such as pesticides, and commercial and industrial waste products, particularly solvents, can also find their way into drinking water, with harmful effects. Even sunlight can produce potentially harmful substances in chlorinated water that contains certain kinds of contaminants.

Our real challenge is to ensure that our water supplies remain unpolluted. This is accomplished by preventing unwanted substances from entering our water supplies and removing those that already are present.

B.8 Laboratory Activity: Water Testing

Getting Ready

Chemists use a variety of methods for detecting and identifying ions in aqueous solutions. In this activity you will use tests that a chemist might use to check for the presence of certain ions in water solution. Positively charged ions have a deficiency of electrons and are called **cations;** negatively charged ions have an excess of electrons and are called **anions.** You will investigate two cations and two anions.

The tests you will perform are confirming tests. In each test you will look for a change in solution color, or the appearance of an insoluble material called a precipitate. If the test is positive you can be sure the ion in question is present. However, a negative test (no color or precipitate) does not necessarily mean the ion in question is not present. The ion may simply be present in such a small amount that the color or precipitate cannot be seen.

You will investigate the iron(III) cation (Fe^{3+}), the calcium cation (Ca^{2+}), the chloride anion (Cl^-), and the sulfate anion (SO_4^{2-}).

Each test will be performed on three different samples:

- a reference solution (known to contain the ion of interest)
- tap water (which may or may not contain the ion)
- a control (distilled water, known *not* to contain the ion).

In your laboratory notebook, prepare a data table similar to the one shown below:

Data table			
Solutions	**Color**	**Precipitate**	**Is ion present?**
Fe^{3+} reference			
Tap water			
Control			
Ca^{2+} reference			
Tap water			
Control			
Cl^- reference			
Tap water			
Control			
SO_4^{2-} reference			
Tap water			
Control			

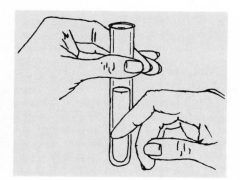

Figure I.15 Tapping a forefinger against a test tube mixes its contents.

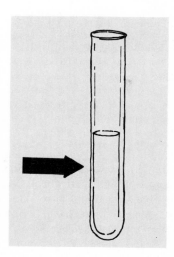

Figure I.16 Look through the side of the test tube to check for color.

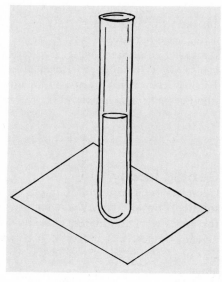

Figure I.17 Hold test tube over white paper to check for color.

Following is a list of hints to provide guidance in completing the ion analysis:

1. If the ion is present in tap water, it probably will be in a much lower concentration than in the reference solution. Therefore, the color or amount of precipitate produced will be less obvious in the tap water sample than in the reference solution.

2. When carrying out an ion test, mix the contents of the test tube thoroughly, unless the directions provide other guidance. Look at the mixing procedure illustrated in Figure I.15.

3. In a test based on change of color, so few color-producing ions may be present that you cannot be sure that the reaction has occurred. There are several ways you can tell whether the expected color is actually present.

   • Look through the side of the tube (Figure I.16). Place a sheet of white paper behind or below the test tube to make any color more visible (Figure I.17).

   • Compare the color of the control (distilled water) test to that of tap water. Distilled water contains none of the ions for which you are testing. Thus, even a faint color in the tap water is evidence that the ion is present.

4. In an ion test involving a precipitate, you may not be able to observe one even after thoroughly mixing the solutions. In this case shine a light beam through the tube to see if light is scattered (a Tyndall effect test; see Part B.3). Such light scattering confirms the presence of a precipitate in the form of colloidal particles.

Procedure

1. Rinse three test tubes with distilled water.

2. Use a graduated cylinder to measure 2 mL of tap water; pour the water into a test tube. Mark the test tube with a grease pencil at the 2-mL level. Mark two other test tubes with a line at the same level. Label the three test tubes Reference, Tap Water, and Control.

3. Carry out each of the following four tests on the reference solution provided by your teacher, on tap water, and on a control sample of distilled water.

Jon Jacobson

There are about 3×10^{25} molecules of water
(30,000,000,000,000,000,000,000,000 molecules) in this measuring cup.

Iron(III) Ion Test (Fe^{3+})

1. Pour 2 mL of iron(III) reference solution into the clean test tube labeled "Reference."
2. Add three drops of potassium thiocyanate (KSCN) solution to the test tube.
3. Mix the test tube contents thoroughly.
4. Record the results in your data table.

   The reaction that takes place can be represented as follows:

Iron(III) ion (reference solution)		Thiocyanate ion (test solution)		Iron(III) thiocyanate ion (red color)
$Fe^{3+}(aq)$	$+$	$SCN^-(aq)$	$\rightarrow$	$Fe(SCN)^{2+}(aq)$

Because there are two types of iron ions, we use iron(II) for Fe^{2+} and iron(III) for Fe^{3+}.

Only ions that take part in the reaction are included in this type of equation.

5. Repeat this iron(III) ion test on a 2-mL sample of tap water and a 2-mL sample of distilled water, placing each sample in its properly labeled test tube. Record your results.
6. Discard the solutions in your test tubes. Wash the tubes thoroughly with tap water and rinse with distilled water before going on to the next test.

Calcium Ion Test (Ca^{2+})

1. Pour 2 mL of calcium ion reference solution into the clean test tube labeled "Reference."
2. Add three drops of dilute acetic acid.
3. Add three drops of sodium oxalate ($Na_2C_2O_4$) solution to the test tube.
4. Mix the contents of the test tube. Record your results. The reaction that takes place can be represented as follows:

Calcium ion (reference solution)		Oxalate ion (test solution)		Calcium oxalate (precipitate)
$Ca^{2+}(aq)$	$+$	$C_2O_4{}^{2-}(aq)$	$\rightarrow$	$CaC_2O_4(s)$

5. Repeat this calcium ion test on a 2-mL sample of tap water and a 2-mL sample of distilled water, placing each sample in its properly labeled test tube. Record your results.

6. Discard the solutions in your three test tubes. Wash the test tubes thoroughly with tap water and rinse with distilled water before going on to the next test.

Chloride Ion Test (Cl⁻)

1. Pour 2 mL of chloride ion reference solution into the clean test tube labeled "Reference."

2. Add three drops of silver nitrate ($AgNO_3$) test solution. Avoid contact with skin.

3. Mix the contents of the test tube thoroughly.

4. Record the results in your data table. The reaction that takes place can be represented as follows:

Silver ion (test solution)		Chloride ion (reference solution)		Silver chloride (precipitate)
$Ag^+(aq)$	$+$	$Cl^-(aq)$	$\rightarrow$	$AgCl(s)$

5. Repeat this chloride ion test on a 2-mL sample of tap water and a 2-mL sample of distilled water, placing each sample in its properly labeled test tube. Record your results.

6. Discard the solutions in your three test tubes. Wash the tubes thoroughly with tap water and rinse with distilled water before going on to the next test.

Sulfate Ion Test (SO₄²⁻)

1. Pour 2 mL of sulfate ion reference solution into the clean test tube labeled "Reference."

2. Add 3 drops of barium chloride ($BaCl_2$) test solution to the test tube.

3. Mix the contents of the test tube thoroughly.

4. Record the results in your data table. The reaction that takes place can be represented as follows:

Barium ion (test solution)		Sulfate ion (reference solution)		Barium sulfate (precipitate)
$Ba^{2+}(aq)$	$+$	$SO_4^{2-}(aq)$	$\rightarrow$	$BaSO_4(s)$

5. Repeat this sulfate ion test on a 2-mL sample of tap water and a 2-mL sample of distilled water, placing each in its properly labeled test tube. Record your results.

6. Discard the solutions in your three test tubes. Wash the tubes thoroughly with tap water and rinse with distilled water.

Questions

1. Why was a control used in each test? Why was distilled water chosen as the control?

2. What kinds of difficulties are associated with the use of qualitative tests?

3. These tests cannot absolutely confirm the absence of an ion. Why?

B.9 *You Decide:* Analyzing the Riverwood Mystery

Your teacher will divide the class into groups composed of four or five students. Each group will complete this decision-making activity. When all groups have finished, the entire class will compare and discuss the answers obtained by each group.

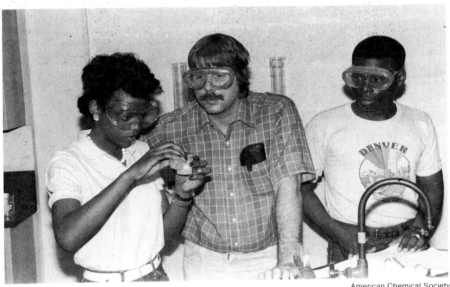

American Chemical Society

In a *ChemCom* lab.

At the beginning of this unit, you read newspaper articles describing the Riverwood fish kill and several citizens' reactions to it. Among those interviewed were Harmon Lewis, a longtime resident of Riverwood, and Dr. Margaret Brooke, a water-systems scientist. These two individuals had very different reactions to the fish kill. Harmon Lewis was angry, certain that human activity had caused the fish kill—probably some sort of pollution. Dr. Brooke refused even to speculate about the cause of the fish kill until she had run some tests. Which position comes closer to your own reaction?

Let's investigate this issue further.

1. Reread the newspaper accounts of the fish kill located at the beginning of Parts A and B. List all *facts* (not opinions) concerning the fish kill in the newspaper stories. Scientists often refer to facts as **data.** Data are objective pieces of information. They do not include interpretation.

2. After listing facts concerning the fish kill, list the questions you would want answered before you could decide the cause of the fish kill. Some typical questions might include: Do barges or commercial boats travel on the Snake River? Were any shipping accidents on the river reported recently?

3. Look over your two lists—one of facts and the other of questions. At this point, can any possible causes of the fish kill be ruled out as unlikely? Can you suggest any probable cause? Be as specific as possible. You will have an opportunity later in the unit to test the reasoning you used to answer these questions.

B.10 What Are the Possibilities?

The activities you have just completed (gathering data, seeking patterns or regularities among the data, suggesting reasons that attempt to account for the data) are typical of approaches used by scientists when they attempt to solve problems. Such scientific methods are based on a combination of systematic, step-by-step procedures and logic, as well as occasional hunches and guesses.

A fundamental and difficult part of scientists' work is knowing what questions to ask. You have listed some questions that must be asked concerning the cause of the fish kill. These types of questions help focus a scientist's thinking. Often a large problem can be reduced to several smaller problems or questions, each of which is more easily managed and solved.

The number of possible causes for the fish kill is large. The scientists investigating the problem must find ways to eliminate some possible causes and zero in on those that are most likely. They try either to eliminate all but one cause or to come up with conclusive proof of a specific cause.

Water-systems analyst Brooke reported that suspended materials had already been eliminated as possible causes of the fish kill. She concluded, therefore, that if the fish kill cause was water-related, it would be due to something dissolved in the water.

We will devote the next part of this unit to examining several major categories of water-soluble substances and considering how they might be involved in the fish kill. The mystery of the Riverwood fish kill will be confronted at last!

PART B
SUMMARY *QUESTIONS*

1. List three unusual properties of water and briefly describe their importance to life on this planet.

2. Identify each of the following as either a solution, suspension, or colloid.
   a. A medicine that says "shake before using"
   b. Rubbing alcohol
   c. Italian salad dressing
   d. Mayonnaise
   e. A cola soft drink
   f. An oil-based paint
   g. Milk

3. Using what you know about chemical notation, which of the following is an element, and which is a compound?
   a. CO
   b. Co

4. Interpret the following chemical equation, which represents burning methane (CH_4), in terms of molecules and atoms.

$$CH_4 + 2\,O_2 \rightarrow CO_2 + 2\,H_2O$$

5. Name the elements in each of the following substances. List the number of atoms of each element shown in the substance's formula.
   a. Phosphoric acid, H_3PO_4 (used in some soft drinks and in the production of some types of fertilizer)
   b. Sodium hydroxide, NaOH (found in some drain cleaners)
   c. Sulfur dioxide, SO_2 (a by-product from burning some grades of coal)

6. A friend of yours insists that citizens ought to force their local governments to supply them with 100% pure, "chemical-free" water. Based on what you've learned thus far, how would you respond to this demand? (*Hint:* Is 100% pure, chemical-free water ever possible? What chemical and economic factors limit water purity? What do we really want when we ask for pure water?)

EXTENDING *YOUR KNOWLEDGE (OPTIONAL)*

- The Celsius temperature scale is used in scientific work in all parts of the world, and is used in normal activities by most of the world's citizens. However, Fahrenheit temperatures are still used in weather reports in this country. From the normal freezing and boiling points of water expressed in these two scales, try to develop an equation that converts a Celsius temperature to its Fahrenheit equivalent. (*Hint:* To start, recall that there are 180 Fahrenheit degrees but only 100 Celsius degrees between the freezing point and boiling point of water.)
- The density of petroleum-based oil is approximately 0.9 g/mL. By contrast, the density of water is about 1.0 g/mL. What implications does this density difference have for an "oil spill" in a body of water? Consider the implications for aquatic life, oil spill cleanup operations, and the possibility of an oil fire.
- For those elements in Table I.3 (page 25) with symbols not based on their names, look up the names on which the symbols are based and their origins.

Department of the Interior

This land in Arizona would be desert without irrigation.

C INVESTIGATING THE CAUSE OF THE FISH KILL

The immediate problem facing those investigating the Riverwood water crisis is to determine if a dissolved substance was responsible for the fish kill. They must search for evidence of an intolerably high amount of a dissolved substance toxic to fish, or possibly a shortage of dissolved oxygen.

C.1 Solubility

Solubility of Solids

How much of a substance will dissolve in a given amount of water? Imagine preparing a water solution of potassium nitrate (KNO_3). You pour water into a beaker and then add a scoopful of solid, white potassium nitrate crystals. As you stir the water, the solid crystals disappear. The liquid remains colorless and clear. In the resulting solution, water is the solvent, and potassium nitrate is the solute.

If you add a second scoopful of potassium nitrate crystals to the same beaker and stir, these crystals will also dissolve. But if you continue adding the solid, eventually some crystals will remain on the bottom of the beaker, no matter how long you stir. There is a maximum quantity of potassium nitrate that will dissolve in a beaker of water at room temperature.

The **solubility** of a substance in water refers to the maximum quantity of substance, expressed, for example, in grams, that will dissolve in a certain quantity of water (e.g., 100 g) at a certain temperature. The solubility of potassium nitrate, for example, might be expressed in units of "grams per 100 g water" at the specified temperature.

The term "soluble" is actually a relative term, since everything is soluble in water to some extent. The term "insoluble," therefore, really refers to substances that are only very, very slightly soluble in water. Chalk, for example, is insoluble in water.

The size of the solute crystals and the vigor and duration of stirring help determine how long it takes for a solute to dissolve. However, these factors do not affect how much substance will eventually dissolve.

When a solvent holds as much of a solute as it normally can at a given temperature, we say that the solution is **saturated.** Any lesser amount of dissolved solute at that temperature produces an **unsaturated** solution.

Figure I.18 shows the maximum mass (in grams) of various ionic solutes that will dissolve in 100 g of water at temperatures from 0 °C to 100 °C. The plotted line for each solute is called a solubility curve.

Note that the solubility curve for sodium chloride (NaCl) is essentially a horizontal line. This tells us the solubility of sodium chloride is not appreciably affected by changes in water temperature. By contrast, the curve for potassium nitrate (KNO_3) turns upward steeply as temperature increases, showing that the solubility of potassium nitrate in water is greatly influenced by the water temperature.

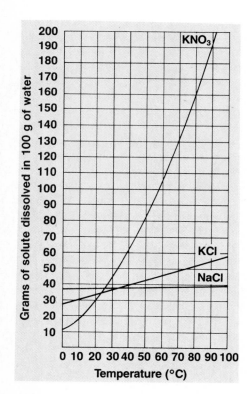

Figure I.18 Relationship between solubility and temperature for three salts in water.

Table I.4   *Solutions of KNO$_3$ (at 20 °C the solubility of KNO$_3$ is 30 g/100 g of water)*

Solution description	Amount of solute/solvent
Unsaturated KNO$_3$ solution (at 20 °C)	Less than 30 g/100 g water
Saturated KNO$_3$ solution (at 20 °C)	30 g/100 g of water
Supersaturated KNO$_3$ solution (at 20 °C)	More than 30 g/100 g of water

Each point on a solubility curve represents a saturated solution. For example, the graph shows that 39 g of sodium chloride dissolved in 100 g of water at 100 °C produces a saturated solution.

Any point below a solubility curve represents an unsaturated solution. For example, a solution containing 80 g of potassium nitrate and 100 g of water at 60 °C is an unsaturated solution. If you were able to cool this solution to 40 °C without forming any solid crystals, you would have a solution of potassium nitrate that is **supersaturated** at this lower temperature. A supersaturated solution contains more dissolved solute than a saturated solution. Any jarring, however, would cause 18 g of potassium nitrate crystals to appear and settle. The remaining liquid would then contain 62 g of solute per 100 g water—a stable, saturated solution. Table I.4 gives the amounts of potassium nitrate in saturated, unsaturated, and supersaturated solutions at 20 °C.

Solubility of Gases

We have seen that the solubility of a solid in water often decreases when the water temperature is lowered. The solubility behavior of gases is quite different. As water temperature decreases, a gas becomes more soluble! Because of its importance to aquatic life, let's see what happens to oxygen's solubility when water temperature changes.

Figure I.19 shows the solubility of oxygen gas at various water temperatures, reported as milligrams of oxygen gas dissolved per 1000 g of water. Note that the solubility of oxygen gas at 0 °C is about twice its solubility at 25 °C. The values for oxygen solubility are much smaller than the values shown in Figure I.18 for solid solutes. For example, at 24 °C, about 37 g of sodium chloride will dissolve in 100 g of water. At the same temperature, somewhat less than 9 mg of oxygen gas will dissolve in 1000 g of water. It's clear that gases are far less soluble in water than are many ionic solids.

Be sure to note differences in axis labels when you compare graphs.

The solubility of a gas depends not only on the water temperature, but also on gas pressure. Gas solubility is proportional to the pressure of the gas above the liquid. That is, if the pressure of the gas were doubled, the amount of gas that dissolves would also double. You experience this effect every time you open a bottle or can of carbonated soft drink. Dissolved carbon dioxide gas (CO_2) escapes from the liquid in a rush of bubbles. The gas was originally forced into the container at high pressure just before it was sealed, to increase the amount of carbon dioxide dissolved in the beverage. When it is opened, the pressure inside drops to atmospheric pressure. Dissolved carbon dioxide gas escapes from the liquid until it reaches its lower solubility at this lower pressure.

The following questions will help you become more familiar with the information found in the solubility graphs in Figures I.18 and I.19. Refer to the appropriate graph to answer each question.

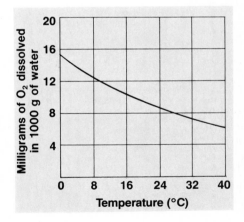

Figure I.19   Solubility curve for O$_2$ gas in water in contact with air.

YOUR*TURN*

I.5   Solubility and Solubility Curves

What is the solubility of potassium nitrate at 80 °C? The answer is found by locating, in Figure I.18, the intersection of the potassium nitrate curve with the vertical line representing 80 °C. The solubility is found by following the horizontal line to the left. Thus, the solubility of potassium nitrate in water at 80 °C is 160 g per 100 g of water.

At what temperature is the solubility of dissolved oxygen gas 11 mg per 1000 g of water? See Figure I.19. Think of the space between 8 and 12 mg/1000 mg on the axis in Figure I.18 as divided into four equal parts, follow the horizontal line at "11 mg/1000 g" to its intersection with the curve, follow a vertical line down to the axis, mentally divide the space between 8 °C and 16 °C into eight parts, and "read" the desired temperature as 11 °C.

It is possible to calculate the solubility of a substance in various amounts of water. We found from the solubility curve that 160 g of potassium nitrate will dissolve in 100 g of water at 80 °C. How much potassium nitrate will dissolve in 200 g of water at this temperature? The arithmetic looks like this:

$$\left(\frac{160 \text{ g KNO}_3}{100 \text{ g H}_2\text{O}}\right) = \left(\frac{x \text{ g KNO}_3}{200 \text{ g H}_2\text{O}}\right)$$

$$x = \left(\frac{160 \text{ g KNO}_3}{100 \text{ g H}_2\text{O}}\right) \times (200 \text{ g H}_2\text{O}) = 320 \text{ g KNO}_3$$

1. a. What mass (in grams) of potassium nitrate (KNO_3) will dissolve in 100 g of water at 50 °C?
    b. What mass of potassium chloride (KCl) will dissolve in 100 g of water at this temperature?

2. a. If we dissolve 25 g of potassium nitrate in 100 g of water at 30 °C, how many additional grams of potassium nitrate must be added at this temperature to produce a saturated solution?
    b. What is the minimum quantity of 30 °C water needed to dissolve 25 g of potassium nitrate?

3. a. What mass of oxygen gas can be dissolved in 100 g of water at 24 °C? At 20 °C?
    b. What mass of oxygen gas can be dissolved in 1.0 g of water at 20 °C?

C.2   Solution Concentration

Some substances dissolved in water cause no problems at low levels of concentration, and may even be beneficial. However, these same substances dissolved in larger quantities may be harmful. For example, the level of chlorination in a swimming pool and the amount of fluoridation in a municipal water system must be carefully measured and controlled.

Solution concentration refers to the quantity of solute dissolved in a specific quantity of solvent or solution. You have already worked with one type of concentration expression. The water solubility graphs include solution concentrations as a mass of a substance dissolved in a given mass of water. Another way to express concentration is with percentages.

Dissolving 5 g of table salt in 95 g of water produces 100 g of solution, or a 5% salt solution (by mass).

$$\left(\frac{5 \text{ g salt}}{100 \text{ g solution}}\right) \times 100\% = 5\%$$

This solution concentration could also be expressed as five parts per hundred of salt, or 5 pph salt. After all, "percent" means parts per hundred parts. To prepare 10 times as much salt solution of the same concentration, you would need to dissolve 50 g of salt in 950 g of water to make 1000 g of solution.

$$\left(\frac{50 \text{ g salt}}{1000 \text{ g solution}}\right) \times 100\% = 5\%$$

This solution can be described as containing 50 parts per thousand of salt (50 ppt salt), or as 5 pph salt.

5 pph = 50 ppt

$$\frac{5}{100} = \frac{50}{1000}$$

For solutions involving much smaller quantities of solute (such as dissolved gases in water), concentration units of parts per million, ppm, are useful. What would be the concentration of the 5% salt solution if it is expressed in ppm? Since 5% of 1 million is 50,000, a 5% salt solution is 50,000 parts per million.

The notion of concentration is part of your daily life. Interpreting recipes, adding antifreeze to an automobile, or mixing a cleaning solution all involve solution concentrations. The following problems will allow you to review the terminology and ideas of solution concentration. These problems will also give you experience with the chemist's view of this concept.

YOUR*TURN*

I.6 Describing Solution Concentrations

Solution concentrations can be used in calculations exactly as illustrated in Your Turn I.5 for solubilities. For example, 25 g of fertilizer is dissolved in 75 g of water. To find the concentration of this solution in grams of fertilizer per 100 g of solution, the arithmetic is as follows:

$$\frac{25 \text{ g fertilizer}}{25 \text{ g fertilizer} + 75 \text{ g water}} = \frac{25 \text{ g fertilizer}}{100 \text{ g solution}} \text{ or 25 pph fertilizer}$$

The concentration of this solution can be expressed as 25 g of fertilizer/ 100 g of solution. The concentration of this solution in mass percent is found as follows, using the total mass of the solution, which is 100 g (25 g of fertilizer + 75 g of water):

$$\left(\frac{25 \text{ g fertilizer}}{100 \text{ g solution}}\right) \times 100\% = 25\%$$

The solution is 25% by mass or the concentration could be given as 25 pph, 250 ppt, or 250,000 ppm.

Consider this second example: If one teaspoon of sucrose, which has a mass of 10 g, is dissolved in 240 g of water, what is the concentration of the solution in grams of sucrose per 100 g of solution (percent sucrose by mass, or pph)? What is the concentration in ppt?

Since there are 10 g of sucrose and 240 g of water, there would be 250 g of solution.

$$\left(\frac{10 \text{ g sucrose}}{250 \text{ g solution}}\right) \times 100\% = 4\% \text{ sucrose by mass (4 pph sucrose)}$$

Since 4% of 1000 is 40, this solution would be 40 ppt sucrose.

1. A level teaspoon of table sugar (sucrose) is dissolved in a cup of water. Identify the solute, the solvent, and the solution.
2. If 17 g of sucrose is dissolved in 183 g of water, what is the concentration of this solution in pph? If 34 g of sucrose is dissolved in 366 g of water, what is the concentration of this solution in pph?
3. What does the term "saturated" mean?
4. A sample of water, in an open vessel, containing 8.8 ppm of dissolved oxygen gas at 22 °C is heated to a higher temperature. Would the concentration of dissolved oxygen in the warmer solution be greater than or less than that in the original solution? Why?

C.3 Oxygen Supply and Demand

All animals need oxygen gas to survive. Although oxygen is part of all water molecules, animals cannot extract oxygen from these molecules. Aquatic organisms such as fish, frogs, insect larvae, and bacteria must have a continuous supply of oxygen gas dissolved in the water in which they live.

Was a shortage of dissolved oxygen gas in the Snake River responsible for the Riverwood fish kill? To explore this possibility, we need to consider many factors. How much oxygen gas (or other substances) will dissolve in water? How does water temperature affect the amount of dissolved oxygen? How much oxygen do various aquatic creatures actually consume?

Some of the oxygen used by fish and other creatures that live in water dissolves directly from the air above the water.

Additional oxygen gas is mixed into the water through **aeration,** which takes place when water plunges over a dam or flows across boulders in a stream, forming a water-air "froth." Oxygen gas is also added to natural waters through **photosynthesis,** the process by which green plants and ocean plankton make sugars

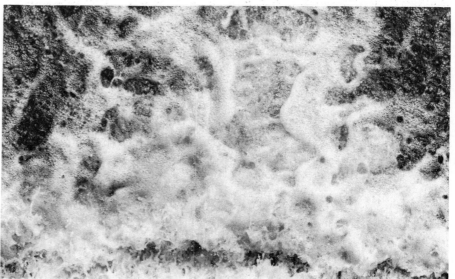

Jon Jacobson

"Frothy" water is a mixture of air and water. This is one way that oxygen gas becomes dissolved in water.

from carbon dioxide and water in the presence of sunlight. During daylight hours, aquatic green plants constantly produce glucose. Oxygen gas is also produced during photosynthesis, and is released from the aquatic green plants to the surrounding water. The overall chemical equation for the formation of glucose ($C_6H_{12}O_6$) and oxygen through photosynthesis is

$$\text{Energy} + 6\,CO_2 + 6\,H_2O \rightarrow C_6H_{12}O_6 + 6\,O_2$$

Organisms living in a water environment continuously compete for the available oxygen. Oxygen-consuming bacteria (called **aerobic bacteria**) feed on solid wastes of larger animals and on their remains after they die. They also feed on certain man-made substances found in the water. Such **biodegradable** substances are broken down to simpler substances by these aerobic bacteria.

A biodegradable substance can be broken down by organisms in the environment.

If the water contains large amounts of biodegradable materials, bacteria thrive and multiply. The resulting bacterial "population explosion" places greater demands on the available dissolved oxygen. Aquatic creatures needing the largest amounts of dissolved oxygen are at greatest risk if the bacterial population gets too large. Their survival is then in question.

Dissolved oxygen in water is accessible to fish but not to humans.

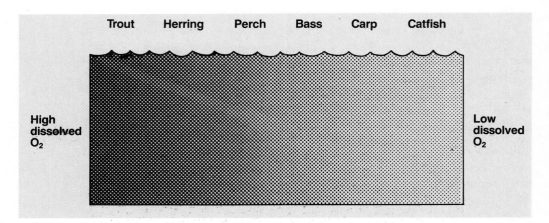

Figure I.20   Dissolved oxygen required for various species of fish.

The minimum concentration of dissolved oxygen (abbreviated DO) needed to support aquatic life depends on the type of animal being considered. Fish cannot live where dissolved oxygen is less than 0.004 grams per 1000 g of solution. This concentration could be expressed as 0.004 parts per thousand (ppt), but it is more conveniently expressed as four parts per million, 4 ppm.

Stop for a moment to think about how small this number is. A concentration as small as four parts per million is difficult to visualize. Assume that a sample of water is represented by a million pennies, stacked one on top of the other. The stack would rise 1.6 kilometers (one mile) high! Four pennies in this stack represent the minimum amount of dissolved oxygen needed for fish to survive. It is a very small amount, but absolutely essential!

If the dissolved oxygen concentration decreases, fish species requiring the most oxygen will migrate to other water regions or die. Such species unfortunately include desirable sport fish, such as brook trout. Figure I.20 summarizes the relative dissolved oxygen requirements of several fish species.

When studying systems in nature, we need to consider many factors. This is particularly true in exploring possible reasons for a community problem such as the fish kill in Riverwood. Can you think of factors that would influence the dissolved oxygen concentration in lakes and rivers in addition to the ones we have considered so far?

C.4 Temperature and Gas Solubility

In Part C.1 we noted that water temperature helps determine the maximum amount of oxygen gas the water can dissolve. And the dissolved oxygen concentration helps to determine water's ability to support oxygen-consuming creatures. Water temperature also affects the amount of oxygen used by organisms living in the water.

Fish are cold-blooded animals. That is, their body temperatures rise and fall with the surrounding water temperature. Body temperature affects the fish's metabolism—the complex series of interrelated chemical reactions that keep the fish alive. The rates or speeds of many chemical reactions are roughly doubled by a 10 °C temperature rise. Cooling a system by 10 °C slows down the rates of such reactions by a similar factor.

If the water temperature increases, the body temperature of a fish will also increase. The chemical reactions inside the fish then speed up and the fish become more active. They eat more and swim faster. As a result, they also use up more dissolved oxygen. The bodily processes of aerobic bacteria become faster in the same way and this increases bacterial oxygen consumption.

Table I.5 *Maximum water temperatures at which fish can survive*

Fish	Temperature	
	°C	°F
Trout	15	59
Perch and pike	24	75
Carp	32	90
Catfish	34	93

During warm summer months, competition for dissolved oxygen among water inhabitants can become quite severe. With rising temperatures, bacteria and fish require more oxygen. But the warmer water is capable of dissolving less oxygen. After a stretch of hot summer days, some streams experience large fish kills, in which hundreds of fish suffocate. In Table I.5 are the maximum water temperatures at which selected fish species can survive.

High lake or river water temperatures can sometimes be traced to human activity. Many industries depend on natural bodies of water for cooling their heat-producing processes. Cool water is drawn into the plant. Devices called "heat exchangers" transfer thermal energy (heat energy) from the processing area to the cooling water. The heated water is then released back into lakes or streams—either directly, or after the water has partially cooled. Industrialists and environmentalists share the concern that released water must not upset the balance of life in natural bodies of water.

Was thermal pollution and the possible depletion of dissolved oxygen responsible for the fish kill? Let's examine the Snake River oxygen concentrations obtained prior to the Riverwood fish kill.

C.5 *You Decide:* Too Much Oxygen or Too Little?

Your teacher will divide the class into groups of four or five students each. Each group will read the following passage and use the information supplied to complete the exercises. When the small groups have finished their work, the class will compare the groups' conclusions.

Joseph Fisker of the County Sanitation Commission has taken measurements of dissolved oxygen in the Snake River for the past 18 months. The Sanitation Commission measures and records dissolved oxygen concentrations to help determine the quality of Snake River water. Fisker takes his daily measurements at 9 A.M. from under the bridge near Riverwood Hospital, at a water depth of one-half meter.

In addition to measuring the dissolved oxygen, Fisker records the water temperature and uses a table to find the concentration of dissolved oxygen that would produce a saturated water solution at that temperature.

Let's examine his Snake River data for last year and also for the summer months this year (Tables I.6 and I.7).

Graphing Hints

Preparing a graph of experimental data often helps in finding regularities or patterns among the values. The information below will help you prepare and interpret such graphs.

Choose your scale so that the graph fills as much of the area of the graph paper as possible.

Table I.6   *Last year's monthly average dissolved oxygen levels, Snake River at Riverwood*

Month	Water temperature (°C)	Dissolved oxygen (ppm)
January	2	12.7
February	3	12.5
March	7	11.0
April	8	10.6
May	9	10.4
June	11	9.8
July	19	9.2
August	20	9.2
September	19	9.2
October	11	10.6
November	7	11.0
December	7	11.0

Table I.7   *This summer's monthly average dissolved oxygen levels, Snake River at Riverwood*

Month	Water temperature (°C)	Dissolved oxygen (ppm)
June	14	10.2
July	16	9.6
August	18	9.6

The scale you select for an axis assigns a given value to each regularly spaced division on the axis. It is not necessary that both axis scales start with a "zero" value, particularly if all the values to be plotted cluster around a narrow range not near zero. For example, if all your plotted values are between 0.50 and 0.60 on the x axis, the x-axis scale can be drawn as shown in Figure I.21.

Label each axis with the quantity and unit being graphed. For example, a scale might be labeled "Temperature (°C)." Give the graph itself a title. Plot each point. Then draw a small circle around each point, like this: ⊙. If you plot more than one curve on the same graph, distinguish the sets of points by enclosing each with a different geometric shape, such as △, ▽, or ⊡.

After the points have been plotted, draw the best smooth line passing through as many points as possible.

1. Graph the average monthly dissolved oxygen levels measured in the Snake River during last year. Label the y axis as the concentration in ppm, and the x axis as the water temperature in °C. Why does the plot have the particular shape it does?

2. On the same graph, plot the dissolved oxygen levels and river temperatures collected during this year's summer months. Distinguish the two sets of points by using different plotting symbols for each set.

3. Compare the average dissolved oxygen concentrations measured in December and June. How can you explain this difference? How can you account for the similar concentrations in March and November?

4. Compare the average dissolved oxygen concentration in August of this year with that of August last year. What reasons might account for the difference?

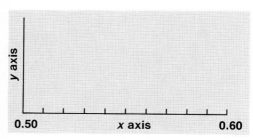

Figure I.21   A possible *x*-axis scale (see text).

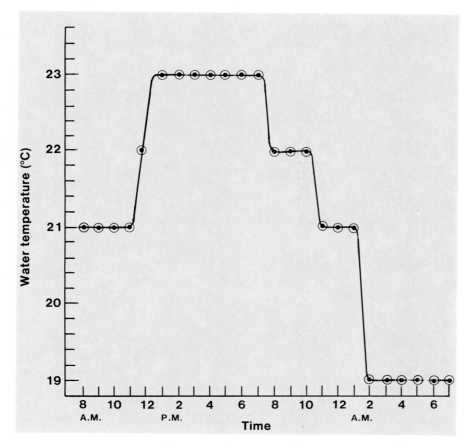

Figure I.22 Changes in water temperature of the Snake River over time.

In September, soon after the fish kill was reported in Riverwood, the County Sanitation Commission invited the Environmental Protection Agency to help with the water analysis. The Environmental Protection Agency sent Marilyn Crocker to make dissolved oxygen measurements in the Snake River hourly for one day. The goal was to detect any short-term changes in either the temperature or the dissolved oxygen concentration. Crocker decided to make the dissolved oxygen measurements at the same location used by Fisker. Her data are given in Table I.8 and plotted in Figures I.22 and I.23.

1. Compare the two graphs. Is any pattern apparent in either graph? Can you explain any pattern that you detect? Compare the dissolved oxygen levels during daylight and nighttime hours. How do you account for this difference?

2. Calculate the average temperature and the average concentration of dissolved oxygen for this one-day period.

3. Since no daily water temperature or dissolved oxygen level was reported for September last year, the only comparison that can be made is between the average of one day in September this year and the monthly average for all of September last year. Is this a valid comparison? Why or why not? Now consider the one-day measurements. Which do you think provides more useful information—the average temperature and dissolved oxygen values or the maximum and minimum values? Give reasons to support your answer.

Table I.8 *Hourly dissolved oxygen values for one day, Snake River at Riverwood*

Time	Water temperature (°C)	Dissolved oxygen (ppm)
8 A.M.	21	9.1
9	21	9.1
10	21	9.1
11	21	9.1
12	22	9.2
1 P.M.	23	9.3
2	23	9.3
3	23	9.2
4	23	9.2
5	23	9.2
6	23	9.2
7	23	9.2
8	22	9.2
9	22	9.2
10	22	9.2
11	21	9.1
12	21	9.1
1 A.M.	21	9.1
2	19	9.0
3	19	9.0
4	19	9.0
5	19	9.0
6	19	9.0
7	19	9.0

Figure I.23 Changes in dissolved oxygen in Snake River over time.

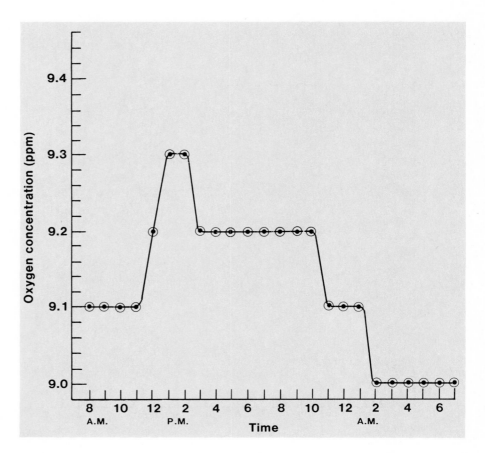

Table I.9 *The concentration of dissolved oxygen needed to produce a saturated water solution at selected temperatures*

Water (°C)	100% Oxygen saturation (ppm)
0	14.6
1	14.2
2	13.9
3	13.5
4	13.2
5	12.8
6	12.5
7	12.2
8	11.9
9	11.6
10	11.3
11	11.1
12	10.8
13	10.6
14	10.4
15	10.2
16	9.9
17	9.7
18	9.5
19	9.3
20	9.2
21	9.0
22	8.8
23	8.7
24	8.5
25	8.4

4. The dissolved oxygen concentrations needed for saturated water solutions at various water temperatures are provided in Table I.9. Use this table to decide whether the dissolved oxygen is below, at, or above the saturation level for each of the measurements in Tables I.6–I.8. You'll also need the following formula:

$$\text{Percent of saturation} = \left(\frac{\text{ppm dissolved oxygen measured}}{\text{ppm dissolved oxygen to saturate solution}}\right) \times 100\%$$

For example, at 8 A.M. during the one-day measurements, the water temperature was 21 °C and the dissolved oxygen concentration was 9.1 ppm. According to the table, 9.0 ppm dissolved oxygen is a saturated solution at 21 °C.

$$\text{Percent of saturation} = \left(\frac{9.1 \text{ ppm}}{9.0 \text{ ppm}}\right) \times 100\% = 101\%$$

So at 8 A.M., the saturation level of dissolved oxygen was 101%—slightly supersaturated.

5. Acceptable and unacceptable dissolved oxygen levels in river water for fish life are given below:

125% or more of saturation:	May be too high for fish species to survive
80–124%:	Excellent for most fish species to survive
60–79%:	Adequate for most fish species to survive
Below 60%:	Too low; most fish species die

Based on this information, is the oxygen concentration in the Snake River within an acceptable range to support fish life?

6. Is the amount of dissolved oxygen in the Snake River a likely cause of the Riverwood fish kill? Explain your answer.

C.6 Acid Contamination

We will now turn to a classification scheme that plays a major role in water quality and the life of aquatic organisms—the acidity or basicity of a water sample.

Acids and **bases** can be identified in the laboratory by certain characteristic properties. For example, the vegetable dye litmus turns blue in a basic solution, and red in an acidic solution. Other vegetable dyes, including red cabbage juice, also have distinctive colors in acid and base solutions.

Many acids are molecular substances. Most have one or more hydrogen atoms that can be detached rather easily. These hydrogen atoms are usually written at the left end of the formula for an acid (see Table I.10). Some compounds lacking the characteristic acid formula still dissolve in water to produce an acidic solution. One of these substances is ammonium chloride, NH_4Cl.

Many bases are ionic substances that include the hydroxide ion (OH^-) in their structures. (This distinguishes bases from alcohols, which have an attached, nonionic, OH group.)

Some materials, such as household ammonia (a water solution of ammonia, NH_3) and baking soda (sodium bicarbonate, $NaHCO_3$) do not contain the OH^- ion but still produce basic water solutions. They do so by reacting with water to generate OH^- ions. Human blood has enough sodium bicarbonate and similar substances dissolved in it to be slightly basic.

Some substances display neither acidic nor basic characteristics. Chemists classify them as **neutral** substances. Water, sodium chloride (NaCl), and table sugar (sucrose, $C_{12}H_{22}O_{11}$) are all neutral compounds.

Table I.10 *Some common acids and bases*

Name	Formula	Use
Acids		
Acetic acid	$HC_2H_3O_2$	In vinegar (typically a 5% solution of acetic acid)
Carbonic acid	H_2CO_3	In carbonated soft drinks
Hydrochloric acid	HCl	Used in removing scale buildup from boilers and for cleaning materials
Nitric acid	HNO_3	Used in the manufacture of fertilizers, dyes, and explosives
Phosphoric acid	H_3PO_4	Added to some soft drinks to give a tart flavor; also used in the manufacture of fertilizers and detergents
Sulfuric acid	H_2SO_4	Largest volume industrial chemical; present in automobile battery fluid
Bases		
Calcium hydroxide	$Ca(OH)_2$	Present in mortar, plaster, and cement; used in paper pulping and dehairing animal hides
Magnesium hydroxide	$Mg(OH)_2$	Active ingredient in milk of magnesia
Potassium hydroxide	KOH	Used in the manufacture of some liquid soaps
Sodium hydroxide	NaOH	A major industrial chemical; active ingredient in some drain and oven cleaners; used to convert animal fats into soap

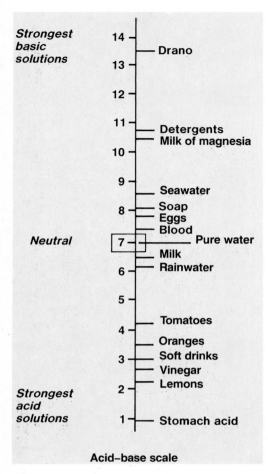

Figure I.24   The pH of some common materials.

When an acid and a base react with each other the characteristic properties of both substances are destroyed. Such a reaction is called **neutralization.**

The acidic, basic, or neutral character of a solution can be measured and reported using the pH scale. pH values commonly range from 1 to 14, although some very basic or acidic solutions may be outside this range. At 25 °C, a pH of 7 indicates a neutral solution. pH values of less than 7 indicate acids; the lower the pH the more acidic the solution. Solutions with pH values greater than 7 are basic; the higher the pH the more basic the solution. The pH values of some common materials are shown in Figure I.24.

Rainwater is naturally slightly acidic. This is because the atmosphere includes substances—carbon dioxide (CO_2) for one—that produce an acidic solution when dissolved in water. When acidic or basic contamination in a body of water poses problems, it is usually due to substances or wastes from human activities such as coal mining or industrial processing.

Most fish can tolerate a pH range from 5 to 9 in lake or river water. Serious fishermen look for freshwater sport fish in water between a pH of 6.5 and 8.2. The pH measurements in the Snake River near Riverwood revealed that the pH of the stream was well within normal limits at the time of the fish kill, ranging from 6.7 to 6.9. Thus, we can dismiss an abnormal pH as the cause of the fish kill.

Our next major candidate for concern in Snake River contamination will be the so-called heavy metal ions. The following overview explains the idea of ions and ionic compounds.

C.7   Ions and Ionic Compounds

We noted earlier that ions are electrically charged particles, some positively charged and others negatively charged. Positive ions are called cations and negative ions are called anions. An ion can be a charged individual atom such as Na^+ or Cl^-, or a group of bonded atoms such as NO_3^-, which possess an electrical charge.

Solid sodium chloride, NaCl, consists of equal numbers of positive sodium ions and negative chloride ions in 3-dimensional networks that form crystals (Figure I.25). An ionic compound such as calcium chloride, $CaCl_2$ (road deicing salt) presents a similar picture. However, unlike sodium ions, calcium ions (Ca^{2+}) each contain a charge of 2+. Table I.11 lists the formulas and names of common positive and negative ions.

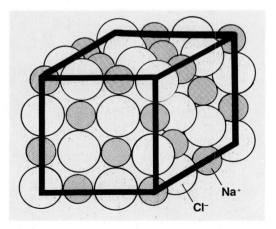

Figure I.25   Sodium chloride crystal.

The name of an ionic compound is composed of two parts. First the positive ion is named, then the negative ion. As the table suggests, many positive ions have the same name as their original elements. Negative ions composed of a single atom, however, have the last few letters of the element names changed to the suffix *-ide*. For example, the negative ion formed from fluorine (F) is fluor*ide*. KF is thus potassium fluoride.

Formulas for ionic compounds can be easily written, if a simple rule is followed. The correct formula contains the fewest positive and negative ions needed to make the total electrical charge zero. In sodium chloride the ion charges are 1+ and 1−. Since one ion of each type results in a total charge of zero, the formula for sodium chloride must be NaCl.

When the two ion charges do not add up to zero, add ions of either type until the charges fully cancel. In calcium chloride, one Ca^{2+} ion has a charge of 2+. Each chloride ion has a charge of 1−; two of these are necessary to equal 2−. Thus two chloride ions are needed for every calcium ion. The subscript 2 written after chlorine's symbol satisfies this requirement—thus we have $CaCl_2$.

Formulas for compounds containing **polyatomic** (many atom) ions follow this same basic rule. However, if more than one polyatomic ion is needed to bring the total charge to zero, the polyatomic ion formula is enclosed in parentheses before the needed subscript is added. Ammonium sulfate is composed of the positive ammonium ion (NH_4^+) and the negative sulfate ion (SO_4^{2-}). Two ammonium ions with a total charge of 2+ are needed to match the 2− charge of sulfate. Thus the formula for ammonium sulfate is written $(NH_4)_2SO_4$. The following exercises will help you recognize ionic compounds and practice naming and writing formulas for them.

Debi Stambaugh

Sodium chloride crystals at 100× magnification—note the characteristic cubic geometry of each crystal.

Table I.11   *Common ions*

Cations

+1 Charge		+2 Charge		+3 Charge	
Formula	Name	Formula	Name	Formula	Name
Na^+	Sodium	Mg^{2+}	Magnesium	Al^{3+}	Aluminum
K^+	Potassium	Ca^{2+}	Calcium	Fe^{3+}	Iron(III)*
NH_4^+	Ammonium	Ba^{2+}	Barium		
		Zn^{2+}	Zinc		
		Cd^{2+}	Cadmium		
		Hg^{2+}	Mercury(II)*		
		Cu^{2+}	Copper(II)*		
		Pb^{2+}	Lead(II)*		
		Fe^{2+}	Iron(II)*		

Anions

−1 Charge		−2 Charge		−3 Charge	
Formula	Name	Formula	Name	Formula	Name
F^-	Fluoride	O^{2-}	Oxide	PO_4^{3-}	Phosphate
Cl^-	Chloride	S^{2-}	Sulfide		
Br^-	Bromide				
I^-	Iodide				
NO_3^-	Nitrate	SO_4^{2-}	Sulfate		
NO_2^-	Nitrite	SO_3^{2-}	Sulfite		
OH^-	Hydroxide	SeO_4^{2-}	Selenate		
HCO_3^-	Hydrogen carbonate (bicarbonate)	CO_3^{2-}	Carbonate		

*Some metals are able to form ions with one charge under certain conditions and a different charge under different conditions. To specify the charge for these metal ions, Roman numerals are used in parentheses after the name of the metal.

YOUR*TURN*

I.7 Ionic Compounds

In writing the formula for an ionic compound, first decide how many of each ion are needed to make their total charges add to zero. Then write the formula for the positive ion followed by the formula for the anion. Add any needed subscripts and parentheses.

Prepare a chart describing the composition of each ionic compound described below. Your chart should have four columns, as shown in the sample. Refer to the table of common anions and cations as needed to complete this exercise.

Data table

	Cation	Anion	Formula	Name
1.	K^+	Cl^-	KCl	Potassium chloride

(Complete this chart for substances 2 through 10.)

1. Potassium chloride is the primary ingredient in "lite salt," designed for people on low-sodium diets.
2. $CaSO_4$ is a component of plaster.
3. A substance composed of Ca^{2+} and PO_4^{3-} ions is found in some brands of phosphorus-containing fertilizer. This substance is also a major component of bones and teeth.
4. Ammonium nitrate, a rich source of nitrogen, is often used in fertilizer mixtures.
5. Iron(III) chloride finds use in some water-purification processes.
6. $Al_2(SO_4)_3$ is another chemical used to purify water in some municipalities.
7. Baking soda is an ionic substance composed of sodium ions and hydrogen carbonate ions.
8. Milk of magnesia is known to chemists as magnesium hydroxide.
9. A compound composed of Fe^{3+} and O^{2-} is a principal component of rust.
10. Limestone and marble are both forms of the substance calcium carbonate.

C.8 Dissolving Ionic Compounds

The dissolving of a substance in water—either from the Snake River or from the tap in your kitchen—is like a tug of war. A solid substance will dissolve if its particles are attracted strongly enough to water molecules to release them from the crystal. To dissolve, attractive forces between particles at the solid crystal surface must be overcome so that the ions separate from the crystal and move into the solvent.

Water molecules are attracted to the ions at the surface of an ionic solid. Water molecules have both an electrically negative region (the oxygen end) and an electrically positive region (the hydrogen end). The water molecule's negative oxygen end is attracted to the crystal's positive ions. The positive hydrogen ends of other water molecules are attracted to the negative ions. When an ionic crystal dissolves in water, the ions leave the crystal and become surrounded by water

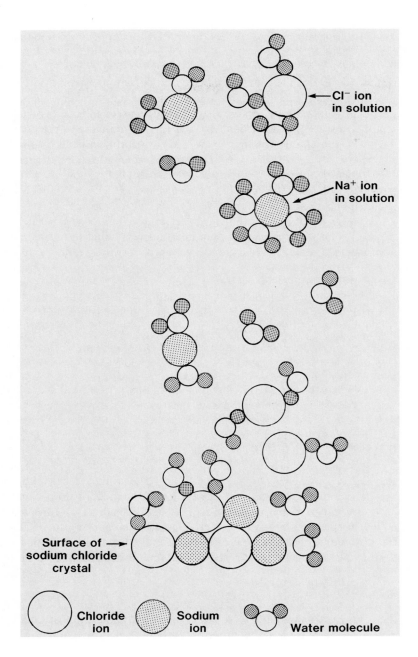

Figure I.26   Sodium chloride dissolving in water.

molecules. That is, they dissolve in the water. Figure I.26 illustrates such a dissolving process. If the attractions among ions in the crystal are sufficiently strong, an ionic substance may be only slightly soluble in water.

With this background on ions in solution, you are now prepared to consider whether certain dissolved metal ions were responsible for the Riverwood fish kill.

C.9 Heavy Metal Ion Contamination

Many ions of metallic elements, including iron (Fe), potassium (K), calcium (Ca), and magnesium (Mg) are essential to human health. As much as 10% of our requirements for these elements is obtained from minerals dissolved in drinking water. Other metallic elements, termed heavy metals because in general their atoms are more massive than those of the necessary metallic elements, can also dissolve in water as ions. The heavy metal ions of greatest concern are those of lead (Pb), mercury (Hg), and cadmium (Cd). Even in small amounts, these elements are toxic. Their ions attach themselves to proteins in our bodies and thereby prohibit the proteins from functioning properly. The effects of heavy metal poisoning are severe. They include damage to the nervous system, kidneys, and liver, probable mental retardation, and even death. Lead, mercury, and cadmium are particularly hazardous because they are widely used, and can build up in the food chain. They become more dangerous as they accumulate in the body.

These metal ions enter streams and rivers primarily in wastewater released by industry and (in the case of lead) from leaded gasoline automobile exhaust. Even when the original heavy metal concentration is as low as two to four parts per billion, these metals can become concentrated within the bodies of fish and shellfish. These aquatic animals are then hazardous to eat.

Heavy metal ions are difficult to detect in water in low concentrations. Their removal from water is very difficult and thus very expensive. The most practical approach is to prevent them from entering waterways in the first place.

Lead (Pb)

Lead is probably the heavy metal most familiar to you. Most lead in our environment comes from human activities. Lead and lead compounds have been used in pottery, automobile electrical storage batteries, solder, cooking vessels, pesticides, and household paints. One compound of lead and oxygen, red lead (Pb_3O_4) is the primary ingredient of paint that protects bridges and other steel structures from corrosion.

Romans constructed lead water pipes more than 2000 years ago, some of which are still in working condition. Lead water pipes were used in this country in the early 1800s, but were replaced by iron pipes after the discovery that water transported through lead pipes could cause lead poisoning. There is a suspicion that lead poisoning may have contributed to the fall of the Roman Empire. Today we use copper or plastic water pipes in our homes, although some older homes may have lead water pipes and shower pans. The symbol for lead, Pb, comes from the Latin name *plumbum,* also the source of the modern word "plumber."

A molecular compound of lead, tetraethyl lead, $(C_2H_5)_4Pb$, has long been added to automobile gasoline to produce a better burning fuel. Unfortunately, the lead enters the atmosphere through auto exhaust. In fact, most of the lead to which we are currently exposed comes from leaded gasoline. As activity at any filling station will confirm, unleaded gasoline is becoming increasingly more common.

On average, U.S. drinking water contains dissolved lead ions at about half the U.S. Environmental Protection Agency allowable limit of 0.05 ppm. However, 1.4% of water systems tested recently exceeded this limit.

Fortunately, most lead we take in is usually excreted in urine fast enough that blood levels are not dangerously high, except in cases of prolonged exposure to high lead concentrations.

Mercury (Hg)

Mercury is the only metallic element that is a liquid at room temperature. In fact, its symbol comes from the Latin word *hydrargyrum,* meaning quick silver or liquid silver. Mercury has a number of important uses, some due specifically to its liquid state. Mercury, an excellent electrical conductor, is used in "silent" light switches. It also is found in fever and weather thermometers, thermostats, mercury-vapor street lamps, fluorescent light bulbs, and in some paints. As a pure liquid element, mercury is not particularly dangerous. However, its vapor is quite hazardous to health. Since liquid mercury slowly evaporates, you should avoid direct exposure to it.

Some mercury compounds are useful as antiseptics, fungicides, and pesticides. You may have used mercurochrome on a wound to kill bacteria. The toxicity of mercury compounds to bacteria extends also to humans. In the 18th and 19th centuries, mercury(II) nitrate, $Hg(NO_3)_2$, was used in making felt hats.

After absorbing this compound for many years, hatmakers often suffered from mercury poisoning. Symptoms included numbness, staggered walk, tunnel vision, and brain damage, giving rise to the expression "mad as a hatter."

Organic compounds containing the methylmercury ion (CH_3Hg^+) are highly poisonous. (Organic compounds are composed of carbon atoms attached to other atoms, predominantly hydrogen.) A danger to humans can arise if mercury-containing industrial wastes in acidic river-bottom sediments are converted by **anaerobic bacteria** (bacteria that do not require oxygen) to these highly toxic compounds. In the late 1950s, villagers near Minamata Bay, Japan, suffered serious brain and nerve damage, and many died from eating fish contaminated with methylmercury formed from discharges from a nearby chemical plant.

Fortunately, the concentration of mercury ion in water in the United States is usually quite low. The danger of mercury poisoning from aqueous sources is more a local problem where waste is discharged into acidic waters.

Cadmium (Cd)

Cadmium has properties similar to zinc (Zn); the two are usually found together. Galvanized steel is electrically plated with zinc; it normally contains about 1% cadmium. Cadmium is used in photography and in the manufacture of paints; it is also a component of nickel-cadmium (NiCad) batteries and certain special solders.

Cadmium is a very toxic element. Some cases of cadmium poisoning have been traced to cadmium-plated food utensils. In low doses it produces headaches, coughing, and vomiting. With extended exposure, cadmium ion can accumulate in the liver and kidneys, damaging them irreversibly. The metal ion may also replace some bone calcium, resulting in painful bone disorders. This form of cadmium poisoning struck several hundred people in northern Japan in the 1960s; zinc mine drainage had added cadmium ion to the local river.

Cadmium creates greater problems when it is inhaled than when it is ingested. Tobacco smoke is the major source of inhaled cadmium. In this country, most drinking water contains very little cadmium. However, the National Academy of Sciences reported in 1978 that our rivers contain an average of 9.5 ppb (parts per billion) of cadmium ion, close to the U.S. Environmental Protection Agency limit of 10 ppb. In addition, cadmium ions can leach from galvanized water pipes found in older homes if the water is slightly acidic.

The low cadmium ion concentrations found in most drinking water supplies seem to cause no harm, although some evidence connects such concentrations to high blood pressure. Caution is certainly justified, however, since cadmium taken into the body remains there. Thus bodily cadmium levels increase slowly year by year.

C.10 *You Decide:* Did Heavy Metal Ions Kill the Fish?

When the Riverwood fish kill occurred, the County Sanitation Commission, together with the EPA and other scientists involved in analyzing the river water, gathered data on the concentrations of specific ions in Snake River water. Table I.12 contains a list of the ions EPA officials decided to measure in the Snake River as possible causes of the fish kill. The table also includes levels of these selected ions measured six months ago, together with their present levels, and EPA limits for freshwater aquatic and human life.

1. Which ions have decreased in concentration in the Snake River during the last six months?
2. Which ions have increased in concentration during the last six months?

Jon Jacobson

Chemists collecting water samples.

Table I.12   *Ion concentrations in the Snake River*

Ion	Concentration six months ago (ppm)	Present concentration (ppm)	EPA limit for freshwater aquatic life (ppm)	EPA limit for humans (ppm)
Arsenic	0.0002	0.0002	0.44	0.05
Cadmium	0.0001	0.001	0.0015	0.01
Lead	0.01	0.02	0.074	0.05
Mercury	0.0004	0.0001	0.0041	0.05
Selenium	0.004	0.008	0.26	0.01
Chloride	52.4	51.6	No limit	No limit
Nitrate	2.1	1.9	No limit	No limit
Sulfate	34.0	35.1	No limit	No limit

3. Calculate an aquatic life "risk" factor for the ions in the Snake River that have increased in concentration. Use this equation:

$$\text{"Risk" factor} = \frac{\text{Present concentration of ion}}{\text{EPA concentration limit}}$$

Any ion having a risk factor larger than one exceeds the EPA limit for freshwater aquatic life. Among ions below the EPA limit, the ion with the highest risk factor is closest to exceeding the EPA maximum value.

4. Which ion has the highest risk factor for freshwater aquatic life?
5. Calculate the risk factor for human life for ions that have increased in concentration.
6. Do you think the residents of Riverwood should be concerned about the increased concentration of ions in relation to their effect on human health? Why or why not?
7. How could Riverwood citizens find out if the present concentration of ions is cause for concern?

Analysis of a more extensive set of Snake River ion concentration data convinced County Sanitation Commission and EPA representatives that the fish kill was not due to excessively high concentrations of any hazardous ions. So the Riverwood mystery continues!

In addition to dissolved ionic substances, another class of solutes could serve as the source of Riverwood's water problem. The presence of certain molecular substances in the Snake River water might provide the answer to the fish kill. These are the next focus of our investigation.

C.11   Molecular Substances in the River

Most molecules are composed of atoms of nonmetallic elements. These atoms are held together by the attraction of the nucleus of one atom for electrons of another atom. However, the difference in electron attraction between the two atoms is too small for electrons to be transferred from one atom to another. Thus ions are not formed, as often happens when metallic and nonmetallic atoms interact.

Unlike ionic substances, which occur as solid crystals at normal conditions, a molecular substance may be a solid, liquid, or a gas. Molecules of substances like oxygen (O_2) and carbon dioxide (CO_2) have little attraction for each other; these substances are gases under normal conditions. Substances like alcohol (C_2H_5OH) and water (H_2O) have larger between-molecule attractions; these are liquids under normal conditions. Other molecular substances such as table sugar (sucrose, $C_{12}H_{22}O_{11}$) have even greater molecular attraction and occur as solids.

The attraction of a substance's molecules for each other compared to their attraction for water molecules helps determine how soluble the substance will be in water. But what causes these attractions? The distribution of electrical charge within the molecules has a great deal to do with it.

We have already observed that the "oxygen end" of a water molecule is electrically negative compared to its positive "hydrogen end." That is, water molecules are polar. Such charge separation is found in many molecules whose atoms have differing attraction for electrons.

The more polar a molecular substance is, the more waterlike it is and the more soluble it will be in water. In essence, "like dissolves like." "Dissolving" for molecular substances is similar to dissolving for ionic solutes, except instead of ions we have polar molecules interacting with solvent water molecules.

One implication of "like dissolves like" is that solvents composed of **nonpolar** molecules are ineffective in dissolving ionic or even polar molecular substances. However, they are very good solvents for other nonpolar substances. For example, nonpolar cleaning fluids are used to "dry clean" clothes. They readily dissolve away nonpolar body oils found in the fabric.

A nonpolar molecule has an even distribution of electric charge.

Were dissolved molecular contaminants present in the Snake River at the time of the fish kill? Most likely yes, in some amount. Whether they killed the fish is another question, however. That depends on what solutes were present and at what concentrations. This in turn depends on how the solutes interact with the polar solvent, water.

In the following laboratory activity we will look at some typical molecular and ionic substances and compare their solubilities in water and in a nonpolar solvent.

C.12 Laboratory Activity: Polar and Nonpolar Solvents

Getting Ready

In this laboratory activity you will investigate the solubilities of seven solutes in two different solvents—water (H_2O), a polar solvent, and vegetable oil, a nonpolar solvent. Your observations will be interpreted in terms of the "like dissolves like" guideline introduced in Part C.11.

Direct contact of chemicals with the skin should be avoided. Mix the contents of the test tubes in this activity as illustrated in Figure I.15. Also, transfer the solid solute samples on the end of a spatula or wooden splint. Be especially cautious in handling iodine, which can irritate the skin and eyes.

In your laboratory notebook, prepare a data table as illustrated below. This table lists the names and chemical formulas of the seven solutes.

Data table		
	Solubility in	
Solute	**Water (H_2O)**	**Vegetable oil**
Urea [$CO(NH_2)_2$]		
Iodine (I_2)		
Ammonium chloride (NH_4Cl)		
Naphthalene ($C_{10}H_8$)		
Copper(II) sulfate ($CuSO_4$)		
Ethanol (C_2H_5OH)		
Sodium chloride ($NaCl$)		

Procedure

1. Using a graduated cylinder, measure and pour 5 mL of water into a test tube. Mark the height of this volume on your test tube with a marking pencil. Mark the other six test tubes at the same height. This will make it easy to measure out 5-mL volumes without using the graduated cylinder.
2. Add 5 mL of water to each test tube.
3. Test the solubility of each of the seven solutes in water by adding a different solute to each test tube. For liquid solutes, add 5 mL. For solid solutes, add a sample the size of a matchhead, using a spatula or a wooden splint to transfer the solid. Be sure to use a wooden splint for iodine and discard the splint after use.
4. Gently mix the contents of each test tube by firmly tapping the test tube as illustrated in Figure I.15.
5. Judge the extent to which each solute dissolved in the polar solvent water. Record your observations using the following key: S = soluble; SS = slightly soluble; IN = insoluble.
6. Discard the contents of the test tubes, following your teacher's directions.
7. Wash and thoroughly dry the test tubes.
8. Repeat steps 3 through 7, substituting the nonpolar vegetable oil for water.

Questions

1. Which solutes were more soluble in water than in vegetable oil?
2. Which were more soluble in vegetable oil than in water?
3. Explain the observations summarized in your answers to Questions 1 and 2.
4. Did any solutes produce unexpected results? If so, briefly describe these results. Can you suggest reasons for this behavior?

PART C
SUMMARY *QUESTIONS*

1. Explain why a bottle of warm soda fizzes more than a bottle of cold soda when opened.
2. Explain the phrase "like dissolves like."
3. Why does table salt (NaCl) dissolve in water but not in cooking oil?
4. From each pair below, select the water source containing the greater amount of dissolved oxygen. Try to give a reason for each choice.
   a. A river with rapids or a quiet lake?
   b. A lake in spring or the same lake in summer?
   c. A lake with only catfish or a lake containing trout?
5. Refer to Figures I.18 and I.19 to answer the following questions.
   a. How much potassium nitrate, KNO_3, must be dissolved in 100 mL of water at 50 °C to make a saturated solution?
   b. Is a solution of potassium nitrate that has 50 g dissolved in 100 mL of water at 30 °C saturated, unsaturated, or supersaturated? How would you describe the same solution if it were heated to 60 °C?

Since the density of water is 1.00 g/mL, 1 g H_2O = 1 mL H_2O.

6. Name the following compounds.
   a. $NaNO_3$ (used in meat processing)
   b. $MgSO_4$ (Epsom salt)
   c. Al_2O_3 (aluminum "rust" which adheres to an aluminum surface and protects the underlying metal)
   d. $BaSO_4$ (used in making X rays of the gastrointestinal system)
7. A 35 g sample of ethanol is dissolved in 115 g of water. What is the concentration of the ethanol, expressed as g per 100 g solution?
8. What are heavy metals? Why are they such a problem in the environment? Name some general effects of heavy-metal poisoning.

EXTENDING *YOUR KNOWLEDGE (OPTIONAL)*

• Organic pesticides such as DDT can become concentrated in the fatty tissues of animals. Explain this effect using the "like dissolves like" rule. Why don't water-soluble substances become concentrated in fatty tissues in a similar way?
• Prepare a report on the biological magnification (or concentration) of DDT in food chains, and the banning of DDT from use in this country.

Fish Kill Remains a Mystery

In a brief communication to the *Herald*, Dr. Harold Schmidt, the EPA consultant called in to help investigate the recent Snake River fish kill, reported more negative results. Apparently, extensive chemical tests failed to find unusual levels of any organic compounds in the water. Thus, pesticides, fertilizers, and industrial wastes have been ruled out as culprits in the mysterious death of the fish. More details will be reported as they become available.

Monty Clark, N.Y. State Dept. of Environmental Conservation

Monitoring a river for water pollution.

D WATER PURIFICATION AND TREATMENT

By now you probably share an interest with Riverwood residents in resolving the mystery of the Snake River fish kill. Of course, the quality of your own community's water supply is of greater immediate importance. In this unit we will temporarily leave Riverwood to discuss how natural and manmade purification systems can together ensure the safety of community water supplies, including those in your own community.

Until late last century, Americans obtained water from local ponds, wells, and rainwater holding tanks. Wastewater was discarded in dry wells, leaching cesspools (pits lined with broken stone), or was just dumped on the ground. Human wastes were usually thrown into holes or receptacles lined with brick or stone. Periodically, these were either replaced or emptied.

By 1880, about one-quarter of urban households in the United States had flush toilets; municipal sewer systems were soon constructed. However, as recently as 1909, nearly all sewer wastes were released without treatment into streams and lakes from which others drew their water supplies. Many believed natural waters would purify themselves indefinitely.

As you might expect, waterborne diseases increased. Filtration and chlorination of municipal water supplies soon began. However, municipal sewage, the combined waterborne wastes of a community, remained generally untreated. Today, given the quantity of sewage generated and greater recreational use of natural waters, sewage treatment has become essential.

To act intelligently about water use—whether in Riverwood or in our own communities—we need to know how clean our water is, how it can be brought up to the quality we require, and how waterborne community wastes can be treated. It should not take an emergency to focus our attention on these issues. Let's look first at the ways in which water is naturally purified.

D.1 Natural Water Purification

We noted that many early community leaders believed natural waters would, if left alone, purify themselves. Under some conditions they do!

Nature's water cycle, the hydrologic cycle, was briefly described in Part A.6. Recall that thermal energy from the sun causes water to evaporate from oceans and other water sources, leaving behind dissolved minerals and other substances carried by the water. Water vapor rises, condenses to tiny droplets in clouds, and eventually falls as rain or snow depending on the temperature. It then joins surface water or seeps into the ground to become groundwater. Eventually groundwater may become surface water and evaporate again, continuing the cycle.

Raindrops and snowflakes are nature's purest form of water, containing only dissolved atmospheric gases. Unfortunately, human activities release a number of harmful gases into the air, making present-day rain less pure than it was in earlier times.

When raindrops strike the Earth, water quickly loses its relative purity. Organic substances deposited by living species become suspended or dissolved in the rainwater. A few centimeters below the soil surface, bacteria "feed" on these substances, converting the organic materials to carbon dioxide, water, and other simple compounds. These bacteria thus help re-purify the water.

As it seeps deeper into the ground, water usually passes through gravel, sand, and even rock. Your first laboratory activity in this unit (Part A.2) demonstrated how gravel and sand can act as a water filter. In the ground, bacteria and any suspended matter in the water are removed by such filtration.

In summary, three basic steps make up nature's water purification system:

- First is **evaporation,** followed by **condensation.** These processes remove nearly all dissolved substances.
- Next is bacterial action. Microscopic organisms convert dissolved organic contaminants to a few simple compounds.
- Finally comes filtration through sand and gravel. This process removes nearly all suspended matter from the water.

Given appropriate conditions, we could depend solely on nature to purify our water. "Pure" rainwater gives us our best supply of clean water. If water seeping through the ground encounters enough bacteria for a long enough time, all natural organic contaminants can be removed. Flowing over sufficient sand and gravel will remove suspended matter. However, nature's system cannot be overloaded if it is to work well.

If groundwater is slightly acidic (pH less than 7) and filters through rocks containing slightly soluble magnesium and calcium minerals, a problem arises. Chemical reactions with these minerals may add substances to the water rather than removing them. In this case the water may contain too high a concentration of dissolved minerals. Nature does not always produce water as pure as we want.

Sometimes water contains an excess of calcium (Ca^{2+}), magnesium (Mg^{2+}), or iron(III) (Fe^{3+}) ions. This water does not form a soapy lather easily and is therefore called **hard water.** Because hard water can cause a variety of problems (described in detail later), it is important to remove these ions from solution. This process of removing Ca^{2+}, Mg^{2+}, or Fe^{3+} from water is called **water softening** and results in water that readily forms a lather with soap.

D.2 Laboratory Activity: Water Softening

Getting Ready

In this laboratory activity you will explore several ways of softening water. You will be supplied with a sample of hard water containing Ca^{2+} ions. You will compare the effectiveness of three water treatments for removing the calcium ion: sand filtration, treatment with Calgon, and treatment with an ion-exchange resin.

Calgon (which contains sodium hexametaphosphate, $Na_6P_6O_{18}$) and similar commercial products "remove" hard-water cations by causing them to become part of larger soluble anions, for example:

$$2\ Ca^{2+}(aq) \quad + \quad P_6O_{18}{}^{6-}(aq) \quad \longrightarrow \quad Ca_2(P_6O_{18})^{2-}(aq)$$

Calcium ion from hard water	Hexametaphosphate ion from Calgon	Calcium hexametaphosphate ion

Calgon also contains sodium carbonate, which softens water by removing hard water cations as precipitates such as calcium carbonate, as shown below. The solid particles of calcium carbonate are washed away with the rinse water.

Another water-softening method involves a process called "ion exchange." Hard water is passed through an ion-exchange resin like those found in home water-softening units. Hardness-causing cations are retained on the ion-exchange resin, and cations that do not cause hardness (usually Na^+) are released from the resin into the water to take their place. We will consider these softening procedures in greater detail after this laboratory activity.

Two tests will be used to determine whether or not the water has been "softened." The first involves the reaction between calcium cation and carbonate anion (added as sodium carbonate, Na_2CO_3, solution), which results in the formation of a precipitate of calcium carbonate:

$$Ca^{2+}(aq) \quad + \quad CO_3^{2-}(aq) \quad \longrightarrow \quad CaCO_3(s)$$

| Calcium ion in hard water | Carbonate ion from sodium carbonate | Calcium carbonate precipitate |

The second is the effect of adding soap to the water to form a lather.

In your laboratory notebook, prepare a data table as illustrated below:

Data table	Filter paper	Filter paper and sand	Filter paper and Calgon	Filter paper and ion-exchange resin
Reaction with sodium carbonate (Na_2CO_3)				
Degree of cloudiness (turbidity) with Ivory brand soap				

Procedure

1. Prepare the equipment as pictured in Figure I.27. Lower the tip of each funnel into a test tube supported in a test tube rack.
2. Fold four pieces of filter paper; insert one in each funnel. Number the funnels 1 to 4.

Figure I.27   Filtration apparatus.

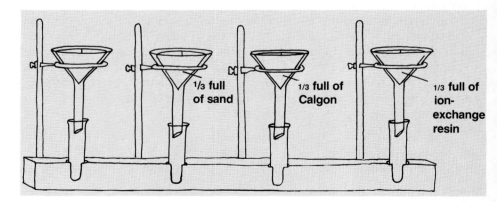

3. Funnel No. 1 serves as a control and should contain only the filter paper. (Hard water ions in solution definitely will not be removed by filter paper.) Fill funnel No. 2 one-third full of sand. Fill funnel No. 3 one-third full of Calgon. Fill funnel No. 4 one-third full of ion-exchange resin.

4. Pour about 5 mL of hard water into each of the four funnels. Do not pour any water over the top of the filter paper or between the filter paper and the funnel wall.

5. Collect the filtrates in the test tubes. *Note:* The Calgon filtrate may appear blue due to other additives in the softener. This will cause no problem. However, if the filtrate appears cloudy, some Calgon powder may have passed through the filter paper. In this case, replace the filter paper with a new piece of filter paper and re-filter the liquid in the test tube.

6. Add 10 drops of sodium carbonate (Na_2CO_3) solution to each filtrate. Does a precipitate form? Record your observations. A cloudy precipitate is evidence that the Ca^{2+} ion (a hard-water cation) was not removed.

7. Discard the test tube solutions. Clean the test tubes thoroughly with tap water and rinse with distilled water.

8. Pour another 5-mL hard water sample through each funnel, collecting the filtrates in clean test tubes. Each filtrate should be the same volume.

9. Add a piece of Ivory brand soap no larger than a pea to each test tube. The pieces should be as nearly the same in size as possible.

10. Crush the soap into smaller pieces with a stirring rod. Stir gently. Wipe the stirring rod before inserting into another test tube.

11. Compare the cloudiness (turbidity) of the four soap solutions. Record your observations. The greater the cloudiness (turbidity), the greater the amount of soap that dispersed. The amount of soap that dispersed determines the cleaning effectiveness of the solution.

12. Shake each test tube vigorously as shown by your teacher. The greater the height of the suds that form, the softer the water. Measure the height of the suds in each test tube and record your observations.

Questions

1. Which was the most effective water-softening method? Suggest why this worked best.

2. What relationship can you find between the amount of hard-water ion (Ca^{2+}) remaining in the filtrate and the solubility of the Ivory brand soap?

3. What effect does this relationship have on the cleansing action of the soap?

4. Explain the advertising claim that Calgon prevents "bathtub ring." Base your answer on observations made in this laboratory activity.

D.3 Hard Water and Water Softening

In the just-completed laboratory activity you investigated several ways to soften hard water, using the calcium ion (Ca^{2+}) as a typical hard-water ion. River water usually contains low concentrations of iron(III), calcium, and magnesium ions. Groundwater, flowing over rock formations containing limestone, chalk, and other calcium-, magnesium-, and iron-containing minerals, often has much higher concentrations of these hard-water ions (see Figure I.28 and Table I.13).

Jon Jacobson

The horizontal band is bathtub scum. The vertical stains are likely mineral deposits from dripping water.

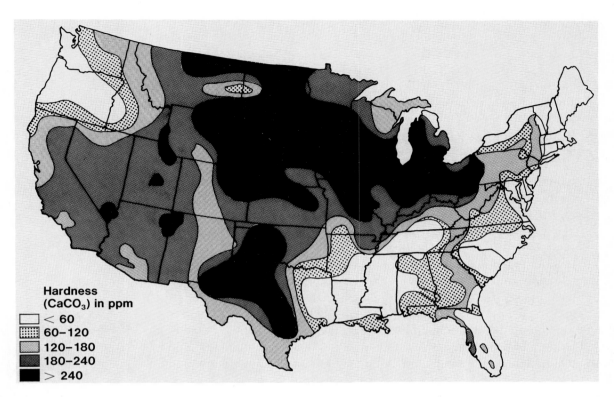

Figure I.28   Hard water areas of the United States.

Table I.13   *Some minerals contributing to hard water*

Mineral	Chemical name	Chemical formula
Limestone or chalk	Calcium carbonate	$CaCO_3$
Magnesite	Magnesium carbonate	$MgCO_3$
Gypsum	Calcium sulfate	$CaSO_4 \cdot 2H_2O$
Dolomite	Calcium carbonate and magnesium carbonate combination	$CaCO_3 \cdot MgCO_3$

What household problems are caused by hard water? Questions 2 and 3 in the laboratory activity addressed some of these. First, hard water interferes with the cleaning action of soaps. When soap mixes with soft water, it disperses to form a cloudy solution complete with a sudsy layer on top. However, when soap is added to hard water, the hard-water ions react with the soap to form insoluble compounds (precipitates) which appear as solid flakes or a sticky scum—thus the "bathtub ring"! This precipitated soap is not available for cleaning. Worse yet, the scum leaves deposits on clothes, skin, and hair. The substance formed by soap and a hard-water calcium ion is shown in Figure I.29.

If hydrogen carbonate (bicarbonate, HCO_3^-) ions are present in hard water, boiling the water causes solid calcium carbonate ($CaCO_3$) to form. This rids the water of undesirable calcium ions and thus softens it. The solid calcium carbonate, however, forms a scale inside tea kettles and household hot water heaters. This rock-like scale (composed of the same substance found in marble and limestone) acts as thermal insulation. Heat flow to the water is partially blocked, and more time and energy are required to heat water to the desired temperature. Such deposits can also form in home water pipes. In older homes where this has occurred the flow of water can be greatly reduced.

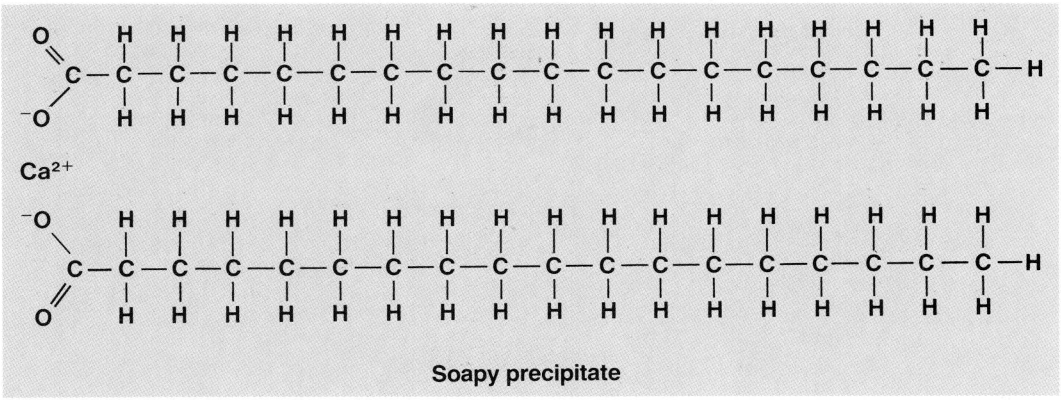

Soapy precipitate

Figure I.29 A typical scum, composed of long chains of carbon atoms with attached hydrogen atoms and negatively charged oxygen at one end.

Fortunately, as you found in the laboratory activity, some of the calcium, magnesium, and iron(III) ions can be removed from the water to soften it. Adding sodium carbonate to the water, as you did in the laboratory activity, was an early method for softening water. The sodium carbonate, known as washing soda, was added to the wash water along with the clothes and the soap. The hard-water ions were precipitated as calcium and magnesium carbonate and washed away with the rinse water. Other water softeners in common use are borax, trisodium phosphate, and Calgon. As you learned in the laboratory activity, Calgon ties up the hard-water ions not as a precipitate, but in an ion that does not react with soap.

The development of synthetic detergents was a great advance in the history of cleaning agents. Synthetic detergents act like soap, but do not form insoluble compounds with hard-water ions. Most cleaning products sold today are such detergents. Unfortunately, many early detergents were not easily decomposed by bacteria in the environment—that is, they were not biodegradable. At times, mountains of foamy suds were observed in natural waterways. These early detergents also contained phosphate ions (PO_4^{3-}), which encouraged extensive algae growth, choking lakes and streams. Detergents used today are biodegradable and are generally phosphate-free; they do not cause these problems.

If you live in a hard-water region, a water softener may be attached to your home plumbing. As water enters the home, it flows through a large tank filled with ion-exchange resin similar to the resin you used in the water-softening laboratory activity. The resin consists of millions of tiny, insoluble, porous beads possessing an attraction for positive ions. Initially, the resin is filled with sodium ions. Calcium and magnesium ions in the entering hard water are attracted to the resin and become attached to it. At the same time, sodium ions leave the resin to dissolve in the water. Thus, undesirable ions are exchanged for sodium ions (Figure I.30). The sodium ions form neither insoluble deposits with soap nor scale in water pipes.

Eventually, of course, the resin fills with hard-water ions and must be regenerated. This is accomplished by allowing concentrated saltwater (containing sodium ions and chloride ions) to flow through the resin. This process replaces the hard-water ions held on the resin with Na^+ ions. The released hard-water ions are washed down the drain with the excess salt water. Since this process takes several hours, it is usually done at night. Once the resin is regenerated, the valves are reset and the softener is ready to continue exchanging ions in the incoming water.

Water softening is often done on a home-by-home basis. Other water-treatment processes occur at a municipal level, both in Riverwood and other cities. How are community water supplies made drinkable? How is wastewater treated before it is returned to the environment? Such questions are our next concern.

Figure I.30   Ion exchange water
softener.

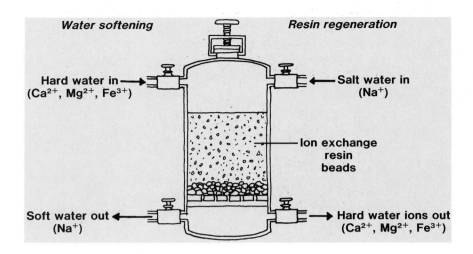

D.4 Municipal Water Purification

Today, many rivers are both a source of municipal water and a place to dump wastewater. So water must be cleaned twice—once before we use it, and again after we use it. Pre-use cleaning, called water treatment, occurs at a municipal filtration and treatment plant. Figure I.31 diagrams typical water treatment steps. Each numbered step in the figure is briefly described below:

- *Screening.* A metal screen prevents fish, sticks, soda cans, and other large objects from entering the water treatment plant.
- *Pre-chlorination.* Chlorine, a powerful disinfecting agent, is added to kill disease-causing organisms.
- *Flocculation.* Crystals of alum, aluminum sulfate, $Al_2(SO_4)_3$, and slaked lime, calcium hydroxide, $Ca(OH)_2$, are added to remove particles in the water such as colloidal clay. Suspended particles give water a murky appearance. The added substances react to form aluminum hydroxide, $Al(OH)_3$, a sticky, jellylike material which traps the colloidal particles.
- *Settling.* During this process the aluminum hydroxide with trapped colloidal particles and other solids remaining in the water settle to the bottom of the tank.
- *Sand filtration.* Any remaining suspended materials that did not settle out are removed here. (This process should remind you of a procedure used to purify your foul-water sample.)
- *Post-chlorination.* The chlorine concentration is adjusted so that residual chlorine remains in the water, protecting it from bacterial infestation.
- *Optional further treatment.* Depending on the community decision, one or more of the following steps might also be carried out before water leaves the treatment plant:

  - *Aeration.* Sometimes water is sprayed into the air to remove odor and improve its taste.
  - *pH adjustment.* Well water may be acidic enough to dissolve metallic water pipes slowly. This not only shortens the life of the pipes, but may cause cadmium (Cd^{2+}) and other undesirable ions to enter the water supply. Calcium oxide (CaO), a basic substance, is added to neutralize such acidic water.
  - *Fluoridation.* Up to about 1 ppm of fluoride ion (F^-) may be added to the treated water. At this low concentration, fluoride ion can reduce tooth decay, and also reduce causes of osteoporosis (bone-calcium loss among older adults) and hardening of the arteries.

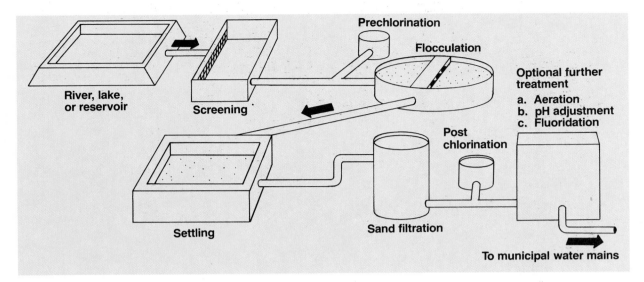

Figure I.31   Diagram of a municipal water purification plant.

Post-use cleaning of municipal water occurs at a **sewage treatment plant.** The major goal of wastewater treatment is to prevent bacteria and viruses found in human waste from infecting the public. However, sewage contains other undesirable materials. These can include garbage-disposal scraps; used wash water; slaughterhouse and food-packing plant scraps; and organic solvents and waste chemicals from homes, businesses, and industry. Ideally, all these should be removed before "used" water is returned to our rivers and streams. Figure I.32 is a schematic drawing of the main steps in sewage treatment. Each step is outlined below.

- *Screening and grit removal.* Sand and gravel are allowed to settle out; other large objects are removed. Smaller debris is ground. The solid residues are taken to an incinerator or landfill for burial.
- *Primary settling.* Floating grease and scum are skimmed off and solids are allowed to settle out as sludge.
- *Aeration.* In one method, the sewage filters through sludge held on baseball-sized rocks (or plastic baffles) in an aeration tank. Air circulates between the rocks; aerobic bacteria multiply into colonies that digest complex organic substances.
- *Final settling.* More sludge settles out. Most of the sludge is aerated, chlorinated, dried, and sent to an incinerator or landfill. Some sludge may be sent back to the aeration tank.
- *Disinfection.* Chlorine or other substances are added to kill germs.
- *Optional further treatment.* The pH of the water may be lowered with carbon dioxide, CO_2. When dissolved in water this gas forms carbonic acid (H_2CO_3), which neutralizes basic compounds in the cleaned-up sewage. In some systems, phosphate ions (PO_4^{3-}) are also removed by precipitation. Heavy metal ions may be removed.

Gas is produced during sludge aeration and digestion. This "sludge gas" contains about 65% methane (CH_4) and 25% carbon dioxide (CO_2). Methane is a good fuel—it is probably the major ingredient of the natural gas you are using in your Bunsen burner. In some treatment systems it is collected and burned to heat and dry the sludge residue.

Of all the chemicals involved in municipal water treatment, chlorine is probably the best known and most common additive. It not only appears in community water supplies, but also in swimming pools. Let's examine its use in greater detail.

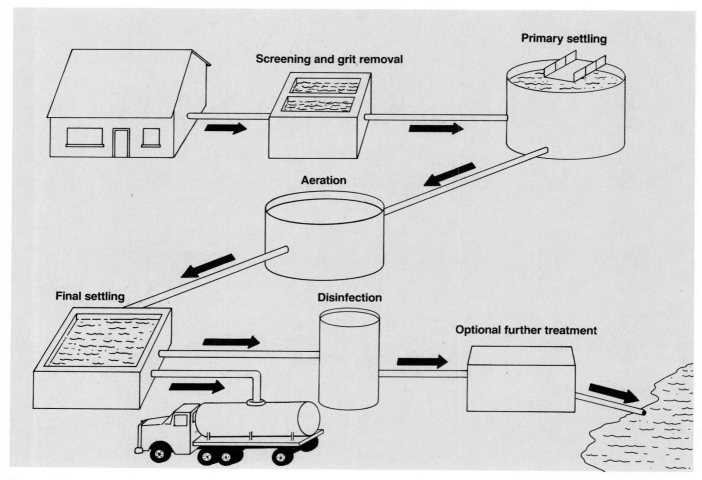

Figure I.32 Wastewater moves through underground sewer pipe and through a sewage treatment plant.

D.5 Chlorine in Our Water

Chlorine has served as a water disinfectant for decades. When added to water, it kills disease-producing microorganisms. Without doubt, adding chlorine to public water supplies has saved countless lives by controlling waterborne diseases. The most common cause of illness throughout the world is unhealthy water supplies.

In most municipal water treatment systems, chlorination takes place in one of three ways:

- Chlorine gas (Cl_2) is bubbled into the water. Although chlorine gas, a nonpolar substance, is not very soluble in water, it reacts with water to produce a water-soluble, chlorine-containing compound.
- A water solution of sodium hypochlorite (NaOCl) is added to the water. (Laundry bleach is also a sodium hypochlorite solution.)
- Calcium hypochlorite, $Ca(OCl)_2$, is dissolved in the water. Available as a powder and as small pellets, it is often used in swimming pools.

Regardless of the source, chlorine's active form in water is believed to be hypochlorous acid, HOCl. This substance is created whenever chlorine, sodium hypochlorite, or calcium hypochlorite dissolves in water.

There is at least one potential problem associated with the addition of chlorine to municipal water systems. The following Chem Quandary provides the background.

CHEM*QUANDARY*

Under some conditions, chlorine in the water can react with organic compounds produced by decomposing plant and animal matter, forming substances harmful to human health. A group of these substances is known as trihalomethanes (THMs). One common THM is chloroform ($CHCl_3$). Chloroform causes cancer in rats. Due to concern over possible harmful effects of THMs, the Environmental Protection Agency has placed a limit of 100 ppb (parts per billion) on the total THM concentration permitted in our water supplies. Some solutions to the THM problem are available, but each has disadvantages:

- Water in the treatment plant could be passed through an activated charcoal filter. Activated charcoal can remove most organic compounds from water, including THMs. *Disadvantage:* Charcoal filters are expensive to install and expensive to operate.
- Chlorine could be eliminated altogether; ozone (O_3) or ultraviolet light could be used to disinfect the water. *Disadvantage:* These methods would not protect the water once it leaves the treatment plant. The water could be infected by a later addition of bacteria—for example, through faulty water pipes. Also, ozone can be toxic if not used properly, as we shall see.
- The pre-chlorination step could be eliminated. Chlorine would be added only once, after the water had been filtered and much of the organic material removed. *Disadvantage:* The chlorine added in post-chlorination could still promote the formation of THMs, but to a lesser extent than with pre-chlorination. A decrease in chlorine concentration might also make the water susceptible to bacterial infestation.

1. Consider each of the listed alternatives. Are any of these choices preferable to standard chlorination procedures? Explain your reasoning and make a list of benefits and problems that might result from your choice.
2. Can you think of any other alternatives?

The quality of Snake River water was somehow responsible for the fish kill and the resulting concern of the Riverwood community. Yet our exploration of the most common causes of water contamination has not revealed the source of the problem. Tests have verified that the water is totally safe for human use and contains enough oxygen to support aquatic life. However, the fish kill remains unexplained. Perhaps tomorrow's Riverwood newspaper will finally bring an answer to the mystery!

PART D
SUMMARY*QUESTIONS*

1. Explain the basic steps involved in nature's purification system.
2. How are municipal water purification and sewage treatment similar to nature's "system"? How are they different?
3. What are the advantages of chlorinated drinking water over untreated water? What are its disadvantages?

EXTENDING *YOUR KNOWLEDGE (OPTIONAL)*

- During the past century, water-quality standards have become increasingly strict. Discuss several reasons for this trend.
- In recent years many communities have invested in tertiary sewage treatment. Investigate the purpose, design features, advantages, and disadvantages of tertiary treatment. Prepare a written statement to "sell" such a treatment to a community.
- High concentrations of iron(III) ions are undesirable in drinking water. Write a balanced equation showing how these ions might be removed by a sodium ion-exchange resin.
- Prepare a report on the growing controversy over the use and abuse of groundwater supplies within the United States.

U.S. Public Health Service

Water cleaned by nature is not always safe to drink.

E PUTTING IT ALL TOGETHER: FISH KILL IN RIVERWOOD— WHO PAYS?

Fish Kill Cause Found; Meeting Tonight

The massive fish kill in the Snake River was caused by "gas bubble disease," announced Mayor Edward Cisko at a news conference early today. Since the disease is noninfectious, humans are at no risk from the water.

With Mayor Cisko at the conference was Dr. Harold Schmidt of the Environmental Protection Agency laboratory. Dr. Schmidt explained that the disease is caused by an excess of air dissolved in the river water. "The excess dissolved air, mostly oxygen and nitrogen, passes through the fish's gills, where it forms gas bubbles. Consequently, less oxygen cir-

culates through the fish's bloodstream. The fish usually die within a few days if the situation is not corrected."

Dr. Schmidt dissected sample fish within a short time after death and found evidence of the gas bubbles, the only positive identification of the disease.

Dr. Schmidt gave assurances that river water containing excess air is not harmful to human health, and that the town's water supply is "fully safe to drink."

Mayor Cisko refused comment on the reasons for the water condition, saying, "The cause is still under investigation."

But an informed source close to the mayor's office stated that "the most likely cause is the power company's release of water from the dam upstream of Riverwood." The mayor's secretary confirmed that power company officials will meet with the mayor and his staff later today.

Mayor Cisko also announced that there will be a special public Town Council meeting at 8 P.M. tonight in the Town Hall. The council will discuss who is responsible for the fish kill, and who should pay for the costs associated with the three-day water shutoff. Several area groups plan to make presentations at tonight's meeting.

Editorial: Attendance Urged at Special Council Meeting

Tonight's special Town Council meeting could result in important decisions affecting all Riverwood citizens. The meeting will address two primary questions: Who is responsible for the fish kill and who should pay for the water that was trucked into Riverwood during the three-day water shutoff? These questions have financial consequences for all town taxpayers.

Those testifying at tonight's public meeting include power company officials, scientists involved in the river water anal-

yses, and engineers from an independent consulting firm familiar with power plant design. Chamber of Commerce members representing Riverwood store owners, representatives from the County Sanitation Commission, and the Riverwood Taxpayers Association will also make presentations.

We urge you to attend this meeting. Many unanswered questions remain. Was the fish kill an "act of nature" or was some human error involved? Was there negligence? Should the town's business com-

munity be compensated, at least in part, for financial losses resulting from the fish kill? If so, how should they be compensated, and by whom? Who should pay for the special drinking water brought into Riverwood? Can this situation be prevented in the future? If so, at what expense? Who will pay for it?

This newspaper will devote a large portion of its "Letters to the Editor" column in the coming days to your comments on these and other issues related to the community's recent water crisis.

Jon Jacobson

Seeking consensus at a town council meeting.

You will be assigned to one of six "special interest" groups who will testify at the special meeting of the Riverwood Town Council. You will receive some suggestions on information to include in your group's presentation. Consider these suggestions only as a starting point. Identify other points to stress in your presentation.

Use your planning time to select a group spokesperson and to organize the presentation. You may wish to prepare written notes to use. Each group will have two minutes to present its position and one minute for rebuttal. Failure to stay within the presentation time limits will result in loss of rebuttal time. Students assigned to the Town Council group will act as official timekeepers.

Following the meeting, each group (or, alternatively, each student) will write a letter to the editor of the Riverwood newspaper suggesting answers to questions posed in the editorial reprinted in this section.

As an alternative to preparing a letter to the editor, your teacher may ask each group to prepare for a simulated television interview. In this case, one spokesperson from each group will be questioned by a television interview team. Questions should be based, at least in part, on those raised in the newspaper editorial.

After preparing the letters to the editor or holding the television interviews, the different points of view contained in the letters or interviews will be compared and discussed by the entire class.

E.1   Directions for Groups Making Town Council Meeting Presentations

Town Council Members (Two Students)

Your group is responsible for conducting the meeting in an orderly manner. Be prepared to:

1. Decide and announce the order of presentations at the meeting. Groups presenting factual information should be heard before groups voicing opinions.
2. Explain the meeting rules and the penalties for violating those rules (see below).
3. Recognize each special interest group at its assigned presentation time.
4. Enforce the two-minute time limit on presentations. One way to do this is to prepare time cards with one minute, one-half minute, and zero minutes written on them. These cards, placed in each speaker's line of sight, will serve as adequate warnings to the speaker.

Meeting Rules and Penalties for Rule Violations

1. The order of presentation is decided by council members and announced at the start of the meeting.
2. Each group will have two minutes for its presentation. Time cards will notify the speaker of time remaining.
3. If a member of another group interrupts a presentation, the offending group will be penalized one-half minute for each interruption to a maximum of one minute. If the group has already made its presentation, it will forfeit its rebuttal time.

Power Company Officials

The following will help with your presentation:

The release of water from the dam is a standard procedure to prevent flooding. The potential for flooding was increased due to the unusually heavy rains experienced in the area this past summer. The last time it was necessary to release such a large volume of water from the dam was 30 years ago. A fish kill was reported then but the cause remained unknown. On that occasion, Riverwood and the surrounding area also had experienced an unusually wet summer. Normally, only small volumes of water are released from the dam at any particular time.

The dam was constructed in the 1930s using the most current design of the time. Its basic design has not been altered since it was constructed.

Scientists

The following will help with your presentation:

Gas bubble disease is a noninfectious disease that has only recently been identified. It is caused by excessive gas dissolved in the water. When the total amount of dissolved gases, primarily oxygen and nitrogen, reach a *combined* total of 110–124% of saturation, symptoms of gas bubble disease can occur in fish. There are no known harmful effects of such water to humans.

The most dangerous component is the excess nitrogen dissolved in the water. Fish metabolism can partially reduce the effect of excess oxygen through hemoglobin-oxygen transport, but there is no such mechanism for transport of nitrogen in blood.

Fish die because the supersaturated gases in the water produce gas bubbles in their blood and tissues. These bubbles often form in blood vessels of the gills and heart. Death results since blood is unable to circulate throughout the fish's bodies. Some fish varieties also develop distended (bloated) air bladders. Fish death can occur from a few hours to several days after the formation of the gas bubbles.

A definitive indicator of gas bubble disease is the presence of gas bubbles in the gills of dead fish. However, some gas bubbles disappear rapidly after fish die, so prompt dissection and analysis are required.

Supersaturation of the water with oxygen and nitrogen gas often occurs near dams and hydroelectric projects whenever water is released and forms "froth," trapping large amounts of air. Water at the base of the dam may have oxygen and nitrogen dissolved at 139% of saturation, while 90 km (about 56 miles) downstream, the supersaturation may still be as high as 111% of saturation. The Environmental Protection Agency limit for combined oxygen and nitrogen supersaturation in rivers is 110%. Specially designed spillways providing more gradual release of water from dams may substantially lessen or even prevent supersaturation of the released water.

Engineers

The following will help with your presentation:

Engineers can predict whether large amounts of air will be trapped in water released from a dam spillway. This involves knowledge of the physical structure of the spillway and the volume of water that will be released.

The U.S. Corps of Engineers has conducted research on whether operational or structural changes in dams might reduce the chance of gas supersaturation in released water. Their main goal has been to find ways of reducing the volume of water released from spillways and preventing the released water from plunging to great depths beneath the river surface. When water plunges to great depths the increased pressure can force greater amounts of air to dissolve in the water (see Part C.1).

Three specific suggestions could help Riverwood. The first is to enlarge the reservoir upstream from the dam. This would provide greater water storage capacity during times of heavy rain and runoff. Water could thus be released from the spillway in smaller quantities, decreasing the chance of high gas supersaturation.

The second suggestion is to launch a major fish-collecting operation upstream from the dam. The fish could then be trucked around the dam and released at a downstream location where the supersaturation level was low enough to ensure fish survival.

The third suggestion is to install deflectors on the downstream side of the spillway. Spillway deflectors avoid creating high levels of dissolved air by preventing released water from plunging to great depths (see Figure I.33). Instead, they release the water along the river surface where the chance of large quantities of air dissolving is reduced.

Chamber of Commerce

The following will help with your presentation:

Canceling the annual fishing tournament cost Riverwood merchants a substantial sum. Nearly 1000 out-of-town participants were expected to have taken part in the tournament. Many participants would have rented rooms for at least two nights and eaten at local restaurants and diners. In anticipation of this business, arrangements were made for extra help and food supplies. Fishing and sporting goods stores stockpiled extra fishing supplies. Some businesses have had to apply for short-term loans to help pay for their extra, unsold inventories.

Jon Jacobson

Spillway and deflector.

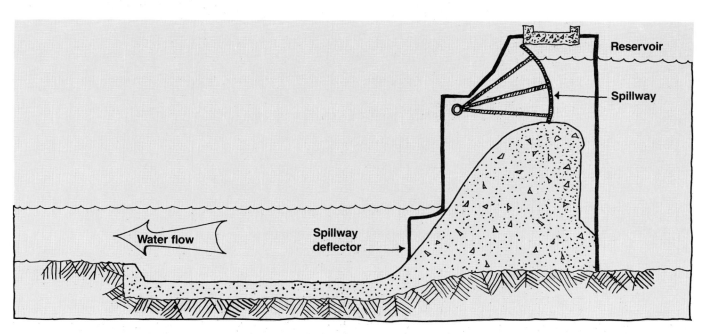

Figure I.33   Spillway and deflector.

Local churches and the high school planned family social activities as revenue-makers during the tournament. The school band, for instance, planned a benefit concert for the tournament weekend. The concert would have raised money to send band members to the spring state band competition.

The public will likely remember the fish kill in future years. Tournament organizers predict that revenues from future fishing competitions in Riverwood will be substantially reduced due to the adverse publicity generated this year. Thus the total financial losses due to the water emergency may be much higher than currently projected.

County Sanitation Commission

The following will help with your presentation:

The Snake River water analysis following the fish kill verified that Riverwood drinking water is safe according to Environmental Protection Agency guidelines. However, one water contaminant, selenium, has significantly increased since earlier river tests. Despite its increase in concentration, selenium's 0.008-ppm level is still below the EPA's 0.01-ppm limit.

The main source of selenium in water is soil runoff. The concentration of selenium in soil varies by region, depending on the source of the soil. Selenium-containing soil near Riverwood came from the debris of prehistoric volcanic eruptions which carried selenium from within the Earth's crust to its surface.

Selenium is essential to human and animal health in trace amounts. However, if ingested in too great amounts, its toxic effects are similar to those of arsenic poisoning.

The recommended human dose of selenium is 0.05 mg to 0.20 mg per day. It is contained in foods such as wheat, asparagus, and seafood. The body needs selenium to assist enzymes in protecting and repairing cell membranes. Due to this action, it is thought by some authorities—at least in trace amounts—to help prevent cancer.

Riverwood Taxpayer Association

The following will help with your presentation:

Who will pay for the water that was brought into the town during the water shutoff?

Will taxes be increased to compensate local business people for the financial losses they have experienced? (Keep in mind that the local merchants are most likely Riverwood taxpayers themselves!)

If the power company redesigns the dam's spillway, will the cost of construction be passed on to the taxpayers? If so, how?

How much (if at all) should the information presented by the other groups influence your position concerning who pays? If possible, you may wish to obtain written briefs from the other groups before the town meeting. What other sources of information might be useful?

E.2 Looking Back and Looking Ahead

The Riverwood water mystery has finally been solved. It is ironic that the water "contaminants" responsible for the fish kill and for the town's understandable concern are just excessive amounts of oxygen gas and nitrogen gas dissolved in the water. Neither substance qualifies as toxic or dangerous—after all, we live immersed in an atmosphere of these gases.

However, deep sea divers have long feared and respected the hazard known as the "bends"—the formation of nitrogen gas bubbles in a diver's blood if bodily pressure is lowered too rapidly in moving back to the water surface. Thus, even for humans, a substance as seemingly harmless as nitrogen gas can pose life-threatening risks under certain conditions.

Although the analogy is not perfect, the gas bubble disease that killed the fish can be considered a form of the bends. In fact, the same scientific principle that explains the fizzing of a carbonated beverage accounts for both of these hazardous situations.

Did all of the earlier water analyses in the Snake River represent a waste of time and money? Of course not. Even though the tests failed to locate a probable cause for the fish kill, they eliminated several major possibilities, and thus narrowed the field of investigation. In scientific research negative results may be as important and useful as positive ones.

In the case of the Riverwood investigation, one unexpected finding has given chemists an "early warning" of a possible future water-quality problem. The selenium concentration in the Snake River, although not responsible for the fish kill, has increased enough over the past few months to merit serious attention and action by the authorities. If the fish kill had not happened, would this potential problem have been identified this soon? Possibly. But it's not unusual for a systematic search for a solution to one scientific or technological problem to uncover one or more new problems. In fact, this is partly why scientific work is considered so challenging and interesting by those who work as scientists and technicians.

Of course, Riverwood and its citizens only exist on the pages of this book. Their problem, however, could be real. Certainly the chemical facts, principles, and procedures that helped us understand their problem and its solution directly apply to a wide range of experiences in your own home and community.

Although we are now prepared to leave Riverwood, our exploration of chemistry has only just begun. There are many issues involving chemistry in the community to investigate. Water and its chemistry are only a part of a larger story.

N. B. Neely

. . . and Riverwood returned to its favorite pastime.

UNIT *TWO*

Conserving Chemical Resources

CONTENTS

INTRODUCTION

Ancient societies lived off nature's bounty, using only tiny fractions of natural resources such as forests, metal ores and minerals, and animals, fish, and plants. As humans gained additional knowledge and skills in agriculture, animal husbandry, metallurgy, crude manufacturing, and medicine, longevity increased and human populations grew. In these earlier times, the chemical resources removed from the earth were miniscule compared with the amount that remained.

Gradually people began to organize their discoveries about the natural world, and to apply this organized knowledge to the invention of devices and techniques that would make life easier. The process of gathering, analyzing, and organizing knowledge about the natural world is known as **science.** In contrast, **technology** represents the application of science in converting natural resources into goods and services.

Science and the accompanying technology have advanced rapidly. Today, it is estimated that scientific knowledge doubles every nine to ten years. Technology appears to be changing even more rapidly. Scientific and technological advances have given us stainless steel and polyester fiber, headset radios and computers, Boeing 747s and brain scanners, cocaine and Agent Orange, fast food and diet soft drinks.

The industries that make these products have grown rapidly. In the United States, 5% of the world's population uses more than half of the world's processed resources. In fact, during the last 40 years, the United States has consumed more fossil fuels and metal ores than were used by all the Earth's inhabitants up to that time.

Let's illustrate what this consumption means on a personal level. It has been estimated that within a lifetime, a typical U.S. citizen requires some 26 million gallons of water, 52 tons of iron and steel, 6.5 tons of paper, 1200 barrels of petroleum, 21,000 gallons of gasoline, 50 tons of food, 5 tons of fertilizer, plus a wide variety of other chemical resources. These huge quantities can be put into perspective by focusing on energy, which must always be used in processing resources.

Egyptian pharaohs used the energy of 100,000 laborers to build the Pyramids. In building the Great Wall, Chinese emperors used the energy of two million workers. To keep you warm and clothed, grow and process your food, transport you and your necessities, and to entertain you during leisure hours, you have at your personal service enough energy to equal the labor of 200 full-time workers.

Jon Jacobson   Jon Jacobson

Resources are directed toward production of a variety of goods.

These services are costly. Our growing population has greatly increased the demand for resources. We have taken vast amounts of resources from the Earth and, in the process, have greatly altered it. Also, we have generated large quantities of waste materials. For example, a typical U.S. citizen will discard about 126 tons of garbage in one lifetime. The combined effects of mining, processing, using, and discarding materials have caused environmental damage.

We need to become more aware of the consequences of using resources. We must learn to balance our withdrawals by returning materials to the environment in useful, or at least not harmful, forms. If we do this, the Earth's inhabitants can continue to enjoy the benefits of a rich bounty.

In this unit, you will explore some issues surrounding our use of resources. You will become more familiar with some of the materials that add richness or discomfort to your life, and you will learn how you can personally help to conserve valuable materials.

The many goods available in this mall are brought to you by the work of chemists.

A USE OF RESOURCES

How much is a penny worth? You will probably answer "one cent." Well, that's certainly correct. But then again, maybe it's not. It depends on the year the penny was produced. Confused? Then read the following article.

Zinc Makes More Cents

After remaining virtually unchanged since it was first issued in 1909, in 1982 the Lincoln Head penny lost a full 20% of its mass. The change was made as an economy measure. The mass loss was due to the partial substitution of less expensive and lower density zinc for the original copper. Copper prices had risen to the point at which the metal in the penny was worth more than one cent.

When the material value of a coin becomes greater than its face value, two undesirable things can happen. First, the U.S. Treasury begins to lose money in manufacturing the coin. (When the con-

tent of the penny was changed in 1982, it was estimated that the United States would save $25–50 million annually.)

Second, individuals may remove the coins from circulation to sell them for their metal content.

Chemists are often called upon to find ways to substitute less costly, more plentiful resources for scarce and expensive ones, without sacrificing the advantages of those resources. The old penny was 95% copper and 5% zinc. The new penny is 97.6% zinc, coated with a thin electroplating of copper. It is almost as durable as the old penny, since the strong copper plating protects the more chemically reactive zinc from the wear and tear of daily use.

How much is a penny really worth? If "worth" means the value of the metals in a coin, a penny issued from 1944 to 1981 is worth more today than one cent. A penny minted after 1982 is worth less than a cent. As money, of course, a penny is still just a penny.

The U.S. Mint is able to make a zinc coin look like copper. Let's see if you too can alter the appearance of a metallic coin.

A.1 Laboratory Activity: Striking It Rich with Chemistry

Getting Ready

Seeing is believing—or so it is said. In this activity you will observe how the properties of a metal can be changed. Copper (Cu), the familiar metal of pennies, will be changed in properties by heating it with zinc (Zn) in the presence of a solution of sodium hydroxide (NaOH).

In your laboratory notebook prepare a table like that below, leaving plenty of room for your observations.

Data table	Copper penny	Copper foil
Untreated		
Treated with Zn + NaOH		
Treated with Zn + NaOH and heated		

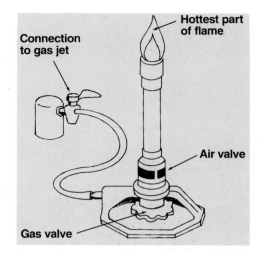

Figure II.1   A Bunsen burner.

A Bunsen burner will be used in heating the copper. Before you begin the lab procedure, examine your burner and identify the parts shown in Figure II.1. Then practice lighting and adjusting the burner as follows:

1. Attach the burner hose to the gas outlet (which should be closed).
2. Close the air valve and the gas valve on the burner.
3. Open the valve on the gas outlet.
4. Light a match or have your striker ready.
5. Open the gas valve on the burner and light the burner by bringing the lighted match to the top of the barrel or sparking the striker.
6. Adjust the height of the burner flame with the gas valve.
7. Adjust the flame temperature by rotating the air valve. The hottest part of the flame is just above the inner blue cone, which is about 2–3 cm (1 inch) high with a relatively high air setting. Cooler flames (lower air settings) have a smaller or undefined inner cone and often include orange-colored regions.
8. Close the gas outlet to extinguish the flame.

Procedure

1. Obtain three pennies and three pieces of copper foil.
2. Assemble a ring stand with a ring clamp and wire gauze. As illustrated in Figure II.2, place a beaker on the wire gauze and surround the beaker with a second ring clamp so that the beaker is prevented from tipping over.
3. Weigh a 0.5 g sample of granulated zinc (Zn). Pour it into the beaker.
4. Carefully pour into the beaker 15 mL of sodium hydroxide (NaOH) solution.
5. Heat the beaker gently with the Bunsen burner until the solution just begins to bubble. Then adjust the burner flame to continue gentle bubbling. *Caution:* Do not allow the solution to boil vigorously. Hot sodium hydroxide solution is very caustic, that is, it damages the skin. If any solution contacts your skin, immediately wash the affected area with cold tap water. Notify your teacher.
6. Using forceps or tongs, carefully add two pennies to the hot sodium hydroxide solution. Do not drop the coins into the solution so that you cause a splash. Set the third penny aside as a control—an untreated sample that can be compared with the treated coins.
7. Observe and record any changes in the appearance of the coins until no further changes are noted.
8. Fill two beakers with distilled water.
9. With forceps or tongs, remove the two pennies from the solution. Place them both in one of the beakers of distilled water. Remove heat from the beaker of sodium hydroxide, but do not discard the solution.

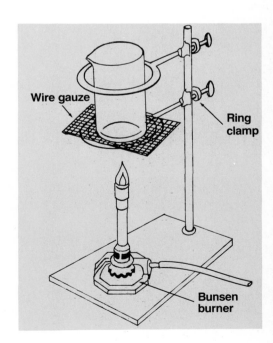

Figure II.2   Setup for reaction between zinc and sodium hydroxide. The beaker rests on the wire gauze and is prevented from tipping by a ring clamp of the proper size.

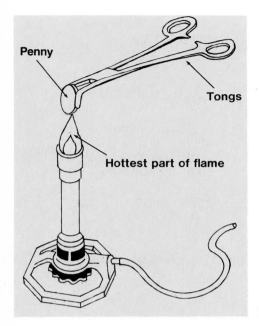

Figure II.3 Heating zinc-sodium hydroxide treated coin. The coin should be heated in the outer cone of the burner flame.

10. Using forceps or tongs, remove the coins from the beaker of water. Rinse them under running tap water. Dry the coins with a paper towel. Set one treated coin aside to be used for later comparisons.

11. Gently heat the other treated, dried coin in the outer cone of the burner flame, holding it vertically with the forceps or tongs as shown in Figure II.3.

12. Continue heating the coin for three seconds after its appearance changes. *Do not overheat it.* Immediately immerse the coin in the second beaker of distilled water. Record your observations.

13. Remove the coin from the beaker of water. Dry it with a paper towel.

14. Observe the appearance and flexibility of the three pennies and record your observations in the table.

15. Empty, rinse, and refill the two beakers with distilled water.

16. Repeat steps 5 through 14, replacing each coin with one of the pieces of copper foil and using the reserved zinc/sodium hydroxide solution. When finished, discard the sodium hydroxide solution as directed by your teacher.

17. Observe the appearance and flexibility of the three pieces of copper foil and record your observations in the table.

Questions

1. Compare the color of the three coins (untreated, heated in sodium hydroxide solution, heated in sodium hydroxide solution and in burner flame). Do any of the treated coin appearances remind you of other metals?

2. How could you verify whether you had changed the copper metal to another metal?

3. Which sample of copper foil is more flexible—the treated or the untreated piece?

4. What other properties of the copper foil were changed by the treatment?

5. Can you think of any practical uses for the metallic changes you observed in this activity?

What happened to the copper atoms originally present in the treated pennies? Were the copper atoms used up or destroyed? Could we convert the treated pennies back to normal coins? Think about these questions as we continue our exploration of chemical resources.

A.2 Using Things Up

In the laboratory activity you just completed, copper seemed to disappear. Many things we use every day seem to disappear. The fuel in the car's gasoline tank disappears as we drive down the road. The ice cream we eat disappears—often quickly. A pencil eraser gets shorter and shorter. Steel in automobile bodies rusts away.

Even though such materials do disappear when we use them, the atoms composing them do not. In the laboratory activity, the copper became coated (plated) with zinc. Upon heating, the copper atoms mixed with zinc atoms to form brass. The original copper atoms, although not visible, were still present.

Gasoline burns (reacts with oxygen gas from the air), producing energy to propel our cars. During the burning, carbon and hydrogen atoms from gasoline and oxygen atoms from air react to form carbon dioxide (CO_2) and water (H_2O). These products exit through the exhaust system.

As ice cream is digested, atoms from sugars and fats in the ice cream combine with other substances and in the process provide both energy and new compounds needed for bodily functions. Particles from the pencil eraser rub off, spread over the paper, and are brushed away. The iron atoms originally in the car's steel frame are still present in the rust.

Nothing is ever really lost when atoms are counted. "Using things up" means changing resources rather than destroying them. Sometimes the atoms and molecules of resources can be reclaimed, and sometimes they become so widely dispersed that they cannot be efficiently collected again.

The law of conservation of matter, like all scientific laws, summarizes what has been learned by observation of nature: *In a chemical reaction matter is neither created nor destroyed.* Matter at the level of individual atoms is always fully accounted for. Nature is an exacting bookkeeper. This is why chemical equations must always be balanced. Balanced equations allow us to represent on paper how nature accounts for all atoms in every chemical reaction.

A.3 Keeping Track of the Atoms

Coal is mostly carbon (C); when carbon burns it combines with oxygen (O_2) from the air to produce carbon dioxide (CO_2). Writing the formulas for the reactants (C and O_2) on the left and those for the product (CO_2) on the right, and adding the symbols for their states gives

$$C(s) + O_2(g) \rightarrow CO_2(g)$$

In equations, (s), (l), or (g) tell us the state—solid, liquid, or gas—of the substance at the reaction conditions.

This statement is an equation. In addition to stating what substances react and what substances are formed, this equation makes a bookkeeping statement. All atoms in the product are accounted for in the reactants. To form one molecule of carbon dioxide, CO_2, requires one atom of carbon and two atoms of oxygen. The two atoms of oxygen are supplied by one diatomic oxygen molecule.

When copper (Cu) is exposed to the atmosphere, it takes part in a number of chemical reactions, one of which is the formation of copper(I) oxide (Cu_2O). An ionic compound, copper(I) oxide contains no molecules. We refer to the combination of ions in its formula as a *formula unit.*

The statement

$$Cu(s) + O_2(g) \rightarrow Cu_2O(s)$$

is not an equation. It states what the products and reactants are, but it does not fulfill the bookkeeping function. For each molecule of diatomic oxygen that reacts, two formula units of Cu_2O form.

$$Cu(s) + O_2(g) \rightarrow 2\ Cu_2O(s)$$

Now consider the number of copper atoms needed to form two formula units of Cu_2O. One formula unit requires two copper atoms, so formation of two units requires four atoms.

$$4\ Cu(s) + O_2(g) \rightarrow 2\ Cu_2O(s)$$

coefficient
↓
3 CO₂
↑
subscript

The above statement is the equation for the chemical reaction of copper with oxygen to give copper(I) oxide. The numbers, 2 and 4, placed before the symbol or formula are called *coefficients.*

To check the bookkeeping, count the atoms of each element on both sides of the equation.

Reactants side:	*Products side:*
4 atoms copper	2 formula units Cu_2O
1 molecule O_2	(made from a total of four copper
(containing two oxygen atoms)	and two oxygen atoms)

Equations represent what actually happens in a chemical reaction. Statements that are not balanced cannot represent reality, and are not equations.

In the following exercises, you will practice recognizing equations and unbalanced statements. Then in a laboratory activity you will complete another experiment in which copper seems to disappear. By observing the products of a chemical reaction, however, you will discover the fate of all of the reactant atoms.

2 Cu₂O includes 4 Cu atoms and 2 O atoms

YOUR *TURN*

II.1   Balanced Equations

1. For each of the following chemical statements, first interpret the statement in words. Then list all of the atoms in the reactants and products of the statement as written. Decide whether or not the statement is an equation. The first one is done for you to illustrate further how to deal with combinations of coefficients and subscripts.

   a. The reaction between propane, C_3H_8, and oxygen, O_2, is a common source of heat for campers, recreational vehicle users, and others using liquid propane fuel (LPG). This reaction can be represented by

$$C_3H_8(g) + O_2(g) \rightarrow CO_2(g) + H_2O(g) + \text{Thermal energy}$$

   Interpreted in words, we say:

   Propane gas reacts with oxygen gas to give carbon dioxide gas, water vapor, and energy. Listing the atoms in reactants and products, we find

   Reactant side: *Product side:*
   3 carbon atoms   1 carbon atom
   8 hydrogen atoms   2 hydrogen atoms
   2 oxygen atoms   3 oxygen atoms

   Since the number of carbon, hydrogen and oxygen atoms is not the same in reactants and products, the representation above is not an equation. To balance the statement above, note that the three carbon atoms of the reactants each require one oxygen molecule to form CO_2. Also, the eight hydrogen atoms of the reactants can form four water molecules if atoms from two oxygen molecules are available. In all, five oxygen molecules are needed to accommodate the three carbon and eight hydrogen atoms in one molecule of propane. Therefore, the equation is:

$$C_3H_8(g) + 5\,O_2(g) \rightarrow 3\,CO_2(g) + 4\,H_2O(g) + \text{Thermal energy}$$

   Checking the atom balance in the equation, we find

   Reactant side: *Product side:*
   3 carbon atoms (in C_3H_8)   3 carbon atoms (in 3 CO_2)
   8 hydrogen atoms (in C_3H_8)   8 hydrogen atoms (in 4 H_2O)
   10 oxygen atoms (in 5 O_2)   10 oxygen atoms
                                         (3 CO_2; 4 H_2O)

   b. The burning of wood or paper can be represented by:

$$C_6H_{10}O_5(s) + 6\,O_2(g) \rightarrow 6\,CO_2(g) + 5\,H_2O(g) + \text{Thermal energy}$$

c. The decomposition of nitroglycerine when dynamite explodes can be represented by:

$$4 \, C_3H_5(NO_3)_3(l) \longrightarrow 6 \, N_2(g) \, + \, O_2(g) \, + \, 12 \, CO_2(g) \, + \, 10 \, H_2O(g)$$

d. Combining metallic silver with hydrogen sulfide and oxygen gases in the air to form silver tarnish (silver sulfide is black):

$$4 \, Ag(s) \, + \, 4 \, H_2S(g) \, + \, O_2(g) \longrightarrow 2 \, Ag_2S(s) \, + \, 4 \, H_2O(l)$$

e. Forming an aluminum hydroxide precipitate is used to help remove suspended matter from public water supplies. In practice, aqueous solutions of aluminum sulfate, $Al_2(SO_4)_3$, and calcium hydroxide, $Ca(OH)_2$, are added to the water supply. They mix and a gelatinous precipitate of aluminum hydroxide, $Al(OH)_3$, forms. The precipitate slowly settles, carrying suspended matter with it, thereby removing this material from the water supply.

   The aqueous solution of aluminum sulfate contains Al^{3+} and SO_4^{2-} ions. The aqueous solution of calcium hydroxide contains Ca^{2+} and OH^- ions. The only observable product of mixing these solutions is aluminum hydroxide. Therefore the process is represented as a reaction between the ions needed to form the product:

$$Al^{3+}(aq) \, + \, 3 \, OH^-(aq) \longrightarrow Al(OH)_3(s)$$

The Ca^{2+} and SO_4^{2-} ions, while present in solution, are not involved in the reaction. But, if water is evaporated from this solution, the reaction

$$Ca^{2+}(aq) \, + \, SO_4^{2-}(aq) \longrightarrow CaSO_4(s)$$

will occur, and a solid residue of calcium sulfate ($CaSO_4$) will remain. In balancing chemical statements involving ions, the net charge on the left of the arrow must be the same as that on the right of the arrow.

   Using the preceding information, write an equation for the reaction that occurs when aqueous solutions of aluminum sulfate and calcium hydroxide are mixed. Interpret your equation in words.

2. Since all the atoms of reactants appear as atoms of products in a chemical reaction, how should the total mass of products compare to the total mass of reactants? Why?

3. How would you verify your answer to Question 2 regarding the masses of reactants and products? If the reactants or products were gases, how could the answer to Question 2 be verified?

4. Someone has remarked that our planet and its surrounding atmosphere are similar to an immense, sealed flask. In what way is this true? In what way is this not true?

A.4 Laboratory Activity: Using Up a Metal

Getting Ready

In this activity you will observe the chemical reaction between nitric acid (HNO_3) and copper (Cu) metal. This reaction is an example of **corrosion,** a term applied to any reaction that causes a material to deteriorate or be worn away. Many metals are corroded by acids. *Caution:* Skin also is corroded by acids.

Procedure

1. Obtain a copper wire sample and clean it by rubbing it with steel wool.
2. Bend the wire in half and drop it into an empty test tube.
3. Carefully add enough nitric acid (HNO_3) to the test tube to cover the copper wire. *Caution:* Nitric acid is corrosive to skin. If any acid accidentally spills on you, wash the affected area with tap water for several minutes. Notify your teacher.
4. Place a sheet of white paper behind the test tube. (This will make it easier to observe the reaction.)
5. Observe the reaction for five minutes. Record all observed changes in the wire, the solution, and in the test tube contents.
6. Discard the test tube contents according to your teacher's directions.

Questions

1. You cleaned your original copper wire with steel wool. In terms of atoms, what actually happened during this step? Was what happened a chemical reaction? Explain.
2. What do you think caused the formation of color in the test tube during the reaction? What happened to the copper as the reaction proceeded?
3. A chemical equation for the reaction you just observed is given below. Use the equation and your original observations in answering these questions: You observed several color changes during the reaction. What is the color of each substance shown in the balanced equation? Where did the copper atoms from the wire go? What elements were in the colored gas molecules released by the reaction? Where did these atoms come from? Where did the atoms in the product water come from?

Copper + Nitric acid $\longrightarrow$ Copper(II) nitrate + Nitrogen dioxide + Water

$$Cu(s) + 4\,HNO_3(aq) \longrightarrow Cu(NO_3)_2(aq) + 2\,NO_2(g) + 2\,H_2O(l)$$

The equation given above is not a complete representation of the reaction, because it does not show the ions present in the solution and their involvement in the reaction. In the solution, nitric acid is present as $H^+(aq)$ and NO_3^- ions. Upon reaction, copper atoms form Cu^{2+} ions. A better representation of the reaction is:

$$Cu(s) + 4\,H^+(aq) + 2\,NO_3^-(aq) \longrightarrow Cu^{2+}(aq) + 2\,NO_2(g) + 2\,H_2O(l)$$

If water is evaporated from the solution after the reaction is complete, blue crystals of copper(II) nitrate will appear. How do you account for this? How is it related to the original equation for the reaction given above?

A.5 Resources and Waste

As scientific and technological knowledge increase, our society uses resources at an ever-increasing rate. To satisfy the needs of an average U.S. citizen, some 23,000 kg (25 tons) of various resources must be withdrawn from the Earth each year.

Jon Jacobson

Waste and resources share a common fate at a landfill.

Using or obtaining a resource often results in changing one material into another that is unwanted. Burning coal generates corrosive gases that enter the atmosphere. Extracting a metal from an ore often leaves behind solid by-products that must be discarded.

Coal contains sulfur. The corrosive gases SO_2 and SO_3 are formed in burning.

We also generate waste when we use consumer products so popular in our society. The foil wrapper becomes waste when we use a stick of chewing gum. Some items become waste when we tire of them. Others, such as electric coffee pots, become waste when we discover it is cheaper to buy a new one than to repair an old one. When we throw such materials away, we don't really get rid of them. At the atomic level, there is no "away." The chemical elements combined as our trash may not be useful to us in that form, but they are still there—and must be dealt with.

More and more our society is faced with problems associated with **discards**—things we no longer want or need. We generate awesome quantities of discards. Each person in this country throws "away," on average, nearly 2 kg (4 lbs) of unwanted materials daily. About half of this is paper and other combustibles. Combined, the materials discarded by U.S. citizens would fill the New Orleans Superdome from floor to ceiling twice each day! And this does not include the far larger amounts of discards generated in producing the original consumer items.

Discards have earned several names depending on where we deposit them. Materials that we gather and throw away in a systematic manner by tossing them into waste cans or garbage disposal units are called "trash" or "garbage." "Pollution" is often made up of unwanted, sometimes harmful materials, discarded carelessly.

Many pollutants are actually "resources out of place." For example, glass bottles and aluminum cans resting on river bottoms or randomly scattered on roadsides need not be discards. Sturdy glass bottles can be reused. By **reuse** we mean processing (e.g., collecting, sterilizing, and refilling bottles) manufactured items so they can be used again. Aluminum cans and glass bottles can also be recycled, sometimes at lower cost than making new containers from original raw

The Louisiana Superdome. U.S. citizens discard a Superdome of trash every 12 hours.

materials. **Recycling** means reprocessing the materials in manufactured items to make new manufactured items (e.g., using the glass from old bottles to make new ones).

What do you do with discards generated by your daily activities? You probably throw many of them into wastebaskets or trash cans. But where do they go from there? Read on.

A.6 Disposing of Things We No Longer Need

The graph in Figure II.4 shows what happens to discards after they leave our trash cans. The top line represents the total tons of solid waste handled by municipalities each year. The amounts recovered for recycling or burned to produce useful energy are also shown. The rest, the net discards, are deposited in landfills and dumps or incinerated. The plots have been projected to the year 2000 based on trends in industrial production of materials.

Increased attention to waste disposal is important for us as individuals, communities, nations, and planetary inhabitants. Table II.1 shows our major types of waste materials and a projection of the amounts in the year 2000. Study this table and Figure 11.4. What benefits could come from more emphasis on by-product reuse, recycling, or generation of energy from waste?

Changes in our habits might, of course, change what happens in the future. Research into new uses of waste is under way. Compacted waste can be coated with asphalt to produce building materials, according to Japanese scientists. A process developed by the U.S. Bureau of Mines can convert 1000 kg of organic waste materials (those with high amounts of carbon and hydrogen) into 250 kg of oil. Crushed glass and shredded rubber are used in road construction.

Let's consider ourselves. What do we use on a daily basis? What chemical resources are used up to support our routine activities? What items do we throw away? What happens to them? The following *You Decide* will give you an opportunity to consider such questions.

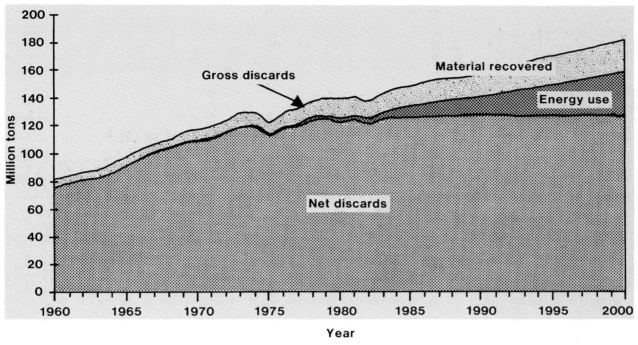

Figure II.4 Municipal solid waste. The total amount discarded (gross discards) and the amounts recovered for recycling or burned to produce useful energy are shown. The remainder (net discards) is disposed of by landfill, dumping, or incineration. *Source: Characterization of Municipal Solid Waste in the United States, 1960–2000.* Franklin Associates, Ltd., Prairie Village, Kansas, 1986. Prepared for U.S. Environmental Protection Agency, Office of Solid Waste and Energy Response, Washington, D.C. (WH–565E).

Table II.1   *Materials discarded as municipal waste*

Materials	1984		2000	
	Millions of tons	%	Millions of tons	%
Paper and paperboard	49.4	37.1	65.1	41.0
Glass	12.9	9.7	12.1	7.6
Metals	12.8	9.6	14.3	9.0
Plastics	9.6	7.2	15.5	9.8
Rubber and leather	3.3	2.5	3.8	2.4
Textiles	2.8	2.1	3.5	2.2
Wood	5.1	3.8	6.1	3.8
Other	0.1	0.1	0.1	0.1
Food wastes	10.8	8.1	10.8	6.8
Yard wastes	23.8	17.9	24.4	15.3
Miscellaneous inorganic wastes	2.4	1.8	3.1	2.0
TOTAL	133.0	100.0	158.8	100.0

Source: Characterization of Municipal Solid Waste in the United States, 1960–2000. Franklin Associates, Ltd., Prairie Village, Kansas, 1986. Prepared for U.S. Environmental Protection Agency, Office of Solid Waste and Energy Response, Washington, D.C. (WH-565E)

A.7   *You Decide:* Resource Junkies

We each use many natural and manufactured items daily. We rarely think about the variety of things we use, or about resources that helped make them. It's time to take stock!

"Resources" are materials that can be withdrawn from our natural environment such as plants, animals, minerals or rocks, or gases from the air.

The Earth is, in many ways, like any other spaceship. The resources "on board" are all we can count on for the duration of our "trip." Some of our spaceship's resources, such as fresh water, air, fertile soil, plants, and animals, can be

Don Green, Kennecott Copper Corporation

The total quality of copper available to us is constant.

American Chemical Society

Unlike copper, this wood is a renewable resource.

replenished over relatively short times by natural processes such as (for water) the hydrologic cycle or (for animals) reproduction. These are **renewable resources**—if we are careful, nature will help us keep up our supplies of these materials. Our main concerns are to avoid using renewable resources faster than nature can replenish them, or to avoid creating serious environmental damage by using them carelessly.

Other materials such as metals, natural gas, coal, and petroleum are **nonrenewable resources.** The natural processes that introduced them to our planet are not likely to be repeated. Since nonrenewable resources cannot be replenished, they can be "used up." What happens, of course, is that many become so widely dispersed that we can't collect them again at an affordable cost.

In this activity you are to think about several items that you use each day, and consider the resources of which they are made or the resources consumed in their manufacture.

You may use a television set each day, but we suggest you choose simpler items. By the time you would have analyzed the parts of a television set, you would have mentioned just about every type of natural resource.

Let's say you used a pencil today. What resources are combined in the pencil? If it is a common wooden lead pencil, it is made of wood and graphite (a form of the element carbon produced from wood or other natural materials), and probably also paint. The paint might include some natural or synthetic (i.e., manmade) pigments (coloring materials) and, before being applied it was dispersed in a solvent (possibly from petroleum). The pencil may have an eraser made of rubber (which could be from a plant or could be synthetic) attached with a metal collar. Of these materials, wood, graphite, natural rubber, and plant pigments come from renewable resources, while synthetic pigments and solvents, and the metal come from nonrenewable resources.

Perhaps you used a disposable automatic pencil. Here, wood that ordinarily holds the graphite has been replaced by plastic. Most plastics are made from chemicals obtained from petroleum. While you may prefer this newer type of pencil, it results from replacement of a renewable resource, wood, with plastic made from petroleum, a nonrenewable resource.

You should also consider waste materials generated by using items on your list. What about the pencils? If you used the eraser, you probably just brushed the eraser crumbs aside and they settled into the general dust in the room. Once the wooden pencil gets too short to hold or the lead in the automatic pencil is used up you probably will throw the pencil into the waste basket.

1. List 10 simple things you used or used up during the past 24 hours.
2. For each listed item, answer these two questions:
    a. What resources were used in its manufacture?
    b. How did you dispose of unwanted materials associated with its use?
3. Classify each resource in your answers to Question 2a as renewable or nonrenewable.

    Your class will divide into small groups to discuss the remaining questions. A full-class discussion will then highlight major points developed by the groups.

4. Summarize the resources listed by everyone in the group in answering Question 2a. What percent of the items are made from renewable resources?

5. Consider at least four of the listed items that are made mainly of nonrenewable resources. Try to think of a substitute for each of these items that would involve only renewable resources. Make a list of these replacement items.

6. Now summarize the waste disposal methods listed in answering Question 2b. If everyone in this country used these same disposal methods, what benefits or burdens would there be for your community? For our country? For the planet?

7. Examine the title of this *You Decide* activity. Describe two possible meanings of the title. Are both meanings appropriate? Why?

We use resources in many ways. But how do we decide which resource to select for which use? Clearly, this depends on knowing several things—the requirements of the intended use, the properties of the materials available, and their cost. Two of these concerns involve chemical knowledge, as we will discover in the next part of this unit.

PART A
SUMMARY *QUESTIONS*

1. State the law of conservation of matter. How is such a scientific law different from a law created by the government?

2. Inventory the atoms to determine if each of the following equations is balanced.

   a. The preparation of tin(II) fluoride (a component of some toothpastes, referred to on the label as "stannous fluoride"):

   $$Sn(s) + HF(aq) \rightarrow SnF_2(aq) + H_2(g)$$

   b. The synthesis of carborundum (SiC) for sandpaper:

   $$SiO_2(s) + 3\ C(s) \rightarrow SiC(s) + 2\ CO(g)$$

   c. The reaction of an antacid with stomach acid:

   An antacid is a mild base.

   $$Al(OH)_3(s) + 3\ HCl(aq) \rightarrow AlCl_3(aq) + 3\ H_2O(l)$$

3. In what way are phrases such as "using up" and "throwing away" inaccurate from a chemical viewpoint?

4. Briefly explain the Spaceship Earth analogy. In what ways is this analogy useful? In what ways is it misleading?

5. Describe at least two benefits of discarding less and recycling more of our wastes. Consider the law of conservation of matter and the resources available on Spaceship Earth in forming your answer.

6. What advantages, if any, does reuse have over recycling?

7. List four renewable resources and four nonrenewable resources.

B WHY WE USE WHAT WE DO

The Statue of Liberty is one of many historic objects that have undergone restoration. Paintings, furniture, tools, and machinery once relegated to the nation's attics are often restored. Such items may be put back into use or they may, like the Statue of Liberty, be restored because they are beautiful and of historical value.

Every object, old or new, is constructed from materials chosen because their characteristics or properties are suitable. What makes specific materials best for each use? We can begin to answer this question by looking at some properties of materials.

B.1 Properties Make the Difference

The Bettmann Archive

A knowledge of chemistry guided the recent renovation of the Statue of Liberty.

The Statue of Liberty had to be strong yet flexible to withstand the winds of New York Harbor. It had to be made of material that could be shaped and would maintain a pleasing appearance. The materials had to be readily available at reasonable cost. It was the job of the artist and the architect to know the characteristics of available materials and to select those used to build the statue and its support system.

The unique properties of materials make them useful for specific purposes. The desired properties may be physical properties such as color, density, or odor. Specific **physical changes** such as melting or boiling at certain temperatures may also be desirable characteristics. In a physical change, the identity of a substance is not changed.

Chemical properties of a material may also play an important role in its usefulness. A chemical property might be, for example, the reactivity of a substance with oxygen or with acids. In a **chemical change** (i.e., a chemical reaction), the identity of one or more substances changes, and one or more new substances are formed. A chemical change can often be detected by observing the formation of a gas, the formation of a solid, a color change, a change in the surface of a solid material, or a temperature change (indicating that heat has been absorbed or evolved).

As you will see in the following exercise, common properties of materials can be classified as physical and chemical properties.

YOUR TURN

II.2 Properties: Physical or Chemical?

In this exercise, classify each statement as describing a physical or a chemical property. A single question will help you: Is a change in the *identity* of a substance involved? If the answer is "no," then it is a physical property; if "yes" it is a chemical property. Consider the following statement:

Copper compounds are often blue or green in color.

Color is one of the characteristic properties of individual chemical compounds. Clearly, a green copper compound in a jar on the shelf is undergoing no change in identity. Color is, therefore, a physical property. Note, however, that a *change* in color often indicates a change in identity and therefore may represent a chemical property.

1. Some metals may become dull when exposed to air.
2. Metals, when pure, have a high luster (are shiny and reflect light).
3. Mercury's high density and liquid state at room temperature make it useful in barometers.
4. Archaeologists uncover ancient gold artifacts that are untarnished, while iron artifacts are often corroded.
5. The hardness of diamonds enables them to be used on drill bits.
6. Metals are typically ductile (can be drawn into wires).
7. You shouldn't use silver utensils to handle sulfur-containing foods such as eggs or mustard, since the silver will tarnish.
8. The high melting point of tungsten makes it useful for light bulb filaments.
9. Metals are typically much better conductors of heat and electricity than are nonmetals.
10. The magnesium ribbon of a photo flashcube ignites in the oxygen around it when you snap a picture.

Sometimes the substance needed for a particular use is either not available or is too expensive. Or a substance may have some undesirable chemical or physical properties that overshadow its desirable ones. What can be done in such situations? Often another substance that has most of the important properties of the original substance can be found. This new substance is then used instead.

Jon Jacobson

A blacksmith modifies properties of a metal sample through a variety of treatments.

Table II.2 *Common elements*

Element	Symbol
Aluminum	Al
Antimony	Sb
Argon	Ar
Barium	Ba
Beryllium	Be
Bismuth	Bi
Boron	B
Bromine	Br
Cadmium	Cd
Calcium	Ca
Carbon	C
Cesium	Cs
Chlorine	Cl
Chromium	Cr
Cobalt	Co
Copper	Cu
Fluorine	F
Gold	Au
Helium	He
Hydrogen	H
Iodine	I
Iron	Fe
Krypton	Kr
Lead	Pb
Lithium	Li
Magnesium	Mg
Manganese	Mn
Mercury	Hg
Neon	Ne
Nickel	Ni
Nitrogen	N
Oxygen	O
Phosphorus	P
Platinum	Pt
Potassium	K
Silicon	Si
Silver	Ag
Sodium	Na
Sulfur	S
Tin	Sn
Tungsten	W
Uranium	U
Zinc	Zn

That's what the U.S. Mint did when copper became too expensive to serve as the metal for pennies. Zinc metal is about as hard as copper and its density, although somewhat less, is still near that of copper. It is also readily available and is much less expensive than copper. For these reasons, zinc was chosen to replace copper for all post-1982 pennies. However, zinc is chemically more reactive than copper. Zinc pennies made during World War II had no protective coating and quickly corroded. Post-1982 pennies are plated with copper to increase their durability and also to maintain the familiar appearance of earlier coins.

Whether it be the copper or zinc in a penny, or the magnesium in a photo flashcube, each substance has its own specific chemical and physical properties. With the millions of substances available, how can we even begin to wade through the vast array to identify a particular substance for a given need? Luckily, nature has simplified things for us. All substances are made of a relatively small number of building blocks—atoms of the different chemical elements. Knowledge of similarities and differences among common elements can greatly simplify the challenge of matching substances to uses. We will learn more about the elements in the next section.

The next activity will help you become more familiar with the common elements listed in Table II.2.

YOUR *TURN*

II.3   Chemical Elements Crossword Puzzle

Your teacher will distribute a crossword puzzle that you should complete. Clues for the puzzle, which appear at the end of this Unit (page 132), are descriptions of the properties and uses of the elements listed in Table II.2. Use this table as a guide in completing the puzzle.

B.2   The Chemical Elements

Earlier (Unit One, Part B.4) we learned that all matter is composed of atoms and that atoms of an element differ from those of other elements in their properties. Over 100 chemical elements are known. However, only about one-third are important to us on a daily basis. Table II.2 lists some common elements and their symbols.

The elements, as shown by Table II.3, have properties that vary over wide ranges. Some, such as magnesium and aluminum, are very similar and others, such as iodine and gold, are very different. Often, chemical compounds composed of similar elements have similar properties.

Table II.3 *Some properties of the elements*

Property	From	To
Density		
Metallic elements	0.53 g/mL (Li)	22.6 g/mL (Os)
Nonmetallic elements	0.0008 g/mL (H_2)	4.93 g/mL (I_2)
Melting point		
Metallic elements	−33 °C (Hg)	3410 °C (W)
Nonmetallic elements	−249 °C (Ne)	3727 °C (C)
Reactivity		
Metallic elements	Low (Au)	High (Cs)
Nonmetallic elements	None (He)	High (F_2)

Elements can be grouped or classified in many ways according to similarities and differences in their properties. Two major classes are metals and nonmetals. Everyday experience has given you some knowledge of the properties of metals. In the next laboratory activity you will have a chance to explore further the properties of metals and nonmetals.

A small number of elements have properties intermediate between those expected for metals and nonmetals. These elements are referred to as **metalloids.** In some properties metalloids are like metals and in others they are like nonmetals. Every element can be classified as a metal, a nonmetal, or a metalloid. You will now discover some properties that make this classification possible.

B.3 Laboratory Activity: Metal or Nonmetal?

Getting Ready

In this activity you will explore the properties of eight elements with the goal of classifying them as metals, nonmetals, or metalloids. You will examine the appearance of the elements to observe the physical properties of color, luster, and the form of the sample. (Is it crystalline like table salt?) By tapping the sample with a hammer, you will determine whether it is malleable or brittle. You may also test for the physical property of electrical conductivity. (As an alternative, your teacher may demonstrate this test.)

Two chemical reactions will be used to show differences in the chemical properties of the elements. For each sample, you will discover whether or not chemical reactions occur with hydrochloric acid, HCl(*aq*), and with a copper(II) chloride (CuCl$_2$) solution.

Prepare a data table in your notebook, leaving plenty of space to record the properties of the eight elements, which have been coded with letters *a* to *h*.

Data table					
Element	**Appearance**	**Result of tapping**	**Reaction with acid**	**Reaction with CuCl$_2$(*aq*)**	**Conductivity (optional)**
a. *b.* *c.* *d.* *e.* *f.* *g.* *h.*					

Caution: Do not touch element *h* with your hands. Use forceps or tweezers to manipulate crystals of this sample. If the element comes in contact with skin, wash affected area with water.

Procedure

Physical Properties
1. *Appearance:* Observe and record the appearance of each element. Include physical properties such as color, luster, and also the form.
2. *Tapping:* Gently tap each element except sample *h* with a hammer and describe its property as malleable or brittle. A material is **malleable** if it flattens without shattering. A sample is **brittle** if it shatters into pieces when struck. Your teacher will demonstrate the result of tapping sample *h*.

Nonconductors are sometimes used as insulators.

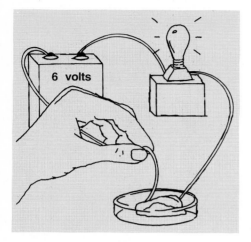

Figure II.5   Testing for conductivity.

3. *Conductivity (optional):* If the conductivity apparatus is available, use it to test the eight samples. *Caution:* Avoid touching the electrodes with your hands; an electric shock may result.

Touch both electrodes to the element being tested. If the bulb lights, the element sample has allowed electricity to flow through it. Such a sample is termed a **conductor.** If the bulb fails to light, the material is a **nonconductor** (see Figure II.5).

Chemical Properties

1. Test each sample for reactivity with acid as described below. The formation of gas bubbles indicates that a chemical reaction has taken place.
   a. Prepare eight test tubes labeled *a* to *h*. Place 5 mL of water in one test tube. With a grease pencil mark each test tube with a line at the height of the 5 mL of water. Pour out the water.
   b. Place a sample of each of the eight elements in the appropriately labeled test tube. The sample should be a 2-cm length of wire or ribbon, or 0.5–1.0 g of solid.
   c. Add 5 mL of hydrochloric acid (HCl) to each test tube.
   d. Observe and record each result.

2. Test each sample for reactivity with copper(II) chloride ($CuCl_2$) solution as described below. Changes in the appearance of any element sample indicate a chemical reaction has taken place.
   a. Prepare eight test tubes and add element samples as described in steps 1a and b above.
   b. Add approximately 5 mL of $CuCl_2$ solution to each test tube.
   c. Observe the test tubes for five minutes; changes may be slow.

Questions

1. Sort the eight coded elements into two groups, based on similarities in their physical and chemical properties.
2. Which elements could fit into either group based on certain properties?
3. Based on the following information, reclassify each element as a metal, a nonmetal, or a metalloid. Metals are elements that have a luster, are malleable, and conduct electricity (physical properties). Many metals react with acids and with copper(II) chloride solution (chemical properties). Nonmetals are usually dull in appearance, brittle, and do not conduct electricity (physical properties). Most nonmetals do not react with acids or with copper(II) chloride solution (chemical properties). Elements that have some properties of both metals and nonmetals are metalloids.

Metalloids are often used in the manufacture of electronic devices such as computers and digital watches.

Even though we have narrowed our view of all known substances to slightly more than 100 chemical elements, the amount of information on each element is still immense. Nature has again come to our rescue. Elements can be organized very nicely into a manageable system.

B.4 The Periodic Table

Scientists always search for patterns and regularities in nature. If an underlying pattern can be found, information can be organized in ways that make it more understandable and useful.

By the mid-1800s about 60 elements were known. Five then-known nonmetallic elements—hydrogen (H), oxygen (O), nitrogen (N), fluorine (F), and chlorine (Cl)—exist at room temperature as gases. Two elements are liquids—the metal mercury (Hg) and the nonmetal bromine (Br). The remaining elements known at that time are solids with widely differing properties.

The gaseous elements discovered first were all diatomic: H_2, O_2, N_2, F_2, and Cl_2.

During this period several scientists, working independently, attempted to devise a classification system that placed elements with similar properties near each other on a chart. Such an arrangement is termed a **periodic table.** Dimitri Mendeleev, a Russian chemist, in 1869, published a periodic table very similar to that of today. The table serves a function not unlike a calendar in which all the Sundays are in one column, all the Mondays in the next, and so on, and all the days in the same week are in the same row.

Among the properties used in devising the first periodic tables are the masses of the atoms and their abilities to combine with atoms of other elements. Gradually it had become clear that atoms of different elements differ in mass. For example, hydrogen atoms are the lightest of all, oxygen atoms are about 16 times as heavy as hydrogen atoms, and sulfur atoms are about twice as heavy as oxygen atoms (making them about 32 times as heavy as hydrogen atoms). By such comparisons **atomic masses** can be assigned to atoms of all elements.

Atoms of the elements also differ in how many atoms of other elements they will combine with. For example, atoms of some elements combine with no more than one atom of chlorine, giving compounds with the general formula ECl (E represents the second element). Others combine only with two, or three, or four chlorine atoms, giving ECl_2, or ECl_3, or ECl_4 compounds. Because oxygen and chlorine each combine with a large number of elements, the search for patterns among the elements extended to examination of the "combining power" with oxygen and chlorine.

In the first periodic tables, elements with similar properties were placed in vertical groups. Rather than telling one of the great scientific detective stories, we invite you to follow a similar path.

Dimitri Mendeleev (1834–1907) published the first useful periodic table.

YOUR*TURN*

II.4 Grouping the Elements

You will be given a set of element data cards. Each card lists some properties of one of the first 20 elements. First, arrange the cards in the order of increasing atomic mass. Then place the cards in a number of different groups. Each group should include elements with similar properties. For example, you might put together all elements with boiling points below 0 °C and in another group all elements with boiling points above 0 °C. Or you might group all elements by the number of chlorine atoms in their chlorides. Next examine the cards within each group for any patterns. Arrange the cards within each group in some logical sequence. Then observe how particular properties vary from group to group. Arrange all the card groups into some logical sequence.

When you have found patterns within and among the card groups that appear to be reasonable and useful, tape the cards onto a sheet of paper to preserve your pattern for classroom discussion.

Early periodic tables were very useful, but they gave no insight into why similarities occur in the properties of the elements. The reason for these similarities was discovered about 50 years later. It is the basis for the modern periodic table. Recall that atoms are composed of smaller particles, including equal numbers of positively charged protons and negatively charged electrons (Unit One, Part B.6). One essential difference between atoms of different elements is in the number of protons present—the **atomic number.** Every sodium atom contains 11 protons, and every carbon atom contains six protons. If the number of protons in an atom is 9, it is a fluorine atom; if 12, it is a magnesium atom. An atom of hydrogen contains one proton; hydrogen has an atomic number of 1. An atom of helium contains two protons and thus has an atomic number of 2.

Placing all elements in sequence according to their atomic numbers is a key feature of the modern periodic table. This table also reflects the arrangement of electrons in atoms. As we shall see, electron arrangement is closely related to the properties of atoms.

Patterns are sometimes discovered when graphs are prepared from data. In the next exercise you will explore the relationship between atomic numbers and the groupings of elements with similar properties.

YOUR *TURN*

II.5   Periodic Variation in Properties

Your teacher will give you the atomic numbers of the 20 elements that you arranged in Your Turn II.4. Use these atomic numbers and the information on the element cards to prepare the two graphs described below. It will be helpful if you label each point on the graphs with the symbol of the element that it represents.

Graph 1. Trends in a chemical property. Label the x axis with the atomic numbers from 1 to 20. Select the formulas of either the oxides or the chlorides and label the y axis for the formulas given on the cards. To plot the data for the chlorides, label the y axis with 0 for formation of no chlorides, 1 for ECl compounds (representing 1 chlorine atom per E atom), 2 for ECl_2, 3 for ECl_3, and 4 for ECl_4. To plot the data for the oxides, label the y axis with 0 for formation of no oxide, 0.5 for E_2O (representing 0.5 0 atom per E atom), 1 for EO, 1.5 for E_2O_3, 2 for EO_2, and 2.5 for E_2O_5. Plot the data from the element cards.

Graph 2. Trends in a physical property. Label the x axis with the atomic numbers from 1 to 20. Select either the melting point or boiling point and label the y axis as shown in the accompanying figure. Use as much of the space on your graph paper as possible. Plot the data from the element cards, but do not include data for the element with atomic number 6, carbon, which will be too far off the scale of the y axis.

Connect adjacent points on both graphs with straight lines. Answer the following questions.

1. Does either graph reveal a cyclic or recurring pattern? (*Hint:* Focus attention on those elements appearing in the peaks or valleys. Are these graphs consistent with your earlier grouping of the elements? Why or why not?

2. Based on these graphs, comment on why the chemist's organization of elements is called the *periodic* table.

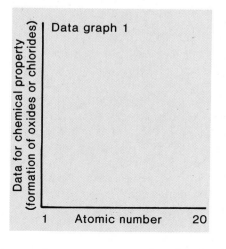

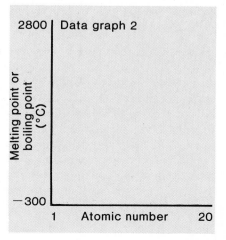

The periodic relationship among elements is summarized in the modern periodic table (see inside back cover). When elements are listed in order by their atomic numbers, and grouped according to common properties, they form seven horizontal rows, called **periods.** The vertical columns each contain elements with similar properties. These are called **groups** or **families** of elements. The lithium (Li) family, for example, consists of the six elements in the first column at the left-hand end of the table. These elements are all highly reactive metals that form ECl chlorides and E_2O oxides. Like sodium chloride, all chlorides and oxides of lithium family elements are ionic compounds. The helium family, at the right-hand end of the table, by contrast, consists of very unreactive elements (only xenon and krypton are known to form any compounds at all). The recurrence of similar properties at regular intervals when elements are arranged in order of increasing atomic number is sometimes referred to as the **periodic law.**

To become more familiar with the periodic table, locate the 20 elements you classified earlier. How do their relative positions compare with their locations in your chart?

The arrangement of elements in the periodic table provides an orderly summary of the key characteristics of elements. If we know the major properties of a certain chemical family, then we can predict some of the behavior of any element in that family. Try your hand at making some predictions based on this important chemical classification scheme.

He family elements are known as noble gases.

Based on his table, Mendeleev correctly predicted the properties of several then-unknown elements.

YOUR*TURN*

II.6 Periodic Table

Properties of an element can, in some cases, be estimated by averaging properties of the preceding and following elements in the same periodic table group. This was how Mendeleev predicted the properties of elements unknown in his time. He was so certain of his conclusions, that he left gaps in his periodic table for missing elements with the predicted properties. Mendeleev's fame rests largely on the correctness of these predictions. When the elements were discovered, they fit in exactly as he had expected.

As an example, suppose that krypton is unknown and you want to answer the following question:

Estimate the boiling point of krypton, given that the boiling point of argon is -186 °C and that of xenon is -112 °C.

In its periodic table group, krypton is preceded by argon and followed by xenon. Taking the average of the boiling points of these elements gives

$$\frac{(-186 \text{ °C}) + (-112 \text{ °C})}{2} = -149 \text{ °C}$$

The estimated boiling point of krypton, -149 °C, is within 5% of the known boiling point, which is -157 °C.

As another example, consider the prediction of the formulas of chemical compounds based on periodic table relationships.

What formula would you predict for the compound formed between carbon and sulfur? Keep in mind that carbon and oxygen form carbon dioxide (CO_2).

Consulting the periodic table shows that sulfur (S) and oxygen (O) are in the same family. Knowing that carbon and oxygen form CO_2, the best prediction is that the compound in question will be carbon disulfide (CS_2) (a correct prediction).

1. One of the elements undiscovered in Mendeleev's time was germanium. Given that the melting points of silicon and tin are 1410 °C and 232 °C, respectively, estimate the melting point of germanium.

2. Estimate the melting point of rubidium. The melting points of potassium and cesium are 64 °C and 29 °C, respectively. Would you expect the melting point of sodium to be higher or lower than that of rubidium?

3. These are formulas for known compounds: NaI, $MgCl_2$, CaO, Al_2O_3, and CCl_4. Predict the formula of a compound formed from each pair of elements: (a) Si and F, (b) Al and S, (c) K and Cl, (d) Ca and Br, (e) Ba and O.

4. Which family of elements is so lacking in chemical reactivity that its elements were originally regarded as "inert"?

B.5 Chemical Reactivity

Magnesium and aluminum react with oxygen. In fact, they react so quickly that we seal small samples of magnesium with oxygen gas in photo flashbulbs. When the metal is heated by electricity from the camera battery, it ignites, producing a blinding flash. The equation for the reaction of magnesium with oxygen is given below:

$$2\ Mg(s)\ +\ O_2(g) \longrightarrow 2\ MgO(s)$$

Look for the magnesium oxide (MgO), a white powder, the next time you've taken a flash picture.

Iron reacts with oxygen also, but it does so much more slowly. Rusting is the chemical combination of these two elements. Rusting (a form of corrosion) includes a complex series of reactions involving water as well as oxygen gas. It's

Jon Jacobson

The reactivity of oxygen and iron is destroying this car.

commonly known, for example, that dry iron utensils do not rust. And cars rust faster on the coast than in the desert. To a chemist, "rust" is a combination of a number of iron-containing compounds including Fe_2O_3.

Gold does not react with oxygen in the air. This is one reason gold is valuable as a material for decorative objects we want to keep for a long time (like the Statue of Liberty torch). Gold-plated electrical contacts are dependable because nonconducting oxides do not form on their surfaces.

By observing the ease with which metals react with oxygen, we learn something about the reactivities of the metals. In the following laboratory activity you'll investigate another method of comparing the relative chemical reactivities of metals and their ions.

B.6 Laboratory Activity: Metal Reactivities

Getting Ready

In this activity you will observe and compare some chemical reactions of several metallic elements. The reaction to be studied occurs between the metal and a solution that contains the ions of a different metal. You will carry out the reaction of each of three metals (copper, magnesium, and zinc) with water solutions of ionic compounds that contain metal ions (copper, magnesium, zinc, and silver nitrates).

In your laboratory notebook, prepare a data table like the one below.

Data table: Relative reactivities of metals

Metal	Solutions			
	Cu(NO$_3$)$_2$	Mg(NO$_3$)$_2$	Zn(NO$_3$)$_2$	AgNO$_3$
Cu	—			
Mg		—		
Zn			—	
Ag	NR	NR	NR	NR

We have filled in the results for reactions of silver metal (too expensive!). NR stands for "no visible reaction." The dashes indicate tests that are not needed.

Procedure

1. Obtain four strips (approx. 3 cm $\times$ 0.5 cm) of each of the three metals to be tested.

2. Clean the shiny surface of each metal strip by rubbing it with sandpaper or emery paper. Record your observations on the appearance of the metals.

3. Label four test tubes for the four solutions to be used. Measure out 5 mL of water in one and with a grease pencil mark each test tube to show the height of 5 mL.

4. Place 5 mL of each of the test solutions in the appropriately labelled test tubes.

5. Add a copper strip to each solution as appropriate. Observe the results for three to five minutes. If no reaction is observed, write NR on your data table. When you observe a reaction, record the observed changes (see Figure II.6).

6. Remove the copper strips from the test tubes. Dry the strips with a paper towel and clean them with sandpaper so they will be ready for the next group of students.

Figure II.6 Testing copper for its
reactivity. The test tubes each contain
5 mL of the test solutions. A copper strip
should be placed in each test tube and
the results observed.

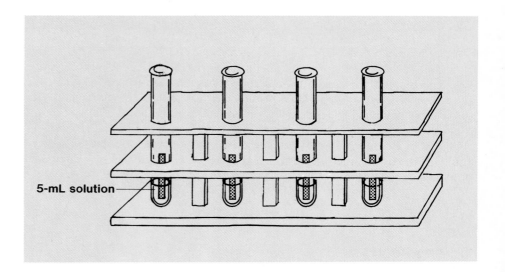

5-mL solution

7. Discard the used test tube solutions as directed by your teacher. Wash the used test tubes.

8. Repeat steps 4 through 7 with each of the other two metals and complete all entries in the data table.

Questions

1. Which metal reacted with the most solutions?

2. Which metal reacted with the fewest solutions?

3. List the four metals in order, placing the most reactive metal first (the one that reacted with the most solutions) and proceeding in order to the least reactive metal (the one that reacted with the fewest solutions). Such a ranking of elements in order of chemical reactivity is called an **activity series.**

4. Refer to your metal activity list in Question 3. Based on the list, can you tell why the Statue of Liberty was made with copper instead of zinc?

5. What material that you observed in this activity might have been a better choice for the statue than copper? Why wasn't it chosen?

6. Given your knowledge of relative chemical activity, which one metal on your list is most likely to be found in an uncombined or "free" state in nature? Which metal would be least likely to be found uncombined with other elements?

B.7   What Determines the Properties of Substances?

What causes differences in the reactivities of the metals? Or in the many other properties that vary from element to element? Recall that atoms of different elements differ in the number of protons (atomic numbers). Therefore, they also differ in the number of electrons. Many properties of elements are determined largely by the number of electrons in their atoms and how the electrons are arranged. (In the next unit, during our study of the molecules in petroleum, we will look more closely at electron arrangements.)

In atoms: No. of electrons = no. of protons (atomic number)

Consider metal reactivities, which you just investigated in the laboratory. The major distinction between metals and nonmetals is that metal atoms lose their outer electrons much more easily than do nonmetal atoms. Under suitable conditions, these outer electrons can be transferred to other atoms or ions. In your laboratory activity, for example, magnesium atoms (Mg) each transferred two electrons to positively charged zinc ions (Zn^{2+}),

$$Mg(s) + Zn^{2+}(aq) \longrightarrow Mg^{2+}(aq) + Zn(s)$$

The NO_3^- ion is unchanged in this reaction.

and similar reactions occurred between other pairs of metals. The more active metals lose their electrons more easily, and so give them up to the ions of less active metals.

Some physical properties of metals depend on attractions between atoms. For example, the stronger the attraction between atoms, the higher the melting point of the metal. Since magnesium has a higher melting point than sodium, we can infer that the between-atom attractions are stronger in magnesium metal than in sodium metal.

Chemical and physical properties of substances other than metals can also be explained by the structure of their atoms, ions, or molecules and by the attraction between these particles. As we pointed out earlier, water's unusually high melting and boiling points are due to the strong attraction between water molecules.

Understanding the properties of atoms enables chemists to predict and correlate the behavior of substances. This information, often combined with a bit of imagination, allows us to extend the uses of materials and enables chemists to create new chemical compounds to meet specific needs.

B.8 Modifying Properties to Fit Intended Uses

Throughout history—first by chance and more recently guided by science—we have greatly expanded the range of materials available for our use. We have learned to modify the properties of matter either by physically blending or chemically reacting two or more substances. Sometimes only slight changes in the properties of the individual substances are desired. And sometimes chemists create new materials with greatly different properties.

For example, the writing material in a black "lead" pencil is mainly graphite, a natural form of the element carbon. (When first discovered, graphite was mistakenly believed to be a form of lead, and the name has stuck.) Pencil lead is available in a range of hardnesses. To modify the hardness of pencil lead, clay is mixed with graphite in varying amounts. This produces harder pencil lead (less graphite can be rubbed off onto the paper). Hard pencil lead, No. 4, makes a very light line. Softer writing lead (such as No. 1) makes very black, easily smudged lines on paper.

In the first laboratory activity in this unit (Part A.4), you saw an example of how the properties of metals can be modified by creating **alloys,** solid mixtures of atoms of different metals. Brass, which formed when you heated the zinc-coated penny, is an alloy of copper with from 10 to 40% zinc. Brass is harder than copper and has an attractive gold color, unlike either copper or zinc.

Examples of compounds designed to fit specific purposes are everywhere. Most plastics are essentially custom-designed materials made up of very large molecules. The action of many drugs depends on very specific molecular shapes. Penicillin, for example, is an antibiotic produced in nature by a mold. The penicillin molecule has been modified to give a family of "semisynthetic" penicillins with improved or more specific effectiveness.

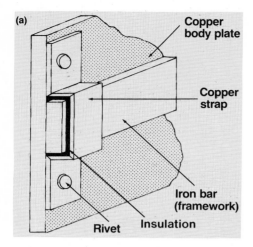

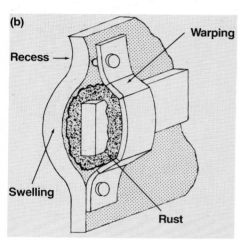

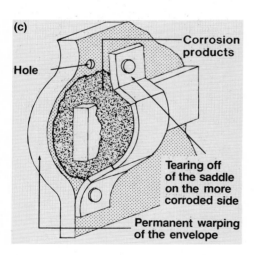

Source: Adapted from Nielson, N. "Keeping the Torch Lit." *Materials Performance*, 1984, 24 (4), p. 80.

Figure II.7   (a) A Statue of Liberty body plate—iron framework connection (as originally constructed). (b) and (c) Corrosion of the statute framework.

B.9 *You Decide:* Restoration of the Statue of Liberty

President Ronald Reagan announced the decision to restore the Statue of Liberty on May 18, 1982. Several questions faced the restoration experts, including what caused the statue to deteriorate, how the damage could be repaired, and what action should be taken to prevent further deterioration.

The body of the statue is composed of 300 individual copper plates. Each plate was originally connected to an iron-bar framework by riveted copper straps, diagrammed in Figure II.7a. When two different metals such as copper and iron are in contact with each other in the presence of moisture and dissolved ions, the metals react. (A similar reaction between copper and zinc can be demonstrated easily with a post-1982 penny. Your teacher will provide you with instructions for a take-home experiment using pennies that demonstrates corrosion of metals in contact in such an environment.)

The statue builders did attempt to prevent copper from coming in contact with the iron framework, which would cause corrosion. They placed shellac-soaked asbestos between copper and iron at their junctions. Unfortunately, this was inadequate protection. Over the years, condensed water vapor and rain collected at the junctions. The humid interior of the statue, which was far from waterproof, also hastened corrosion of the iron. The iron bars rusted and swelled; some lost a large portion of their mass. As a result of the swelling, more than 40% of the 450,000 rivets pulled loose. This left holes in the copper and allowed the plates to sag (Figure II.7b and c).

In addition to internal structural damage, there was concern that the statue's copper exterior might have suffered the effects of air pollution. Copper metal reacts with substances in the air to form a compound that provides a stable, attractive, green coating or **patina,** on the exposed copper surface. The patina protects the underlying copper from further deterioration by reaction with substances in the air.

Acidic pollutants can convert copper patina into a related substance that is more soluble in water. As rainwater dissolves this new substance, more copper metal is exposed and can undergo further corrosion.

In summary, three major sources of deterioration of the statue had to be considered in planning the repairs:

- Corrosion of the iron framework at contact points between the iron and copper.
- The humid atmosphere inside the statue, which hastened the corrosion of iron.
- Removal of the protective patina coating on the copper exterior of the statue due to airborne pollution.

A further problem was created by the multiple coats of paint and tar applied to the statue's interior over the years. The damage due to corrosion could not be fully assessed and repairs made until the paint and tar were removed.

How would you have tried to solve some of Liberty's restoration problems? Using common experience and your knowledge of chemistry, propose one or more solutions to each problem identified above. If substitution of materials is involved in your proposed action, consider factors such as the chemical and physical properties of the materials you propose using, their cost, and the need to preserve the original design of the statue. You will share your ideas with the class and compare them to the solutions chosen by the restoration committee.

PART B
SUMMARY *QUESTIONS*

1. What characteristic chemical or physical property can be used to distinguish between each of the following pairs of substances?
    a. Brass from gold
    b. Hydrogen from helium
    c. Tungsten from iron
    d. A lithium family metal from silver

2. What two properties do nonmetals lack that make them unsuitable for electric wiring?

3. Given the correct formulas Al_2O_3 and $BeCl_2$, predict the formulas for the compounds containing
    a. Mg and F   b. B and S

4. For medical reasons, people with high blood pressure are advised to limit the amount of sodium ions in their diet. Normal table salt (NaCl) has a commercially available substitute: potassium chloride. Write the formula for potassium chloride. Why are its properties similar to sodium chloride?

5. For each of the following, determine whether the set of elements belongs to the same family; if not, identify the element that does not belong with the other two.
    a. Sodium, potassium, magnesium
    b. Helium, neon, argon
    c. Oxygen, arsenic, sulfur
    d. Carbon, nitrogen, phosphorus

6. Explain how a graph that plots melting points vs. atomic numbers lends support to the idea of the periodic table.

7. Why is it inaccurate to talk of the chemically "perfect" or "best" metal?

8. If two dissimilar metals are used in construction, why is it desirable to separate the two with a nonconducting material?

Jon Jacobson

This gold plated jewelry will not corrode. This property plus its pleasing appearance, and its malleability and ductility make gold an ideal ornamental metal.

C CONSERVATION IN NATURE AND THE COMMUNITY

In this section we will explore the chemical "supplies" aboard Spaceship Earth. We will also consider how nature conserves resources. Then we will look at the need for conservation at the human level and some possible ways it can be achieved.

C.1 Sources of Our Resources

Despite advances in space travel, our resource needs must continue to be met by the chemical "supplies" located on Spaceship Earth. These supplies or resources are often inventoried in terms of where they are found. Table II.4 indicates the composition of our planet.

The atmosphere, the hydrosphere, and the outer portion of the lithosphere are the sources of *all* resources for *all* our activities. We draw nitrogen, oxygen, neon, argon, and a few other gases from the atmosphere. We take water and some

Table II.4 *The Earth's composition*

Layer of planet	Thickness (average)	Composition (decreasing order of abundance)
Atmosphere	100 km	N_2 (78%), O_2 (21%), Ar (0.9%), He + Ne (<0.01%) variable amounts of H_2O, CO_2, etc.
Hydrosphere	5 km	H_2O, and in the oceans that cover some 71% of the Earth's surface, approximately 3.5% NaCl and smaller amounts of Mg, S, Ca, and other elements as ions
Lithosphere:	6400 km	
Crust	Top 40 km	Silicates (compounds formed of metal, Si, and O atoms). Metals include Al, Na, Fe, Ca, Mg, K, and others
		Coal, oil, and natural gas
		Carbonates such as $CaCO_3$
		Oxides such as Fe_2O_3
		Sulfides such as PbS
Mantle	40–2900 km	Silicates of Mg and Fe
Core	2900 km to Earth's center	Fe and Ni

dissolved minerals from the hydrosphere. However, we rely on the lithosphere, the solid part of the Earth, for most of our chemical resources. It is here that we find petroleum and metal-bearing **ores.** (An ore is naturally occurring rock or mineral from which it is profitable to recover a metal or other material.) Our deepest mines barely scratch the surface of the Earth's crust. If the Earth were the size of an apple, all accessible resources would be concentrated in the apple skin. From this thin band of soil and rock on Earth we must obtain almost all the raw materials we use to construct homes, automobiles, appliances, computers, cassette tapes, records, and tennis rackets—in fact, all manufactured objects.

These chemical supplies are well suited to support complex life forms. However, many important resources are not distributed uniformly. There is no correlation between the abundance of these resources and either land area or population. For example, the Republic of South Africa has only 0.6% of the world's population but, as shown in Table II.5, extraordinary amounts of many important elements are located there.

Many nations have a surplus of one or more chemical resources but a deficiency of others. Throughout history, unequal distribution of resources has motivated both great achievements and brutal wars. Much of the development of the United States has been due to the quantity and diversity of our chemical resources. Yet, in recent years the United States has imported increasing amounts of certain chemical resources. Table II.6 illustrates this quite clearly.

In addition to the land, which provides most of our chemical resources, the oceans contain significant dissolved amounts of compounds of some 17 metals. Also, solid nodules discovered on the ocean floor contain as much as 24% manganese (Mn), 14% iron (Fe), and trace amounts of copper (Cu), nickel (Ni), and cobalt (Co). The availability of minerals from seawater and from underwater nodules raises hope that these and perhaps other metal-rich sediments can someday be "aqua-mined."

Table II.5 *South Africa's resources*

Resource	Percent of world's known supply of given resource
Land area	0.8
Population	0.6
Pt group metals (Pt, Pd, Ir, Rh, Ru, Os)	75
Chromium	68
Gold	51
Gemstones (diamonds, etc.)	34
Titanium	25

Table II.6   *Some essential materials and sources of U.S. supply*

Material and uses	Percent imported		Major foreign sources
	0 25 50 75 100		
Mica (sheet) Electrical insulators; filler (plasterboard, rolled roofing, shingles)	100	▬▬▬▬▬▬	India, Brazil, Malagasy Republic
Manganese Steel, alloys	99	▬▬▬▬▬	Brazil, Gabon, Australia, South Africa
Cobalt Alloys, catalysts, ceramics, pigments	98	▬▬▬▬▬	Zaire, Belgium, Luxembourg, Finland, Norway, Canada
Chromium Steel (up to 25%), alloys, decorative plating	91	▬▬▬▬	South Africa, Soviet Union, Turkey, Rhodesia
Aluminum (ores and metal) Building materials, powerlines, vehicle parts, packaging	85	▬▬▬▬	Jamaica, Surinam, Australia, Dominican Republic
Fluorine Uranium production, specialty chemicals	82	▬▬▬▬	Mexico, Spain, Italy
Platinum group metals Catalysts, electronics, jewelry, medical and dental applications	80	▬▬▬▬	South Africa, United Kingdom, Soviet Union
Tin Plated food cans, solder, bronze, bearing metals	75	▬▬▬	Malaysia, Thailand, Bolivia
Mercury Agriculture (e.g., pesticides), electrodes in Cl_2 production, street lights, gauges	73	▬▬▬	Canada, Algeria, Mexico, Spain
Selenium Tinted glass, xerography, electronic devices, photoelectric cells	58	▬▬▬	Canada, Japan, Mexico

Even if aqua-mining were to become a major new source of minerals, the total supply of nonrenewable resources aboard our spaceship would remain unchanged. The possibility of the supply of nonrenewable resources running out might be postponed, not avoided. The real question is, how can we deal wisely with the resources of the Earth? Conservation is the best answer.

C.2 Conservation Is Nature's Way

The law of conservation of matter is based on the notion that the basic "stuff" of our world is indestructible. Chemists explain observable phenomena in terms of atoms. All the changes we observe in matter can be interpreted as rearrangements among atoms.

Determining the amount of an element or a chemical compound that can be obtained from a natural resource usually begins with a chemical equation. Earlier (Part A.3) you practiced distinguishing chemical statements from chemical equations. Now you will learn how to turn such statements into equations.

Let's consider the simple example of the reaction of hydrogen with oxygen to give gaseous water. First, write the reactant formula(s) to the left of the arrow and the product formula(s) to the right.

$$H_2(g) + O_2(g) \longrightarrow H_2O(g)$$

Some rockets are powered by the reaction between liquid hydrogen and liquid oxygen.

Now count atoms. There are two hydrogen atoms on the left and two on the right. Hydrogen atoms are balanced. But there are two oxygen atoms on the left and only one on the right. Since oxygen is not balanced, the equation as a whole is not balanced. Coefficients must be added so that the numbers of atoms of each kind are balanced.

To have as many oxygen atoms in the product molecules as in the reactant molecules, we write a 2 in front of the formula for water.

$$H_2(g) + O_2(g) \longrightarrow 2 H_2O(g)$$

Now there are two oxygen atoms on each side. But hydrogen is no longer balanced. We correct this by placing a 2 in front of the formula for the hydrogen molecule. The balanced equation is:

$$2 H_2(g) + O_2(g) \longrightarrow 2 H_2O(g)$$

(Note that the coefficient 1 is understood and need not be written.)

This is a correct symbolic statement of the reaction and of nature's conservation of atoms. When two molecules of hydrogen gas react with one molecule of oxygen gas, two molecules of gaseous water are formed.

The formula for a chemical compound reflects its composition. Thus we cannot balance the equation above by writing the subscript 2 after the oxygen atom in the water molecule. The formula H_2O_2 represents a different compound, hydrogen peroxide, which is *not* produced in this reaction. Consequently, the only way to balance an equation is by placing proper coefficients in front of appropriate formulas.

H_2O_2 in dilute water solution is used as an antiseptic.

Here are some additional rules of thumb to help you balance equations:

- Treat polyatomic ions, such as NO_3^- and CO_3^{2-}, as units rather than balancing their atoms individually.
- If water is present in an equation, balance hydrogen and oxygen atoms last.
- Recount all atoms when you believe an equation is balanced—just to be sure!

YOUR*TURN*

II.7 Balancing Equations

As an example of turning a chemical statement into an equation consider the following:

The reaction of methane (CH_4) with chlorine (Cl_2) occurs in sewage water plants and often in chlorinated water supplies. A common product is chloroform ($CHCl_3$). This product also is made by the chemical industry for use in certain pharmaceutical preparations. A chemical statement describing this reaction is

$$CH_4(g) + Cl_2(g) \longrightarrow CHCl_3(l) + HCl(g)$$

To make this an equation, we proceed as follows: There is one carbon atom on each side of the arrow, so, for the moment, the statement is balanced on carbon. There are four hydrogen atoms on the left, but only two on the right. If the two, thus far unaccounted for, hydrogen atoms react with chlorine atoms, two more hydrogen chloride (HCl) molecules will form, and we can write:

$$CH_4(g) + Cl_2(g) \longrightarrow CHCl_3(l) + 3\ HCl(g)$$

Now that atoms of carbon and hydrogen are in balance, we note that there are two chlorine atoms on the left and six on the right of the arrow. These six chlorine atoms must have come from three chlorine (Cl_2) molecules, so we can write the equation:

$$CH_4(g) + 3\ Cl_2(g) \longrightarrow CHCl_3(l) + 3\ HCl(g)$$

Examine each of the following and balance any that is not balanced.

1. Two blast furnace reactions used to obtain iron from its ore:

$$C(s) + O_2(g) \longrightarrow 2\ CO(g)$$
$$Fe_2O_3(s) + CO(g) \longrightarrow Fe(l) + 3\ CO_2(g)$$

Electric furnace at the Indiana Harbor Works of the Inland Steel Company.

2. Two reactions in the refining of a copper ore:

$$Cu_2S(s) + O_2(g) \rightarrow CuO(s) + SO_2(g)$$
$$CuO(s) + C(s) \rightarrow Cu(s) + CO_2(g)$$

3. The reaction of ammonia (NH_3) with oxygen gas (O_2) occurs continuously in the soil. It also is used extensively in the chemical industry to make intermediates for the manufacture of drugs, explosives, fibers, and other products.

$$NH_3(g) + O_2(g) \rightarrow NO_2(g) + H_2O(l)$$

4. Combustion in an automobile engine can be represented by:

$$C_8H_{18}(l) + O_2(g) \rightarrow CO_2(g) + H_2O(g)$$

C.3 Counting and Weighing Atoms, Molecules, and Ions

In the answer to Question 2 above, you obtained the balanced equation

$$Cu_2S(s) + 2\ O_2(g) \rightarrow 2\ CuO(s) + SO_2(g)$$

which can be interpreted as follows: One formula unit of copper(I) sulfide plus two molecules of oxygen react to give two formula units of copper(II) oxide and one molecule of sulfur dioxide. This information is not too useful to a metal refinery owner who wants to know how much sulfur dioxide air pollutant will be released by roasting a certain amount of copper(I) sulfide ore.

Chemists have devised a counting unit called the **mole** (symbolized mol) that helps the refiner solve his problem. You are familiar with the counting units "pair" or "dozen." Just as one dozen water molecules means 12 water molecules, to a chemist one mole of water molecules means 6.02×10^{23} molecules. This is a very large number! Suppose you could string a mole of paperclips (6.02×10^{23} paperclips) together and wrap the string around the Earth. It would circle the Earth more than 5×10^{16} (50 trillion) times.

But, as large as one mole of molecules is, drinking this amount of water would still leave you thirsty on a hot day. One mole of water is less than one-tenth of a cup of water—only 18 g (or 18 mL) of water. This shows why the mole is so useful in chemistry. It represents a number of atoms, molecules, or formula units large enough to be conveniently weighed. Furthermore, the atomic masses (atomic weights) of the elements can be used to find the mass of one mole of any substance, called the **molar mass.**

The mass of one mole of atoms of an element is the quantity in grams equal to its atomic mass. To find the molar masses of the elements sulfur (S) and copper (Cu), for example, we first find their atomic masses in the periodic table (inside the back cover). For sulfur the atomic mass is 32.07 and for copper it is 63.55. Therefore,

$$1 \text{ mol S} = 32.07 \text{ g} \qquad 1 \text{ mol Cu} = 63.55 \text{ g}$$

For $O_2(g)$ the molar mass is twice the atomic mass; one mol is 32.00 g.

The molar mass of a compound is the sum of the molar masses of the atoms (found in the formula for that compound). Let's use two compounds of interest in the refinery owner's equation, copper sulfide (Cu_2S) and sulfur dioxide (SO_2), for examples. One mole of copper(I) sulfide (Cu_2S) contains two moles of copper atoms and one mole of sulfur atoms. Using the molar mass of copper and that of sulfur gives

$$2 \text{ mol Cu} \times \frac{63.55 \text{ g Cu}}{1 \text{ mol Cu}} = 127.10 \text{ g Cu}$$

$$1 \text{ mol S} \times \frac{32.07 \text{ g S}}{1 \text{ mol S}} = \underline{32.07 \text{ g S}}$$

$$\text{Molar mass of } Cu_2S = 159.2 \text{ g } Cu_2S$$

The molar mass of sulfur dioxide, or any other compound, is found similarly.

$$1 \text{ mol S} \times \frac{32.07 \text{ g S}}{1 \text{ mol S}} = 32.07 \text{ g S}$$

$$2 \text{ mol O} \times \frac{16.00 \text{ g O}}{1 \text{ mol O}} = \underline{32.00 \text{ g O}}$$

$$\text{Molar mass of } SO_2 = 64.07 \text{ g } SO_2$$

In brief, the molar mass of a compound is found by first multiplying the moles of each element present in the formula by the molar mass of the element. Then the total element molar masses are added to give the compound's molar mass. Check your understanding of this procedure by completing the following exercise.

YOUR *TURN*

II.8 Molar Masses

Determine the molar mass of each substance:

1. Nitrogen gas: N_2
2. Sodium chloride (table salt): $NaCl$
3. Sucrose (table sugar): $C_{12}H_{22}O_{11}$
4. Chalcopyrite: $CuFeS_2$
5. Malachite: $Cu_2CO_3(OH)_2$ (*Hint:* This formula shows 5 mol of oxygen atoms)
6. Azurite: $Cu_3(CO_3)_2(OH)_2$

Now we can return to the refiners' problem. The mole unit makes it possible to calculate the mass of sulfur dioxide released during refining. The coefficients in a chemical equation show the numbers of moles of reactants and products. Therefore,

$$Cu_2S(s) \quad + \quad 2 O_2(g) \quad \rightarrow \quad 2 CuO(s) \quad + \quad SO_2(g)$$
$$\text{1 mol} \qquad\qquad \text{2 mol} \qquad\qquad \text{2 mol} \qquad\qquad \text{1 mol}$$

for every one mole of Cu_2S that reacts, one mole of SO_2 will be formed. Using the molar masses found above shows that for every 159.2 g of Cu_2S processed, 64.07 g of SO_2 will be generated.

Many chemical reactions take place in water solution. The mole concept is helpful here too. Chemists often use the unit called **molarity** (symbolized *M*) to express the concentration of a solution. The molarity (or molar concentration) of a solution equals the total moles of solute that would be contained in one liter of the solution.

For example, a 1.0 M solution of sucrose could be prepared by dissolving one mole of sucrose molecules in enough water to make a one-liter solution. A one-molar (1 M) solution of magnesium chloride would have one mole of formula units of $MgCl_2$ dissolved in enough water to make one liter of solution. A 0.1 M solution of alcohol would have 0.1 mole of alcohol ($0.1 \times 6.02 \times 10^{23}$) molecules dissolved in enough water to make a liter of solution.

Molarity = $\dfrac{\text{Moles of solute}}{\text{Liters of solution}}$

Suppose we wish to have hydrochloric acid (HCl) in solution at a concentration of 1 M react completely with sodium hydroxide (NaOH) in solution:

$$HCl\ (aq) + NaOH(aq) \rightarrow NaCl(aq) + H_2O(l)$$

The equation shows that each mole of the acid reacts with one mole of NaOH. Therefore, we know that the acid in, say, 1 L of 1 M solution will react completely with 1 L of 1 M NaOH. In fact, any equal volumes of solutions of HCl and NaOH with the same molar concentrations will react completely.

1 L of a 1 M solution of NaOH contains 1 mol of Na^+ ions and 1 mol of OH^- ions.

The following exercise will give you some practice in understanding the meaning of solution concentrations expressed as molarity.

YOUR*TURN*

II.9 Molarity

Consider the following question:

> How many moles of sodium chloride (NaCl) are present in 0.50 L of a 0.20 M solution?

The solution contains 0.20 mol of NaCl in each liter of solution, or 0.20 mol/L. We want to know how many moles of NaCl are in 0.50 L. Therefore:

$$\left(\frac{0.20\ \text{mol NaCl}}{1\ \text{L}}\right)(0.50\ \text{L}) = 0.10\ \text{mol}$$

The 0.50 L of the 0.20 M solution contains 0.10 mol of NaCl. The molar mass of sodium chloride can be used to find the mass (in grams) of sodium chloride present:

$$(0.10\ \text{mol NaCl}) \times \left(\frac{58.44\ \text{g NaCl}}{1\ \text{mol NaCl}}\right) = 5.8\ \text{g NaCl}$$

Now consider the reverse type of problem:

> What is the concentration expressed as molarity of a solution that contains 1.0 mol of sucrose in 4.0 L of solution?

$$\text{Molarity} = \left(\frac{\text{mol}}{\text{L}}\right) = \left(\frac{1\ \text{mol sucrose}}{4.0\ \text{L}}\right) = \frac{0.25\ \text{mol sucrose}}{1.0\ \text{L}}$$

The solution is 0.25 M sucrose.

Now try answering the following questions.

1. A bottle of hydrochloric acid (HCl) is labeled 0.10 M HCl. What does this mean?

2. How many moles of sodium chloride (NaCl) are present in 1.0 L of a 0.75 M solution? In 500 mL of a 0.75 M solution? In 2.0 L of a 0.75 M solution?

3. How many grams of sodium chloride are present in each solution mentioned in Problem 2 above?

4. Suppose that the volume of a sample of 0.20 M sucrose solution is doubled by adding water, but without adding any more sucrose. What is the molarity of the new sugar solution? How many moles of sucrose would be present in 10 mL of this solution?

5. What is the concentration expressed as molarity of 500 mL of solution that contains 50.5 g of KNO_3? How many moles of K^+ ions are present in this solution? How many moles of NO_3^- ions are present?

6. A solution of barium hydroxide, $Ba(OH)_2$, is labeled 0.0010 M. How would you prepare such a solution from solid $Ba(OH)_2$ and water?

With the help of the mole, chemical equations allow chemists to account for the masses of elements and compounds involved in chemical reactions. Monitoring and accounting for resources used in manufactured items is not as easy.

C.4 Conservation Must Be Our Way

If nature always conserves, then why is it sometimes reported that a resource is "running out"? In what sense can we "run out" of a resource?

One can talk about depleting a resource in two related ways. First, remember that nature conserves atoms, but not necessarily molecules. Nature's rate of production of molecules, such as those which compose petroleum, is negligible compared to the rate at which we extract and burn them.

A second sense in which we can deplete a resource applies to metals. For profitable mining, an ore must contain some minimum concentration of metal. (This minimum value depends on the metal ore—from as high as 30% for aluminum to less than 1% for copper or 0.001% for gold.) As sites with high metal concentrations are depleted, lower concentration sites are developed. Meanwhile, through use, we disperse the originally concentrated resource. At some future

Reynolds Metals Co., ALCOA

Consumers can exchange used aluminum cans for money at this automatic recycling unit which operates 24 hours a day.

time our economy may not be able to support further extraction of such a metal for general use. For practical purposes, we will have depleted our supply of this resource.

Can we keep from doing this? Nature conserves automatically at the atomic level. Let's look at what conservation means in human terms.

How can we conserve our resources? That is, how can we slow down the rate at which we use them? The "three R's" of conservation are replace, reuse, and recycle. To replace a resource requires finding substitute materials with similar properties, preferably materials from renewable resources.

Gathering, processing, and using resources generates unwanted materials. We must also manage these materials. The waste and dispersion of nonrenewable resources may eventually pose serious threats to the well-being of our society. It is preferable that the by-products of what we use be gathered and stored or disposed of wisely.

Some manufactured items could be prepared for reuse rather than sent to the dump. Unwanted or outgrown clothing could be redistributed to others. Broken equipment could be repaired. Some items that wind up as trash could be recycled by reprocessing so that the materials present in them could be used again.

Many communities realize the wisdom of this aspect of resource management. How is a recycling program planned and organized? Let's consider such an activity in detail.

C.5 *You Decide:* Recycling Drive

Our nation has been called a "throwaway" society. It is true, for example, that 30% of the country's production of major materials is eventually discarded. In 1980 alone, waste disposal cost U.S. taxpayers $4 billion. Ten percent of the nation's energy use is devoted to handling discarded materials.

Some critics say that our society overpackages food and consumer items. For example, think about the single-use packaging involved in one fast-food meal. The packaging inventory would include a plastic or paper hamburger container, plastic-coated cup, plastic lid, plastic straw, paper french fry bag, plastic catsup pouch, paper packages for the salt and pepper, paper napkin, and even a paper bag to hold the meal!

Some packaging is necessary. Packaging protects ingredients, keeps small items together, and in many instances promotes cleanliness and safety. But even a simple ballpoint pen is often packaged in plastic and cardboard, and is placed in a bag by the cashier for you to take home. (And, like many other consumer items, the ballpoint pen may be designed to be discarded rather than refilled or reused.)

Do you buy milk in a plastic container, glass bottle, or cardboard container? What do you do with a pocket radio or calculator when it breaks? Do you have it repaired or toss it out and buy another? How many used batteries did your family discard in the past year? Do you mend worn socks or throw them away?

What are the alternatives? One is to use less. Another is to buy in bulk to use less packaging material. Other alternatives are to use items for a longer time or to reuse or recycle them. Recycling requires considerable work. What are its benefits? To find answers, let's examine three materials: paper, aluminum, and glass.

Paper. This is an important renewable resource. Since paper is made from tree pulp, new seedlings can be planted to replace trees cut down. However, it takes about 25 years for the seedlings to grow large enough to be economically useful. The "renewing" of this resource takes time! About 17 trees are needed to produce a ton of paper. That is just enough to supply two average citizens with the paper they use in one year!

Energy is required to make paper from a tree. Less than half as much energy is needed to process recycled paper as is used in making new paper. Unfortunately, only about 20% of the paper we use is currently recycled.

Aluminum (Al). This is a nonrenewable chemical resource—the number of aluminum atoms on Earth is, for all practical purposes, fixed. That is all we can expect to have.

Aluminum is the most abundant metal in the Earth's crust (8%). However, much of this aluminum is in the form of silicates, from which it is not easily extracted. Our national demand for aluminum is so great that our own supplies of the ore, bauxite, cannot meet our needs. We import approximately 85% of the aluminum used in this country. Producing aluminum even from bauxite requires considerable energy. Recycling used aluminum consumes only one-twentieth of the energy needed to produce it from aluminum-containing ore. At one time we discarded 50 billion aluminum cans yearly. Thanks to organized national efforts, we now recycle about half of our used aluminum.

Glass. A simple glass is made by melting together, at high temperatures, sand (silicon dioxide, SiO_2), soda ash (sodium carbonate, Na_2CO_3) and limestone (calcium carbonate, $CaCO_3$). All three materials are nonrenewable but plentiful. Glass recycling uses so much energy that it is more efficient to reuse old containers than it is to make new ones from used glass. In the not-too-distant past, most milk, juice, and carbonated beverages were sold in returnable (reusable) glass containers.

Working in small groups, discuss possible answers to the following questions. Your group's answers will be discussed later by the entire class.

1. Which of the three materials described above is the most important to recycle for economic reasons? For political reasons? For environmental reasons? Explain your answers.

2. If recycling is important, should the federal government require that certain materials be recycled? If so, identify some materials that should be recycled under such a law. How could such a law be enforced?

3. As individuals, we can conserve, reuse, or recycle materials in many different ways. For example, we can use both sides of paper for writing, or, when given a choice, purchase beverages in returnable bottles and return them. Identify at least five other ways we, as individuals, can conserve, reuse, or recycle certain materials.

4. Describe three everyday routines you would be willing to change to reduce the problems of solid waste disposal.

5. We plant forests to supply our paper needs. Assume that all printed or typewritten communication is replaced in the future by computer-based networks. What current uses of paper would cease? What occupations or jobs would be eliminated? What would you be reading in place of this paper chemistry textbook? How else would your daily routine be changed by this technological advancement?

PART C
SUMMARY *QUESTIONS*

1. List and briefly describe the three regions of the Earth. Which of these regions serves as the main "storehouse" of chemical resources used in manufacturing consumer products?

2. What is the promise of aqua-mining?

3. Balance the following chemical statements:
   a. The preparation of phosphoric acid (which is used in making soft drinks, detergents, and other products) from phosphate rock and sulfuric acid:

   $$Ca_3(PO_4)_2(s) + H_2SO_4(aq) \rightarrow H_3PO_4(aq) + CaSO_4(s)$$

   b. The preparation of tungsten from its ore:

   $$WO_3(s) + H_2(g) \rightarrow W(s) + H_2O(l)$$

   c. The heating of lead sulfide ore in air:
   $$PbS(s) + O_2(g) \rightarrow PbO(s) + SO_2(g)$$

4. Determine the molar mass of each substance:
   a. Epsom salt, $MgSO_4$
   b. Lye drain cleaner, $NaOH$
   c. Penicillin, $C_{16}H_{18}O_5N_2S$

5. In one method of producing chromium metal, the final step is the reaction of chromium(III) oxide with silicon at high temperature, as follows:

   $$2\ Cr_2O_3(s) + 3\ Si(s) \rightarrow 4\ Cr(s) + 3\ SiO_2(s)$$

   a. How many moles of each reactant and product are represented by this chemical equation?
   b. What mass (in grams) of each reactant and product is represented by this equation?
   c. Show how this equation illustrates the law of conservation of mass.

6. If 40.0 g of NaOH are dissolved in enough water to make 1.00 L of solution, the resulting concentration is 1.00 M. What would be the molar concentration of a solution prepared by dissolving half as much NaOH (20.0 g of NaOH) in enough water to make 1.00 L of solution? What is the molarity if we used 20.0 g in 0.50 L?

D METALS: SOURCES AND REPLACEMENTS

Technological advances and changes in life-styles can trigger rapid changes in the resources we need. Even though these changes are difficult to predict, we must be prepared to deal with them.

Copper is useful as a case study in considering present and projected uses of a vital chemical resource. We will consider the sources of our copper supply, the form in which copper is found, and how the source material is transformed into pure copper. You will produce a sample of metallic copper. Finally, we'll look at some possible replacements for this resource.

D.1 Copper: Sources and Uses

Copper resources are widely (but unevenly) distributed throughout the world. The United States has been a major world supplier of copper ore. Canada, Chile, Peru, and Zambia also have significant supplies of copper ore.

Whether an adequate profit can be earned from mining a particular metallic compound at a particular site depends on several factors:

- the relative supply of and demand for the metal
- the type of mining and processing required to obtain the metal
- the amount of useful ore at the site
- the percentage of metal in the ore.

When copper was first mined, the rich ores obtained contained 35–88% copper. Such ores are no longer available. In fact, it is now economically feasible to mine ores containing less than 1% copper. The ore is processed chemically to produce metallic copper. The resulting copper is then formed into a variety of useful materials. Figure II.8 summarizes the copper cycle from sources to uses to waste products.

Will future developments increase or decrease the need for copper? Are we doomed to deplete the rich deposits of this valuable resource? Do we have any alternatives to copper? The following activity will help you answer these questions.

Properties of copper
Easily shaped and formed (malleable and ductile)
High electrical conductivity
High thermal conductivity
Relatively unreactive
Resistant to corrosion
Attractive color and luster

YOUR*TURN*

II.10 Uses of Copper

Some properties of copper are listed in the margin. Let's consider how these properties make copper suitable for some of its many uses.

What properties of copper make it suitable for use in electrical power generators? Certainly its malleability and ductility allow copper to be formed into the necessary loops for a generator armature. And its high

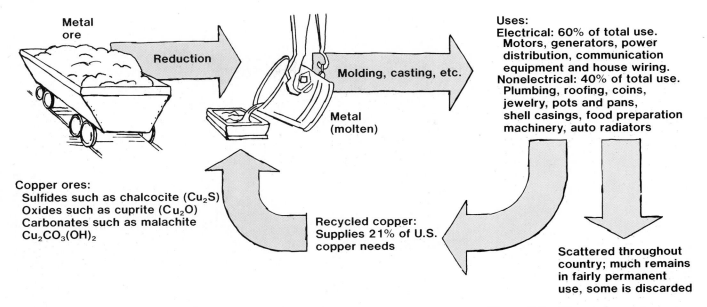

Figure II.8   The copper cycle.

electrical conductivity is essential to this application. Resistance to corrosion is also an asset in such large and expensive machinery.

1. For each of the remaining copper uses listed in Figure II.8, give the properties of copper that make it appropriate for that use.

2. How would increased recycling of scrap copper affect the future availability of this metal? Is there a limit to the role recycling can play? Why?

3. For each present-day use of copper listed below, describe a technological change that could decrease the need for copper in that field:
    a. Communication
    b. Coins
    c. Power generation
    d. Wiring within appliances

D.2   Evaluating an Ore

How do geologists know the percent of copper or other metal in a particular ore? Some fundamental chemical ideas apply to this problem. Once again the mole and molar mass come to the rescue.

In a compound, the relative number of atoms of each element is indicated by the compound's formula. For example, the mineral chalcocite, copper(I) sulfide (Cu_2S), contains two copper atoms for each sulfur atom. Such information is helpful in finding the amount of copper contained in a sample of this or any other species for which we know a chemical formula.

The percent of metal in a given ore is of great importance in helping decide whether a particular site is worth mining. Apply your knowledge regarding the composition of compounds by completing the following exercise.

A mineral is a chemical compound. An ore is usually a mixture of minerals, some useful, some not.

YOUR*TURN*

II.11 Percent Composition

Some copper-containing minerals are listed in Table II.7. Find the percent copper in chalcocite, Cu_2S, and the percent copper in an ore that contains 5.0% chalcocite.

Table II.7 *Copper-containing minerals*

Common name	Formula
Chalcocite	Cu_2S
Chalcopyrite	$CuFeS_2$
Malachite	$Cu_2CO_3(OH)_2$
Azurite	$Cu_3(CO_3)_2(OH)_2$

We must begin with the molar mass of Cu_2S, which is 159.2 g. From the formula we know (as shown in the margin) that a mol of Cu_2S contains 2 mol or 127.1 g, of Cu. Therefore,

$$\% \ Cu = \left(\frac{\text{Mass of Cu}}{\text{Mass of } Cu_2S} \right) \times 100 = \left(\frac{127.1 \text{ g Cu}}{159.2 \text{ g } Cu_2S} \right) \times 100 = 79.85\% \ Cu$$

A similar calculation would confirm that Cu_2S contains 20.15% sulfur. (Try this calculation for practice. Note that the sum of percent copper and percent sulfur equals 100.00%. Why? To find the percent of copper in the ore, assume that we have 100 g of the ore. As the ore is 5.0% chalcocite, 100 g will contain 5.0 g of chalcocite (0.050 × 100 g = 5.0 g). From the calculation above, we know that 79.85% of this mass is copper. Thus

$$5.0 \text{ g } Cu_2S \times 0.7985 = 4.0 \text{ g Cu}$$

With 4.0 g of copper in 100 g of ore, the ore is 4.0% copper, (4.0 g/100 g) × 100 = 4.0%.

1. Calculate the percent copper in the last three copper minerals listed in Table II.7. Assuming that each mineral were present in an ore at the same percent and that copper could be extracted from each at the same cost, which ore could be mined most profitably?

2. Two common iron-containing minerals are hematite (Fe_2O_3) and magnetite (Fe_3O_4). If you had an equal mass (such as 1 kg) of each, which sample would contain the greater amount of iron? Support your answer with calculations.

3. Small samples of ore are analyzed to find the percent metal contained in the ore at a given site. Assume that a 100 g sample of iron ore from Site A contained 20 g of Fe_2O_3, while a 100 g sample from Site B contained 15 g of Fe_3O_4. What is the mass of iron in each sample? Which ore contains the larger percent of iron?

Grams of Cu in one mol Cu_2S:

$(2 \text{ mol Cu}) \left(\dfrac{63.55 \text{ g Cu}}{1 \text{ mol Cu}} \right) = 127.1 \text{ g Cu}$

Once an ore is mined, it must be processed. How do we get, or win, copper from its compounds? To answer this question we must explore the chemistry of metallurgy.

D.3 Winning Metals from Ores

Humans have been described as "tool-making animals." Stone, wood, and natural fibers were easily available and became the earliest tool materials. While a variety of useful implements can be made from such naturally occurring materials, the discovery that fire would transform certain rocks into a strong, malleable material prompted a dramatic leap in the growth of civilization.

Gold, and then silver, were probably the first metals to be used. Found in their uncombined states they were used to make decorative objects. It is estimated that copper has been in use since 8000 B.C. for making tools, weapons, utensils, and decorations. It was about 3800 B.C. when bronze, an alloy of copper and tin, was invented. Thus humans moved from the Stone Age into the Bronze Age. Eventually the metallurgy of iron was developed, and more than 3000 years ago the Iron Age began. In time, as humans learned more about chemistry and about fire, a wide variety of metallic ores were transformed into ever more useful materials.

Copper, gold, and silver are not the most abundant metals. Aluminum, iron, and calcium are all more plentiful on this planet. Why then were copper, gold, and silver among the first metallic elements discovered? And what happens to certain "rocks" when they are heated over a wood fire? As you might suspect, chemistry provides answers to these questions.

In fact, you have already explored some of this chemistry in the laboratory activity on metal reactivity (Part B.6). You discovered, for example, that copper is more reactive than silver, but less reactive than magnesium. A more complete activity series is given in Table II.8, which includes brief descriptions of the methods by which these metals are retrieved from their ores.

The most reactive metals are at the top of the list; the less reactive metals are closer to the bottom. As you might guess, once metals have reacted and formed ionic compounds, the most reactive metals are more difficult to retrieve than the less active metals.

One way an activity list is useful is in predicting whether or not reactions are likely to occur. For example, you discovered in the laboratory that zinc metal, which is more reactive than copper, will react with copper ions in solution. However, zinc will not react with magnesium ions in solution, for zinc is less reactive than magnesium. In general, a more reactive metal will release a less reactive metal from its compounds.

Use Table II.8 and the periodic table to complete the following exercise.

Table II.8 *Metal activity series**

Metal	Metal ion	Reduction process in metallurgy
Lithium	Li$^+$	
Potassium	K$^+$	
Calcium	Ca^{2+}	Sending electric current through the molten salt (electrolysis)
Sodium	Na$^+$	
Magnesium	Mg^{2+}	
Aluminum	Al^{3+}	
Manganese	Mn^{2+}	
Zinc	Zn^{2+}	
Chromium	Cr^{2+}, Cr^{3+}	Heating with coke (carbon) or carbon monoxide (CO)
Iron	Fe^{2+}, Fe^{3+}	
Lead	Pb^{2+}	
Copper	Cu^{2+}	
Mercury	Hg^{2+}	Element occurring free or easily obtained by heating in air (roasting)
Silver	Ag$^+$	
Platinum	Pt^{2+}	
Gold	Au$^+$, Au^{3+}	

*Listed in order of decreasing reactivity (most active metal first).

YOUR *TURN*

II.12 Metal Reactivity

1. Despite their relative scarcity, copper, silver, and gold were discovered and used long before the much more abundant metal iron. Why? In fact, the metals at the top of the activity list were not isolated in their pure form until after 1780. What reasons can you give to explain this?

2. What trend in metallic reactivity do you find as you move from left to right across a given horizontal row (period) of the periodic table?

   To help you answer this question, compare the reactivities of sodium, magnesium, and aluminum. In which part of the periodic table are the most reactive metals found? Which side of the periodic table contains the least reactive metals?

3. Will iron (Fe) metal react in a solution of lead nitrate, $Pb(NO_3)_2$? Will platinum (Pt) react in a lead nitrate solution? Explain your answers.

4. Compare the three processing methods described in the activity table. Which would you expect to require the greatest quantity of energy? Which is likely to be the most expensive? Why?

5. The least reactive metals are easiest to obtain from their ores. Would these necessarily be the cheapest metals? If not, what other factor(s) influence the market value of a given metal? Use specific examples from the activity chart in your explanation.

What happens at the atomic level when rocks containing easily obtained metals are heated? What happens when a metal is set free from any ore? The process of converting a combined metal (usually a metal ion) in a mineral into a free metal is referred to as **reduction.** The term has a very specific chemical meaning. For metal ions to be converted to metal atoms, the ions must gain electrons. *Any* process in which electrons are gained by a species is called "reduction." The reduction of one copper(II) ion requires two electrons:

$$Cu^{2+} + 2e^- \rightarrow Cu$$

The reverse process, in which an ion or any other species loses electrons is called **oxidation.** Under the right conditions copper *atoms* can be oxidized:

$$Cu \rightarrow Cu^{2+} + 2e^-$$

(*Note:* A good way to keep this straight is to remember that "LEO the lion goes GER": *L*oss of *E*lectrons is *O*xidation, *G*ain of *E*lectrons is *R*eduction.)

We live in an electrically neutral world. Therefore, whenever one species gains electrons another must have lost them. Oxidation and reduction never occur separately. They occur together in what chemists call oxidation-reduction, or **redox** reactions.

You have already carried out several redox reactions. In the laboratory activity on metal reactivities (Part B.6), the elemental metals were oxidized. For example, in the reaction

$$Cu(s) + 2 Ag^+(aq) \rightarrow 2 Ag(s) + Cu^{2+}(aq)$$

copper atoms were oxidized (converted to Cu^{2+} ions) and silver ions from $AgNO_3$ in solution were reduced (converted to Ag atoms). In the same activity you demonstrated that copper ions could be recovered from solution by reaction with magnesium, a more active metal than copper. Here, magnesium atoms are oxidized, copper ions are reduced.

$$Mg(s) + Cu^{2+}(aq) \rightarrow Cu(s) + Mg^{2+}(aq)$$

In some circumstances this might be a useful way to obtain copper metal. However, as is always the case, in obtaining the desired product, something else was used up—in this case an equally desirable metal, magnesium.

What causes redox reactions to occur? Many metallic elements are found in nature as ions (components of minerals) because they combine readily with other elements to form ionic compounds. Obtaining a metal from its mineral usually requires the addition of energy as well as a source of electrons, known as a reducing agent. As Table II.8 shows, a variety of techniques are used, depending on the chemical reactivity of the metal ion in the ore, the availability of reducing agents, and the energy resources available. Let's consider the methods used.

Pyrometallurgy is the treatment of metals and their ores by heat, such as in a blast furnace. It is used in two of the three reduction processes given in the table: heating an ore in air (roasting) or heating it with an added reducing agent. Carbon (coke) and carbon monoxide are commonly used, since they are inexpensive and readily available. A more active metal can be used if neither of these will do the job. Pyrometallurgy is the most important and oldest extractive process.

Electrometallurgy is the processing of metals by methods requiring electricity, including electroplating, electrorefining, and use of an electric arc furnace to make steel. It is used in cases where no adequate reducing species is available or where very high metal purity is needed. Typically, the electric current supplies electrons to the metal ions, thus reducing them.

Hydrometallurgy is the treatment of ores and other metal-containing materials by wet processes involving reactants in water solution. You used this type of procedure when you compared the reactivity of four metals in Part B.6. Hydrometallurgy has not been commonly used on an industrial scale due to the high cost of the more active metal. However, as the ores mined become less concentrated in the desired metal, it is becoming economically feasible to turn to this and other wet methods for processing many minerals that can be dissolved in water.

In the following laboratory activity you will try your hand at electrometallurgy.

Reynolds Metals Co., ALCOA

Workers prepare to draw molten aluminum metal from electrolytic cells at ALCOA's Badin (N.C.) Smelting Works.

Figure II.9 Apparatus for electrolysis of copper(II) chloride solution.

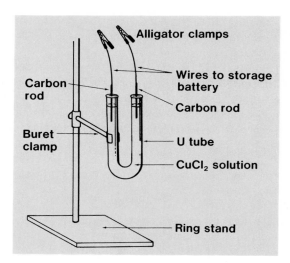

D.4 Laboratory Activity: Electrolysis of a Salt

Getting Ready

In this activity you will produce copper from a solution of copper(II) chloride ($CuCl_2$) by electrolysis. You will use a storage battery as a source of electricity.

Electrolysis on an industrial scale uses very large quantities of electrical energy, making it an expensive, although effective, method of obtaining or purifying metals. In the industrial method of copper refining used today, pure copper is produced by electrometallurgy from less pure copper produced by pyrometallurgy.

Procedure

1. Obtain two carbon rods and clean them with sandpaper or emery paper.
2. Set up the electrolysis apparatus shown in Figure II.9. Connect the alligator clamps to the carbon rods, but do not connect them yet to the storage battery.
3. Put enough copper(II) chloride ($CuCl_2$) solution into the U-tube so that the carbon rods are one-fourth to one-half immersed in the solution.
4. Have your teacher approve the set up.
5. After your teacher has approved the set up, attach the wires to the storage battery.
6. Observe the reaction for approximately five minutes and record your observations in your notebook.
7. *Cautiously* sniff each carbon rod.

Questions

1. Describe the changes that occurred during the experiment.
2. One electrode, called the cathode, is the place where reduction takes place.
    a. What change did you observe at the cathode in this reaction?
    b. At the cathode, were electrons added to or released by ions in solution?
    c. Which electrode was the cathode in the experiment?
3. The other electrode, called the anode, is where oxidation takes place.
    a. What change took place at the anode in this reaction? What product was formed here?
    b. At the anode, were electrons added to or released by ions in solution?
    c. Which electrode was the anode in the experiment?
    d. Write the balanced equation for the overall chemical reaction that took place in this electrolysis reaction. (The oxidation product is gaseous chlorine, $Cl_2(g)$.)

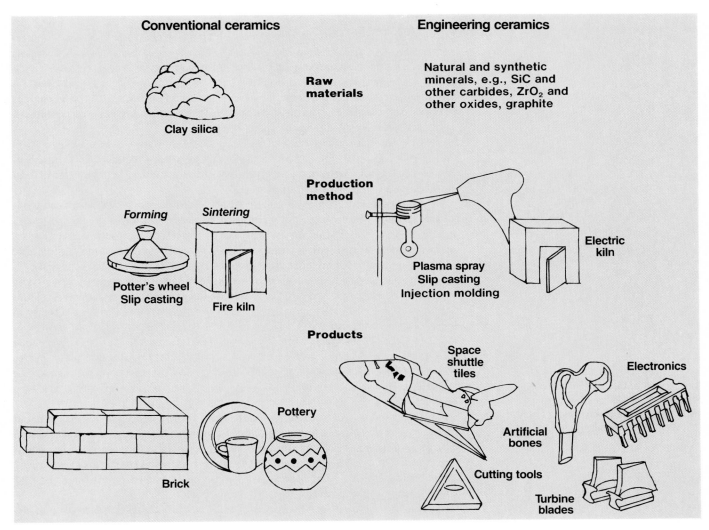

Conventional ceramics

Engineering ceramics

Raw materials

Clay silica

Natural and synthetic minerals, e.g., SiC and other carbides, ZrO$_2$ and other oxides, graphite

Production method

Forming

Sintering

Potter's wheel
Slip casting

Fire kiln

Plasma spray
Slip casting
Injection molding

Electric kiln

Products

Brick

Pottery

Space shuttle tiles

Artificial bones

Cutting tools

Turbine blades

Electronics

Figure II.10 Conventional ceramic products such as bricks and pottery are produced from clay. Engineering ceramics, which may be, for example, higher melting, stronger, or less brittle than conventional ceramics, are produced from various types of natural and synthetic minerals.

D.5 Materials of the Future

As we continue to extract and use, but not recover, chemical resources from Spaceship Earth, we are sometimes forced to consider alternatives. One option is to find new materials that can substitute for less-available resources. An ideal substitute would satisfy three requirements: Its properties would match or exceed those of the original material; it would be plentiful; and, of course, it would be inexpensive. Substitute materials seldom meet all these conditions completely. Thus, one usually must balance the benefits and burdens involved in such substitutions. We will consider the promise and challenge of some new materials in this section.

One of the most plentiful materials on this planet is clay. Clays are mainly composed of silicon, oxygen, and aluminum, along with magnesium, sodium, and potassium ions and water molecules. Early humans found that clay mixed with water, then molded and heated, formed useful ceramic products such as pottery and bricks.

In more recent times, researchers have found that if other common rock materials are heated to high temperatures, useful "fired" compounds, also called ceramics, can be formed. Figure II.10 shows the sources, processing, and products from conventional ceramics and the newer, stronger engineering ceramics.

The Bettmann Archive

The experimental aircraft, Voyager, which completed the first non-stop round the world flight without refueling, is made of light-weight composite materials.

What properties made original ceramics useful for pottery and bricks? Certainly, characteristics such as hardness, rigidity, low chemical reactivity, and resistance to wear are among them. The main attraction of ceramics for future use, however, is their high melting point and their strength at high temperatures. They might serve, in fact, as attractive substitutes in some steel applications. For example, scientists believe ceramic construction may allow diesel or turbine engines to operate at higher temperatures. Such high-temperature engines would run with increased efficiency, reducing fuel consumption.

The major problem still facing researchers, however, is that ceramics are brittle and fracture if exposed to rapid temperature changes, as during hot-engine cool-down. Great hope remains, however, for the future of ceramics. They could become vitally important materials.

Plastics are already used in many applications where metals were once used. These synthetic substances are composed of complex chains of carbon atoms having hydrogen and other atoms attached. They offer decreased weight and can be designed to be resilient in situations where metals would become dented. The plastic bumpers on many current automobiles provide an excellent example.

Plastics can be created with a very wide range of properties from soft and flexible to hard, rigid, and brittle. Unfortunately, plastics are composed of materials derived from petroleum, an important nonrenewable resource already in great demand as a fuel.

Optical fibers have already revolutionized communications. Telephone messages are now being sent through these specially designed glass tubes as pulses of light. Not only have the optical fibers replaced the metal resources used in traditional phone lines, but a fundamentally new way of sending signals has been created.

Increased use of substitutes made from locally available resources could make the United States less dependent on imports for essential metals. Would this be an advantage for our country? Would it be an advantage for other countries? What factors are involved in the importing and exporting of resources? What would we do if the supply of an essential imported metal were cut off? Think about these questions.

In the next exercise you can try your hand at selecting alternative materials. In the *Putting It All Together* section at the end of this unit, keep these factors in mind.

YOUR*TURN*

II.13 Alternatives to Metals

1. Look back at Figure II.8 and the uses for copper listed there. Choose four or more uses and for each try to suggest an alternative material that could serve the same purpose. Draw your suggestions from both conventional materials and possible new materials.

2. Suggest some common items that might be replaced by ceramics or plastics, with resultant savings in the use of metals.

3. Suppose silver were to become as inexpensive as copper. In what uses would silver most likely replace copper? Justify your choices.

PART D
SUMMARY *QUESTIONS*

1. Give at least two reasons that projections of future resource availability have a great degree of uncertainty.

2. Why is recycling of metal resources important? Does it guarantee that we will always have sufficient supplies of a given resource? Why or why not?

3. In attempting to meet specific needs, chemists and engineers think in terms of a set of desired properties. List three applications of copper metal and the corresponding property or properties that explain its use for that particular application.

4. Give the chemical name and determine the percent metal (by mass) in each compound:
   a. Ag_2S
   b. Al_2O_3
   c. $CaCO_3$

5. A 100 g sample of ore contained 10 g of lead(II) sulfate ($PbSO_4$). What is the percent lead in this ore?

6. Consider the following two equations. Which represents a reaction that is more likely to occur? Why?
   a. $Zn^{2+}(aq) + 2 Ag(s) \rightarrow 2 Ag^+(aq) + Zn(s)$
   b. $2 Ag^+(aq) + Zn(s) \rightarrow Zn^{2+}(aq) + 2 Ag(s)$

7. Would it be a good idea to use an iron spoon to stir a solution of lead nitrate? Why or why not? (Supply a chemical equation as part of your explanation.)

8. Based on what you now know, which two families of elements contain the most active metals?

9. Name and briefly describe the three classes of reduction processes used in the processing of metallic ores. Under what conditions is each used?

General Electric Company

This graphite-composite bat has the durability and light weight of aluminum, yet is made from a graphite-reinforced XENOY resin.

E PUTTING IT ALL TOGETHER: HOW LONG WILL THE SUPPLY LAST?

E.1 Metal Reserves: Three Projections

The change from an agricultural to an industrial society puts great demands on a country's chemical resources. Industrial nations often must supplement their own chemical resources with imports from other countries. As technology spreads worldwide, additional nations compete for the world's limited supply of minerals. Technology is at least partly responsible for this competition. But it can also aid in better use or reuse of resources already secured.

In Figure II.11 the amount of world reserves of metal ore is plotted versus time. All lines begin at the same point on the left side of the graph. This point represents the total amount of reserves known at the present. By "reserves" we refer to ores from which we are sure metals can be extracted at an economically competitive cost using known technology.

Each curve represents a different possible scenario, or overall rate at which we might consume reserves as time passes. Plot I is a straight line. In this case, we would continue to use ore reserves at the same rate they are used today. The reserves still available decrease by the same amount each year.

Plot II would result if we use metal reserves at an increasingly faster rate over the years. Each year the reserves used would be more than the year before.

Figure II.11 Possible depletion scenarios for metal resources.

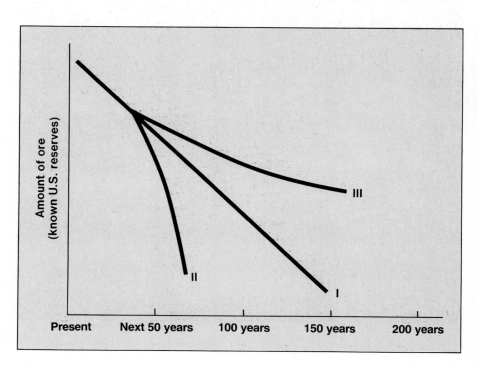

If instead, the rate at which we consume metal reserves gradually slows down, then Plot III would result. Each year the reserves used would be somewhat less than the year before. The reserves would last longer.

What control do we have over which type of plot will apply to a given resource in the future? In the next section you will examine the facts bearing on the use of a single metal, aluminum. You will consider possible conservation measures and their influence on the rate of aluminum use. Finally, you will select from among the possibilities those that seem most likely to succeed in conserving aluminum.

E.2 Aluminum Supply and Demand

Aluminum is the most abundant metal on the Earth's surface. Unfortunately, much of it is in clay. No economically feasible, large-scale methods are currently available for extracting aluminum from clay. Currently, the most important aluminum-producing ore is bauxite, mainly $Al_2O_3 \cdot 2\,H_2O$. Aluminum ore mining has been all but shut down in the United States. It is less expensive to import high-grade aluminum ore from other countries. Even if a reasonable source of high-grade aluminum ore were discovered in this country, it would take at least seven years to establish a productive mine.

The properties that make aluminum so useful are listed in Table II.9. Except for iron, aluminum is the most used metal in this country. Both the automobile and airplane industries now use aluminum as a structural component due to its strength and low density. The weight savings due to aluminum in cars and planes have substantially reduced our total national fuel consumption.

Aluminum is an excellent conductor of electricity, a given mass being more than twice as conductive as the same mass of copper. Most overhead power transmission lines are made of aluminum. The uses of aluminum are summarized in Figure II.12.

Table II.9 *Properties of aluminum*

Silvery white, attractive metal
   Takes high polish. Surface oxide layer can be dyed (anodized aluminum)
Light (low density)
Easily shaped and formed
   Highly malleable and ductile
High electrical conductivity
High thermal conductivity
Forms strong alloys
Corrosion resistant due to surface oxide layer
Not toxic to humans

Figure II.12   Uses of aluminum in the United States.

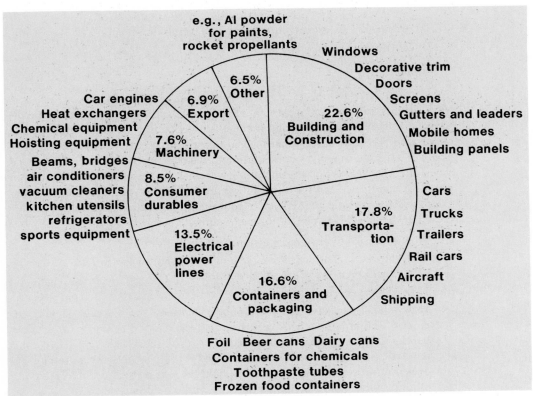

E.3   A Case Study in Options and Opportunities

Refer to the information on the properties and uses of aluminum, and to the plots in Figure II.11 in answering the following questions. Later, you will use your answers in group and classroom discussions.

1. Do you think Plot I in Figure II.11 is a good prediction for the future use of aluminum?

2. What might happen to cause aluminum reserves to be used as represented in Plot II?

3. What might happen to cause aluminum reserves to be used as represented in Plot III?

4. Suppose technology were developed that would allow extraction of aluminum from clay at a reasonable cost. What effect would this have on Plot I? Plot II? Plot III?

5. Next, consider how best to conserve aluminum. In answering the questions below, consider the uses of aluminum listed in Figure II.12 and any others that you might think of. The goal here is to choose the combinations of uses and conservation methods that have the best chance of success and would be most effective. In making the choices, take into account the effects on economics, lifestyles, and the environment. For example, replacing aluminum cookware with stainless steel cookware would be an economic change for individuals, because aluminum cookware is less expensive than stainless steel; it would be a change in lifestyle, because some cooks would have to change their preferences. It might not be the most effective conservation method, as aluminum pots last a long time if properly cared for.

   a. Identify one or two uses from which the aluminum could be collected and reused.

   b. Identify one or two uses that would permit the aluminum to be recycled.

   c. Identify one or two uses in which aluminum could be replaced by alternate materials with similar desirable properties. Suggest what these materials might be (other metals? alloys? plastics? ceramics?).

   d. Identify any uses of aluminum that result in an ultimate loss of aluminum.

E.4   How Can We Influence the Future?

Your teacher will divide the class into small groups. Each group is to review the suggestions made by each group member in completing Question 5 above and choose the possible conservation measures with the greatest chance of success. You will be asked to make a presentation to the class justifying your choices and explaining their effects on the community. In making the choices, consider what would be required to carry out the different conservation measures and also consider the following questions. Then in your final presentation to the class, answer these questions as best you can for each method chosen.

1. How expensive is the conservation method likely to be?

2. Will this method affect all people equally? If not, what portion of the population will bear the greatest burden?

3. How will this conservation measure be carried out? Is new technology needed?

4. How will this conservation measure be encouraged or enforced? Should federal or local laws be passed requiring that the method be used? Could a tax be charged on materials discarded instead of recycled or reused by this method? Should higher prices be charged for items not using aluminum recycled or reused by this method? Should laws be passed forbidding the use of aluminum in certain applications where it could be replaced?

E.5 Looking Back and Looking Ahead

As we end the second unit in the *ChemCom* story, we can stop and take stock of what we have learned thus far. To date, we have "uncovered" some of the working language (symbols, formulas, and equations), laboratory techniques, basic laws (law of conservation of matter and the periodic law) and theories (atomic-molecular) of chemistry and how they can help us better understand a few socially relevant issues. Central among these issues is the use and abuse of the chemical resources of Spaceship Earth. Water, metals, petroleum, food, air, our basic industries, and even our health are all resources that need to be wisely managed to obtain maximum benefits for all people, while minimizing environmental costs.

We have also explored some social factors that enter into policy decisions concerning "technological" problems. We have seen that although chemistry is often a crucial ingredient in recognizing and resolving such issues, many problems are too complex to yield only to a technological solution. Tough decisions may be necessary. Issues usually are not black or white, but many shades of gray. As future voting citizens you must continue to be concerned with a variety of issues that require some scientific understanding. The remaining units in *ChemCom* will continue to prepare you for this important role.

Next we will deal with petroleum, a nonrenewable chemical resource so important that it needs a unit all to itself.

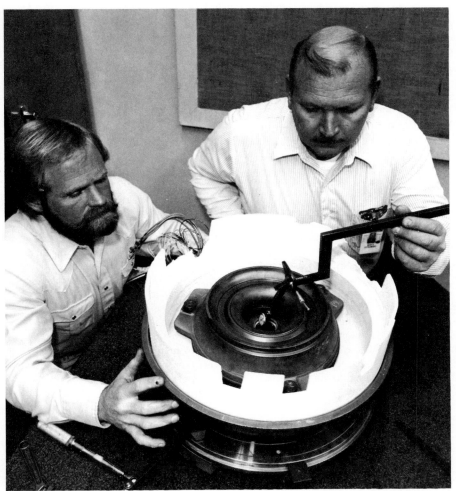

Department of Energy

These engineers are inspecting part of a ceramic engine made from silicon nitride (the turbine shroud) and aluminum silicate (the white insulating case).

To be used with
YOUR TURN
II.3 Chemical Elements Crossword Puzzle Clues (p. 94)

The following are the clues to the crossword puzzle your teacher will distribute.

Down

1. An unreactive, gaseous element that is a product of the nuclear reaction (fusion) of hydrogen atoms. This reaction occurred at the beginning of time and occurs today in stars such as our sun. The second most abundant element in the universe, it is quite rare on Earth. Small concentrations are found in some natural gas deposits. It is used in blimps because of its low density. (Only hydrogen, which is highly flammable, has a lower density). It is also used in cryogenic (low-temperature) work because it can be compressed to a liquid that has a temperature of $-269\,°C$.

2. A reactive, metallic element. Its compounds are used as a medical "cocktail" to outline the stomach and intestines for X-ray examination. Its compounds also give green colors to fireworks.

4. A highly reactive metal. It is used in the manufacture of synthetic rubber and drugs. Recently one of its compounds has been used to successfully treat a certain type of mental illness. It finds limited use in nuclear bombs.

6. A widely distributed nonmetal which is never found in its free, elemental state. It is an essential component in all cell protoplasm, DNA, and various animal tissues and bones. It is also one of the three main elements in fertilizers.

9. An unreactive gas. In the comic book world, a mineral containing this element could weaken Superman. In the real world, a radioactive form of this element is a byproduct of most nuclear explosions and its presence in the atmosphere can indicate which nations are testing nuclear weapons.

10. A reactive metal with a high melting point. It is used in the manufacture of rocket nose cones because it is very strong for its low density.

12. A reactive, silver-white metal that is second in abundance to sodium in ocean water. Due to its low density and high strength, its alloys are often used for structural purposes in the transportation industry, as in "mag" wheels. It is also used in photo flash cubes, fireworks and incendiary bombs because it ignites very readily. Some of its compounds, such as Epsom salt and milk of magnesia, serve medicinal purposes.

14. A component of all living matter and fossil fuels; the black material on a charred candle wick.

18. Nicknamed quicksilver, it is the only metal which is a liquid at room temperature. It is used in thermometers because it expands significantly and regularly when heated. Its high density makes it a practical substance to use in barometers. (*Note:* A barometer is used to measure atmospheric air pressure.) It is a toxic "heavy" metal.

19. The lightest and most abundant element; the fuel of the universe. It is believed that all other elements were originally formed from a series of stellar nuclear reactions beginning with this one. It is found in numerous compounds such as water and most compounds containing carbon.

20. A highly reactive metal of low density. It is one of the three main elements found in fertilizer. Its compounds are quite similar to those of sodium, though typically more expensive.

22. A soft, dense metal used in bullets and car batteries. It was once used extensively both in plumbing and in paints. Concern over its biological effects has caused a ban on its use for these purposes. It is being slowly phased out as a gasoline additive for the same reason.

25. With the highest melting point of any pure element, it is the filament in ordinary (incandescent) lightbulbs. Its one-letter symbol comes from the name wolfram.

27. A metallic element. It is added to steel to increase its strength.

28. A metallic element which serves as the negative pole (electrode) in the common flashlight battery. It is used to plate a protective film on iron objects (as in galvanized buckets). Melted with copper it becomes brass.

29. A metal that is used to make stainless steel. Combined with nickel, it forms nichrome wire which is used in toasters and other devices where high electrical resistance (to produce heat) is desired.

30. This metal has a relatively low melting point and it is used in fire detection and extinguishing devices as well as in electrical fuses.

31. The most chemically reactive metal. Though it is quite rare, it is used in some photoelectric cells and in atomic clocks, which have far greater accuracy than our mechanical or electric clocks.

33. A reddish, lustrous, ductile, malleable metal that occurs in nature in both free and combined states. It forms the body of the Statue of Liberty. Other uses include electrical wiring, pennies, and decorative objects.

34. A magnetic, metallic element used extensively for structural purposes. Your outdoor stair railing at home may be made of this element.

38. A yellow, nonreactive, metallic element that has been highly valued for its beauty and durability since ancient times.

39. A metallic element that is used as a corrosion-resistant coating on the inside of cans used for packaging food, oil, and other substances.

Across

3. A highly reactive, gaseous nonmetal. Its compounds are added to some toothpastes and many urban water supplies to prevent tooth decay.

5. A reactive metal whose compounds make up limestone, chalk, cement, and the bones and teeth of animals. Milk is a good nutritional source of this element.

7. An expensive, silver-white metal used in jewelry. It is also used in some industrial processes to speed up chemical reactions.

8. A solid purple-black nonmetal which changes to a deep purple gas upon heating. An alcohol solution of this element serves as an effective skin disinfectant. A compound of the element is added to sodium chloride (table salt) to prevent goiter.

10. Used in borosilicate (Pyrex) glass, Boraxo soap, drill bits, and control rods in nuclear power plants.

11. One of the three magnetic elements, this metal is used in 5-cent pieces and other coins, in electroplating, and in nichrome wire.

13. The most abundant metal in the Earth's crust, this silver-white element is characterized by its low density, resistance to corrosion, and high strength. It is used for a variety of structural purposes, such as in airplanes, boats, and cars.

14. A hard, magnetic metal used in the production of steel. A radioactive form of this element is used in cancer treatment.

15. A silver-white, lustrous, radioactive metal. Used as fuel in nuclear power plants and in atomic warheads.

16. An unreactive, gaseous element used in advertising signs for the bright reddish-orange glow it produces when an electric current is passed through it.

17. A yellow nonmetal that occurs in both the free and combined states. It is used in making match tips, gunpowder, and vulcanized rubber. Its presence in coal leads to acid (sulfuric acid) rain if it is not removed before the coal is burned.

21. This metal is the best conductor of heat and electricity. Its scarcity prevents it from being commonly used for such purposes. It was used extensively in the past in the manufacture of coins, but has become too expensive. It is used today for fine eating utensils and decorative objects. Some of its compounds are sensitive enough to light to be used in photographic film.

23. A gaseous nonmetal, the most abundant element on Earth. It makes up some 21% of the Earth's atmosphere and is essential to most forms of life for the conversion of food into energy.

24. The second most abundant element in the Earth's crust. It is the principal component of sand and quartz and finds use in solar cells, computer chips, caulking materials, and abrasives.

26. A metallic element used in control rods in nuclear power plants and in Ni-Cad rechargeable batteries.

30. A red, highly reactive, fuming liquid with a foul smell. It finds limited use as a disinfectant. One of its compounds is a component of leaded gasoline.

32. An odorless, colorless, unreactive gas used in most incandescent lightbulbs.

35. An element whose symbol comes from its Latin name. It is used with lead in car batteries.

36. A soft, highly reactive metal whose compounds include table salt, lye, and baking soda.

37. A gaseous nonmetal that makes up 78% of our atmosphere. Its compounds are important components of proteins, fertilizers, and many explosives.

40. A highly reactive, greenish-yellow gas used as a bleach, as a disinfectant (in the purification of water), and as a poison gas.

UNIT *THREE*

Petroleum: To Build or to Burn?

CONTENTS

INTRODUCTION

The first *ChemCom* unit focused on an important renewable resource—water. The second explored some important nonrenewable resources. By now, you should see quite clearly how, as passengers on Spaceship Earth, we must rely on the resources on board.

Petroleum is a vitally important, nonrenewable resource. Our society runs on it. Petroleum in the form of gasoline powers nearly every U.S. automobile on its annual drive of some 10,000 miles. Burning petroleum-based fuel serves as a source of heat and electricity for many U.S. homes and industries.

In a less-visible role, petroleum provides the chemical starting materials for the manufacture of all sorts of products that we each use every day. The title, "Petroleum: To Build or to Burn?," refers to these two roles of petroleum in our society, as fuel and as chemical building material.

Important decisions about how to use petroleum lie ahead. In this unit we will consider how dependent we are on petroleum. Since petroleum is nonrenewable and our present rate of use is quite high, how long are supplies expected to last? An even more fundamental question is: What is it about petroleum's chemical composition that makes it such a valuable resource? The answer to this question will determine our options as supplies dwindle. Can we develop alternatives to serve as substitutes? Or, must we rethink our use of this valuable material and perhaps change the way we live?

Much depends on the degree to which society seeks answers to such questions. Unfortunately, attention to them tends to fluctuate with the price of petroleum, a price strongly dependent on economic and political conditions. Twice during the 1970s the steady flow of imported petroleum to this country was interrupted. In 1973–1974 an embargo on shipments and a price increase were enforced by Organization of Petroleum Exporting Countries (OPEC). U.S. gasoline crept perilously close to $2 per gallon; long lines appeared at gas stations; and many struggled to improve the insulation in their houses to reduce heating oil use. In 1979, a revolution in Iran halted shipments from that country, a major oil producer. These events led government and industry to accelerate research on alternate energy sources.

OPEC is the Organization of Petroleum Exporting Countries.

By the mid-1980s petroleum prices had dropped, and buying gasoline did not leave as large a dent in the pocketbook. Oil was selling in 1986 for as low as $14.50 a barrel and gasoline prices of 70¢ to 90¢ a gallon were common. Interest in alternative energy sources declined even though oil prices are now rising.

Forecasting the future price of petroleum is difficult. The price might remain stable for years. Or it could rise to new heights or drop to new lows in response to changing political and economic conditions. A sensible view of its future requires looking hard at factors other than the price at the moment. We must focus on the supplies available and the rate of consumption.

A PETROLEUM IN OUR LIVES

We burn petroleum for fuel, but the variety of things we make from it is incredible. Let's look at some products that we use daily which are made directly from petroleum or from substances obtained from it.

A.1 *You Decide:* It's a Petroleum World

Study Figure III.1. List the items in the figure that consume petroleum or are made from it. When you think that you have listed everything, turn to the last page of this unit. There you will find a version of Figure III.1 in which all the items that consume petroleum or are made from it are removed. Compare the two figures and add to your list those items you have missed. How many petroleum-based products did you overlook?

Suppose there were a severe petroleum shortage. Which five uses of petroleum-based products shown in the first figure would you be most willing to do without? Which five would you be least willing to give up?

Figure III.1 Life with petroleum.

Gasoline lines in California. Will this scene be repeated?

**13%
Building**

**87%
Burning**

Based on 1983 figures

Figure III.2   Petroleum: Burning and building.

How important do you expect petroleum to be in your life when you reach the age of 40?

Were you surprised by all the items that use or are made from petroleum? Often we don't realize how important something is until we try to imagine life without it. Petroleum and things made from it have become such an integral part of modern life that we tend to take them for granted. However, we must face the reality that we are using our limited supply of petroleum at such a rapid rate that we must ask an important question.

A.2   How Long Can Petroleum Fuel Our Economy?

The United States consumes about 17 million barrels of petroleum per day. If this is divided evenly among citizens, your daily "share" would be about three gallons. What have you done with your portion?

Most of the nation's petroleum is burned as an energy source for heating, electricity, and transportation. The rest is used for building plastics, fabrics, synthetic vitamins, and many other things that greatly affect our lives.

Figure III.2 shows—on average—how much of a barrel of petroleum is used for burning (as an energy source) and for building (as a source of chemical reactants to produce other useful substances).

Some petroleum experts predict that world oil production from known petroleum reserves will reach its peak around 1995 (see Figure III.3). After that, they predict a sharp decline in petroleum production as reserves dwindle. In less than 100 years production of petroleum from presently known reserves is expected to be as low as it was in 1910. At that time, petroleum was used only for illumination to replace the limited supply of whale oil.

The price of petroleum is expected to increase steadily as it becomes increasingly scarce. It will gradually become too costly for many of today's common applications.

In a time of petroleum scarcity, how would you decide to use this resource? Would you burn it for its energy or build other substances from it? Dimitri Mendeleev, the Russian chemist who proposed the arrangement of elements in the

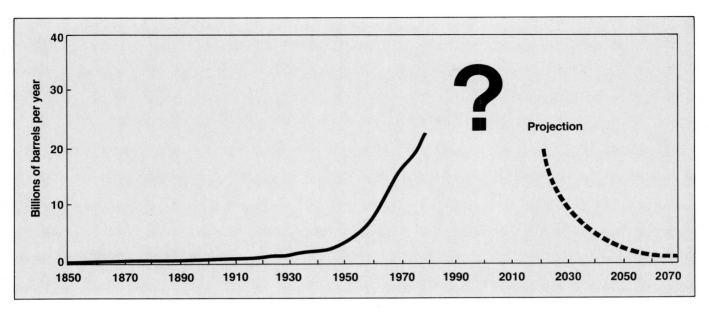

Figure III.3 Estimated production from known petroleum reserves (shown by solid line). Projected consumption of reserves (dashed line).

periodic table in 1869, recognized petroleum's value as a raw material for industry. He advised that burning petroleum as a fuel "would be akin to firing up a kitchen stove with bank notes." The great supply of petroleum, its ease of storage and handling as a fuel, and its relatively low cost have led us to disregard his advice.

A time will come, however, when the choice of whether to build or to burn will confront all nations. The decisions required then will depend on knowing the sources of petroleum, how it is used, and what alternatives are available.

Let's start our exploration of petroleum by asking, Where do we get our national supplies of this important resource?

A.3 *You Decide:* Oil, Oil—Who's Got the Oil?

Like many other chemical resources, petroleum is unevenly distributed on the planet. Large amounts are often concentrated in small areas. In addition, nations with large reserves do not necessarily consume large amounts of this resource. That is, the geographic distribution of demand does not correspond with the location of petroleum reserves. Consequently, exporting and importing arrangements, known as trade agreements, are often made between countries.

Examine Figure III.4a to see where the world's known supplies of petroleum are located. The proven petroleum reserves are shown by region. A proven reserve can be tapped by available technology at costs consistent with current prices for the resource. Figure III.4b shows the regional distribution of world land. Use both charts to answer these questions:

1. Which region has the most petroleum relative to its land area?
2. Which region has the least petroleum relative to its land area?

V. Rankin, Photographer, FLUOR CORP.

Offshore drilling rig designed to operate in water depths up to 350 ft (110 m). The rig can drill up to six 30,000 ft (9 km) wells from one location.

Figure III.4a. Distribution of world's proven petroleum reserves.

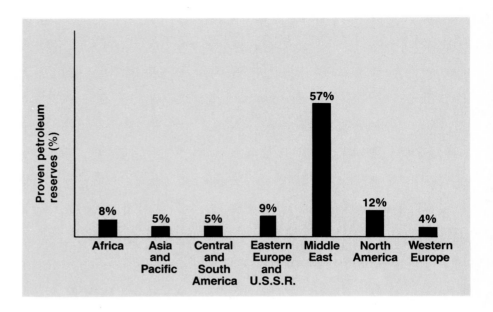

Figure III.4b. Distribution of world's land.

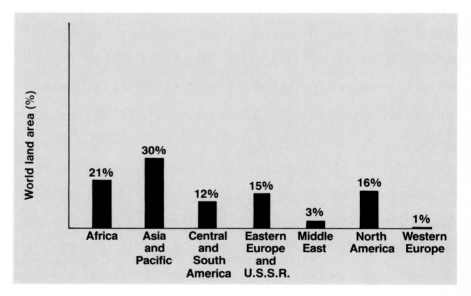

Figure III.4c. World consumption of petroleum.

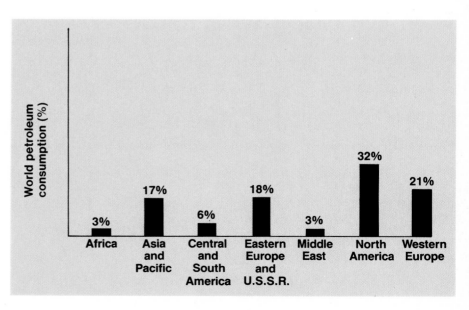

Now examine Figure III.4c, which shows the distribution of the world's consumption of petroleum by region. Use this figure along with Figures III.4a and b to answer these questions:

3. Which regions consume a greater percent of the world's supply of petroleum than they possess?
4. Which regions consume a smaller percent of the world's supply of petroleum than they possess?
5. Which regions are likely to have petroleum to export?
6. Which regions are likely to import petroleum?
7. List several pairs of regions that might make petroleum trade agreements. (A given region may be used more than once.)
8. Not all possible trade agreements are actually made. What factors might prevent trade relationships between regions?
9. What two regions are the major consumers of petroleum?
10. Why do these two regions consume the largest amounts of the world's petroleum supply?
11. Compare North America and the Middle East in terms of land area, oil reserves, and oil consumption. What conclusions can you draw from this comparison?
12. If one assumes that (a) the world's supply of petroleum is limited, and (b) world consumption of petroleum will increase at least to the end of this century, what responsibility, if any, should major petroleum-consuming regions have regarding the rest of the world? Explain your answer.

Thus far in our study, we have recognized how greatly we depend on petroleum. Society's increasing reliance on this nonrenewable and limited resource must be considered with great care. However, before we can approach such issues constructively, we need a better understanding of petroleum itself. What features of petroleum make it so valuable for both building and burning? In the next part we will tackle this question.

PART A
SUMMARY *QUESTIONS*

1. Nearly 90% of the petroleum consumed in the United States is burned as fuel, yet the 10% used for "building" purposes has great impact on our lives.
   a. Support this claim by listing 10 household items made with petroleum.
   b. Knowing that the United States uses 17 million barrels of petroleum per day, how many of these can we assume are burned? How many are used to build?
2. Suppose the cost of petroleum increased by 10% and the supply was reduced so that this country could use only 15 million barrels each day. Would you expect the price of fuel and nonfuel petroleum products also to increase by 10%? If not, which percent value is likely to be greater?
3. What type of trade relationship is likely between North America and the Middle East? If other regions of the world become more industrialized and oil supplies continue to dwindle, how might this relationship change?
4. The traditional unit of measure for petroleum, the barrel, is equal to 42 gallons. Assume that each barrel of petroleum yields 21 gallons of gasoline (after modification of some molecules). Also assume that your car runs 18 miles on each gallon of gasoline and that you travel 10,000 miles per year. How many barrels of petroleum must be processed to operate your car for one year?

B PETROLEUM: WHAT IS IT? WHAT DO WE DO WITH IT?

Amer. Petro. Institute Photographic & Film Service

A "gusher" of crude oil.

Distillation was mentioned as a water purification technique in Unit One.

Petroleum has been called "black gold." Why is it so valuable? How does it differ from other valuable resources such as the ores from which aluminum, iron, or copper are obtained?

Petroleum is chemically very different from metal ores, for it provides many hundreds of useful products, rather than one or two. Petroleum is a mixture containing hundreds of molecular compounds. These compounds have two desirable chemical properties in common. First, they are rich in energy that is released when the molecules undergo combustion—the "burning" use of petroleum. Second, the molecules can be chemically linked together or modified in many ways to produce a vast variety of useful materials—the "building" use of petroleum.

Chemists have learned how to combine small molecules from petroleum into the giant, chainlike molecules that are the raw materials for films, fibers, artificial rubber, and all kinds of plastics. They have also learned to convert petroleum into the molecules contained in perfumes, explosives, and drugs, including aspirin, Tylenol, and codeine. To chemists, petroleum has always been far more exciting and challenging than its black, sometimes gooey appearance suggests. What kinds of molecules make petroleum the treasure that it is? How can these molecules be separated from each other?

B.1 Working with Black Gold

Petroleum as it is pumped from underground is called **crude oil.** It is a greenish brown to black liquid that can be thin like water or quite thick. Crude oil is transported by pipeline, train, tanker truck, barge, or ocean tanker to oil refineries. There it is separated into simpler mixtures, some ready for use and others to undergo further chemical treatment.

Any salts (ionic compounds) or acids that might be present are the first things removed from crude oil. Most of the remaining substances are **hydrocarbons.** These molecular compounds are composed of only two elements—hydrogen and carbon. The hydrocarbons are separated by distillation into groups of substances having similar boiling points.

Rather than just reading about distillation, you can separate a mixture into two substances by distillation in the laboratory. Although petroleum refining is a far more complicated process, the same general principle of separation applies.

B.2 Laboratory Activity: Separation by Distillation

Getting Ready

Distillation is a method of separating substances according to their boiling points. The vapors rising from the boiling mixture at different temperatures are cooled and condensed into liquids, called **distillates,** which can be collected separately.

You will be given a mixture of two substances (A and B) and asked to separate them by distilling the lower boiling substance away from the higher boiling one. By measuring the mass and volume of your distillate, you can determine its density, a property that helps to identify the distillate.

To further assist you in identifying the components of your mixture you can observe the colors formed when various substances are dissolved in pure samples of A and B. Table III.1 lists the possible components of your mixture, their densities, and the colors each would give in the identifying tests. Prepare a table in your notebook like that below.

Data table

	Color observed in test with:		
	I_2	$CoCl_2$	$CuSO_4$
Sample A			
Sample B			
Distillate			

Density of distillate: _____

Identity of sample A: _____

Identity of sample B: _____

Identity of distillate: _____

Table III.1   *Experimental data: Properties of Possible Components of Unknowns*

Substance	Formula (boiling pt., °C)	Density (g/mL)	Result of identifying test with		
			I_2	$CoCl_2$	$CuSO_4$
Isopropyl (rubbing) alcohol	C_3H_8O (82.4)	0.78	Brown solution	Dark blue solution	Colorless
Xylene (cleaning solvent)	C_8H_{10} (144)	0.88	Red solution	Does not dissolve	Colorless
Water	H_2O (100)	1.00	Dissolves slightly— light yellow	Pink solution	Blue
Ethylene glycol (antifreeze)	$C_2H_6O_2$ (198)	1.11	Yellow-brown solution	Dissolves slightly— purple crystal	Colorless
TTE (Freon-113)	$C_2Cl_3F_3$ (45.8)	1.58	Violet solution	Does not dissolve— crystal remains red	Colorless

Procedure

1. Wash and dry a 25-mL graduated cylinder. When the cylinder is completely dry, weigh it, and record its mass. You will use this cylinder to collect the distillate.

2. Assemble the apparatus illustrated in setup I or setup II in Figure III.5. Follow the assembly procedure demonstrated by your teacher. *Be sure to exercise caution if you must insert glass tubes into stoppers.*

3. Obtain an unknown mixture sample. Record its code number. Pour 100 mL of the sample into the distillation flask in your setup and drop a boiling chip into the flask. Connect the flask to the condenser using a stopper as shown. Check all connections and clamps to ensure that the distillation setup is secure and will not leak. Wait for your teacher to check your apparatus. While waiting, complete the identifying tests in Step 4.

4. Identifying tests:

   a. Take six clean test tubes and label three "A" and three "B." Mark one test tube with a grease pencil at the 2-mL level. Then place three 2-mL samples of unknown A and three 2-mL samples of unknown B in the appropriate labeled test tubes.

   b. Using forceps, add one small iodine (I_2) crystal to a sample of A. Record your observations. Repeat this procedure with a sample of B.

   c. Using forceps, add one small cobalt chloride ($CoCl_2$) crystal to one of the remaining A samples. Record your observations. Repeat this procedure with a B sample.

   "Anhydrous" means without water. The "hydrated" form is $CuSO_4 \cdot 5 H_2O$.

   d. Using a spatula, add a small quantity (0.05 g) of anhydrous copper(II) sulfate ($CuSO_4$) to the last A sample. Record your observations. Repeat this procedure with the remaining sample of component B.

   e. Compare your results with Table III.1. Based on your observations, identify components A and B. Record their identities.

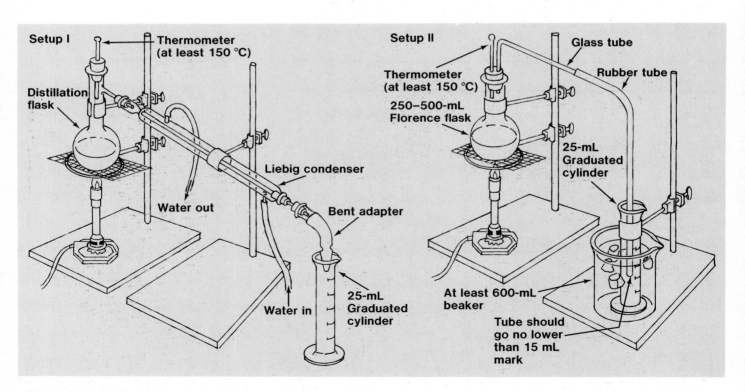

Figure III.5 Distillation apparatus. Two setups are shown; their use depends on the available equipment.

5. After your setup has been checked, begin heating your distillation mixture slowly. Note and record the vapor temperature at which the mixture begins to boil.

6. Record the vapor temperature when the first drop of distillate enters the graduated cylinder. Adjust the Bunsen burner flame so that the mixture boils gently and at an even rate. Keep the vapor at about the same temperature by passing the burner flame back and forth under the flask. *Do not allow the temperature to exceed 130 °C.* Uncontrolled boiling or allowing all of the liquid to boil away could cause the glassware or the thermometer to break.

7. Collect 6–10 mL of distillate. Turn off the burner. Replace the graduated cylinder with an empty beaker to capture any further distillate.

8. Dry the outside of the graduated cylinder and reweigh it. Calculate the total mass of distillate collected.

9. Record the volume of distillate in the graduated cylinder to the nearest 0.1 mL.

10. Place about 2 mL of distillate in each of three test tubes. Repeat the identifying tests described in Step 4.

11. Calculate the density of your distillate in units of grams per milliliter (g/mL) and record this value.

$$\text{Density} = \frac{\text{Mass of distillate (g)}}{\text{Volume of distillate (mL)}}$$

12. Compare your calculated density and the results of the identifying tests with Table III.1. What is the identity of your distillate?

13. Dismantle and clean the distillation apparatus as directed by your teacher.

Questions

1. What were the two components in your starting mixture?

2. Based on the density and identifying tests performed on the distillate, is the distillate a mixture of the original two components or a single substance? If it is a pure substance, which component is it?

3. What laboratory tests could you perform to determine whether the liquid left behind in the flask is a mixture or a pure substance?

Unlike your laboratory mixture, crude oil is composed of hundreds of different hydrocarbon compounds. This is a much more complicated distillation challenge! The refining process described in the next section does not result in the separation of each substance in crude oil, but produces several usable mixtures.

B.3 Petroleum Refining

The refining process separates crude oil by distillation into **fractions,** which are mixtures of hydrocarbons of similar boiling points and other properties. Figure III.6 illustrates the distillation, or fractionation, of crude oil. During distillation the smallest molecules vaporize first and move toward the top of the distilling column. Each arrow pointing to the right is labeled with the name of a fraction and its boiling point range. The higher boiling point fractions contain the largest molecules. The names given to various fractions and their boiling ranges vary, but the refining of crude oil is in general always as illustrated.

Crude oil is heated to about 400 °C (750 °F) in the furnace. Then it is pumped into the distilling column, a steel column more than 30 m (100 ft) tall. Sets of trays are arranged at different heights inside the column.

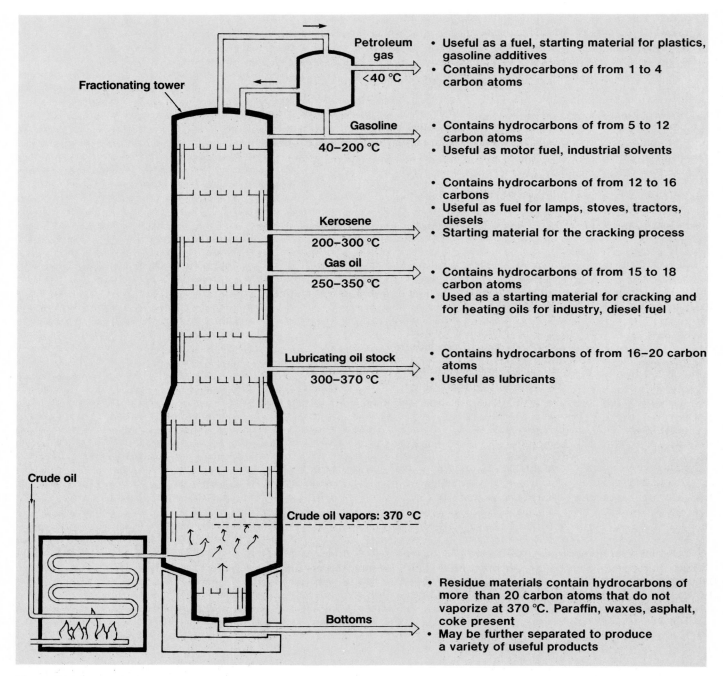

Fractionating tower

Petroleum gas
<40 °C
- Useful as a fuel, starting material for plastics, gasoline additives
- Contains hydrocarbons of from 1 to 4 carbon atoms

Gasoline
40–200 °C
- Contains hydrocarbons of from 5 to 12 carbon atoms
- Useful as motor fuel, industrial solvents

Kerosene
200–300 °C
- Contains hydrocarbons of from 12 to 16 carbons
- Useful as fuel for lamps, stoves, tractors, diesels
- Starting material for the cracking process

Gas oil
250–350 °C
- Contains hydrocarbons of from 15 to 18 carbon atoms
- Used as a starting material for cracking and for heating oils for industry, diesel fuel

Lubricating oil stock
300–370 °C
- Contains hydrocarbons of from 16–20 carbon atoms
- Useful as lubricants

Crude oil

Crude oil vapors: 370 °C

Bottoms
- Residue materials contain hydrocarbons of more than 20 carbon atoms that do not vaporize at 370 °C. Paraffin, waxes, asphalt, coke present
- May be further separated to produce a variety of useful products

Figure III.6 A fractionating tower. The cracking process referred to is a method for converting larger hydrocarbon molecules into smaller ones more suitable for gasoline.

As the hot crude oil enters the tower, molecules of substances with lower boiling points gain enough energy to break away from the liquid and rise into the cooler portions of the tower. As they rise they cool. Substances with the lowest boiling points remain in the vapor state and rise to the top of the tower. There they are drawn off as gases. Some substances condense and fall into trays located at different tower heights. These are drawn off as liquid fractions, each with its own boiling point range. By contrast, substances with very high boiling points remain as liquids through the entire procedure. These thick (viscous) liquids are drained from the bottom of the column.

You are already familiar with the names of some of these petroleum distillation fractions, such as gasoline, kerosene, and lubricating oils. In the following activity you'll have the chance to examine some of petroleum's component fractions in detail.

B.4 Laboratory Activity: Physical Properties

Getting Ready

In this laboratory activity you will observe the differences in the physical properties of several petroleum-based materials by measuring their densities and relative viscosities. For comparison, you will measure these properties for water also.

To determine densities, you will measure masses and volumes of liquid and solid samples.

Viscosity is the term for resistance to flow. A material with a high viscosity flows slowly and with difficulty, like honey. A material with a low viscosity flows readily, like water. You will determine relative viscosities, which means ranking materials on a range from the most to the least viscous.

In your laboratory notebook, prepare a data table like the one below, which you will use for reference.

Data table—Sample examination

Material	Carbon atoms per molecule	State at room temperature (solid, liquid)
Mineral oil	12–20	
Asphalt	More than 34	
Kerosene	12–16	
Paraffin wax	More than 19	
Motor oil	15–18	
Household lubricating oil	14–18	

Also prepare the data tables below:

Data table—Density measurements

Average mass of capped tube: _____
Average mass of plastic bead: _____
Average volume: _____

Liquid	Mass of capped tube, bead, and liquid (g)	Calculated mass of liquid (g)	Calculated density of material (g/mL)
Water			
Mineral oil			
Kerosene			
Motor oil			
Household lubricating oil			

Solid	Mass of sample (g)	Volume increase (mL)	Calculated density of material (g/mL)
Paraffin wax			
Asphalt			

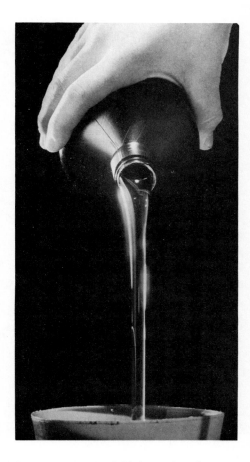

The viscosity of a fluid determines how fast it can be poured.

Data table—Viscosity measurements		
Material	**Average time for bead to fall (s)**	**Relative viscosity**
Water Mineral oil Kerosene Motor oil Household lubricating oil		

Procedure

Sample Examination
1. Obtain samples of the six materials listed in your sample examination table.
2. Record the state (solid or liquid) of each sample.
3. Based on your knowledge of petroleum fractions (see Figure III.6), which material would you expect to have the lowest boiling point? The highest boiling point?

Density Measurement
Liquid Samples
1. Your teacher will give you the average values for the mass of an empty capped tube, the mass of a plastic bead, and the volume of liquid in a sample tube. For convenience, record these values at the top of your data table.
2. Weigh the capped tubes containing each of the petroleum product samples and also one containing water. Record the masses.

Solid Samples
1. Fill a 25-mL graduated cylinder to the 10-mL mark with water.
2. Weigh each solid sample carefully. Record the masses.
3. Carefully drop the first weighed solid sample into the water in the cylinder. Measure the increase in volume and record this value.
4. Repeat Step 3 for the other solid sample.

Density Calculations
Liquid Samples
1. Calculate the mass in grams of each liquid sample, using the total masses of the samples, their containers, and the beads obtained in Step 2, above:

Sample mass = Total mass − (avg. capped tube mass + avg. bead mass)

Record the mass of each liquid sample.
2. Using the average volume of liquid in each capped tube and your calculated sample mass, calculate the density of each sample in grams per milliliter. Record the values.

For example, suppose the sample mass is 40.2 g and the average volume is 36.7 mL:

$$\text{Sample density} = \frac{\text{sample mass}}{\text{average volume}} = \frac{40.2 \text{ g}}{36.7 \text{ mL}} = 1.10 \text{ g/mL}$$

Solid Samples

1. Using the sample masses and the increases in volume that you found above, calculate the sample densities in grams per milliliter. The calculation is the same as illustrated for the liquids, with the increase in volume replacing the average tube volume.

Relative Viscosity

1. Determine the average time for a bead to fall from top to bottom within the capped tube containing water. Follow this procedure:
   a. Hold the capped tube upright until the ball is at the bottom.
   b. Gently turn the tube horizontally. (The bead will stay at one end.)
   c. Quickly turn the tube upright so the bead is at the top.
   d. Determine the number of seconds required for the bead to fall to the bottom of the tube.
   e. Repeat this procedure three more times. Calculate the average time required for the bead to fall.
2. Repeat the Step 2 procedure for each liquid petroleum-based sample.
3. Rank your samples in order of relative viscosity, assigning the number 1 to the least viscous material (the one in which the ball fell fastest).

Questions

1. The density of oil is a major factor both in oil spills and oil fires. Explain.
2. Propose a rule based on observations made in this activity regarding the relative number of carbon atoms per molecule and the resulting viscosity of the material.
3. Suppose that a fellow classmate suggested that petroleum fractions could be separated at room temperature on the basis of viscosity. Do you agree? Explain your answer. What would be some advantages of such a separation procedure?
4. Petroleum refiners and distributors must consider both the ease of evaporation and viscosity of their products when shipping gasoline and motor oils to different parts of the country. Explain why the gasoline shipped to a northern state (say Alaska) in winter must be different from that shipped to a southern state (say Florida) in summer.

   The petroleum fractions you have investigated represent just a few of the great number of materials present in petroleum. The next activity will outline in greater detail the substances we get from each fraction and what we do with them.

B.5   *You Decide:* From Crude Oil to Products

In Figure III.7 five hydrocarbon fractions are listed in order of increasing boiling point range. The low-boiling petroleum gas is at the top, and the high-boiling residues are at the bottom. Next to each fraction, arrows point to the refinery products from that fraction. These products are sold to users or processors. Some of the ultimate uses of these products are also listed. The box at the bottom illustrates the wide variety of consumer products made from petrochemicals (see Part D.4).

Petrochemicals are materials made from petroleum.

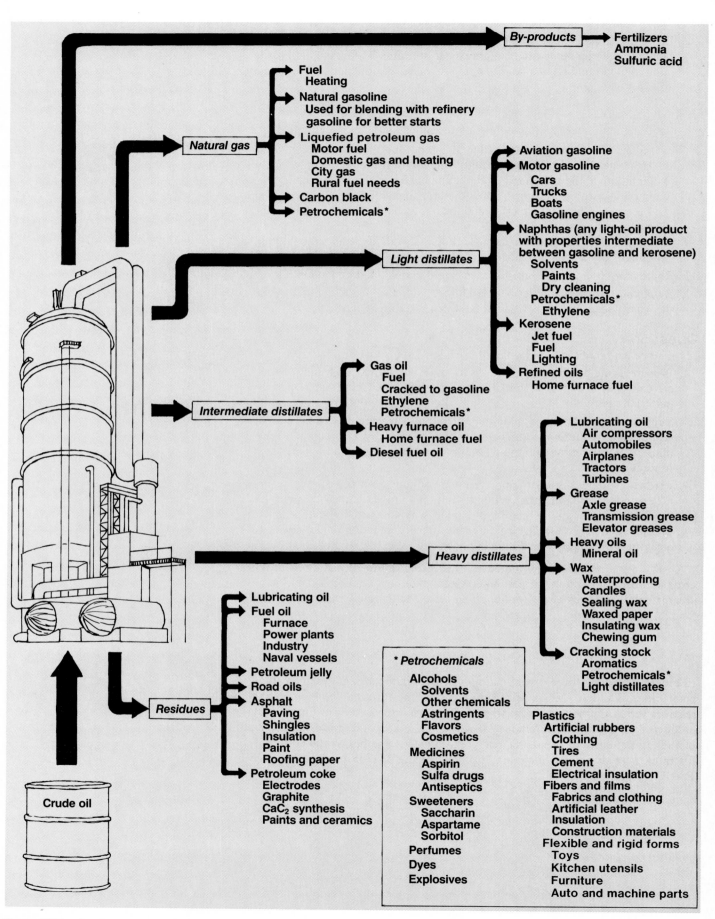

Figure III.7 From crude oil to products.

Use the figure to answer the following questions:

1. Do any of the five fractions represent petroleum's use only as an energy source for burning? If so, identify them.

2. Do any fractions represent petroleum's use only as a source of materials to build new substances? Name them.

3. Identify the fractions that include both burning and building uses of petroleum.

4. Choose a branch (fraction) on the petroleum pipeline. Describe how life might change if this branch and its resulting products were eliminated during a petroleum shortage.

5. Identify two major petroleum uses you consider important enough to continue even during a severe petroleum shortage. Give your reasons.

6. Based on your answers to the questions above, which do you believe is the more important use of petroleum—burning it to generate energy or building new substances from it?

The samples of refined petroleum fractions you investigated earlier in this unit were originally separated from petroleum by distillation. Each fraction has different physical properties. What explains these differences?

In the following sections, we will look in greater detail at the composition and structure of the types of molecules found in petroleum. We will see that here, too, the properties of substances are related to molecular structure.

B.6 A Closer Look at Petroleum Molecules

The gaseous fraction of crude oil contains compounds with the lowest boiling points. These hydrocarbons readily separate from each other and rise to the top of the distillation column as gases. Apparently their molecules have relatively little attraction for each other and for other molecules in petroleum. These gaseous hydrocarbon molecules contain from one to four carbon atoms.

The distillate fractions that are liquids at room temperature, including gasoline, kerosene, and the heavier oils, consist of molecules with 5 to about 20 carbon atoms. The greasy-solid fraction, which doesn't vaporize even at high distilling temperatures (at one atmosphere pressure) contains molecules with even greater numbers of carbon atoms. These substances apparently have the strongest forces of attraction between molecules.

Complete the following *Your Turn* to learn more about the physical properties of the hydrocarbons.

YOUR*TURN*

III.1 Hydrocarbon Boiling Points

The work of chemists often involves determining the physical and chemical properties of substances. Such data can be organized in a variety of ways. The most useful ways are those that lead to the discovery of patterns among the experimental values. Such patterns often stimulate searches for explanations of the regularities. The development of the periodic table is an outstanding example of the value of this approach (Unit Two, Part B.4). Recall how you were able to predict a property of one element in a family from values of the same property for the other elements.

Here we will explore the organization of boiling point data for some hydrocarbons. During evaporation and boiling, individual molecules in the liquid state gain enough energy to pull away from the attraction of neighboring molecules and enter the gaseous state.

Table III.2 *Various hydrocarbon boiling points*

Hydrocarbon	Boiling point (°C)
Butane	−0.5
Decane	174.0
Ethane	−88.6
Heptane	98.4
Hexane	68.7
Methane	−161.7
Nonane	150.8
Octane	125.7
Pentane	36.1
Propane	−42.1

Answer the following questions about the organization and patterns of the boiling point data given in Table III.2.

1. In what pattern or order are the data in Table III.2 organized? Is this a helpful way to present the information? Why?

2. If we wish to search for a trend or pattern among these boiling points, can you think of a more useful way to list these data? Rewrite the summary of data, organizing it according to your idea.

3. Use your new data table to answer these questions:
   a. Which substance(s) are found as gases (i.e., have already boiled) at room temperature (22 °C or 72 °F)?
   b. Which substance(s) are found as liquids at room temperature, but boil below body temperature (37 °C or 98.6 °F)?

4. What can you infer about the intermolecular forces of attraction in decane compared with those in butane?

5. Do you think attractive forces might relate to other properties of liquids such as viscosity or freezing point? Make a guess and rank pentane, octane, and decane in order of increasing viscosity. Give the number 1 to the least viscous of the three substances. Then check with your teacher to see if you are correct.

B.7 Chemical Bonding

Hydrocarbons and their derivatives are the focus of an entire branch of chemistry known as **organic chemistry.** These compounds are described as "organic" compounds because in the early days of chemistry it was thought that such compounds could only be made by plants or animals. Today chemists know how to make many of them.

Hydrocarbons are molecular compounds. In molecules of many hydrocarbons, carbon atoms are joined together to form a backbone known as a **carbon chain.** Hydrogen atoms are attached to this chain. As you will soon see, the ability of carbon atoms to form chains helps to explain the vast number of known hydrocarbons. Also, hydrocarbons are the parents of an even larger number of compounds.

Atoms are held to one another by chemical bonds.

To find out how atoms are held together, we must first examine the arrangement of electrons in atoms. We have seen that atoms are made up of neutrons, protons, and electrons. In every atom the neutrons and protons are located in a dense central region known as the **nucleus.** Studies have shown that electrons occupy different energy levels in the space surrounding the atomic nucleus. Each energy level can hold only a certain number of electrons.

Consider atoms of the noble gas helium (He). Each helium atom has two protons in its nucleus and two electrons surrounding the nucleus. The two electrons occupy the first, or innermost, electron energy level and this is as many electrons as this level can hold.

The next noble gas, neon, has atomic number 10 (Unit Two, Part B.4); its atoms each contain 10 protons and 10 electrons. Only two of the electrons can occupy the first energy level. The remaining eight reside in the second energy level, and it is also full, since the maximum number of electrons for this level is eight.

Helium and neon are both chemically unreactive—their atoms do not combine with those of other atoms to form compounds. Sodium atoms, however, with atomic number 11, and therefore just one more electron than neon, are extremely reactive. Fluorine atoms with one less electron than neon also are extremely reactive. The differences in the reactivities of all elements are accounted for by the electron arrangements in their atoms.

Let's look for a moment at ionic compounds, before returning to the hydrocarbons and other molecular compounds.

In a sodium atom, 10 electrons fill the first and second levels, leaving a single electron to occupy the third and outermost level. Eight electrons in a filled outer energy level is a stable arrangement, but one electron in such a level is not. The sodium atom readily loses its outermost electron to produce Na^+, which has the stable filled outer energy level. Sodium ions are present in many compounds.

In fluorine atoms (atomic number 9), the outer energy level contains seven electrons, and is one electron short of the stable eight. Losing seven electrons is very difficult, but gaining one is easy for fluorine atoms. Fluorine is a very reactive element. Its atoms readily form the fluoride ion, F^-, in which the outer energy level is filled to capacity because one electron has been added.

When sodium and fluorine atoms react with each other, each sodium atom donates an electron to a fluorine atom. In this process, sodium and fluoride ions are formed and attract one another. This results in the crystalline ionic compound known as sodium fluoride. We say that **ionic bonds** hold the ions together. Many ionic compounds are formed between metals that easily lose electrons and nonmetals that easily gain them.

In molecular substances, atoms have not formed ions, but they have acquired filled outer energy levels, in this case by sharing electrons. Many molecular substances form between nonmetal atoms, those that do not easily lose electrons.

The hydrogen molecule (H_2) provides a simple example. Each hydrogen atom contains one electron. It's clear that one additional electron is needed to fill the single energy level in a hydrogen atom. Two hydrogen atoms can accomplish this by sharing their electrons. If each electron is represented by a dot ($\cdot$), then the formation of a hydrogen molecule can be written in this way:

$$H\cdot \; + \; \cdot H \rightarrow H:H$$

The chemical bond formed by the sharing of electrons between two atoms is called a **covalent bond.** Through such sharing, both atoms achieve filled outer electron energy levels.

A carbon atom, atomic number 6, has six electrons—two in the innermost level and four in the outer level. Four more electrons are needed to fill the outer energy level. This can be accomplished through covalent bonding. Consider the simplest hydrocarbon molecule, methane (CH_4). In this molecule, each hydrogen atom shares its single electron with a carbon atom as the following representation suggests:

$$4\,H\cdot \; + \; \cdot \overset{\displaystyle\cdot}{\underset{\displaystyle\cdot}{C}} \cdot \quad \rightarrow \quad H : \overset{\displaystyle H}{\underset{\displaystyle H}{\overset{\displaystyle\cdot\cdot}{\underset{\displaystyle\cdot\cdot}{C}}}} : H$$

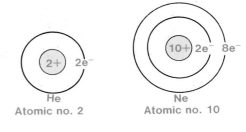

He
Atomic no. 2

Ne
Atomic no. 10

Ionic compounds and their solubility were introduced in Unit One.

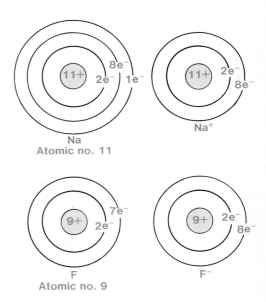

Na
Atomic no. 11

Na^+

F
Atomic no. 9

F^-

The dots in the structures in this equation represent only outer electrons for each atom. Such structures are called **electron-dot formulas.** The two electrons in each covalent bond "belong" to both of the bonded atoms. Count the dots surrounding each symbol. Those between two symbols represent the electrons shared by those atoms. Notice that each hydrogen atom in methane has a filled outermost energy level (two electrons in the first level) and the carbon atom has a filled outermost energy level (eight electrons in the second level).

For convenience, each pair of electrons in a covalent bond is replaced by a dash, leading to another common way of representing covalently bonded substances. This is called a **structural formula:**

$$
\begin{array}{ccc}
& H & \\
& \overset{..}{\underset{..}{H:C:H}} & \\
& H &
\end{array}
\qquad\qquad
\begin{array}{c}
H \\
| \\
H-C-H \\
| \\
H
\end{array}
$$

Electron dot structure   Structural formula

The arrangements of covalently bonded atoms in a molecule create distinctive three-dimensional structures. These structures help to determine the properties of molecular substances and how molecules interact with each other. A good way to visualize the three-dimensional character of molecules is to build models of them. The following activity will give you a chance to do this.

B.8 Laboratory Activity: Modeling the Alkanes

In this activity you will make models of several simple hydrocarbons. The goal is to relate the three-dimensional shapes of molecules to the names, formulas, and pictures used to represent molecules on paper.

Pictures of two types of molecular models are shown in Figure III.8. Most likely, you will use ball-and-stick models. Each ball represents an atom and each stick represents a covalent bond connecting two atoms. Real molecules are not composed of ball-like atoms located at the ends of stick-like bonds. Evidence shows that atoms are in contact with each other, more like those in the space-filling models. However, the ball-and-stick models are useful, because they make it easy to see the structure and geometry of molecules.

Look again at the electron-dot structure and structural formula that is printed just above for methane (CH_4) the simplest hydrocarbon. Methane is the first member of a series of hydrocarbons known as the **alkanes,** which we explore in this activity. In the alkanes each carbon atom forms covalent bonds with four other atoms. Alkanes are classified as **saturated hydrocarbons,** because each carbon atom is bonded to the maximum number of other atoms (four).

Figure III.8   Three-dimensional models: (a) Ball-and-stick. (b) Space filling.

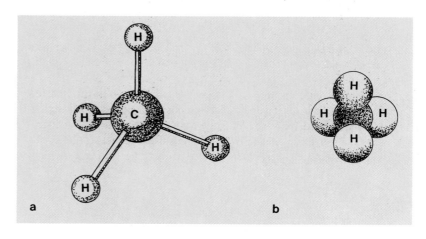

Procedure

1. Build a model of methane (CH_4).

    Compare your model with the electron dot and structural formulas above. Note that the actual angles between the atoms are not 90°, as implied by the formulas.

    Compare the model with the drawings of models in Figure III.8. A box surrounding the CH_4 molecule would have the shape of a triangular pyramid (a pyramid with a triangle as a base), as shown in Figure III.9 This geometric figure is called a **tetrahedron.** One way to account for this shape is to assume that the four pairs of electrons in the bonds surrounding the carbon atom—all possessing negative charges—stay as far away from each other as possible. The bonds point to the corners of the tetrahedron and the angles between the bonds are all 109.5°.

2. Build models of alkane molecules containing two and three carbon atoms. Remember that in each alkane the carbon atoms must be bonded to four other atoms.

    How many hydrogen atoms are present in the two-carbon alkane? In the three-carbon alkane? Try to draw a picture like that in Figure III.8 of the two-carbon alkane.

3. Draw electron dot and structural formulas for the two- and three-carbon alkanes. The molecular formulas for the first two alkanes are CH_4 and C_2H_6. What is the molecular formula of the third?

    Examine your three-carbon alkane model and the structural formula you drew for it. Note that the middle carbon atom is attached to two hydrogen atoms, while each end carbon atom is attached to three hydrogen atoms. This molecule can be represented as $CH_3 — CH_2 — CH_3$ or $CH_3CH_2CH_3$, which are examples of **condensed formulas.** Condensed formulas provide more information about molecular structure than molecular formulas such as C_3H_8.

    For each carbon atom added to an alkane chain, two hydrogen atoms must also be added. The molecular formula for any alkane molecule is represented by C_nH_{2n+2}, where n is the number of carbon atoms in the molecule.

4. Use the general alkane formula to write the molecular formulas for the first 10 alkanes. The condensed formulas for these 10 alkanes are given in Table III.3. Compare your molecular formulas with the condensed formulas and verify that the predictions are correct.

    The names of the first 10 alkanes are also given in Table III.3. The names are all composed of a "root" and the ending *-ane*. The root of each alkane name refers to the number of carbon atoms in the molecule's carbon chain or backbone. To a chemist, *meth-* means one carbon atom, *eth-* means two, and *prop-* means three.

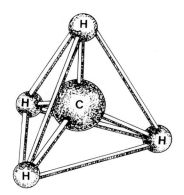

Figure III.9   The tetrahedral shape of methane molecules.

Table III.3   *Some members of the alkane series*

Name	Number of carbons	Formula
Methane	1	CH_4
Ethane	2	CH_3CH_3
Propane	3	$CH_3CH_2CH_3$
Butane	4	$CH_3(CH_2)_2CH_3$
Pentane	5	$CH_3(CH_2)_3CH_3$
Hexane	6	$CH_3(CH_2)_4CH_3$
Heptane	7	$CH_3(CH_2)_5CH_3$
Octane	8	$CH_3(CH_2)_6CH_3$
Nonane	9	$CH_3(CH_2)_7CH_3$
Decane	10	$CH_3(CH_2)_8CH_3$

5. Write structural formulas for butane and for pentane.
6. Name the alkanes with the following formulas:
   a. $CH_3CH_2CH_2CH_2CH_2CH_2CH_3$
   b. $CH_3CH_2CH_2CH_2CH_2CH_2CH_2CH_2CH_3$
7. Write the molecular formulas for the 11, 12, and 13 carbon alkanes. The roots representing 11, 12, and 13 carbon atoms are *undec-, dodec-, and tridec-.* Write the names for these alkanes.
8. Name alkanes that have the molar masses (a) 30 g/mol, (b) 58 g/mol.

YOUR*TURN*

III.2 Alkane Boiling Points: Trends

Based on what you know about the properties, formulas, names, and chemical bonding in alkanes, work out the following:

1. Without using specific data, sketch your idea of the appearance of a graph showing the boiling points of alkanes (y axis) and the number of carbon atoms present (x axis). Describe the graph line you sketched. Compare your sketch with those of two other classmates. Briefly discuss any similarities and differences.

2. Now prepare the same kind of graph using the boiling point data from Table III.2 (Part B.6). The x-axis scale should range from 1 to 13 atoms (even though you will initially plot data from 1 to 10 carbon atoms); the y-axis scale should extend from -200 °C to $+250$ °C.

   a. Compare this graph line with the one you sketched in Question 1 above. Was your sketch on the right track?

   b. From your graph, estimate the average boiling point change (in degrees Celsius) when one carbon atom and two hydrogen atoms ($-CH_2-$) are added to a given alkane chain.

   c. The pattern of boiling points among the first 10 alkanes allows the prediction of boiling points of other alkane chains. From your graph, estimate the boiling points of undecane ($C_{11}H_{24}$), dodecane ($C_{12}H_{26}$), and tridecane ($C_{13}H_{28}$). To do this, extend your graph in the direction it is headed with a dashed line (this is called extrapolation). Then read on the y axis the predicted values for the C_{11}, C_{12}, and C_{13} hydrocarbon boiling points. Compare the predicted boiling points to actual values provided by your teacher.

   d. We observed earlier that the boiling point of a substance varies with the extent of attraction among the substance's molecules. For the alkanes you have studied, how are these attractions related to the total number of carbon atoms per molecule?

B.9 Laboratory Activity: Alkanes Revisited

Getting Ready

The alkane molecules that we have considered so far are **straight-chain alkanes** in which each carbon atom is linked to no more than two other carbon atoms. Many other arrangements of carbon atoms in alkanes are possible. Alkanes in which one or more carbon atoms are linked to either three or four other carbon atoms are **branched-chain alkanes.**

In this activity you will use the ball-and-stick molecular models to discover some of the possible variations in alkane structures.

A straight carbon chain
C — C — C — C — C

A branched carbon chain
C — C — C — C
         |
         C

Procedure

1. Construct a ball-and-stick model of butane (C_4H_{10}). Compare your model with those built by other groups. How many different arrangements of the atoms in C_4H_{10} are possible?

   Molecules that have the same molecular formula but different arrangements of the atoms are called **isomers.** By comparing models, convince yourself that there are two isomers of butane. The formation of isomers helps to account for the very large number of known compounds containing chains or rings of carbon atoms.

2. Draw electron-dot formulas for the two butane isomers. Write the structural formulas for both butanes.

3. Working in groups of two, draw structural formulas for the isomers of hexane (C_6H_{14}). Compare your structures with those of other groups. How many hexane isomers are there?

4. Groups will be assigned to build each of the hexane isomers. Compare the three-dimensional models with the structures that you drew on paper.

Alkane formulas with four or more carbon atoms have more than one possible structure. Your experience with hexane (six carbon atoms) should suggest that the number of different structures increases rapidly as the number of carbon atoms increases. Because each isomer is a different substance, each has characteristic properties. Let's examine boiling point data for some alkane isomers.

YOUR*TURN*

III.3 Alkane Boiling Points: Isomers

You have already observed that the boiling points of straight chain alkanes are related to the number of carbon atoms in their molecules. Increased intermolecular attractions are related to the greater molecule-to-molecule contact possible for larger alkane molecules. Let's consider the boiling points of isomers.

1. The boiling points of two sets of isomers are listed in Table III.4. Within a given series, how does the boiling point change as the number of carbon side chains increases?

2. Match each boiling point to the appropriate C_7H_{16} isomer: 98.4 °C, 92.0 °C, 79.2 °C

   a. $CH_3 — CH_2 — CH — CH_2 — CH_2 — CH_3$
                          |
                         CH_3

                         CH_3
                          |
   b. $CH_3 — CH_2 — CH_2 — C — CH_3$
                            |
                          CH_3

   c. $CH_3 — CH_2 — CH_2 — CH_2 — CH_2 — CH_2 — CH_3$

3. Below is the formula of a C_8H_{18} isomer.
   a. Compare it with the C_8H_{18} isomers listed in Table III.4 and predict whether it should have a higher or lower boiling point than each of the three given in the table.

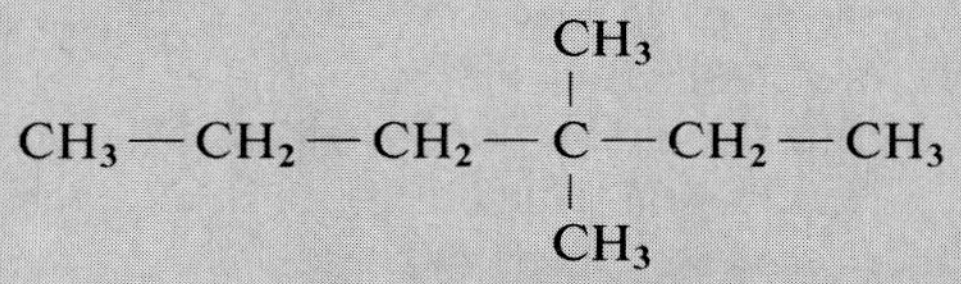

$$
\begin{array}{c}
CH_3 \\
| \\
CH_3-CH_2-CH_2-C-CH_2-CH_3 \\
| \\
CH_3
\end{array}
$$

   b. Would you expect the C_8H_{18} isomer shown above to have a higher or lower boiling point than each of the three C_5H_{12} isomers shown in Table III.4?

Table III.4 *Alkane isomers*

Alkane	Structure	Boiling point (°C)
C_5H_{12} isomers	$CH_3-CH_2-CH_2-CH_2-CH_3$	36.1
	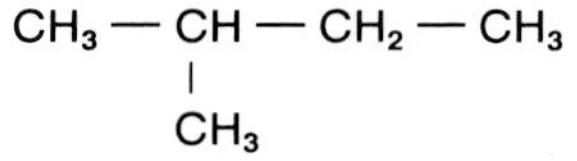 $CH_3-CH-CH_2-CH_3$ with CH_3 branch	27.8
	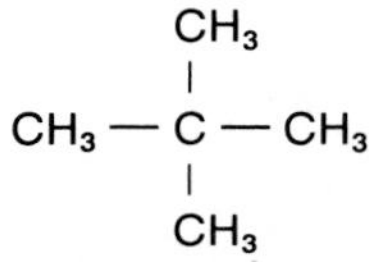 CH_3-C-CH_3 with two CH_3 branches	9.5
Some C_8H_{18} isomers	$CH_3-CH_2-CH_2-CH_2-CH_2-CH_2-CH_2-CH_3$	125.6
	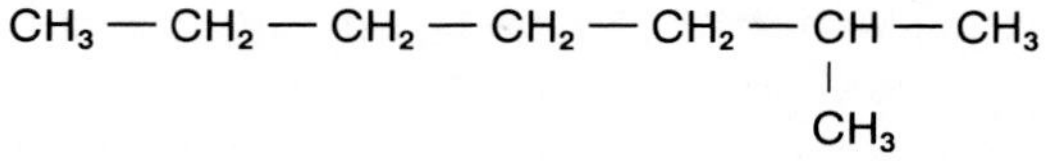 $CH_3-CH_2-CH_2-CH_2-CH_2-CH-CH_3$ with CH_3 branch	117.7
	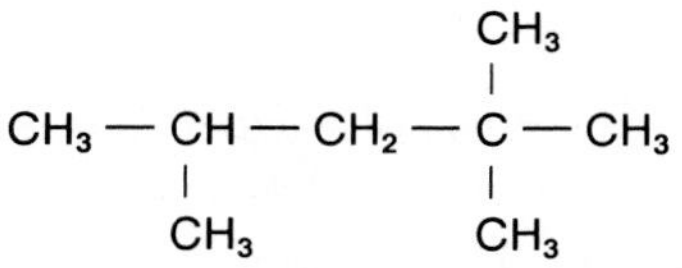 $CH_3-CH-CH_2-C-CH_3$ with CH_3 branches	99.2

Knowledge of petroleum's varied molecular components enables chemists to separate this complex mixture into a variety of potentially useful substances. However, since petroleum is a nonrenewable and limited resource, how can we make best use of various petroleum fractions? Should we use them to build or to burn? Or, if for both, how much should be directed to each use? What alternatives might be available in the future to decrease our dependence on petroleum? These questions will be explored in the following pages. Most petroleum currently used is burned as fuel; therefore, this use serves as our focus in Part C.

PART B
SUMMARY *QUESTIONS*

1. In what sense is petroleum similar to metallic resources such as copper ore? In what sense is it different from them?

2. A 50.0-mL sample of octane has a mass of 35.1 g.
   a. What is the density of octane?
   b. What is the mass of a 100-mL sample of octane?
   c. What is the mass of 3.78 L (1 gallon) of octane? (*Hint:* Rearrange the equation $d = m/V$ to solve for mass: $m = d \times V$. Be sure that the units work out properly.)

3. In what way(s) is petroleum refining similar to the distillation you performed in the laboratory? How is it different?

4. Identify two broad categories of petroleum use. List two examples for each category.

5. Among the main components of paraffin wax used to make candles is a group of alkanes containing 25 carbon atoms per molecule. Write the molecular formula for members of this group.

6. Experimental evidence confirms the tetrahedral shape of a molecule of methane (CH_4). How do chemists explain this observation? How does your molecular model kit allow for this fact?

7. List two features of molecular structure that determine the relative boiling points of hydrocarbons. How do these features influence boiling points?

8. Define the term "isomer" and illustrate this definition by drawing structural formulas for at least three isomers of C_7H_{16}.

9. You are drawn into a discussion between two classmates. One contends that the two isomers of butane each contain 10 hydrogen atoms and 10 covalent bonds. The other says that one isomer contains 10 hydrogen atoms and 13 covalent bonds, but that the other contains 10 hydrogen atoms and 10 covalent bonds. Can you clarify the situation?

EXTENDING *YOUR KNOWLEDGE* (OPTIONAL)

- Investigate the different compositions of gasoline sold in various parts of the country. Does the time of year relate to gasoline composition? If so, what factors help to determine the optimum composition for various times of the year?
- The hydrocarbon boiling points listed in Table III.2 were measured under normal atmospheric conditions. How would the boiling points change if atmospheric pressure were increased or decreased? (*Hint:* Consider the fact that butane appears as a liquid in butane lighters, yet escapes through the lighter nozzle as gas.)
- Dissolving a solute such as salt in a pure liquid will raise the liquid's boiling point and also lower its freezing point. However, salt is undesirable as an additive for car radiators, while ethylene glycol is a suitable additive. Why? (*Hint:* contrast the structure and properties of the two substances.)

Ethylene glycol

C PETROLEUM AS A SOURCE OF ENERGY

No one knows exactly how petroleum was first formed. Most evidence indicates that it originated from plants and animals that lived in ancient seas some 500 million years ago. These organisms died and eventually were covered with sediments. Pressure, heat, and microbes converted what was once living matter into petroleum, now trapped in porous rocks. Very likely, petroleum is continuously being formed, even today, from organic sediments. But its rate of formation is too slow to make it a renewable resource.

Petroleum use can be traced back almost 5000 years. Ancient Middle Eastern civilizations collected petroleum that seeped from the ground and used it to waterproof ships and canals and to pave roads. By A.D. 1000, Arabs processed petroleum to obtain kerosene for lighting. Eleventh-century Chinese extracted oil from wells more than a half-mile deep. Marco Polo described oil fields he observed in travels through Persia in the thirteenth century.

The first oil well in the United States was drilled in 1869 in Titusville, Pa. In the century and a quarter since this drilling, our way of life has been greatly altered. The following activity will help you realize just how much life has changed during the more recent history of our petroleum use.

C.1 *You Decide:* Were They the Good Old Days?

Earlier in this century, petroleum was used far less than it is now. To investigate what life was like then, you will serve on a team to interview someone who remembers this period of our country's past.

First, however, your class should decide what questions should be included in all interviews. Sample questions are given below. You may use these or develop your own set of 10–12 key questions. The same basic questions should be used by all interview teams, so results can be compared later.

Sample Interview Questions

1. How would you describe where you lived as a child—urban, suburban, or rural?
2. What was the main source of heat in your home at that time?
3. How was this source of heat supplied? Did you obtain the fuel yourself or was it delivered to your home?
4. In terms of cleanliness, convenience, and quantity of heat produced, how would you rate the older source of heat to that used today?
5. What was the main source of lighting in your home? What source of energy was used to provide the lighting?
6. What, if any, was the main means of public transportation? What provided the energy for this transportation?
7. What was the main source of private transportation? How prevalent was this method of transportation? What was its source of energy?
8. What fuel was used for cooking?
9. If you bought your food, as opposed to growing or raising it yourself, how was it packaged?

10. In what kind of container was milk obtained?

11. What kind of soap was used to wash clothes? How did its effectiveness compare to that of today's soaps and detergents?

12. What were the main fabrics used in clothes? From what were the fabrics made?

13. Were clothes easier or harder to care for than they are now? Please explain.

After deciding which questions to include in the interviews, your class will form a number of interview teams. Each team should arrange to talk with a team member's grandparent, a neighbor more than 70-years old, or a resident of a local retirement center. One interview should be conducted per team.

Before conducting the actual interview, each team should interview one of its own members. The practice interview will provide current information for comparison and will give the team useful interviewing practice. Summarize all questions and answers in a written outline or chart after each interview is completed.

All team results should be tabulated on a single class poster or bulletin board. The questions can be written in a vertical row; the most frequent answers can become column headings. Each team can then place a check mark in the appropriate column for each question. Information obtained in the interviews that cannot be added to this chart should be introduced during the class discussion.

Here are some suggested topics for the class discussion that will follow this activity:

1. What are the main differences between earlier years and the present day regarding the items listed below:

   a. Home heating   e. Cooking
   b. Lighting   f. Food packaging
   c. Public transportation g. Clothes washing
   d. Private transportation h. Clothing material

Jon Jacobson

A portable but inefficient light source from an earlier era.

2. Would a return to "the good old days" be desirable? Why or why not?

3. If current energy sources become used up, must we return to a lifestyle similar to that of the past? Why or why not?

Would you want to live in the "good old days"? Since we do live in the here and now, we must give serious thought to making the best possible use of our remaining energy sources—petroleum being a major one. To help us forecast our energy future, we will first examine the energy sources that have powered our society during the past century.

C.2 Energy: Past, Present, and Future

The sun is our primary energy source. Through **photosynthesis,** radiant energy from the sun is stored as chemical energy in plants. Animals eat these plants, again storing the energy in **biomolecules,** the molecules of living systems.

Solar energy and the energy stored in biomolecules are the basic energy sources essential to life on our planet. Since the discovery of fire, our ability to use various forms of stored solar energy has been a major influence in the development of civilization. The specific forms, availability, and price of energy strongly influence where and how people live, as your interviews probably suggested.

In the past, our nation had abundant supplies of inexpensive energy. Until about 1850, wood, water, wind, and animal power satisfied all of our slowly growing energy needs. Wood, the predominant energy source, was readily available due to the conversion of forests to farmland. Wood served as an energy source for heating, cooking, and lighting. Water, wind, and animal power provided transportation and "fueled" our machinery and industrial processes. In the next activity, you can see just how much has changed over the years.

In 1920, the U.S. population was 106 million. Today it is more than 241 million.

1 exajoule is 10^{18} joules or roughly the total energy used in the U.S. in 3.5 days.

YOURTURN

III.4 Fuel Consumption Over the Years

Figure III.10 shows how energy consumption has changed in the United States during the past 130 years. It also shows the quantity of energy produced from various fuel sources, such as coal, wood, and petroleum, during any given time period between 1850 and the 1980s. For example, in 1920 when a total of about 22 exajoules (EJ) was used, coal use was at its peak—coal was by far the major energy source. Oil was second in importance, and lesser quantities from wood, natural gas, and hydropower, geothermal and other sources were used.

Use Figure III.10 to answer the following questions.

1. Since 1850 has our overall use of energy remained constant, increased at a fixed rate, or accelerated (grown at an increasing rate)? Describe at least two factors that might explain this trend.

2. Did overall energy use decrease at any time over the past 130 years? If so, when did this occur? Why?

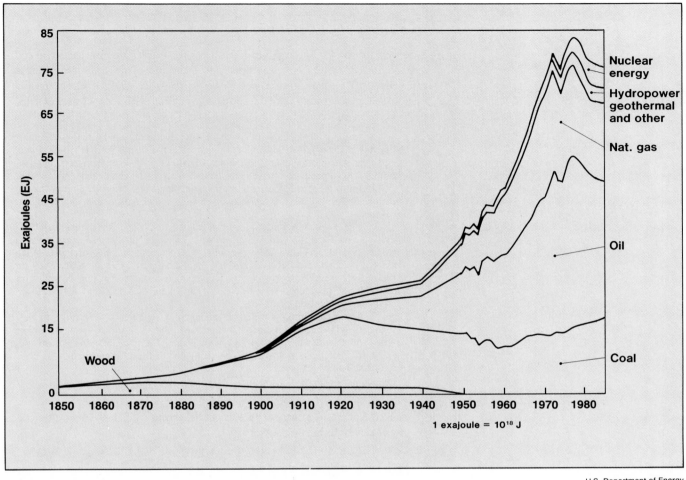

U.S. Department of Energy

Figure III.10 U.S. energy consumption by fuel type, 1850–1980.

3. Over what time period did wood supply more than 50% of our overall energy needs? What was the chief form of long-distance transportation during this period?

4. What factors might explain the declining use of wood after this period? What energy source was the next to rise in importance?

5. Compared to other energy sources, only a small quantity of petroleum was used prior to 1910. What do you think was petroleum's main use at that time?

6. Oil became increasingly important about the same time that the use of coal reached its peak. When did this occur? What can explain the growing use of petroleum after this date?

7. What is the most recent energy source to enter the picture? What is the major use of this energy source?

Obviously changing demands for, and supplies of, various energy sources have played a large role in determining our country's history. But what about the future—your future? What will the energy picture look like as we enter the twenty-first century? For one possible version of the future, read on!

Chem_Quandary_

What would life be like without petroleum for fuel? _Time_ magazine asked science fiction writer Isaac Asimov to describe such a world. Asimov chose the year 1997 as a target date. By 1997 you will be a part of the public responsible for helping make decisions and dealing with their consequences.

Here is an excerpt from Asimov's story.

> Anyone older than 10 can remember automobiles. They dwindled. At first the price of gasoline climbed—way up. Finally only the well-to-do drove, and that was too clear an indication that they were filthy rich, so any automobile that dared show itself on a city street was overturned and burned. Rationing was introduced to "equalize sacrifice," but every three months the ration was reduced. The cars just vanished and became part of the metal resource.
>
> There are many advantages, if you want to look for them. Our 1997 newspapers continually point them out. The air is cleaner and there seem to be fewer colds. Against most predictions, the crime rate has dropped. With the police car too expensive (and too easy a target), policemen are back on their beats. More important, the streets are full. Legs are king in the cities of 1997, and people walk far into the night. Even the parks are full, and there is mutual protection in crowds.
>
> As for the winter—well, it is inconvenient to be cold, with most of what furnace fuel is allowed hoarded for the dawn; but sweaters are popular indoor wear and showers are not an everyday luxury. Lukewarm sponge baths will do, and if the air is not always very fragrant in the human vicinity, the automobile fumes are gone.

"The Nightmare of Life without Fuel." _Time,_ 1977, April 25, p. 33. Reprinted with permission.

1. Based upon this story, write a short description of how your daily life would change in such a world.
2. What change would involve the hardest adjustment for you? Why?
3. Which would be the easiest? Why?
4. Can you suggest any action we might take as individuals to prevent this hypothetical situation from becoming a reality?
5. Could government action now help prevent this from happening? Explain.

Are we doomed to run short of energy? In considering this question, we must first develop a clearer understanding of how energy is stored in fuels and the various means we use to convert this chemical energy into other, more useful forms.

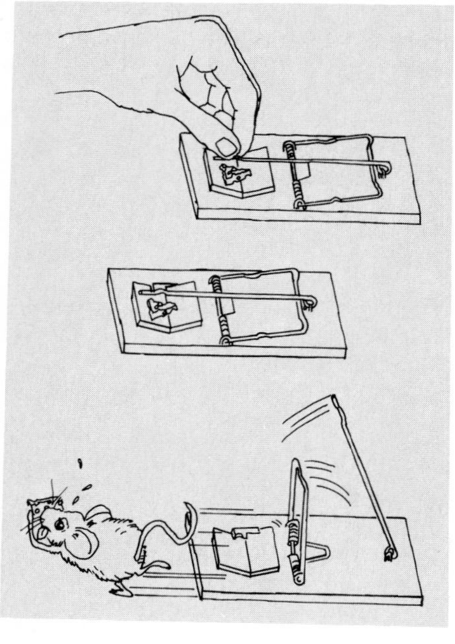

C.3   Energy and Fossil Fuels

Petroleum, natural gas, and coal—the **fossil fuels**—can be considered forms of buried sunshine. Fossil fuels probably originated from the biomolecules of prehistoric plants and animals. The stored energy released from burning fossil fuels is energy originally captured from sunlight during photosynthesis. Think of it as similar to the energy stored in a loaded mousetrap (Figure III.11). Energy must be supplied to coil the spring. Most of that energy is stored in the new arrangement of the mousetrap parts. When the trap is sprung, these parts rapidly rearrange and the trap returns to a more stable state. The stored energy is released during this process.

Figure III.11   Energy: Capture and release.

Chemical energy is stored in chemical compounds. When chemical reactions occur and atoms rearrange to form more stable structures, as during the burning of fuels, some of the stored energy is released as thermal energy and light. The formation and decomposition of water will illustrate how chemists look at the energy involved in chemical reactions. The equation for the formation of water from its elements is

$$2\ H_2 + O_2 \rightarrow 2\ H_2O$$

Think of this reaction as occurring in a series of imaginary bond-breaking and bond-making steps (Figure III.12). In the first imaginary step (*a* in the figure) all the bonds in the reactant molecules are broken to form the free atoms. This step, bond breaking, takes up energy and is an **endothermic** process. The next step (*c*) is the formation of new bonds, producing the two water molecules. The formation of bonds gives off energy, an **exothermic** process. The entire change (step *a* + step *c*) is exothermic because the sum of the energy needed to break the bonds of the reactants is less than the total energy released by the formation of the bonds in the product. Once an exothermic reaction has begun, it continuously releases energy.

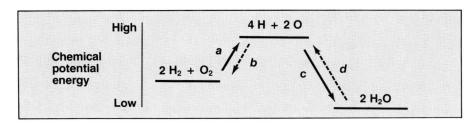

Figure III.12   In step *a*, bonds are broken, a process that requires energy. In step *c*, bonds are formed, a process that releases energy. Since more energy is released in step *c* than is required in step *a*, the formation of water from H_2 and O_2 is exothermic.

By contrast, the reverse reaction, the decomposition of water (step *d* + step *b*), is an endothermic reaction.

$$2\ H_2O \rightarrow 2\ H_2 + O_2$$

In this process, H—O bonds are broken, requiring energy, and H—H and O—O bonds are formed, releasing energy. More energy is needed to break the bonds in water molecules than is released in forming the bonds of the product molecules. Thus energy is needed for the overall process. An endothermic reaction can proceed only if energy is continuously supplied.

Fuel-burning reactions release thermal energy, or heat. Scientists and engineers have greatly increased the usefulness of this energy by developing devices that can convert it into other forms. In fact, much of the energy we use has undergone several conversions.

Try being an "energy detective" in the following activity by tracing energy conversions, first in a hair dryer and then in an automobile.

YOUR*TURN*

III.5 Energy Conversion

Let's look at the energy conversion steps necessary to dry your hair with a hair dryer as represented by the drawings in Figure III.13. Starting at the fossil fuel end, let's examine the types of energy utilized at each step in Figure III.13.

A fossil fuel has stored (A) chemical energy. In a power plant, the fossil fuel is burned to generate (B) thermal energy. The power plant generator converts thermal energy to (C) electrical energy. When the electricity reaches the hair dryer it is converted to (D) the thermal energy used

Figure III.13   Tracing energy sources and conversion in a hair dryer.

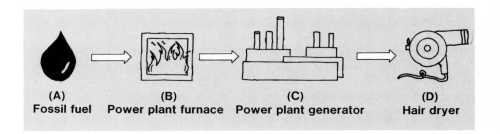

(A) Fossil fuel   (B) Power plant furnace   (C) Power plant generator   (D) Hair dryer

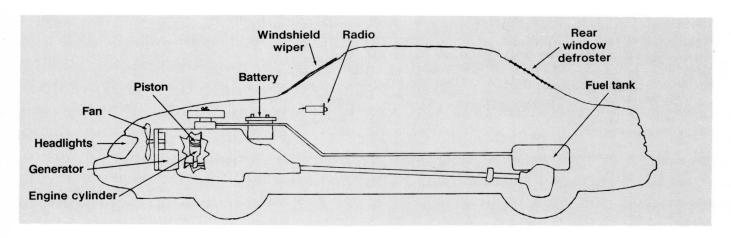

Figure III.14   Some of the energy storage and conversion devices in an automobile.

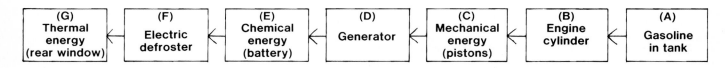

(G) Thermal energy (rear window) ← (F) Electric defroster ← (E) Chemical energy (battery) ← (D) Generator ← (C) Mechanical energy (pistons) ← (B) Engine cylinder ← (A) Gasoline in tank

Figure III.15   Tracing energy conversion in an automobile.

to dry your hair plus the mechanical energy of a small fan to blow out the hot air.

Now that we have given you an example, you can tackle the energy pathway in a more complex system.

An automobile is a self-contained system of numerous energy converters and energy-using devices, some of which are shown in Figure III.14. Name the types of energy missing in the diagram in Figure III.15, which traces energy from the gasoline in the tank to the rear window defroster.

Although energy-conversion devices have certainly increased the usefulness of petroleum and other fuels, some of these devices have produced their own problems. Pollution problems sometimes accompany energy conversion steps. More fundamentally, some useful energy is always "lost" when energy is converted from one form to another. That is, no energy conversion is totally efficient; some energy always becomes unavailable to do useful work. For example, consider an automobile that starts with 100 units of chemical energy in the form of gasoline (Figure III.16).

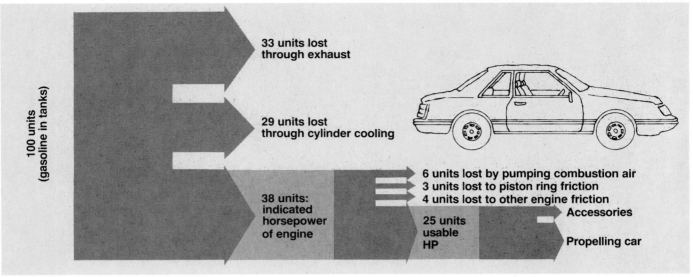

33 units lost
through exhaust

29 units lost
through cylinder cooling

100 units
(gasoline in tanks)

6 units lost by pumping combustion air
3 units lost to piston ring friction
4 units lost to other engine friction

38 units:
indicated
horsepower
of engine

25 units
usable
HP

Accessories

Propelling car

Journal of Chemical Education, v56 n1, 43, Fig. 1.

Figure III.16   Energy conversion
efficiency of an automobile.

Even a well-tuned automobile can convert only about 25% of the chemical
energy in the fuel to useful mechanical energy (motion). The remaining 75% of
the original chemical energy is lost to the surroundings as heat. In the following
Your Turn, you will see what this means in terms of gallons of gasoline, and also
dollars and cents.

YOUR*TURN*

III.6 Energy Conversion Efficiency

Assume your family drives an average of 225 miles per week and that
your car travels 19.0 miles per gallon. How much gasoline does your
car use each year?

Questions such as this can be answered by using simple arithmetic. One
approach is to carefully use "units" and cancel them properly. The information given in the problem above can be set up as follows

$$\frac{225 \text{ miles}}{1 \text{ week}} \qquad \frac{19.0 \text{ miles}}{1 \text{ gal}}$$

or, if needed, as inverted:

$$\frac{1 \text{ week}}{225 \text{ miles}} \qquad \frac{1 \text{ gal}}{19.0 \text{ miles}}$$

The desired answer must have the units:

$$\frac{\text{gal}}{\text{year}}$$

Calculating the desired answer requires supplying information that you
know—there are 52 weeks in one year, $\frac{52 \text{ weeks}}{1 \text{ year}}$. It also requires using
the second factor above in the "upside down" version so that units will cancel
to give the desired answer:

$$\left(\frac{225 \text{ miles}}{1 \text{ week}}\right)\left(\frac{1 \text{ gal}}{19.0 \text{ miles}}\right)\left(\frac{52 \text{ weeks}}{1 \text{ y}}\right) = 616 \text{ gal/y}$$

1. How much gasoline does your family use each year averaging 200 miles per week?

2. If gasoline costs $1.10 per gallon, how much would your family spend on gasoline per year?

3. Given that a car engine uses only 25% of the available energy released by the burning gasoline, how much gasoline is wasted each year due to your car's inefficiency? How much does this wasted gasoline cost your family if gasoline is $1.10 per gallon?

4. Suppose you trade the family car for one that averages 40.0 miles per gallon. How much gasoline will this car use per year? How much less gasoline is this than your old car used? How much money would you save on gasoline per year?

5. If continued research leads to design of a car engine with an efficiency of 50% that averages 50.0 miles per gallon, how much gasoline and money could your family save per year over a car that was 25% efficient and averaged 19.0 mpg?

Because petroleum supplies are neither limitless nor inexpensive, increased energy efficiency is important if we wish to gain maximum benefits from our supplies. One way to increase overall energy efficiency is to reduce the number of energy conversions between the fuel and its final use. We can also try to increase the efficiency of the energy conversion devices we use.

Unfortunately, devices that convert chemical energy to heat and then to mechanical energy are typically less than 50% efficient. Solar cells (solar energy → electrical energy) and fuel cells (chemical energy → electrical energy) hold great promise either for replacing petroleum for some uses or for greatly increasing the efficiency of its use. But, for the foreseeable future, we will continue to burn petroleum to meet energy needs.

But what is burning? What are the products formed when petroleum-based fuels burn? How much energy is involved? We'll investigate these questions next.

C.4   The Chemistry of Burning

You strike a match and a hot yellow flame appears. You hold it to a candle wick. The candle lights and burns. These events are so commonplace that you may not realize that you are observing complex chemical reactions.

Candle-burning involves chemical reactions of the wax (composed of long-chain alkanes) with oxygen gas at elevated temperatures. Many chemical reactions are involved in such "burning," or combustion. For simplicity, chemists usually consider the overall changes involved. For example, the reaction for the burning of one of the components of the wax can be described by this overall equation.

$$C_{25}H_{52}(g) \ + \ 38\ O_2(g) \ \rightarrow \ 25\ CO_2(g) \ + \ 26\ H_2O(g) \ + \ \text{Thermal}$$

Wax (alkane)   Oxygen gas   Carbon   Water vapor   energy
                                  dioxide gas

The reaction is exothermic. The energy given off in the formation of the bonds in product molecules (carbon dioxide gas and water vapor) is greater than the energy needed to break the bonds in the wax and the oxygen gas reactant molecules.

Fuels are useful because they provide energy as they burn. But how much energy is obtained? How can the quantity of released energy be measured? You will have a chance to find out for yourself in the following activity.

C.5   Laboratory Activity: Heats of Combustion

Getting Ready

Earlier we discovered that hydrocarbon boiling points are related to the number of carbon atoms per molecule (and thus to molecular and molar masses). Is the quantity of thermal energy released when hydrocarbons burn also related to the number of carbon atoms per molecule?

The quantity of thermal energy given off when a certain amount of a substance burns is its **heat of combustion.** When one mole of the substance burns, the thermal energy released is called its **molar heat of combustion.** In this activity you will investigate relationships between the thermal energy released when a hydrocarbon burns, and its molar mass. You will determine the heat of combustion of a candle (paraffin wax) and compare this quantity with the literature values for other hydrocarbons.

Prepare a data table similar to the one that follows.

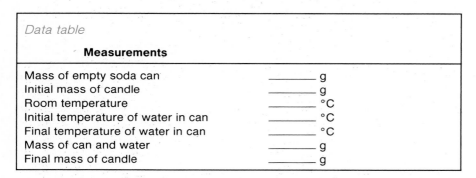

Data table

Measurements	
Mass of empty soda can	_____ g
Initial mass of candle	_____ g
Room temperature	_____ °C
Initial temperature of water in can	_____ °C
Final temperature of water in can	_____ °C
Mass of can and water	_____ g
Final mass of candle	_____ g

Procedure

1. Determine and record the mass of an empty 12-oz soda can.

2. Add 90–100 mL of water to the soda can. Drop small pieces of ice into the soda can a few at a time until the temperature of the water is lowered to 9° to 10 °C below room temperature. Be very careful not to allow the temperature to fall any lower than this. Remove any unmelted ice.

3. Weigh the can plus the water. Record this mass.

4. Set up the apparatus shown in Figure III.17. Adjust the soda can height so the candle is within 2 cm of the can bottom.

5. Prepare the candle for the experiment by holding a lighted match near the candle base so some melted wax falls onto a glass plate. Immediately push the candle into the melted wax and hold it there for a moment, to fasten it to the glass surface.

6. Determine the mass of the candle (attached to the glass plate). Record the value.

7. Measure the temperature of the water to the nearest 0.2 °C. Record this value.

8. Place the candle under the can of water and light the candle. Stir the water gently with a stirring rod as it heats.

9. As the candle burns you may need to lower the soda can so the flame remains just below the can bottom. Do this with caution.

Figure III.17   Heat of combustion apparatus.

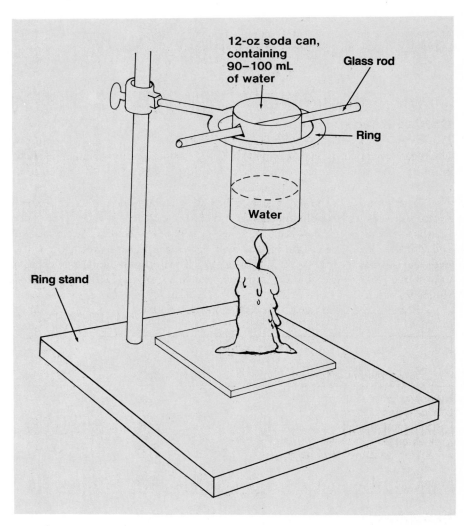

10. Continue heating until the temperature rises as far above room temperature as it was below room temperature at the start of the experiment. (Example: If the water was 15 °C before you began to heat it and room temperature was 25 °C, then you would heat the water 10 °C higher than room temperature, or to 35 °C). When the desired temperature is reached, extinguish the flame.

11. Continue stirring the water until its temperature stops rising. Record the highest temperature the water reached.

12. Determine the mass of the cooled candle and glass plate, including all wax drippings.

Calculations

One characteristic property of a substance is its **specific heat,** the quantity of heat needed to raise the temperature of 1 g of the substance by 1 °C. The specific heat of water is 4.184 J per gram. Therefore, for each degree Celsius that the temperature of the water has been raised, we know that the water has absorbed 4.184 J per gram. Suppose that 10 g of water has increased in temperature by 5.0 °C. The thermal energy absorbed by the water, represented by q, is found from the following calculation:

$$q = (10 \text{ g}) \left(\frac{4.184 \text{ J}}{\text{g} \cdot {}^\circ\text{C}} \right) (5.0 \text{ }^\circ\text{C}) = 210 \text{ J}$$

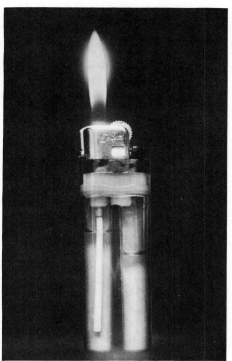

Butane is stored in the barrel of this lighter as a liquid. The butane vaporizes to a gas as pressure is released at the valve.

Jon Jacobson

Note the units. This calculation can be represented by the equation, $q = m_w \times c \times \Delta t$, where m_w is the mass of the water (in grams), c is the specific heat of the water (4.184 joules per gram per degree Celsius), and Δt is the change in temperature of the water (in degrees Celsius).

The heat of combustion of a substance can be expressed as either the heat released per gram of substance burned or per mole of substance burned. To calculate the molar heat of combustion (usually given in kilojoules per mole) from your experimental data, you must first find the heat of combustion per gram.

For paraffin wax, use the data you found in the laboratory activity and complete the following calculations.

1. Calculate the mass of water heated (m_w).
2. Calculate the mass of paraffin burned (m_p).
3. Calculate the temperature change, Δt, which is equal to the final water temperature minus the initial water temperature.
4. Use the values from steps 1–3 in the equation $q = m_w \times c \times \Delta t$ as illustrated above to find the thermal energy absorbed by the water.
5. Assume that the thermal energy absorbed by the water is exactly equal to the thermal energy released by combustion of the entire mass of paraffin that burned. Calculate the heat of combustion per gram of paraffin by dividing q as calculated in 4 by m_p, the mass of paraffin burned. For example, if $q = 500$ J for the combustion of 5.0 g of compound x, then

$$\text{Ht. of combustion} = \frac{q}{m_x} = \frac{500 \text{ J}}{5.0 \text{ g}} = 100 \text{ J/g}$$

6. Convert the heat of combustion in units of joules per gram (J/g) to the molar heat of combustion in kilojoules per mole (kJ/mol). Since the molar mass of paraffin ($C_{25}H_{52}$) is 352 g/mol, the calculation takes the following form:

$$\text{Molar ht. of combustion} \left(\frac{\text{kJ}}{\text{mol}}\right) = \left(\text{Ht. of combustion, } \frac{\text{J}}{\text{g}}\right)\left(\frac{1 \text{ kJ}}{1000 \text{ J}}\right)\left(\frac{352 \text{ g}}{\text{mol}}\right)$$

Questions

Your teacher will collect all heats of combustion and molar heats of combustion data. Use the combined class values to answer the following questions.

1. How does the heat of combustion (in joules per gram) for paraffin wax compare to the literature value for butane (see Table III.5)? You will need to calculate the J/g value for butane from its kJ/mol value.

2. How do the molar heats of combustion (in kilojoules per mole) for these two materials compare?

3. Explain any differences noted in your answers to Questions 1 and 2.

4. Which of these two hydrocarbons is the better fuel? Explain your answer.

5. From the class data, estimate the molar heat of combustion for an alkane with one carbon atom per molecule (methane) and for one with eight carbon atoms per molecule (octane).

6. In calculating heats of combustion you assumed that all the thermal energy from the burning fuel went to heating the water. Was this a good assumption? What other experimental conditions or assumptions would introduce errors in your calculated values?

C.6   Using Heats of Combustion

Assuming that there is sufficient oxygen and that complete combustion occurs, the burning of a hydrocarbon can be described by the equation

Hydrocarbon + Oxygen → Carbon dioxide + Water + Thermal energy

in which energy is treated as a product of the reaction. As you discovered in the previous laboratory activity, this energy can be expressed in terms of kilojoules per mole (or per gram) of fuel burned.

The equation for the combustion of ethane is

$$2\ C_2H_6 + 7\ O_2 \rightarrow 4\ CO_2 + 6\ H_2O + ?\ kJ\ thermal\ energy$$

To complete this equation by supplying the value of the thermal energy, a table of data like that given in Table III.5 must be consulted. We see that the heat of combustion of ethane is 1560 kJ per mole. Note the "per mole." As a reaction product, thermal energy must be balanced, just like the other products. Because the balanced equation shows the combustion of *two* moles of ethane, the amount of thermal energy is twice that for one mole, that is, twice the molar heat of combustion:

$$(2\ mol\ ethane)\left(\frac{1560\ kJ}{1\ mol\ ethane}\right) = 3120\ kJ$$

Therefore, the complete combustion equation is

$$2\ C_2H_6 + 7\ O_2 \rightarrow 4\ CO_2 + 6\ H_2O + 3120\ kJ\ thermal\ energy$$

We could also write a balanced equation for the combustion of one mole of ethane as follows:

$$C_2H_6 + 3.5\ O_2 \rightarrow 2\ CO_2 + 3\ H_2O + 1560\ kJ\ thermal\ energy$$

The point is that the balanced equation shows the relative amounts of reactants, products, *and* energy. If more or less ethane is burned, the other amounts change proportionately.

Table III.5   *Hydrocarbon heats of combustion*

Hydrocarbon	Formula	Heat of combustion (kJ/mol)
Methane	CH_4	890
Ethane	C_2H_6	1560
Propane	C_3H_8	2200
Butane	C_4H_{10}	2859
Pentane	C_5H_{12}	3510
Hexane	C_6H_{14}	4141
Heptane	C_7H_{16}	4817
Octane	C_8H_{18}	5450

As you discovered in the previous laboratory activity, heat of combustion can also be expressed as the heat produced per gram of hydrocarbon burned. Finding the heat of combustion per gram from the molar heat of combustion requires knowing the molar mass (grams per mole) of the compound, and using it in a calculation like the following for octane.

$$\frac{5450 \text{ kJ}}{1 \text{ mol } C_8H_{18}} \times \frac{1 \text{ mol } C_8H_{18}}{114 \text{ g}} = 47.8 \text{ kJ/g}$$

Such heat values can be used to calculate the thermal energy released in the combustion of any mass of a substance. For example, combustion of 12.0 g of octane

$$(12.0 \text{ g octane}) \left(\frac{47.8 \text{ kJ}}{1 \text{ g octane}} \right) = 574 \text{ kJ}$$

produces 574 kJ of thermal energy.

YOUR *TURN*

III.7 Heats of Combustion

To better understand the energy associated with reactions such as the burning of hydrocarbons, use Table III.5 to answer the following questions. The solution given for the first question, plus the sample calculations in the preceding section, can guide you to answer all of these questions.

1. How much thermal energy (in kJ) is released in the complete combustion of 25 mol of hexane?

    The molar heat of combustion of hexane is 4141 kJ. Therefore, for 25.0 mol

    $$(25.0 \text{ mol } C_6H_{14}) \left(\frac{4141 \text{ kJ}}{1 \text{ mol } C_6H_{14}} \right) = 104{,}000 \text{ kJ}$$

    complete combustion yields 104,000 kJ of thermal energy.

2. Write a chemical equation, including thermal energy, for the complete combustion of each of the following alkanes:
    a. Methane (main component of natural gas)
    b. Butane (variety of uses, including lighter fluid)
3. How do the heat of combustion values given in Table III.5 vary with the number of carbon atoms in each hydrocarbon molecule?

Lockheed—California Co.

The Lockheed SR-71A is the world's fastest and highest flying operational aircraft. It uses high-grade jet fuel processed from petroleum.

4. Below are given the heats of combustion in kilojoules per gram for some of the alkanes listed in Table III.5. Calculate the missing values. How does the trend in heats of combustion in kJ/g compare with those in kJ/mol for the hydrocarbons listed?

	Ht. of combustion (kJ/g)
CH_4	55.6
C_2H_6	—
C_3H_8	50.0
C_4H_{10}	—
C_5H_{12}	—
C_6H_{14}	48.2
C_7H_{16}	48.2
C_8H_{18}	47.8

5. The combustion of octane, a major component of gasoline, can be taken as representing the combustion of gasoline.
   a. How much thermal energy would be produced by the combustion of 2 mol of octane?
   b. How much thermal energy would be produced by burning 1 gallon (2.66 kg) of octane? (*Hint:* The answer should have the units of kJ/gal).
   c. Suppose that your car operates so that 16% of the energy released in burning fuel is converted to mechanical energy to turn the wheels. How much useful energy would you get per 20-gallon tank of gasoline (assuming that octane combustion is equivalent to gasoline combustion)?

6. The heat of combustion of coal (as a rough approximation, we assume coal is 100% carbon) is 394 kJ/mol carbon. Write the equation for this reaction, including the quantity of thermal energy produced. Gram for gram, which is the better fuel—coal or octane? In what applications might coal serve as a substitute for petroleum? Describe one application in which coal would be a poor substitute for a petroleum product.

Knowing the structures of molecules and properties such as the heat of combustion, chemists can make new molecules that may better fit particular needs. For example, once the automobile became popular the demand for gasoline increased rapidly. Researchers looked for ways to increase the amount of gasoline (normally about 18%) that could be obtained directly from a barrel of crude oil. One way they succeeded was by altering molecular structures of some of the petroleum hydrocarbons. This important chemical technique deserves further attention.

C.7   Altering Fuels

With the invention of the electric light at the start of this century, the use of kerosene lanterns began to decline rapidly. The kerosene fraction from refined petroleum, composed of hydrocarbons with 12 to 16 carbon atoms per molecule, became a surplus commodity.

By 1913, chemists developed a process for cracking molecules in kerosene into smaller (gasoline-sized) molecules by heating the kerosene to 600–700 °C.

Atlantic Richfield Co.

The tall catalytic cracking units ("cats") in the center of the photo break crude oil down into valuable and useful products such as gasoline and kerosene.

(Recall that the gasoline fraction obtained from refining includes hydrocarbons with 5 to 12 carbon atoms per molecule.) For example, a 16-carbon molecule might be cracked to produce two 8-carbon molecules:

$$C_{16}H_{34}(g) \xrightarrow{700\ °C} C_8H_{16}(g) + C_8H_{18}(g)$$

At this high temperature all three hydrocarbons are in the gaseous state. Examine the product formulas. You should recognize one of them as an alkane—octane, C_8H_{18}. (The other product, also a hydrocarbon, represents another family of compounds we will consider later.)

In practice, products containing from 1 to 14 or more carbon atoms are produced through cracking. Those product molecules containing 5 to 12 carbons are particularly useful as components of gasoline. Some of the C_1–C_4 product molecules formed during cracking are burned, supplying heat needed to keep the temperature high enough for more cracking to occur.

More than one-third of all crude oil is currently subjected to cracking. The process has been modernized by adding catalysts, such as aluminum oxide (Al_2O_3). The catalyst increases the speed of the cracking reactions but is not itself used up. Catalytic cracking is more energy efficient because it takes place at a lower temperature—500 °C rather than 700 °C.

Gasoline comes in a variety of standards (and prices), as you may know. Gasoline composed mainly of straight-chain alkanes, such as hexane (C_6H_{14}), heptane (C_7H_{16}), and octane (C_8H_{18}) burns very rapidly. This rapid burning causes engine knocking and may contribute to engine problems. Branched-chain alkanes burn more satisfactorily in automobile engines. The structural isomer of octane shown below has particularly attractive combustion properties.

$$
\begin{array}{c}
\quad\quad\ CH_3 \\
\quad\quad\ | \\
CH_3-C-CH_2-CH-CH_3 \\
\quad\quad\ |\quad\quad\quad\ | \\
\quad\quad\ CH_3\quad\quad CH_3
\end{array}
$$

A rating scale has been devised in which this hydrocarbon is assigned a rating (called **octane number**) of 100. Straight-chain heptane, a fuel with very poor performance, is assigned a value of zero. The higher the octane number, the better are the anti-knock characteristics of a given gasoline sample.

A relatively inexpensive way to increase the octane rating of gasoline is to add a substance such as tetraethyl lead, $(C_2H_5)_4Pb$, to the fuel. It slows down the burning of the straight-chain gasoline molecules, and adds approximately three points to the octane rating of the fuel.

The lead from such gasoline additives discharges with the auto exhaust into the atmosphere. Because of the harmful effects of lead in the environment, laws have been passed to phase out the use of lead-based gasoline additives.

Since branched-chain hydrocarbons burn more satisfactorily, isomerization processes have been developed for use in refineries. Hydrocarbon vapor is heated with a catalyst in a reaction such as this:

$$CH_3-CH_2-CH_2-CH_2-CH_2-CH_3 \xrightarrow{\text{Catalyst}} CH_3-\underset{\underset{CH_3}{|}}{\overset{\overset{CH_3}{|}}{CH}}-CH-CH_3$$

The branched-chain alkanes produced are blended with gasoline-sized molecules from cracking and distillation to give good-quality nonleaded gasoline. Cracked and isomerized molecules can improve the combustion properties of gasoline, but they also increase its cost. One reason is that extra fuel is consumed in manufacturing the gasoline.

We have examined petroleum's use as a source of energy—as a fuel. In Part D we will turn to petroleum's role as a builder—as a source of chemicals from which a wide variety of useful substances and items can be produced.

PART C
SUMMARY *QUESTIONS*

1. Petroleum has become a major energy source only in recent history. List at least three technological factors that might explain this fact.

2. Compare the use of wood and petroleum as fuels. Identify some advantages and disadvantages of each.

3. From a chemical perspective, how can petroleum be considered "buried sunshine"?

4. Complete an energy trace that shows the energy conversions and devices that are encountered between the chemical energy in an automobile gas tank and the mechanical motion of the windshield wiper.

5. A typical gallon of gasoline will produce about 132,000 kJ of energy when burned. Assuming that the automobile is 25% efficient at converting this energy into useful work, how much energy is "wasted" for each gallon of gasoline burned?

6. Explain the meaning of the phrase "energy efficiency."

7. Write a balanced equation for the combustion of propane (bottled gas).

8. Water gas (a mixture of 50% CO and 50% H_2) is made by the reaction of coal with steam. Since the United States has substantial reserves of coal, water gas might serve as a substitute for natural gas in some applications. Its use as a fuel can be represented by this equation:

$$CO + H_2 + O_2 \rightarrow CO_2 + H_2O + 525 \text{ kJ}$$

How does water gas compare to natural gas in terms of thermal energy produced? If a water gas mixture containing 10 mol CO and 10 mol H_2 were burned, how much thermal energy would be produced?

9. The combustion of acetylene, C_2H_2 (used in a welder's torch), can be represented as:

$$2 C_2H_2 + 5 O_2 \rightarrow 4 CO_2 + 2 H_2O + 2512 \text{ kJ}$$

a. What is the heat of combustion of acetylene in kilojoules per mole? In kilojoules per gram?

b. If 2.5 kg of acetylene is burned, how much thermal energy is produced?

10. List two factors that would help determine which of two hydrocarbon fuels would be preferred for a given use.

11. Explain the meaning of the "octane rating" of a fuel. List two ways to increase a fuel's octane rating.

EXTENDING *YOUR KNOWLEDGE (OPTIONAL)*

Both methanol (CH_3OH) and ethanol (CH_3CH_2OH) have been used as either substitutes for or additives to gasoline. Their respective heats of combustion are 728 kJ/mol (23 kJ/g) and 1370 kJ/mol (30 kJ/g). The heat of combustion of gasoline is approximately equal to that of octane (see Table III.5).

a. In terms of their chemical formulas, how might you account for the fact that the heat of combustion of both methanol and ethanol are considerably less than that of any hydrocarbons we have considered?

b. Would you expect cars running on gasohol (10% ethanol/90% gasoline, by volume) to get more or fewer miles per gallon of fuel than comparable cars operating with 100% gasoline? Why? What other advantages or disadvantages does gasohol have as an automotive fuel?

c. Powdered metals such as aluminum and magnesium can release considerable quantities of heat when burned (their respective heats of combustion are 31 kJ/g and 25 kJ/g). List at least two reasons why they would not be good fuel substitutes for petroleum.

Jon Jacobson

Informed consumers are octane literate. What chemistry information is conveyed by this gasoline pump?

D *MAKING USEFUL MATERIALS FROM PETROLEUM*

Just as an architect uses available construction materials to design a building, a chemist—in a sense a molecular architect—uses available molecules to design others to serve our purposes. Architects must know about the structures and properties of common construction materials. Likewise, chemists must understand the structures and properties of their raw materials, the "builder molecules." In this unit you will explore the structures of some common hydrocarbon builder molecules and some products chemists make from them. In fact, you'll have the chance to make one yourself.

D.1 Laboratory Activity: Modeling the Builder Molecules

Getting Ready

Carbon is a versatile building block atom because of the many ways that it can form bonds to other atoms. In this laboratory activity, you will construct models of two classes of molecules that come directly or with modification from petroleum. Both classes provide important builder molecules for production of materials useful in everyday life.

In the first part of this laboratory activity, you will look at hydrocarbon molecules in which a carbon atom is bonded not to four, but to three other atoms. This series of hydrocarbons is called the **alkenes.** The first member of the alkene series is ethene, C_2H_4.

How can the bonding in alkenes be explained, given that each carbon atom must share eight electrons to fill its outer energy level completely? In a **single covalent bond,** as in the alkanes, just two electrons are shared between two atoms. In a **double covalent bond,** four electrons are shared.

The alkenes are more chemically reactive than the alkanes. Many chemical reactions occur at their double bonds. Compounds that contain double bonds are described as **unsaturated** because not all carbon atoms are bonded to their full capacity of four atoms.

Not all builder molecules are hydrocarbons. Some contain one or more other elements, including oxygen, nitrogen, chlorine, and sulfur. One way to look at the molecules of these substances is to imagine that they are hydrocarbons in which other atoms are substituted for one or more hydrogen atoms.

Adding these other atoms drastically changes the chemical reactivity of the original hydrocarbon molecule. Even molecules composed of the same elements can have quite different properties. The molecules that make up a permanent-press blouse and those of antifreeze (ethylene glycol) each contain only the elements carbon, hydrogen, and oxygen. The astonishing difference in the properties of these two materials is due to the ways these atoms are arranged at the molecular level. In Part 2 you will discover some of the types of molecules formed by carbon, hydrogen, and oxygen atoms.

Single bond $C:C$ *or* $C-C$

Double bond $C::C$ *or* $C=C$

Procedure

Part 1   Alkenes

1. Examine the electron dot and structural formulas for ethene and confirm that each atom has attained an outer energy level filled with electrons.

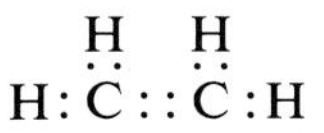

$$\overset{\displaystyle H \quad H}{H:\overset{..}{C}::\overset{..}{C}:H} \qquad \underset{|\quad\;\;|}{H-\overset{\displaystyle H\quad H}{C=C}-H} \qquad H_2C=CH_2$$

Electron dot formula 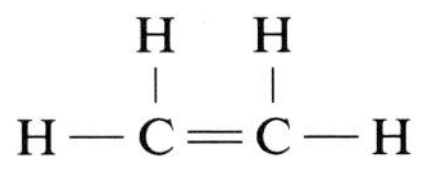   Structural formula   Condensed formula

Note that alkene names follow a pattern similar to that of the alkanes. The same root is used to indicate the number of carbon atoms in the molecule's longest straight carbon chain; each name ends in *-ene*. The first three alkenes are ethene, propene, and butene. For historical reasons, ethene is commonly called ethylene.

2. Examine the molecular formulas of ethene (C_2H_4) and butene (C_4H_8). What general formula for alkenes is suggested by these chemical formulas? (Recall that the alkane general formula is C_nH_{2n+2}.)

3. Build a model of the ethene molecule and one of ethane (C_2H_6).

Compare the atomic arrangements in each model. Note that although you can rotate the two carbon atoms in ethane about the single bond, the two carbon atoms in ethene resist rotation. This is characteristic of all double-bonded atoms.

4. Build a model of butene (C_4H_8). Compare your model of butene with those made by other class members.

How many different arrangements of atoms in C_4H_8 appear possible? Each arrangement represents a different substance—another example of isomers! Do the structural formulas shown below represent structures built by students in your class?

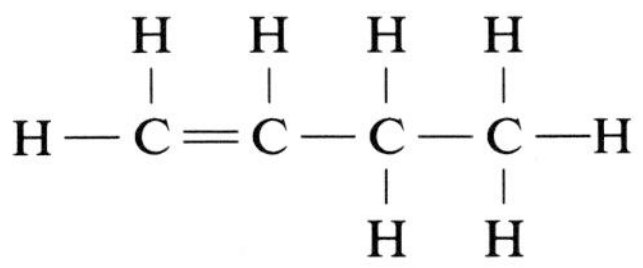

1-Butene, or simply butene 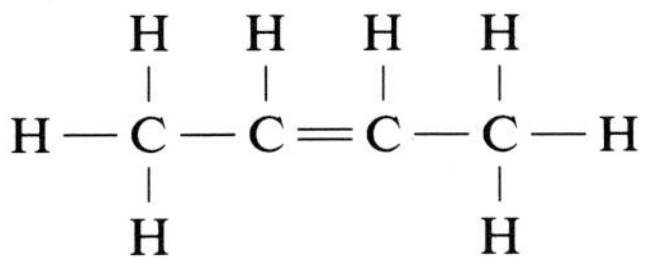   2-Butene

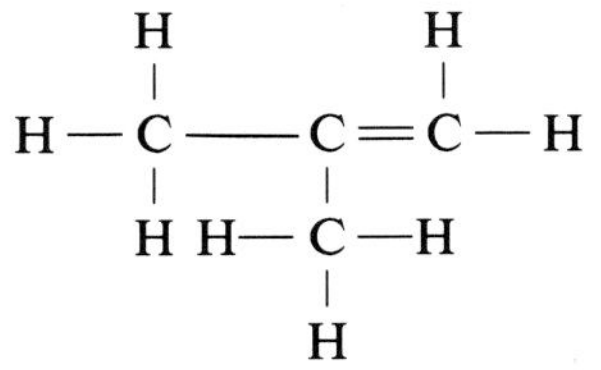

Methylpropene

To distinguish isomers of straight-chain alkenes from one another, the carbon atoms are first assigned numbers so that the double-bonded atoms have the lowest numbers. Then, the number of the first carbon atom that is double-bonded is given at the start of the name, as shown above for 1-butene and 2-butene. Although the third structure above has the butene molecular formula, it is named (systematically) as a methyl-substituted propene.

Organic compounds are named systematically by internationally agreed-upon rules (International Union of Pure and Applied Chemistry, or IUPAC, nomenclature). Some also have common names (like ethylene).

5. Answer the following questions:
   a. Do each of the following pairs represent isomers, or are they the same substance?

   $$CH_2=CH-CH_2-CH_3 \quad \text{and} \quad CH_3-CH_2-CH=CH_2$$

   $$CH_2=\underset{\underset{\textstyle CH_3}{|}}{C}-CH_3 \quad \text{and} \quad CH_3-\underset{\underset{\textstyle CH_2}{||}}{C}-CH_3$$

Triple bond
C∶∶∶C
C≡C

   b. How many isomers of propene (C_3H_6) exist?
   c. Are the following two structures isomers or the same substance?

$$\begin{array}{c} CH_2-CH_2 \\ |\qquad\quad | \\ CH_2\quad\ CH_2 \\ \diagdown\ \ \diagup \\ CH_2 \end{array} \quad \text{and} \quad \begin{array}{c} CH_3-CH-\!-CH_2 \\ |\qquad\quad | \\ CH_2-CH_2 \end{array}$$

6. Based on what you know about molecules with single and double bonds between carbon atoms, build a model of a hydrocarbon molecule that has a triple bond between two carbons.

   Your completed model represents one member of a series known as alkynes. Write the structural formula for
   a. Ethyne, commonly called acetylene
   b. 2-Butyne.

Part 2   Compounds of Carbon, Hydrogen, and Singly Bonded Oxygen

1. Build as many different models of molecules as possible from the following atom inventory: two carbon atoms (each forming four single bonds), six hydrogen atoms (each forming a single bond), and one oxygen atom (forming two single bonds). Diagram each completed structure on paper, indicating how the nine atoms are arranged. Compare your structures with those made by other students. When you are satisfied that all possible structures have been produced, answer these questions:
   a. How many distinct structures have been identified? Write their structural formulas.
   b. Are the substances represented by these structures isomers? Why or why not?

2. The two compounds you may have identified have vastly different physical and chemical properties. Recalling that like dissolves like, which would you expect to be more soluble in water? Which would you expect to have the higher boiling point?

D.2   More Hydrocarbon Builder Molecules

So far, we have looked at just a small part of the inventory of builder molecules that chemical architects have available. Now we look at two important classes of compounds in which carbon atoms are joined in rings.

Picture what happens if one hydrogen atom at each end of a hexane molecule is removed and the two carbon atoms become bonded to each other.

$$CH_3CH_2CH_2CH_2CH_2CH_3$$

Hexane

$$\begin{array}{c} CH_2-CH_2 \\ \diagup\qquad\qquad\diagdown \\ CH_2\qquad\qquad CH_2 \\ \diagdown\qquad\qquad\diagup \\ CH_2-CH_2 \end{array}$$

Cyclohexane

Cyclohexane is representative of the cycloalkanes, saturated hydrocarbons in which the carbon atoms are joined in rings. Like the alkanes, cycloalkanes are relatively unreactive chemically. Cyclohexane is the starting material in the commercial production of nylon.

Oxygen, nitrogen, and sulfur atoms can also be incorporated into rings. You will discover in the next unit that a ring composed of five carbon atoms and one oxygen atom forms the basis of a vitally important class of biomolecules—the carbohydrates.

Benzene (C_6H_6) is the simplest member of a very important class of cyclic builder molecules known as **aromatic compounds.** These compounds make up a separate class because their chemical properties are quite different from those of the cycloalkanes and their derivatives. The pleasant aroma of the first discovered of these compounds gave them their name.

Attempts to draw a cyclic benzene molecule based on what you have learned so far about hydrocarbons might lead to the following structure:

Chemists who first studied benzene proposed this and other structures. But there was a puzzle because carbon-carbon double bonds, which appear in this formula, are very reactive, but benzene did not undergo any of the expected reactions. It took a new understanding of how atoms can be bonded to one another to explain the structure of benzene.

We now know that all carbon atoms and carbon-carbon bonds in benzene are equivalent, a situation arising because certain bonding electrons are shared equally around the ring. To represent the actual benzene molecule on paper we often use the following formula:

Here the dotted line represents the equal sharing of electrons and the unbroken lines represent the bonding of the carbon atoms to one another. The C — H symbols are not included, but each junction between lines represents the location of a carbon and a hydrogen atom.

Small amounts of aromatic compounds are present in petroleum, but large quantities are produced from petroleum-based raw materials. Benzene and other aromatic compounds are present in gasoline, where they increase the octane rating. However, their primary use is as chemical builder molecules.

D.3 Builder Molecules Containing Oxygen Atoms

In making models, you "discovered" two types of compounds containing oxygen that can be represented by:

ROH   ROR   *CH$_3$OH*   *CH$_3$CH$_2$CH$_2$OH*
Alcohol   Ether   *Methanol*   *1-Propanol*

CH₂ — CH₂
CH₂   CH — OH
   CH₂

Cyclopentanol

— OH

Phenol

O
‖
CH₃COH
Acetic acid (present in vinegar)
O
‖
CH₃COCH₃
Methyl acetate (a solvent)

The R's in these formulas represent hydrocarbon portions of the molecules. The —OH and —O— are referred to as functional groups—atoms or groups of atoms that impart characteristic properties to organic compounds. Many compounds containing —OH groups are **alcohols** and have certain properties in common. The —OH group—or other functional group—can be introduced into an alkane, an alkene, a cycloalkane, an aromatic compound (see examples in margin), or into other structures.

Two functional groups, each of which contains two oxygen atoms, are shown below. Note that both have one oxygen atom that is doubly bonded to a carbon atom, and one oxygen atom that is singly bonded to the same carbon atom.

$$\begin{array}{cc} O & O \\ \| & \| \\ R-C-OH & R-C-OR \\ \text{Carboxylic acid} & \text{Ester} \end{array}$$

(also written RCOOH and RCOOR)

Carboxylic acids and **esters** are two more types of versatile builder molecules. Soon you will use an acid as a starting material in making an ester in the laboratory.

There are many other types of functional groups containing atoms of elements such as nitrogen, sulfur, or chlorine. We need not study them all. The essential point is clear. Adding functional groups to the builder hydrocarbons vastly expands the types of molecules that can be built.

D.4   Creating New Options: Petrochemicals

It is difficult to comprehend that less than a century and a half ago, all objects and materials used by society were created directly from naturally occurring materials such as wood or stone, or were crafted from metals, glass, or ceramics drawn from the Earth's crust. Fibers were cotton, wool, linen, and silk. The only plastics were those derived from wood (celluloid) and animal materials (shellac). The available drugs and food additives such as salt, vanilla, and chocolate came from natural sources.

Allied-Signal Inc.

SPECTRA-900 is a low density, supertough polymer fiber, 10 times stronger than steel, developed by Allied Corporation.

Today, many of our objects and materials are synthetic. They are created from oil or natural gas. Such chemical compounds are referred to as **petrochemicals.**

Some petrochemicals, such as detergents, pesticides, drugs, and cosmetic preparations, are put to direct use. Most petrochemicals, however, serve as raw materials (or intermediates) in the production of other synthetic substances, particularly plastics.

Plastics are undoubtedly the industrial masterpiece of the 20th century. They include paints, fabrics, rubbers, insulation materials, foams, glasslike substances, adhesives, and molding and structural materials. The total world production of petroleum-based plastics is five times that of aluminum. Over one-third of the fiber and 70% of the rubber used worldwide is created from petrochemicals.

Apart from their ability to burn, alkanes have little chemical reactivity. Few substances can be built directly from them. By contrast, the alkenes and aromatics are important builder molecules.

Alkenes are found in crude oil and separated during distillation. They are also produced from crude oil alkanes by the cracking process (Part C.7) and collected as by-products of refinery operations. Industrially, the two most important alkenes are ethene (ethylene) and propene. Aromatic substances such as benzene and styrene come from the catalytic cracking and reforming of petroleum. (Reforming of petroleum, like cracking carried out in refineries, produces aromatic compounds from straight-chain alkanes.)

$$CH_2 = CH_2$$
Ethylene

$$H_2C = CHCH_3$$
Propene

$CH = CH_2$ (on benzene ring)

Styrene

Because these builder molecules can be used to make so many different chemicals, it would take a large textbook to present all the relevant reactions. For simplicity, we will focus on ethylene, ethanol, and materials related to ethylene.

Ethylene is readily transformed into a number of useful products because of the high reactivity of its double bond. Two important commercial products made from ethylene are ethanol (ethyl alcohol) and polyethylene.

Ethanol is formed by the acid-catalyzed reaction of a water molecule with the double-bond site of an ethylene molecule. The water molecule "adds" to the double-bonded carbon atoms in a way that eliminates the double bond and leaves each carbon atom bonded to four atoms instead of three. The reaction is called an **addition reaction** and is represented by the following equation:

$$H-\underset{\underset{\text{Ethylene}}{}}{\overset{\overset{H \quad H}{|\quad\;|}}{C=C}}-H \;+\; \underset{\text{Water}}{H-OH} \;\xrightarrow[\text{catalyst}]{\text{Acid}}\; H-\underset{\underset{\underset{\text{Ethanol}}{H \quad OH}}{|\quad\;|}}{\overset{\overset{H \quad H}{|\quad\;|}}{C-C}}-H$$

Ethanol is used extensively as a solvent in varnishes and perfumes, in the preparation of many essences, flavors, drugs, and in alcoholic beverages. It is also used as a fuel.

Polyethylene, used for bags and packaging, is a very important **polymer.** A polymer is a large molecule composed of possibly 500 to 20,000 or more repeating units (residues). In polyethylene the repeating units are ethylene residues. Making polyethylene is similar to making a paperclip chain. A single paperclip is like one molecule of ethylene. And the individual paperclips strung together end to end are like one polyethylene molecule. The chain formed is written

$$-CH_2-CH_2-CH_2-CH_2-CH_2-$$

The chemical reaction is represented as:

$$n\, CH_2 = CH_2 \longrightarrow -CH_2CH_2CH_2CH_2CH_2CH_2-$$

Ethylene   Ethylene residues

Polyethylene

In this reaction, ethylene is called a **monomer**—the small molecule from which the larger polymer molecule is made. This reaction, also, is an addition reaction. Polymers formed in reactions such as this are called **addition polymers.**

A great variety of addition polymers can be made by replacing one or more hydrogen atoms on ethylene molecules with other atoms and then causing these substituted molecules to form polymers. Three examples of common polymers formed from substituted ethylene are polyvinyl chloride, polyacrylonitrile, and polystyrene. Equations representing the formation of these polymers are:

$$n\ CH_2 = CHCl \longrightarrow -CH_2\ CHCH_2\ CHCH_2\ CHCH_2\ CH-$$
$$\qquad\qquad\qquad\qquad\qquad\quad | \qquad\quad | \qquad\quad | \qquad\quad |$$
$$\qquad\qquad\qquad\qquad\qquad\ Cl \qquad Cl \qquad Cl \qquad Cl$$

Vinyl chloride
Cl has replaced H

Polyvinyl chloride (PVC) is used for shoes, leather-like jackets, and plastic pipes.

$$n\ CH_2 = CHCN \longrightarrow -CH_2\ CHCH_2\ CHCH_2\ CHCH_2\ CH-$$
$$\qquad\qquad\qquad\qquad\qquad\quad | \qquad\quad | \qquad\quad | \qquad\quad |$$
$$\qquad\qquad\qquad\qquad\quad CN \qquad CN \qquad CN \qquad CN$$

Acrylonitrile
CN has replaced H

Polyacrylonitrile is used in acrylic fiber for clothes and carpets.

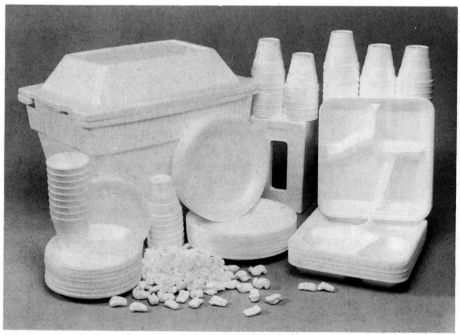

Styrene
Aromatic ring
has replaced H

Polystyrene is used in insulation, coffee cups, coolers, toothbrush handles, and combs.

Jon Jacobson

Why is polystyrene used to make these types of products?

A closer look at polymer molecules will help you understand why plastics and other products made from polymers have some of the properties they do. The arrangement of the covalent bonds in the long stringlike polymer molecules causes the molecules to coil loosely. A group of polymer molecules (such as those in a piece of rubber or molten plastic) intertwine, much like cooked noodles or spaghetti. In this form the material is flexible and soft.

Your skin is composed of biological polymers. Its flexibility is a result of polymeric coiling and intertwining. Gently press the palm of your hand and watch the skin stretch and then move back in place when you remove your finger. Imagine the large molecules uncoiling slightly and sliding a little to allow the skin to stretch under the pressure of your finger and then recoiling again when your finger is removed. You can picture this same kind of event occurring when you stretch and then relax a rubber band or when you push on a piece of soft plastic.

Polymer flexibility can be increased by adding molecules that act as an internal lubricant for the large molecules. Polyvinyl chloride is used without added lubricant for rigid pipes or siding for houses. With added lubricant it becomes flexible enough for raincoats and shoes. Rigidity can be increased by chemically cross-linking the polymer chains so they can no longer move readily. Compare the flexibility of a rubber band with that of a tire tread.

Strength and toughness in a polymer material can be increased by first orienting the polymer chains so they lie generally in the same direction, as you do when you comb your hair. Then the chains are stretched so that they uncoil (see Figure III.18). Polymers that remain uncoiled after this treatment make good films and fibers. Polyethylene makes good film (plastic bags). Polyacrylonitrile makes good fabric (acrylic fiber in your clothes).

Polymer molecules can be formed in ways other than by addition reactions. Proteins, starch, cellulose (in wood and paper), nylon, and polyester are all polymers formed by the loss of water from adjacent monomer molecules. Loss of water in this way is referred to as a **condensation reaction.** The polymers thus formed are known as **condensation polymers.**

Condensation reactions can be used to make small molecules as well as polymers. In the next laboratory activity you will carry out a condensation reaction to make an ester. The reaction is a simple example of how organic compounds are combined to create new substances. Many synthetic flavorings and perfumes contain esters that might be made by similar reactions. Also, this type of reaction, repeated many times over, produces polyester polymers.

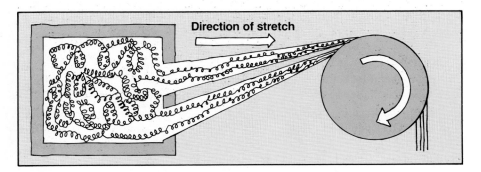

Direction of stretch

Figure III.18 Orienting and uncoiling polymer chains can add strength and toughness to polymer material.

D.5 Laboratory Activity: Making a Petrochemical

Getting Ready

In this activity you will produce a petrochemical by the reaction of an organic acid (an acid derived from a hydrocarbon) with an alcohol to produce an ester that has a pleasing fragrance. Many perfumes contain esters, and the characteristic aromas of many herbs and fruits come from esters in the plants.

The general equation for producing an ester from an organic acid is given below. Note how the acid and alcohol molecules combine by losing a water molecule between them.

$$
\underset{\text{Carboxylic acid}}{R-\overset{\overset{\displaystyle O}{\|}}{C}-OH} \;+\; \underset{\text{Alcohol}}{H-O-R} \;\xrightarrow{H_2SO_4}\; \underset{\text{Ester}}{R-\overset{\overset{\displaystyle O}{\|}}{C}-O-R} \;+\; \underset{\text{Water}}{H-O-H}
$$

Sulfuric acid does not become part of the product. It is a catalyst that makes the reaction proceed faster.

You will carry out the reaction of salicylic acid with methanol to produce the ester named methyl salicylate.

Procedure

1. Set up a ring stand, ring, wire screen, and Bunsen burner.
2. Prepare a water bath by adding about 70 mL of tap water to a 150-mL beaker. Place the water bath on the wire screen above the burner.
3. Take a small test tube to the dispensing table. Pour 2 mL of methanol into the test tube. Next add 0.5 g of salicylic acid to the test tube. Then *slowly and carefully add 10 drops of concentrated sulfuric acid.* As you dispense some of these reagents you may notice their odors. Do not smell any directly. However, record observations of any odors you detect.
4. Return to your desk and place the test tube in the water bath you prepared in Step 1. Light and adjust the burner and heat the beaker and contents.
5. When the water begins to boil, use your test tube tongs to slowly move the test tube in a circle, being careful not to allow the contents to spill out. Notice any color changes. Continue heating until the water bath has boiled strongly for two minutes. Turn off your burner.
6. If you have not by now noticed an aroma, hold your test tube with the tongs and wave your hand across the top to waft the vapors toward your nose. Record your observations about the odor of the product. Compare your observations with those of other class members.

Sulfuric acid and methanol must be kept away from skin and other body parts. If contact occurs flush with large amounts of water.

Questions

1. From a handbook, find the molecular formulas of the acid and alcohol from which you made the ester and write the equation for its formation.
2. Write the formula for amyl acetate, an ester formed from pentanol ($C_5H_{11}OH$) and acetic acid (CH_3COOH). (Amyl acetate has a pear-like odor and flavor, and has many uses in products ranging from syrups to paints and shoe polish.)
3. Classify the following organic compounds as carboxylic acids, alcohols, or esters:
   a. $HOCH_2CH_2CH_2CH_3$
   b. $CH_3OOCCH_2CH_3$
   c. $CH_3\,CHCH_2CH_3$
      |
      CH_2COOH
   d. $CH_3\,\overset{\overset{\displaystyle O}{\|}}{C}OH$

PART D
SUMMARY *QUESTIONS*

1. State the general formula and give at least one specific example (name and formula) of
   a. an industrially important alkene;
   b. an industrially important aromatic compound.

2. Write an equation for the cracking of hexane into two smaller hydrocarbon molecules.

3. State the names and structural formulas for molecules of an organic acid, ether, ester, and alcohol, each of which contains two carbon atoms. Circle the part of the structural formula that is the functional group in that class of compound.

4. How does benzene differ from other cyclic hydrocarbons?

5. More than 90% of known chemical compounds are organic (hydrocarbons or substituted hydrocarbons). Based on your experience with molecular models, identify at least two characteristics of carbon atoms that account for this large number of carbon-based substances.

6. In your own words describe the term "polymerization." As part of your explanation give an example of a "monomer → polymer" synthesis.

7. Why is petroleum such a rich resource for building new substances?

8. Chemical synthesis is one of the many branches of chemistry. Try your hand at planning some syntheses in the problems below. One molecule is missing in each equation. Supply a small molecule that might react with the reactant molecule to produce the given product or products.
   a. A major alkane reaction, other than burning. The organic product, ethyl chloride, is used to make the fuel additive tetraethyl lead.

   $$CH_3-CH_3 + ? \longrightarrow CH_3-CH_2-Cl + HCl$$

   b. The major way of making isopropyl alcohol for rubbing alcohol.

   $$CH_3-CH=CH_2 + ? \longrightarrow CH_3-CH-CH_3$$
   $$\underset{OH}{|}$$

   c. The conversion of a long-chain organic acid to soap

   $$CH_3CH_2CH_2CH_2CH_2CH_2COOH + ? \longrightarrow CH_3CH_2CH_2CH_2CH_2CH_2COO^- Na^+ + H_2O$$

General Electric Company

This is North America's first commercial plastic hockey rink. It is made from polyethylene plastic that looks and performs as ice, but reduces energy and maintenance costs by about 60%.

E ALTERNATIVES TO PETROLEUM

Petroleum is a nonrenewable resource—at least in relation to the time humans have inhabited this planet. You have seen in the previous sections how important it has become to us. Alternatives are already being investigated to replace petroleum both to burn and to build.

E.1 Alternative Energy Sources

The way we live—our life-styles, homes, agriculture, and industries—requires considerable quantities of energy. Earlier (Part C.2) you discovered that the exact mix of energy sources upon which our country has relied has changed over time. As our energy needs grew, we relied on a greater variety of fuels, but principally on the nonrenewable fossil fuels: coal, then oil and natural gas. What is the future for fossil fuels, or in particular, for petroleum?

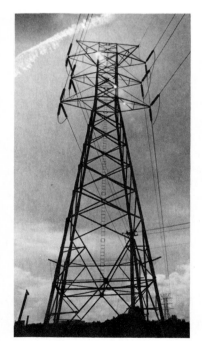

Jon Jacobson

Department of Energy

Jon Jacobson

Electricity is also generated from sources other than petroleum—such as nuclear and hydroelectric power.

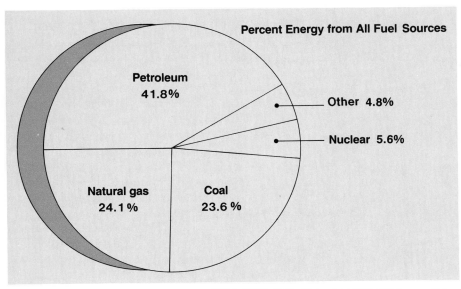

Figure III.19   Percent of energy used from all fuel sources.

Source: Monthly Energy Review, Sept. 1985–1986 Summary Data.

YOUR*TURN*

II.8 Energy Dependency

To answer our concerns, let's start by getting a clear picture of our energy dependency. Here again, examining the facts in a community issue of importance requires interpreting numerical data. Consider the pie chart in Figure III.19.

1. Which fuel is the No. 1 energy source?
2. What percent of our energy needs are currently met by fossil fuels?
3. What percent of our energy needs are currently met by renewable energy sources?

   Of course, the important question concerning the data in the pie chart is how they relate to our supplies of these fuels. Unfortunately, the answer to this question is not quite so straightforward. We find a variety of conflicting estimates of the amounts of fossil fuels we have left. For purposes of discussion we will consider data published in the 1980 report, *Energy in America's Future: The Choice before Us* (Table III.6). The data represent a somewhat optimistic estimate of extractable supplies of fossil fuel.

Table III.6   *Available energy from fossil fuels*

Source	Exajoules (EJ)[a]
Oil and natural gas liquids	1,000
Natural gas	
Conventional sources	1,000
Unconventional sources	700
Coal	40,300

[a]1 exajoule = 10^{18} J.

4. It has been estimated that in the years between 1980 and 2000 the United States will use 2000 exajoules (EJ) of energy (an average of 100 EJ per year). If we continue to rely on petroleum for 42% of our total energy needs, and we consume only U.S. oil (no imports), we will use 840 EJ of our available energy from petroleum by the year 2000 (0.42 × 2000 EJ). How much of our extractable supply of petroleum would be left by the year 2000? by the year 2005?

5. Complete the calculations described in Question 4 for natural gas (including both conventional and unconventional sources) and coal, using the data from Figure III.19 and Table III.6.

Such calculations of the lifetime of a certain fuel are of course just estimates. The rate of use of petroleum, or any other fuel, would slow and the fuel would probably become more expensive as supplies neared exhaustion. Also, the estimates of extractable supplies and of our projected needs are just that—estimates. They are subject to change. However, despite these limitations, your calculations are useful in illustrating the broad picture. Given our relative rates of consumption and available supplies of the various fossil fuels, petroleum presents us with a real problem. Coal has a more promising future. But what about coal as a fuel? Can it provide an alternative to our dwindling supplies of petroleum? Are the two fuels interchangeable? Setting aside, for the time being, possible environmental issues, we need to look at how petroleum is actually used as a fuel. Consider Table III.7.

Table III.7   *Petroleum use by sector (1983)*

End-use sector	Millions of barrels/day	Percent of total use
Transportation	9.31	61.3
Industrial	4.01	26.4
Residential/commercial	1.19	7.8
Electric utilities	0.68	4.5

6. What percent of petroleum is used at fixed-point (stationary) sites?

7. Could coal more readily substitute for petroleum in stationary sites or mobile ones? Why?

The United States is a society "on the go." More than in any other country, private automobiles are the main energy consumer in the U.S. transportation sector. While efforts to revitalize and improve our public transportation systems certainly merit attention, most experts predict that we will continue to rely on the automobile at least until the turn of the century. Given this assumption, what options does chemistry offer us to extend, supplement, and perhaps eventually replace petroleum as a source of energy?

Although we must reduce our total use of petroleum, discovery of new supplies would help extend the availability of petroleum. Offshore oil wells have become common as we tap previously unknown supplies of petroleum locked beneath the ocean floor.

The extraction of "solid petroleum" from tar sands and oil shale offers additional promise. Unfortunately, these sources are very expensive prospects, since the technology is not adequately developed. Vast quantities of sand or rocks must be processed to recover this fuel. Major deposits of oil shale are located west of the Rocky Mountains. These rocks, formed originally from mud, contain kerogen, partially formed oil. When the rocks are heated, the kerogen decomposes to a substance quite similar to crude oil. These shale rocks contain a larger quantity of "pre-oil" than the world's known reserves of conventional petroleum, according to current estimates.

Shale oil processing has serious problems. The biggest of these is the cost of production. Others include securing access to the oil shale lands (80% are owned by the federal government), supplying the large amounts of water needed in processing, dealing with the pollution generated by the processing, and planning for the influx of project workers. Given adequate funding, these problems may be resolved. Presently, research continues toward making shale oil processing a commercial reality in the future. The price and availability of crude oil are important factors in the decision to move ahead with shale oil production.

Another possible alternative to petroleum is the production of liquid fuel from coal. As you have seen, our country's coal supply is much greater than our supply of petroleum. The technology for conversion of coal to liquid fuel (and also to builder molecules) has been available for decades. Germany fueled its military machines in this way during World War II. The U.S. technology is well developed. At present, the expense involved in mining and converting coal to liquid fuel is considerably greater than the cost of producing the same quantity of fuel from petroleum. However, as petroleum prices increase, obtaining liquid fuel from coal may become a more attractive prospect.

The concept of "petroleum plantations" has also been suggested. Some 2000 varieties of plants of the genus *Euphorbia* capture and store solar energy in the form of hydrocarbon compounds, rather than as carbohydrates. Can these compounds be extracted and used as a petroleum substitute? Future research will answer this question.

Other forms of energy currently in use or being investigated are hydropower (water power), nuclear fission and fusion, solar, wind, and geothermal energies, and the burning of trash. All these energy options hold promise for replacing the petroleum used for space heating and generating electricity at stationary sites. But, unfortunately, at present they are not practical replacements for transportation uses of petroleum.

Energy from nuclear fuels is discussed in Unit Five.

We have identified several options to extend petroleum's use as an energy source without altering our life-styles drastically. We can improve on our technology (build more energy-efficient buildings and machines, for example) so less petroleum is consumed. We can also change our technology so other fuels can replace petroleum. But what can replace petroleum's role as a source of chemical building materials?

E.2 Alternative Sources of Builder Molecules

As supplies of petroleum continue to decrease, it is likely that at some future time petroleum's use as a fuel will be curtailed as more of each barrel is reserved for manufacturing petrochemicals. However, alternatives to petroleum as a source of builder molecules must be found since petroleum supplies will some day be gone.

Experts in industrialized countries are turning their attention to coal as a chemical raw material in addition to its role as fuel. Essentially, coal is composed of carbon. Thus, much of our chemical knowledge of the reactions of carbon compounds can be used in developing the chemistry of coal. In principle, all products now manufactured from oil can also be obtained from coal and water. However, the investment of money and time needed to open up new coal mines and to build conversion plants prevents any rapid conversion to coal. In addition, the separation and purification processes necessary for coal are more costly (both

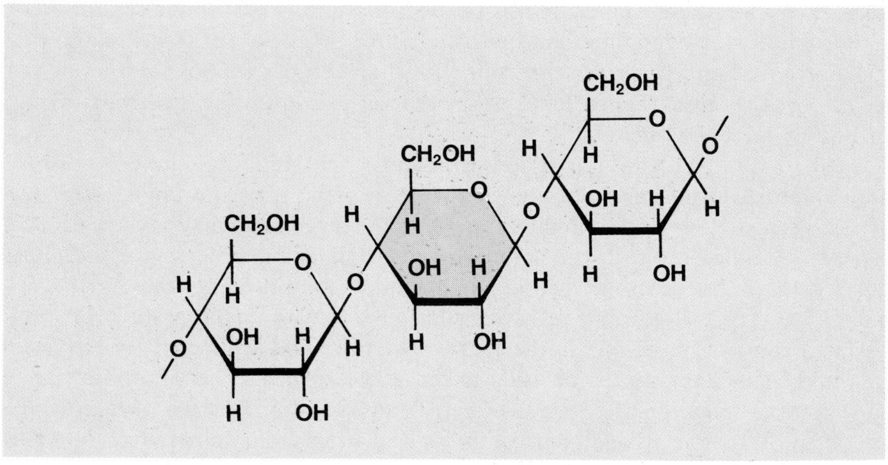

Figure III.20   A portion of a cellulose molecule showing repeating glucose units.

financially and environmentally) than those for petroleum. Thus products derived from coal will cost more—at least until petroleum becomes so scarce that the prices of coal-based items become competitive.

The next available sources of carbon and hydrogen as petroleum substitutes will probably be plant matter—biomass. The major part of most biomass is cellulose, the chief component of wood, leaves, and plant stems. Cellulose is a polymer of repeating glucose units (see Figure III.20). Glucose is a carbohydrate and an important part of your diet (discussed in the next unit).

Cellulose molecules contain the basic carbon structure that can be used to build petrochemicals. One future scenario includes intensive forestry and cultivation of fast-growing plants, as well as use of organic wastes from our homes and industries. Ethanol and other builder molecules are already being produced from sugar cane.

Using biotechnology to aid us, we can indirectly exploit solar energy to convert living plant matter into raw materials from which petrochemicals can be synthesized. The techniques of bioengineering are still in their infancy. However, the use of **enzymes** (biochemical catalysts for specific reactions) for production of specific compounds is already under way. In fact, biological production processes suitable for large-scale use have been developed for six basic chemical compounds, including ethanol and acetic acid. They are, of course, more costly than petroleum-based petrochemicals. However, as the cost of petroleum-based chemicals increases, biomass-based materials will become increasingly important. It is probable that for some time to come petrochemicals will be based on oil, coal, and biomass. The combination at any particular time will depend on economic circumstances within individual countries.

Thus, we can see that while we must face difficult decisions concerning our use of petroleum, chemistry can provide us with other means of accomplishing the important tasks of building and burning. At the present time, however, most alternatives are not fully developed and are expensive. Conservation—making more efficient use of what we have, using items longer, and recycling what we can (motor oil, for example)—is the key to providing us with more time to develop necessary replacements so no drastic shocks disturb our life-styles. Beyond this immediate self interest, conservation is also an ecologically sound strategy and takes into account the needs of all who live on our planet. The concluding section of this unit will give you a chance to examine alternate points of view of how best to promote conservation of the valuable resource called petroleum.

PART E
SUMMARY *QUESTIONS*

1. Describe two major problems posed by our present use of energy sources.

2. Many experts feel that we must explore ways to make use of more renewable sources of energy such as hydro-, solar, and wind power in place of nonrenewable fossil fuels.
   a. Why might this be a wise policy?
   b. For which major end use are these nonrenewables least likely to replace fossil fuels? Why?
   c. Describe what you imagine your community would look like if it decided to install wind and solar power devices on a large scale.

3. Describe some of the promise and problems of using each of the following as a petroleum substitute:
   a. Coal
   b. Oil shale
   c. Hydrocarbons from plants.

4. Coal contains no ethane or ethylene. It is made chiefly of carbon. Suggest the kinds of reactions chemists should try to make ethylene from coal.

5. Of the two broad uses of petroleum (as a fuel and as a raw material), which is likely to be curtailed first as supplies dwindle? Why?

6. What alternative chemical raw materials are available to supplement or replace petroleum? In terms of molecular structure, what types of compounds do chemists seek when looking for petroleum substitutes?

Department of Interior

Like petroleum, coal can be used to produce energy or a range of organic chemicals.

F PUTTING IT ALL TOGETHER: CHOOSING PETROLEUM FUTURES

Petroleum is versatile. As a fuel, it can be used to produce heat and electricity. Unlike other fuels, it is also a convenient, and thus predominant, energy source for transportation. In addition to its use as fuel, petroleum is also an alchemist's dream come true. Although it cannot be converted into gold, the black liquid is routinely converted into more than 3000 products, including synthetic fibers, plastics, detergents, medicines, dyes, and pesticides.

Unfortunately, we are rapidly exhausting our known supplies of petroleum. However, since we can foresee these future shortages, we have the advance opportunity to develop new technologies and policies to supplement, extend, or replace many of our uses of it.

Given its importance in our lives, the decisions we make about petroleum as consumers and citizens will help influence the quality of life in future years. A common theme of all *ChemCom* units is that decisions should be based on the best available information and should be constantly reevaluated in light of new facts. In the following activity you will develop a position on a policy question related to petroleum, using scientific facts as well as opinion to support your position.

F.1 Confronting the Issues

For two class days, you will become a member of a team of experts on the impending energy crisis. For the purpose of this activity, you are asked to accept as fact the following statement, which is to form the basis for discussion and decisions about government action:

> The technology needed to provide alternate sources of energy and builder molecules will not be adequately developed before the year 2100. Studies have shown that by 1995 domestic petroleum supplies will be shrinking and imported oil costs will be rising sufficiently to cause an "energy crisis." The government has settled on three possible courses of action to conserve petroleum and hold off the "crisis" until the time when alternatives to petroleum are available. After further study, one or more of the following will be mandated by law:
>
> 1. The federal government will influence the market by imposing restraints (such as higher taxes) on the fuel applications of petroleum.
> 2. The nonfuel use of petroleum will be limited to the manufacture of long-lasting (lifetime of at least two years) and/or reusable or recyclable consumer products.
> 3. The government will subsidize the development of a national system of mass transportation, and automobile use will be restricted to those locations where the system is not yet completed.

Three teams of experts are to present a panel discussion before a group of government representatives and influential citizens on the three proposed actions. Each team will support and defend one of the three proposals.

You will be assigned to a team that will prepare a presentation on one of the proposals. Your team will select two of its members to speak on the panel. Their presentation, prepared during the first class period, should be based on individual reading assignments (or library research), what you have learned in this *ChemCom* unit, and personal opinion. Facts that you have uncovered and also arguments on why the action that you support will assure a more satisfactory future for society should be included. During the preparation period, the members of the team who will make up the audience should prepare notes on some challenging questions for those supporting alternative proposals.

In preparing for the panel discussion and question period, it is important to keep in mind the following points:

- Agreeing on a set of scientific facts does not necessarily mean that individuals will have the same views on a policy related to these facts. Personal and social concerns also play roles in developing positions.
- Scientists may disagree among themselves on what to expect from future research and technological developments, based on their own personal beliefs and ideas.
- Given these realities, all citizens in a democracy should educate themselves on issues, form their own opinions, and attempt to influence public policy in light of their views.

Since the issues to be considered do not necessarily lead to "right" or "wrong" answers, you will be judged on your use of evidence and logic to support your position and on the clarity of your presentations. You may decide to divide the work evenly into specific tasks within your group, splitting into smaller groups to prepare material on different aspects of the proposal. Also, you may wish to divide the issues so that each of your two panel members is an expert on certain aspects of the problem, for example, technical and social issues.

The panel discussion will have the following format:

1. The six panel members will each have three minutes to present arguments in favor of the proposal that they support.

2. For five minutes, the panel members will participate in an open question and answer period on the issues, directed by a moderator (or the teacher). The moderator must prevent any panel member from dominating the discussion, and must halt it after the time has passed.

3. Questions will then be received from the audience until five minutes remain in the class period.

4. A straw vote will be taken among the audience to determine which of the three proposals has the most support. Because the government may enact more than one option, everyone will vote again for their second choice proposal.

As the final part of this activity, for homework, each class member will prepare a letter to the editor (roughly 300 words long) of a newspaper, either supporting or criticizing an issue raised during the panel discussion.

F.2 Looking Back and Looking Ahead

In this unit, we have once again seen how an understanding of chemistry can help us deal with important personal and social issues involving resource use and abuse on this planet. Clearly, individual and government decisions that ignore or attempt to refute nature's laws are likely to have "costs" much higher than any desired benefits. Chemistry does not provide any single, "right" answer to such major problems, but it does help us to ask important questions and it provides us with various options to consider. Such knowledge can help us make more intelligent decisions on these complex issues.

In the next unit you will encounter another issue that is scientifically complex and that involves both personal and social dimensions. You will discover that this unit's theme, "to build or to burn," also applies to food and nutrition. It's food for thought.

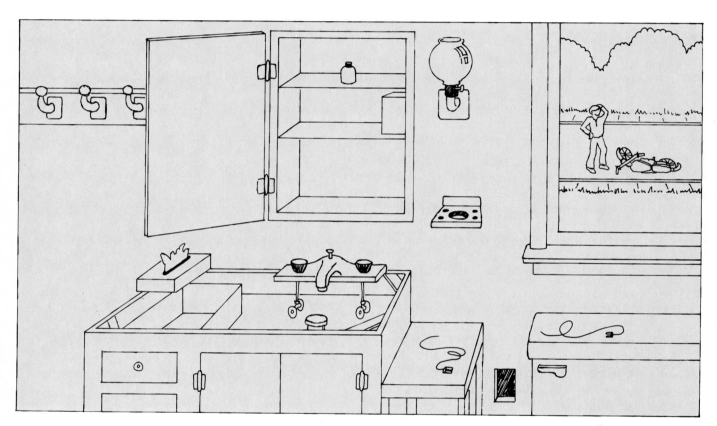

Figure III.21   Life without petroleum. The items in Figure III.1 that consume or are made from petroleum have been removed.

UNIT *FOUR*

Understanding Food

CONTENTS

INTRODUCTION

In the preceding unit, you learned that petroleum provides the raw materials for building many products or for burning as fuel. Our foods are also building materials, as well as fuel. Molecules from food are the materials from which our bodies build new cells, blood, and body tissues that are routinely replaced. Molecules from food are also the fuel that is "burned" in the body to provide the energy needed for all bodily activities from moving around, to thinking, and to maintaining body temperature.

Your body uses chemical reactions to release energy from foods and to build or rebuild itself.

Almost any food can provide energy, although some, notably carbohydrates (sugars and starches), are more efficient energy sources than others. The requirements for building are much more specific than those for providing energy. The major building block molecules for body growth and development are proteins and fats. Vitamins and minerals are also absolutely necessary, although in very small quantities, somewhat like specialized parts in the building of a car.

Different cultures throughout the world have developed widely varying diets. Almost all of these diets supply the same basic balanced nutrition. For example, Mexicans get much of their protein from beans and rice, Americans obtain much protein from beef, and Italians obtain it from pasta (which is processed grain) and cheese. Each culture has its own traditional sources of vitamins and minerals as well. These foods may appear very different, but once they are digested their chemistry is very similar.

In fact, in most cultures, diets that provide balanced nutrition have evolved without anyone having to think about it. The differences in diets in different cultures arise mainly from the kinds of food crops that can be grown in different parts of the world.

For those who get enough to eat, most of the world's traditional diets are balanced. But people in many parts of the world are starving. Most of the world's hunger occurs in the so-called **developing world,** the countries that have not become fully industrialized. In the **developed world,** where industry has matured, hunger is considerably less common. The developed world includes the United States, Canada, most of Europe, Australia, New Zealand, and parts of Asia and South America. In the developed and developing world, poverty is responsible for most of the hunger.

To understand hunger, one must realize that there are two ways to go hungry based upon building and burning.

First, people who don't get enough to eat have too little to burn. This is called **undernourishment.** Second, it is possible to get enough fuel from the food without getting all the building block substances the body needs to grow and to maintain itself. This is called **malnourishment,** or malnutrition. Malnourishment is like trying to build a house with some of the materials missing. You can have all the bricks needed, but if you run out of mortar, you cannot finish the job. A person can be overweight and malnourished at the same time.

You Decide: Your Diet, Part 1—Keeping a Food Diary

Keep a complete diary of everything you eat for three days. This information will be used later when we consider nutrition and food nutrients. Keep your diary either for a Thursday, Friday, and Saturday or for a Sunday, Monday, and Tuesday. Record each food item you eat and estimate its quantity. Include all beverages, except carbonated water or tap water. Include snacks, too. Express your estimates of quantity as volume (such as milliliters, pints, tablespoons, and cups), mass (such as grams or pounds), or count (slices or units such as number of eggs or bananas).

Your teacher will collect your completed diaries and redistribute them when it's time to analyze your diet.

Analyzing what you eat is one way to confirm whether or not you are adequately nourished. You have probably been told many times to eat the right kinds of foods in the proper amounts. But what are the right kinds of foods? What does each do for us? We will begin to address these questions in the next section.

World Bank

Vegetables such as the ones for sale at this open market in Ubon, Thailand, are becoming more plentiful in the country, thanks to agricultural extension efforts supported by the World Bank.

A FOODS: TO BUILD OR TO BURN?

Breathing, talking, thinking require energy from food; healing, growing hair, and building muscles require building materials from food.

To "understand" food requires examining several fundamental questions: What should we eat and why? and How can the world be properly fed? We must recognize that we have no control over decisions on whether the food we eat will be used to build or burn. These decisions are controlled by our bodies.

To begin our study of food, we will look at the molecules from food that are used for building and burning. This will help us understand how diet can influence health.

A.1 Nutritional Imbalances and Their Consequences

Did it ever occur to you that even in the United States, people might be poorly fed? In 1936, the first food consumption survey of the United States was requested by President Franklin D. Roosevelt. It showed that about one-third of all Americans were poorly fed. Recent surveys by the U.S. Department of Agriculture reveal that only half of U.S. families have diets rated as "good," and that one-fifth eat "poorly."

Are you surprised that people in this "land of plenty" are not properly nourished? Poor nutrition does not necessarily mean that one is underfed. Good nutrition requires consuming proper amounts of all necessary nutrients.

People who are malnourished—those who lack some of the molecular building blocks of the body—may have such physical symptoms as fatigue, drying and yellowing of the skin, deterioration of hair texture, swollen joints, and increased susceptibility to illness. Eventually they may die of malnourishment.

Chris Sheridan, Catholic New York

Food is a necessity for everyone.

Undernourishment—too little energy available from foods in the diet—can have the same results as malnourishment. The immediate problem is that the body does not get enough fuel to meet its needs. The body's energy needs always take priority over building needs, for if the body does not have access to enough energy, it eventually dies. If a person does not eat enough, the body meets its energy needs by using up stores of fat. Once these are gone, if undernourishment continues, the body begins to consume its own structural tissue (largely protein) as fuel. This is equivalent to burning some of the structure of a wooden house to heat it. As undernourishment continues further, various parts of the body, including the brain, begin to function poorly. A person becomes weak and confused.

Small children are most severely damaged by eating poorly, because they are growing. Without proper nutrition they are susceptible to infectious diseases, stunted growth, and early death. Unless there is an extreme shortage of food, adults do not generally die from poor nutrition, but their vitality, health, and ability to work may be greatly diminished.

A.2 *You Decide:* Dimensions of Hunger

Although middle-class Americans have never been undernourished, many poor Americans and large numbers of people in the rest of the world go without enough to eat. Worldwide, 15 million people die every year from hunger and related diseases. This is more than half the population of California. Three quarters of those who die are children.

In the mid 1970s the United Nations Food and Agriculture Organization (FAO) surveyed hunger in 86 developing nations (excluding China). Table IV.1 summarizes the FAO's regional findings.

At that time, populations in 12 nations suffered undernourishment on a vast scale. Estimates of undernourished populations, rounded to millions, were, in India, 201; Indonesia, 33; Bangladesh, 27; Nigeria, 14; Brazil, Ethiopia, and Pakistan, 12 each; the Philippines, 10; Afghanistan, 6; and Burma, Colombia, and Thailand, 5 each. More recent FAO studies (1978–79) showed that 56 of 119 developing nations had per-person food energy supplies below recommended needs.

The FAO identifies undernourishment by a standard of "dietary energy intake." Minimally adequate energy intake is considered 1.2 times the rate an inactive person gives off thermal energy. The 1.2 factor allows for body maintenance and minimum physical activity.

Use the information given here and in the previous text section to help answer the following questions.

Questions

1. Why is the death rate from hunger higher for children than for adults?
2. What effect does undernourishment have on human activity?

Table IV.1 *The magnitude of undernutrition in developing nations*

	Near East	Latin America	Africa	Far East	Total
Total population (in millions)	192	317	320	1090	1919
Number undernourished (in millions)	19	41	72	303	435
Percent undernourished	10	13	23	28	23

3. Malnutrition is defined as inadequate intake of proteins, vitamins, and minerals. Malnutrition may occur even if the food energy intake is adequate. If Table IV.1 gave the number of malnourished people rather than undernourished people, would the totals be larger or smaller? Why?

4. Surveying nutrition levels for an entire country is, at best, difficult. Agencies such as the World Health Organization (WHO) and United Nations International Children's Emergency Fund (UNICEF) judge a country's nutritional situation from its **infant mortality rate.**

An infant mortality rate of 50 means that 50 infants less than one-year old die for every 1,000 live births. A country with an infant mortality rate of 50 or lower is considered adequately meeting the basic needs (including nutrition) of its people. Countries with infant mortality rates higher than 50 are judged to have basic, unresolved hunger and malnutrition problems.

Your teacher will provide you with a blank world map and data on infant mortality rate in various nations. Shade in (with a colored pencil or marker) all countries having infant mortality rates higher than 50. Next to the name of each country, write its infant mortality rate.

a. Do any nations have unexpectedly high or low infant mortality rates? (The higher the rate, the more severe the food problem is assumed to be.) If so, which countries are they? Why did you find their values surprisingly low or high?

b. Based on your completed world map, does world hunger divide along any geographic lines? If so, describe them.

5. It's hard to comprehend numbers as large as 15 million, the number of people that die of hunger every year. In fact, this is equivalent to the result of dropping one atomic bomb of the size that destroyed Hiroshima every three days for a year, each killing 125,000 persons. The death rate from hunger is greater than that during World War II, when some 50 million perished during six years.

Begin with $\dfrac{1.5 \times 10^7 \; deaths}{1 \; year}$ and use the units in your calculations so that they cancel correctly.

If 15 million (1.5×10^7) die yearly directly or indirectly due to hunger, how many perish every minute? Calculate this figure by first determining how many die each day, then how many die each hour.

These statistics are profoundly troubling. Must this situation continue? Can hunger be eliminated? What causes world hunger? The cause is clearly associated with people's inability to obtain suitable food in certain regions of the world. But that doesn't really answer the question, it just restates the problem. Before we can understand the issue of world hunger we must know more about foods and how the body uses them. In Part B we will explore in greater depth how the body uses food as fuel.

PART A
SUMMARY *QUESTIONS*

1. In what way does this *ChemCom* unit encompass the same "to build and to burn" theme as the Petroleum unit? If insufficient food is supplied to the body, which of these uses is given priority? Why?

2. In what sense is the issue of world hunger an "energy crisis"? In what sense is it a national resource crisis?

3. Distinguish between the terms *undernourished* and *malnourished*. Is it possible for a person to be malnourished but not undernourished? Can a person be undernourished without being malnourished?

4. Explain the wisdom of the adage "Variety is the spice of life" in reference to one's diet. Is simple "calorie counting" a wise way to approach dieting? Why or why not?

B FOOD AS ENERGY

Humans burn food to obtain energy. In this section you will learn to measure the energy available from different kinds of food as well as how much energy it takes to perform different activities.

B.1 Food for Thought—and for Energy

Everyone who diets counts Calories. A Calorie is a measure of the energy present in food. For example, a standard serving of french fries (68 g) contains 220 Calories of food energy. The capital letter in Calories indicates that this refers to the dieticians' *energy unit*. Recall that a calorie (with a lower case "c") represents the thermal energy needed to raise the temperature of one gram of water one degree Celsius. The dietician's Calorie (with an upper case "C") is a much larger unit, equal to 1000 calories, or one kilocalorie.

The dieticians' Calorie would increase the temperature of one kilogram (one liter) of water by one degree Celsius.

To keep the two kinds of calories straight, remember the following relationships:

1000 calories (cal) = 1 kilocalorie (kcal) = 1 Calorie (Cal)

But let's get back to that serving of french fries. A 68-g serving delivers 220 kcal to the hungry eater. Where did this energy come from? The answer is simple. All food energy is stored sunlight.

In photosynthesis, plants capture solar energy and use it to make large, energy-rich molecules from smaller, simpler ones. The sun's energy is transformed into chemical energy that is stored in the chemical structures of these molecules. We recover some of this stored energy when we eat the plants or dine on meat and dairy products from animals that have consumed green plants. Thus, we are indirectly energized by solar energy.

Jon Jacobson

Decision-making in the grocery store

Jon Jacobson

Estimate the energy contained in these three servings of french fries.

Figure IV.1 Typical calorimetry apparatus. The food sample is placed in the reaction chamber, which is then filled with oxygen and sealed. The food is ignited by a spark and the rise in the water temperature is recorded.

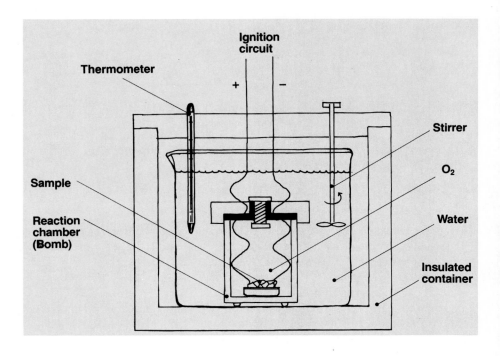

Nutrients are components of food that are needed in the diet.

How do we know how much energy is stored in a food such as french-fried potatoes? Chemists determine this in just about the same way you determined the heats of combustion of butane and candle wax (Unit Three, Part C.5). The food is burned under controlled conditions and the quantity of thermal energy released is carefully measured. This procedure is called **calorimetry,** and the apparatus in which the experiments are carried out is called a calorimeter. (You constructed a simple calorimeter from a soda can.) The type of calorimeter used for foods is illustrated in Figure IV.1.

The energy content of a wide variety of foods has been determined and tables of data published for use in diet planning. The table in Appendix A includes the energy values of common foods as well as their content of food **nutrients**.

Calorie or Joule?

In earlier sections we have used the joule (rhymes with cool) as the standard unit of energy. Now we are using calories. This is not a deliberate attempt to confuse you. Before the modernized metric system (SI) was adopted to standardize measurements, the energy unit often used was the calorie. The joule is the SI unit of energy. It is roughly equivalent to the quantity of energy it takes to lift 100 g (about the weight of a large egg) one meter. Weight-conscious Americans may one day count joules instead of calories. This has not yet happened, so we will use the (upper-case) Calorie as the unit of food energy. However, you can translate (lower-case) calories into joules by using the following relationship:

$$1 \text{ calorie (cal)} = 4.184 \text{ joules (J)}$$
$$\text{also: } 1 \text{ Cal} = 4.184 \text{ kJ}$$

Try the following for some pencil-and-paper practice with calorimetry.

YOUR *TURN*

IV.1 Calorimetry

In a typical calorimetry apparatus, the thermal energy released by burning a sample of food heats a known mass of water. The temperature increase of the water is measured. The heat released by the reaction is then calculated from the same equation you used earlier in a calorimetry experiment (Unit Three, Parts C.5 and C.6):

$$q = m_w \times c \times \Delta t$$

where q = quantity of heat energy (in calories)
   m_w = mass of water (in grams)
   c = specific heat of water (in calories per gram per °C)
   Δt = change in temperature (final − initial, in °C)

Notice that for the thermal energy to have the units of calories, the specific heat of water must have the units of cal/(g °C). In fact, water's specific heat is 1.0 cal/(g °C) and serves as a unit conversion factor in this equation. To see how this equation is used, consider the following example:

> Suppose you wish to warm a cup of water (250 mL or 250 g) from room temperature (22 °C) to just under boiling (99 °C). How much thermal energy will be needed?

$$q = (250 \text{ g}) \times \left(\frac{1 \text{ cal}}{\text{g °C}}\right) \times (99 - 22 \text{ °C}) = 19{,}000 \text{ cal}$$

We could also express this quantity in terms of kilocalories or kilojoules.

$$(19{,}000 \text{ cal}) \times \left(\frac{1 \text{ kcal}}{1000 \text{ cal}}\right) = 19 \text{ kcal}$$

Since 1 kcal = 4.184 kJ,

$$(19 \text{ kcal}) \times \left(\frac{4.184 \text{ kJ}}{1 \text{ kcal}}\right) = 79 \text{ kJ}$$

In the equation given above for quantity of heat there are three quantities that can vary—heat (q), the mass of the water (m_w), and the temperature change (Δt). If any two of these quantities are known, the third one can be found by using the equation. For example, consider the following question:

> One ounce of a popular frosted cereal contains 3 teaspoons (12 g) of sugar, which when burned will release 55.9 Cal. What mass of water could be heated from 22.0 °C to 99.0 °C by burning this much sugar?

First, the known values for the heat released (q) and the temperature change (Δt) are substituted into the equation, along with the factor needed to convert Calories to calories (because c is given calories per gram per °C):

$$(55.9 \text{ Cal}) \times \left(\frac{1000 \text{ cal}}{1 \text{ Cal}}\right) = (m_w) \times \left(\frac{1 \text{ cal}}{\text{g °C}}\right) \times (99.0 \text{ °C} - 22.0 \text{ °C})$$

The answer is found by solving for m_w:

$$m_w = (55{,}900 \text{ cal}) \times \left(\frac{\text{g °C}}{1 \text{ cal}}\right) \times \left(\frac{1}{77.0 \text{ °C}}\right) = 726 \text{ g}$$

The 55.9 Cal of energy will heat 726 g of water from 22.0 °C to 99.0 °C.

Table IV.2 *Energy expenditures for typical activities*[a]

Activity	Energy expended kcal/hour
Lying down or sleeping	80
Sitting	100
Driving automobile	120
Standing	140
Light housework	180
Walking, 2.5 mph	210
Bicycling, 5.5 mph	210
Lawn mowing, power (push) mower	250
Bowling	270
Walking, 3.75 mph	300
Swimming, 0.25 mph	300
Volleyball, rollerskating	350
Tennis	420
Skiing, 10 mph	600
Bicycling, 13 mph	660
Running, 10 mph	900

[a]Based on a 150-pound person

1. A diet drink has an energy content of only six Cal. How many grams of room temperature (22 °C) water could be heated to just under boiling (99 °C) with this quantity of thermal energy?

2. In addition to raising the temperature of a fluid, thermal energy can be converted into mechanical energy to do useful work. Recall that a joule is roughly the quantity of energy needed to lift a large egg (100 g) one meter (i.e., 1 J/m to lift the egg). Calculate how high a large egg could be elevated above the Earth if all of the 6 Cal in Problem 1 could be converted into useful work.

3. Suppose that you consumed six glasses (250 g each) of ice water (0 °C) on a hot summer day. If your body temperature is 37 °C, how many calories of thermal energy did your body supply to heat this water to body temperature? How many Calories is this? How many joules?

4. How many glasses of ice water would you have to drink to "burn off" the 220 Cal of energy you would gain by eating a serving of french fries? Is drinking ice water an efficient way to diet?

What happens to the energy stored in the foods we eat? How much body mass is gained if excess food is consumed? The following activity will help you to estimate this.

B.2 *You Decide:* Energy In—Energy Out

Table IV.2 provides estimates of the energy expended by a 150-lb person in various activities. Use this table to estimate your own daily energy expenditure. List your typical activities over a 24-hour period, estimate the total hours involved with each activity, and then calculate the kilocalories expended. Try to estimate energy expenditures for any activities not given in the table.

From Williams–Harageones–Johnson–Smith, *Personal Fitness: Looking Good/Feeling Good.* Copyright © 1986 by Kendall/Hunt Publishing Company, Dubuque, Iowa. Reprinted with permission.

These runners are expending energy at a rate of about 900 kcal/hr.

An average 15- to 18-year-old female engaged in light activity consumes about 2300 Cal daily. The value for a 15- to 18-year-old male is about 3000 Cal. How does your own estimated energy expenditure compare with these values? In your "energy accounting" compare the total energy you expended with the total food energy you consumed over the same period. To complete this analysis, record all food eaten in a typical day and then calculate all the kilocalories available from it, using an appropriate table. For simplicity in this analysis, we will look at the consumption of an ice cream sundae, to see how much exercise it would take to burn off, or, alternatively, how much weight you would gain from eating it if you didn't exercise.

A pint of ice cream contains 514 kcal and the chocolate topping adds 125 kcal. Consult Table IV.2 to answer the following questions. (You also must know that 1 lb of body fat contains 4000 kcal of energy.)

1. Assume that your regular diet (without the ice cream) just maintains your current body weight. If you eat the ice cream:
   a. How far would you have to walk (at 2.5 mph) to burn it off?
   b. How far must you swim (at 0.25 mph) to burn it?
   c. How many hours of tennis would have the same energy-expending effect?

2. If you choose not to exercise, how much weight will you gain from the ice cream?

3. Now assume that you consume a similar ice cream sundae three times per week for four months. If you don't exercise to burn it off, how much weight will you gain?

4. Of course, another alternative is available—you might decide not to eat the ice cream. Considering the options described so far—eating the sundae (involving either undertaking extra exercise or gaining weight) or not eating the sundae (involving less pleasure)—which would you select? Why?

5. We have implied that eating the ice cream will result in weight gain, unless additional exercise is completed. Can you think of a plan that would allow you to consume the ice cream, do no additional exercise, and still not gain weight? Explain your plan and be prepared to discuss it in class.

It would take 6.39 h of sitting to burn off the sundae:

$$(639 \text{ kcal})\left(\frac{1 \text{ h}}{100 \text{ kcal}}\right) = 6.39 \text{ h}$$

This activity has assumed that—

- If TOTAL ENERGY IN is equal to TOTAL ENERGY OUT, a person will maintain current body weight.
- If TOTAL ENERGY IN is greater than TOTAL ENERGY OUT, a person will gain some body weight (in the form of fat).
- If TOTAL ENERGY IN is less than TOTAL ENERGY OUT, a person will lose some body weight. (See Figure IV.2).

An individual wishing to lose weight must meet the third condition listed above—the total energy consumed must be less than the energy expended. On the other hand, a person wishing to gain weight must take in more energy than is expended.

As wise dieters know, proper nutrition is not just a question of how much is eaten. What we eat also is critical. Some foods provide more energy than others, and some fill you up without providing much energy. In the next section we will examine carbohydrates, a major type of fuel for our bodies.

Figure IV.2 Relationship of food consumption and energy expended to body weight.

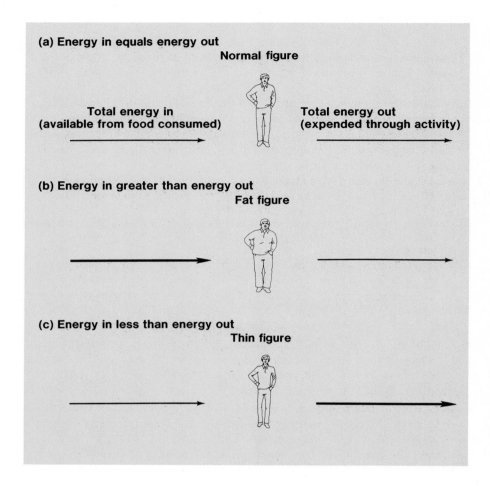

(a) **Energy in equals energy out**

Normal figure

Total energy in
(available from food consumed)

Total energy out
(expended through activity)

(b) **Energy in greater than energy out**

Fat figure

(c) **Energy in less than energy out**

Thin figure

B.3 Carbohydrates: The Energizers

Sugars, starch, and cellulose are all carbohydrates.

Carbohydrates are compounds composed of only three elements—carbon, hydrogen, and oxygen. For example, glucose, the key energy-releasing carbohydrate in biological systems, has the formula $C_6H_{12}O_6$. When such formulas were first discovered, chemists were tempted to write the glucose formula as $C_6(H_2O)_6$—an apparent combination of carbon and water. Hence the term "carbohydrate," suggesting a water-containing carbon compound. We now know that water molecules are not actually present in carbohydrates, but the name has persisted.

Every moment of your life, carbohydrates are oxidized in your body to produce CO_2, H_2O, and energy.

Carbohydrates may be simple sugars such as glucose or composed of two or more simple sugar molecules combined in various ways (Table IV.3). Simple sugars are called monosaccharides. The most common monosaccharide molecules contain five or six carbon atoms bonded to each other. As shown in Figure IV.3, glucose (and most other monosaccharides) can exist either in a chain or a ring form. Do both forms have the same molecular formula? (Check by counting the atoms.)

Sugar molecules composed of two simple sugar units are called disaccharides. Sucrose, ordinary table sugar, is a disaccharide in which the ring forms of glucose and fructose are joined (see Figure IV.4).

Table IV.3 *Classification of carbohydrates*

Classification and examples	Composition	Formula	Common name (source)
Glucose	—		Blood sugar
Fructose	—		Fruit sugar
Galactose	—		—
Disaccharides		$C_{12}H_{22}O_{11}$	
Sucrose	Fructose + glucose		Table sugar
Lactose	Galactose + glucose		Milk sugar
Maltose	Two glucose units		(Germinating seeds)
Polysaccharides	Glucose polymers	—	
Starch			(Plants)[a]
Glycogen			(Animals)[a]
Cellulose			(Fiber, plant structure)

[a]Plants store glucose as starch and animals store glucose as glycogen.

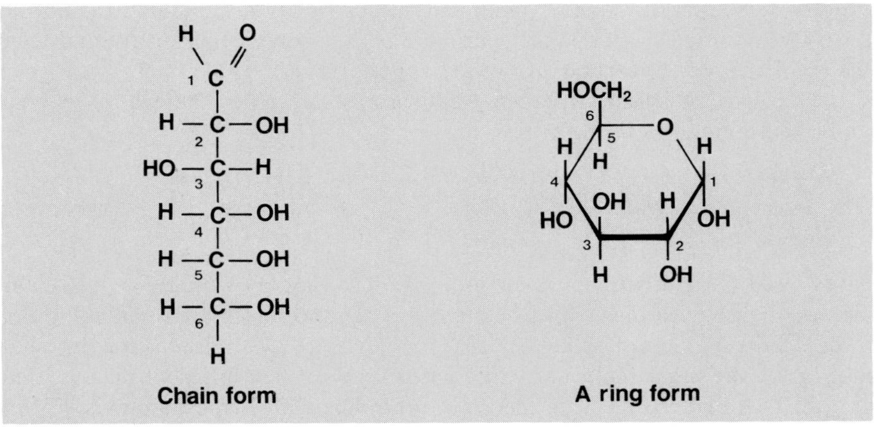

Figure IV.3 Structural formulas for glucose. The chain and ring forms are interconvertible; the ring form predominates in the body.

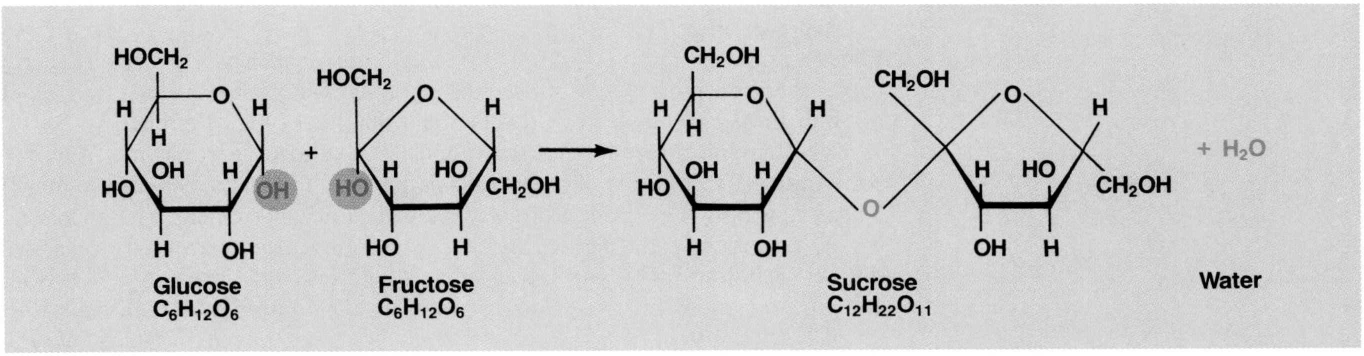

Figure IV.4 Formation of sucrose. The two shaded —OH groups react with the elimination of one H_2O molecule.

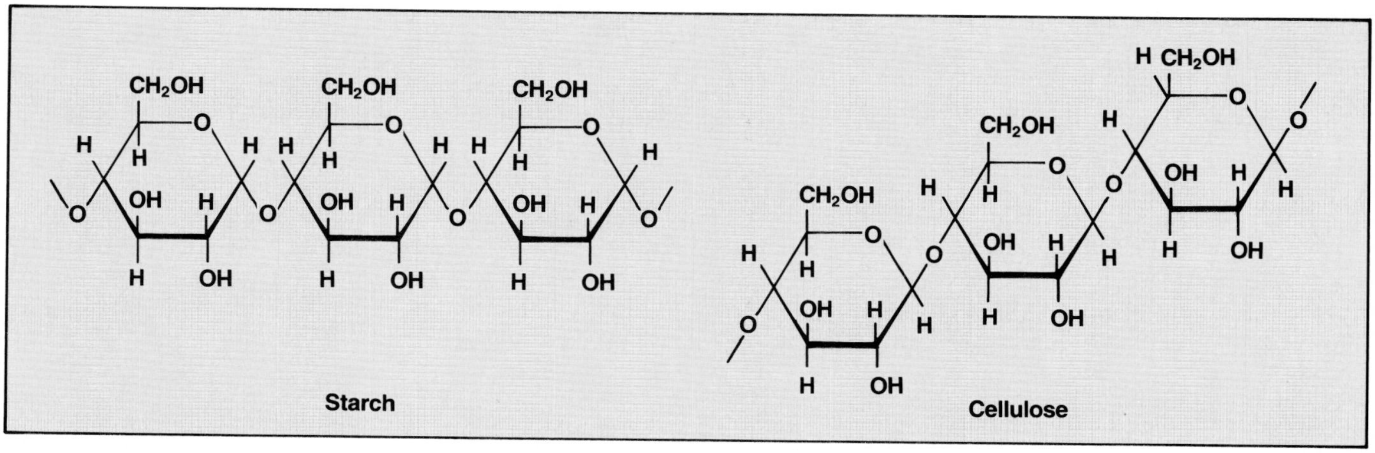

Figure IV.5 *Polysaccharides*. Starch and cellulose are polymers of glucose. They differ in the arrangements of the bonds that join the glucose monomers.

Carbohydrates are all sugars or polymers of sugars.

Polymers composed of simple sugar molecules are called polysaccharides (Figure IV.5). (Recall from our discussion of polyethylene in Unit III, Part D.4, that a polymer is a large molecule in which many smaller molecules have been chemically bonded together.) Starch, a major component of grains and many vegetables, is a polysaccharide composed of glucose units. Cellulose, the fibrous or woody material of plants and trees, is another polysaccharide formed from glucose. The types of carbohydrates are summarized in Table IV.3.

During photosynthesis, green plants produce glucose. The overall reaction can be represented as follows:

$$6\ CO_2 \ + \ 6\ H_2O \ + \ 686\ \text{kcal} \longrightarrow C_6H_{12}O_6 \ + \ 6\ O_2$$

| Carbon dioxide | Water | Solar energy | Glucose | Oxygen |

Plants build the glucose molecules into starch for energy storage, or into cellulose, which is needed to support the plant. Sugars and starch are rapidly digested in your body, making them convenient sources of fuel. Cellulose is not digested. In cellulose the sugar molecules are bonded together in a different manner than in starch (see Figure IV.5), making cellulose indigestible to most animals. (There are exceptions—cows and termites, for example.) Indigestible fiber, however, plays an important role in our diet by keeping the bowels functioning properly.

Sugars and starch are the major energy-delivering substances in our diets. Even the smallest muscle twitch or thinking requires energy. Most of this energy comes from burning glucose molecules obtained from sugars and starch. Each gram of these carbohydrates delivers about 4000 cal (4 Cal) of energy.

4 Cal
1 g carbohydrate

Nutritionists recommend that about 60% of food energy come from carbohydrates. The majority of the world's population obtains carbohydrates mostly by eating grains. The grain is often consumed as rice, corn meal, wheat tortillas, bread, or pasta. In the United States we get our carbohydrates from various sources including fruits, vegetables such as potatoes, and grains. Meats provide a small amount of carbohydrate as glycogen, the form in which animals store glucose. On average, each U.S. citizen consumes more than 90 lb (40 kg) of table sugar per year in beverages, breads, and cakes and as a sweetener. A 12-ounce cola drink contains nine teaspoons of sugar.

YOUR*TURN*

IV.2 Burning Sugars

On average, the quantity of energy released when a carbohydrate reacts completely with oxygen (when it burns), is about 4 kcal per gram. For glucose, this reaction, which is the reverse of the overall photosynthesis reaction, is:

$$C_6H_{12}O_6 \; + \; 6\,O_2 \longrightarrow 6\,CO_2 \; + \; 6\,H_2O \; + \; 686 \text{ kcal/mol glucose}$$

| Glucose | Oxygen | Carbon dioxide | Water | Thermal energy |

The equation represents the combustion of one mole of glucose. Therefore the heat of combustion of glucose is 686 kcal/mol.

1. Use the molar mass of glucose to convert the molar heat of combustion of glucose to the heat of combustion per gram. How does this value compare with the 4 kcal/g average for carbohydrates?
2. It was stated that the average American consumes about 90 lb of table sugar (sucrose) per year. Assuming that all this is beyond the energy needed to maintain constant body weight, calculate the pounds of body fat gained. (*Hint:* 1 lb = 454 g; 1 lb of fat is equivalent to 4000 kcal). Do you think this assumption is valid?

Molar mass is discussed in Unit Two, Part C.3.

B.4 Fats: Stored Energy with a Bad Name

Unlike carbohydrate and protein, the word "fat" has acquired its own general meaning. To most people, "He's too fat" means that the person has an excess of mass (or volume). From the chemist's view, **fats** are a major category of biomolecules that have their own special characteristics and functions, just as carbohydrates do.

Fats are a significant part of our diet. They are present in meat, fish, and poultry; salad dressings and oils; dairy products; and grains.

Like carbohydrates, fats are composed of carbon, hydrogen, and oxygen, but they contain less oxygen than carbohydrates and are more like hydrocarbons. Therefore, in their solubility properties and their greater amounts of stored chemical energy, fat molecules are more like hydrocarbons than carbohydrates. When our bodies take in more food than is needed for energy, much of the excess is converted to fat molecules and stored in the body. If our food intake is not large enough to supply the energy we need, our bodies burn the stored fat.

Fats are members of a class of biomolecules called **lipids.** Some lipids are builder molecules that form cell membranes. Others become hormones, chemical messengers that regulate processes in the body.

Most fat molecules are produced by the combination of one molecule of a simple three-carbon alcohol called **glycerol** with three molecules of compounds known as fatty acids. Fatty acids contain long hydrocarbon chains with a carboxyl group (COOH) at one end. The formation of a typical fat is shown in Figure IV.6. The reaction is similar to one that you carried out in the laboratory (Unit Three, Part D.5) when you made the ester, methyl salicylate. The difference is that a molecule containing three —OH groups reacts with three molecules of acid. Three molecules of water are eliminated to produce a molecule containing three ester groups instead of one. Such a fat is called a **triglyceride.**

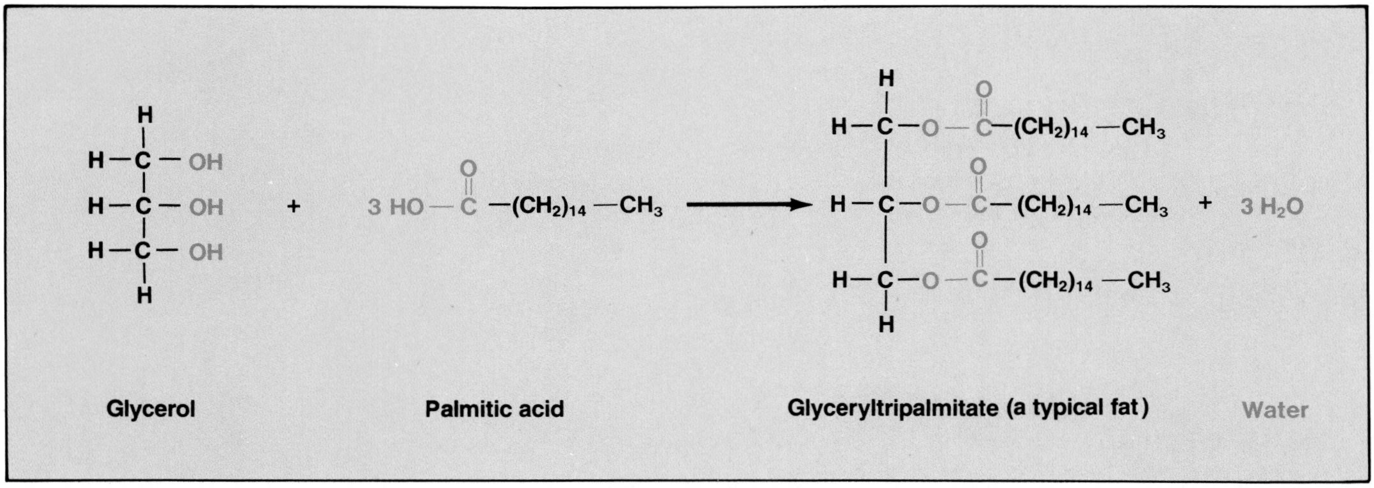

Figure IV.6 Formation of a typical fat, a triglyceride. Glycerol and three molecules of fatty acid combine in a condensation reaction to form a triester and eliminate three water molecules.

Figure IV.7 Typical fatty acids.

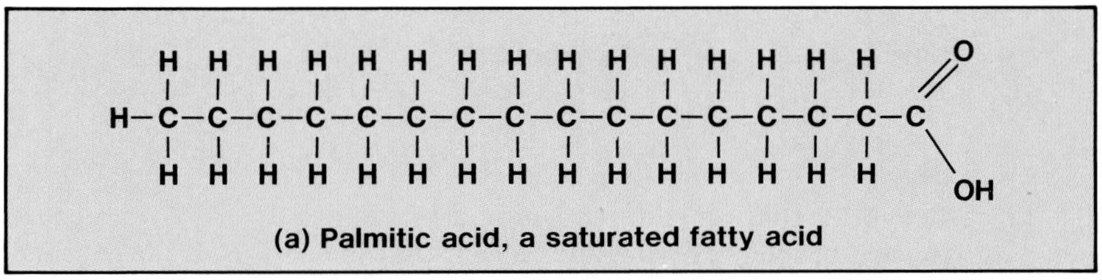

(a) Palmitic acid, a saturated fatty acid

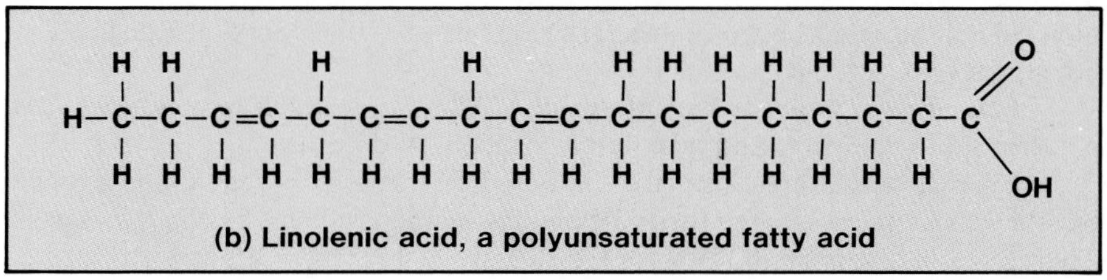

(b) Linolenic acid, a polyunsaturated fatty acid

Recall that hydrocarbons (Unit Three, Parts B.8 and D.2) may be saturated (each carbon atom bonded to four other atoms) or unsaturated (containing double or triple carbon-carbon bonds). The hydrocarbon chains in fatty acids are either saturated (Figure IV.7a) or contain one or more carbon-carbon double bonds ($>C=C<$) (Figure IV.7b). Fats containing saturated fatty acids are called **saturated fats**; fats containing unsaturated fatty acids are called **unsaturated fats**. In fats, carbon-carbon double bonds are reactive sites. Because of the differences in their bonds, saturated and unsaturated fats behave differently in body chemistry. Review the functional groups present in many biomolecules in the following *Your Turn*. Then we will return to the role of fats in the body.

YOUR*TURN*

IV.3 Functional Groups in Biomolecules

As you discovered in the petroleum unit, functional groups strongly influence the properties of organic compounds.

Classes of organic compounds in which various functional groups appear are listed in the margin, where the formulas are written in their more condensed forms (R = hydrocarbon segment).

A molecule may contain more than one functional group. For example, examine the structure of cortisol (a lipid that is not a fat) below. Cortisol, a hormone, released during starvation, stimulates the production of glucose from protein. Cortisol contains several functional groups—three hydroxyl groups, two keto groups, and one carbon-carbon double bond.

1. Refer to the forms of glucose in Figure IV.3 and draw both the chain and the ring structures for glucose. Circle and identify the functional group(s) found in the chain structure. Examine the numbering of the carbon atoms and the functional groups attached to each carbon atom. Which functional groups on which C atoms react to form the ring structure?

2. Examine the straight-chain structure of fructose shown in the margin. Compare this structure with that of glucose.

3. In general, alcohols react with organic (carboxylic) acids to form esters. Using the reaction shown in Figure IV.6 as a guide, write the equation (including structures) for the reaction between stearic acid and glycerol to form glyceryl tristearate. Stearic acid has the following formula:

$$HO - \overset{\displaystyle O}{\overset{\|}{C}} - (CH_2)_{16}CH_3$$

4. Consider the following organic structure:

$$HO - \overset{\displaystyle O}{\overset{\|}{C}} - (CH_2)_7 - \overset{\displaystyle H}{\overset{|}{C}} = \overset{\displaystyle H}{\overset{|}{C}} - (CH_2)_7CH_3$$

Identify the functional group(s). Is this structure a carbohydrate or a fatty acid? How can you tell? Is it saturated or unsaturated? Rewrite the formula to show the carbon atoms in a continuous chain.

ROH
Alcohol

ROR
Ether

$$R - \overset{\displaystyle}{\underset{\displaystyle O}{\overset{\|}{C}}} - H$$

Aldehyde

$$R - \overset{\displaystyle}{\underset{\displaystyle O}{\overset{\|}{C}}} - R$$

Ketone

$$R - \overset{\displaystyle}{\underset{\displaystyle O}{\overset{\|}{C}}} - O - H$$

Carboxylic acid

$$R - \overset{\displaystyle}{\underset{\displaystyle O}{\overset{\|}{C}}} - O - R$$

Ester

$$\begin{array}{c} H \\ | \\ H - C - OH \\ | \\ C = O \\ | \\ HO - C - H \\ | \\ H - C - OH \\ | \\ H - C - OH \\ | \\ H - C - OH \\ | \\ H \end{array}$$

Straight-chain structure of fructose.

Cortisol

Saturated fats appear to contribute to coronary heart disease.

The term "polyunsaturated," often used in food advertising, means that the food contains fats with more than one carbon-carbon double bond per fatty acid molecule. The term has become familiar because evidence is accumulating that saturated fats may contribute to health problems, but some unsaturated fats may not. Saturated fats are associated with formation of plaque (fatlike or fibrous matter) that can block arteries. The result is the condition known as "hardening of the arteries," or atherosclerosis, which is particularly dangerous for coronary (heart) arteries and arteries leading to the brain. If coronary arteries are blocked, a heart attack can result, damaging the heart muscle. If arteries leading to the brain are blocked, a stroke may result, killing brain cells and harming various body functions.

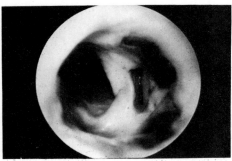

SIU BIOMED

Plaque deposits restrict blood flow in this human artery.

You need about 30% fat in your diet, but too much can be harmful.

The fat molecules in butter and other animal fats are nearly all saturated and are solids at room temperature. Fats from plant sources commonly contain molecules with several carbon-carbon double bonds. At room temperature these "polyunsaturated" fats are liquids, or oils, such as safflower oil (91% unsaturated fat molecules), corn oil (87%), and peanut oil (81% unsaturated).

A process called partial hydrogenation can add enough hydrogen atoms to the double bonds of a fat to convert it to a semisolid, while still allowing some double bonds to remain. The partially hydrogenated molecules are used in margarines and shortening.

Fats are high-energy molecules. One gram of fat can release 9000 cal (9 Cal) of energy—more than double the energy released from an equal mass of carbohydrate or protein. Thus it is not surprising that the body tends to produce fat to store excess food energy efficiently. This also explains why it is so difficult to "burn off" excess fat. Gram for gram, you must run more than twice as far or exercise twice as long to "burn up" fat as you do to burn carbohydrate energy sources.

Currently, Americans get about 40% of their body energy from fats, although the American Cancer Society and the American Heart Association recommend that this be reduced to 30%.

Fat consumption in the United States is decreasing, but is still high compared with the recommended level and with the relative fat intake in developing countries. High consumption of fat is a factor in several "modern" diseases, including obesity, and atherosclerosis. Most of our dietary fat comes from fats and oils present in meat, poultry, fish, and dairy products. Deep-fried items, such as french fries, fried chicken, and potato chips, add even more fat to the diet.

In the following questions, review what you have learned about energy in the body and energy-providing molecules. After you answer these questions, we will consider the nutrients involved in building—the proteins.

PART B
SUMMARY *QUESTIONS*

1. A one-half-ounce serving of raisins provides 40 kcal of thermal energy. If this energy were used to raise the temperature of 100 g of room temperature (22 °C) water, how hot would the water get?

2. People sometimes confuse the terms hydrocarbon and carbohydrate. Define and give an example of each. How are they similar? How are they different?

3. Use Table IV.2 to explain each of the following:
   a. Breakfast is the most important meal of the day. (*Hint:* Estimate how many Calories would be expended by your body between dinner [6 P.M.] and breakfast [8 A.M.].)
   b. Until they are properly fed, starving individuals would have difficulty working for a living even if paying jobs were available.

4. Assume that you require 3000 kcal of food energy per day to maintain your present body weight. If you wished to obtain this energy by consuming the least mass of food, would fats or carbohydrates be your food choice? Calculate how many grams of this nutrient would be needed to supply this quantity of daily energy. Would such a diet be healthy? Why or why not?

5. Is the following structure a hydrocarbon, a carbohydrate, or a fat?

$$H - \overset{\overset{\displaystyle \parallel}{O}}{C} - \overset{\overset{\displaystyle H}{|}}{\underset{\underset{\displaystyle OH}{|}}{C}} - \overset{\overset{\displaystyle H}{|}}{\underset{\underset{\displaystyle OH}{|}}{C}} - H$$

6. It has been estimated that U.S. citizens carry around 2.3 billion pounds of excess body fat.
   a. How many kilocalories of food energy does this represent?
   b. If the excess energy calculated in Question 6a could be diverted to feed the hungry of the world, how many people could be fed for one year? (Assume the average human requires 2650 kcal/day.)

EXTENDING *YOUR KNOWLEDGE (OPTIONAL)*

- Unlike hydrocarbons, simple sugars (carbohydrates) are very soluble in water. Explain why this is so in terms of the molecular structures. You may wish to compare the structure of glucose ($C_6H_{12}O_6$) with that of hexane (C_6H_{14}).
- Assume that you presently consume 3000 kcal/day and that you wish to lose 30 lb of body fat in two months' time. If you intend to lose this weight through dieting alone (i.e., no extra exercise), how many kilocalories would you need to omit from your diet per day to achieve your goal? How many kilocalories per day would you be allowed to consume? Would this be a sensible approach to weight loss? Why or why not?

American Chemical Society

It looks good but think of the Calories!

C FOODS: THE BUILDER MOLECULES

Your body mass is roughly 60% water and 20% fat. The other 20% consists primarily of protein, carbohydrates, and related compounds, and the major bone minerals, calcium and phosphorus.

In the United States, recent generations have grown taller than their parents, on the average. Women today are able to bear children at a much younger age than women who lived 100 years ago. Better nutrition is responsible for these changes. Our genes determine how tall we might possibly grow, but nutrition determines in part how closely we live up to that potential.

In this section you will explore food nutrients as builder molecules. You will discover the critical importance of protein as a body builder.

C.1 Foods as Chemical Reactants

The food we eat supplies the starting molecules for the chemical reactions that allow us to live and function. During digestion, gigantic food molecules are broken down into their building blocks, for example, starches are broken down into glucose. The building blocks are then absorbed from the intestines into the blood, which transports them to the appropriate cells, where they become reactants in chemical changes that keep the body alive and healthy. The branch of chemistry that studies the chemical reactions in living systems is biochemistry.

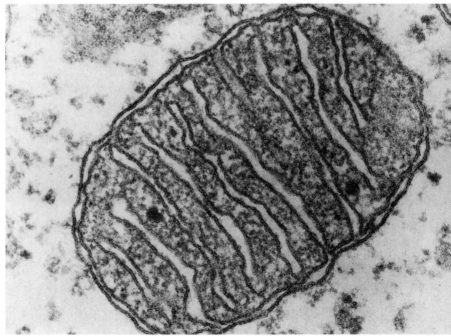

Courtesy of G. E. Palade, Yale Univ. School of Medicine

Much cellular respiration takes place in mitochondria. This photo shows details of a single mitochondrion under an electron microscope.

Biochemical processes are rarely simple. Consider the extraction of energy from disaccharides and polysaccharides. These carbohydrates are broken down by digestion into glucose, $C_6H_{12}O_6$, the primary substance used for energy by most living systems.

As you saw in *Your Turn* IV.2, the overall reaction for burning glucose in the body is the same as the reaction that would occur if you were to burn glucose in air. Obviously, glucose cannot burn with a flame inside the body. Not only would most of the energy escape uselessly as heat, but the resulting temperatures would kill the cells. Yet that burning reaction does, in effect, continuously occur within each human cell. It occurs in a series of at least twenty-two related chemical reactions or steps that, taken as a whole, is called **cellular respiration.**

This process and nearly every other biochemical reaction takes place at body conditions only with the help of molecules called **enzymes** (discussed further in Unit Seven). Enzymes can be thought of as the skilled worker molecules of the body. They help to make and break chemical bonds; each enzyme is as specific to the molecule with which it reacts as a key is to a lock.

*Enzymes are **catalysts**—compounds that help chemical reactions occur by increasing the rate of reaction.*

C.2   Limiting Reactants

The reactions that take place in the body, particularly those that build, require a complete set of ingredients, or reactants. In addition, there must be enough of each ingredient for the reaction to be completed. The situation is like that in baking a cake. Consider this cake recipe:

2 cups flour	1½ tablespoons baking powder
2 eggs	1 cup water
1 cup sugar	⅓ cup oil

The combination of these ingredients will produce one cake. Suppose in the kitchen we find 14 cups of flour, four eggs, 10 cups of sugar, 15 tablespoons of baking powder, 10 cups of water, and 3⅓ cups of oil. How many cakes can be baked? Fourteen cups of flour is enough for seven cakes (two cups flour per cake). And there's enough sugar, baking powder, water, and oil available for 10 cakes (confirm this with the recipe). Yet we cannot make either 7 or 10 cakes with the available ingredients. Why?

We only have four eggs, enough for just two cakes. The eggs have limited the number of cakes we can bake with available ingredients. The excess quantities of the other reactants (flour, sugar, baking powder, water, oil) simply remain unused. If we wish to make more cakes, we must find more eggs.

$$4 \text{ eggs} \left(\frac{1 \text{ cake}}{2 \text{ eggs}} \right) = 2 \text{ cakes}$$

Try the following to practice applying this important principle.

YOUR*TURN*

IV.4   Limiting Reactants

1. Consider the same cake-making example discussed above, but this time assume that you have 26 eggs. How many cakes can be made now if the other ingredients are present in the same quantities as before? Which ingredient is limiting the number of cakes you can make?

2. A booklet is prepared by combining 2 covers, 3 staples, and 20 pages. Assume that we have 60 covers, 120 staples, and 400 pages.
   a. What is the maximum number of booklets that can be prepared with these supplies?
   b. Which is the limiting component in this system?
   c. How many of the other two "reactants" will be left over when the booklet preparation process stops?

In chemical terms, the eggs in our cake-making example would be called the **limiting reactant** (or limiting reagent). The limiting reactant is the starting substance used up first when a chemical reaction occurs. It determines how much (or how little) product is formed.

In chemical reactions, just as in recipes, individual substances react in certain fixed quantities. These relative amounts are indicated in chemical equations.

Let's return to the glucose-burning equation:

$$C_6H_{12}O_6 \; + \; 6\,O_2 \longrightarrow 6\,CO_2 \; + \; 6\,H_2O \; + \; 686$$

| Glucose | Oxygen | Carbon dioxide | Water | kcal/mol glucose |

This equation can be interpreted to mean that one glucose molecule reacts chemically with six oxygen molecules, forming six carbon dioxide molecules and six water molecules. Suppose we had 10 glucose molecules and 100 oxygen molecules. Based on the same equation, which substance is the limiting reactant?

The equation tells us that each glucose molecule requires six oxygen molecules. Thus 10 glucose molecules would require 60 oxygen molecules for complete reaction. However, 100 oxygen molecules are available. So all 10 glucose molecules can be used up, leaving 40 oxygen molecules left over. Because the glucose will be used up first, it is the limiting reactant. Once the 10 glucose molecules are consumed, the reaction can no longer proceed. Additional glucose is needed to continue the chemical change.

YOUR*TURN*

IV.5 Limiting Reactants: Chemical Reactions

A chemical equation can be interpreted in terms not only of molecules, as shown above, but also in terms of moles and grams (as discussed in Unit Two, Part C.3). For the reaction above, 1 mol glucose will react completely with 6 mol oxygen, to give 6 mol of carbon dioxide and 6 mol water. Using molar masses to convert these values to grams shows that 180 g glucose will react completely with 192 g oxygen to produce 264 g carbon dioxide and 108 g water.

If we had one-half as much glucose, or 90 g, one-half as much oxygen, or 96 g, would be required. If we had 90 mg glucose, 96 mg oxygen would be required to react with all of the glucose. Such relationships can be used to identify the limiting reactant.

Ammonia (NH_3) is both an important fertilizer and an intermediate in the production of other fertilizers. It is produced commercially by the following reaction:

$$N_2(g) \; + \; 3\,H_2(g) \xrightarrow[\text{Fe catalyst}]{\text{High temperature and pressure}} 2\,NH_3(g)$$

1. How many moles of each reactant and product are indicated by the equation? How many grams of each reactant and product are indicated by the equation?
2. Assume that a manufacturer has 28 metric tons (one metric ton equals 1000 kg) of nitrogen and 9 metric tons of hydrogen. Also assume that the maximum amount of ammonia is produced from these reactants.
   a. Which reactant would be the limiting reactant?
   b. Which reactant would be left over (i.e., be in excess)? How much of it would be left over?
   c. What is the maximum amount of ammonia that could be made?

The concept of limiting reactants can be demonstrated easily by many common chemical reactions. Your teacher will demonstrate the reaction of hydrochloric acid (HCl) with magnesium metal (Mg):

$$2 \text{ HCl}(aq) \quad + \quad \text{Mg}(s) \quad \longrightarrow \quad \text{MgCl}_2(aq) \quad + \quad \text{H}_2(g)$$

| Hydrochloric acid | Magnesium metal | Magnesium chloride | Hydrogen gas |

This reaction is easy to observe, because hydrogen gas bubbles form as long as the reaction continues. When the gas is no longer produced, we can assume that a reactant (either hydrochloric acid or magnesium metal) has been used up. At this point, the limiting reactant has been fully consumed.

In the demonstration, you will also judge the extent of each reaction. A small balloon placed over the mouth of each test tube will capture the hydrogen gas produced. Thus, the amounts of hydrogen gas formed can be estimated roughly by the sizes of the inflated balloons.

During the demonstration, you will observe two series of reactions:

Part A. Constant amount HCl, variable amount Mg
    Tube 1: 5 mL 3 M HCl + 2.5 cm Mg ribbon
    Tube 2: 5 mL 3 M HCl + 5.0 cm Mg ribbon
    Tube 3: 5 mL 3 M HCl + 10.0 cm Mg ribbon
    Tube 4: 5 mL 3 M HCl + 15.0 cm Mg ribbon
Part B. Constant amount Mg, variable amount HCl
    Tube 5: 2 mL 3 M HCl + 5.0 cm Mg ribbon
    Tube 6: 4 mL 3 M HCl + 5.0 cm Mg ribbon
    Tube 7: 6 mL 3 M HCl + 5.0 cm Mg ribbon
    Tube 8: 8 mL 3 M HCl + 5.0 cm Mg ribbon

M stands for molar concentration or molarity (Unit Two, Part C.3).

Although living systems are much more difficult to study in terms of limiting reactants than are isolated chemical reactions, the shortage of a key nutrient or reactant can severely affect the growth or health of a plant or animal. In many biochemical processes the products of one reaction serve as reactants for other reactions. If one reaction stops because a reactant has been used up (the limiting reactant), an entire series of sequential reactions will also stop.

Fortunately, some life processes have backup, or alternate, reaction pathways available. Often, different substances can be used as reactants if the need arises. For example, in energy production, if the body's supply of glucose is depleted, reactions involved in glucose metabolism cannot occur. One backup system involves the oxidation of fat from the body's reserves instead of glucose. In another, structural protein is broken down and converted to glucose. Once glucose is again available, the glucose metabolism reactions can continue. Producing glucose from protein is much less energy efficient than producing glucose from carbohydrates. But your body will use protein in this way if necessary.

If the intake of a nutrient is consistently below the minimum required by the body, that nutrient may become a limiting reactant in some vital biochemical processes. The results can easily affect one's health.

Plants also must take in the essential nutrients for their growth and metabolism. For example, consider algae, which often pollute lakes and streams. A balanced diet for algae must include carbon, nitrogen, and phosphorus. For every 41 g of carbon, algae require 7 g of nitrogen and 1 g of phosphorus. If any one of these elements is in short supply, it becomes a limiting reactant and affects growth of the algae.

In the following *Your Turn* you will compare limiting reactants in human and plant systems.

Jon Jacobson

Without water and essential nutrients, plants lose their vigor.

YOUR*TURN*

IV.6 Limiting Reactants: Plants and Humans

In Table IV.4 are listed 22 elements currently known to be required in some quantity to support human life.

    For comparison, a list of nutrients needed for the growth of common agricultural crops, such as corn and wheat, is given in Table IV.5. Because crops cannot grow properly without suitable nutrients in sufficient quantities, farmers must be concerned with the limiting reactants in their crop production.

Table IV.4   *Elements known to be needed in human nutrition*

In major biomolecules	Carbon (C)
	Hydrogen (H)
	Oxygen (O)
	Nitrogen (N)
	Sulfur (S)
Major minerals	Calcium (Ca)
	Chlorine (Cl)
	Magnesium (Mg)
	Phosphorus (P)
	Potassium (K)
	Sodium (Na)
Trace minerals[a]	Chromium (Cr)
	Cobalt (Co)
	Copper (Cu)
	Fluorine (F)
	Iodine (I)
	Iron (Fe)
	Manganese (Mn)
	Molybdenum (Mo)
	Nickel (Ni)
	Selenium (Se)
	Zinc (Zn)

[a]Trace minerals are present in amounts of 1 ppm or less. If present in higher concentrations they can be toxic.

Most common fertilizers contain nitrogen, phosphorus, and potassium.

Table IV.5   *Plant nutrients needed by common agricultural crops*

Basic nutrients	Carbon dioxide (CO_2)
	Water (H_2O)
Primary nutrients	Nitrogen (N)
	Phosphorus (P)
	Potassium (K)
Secondary nutrients	Calcium (Ca)
	Magnesium (Mg)
	Sulfur (S)
Micronutrients	Boron (B)
	Chlorine (Cl)
	Copper (Cu)
	Iron (Fe)
	Manganese (Mn)
	Molybdenum (Mo)
	Zinc (Zn)

1. Are any elements required for plant growth not essential nutrients for humans? If so, which ones?

2. Are any elements required for human growth not essential nutrients for plants? If so, name them.

3. Examine the label on a bottle of vitamins that provide 100% of a person's daily requirement of vitamins and minerals. Are all elements listed in Table IV.4 included among the ingredients? If not, which are missing?

4. Which of the plant nutrients are commonly added to increase the productivity of soils in developed nations? If these nutrients can be limiting reactants, what would their nonavailability imply about food production in developing nations?

C.3 Proteins: The Stuff from which Living Systems Are Made

Protein has been described as the primary material of life. The word "protein" comes from the Greek word *proteios,* which means "of prime importance." **Proteins** are the major structural components of living tissue. When you look at another person, everything you see is protein: skin, hair, eyeballs, nails. Bones and cartilage, tendons, and ligaments all contain protein. So do birds' feathers and the fur, hooves, and horns of animals. In addition, all enzyme molecules that help control chemical reactions in the cell are proteins. There are literally tens of thousands of different kinds of proteins in each person. Table IV.6 lists just a few major roles of proteins in the human body.

Table IV.6 *Types and functions of proteins in the body*

Type	Function	Examples
Structural proteins		
Muscle	Contraction, movement	Myosin (muscle)
Connective tissue	Support, protection	Keratin (skin, hair, nails); collagen (tendons, ligaments)
Chromosomal proteins	Part of chromosome structure	Histones
Membranes	Protection, control of influx and outflow, communication	Pore proteins Receptors
Transport proteins	Carriers of oxygen and other substances	Hemoglobin (O_2 carrier in blood)
Regulatory proteins		
Fluid balance	Maintenance of pH, water, and salt content of body fluids	Serum albumin
Enzymes (biological catalysts)	Control of metabolism, other reactions	Proteases (decompose proteins)
Hormones	Regulation of body functions	Insulin (regulates blood glucose), sex hormones
Protective proteins	Antibodies (defense against infection)	Gamma globulin
Any protein	Burned for energy when in excess or in the absence of carbohydrate or fat	Any protein

From Williams–Harageones–Johnson–Smith, *Personal Fitness: Looking Good/Feeling Good.* Copyright © 1986 by Kendall/Hunt Publishing Company, Dubuque, Iowa. Reprinted with permission.

Building body protein.

Figure IV.8   Representative amino acids.

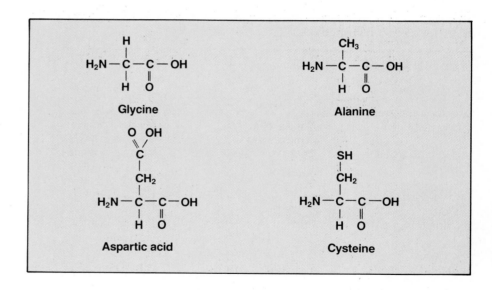

Because protein is such an essential component of our bodies, it is necessary for new growth and for maintaining existing tissue. Our tissues are replaced surprisingly often. Red blood cells must be replaced every month. The cells that line the intestinal tract are replaced weekly. Every time we bathe we wash away dead skin cells.

Proteins are polymers built from small molecules called **amino acids.** Each amino acid contains carbon, hydrogen, oxygen, nitrogen; some also contain sulfur. Just as sugar molecules are building blocks for more complex carbohydrates, 20 different amino acids are the structural units of all proteins. All amino acids have similar structural features, as shown in Figure IV.8. Two functional groups, the amino group ($-NH_2$) and the carboxyl group ($-COOH$), are found in all amino acid molecules.

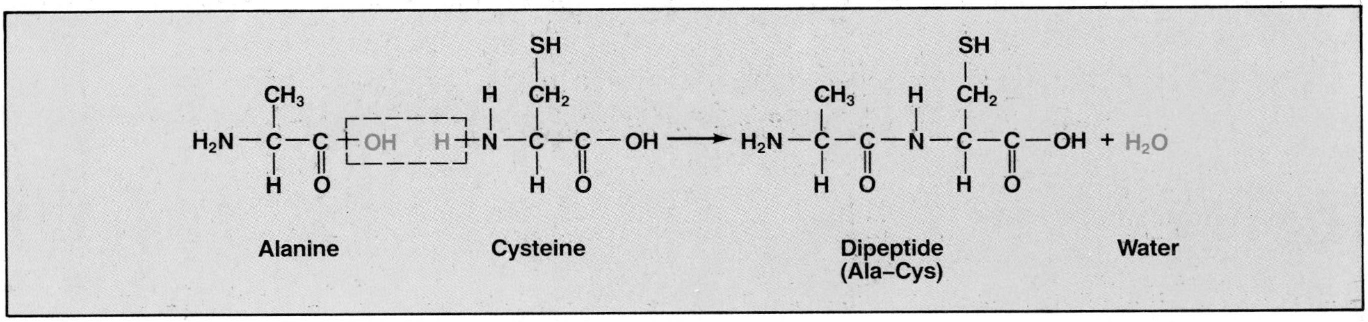

Figure IV.9 Formation of a dipeptide. All proteins contain amino acids linked in this manner.

The combining of two amino acid molecules with loss of one water molecule, as illustrated in Figure IV.9, is a condensation reaction. Like starch, nylon, and polyester (as discussed in Unit Three, Part D.4), proteins are condensation polymers.

Test your skill as a "molecular architect" in the following protein-building activity.

YOUR*TURN*

IV.7 Molecular Structure of Proteins

1. Draw the structures for glycine and alanine (see Figure IV.8) and circle and identify the functional groups in each. How do the two differ?

2. Proteins are polymers of amino acids. If you examine the sample reaction in Figure IV.9, you can see that the amino acid monomers are linked through the amine group on one amino acid and the carboxyl group on another. Each linkage is called a **peptide linkage,** or peptide bond, and is represented by $-\underset{\underset{H}{|}}{N}-\underset{\overset{\|}{O}}{C}-$. The formation of a peptide bond is shown in Figure IV.10. Since each amino acid contains at least one amine group and one carboxyl group, it can form a peptide bond at either, or both, ends. With Figures IV.9 and IV.10 as models, complete the following:

   a. Using structural formulas, write the equation for the reaction between two glycine molecules. Circle the peptide bond in the dipeptide product.

   b. Using structural formulas, write equations for the possible reactions between a glycine molecule and an alanine molecule. Two dipeptides (which contain two linked amino acids) are possible. Identify both and locate their differences.

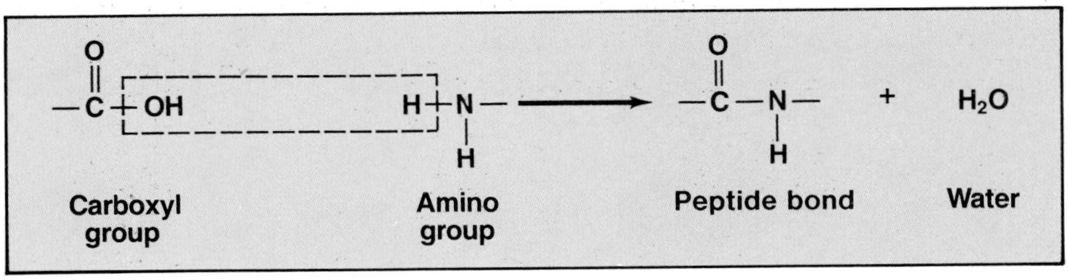

Figure IV.10 Formation of a peptide bond. An amino acid can form peptide bonds with two other amino acids.

Proteins are further discussed in Unit Seven.

3. Examine the formulas of the products in the equations you wrote in answer to Question 2. Note that each product still has a reactive amino group and a reactive carboxyl group. This means that these dipeptides could further react to form additional peptide linkages. In fact, proteins are composed of very long chains of amino acids, and have molecular weights from 5000 to several million. Just as the 26 letters of our alphabet combine in different ways to form different words, so the 20 amino acids can combine in a virtually infinite number of ways to form different proteins.

Hint: Represent each amino acid by a letter, e.g., abc, acb,....

a. How many separate **tripeptides** (three amino acids linked together) could be formed from three different amino acids? For simplicity's sake, first assume that each amino acid can appear only once in the product. (*Note:* Nature does not place this restriction on peptide formation.) If this restriction is removed, how many separate tripeptides can you form?

b. How many tetrapeptides could be formed from four different amino acids? (Consider only the case where each acid is used only once per tetrapeptide.)

c. Given 20 different amino acids and the fact that proteins range in length from about 50 amino acid units to more than 10,000, would the theoretical number of distinct proteins be in the hundreds, thousands, or millions plus? How might this relate to the uniqueness of each organism?

When you eat food that contains protein, the peptide bonds between the amino acids are broken by enzymes called **proteases** in your stomach and small intestine. The freed amino acids then travel through the bloodstream first to the liver and then to the cells. There they are built up into new proteins to meet the body's needs. If you have eaten more protein than your body needs, or, alternatively, if your body needs to burn protein because carbohydrates are in short supply, the amino acids react in the liver. There the nitrogen atoms are removed and converted into urea, which is excreted through the kidneys in the urine. (This helps explain why a high-protein diet can place an extra burden on a person's liver and kidneys.) The remainder of the amino acid molecule is either converted to glucose and burned, or converted to storage fat.

The human body can synthesize 12 of the 20 amino acids. The other eight must be obtained from protein in the diet. Therefore, these eight amino acids are called **essential amino acids.** If an essential amino acid is in short supply in the diet, it can become a limiting reactant in building any protein that contains that amino acid. When this happens, the only way the body can make that protein is by destroying one of its own proteins that contains the limiting amino acid.

Most animal proteins contain all eight essential amino acids in the necessary quantities. Any protein that contains adequate amounts of all essential amino acids is called a **complete protein.** Plant proteins are incomplete; they do not contain adequate amounts of all of the essential amino acids.

Although no single plant protein can provide adequate amounts of all essential amino acids, certain combinations of plant proteins can do so. Such combinations of foods, which are said to contain **complementary proteins** (see Table IV.7), form a part of customary diets in various parts of the world.

The essential amino acids

Isoleucine	*Phenylalanine*
Leucine	*Threonine*
Lysine	*Tryptophan*
Methionine	*Valine*

Histidine (for infants)

Table IV.7 *Examples of foods with complementary proteins*

Foods	Country
Corn tortillas and dried beans	Mexico
Rice and black-eyed peas	Southern United States
Peanut butter and bread	United States
Rice and bean curd	China and Japan
Rice and lentils	India
Spaghetti (wheat) and cheese	Italy

Table IV.8 *Recommended daily allowance for protein*

Age range	g Protein (per lb ideal[a] body weight)
Infants	
0–0.5	1.00
0.5–1	0.90
Children	
1–3	0.81
4–6	0.68
7–10	0.55
11–14	0.45
15–18	0.39
Adults	
19 and older	0.36
Pregnant women	0.62
Nursing women	0.53

[a]The weight recommended for your height and age.

The body cannot store protein, so a balanced protein diet is required daily. The recommended caloric intake from protein is 10–12%. A survey in 1977 found the intake from protein in the United States to average about 17%. Too much protein is as harmful as too little. Excess protein causes overdevelopment of the liver and kidneys, the organs that metabolize protein. Too much protein also increases the body's loss of calcium ions through excretion. Calcium ions are important in nerve transmission and in bone and teeth structures. A protein-heavy diet can even cause dehydration, a problem particularly important to athletes.

How much protein is really needed? The Food and Nutrition Board of the National Academy of Sciences has established recommended dietary allowances (RDAs) for all required nutrients, including protein. Their recommendations regarding protein are given in Table IV.8. Use the information in the table to answer the questions in the following *Your Turn*.

YOUR *TURN*

IV.8 Protein in the Diet

1. According to the table, how many grams of protein should a 105-pound, 12-year-old boy consume per day?

2. How many grams of protein should you eat per day, according to the RDA figures?

3. Why should the RDA values for protein be highest for infants, and progressively lower as a person gets older?

4. What food do young babies consume that provides most of their high protein needs? Can you find any indirect evidence in the table to support your answer?

5. The infant mortality rate in developing nations is higher than in developed nations and, as we have seen, is used as an indicator of nutritional inadequacy. How do the protein requirements relate to this problem? Which groups of persons are most likely to suffer the effects of a nation's inadequate protein supplies? Why?

6. In recent years manufacturers of infant formulas have been criticized for marketing their products in developing countries as substitutes for mother's milk. Why might such formulations be acceptable substitutes in developed nations, but not in developing ones?

A 220 lb adult requires 79 g of protein each day:

$$220 \text{ lb} \left(\frac{0.36 \text{ g protein}}{1 \text{ lb}} \right) = 79 \text{ g}$$

Milk, a baby's first food, has been termed a nearly perfect food. It contains carbohydrate, fat, and protein. And because it is from an animal source, it contains adequate amounts of all the essential amino acids. It is rich in vitamin A, the B vitamins, and, when fortified, vitamin D. It is also a valuable source of calcium.

In the following laboratory activity you will analyze milk to find how much fat, protein, carbohydrate, and energy value it actually contains.

C.4 Laboratory Activity: Milk Analysis

Getting Ready

In this laboratory activity, you will determine the percent protein, fat, carbohydrate, and water in whole milk. Once the composition of milk has been determined, you will calculate its food energy value. Then you will compare the results of your laboratory investigation with the accepted values for milk.

Milk analysis will require two laboratory periods. In the first you will use a technique based on solubility differences to separate fat from the rest of the components of milk. (Fat, like all lipids, is soluble in nonpolar solvents.) Then you will separate protein from the defatted milk by precipitating the protein and filtering off the solid.

On the second day, the quantity of water in whole milk will be found by evaporating the water and weighing the remaining portion of the milk. You will calculate the percent of carbohydrate by difference, that is, once you know the percent fat, protein, and water, assume the rest is carbohydrate.

Procedure, Day 1

Part 1: Extracting and Determining Milk Fat
1. Carefully weigh an empty 50-mL beaker. Record the mass.
2. Add 15 mL of milk to the beaker. Weigh the beaker and milk. Record the mass.
3. Using the results of Steps 1 and 2, calculate the mass of your milk sample.
4. Pour your milk sample into a large test tube. Add 10 mL of nonpolar TTE solvent to the tube. Close the tube tightly with the stopper.
5. Shake the mixture vigorously.
6. Wait one minute. Observe that two liquid phases are formed. Because fats are nonpolar substances, they will tend to dissolve in the nonpolar layer. Can you observe any fat globules in the nonpolar layer?
7. Using a long, dropping pipet (at least 10 cm long), gradually remove the top liquid layer (the nonfat milk) from the tube. Put this removed milk layer in the 50-mL beaker you used in Step 1 above. It is important to remove as much of the white milk layer as possible, without drawing off any of the TTE-fat layer. Perform your final milk removal very carefully!
8. Reweigh the beaker and nonfat milk. Record the mass.
9. Calculate the mass of nonfat milk in the beaker. Use data accumulated in Steps 1 and 8 to complete this calculation.
10. Now calculate the mass of milk fat that was removed in the TTE layer.
11. Calculate the percentage of fat in your original milk sample:

$$\left(\frac{\text{Mass of fat (Step 10)}}{\text{Mass of milk sample (Step 3)}} \right) \times 100\% = \% \text{ Fat in milk sample}$$

12. Add 2 mL of bromine water to the TTE-fat sample in your test tube. Gently mix. If unsaturated fat is present, the brown-orange bromine solution will turn yellow or colorless. Compare the speed of the color change in your sample with that of the two reference samples demonstrated by your teacher. *Caution:* Be very careful not to breathe bromine fumes. Be very careful not to spill any bromine solution on your skin. Wash immediately if you do and inform your teacher.

13. What do your observations from Step 12 suggest about the degree of saturation or unsaturation of milk fat?

14. Discard waste solutions as directed by your teacher.

Part 2: Removal of Milk Protein

1. Add 30 drops of concentrated acetic acid to the beaker containing the nonfat milk. (*Caution:* Keep your nose and face away from the concentrated acetic acid; wash skin immediately if any spills occur.) Swirl briefly, then allow the beaker to sit for five minutes. Observe the precipitate forming in the milk. Acid coagulates milk protein, forming the curd you see here.

2. Weigh one fresh circle of filter paper. Record its mass. Support a short-stemmed funnel on a ring stand above a clean 150-mL beaker. Fold the filter paper and put it in the funnel.

3. Pour the coagulated milk sample into the funnel. Then add 2 mL of water to the empty beaker. With a spatula, attempt to remove as much of the white material clinging to the beaker walls as you can. Pour these loosened particles into the funnel. Repeat this beaker-cleaning step with a second 2 mL of water.

4. The filtration will proceed slowly. Place your name on a paper towel next to your ring stand. In several hours, your teacher will remove the filter paper (with protein) from the funnel so the precipitate can air-dry overnight. The filtrate will also be saved for you to test tomorrow.

Procedure, Day 2

Part 3: Determining Milk Protein, Carbohydrate, and Percent Water

Students at each laboratory table should divide into two groups. Group 1 will test and determine the percent protein in the milk. Group 2 will find the percent carbohydrate and water in the milk. The results from each group will be shared with the other group to provide complete analysis information for the milk sample.

Group 1: Determining and testing milk protein

1. Weigh the filtered, dried protein and filter paper from yesterday's laboratory activity. Record the total mass.

2. Calculate the mass of protein collected.

3. Finally, calculate the percent protein in your milk sample.
To verify that you actually extracted protein from your milk sample, complete the following steps:

4. Label four test tubes 1, 2, 3, and 4. Add 1 mL milk filtrate collected in yesterday's filtration to tubes 1 and 2. Add two chips of the dried milk protein to each of tubes 3 and 4.

5. Add 2 mL of Molish reagent to Tubes 1 and 3, letting it run down the inside walls to the bottom of the tube. Then carefully add 15 drops concentrated sulfuric acid to each tube. (*Caution:* Concentrated sulfuric acid is highly

corrosive to skin, clothing, books, and other materials. Avoid spilling. Immediately flood skin with tap water if any acid is touched.) Observe and record any differences between Tubes 1 and 3. Molish reagent, in the presence of carbohydrate and concentrated sulfuric acid, will produce a purple color near the bottom of the test tube. Based on your observations, which tube contains a high level of carbohydrate?

6. Add 5 mL of Biuret reagent to Tubes 2 and 4. If the solution changes to a purple or purplish blue color, protein is present. If no color develops at room temperature, place the two tubes in a hot-water bath, assembled from a 250-mL beaker containing 150 mL water, supported on a ring stand. Heat the water bath for two minutes (do not allow the water to boil vigorously). Which tube gives a positive protein test?

Share your calculated results with Group 2. Obtain Group 2's calculated results. Then move on to Part 4 below.

Group 2: Determining milk carbohydrate and percent water

1. Determine the combined mass of an empty evaporating dish and stirring rod. Record their combined mass.

2. Add 5 mL fresh milk to the evaporating dish.

3. Weigh the evaporating dish, milk, and stirring rod together. Record their combined mass.

4. Calculate the mass of milk in the evaporating dish.

5. Set the evaporating dish and milk on top of a beaker half full of water. (A 250-mL beaker probably will support the dish securely. Place a boiling chip in the beaker.)

6. Place the beaker-evaporating dish assembly on the wire gauze on a ring stand. Begin heating the water in the beaker to slowly evaporate the liquid from the dish. As a thin "skin" develops on the milk surface, break it with the stirring rod. Prevent the milk from burning by stirring it gently and continuously. Do not allow any milk to be transferred from the evaporating dish—do not set the stirring rod down on the laboratory bench top, for example.

7. As the milk loses its moisture, it may resemble liquid paste. When there is no further change in consistency, stop heating. Allow the evaporating dish to cool. Wipe condensed water from the outside of the dish.

8. Determine the combined mass of the evaporating dish, solid milk residue, and stirring rod. Record this value.

9. Calculate the mass of milk solids in the evaporating dish.

10. Now calculate the mass of water in your original 5-mL milk sample.

11. Finally, calculate the percentage of water in your milk sample.

Obtain the calculated value for the percentage of protein in the milk sample from Group 1. Now calculate the percent carbohydrate in the milk. The total mass of milk is essentially made up of four parts—water, carbohydrate, fat, and protein. (The mass of all mineral matter in milk is only about 1% of the total, and can be ignored.) Move on to Part 4 below.

Jon Jacobson

Milk contains mainly protein, fat, and carbohydrates.

Part 4: Calculating the Energy Value of a Serving of Milk

Fat, protein, and carbohydrate all deliver food energy to the body. The quantity of food energy stored in these three major nutritional categories is as follows:

- Fat: 9 Cal/g (9000 cal/g)
- Protein: 4 Cal/g (4000 cal/g)
- Carbohydrate: 4 Cal/g (4000 cal/g)

You now have laboratory values for the percent fat, percent protein, and percent carbohydrate in a fresh milk sample. From these data, calculate the food energy delivered by a typical serving of milk.

Let's assume we have a 1-cup serving of milk. Assume this has a mass of 244 g. We can first find the mass of each major nutrient category in this milk sample. Then we can convert these masses to the quantity of food energy each contains. Fill in a chart similar to this one:

Data table

Mass of milk	×	% Expressed as decimal fraction	=	Mass of nutrient	Calories per gram nutrient	Calories from each major nutrient
244 g	×	____ Fat	=	____ g Fat	9 Cal/g	_____ Cal
244 g	×	____ Protein	=	____ g Protein	4 Cal/g	_____ Cal
244 g	×	____ Carbohydrate	=	____ g Carbohydrate	4 Cal/g	_____ Cal
				Total Calories per cup (244 g) of milk		_____ Cal

Questions

1. Compare your milk analysis results with the actual values found on a carton of fresh whole fat milk:

Data table	Your laboratory values	Average values in fresh whole fat milk
Percent fat	_____ %	3.3%
Percent protein	_____ %	3.3%
Percent carbohydrate	_____ %	4.5%
Percent water	_____ %	88%
Total Calories/cup	_____ Cal	150 Cal

2. If you add all the "actual" values given in the first question, you will find they do not total 100%. Can you think of any reasons this is so? (Not fair saying that it's due to poor laboratory results!)

3. Now add your "Laboratory" values shown in the first question. They should total 100%. Why?

4. Young children sometimes discover at the breakfast table that they can make their milk curdle if they pour orange juice into it. What is the composition of those milk curds? (*Hint:* Orange juice is rich in citric acid and vitamin C, ascorbic acid.)

5. Do you know the names of the principal protein and the principal carbohydrate in milk? If not, try to find this information in a reference book.

6. Powdered milk is prepared by removing essentially all of the water and fat from fresh milk. Assume that the original milk had a composition similar to that shown in the "Actual values" column of Question 1. What would be the approximate percent protein in the powdered milk? Would the powdered milk qualify as a "high protein" supplement if it were added to other foods?

   Hint: Assume that you started with 100 g of fresh milk; how many grams of water and fat would be lost? How many grams of protein would be present?

PART C
SUMMARY *QUESTIONS*

1. Discuss how the limiting reactant concept applies to your diet and to agriculture.

2. Valine is one of the eight essential amino acids. What does the word "essential" mean in this context? How does the limiting reactant concept apply to essential amino acids?

3. Ammonia (NH_3) can be added directly to soil or converted into other fertilizers. Consider the following reaction to produce ammonium nitrate:

$$NH_3(g) + HNO_3(l) \rightarrow NH_4NO_3(s)$$

If 34 g NH_3 reacts with 63 g nitric acid (HNO_3):
   a. Which species is the limiting reactant?
   b. What is the maximum mass of NH_4NO_3 that can be made?
   c. Which reactant will be in excess and by how much?

4. Proteins form part of all structures in an animal's body, yet a diet of protein alone would be unwise. Why?

5. Diagram the condensation reaction of two alanine molecules. Identify the functional groups in reactants and product.

6. Calculate the total grams of protein a 150-pound, 17-year-old person should consume daily (refer to Table IV.8). Use Appendix A (see page 255) to determine how many ounces of chicken would be needed to supply this quantity of protein. How many cups of milk would supply this same amount?

7. Compare the terms complete protein and incomplete protein and discuss their relevance to your diet.

8. Copy the following structures on your own paper. Circle and identify the functional groups in each structure. Which one represents an amino acid?

a. $CH_3 - CH_2 - C = O$
$$\qquad\qquad\qquad |$$
$$\qquad\qquad\quad OH$$

b. $HS - CH_2 - C - CH_2 - NH_2$
$$\qquad\qquad\qquad\; \| $$
$$\qquad\qquad\qquad\; O$$

c. $\quad\quad\quad\quad H$
$$\quad\quad\quad\quad |$$
$$HO - C - C - CH_3$$
$$\quad\quad\; \| \quad |$$
$$\quad\quad\; O \quad NH_2$$

d. $H_2N - CH_2 - C = O$
$$\qquad\qquad\qquad\; |$$
$$\qquad\qquad\qquad H$$

American Chemical Society

Variety is the essence of good eating.

D SUBSTANCES PRESENT IN FOODS IN SMALL AMOUNTS

Proteins, carbohydrates, and fats form the major building blocks and fuel molecules of life. Other substances—vitamins and minerals—are just as important, even though the body requires only tiny amounts of them. Small but essential quantities of vitamins and minerals are supplied by the foods we eat, or by dietary supplements. What do they do in the body that is so important? Let's first consider vitamins.

D.1 Vitamins: Vital Substances Come in Small Packages

Vitamins perform very specialized tasks in the body. For example, vitamin D moves the calcium ions in the food you eat from your intestines into the bloodstream. Without vitamin D, much of the calcium you ingest would be lost.

By definition, **vitamins** are biomolecules necessary in small amounts for growth, reproduction, health, and life. Despite their importance, the total quantity of all vitamins required per day is only about one-fifth of a gram.

Although the term "vitamin" was coined in the early 20th century, there was evidence long before this century that chemical substances other than fats, proteins, and carbohydrates are required. For example, a disease called scurvy, in which the joints swell, the gums bleed, and the skin is tender, was once common among sailors. As early as the 1500s scurvy was blamed on a food deficiency. After 1753, explorers learned to carry along citrus fruits to prevent it. We now know that scurvy is caused by lack of vitamin C, present in large amounts in citrus fruits. Other health problems are also caused by vitamin deficiencies. About a dozen different vitamins have been identified. Their existence has been determined and proved by synthesizing them in the chemistry laboratory and then testing them in animal diets.

Vitamins can be classified as fat-soluble or water-soluble. The fat-soluble vitamins are A (retinol), D_3 (cholecalciferol), E (alpha-tocopherol), and K (menaquinone). Your body absorbs them into the blood from the intestine with the assistance of fats in the food you eat. These fat-soluble vitamins can be stored in body fat, so it is not necessary to eat them daily. However, because fat-soluble vitamins can accumulate within the body, they can become toxic if taken in large quantities.

Water-soluble vitamins include the eight B vitamins and vitamin C (ascorbic acid). These are not stored in the body, so they must be a part of the daily diet. Cooking can wash them away or destroy them. The B vitamins include B_1 (thiamine), B_2 (riboflavin), niacin, B_6 (pyroxidine), B_{12} (cyancobalamine), folic acid, pantothenic acid, and biotin. The function of B vitamins in body cells is largely related to releasing energy from food. All are cofactors, small nonprotein molecules that assist enzymes in performing their functions.

Table IV.9 illustrates the diverse roles played by vitamins in supporting human life. How much is "enough" of each vitamin? It depends on your age and whether you are male or female. Table IV.10 provides current Recommended Dietary Allowances (RDA's) for selected vitamins for a sampling of different ages and sexes. Use this table to answer the questions in *Your Turn* IV.9.

Table IV.9 *Vitamins: sources, functions, and deficiency conditions*

Vitamin (name)	Main sources	Main functions	Deficiency condition
A (Retinol)	Eggs, butter, cheese, liver, dark green and deep orange vegetables	Development and maintenance of membranes, vision; proper tooth development and bone growth	Inflamed eye membranes, night blindness, scaliness of skin, faulty teeth and bones
B_1 (Thiamine)	Pasta, bread, lima beans, wheat germ, nuts, milk, liver, peas, pork	Energy release from carbohydrates	Beriberi: nausea, severe exhaustion, paralysis
B_2 (Riboflavin)	Milk, meat, eggs, mushrooms, dark green vegetables, pasta, bread, beans, peas	Energy release from carbohydrates, fats, proteins. Maintains mucous membranes	Severe skin problems
Niacin	Meat, enriched or whole grains, poultry, fish, peanuts	Vital to release of energy from glucose	Pellagra: weak muscles, no appetite, diarrhea, skin blotches
B_6 (Pyridoxine)	Muscle meats, liver, whole grains, poultry, fish	Amino acid metabolism, fatty-acid use, hemoglobin synthesis, aids in maintaining blood glucose level	Depression, nausea, vomiting
B_{12} (Cobalamin)	Meat, fish, eggs, milk, kidneys, liver	Formation of red blood cells, functioning of nervous system	Rare except in vegetarians: pernicious anemia; exhaustion
Folic acid	Kidneys, liver, leafy green vegetables, wheat germ, peas, beans	Formation and maturation of red and white blood cells, aids in cell division	Anemia
Pantothenic acid	Found in all plants and animals; nuts; whole-grain cereals and bread	Metabolism of fats, carbohydrates, proteins; formation of hormones and nerve-regulating materials	Anemia
Biotin	Found widely; egg yolk, kidneys, liver, yeast, nuts	Formation of fatty acids, energy release from carbohydrates	Dermatitis
C (Ascorbic acid)	Citrus fruits, melon, tomatoes, green pepper, strawberries, leafy green vegetables	Formation of connective tissues, red blood cells; promotes absorption of iron, protects other vitamins from oxidation	Scurvy: tender skin; weak, bleeding gums; swollen joints
D (Calciferol)	Fish-liver oils, fortified milk	Regulation of body handling of calcium and phosphorus for strong teeth and bones	Rickets: soft bones (bowed legs)
E (Tocopherol)	Wheat germ, whole-grain cereals, liver, margarine, vegetable oil, leafy green vegetables, egg yolk	Prevention of oxidation of vitamin A and fatty acids	Breakage of red blood cells (in premature infants only); oxidation of membranes
K	Liver, cabbage, potatoes, peas, leafy green vegetables	Synthesis of blood-clotting substances; maintenance of bone metabolism	Hemorrhage in newborns; anemia

Table IV.10   *Vitamins: Selected RDAs*

Sex and age	A (RE)[a]	D (μg)[b]	C (mg)	B$_1$ (mg)	B$_2$ (mg)	Niacin (mg)	B$_{12}$ (μg)	K (μg)
Males 11–14	1000	10	50	1.4	1.6	18	3.0	50–100
Males 15–18	1000	10	60	1.4	1.7	18	3.0	50–100
Males 19–22	1000	7.5	60	1.5	1.7	19	3.0	70–140
Males 23–50	1000	5	60	1.4	1.6	18	3.0	70–140
Females 11–14	800	10	50	1.1	1.3	15	3.0	50–100
Females 15–18	800	10	60	1.1	1.3	14	3.0	50–100
Females 19–22	800	7.5	60	1.1	1.3	14	3.0	70–140
Females 23–50	800	5	60	1.0	1.2	13	3.0	70–140

[a]RE = Retinol equivalent units; 1 μg retinol = 1 retinol equivalent.
[b]μg = microgram = 10^{-6} g.

YOUR*TURN*

IV.9   Vitamins in the Diet

1. Carefully planned vegetarian diets can be nutritionally balanced. However, two vitamins pose a problem for people who are strict vegetarians (i.e., those who do not consume any animal products including eggs or milk). Use Table IV.9 to identify these vitamins and briefly describe the result of their absence in the diet. How might strict vegetarians avoid this problem?

2. Complete the following table. Use Tables IV.10 and IV.11 to answer the questions.

Data table

Vegetable (½-cup serving)	No. servings to supply your RDA		Yearly vitamin needs (g)	
	B$_1$	C	B$_1$	C
Green peas	?	?	?	?
Broccoli	?	?	?	?

   a. Would any table entries be different if you were a member of the opposite sex? If so, which one(s)?
   b. Based on your completed table, why do you think variety in diet is essential?
   c. Why might malnutrition (specifically, vitamin-deficiency diseases) be a problem in many developing countries even when people receive adequate supplies of calories in their food?

3. Some people believe that to promote vitality and increase resistance to a variety of diseases, much larger amounts of certain vitamins should be consumed. Of the two broad classes of vitamins, which group is more likely to pose a health problem if consumed in large doses? Why?

4. Nutritionists recommend eating fresh fruit instead of canned fruit and raw or steamed vegetables instead of canned or boiled vegetables. Which class of vitamins are they really concerned with? Why is their advice sound?

Very large vitamin doses are referred to as megadoses.

Table IV.11 *Quantity of thiamine and ascorbic acid in some common vegetables*

Vegetable (½-cup serving)	Vitamin (in mg)	
	B₁ (thiamine)	C (ascorbic acid)
Green peas	0.22	17
Lima beans	0.16	15
Mashed potatoes	0.08	10
Broccoli	0.06	52
Orange juice	0.11	56

To eat a nutritionally balanced diet, one must know which foods deliver needed vitamins for balanced nutrition. However, we must also realize that nutritionists may not yet know all the nutrients necessary for the best health. Fortunately, building a diet around a variety of foods will generally assure consumption of all known and unknown nutrients.

In the following laboratory activity you will find out how the vitamin content of common foods, in this case vitamin C, can be determined.

D.2 Laboratory Activity: Vitamin C Analysis

Getting Ready

Vitamin C, also known as ascorbic acid, is a water-soluble vitamin. It is among the least stable vitamins. It reacts readily with oxygen and its potency can be lost through exposure to light and heat. In this laboratory activity you will investigate the level of vitamin C in a variety of popular beverages, including fruit juices, milk, and soft drinks.

This analysis for vitamin C is based on the chemical properties of ascorbic acid and iodine. Iodine (I_2) solution is capable of oxidizing ascorbic acid, forming the colorless products dehydroascorbic acid, hydrogen ions (H^+), and iodide ions (I^-):

$$I_2(aq) + C_6H_8O_6(aq) \longrightarrow C_6H_6O_6(aq) + 2\,H^+(aq) + 2\,I^-(aq)$$

| Iodine | Ascorbic acid (vitamin C) | Dehydroascorbic acid | Hydrogen ion | Iodide ion |

You will perform a **titration,** a common procedure in chemical laboratories to determine concentrations or amounts of substances in solutions. The general approach is to add known amounts of one reactant gradually from a buret to another reactant until enough for complete reaction has been added. The point of complete reaction is observed by a color change or some other highly visible change that occurs at the **endpoint** of the reaction. Knowing the reaction involved, the unknown amount of one reactant can be calculated from the known amount of the added reactant.

The titration set up is illustrated in Figure IV.11. Complete the procedure as demonstrated by your teacher.

In this analysis, the endpoint is signaled by the reaction of iodine with starch suspension, which produces a blue-black product. Starch is added to the beverage to be tested. An iodine solution is slowly added from the buret. As long as ascorbic acid is present, the iodine is quickly converted to iodide ion, and no blue-black iodine-starch product is observed. However, when all available ascorbic

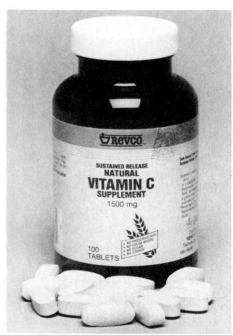

Jon Jacobson

It doesn't matter the source, all samples of vitamin C are the same compound.

Figure IV.11 Titration apparatus.

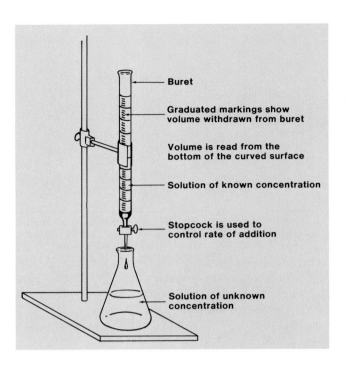

acid has been oxidized, the next drop of added iodine solution reacts with starch to form the expected blue-black color. The endpoint in the titration, then, is the first sign of permanent blue-black color in the beverage-containing flask.

You will first perform a titration with a known vitamin C solution. This will allow you to find a conversion factor that will be useful in your laboratory calculations. This factor specifies the mass of ascorbic acid that reacts with each milliliter (mL) of iodine used in your titration. From these data you can calculate the mass of vitamin C present in 25 mL of each beverage.

Prepare a data table like that below in your laboratory notebook.

Data table: Beverage analysis summary				
Beverage	mL Iodine solution used (from Part 2)	× Conversion factor (from Part 1)	= mg Vitamin C per 25 mL beverage	Rank (highest to lowest in vitamin C)
1.		×	=	
2.		×	=	
3.		×	=	
4.		×	=	
5.		×	=	

Procedure

Part 1: Determining Conversion Factor (Milligrams Vitamin C Per Milliliter Iodine Solution)

1. Measure 25 mL of vitamin C (ascorbic acid) solution into a 125 mL Erlenmeyer flask.

2. Add 10 drops of 1% starch suspension.

3. Fill a clean buret with iodine solution. Record your starting buret volume.

4. Slowly add the iodine solution to the flask as you gently swirl the flask. Continue until the endpoint is reached (the first sign of blue color that remains after at least 20 seconds of swirling). A piece of white paper placed under the flask will help you see the endpoint.

5. Record your final buret volume. Calculate the volume of iodine solution used in the titration.

6. Calculate a conversion factor indicating the number of milligrams of vitamin C corresponding to 1 mL of iodine solution by dividing 25 mg of vitamin C by the volume (in milliliters) of iodine solution used in the titration.

7. Record your calculated value in the "Conversion factor" column of your data table. (The factor has the units mg vitamin C/mL I_2 solution.)

Part 2. Analyzing Beverages for Vitamin C
Follow the procedure below for each of the beverages assigned for analysis by your teacher.

1. Measure 25 mL of beverage into a 125-mL Erlenmeyer flask.

2. Follow steps 2–5 in Part I. Note that a colored beverage may produce an "off-blue" endpoint color. For example, red beverage + blue starch-iodine color → purple endpoint.

3. Write the calculated volume of iodine solution used in your data table. Be sure also to enter the conversion factor value from the data table in Part 1.

4. Perform the indicated multiplication for each beverage to find the mass (mg) of vitamin C present in the 25-mL sample analyzed.

5. Finally, rank by number (1–5) the five beverages, from highest vitamin C level (No. 1) to lowest vitamin C level.

Questions
1. Did any of the vitamin C levels in the foods tested surprise you? Why?
2. What other common foods contain a high level of vitamin C?

Now we are ready to consider the trace substances called minerals. What are they, and what do they do in the body?

D.3 Minerals: An Elementary Part of Our Diet

Some of the most important life-supporting materials in our diet are inorganic substances called minerals. Some of these substances are most likely included in the collection of substances your teacher uses in common laboratory experiments. (But never taste any substances found in the chemistry laboratory.)

Some minerals are built into the body's structural molecules. Some help enzymes do their jobs. Others play vital roles in maintaining the health of heart, bones, and teeth. The thyroid gland, for example, needs a miniscule quantity of iodine (only millionths of a gram) to produce the hormone, thyroxine. The rapidly growing field of bioinorganic chemistry explores ways in which minerals function within living systems.

Of the more than 100 known elements, only 22 are currently believed essential to life. Carbon, hydrogen, nitrogen, and oxygen are so widely present both in living systems and in the environment that they are not included in lists of essential minerals. Essential minerals are commonly divided into two categories for convenience: **macrominerals,** or major minerals, and **trace minerals.** As the name suggests, macrominerals are present in relatively large quantities in the body. There are at least five grams of each macromineral in the body of an average adult human.

Trace minerals are present in relatively small quantities—less than five grams in the average adult. However, they are no less important than macrominerals. Each essential mineral can become a limiting factor, or limiting reactant, if it is not present in sufficient quantity. The minerals, their sources, functions, and deficiency conditions are listed in Table IV.12. Animal feeding studies suggest that in addition, cobalt (Co), nickel (Ni), arsenic (As), and cadmium (Cd) may be essential in trace quantities to human life.

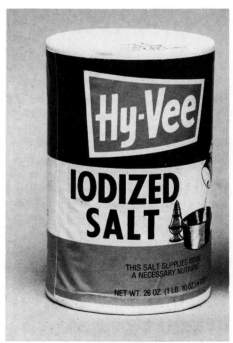

Jon Jacobson

Iodized salt is an important source of the trace mineral iodine.

Table IV.12 *Essential minerals: Sources, functions, and deficiency conditions*

Mineral	Source	Function	Deficiency condition
Macrominerals			
Calcium	Milk, dairy products, canned fish with bones	Essential to bone formation and maintenance, tooth formation; regulates nerve transmission, muscle contraction; involved in blood clotting, collagen maintenance	Rickets in children; osteomalacia and osteoporosis in adults
Phosphorus	Animal protein	Part of bone structure; in genetic code, energy transfer, and cell membrane molecules; helps maintain pH balance of body fluids	Practically unknown; not described
Potassium	Orange juice, bananas, dried fruits, potatoes	Maintenance of heartbeat, water balance, and cell integrity; necessary to nerve transmission, carbohydrate and protein metabolism	Sudden death during fasting; poor nerve function; irregular heartbeat
Chlorine	Meats, salt-processed foods, table salt	Foods digestion (HCl); keeps body fluids electrically neutral by diffusion	—
Sulfur	All proteins	Component of biomolecules and ions	—
Sodium	Meats, salt-processed foods, table salt	Regulation of amount of body fluid; involved in nerve transmission	Headache, weakness, thirst, poor memory, appetite loss
Magnesium	Nuts, legumes, cereal grains, dark green vegetables, seafoods, chocolate, cocoa	Catalyst in synthesis of energy carrier molecules; involved in protein synthesis and energy release, relaxing of muscles	Deficiency is result of fluid loss due to alcoholism or protein malnutrition; heart failure due to spasms
Trace minerals			
Fluorine	Seafoods, fluorinated drinking water	Bone and tooth structure	Dental decay
Chromium	Liver, animal and plant tissue	Necessary for glucose utilization	Loss of insulin efficiency with age
Manganese	Liver, kidney, wheat germ, legumes, nuts, tea	Cofactor for a number of enzymes	Weight loss, occasional dermatitis
Iron	Liver, meats, green leafy vegetables, whole grains	Component of oxygen-carrying proteins (hemoglobin and myoglobin)	Iron-deficiency anemia; tiredness and apathy
Cobalt	Liver, animal proteins	Part of vitamin B_{12}	Anemia
Copper	Liver, kidney, egg yolk, whole grains	Formation of hemoglobin, part of 11 enzymes	Rare
Selenium	Liver, organ meats, grains, vegetables	Part of enzymes; antioxidant that can substitute for vitamin E	Kashan disease, a heart disease found in parts of China
Zinc	Liver, shellfish, meats, wheat germ, legumes	Part of insulin and some 154 enzymes	Anemia; stunted growth
Molybdenum	Liver, kidney, whole grains, legumes, leafy vegetables	Part of enzymes	Unknown
Iodine	Seafoods, iodized salts	Part of thyroxin, regulates rate of energy use	Goiter (enlarged thyroid gland)

Table IV.13   *Selected essential minerals: RDAs*

Sex and age	Calcium (mg)	Phosphorus (mg)	Magnesium (mg)	Iron (mg)	Zinc (mg)	Iodine (µg)[a]
Males 11–14	1200	1200	350	18	15	150
Males 15–18	1200	1200	400	18	15	150
Males 19 and older	800	800	350	10	15	150
Females 11–18	1200	1200	300	18	15	150
Females 19–50	800	800	300	18	15	150
Females 51 and older	800	800	300	10	15	150

[a] µg = microgram = 10^{-6} g.

The suggestion that arsenic—widely known to be poisonous—may be an essential mineral may surprise you. In fact, it is not unusual for substances to be beneficial in low doses but toxic in higher doses. (Even table salt, NaCl, could be quite harmful if consumed in great enough quantities.)

In 1980, RDAs were reissued for various essential minerals. Table IV.13 summarizes these values for several macrominerals and trace elements. Use the values given in Table IV.13 to answer the following questions.

YOUR*TURN*

IV.10   Minerals in the Diet

1. A slice of whole wheat bread contains 0.8 mg iron. How many slices of whole wheat bread must you eat to meet your daily allowance of iron?

2. One cup of whole milk contains 288 mg calcium. How much milk must you drink per day to meet your daily allowance for this mineral?

3. One medium pancake contains 27 mg calcium and 0.4 mg iron. Does a pancake provide a greater percent of your RDA for calcium or for iron? How did you decide?

4. How many grams of calcium and phosphorus would you need on a yearly basis? Why is this figure so much higher than the quantity of other essential minerals listed? (*Hint:* Consider their use.) List several good sources for each of these two minerals. Do you think these sources would be readily available in developing countries? If not, what would you predict as the result of their deficiency? Would any particular age group or sex be especially affected?

5. Most table salt you buy has a small amount of potassium iodide (KI) added to the main ingredient, sodium chloride (NaCl). What is the purpose of this addition? If you follow the advice of many heart specialists and do not add salt to your food, what kinds of food would be good sources of iodine?

For 100% of his RDA of Ca^{2+}, an adult male needs 2.7 cups of milk:

$$(800 \text{ mg Ca}) \left(\frac{1 \text{ cup milk}}{288 \text{ mg Ca}} \right) = 2.7 \text{ cups milk}$$

How is the mineral content of a particular food determined? We'll explore one method in the following laboratory activity.

D.4 Laboratory Activity: Iron Content in Foods

Getting Ready

In this laboratory activity, you will investigate the relative levels of iron found in foods such as broccoli, spinach, raisins, parsley, kidney beans, and cauliflower.

Iron in foods exists as iron(II) or iron(III) ions. These are sometimes called ferrous (Fe^{2+}) and ferric (Fe^{3+}) ions. The iron(II) form is more readily absorbed from the intestine than is iron(III). Thus oral preparations for the treatment of iron-deficiency anemia are almost always iron(II) compounds. The most common ingredient is iron(II) sulfate, $FeSO_4$.

This laboratory activity is based on a very sensitive test for the presence of iron ions in solution. Under the experimental conditions, all iron in the sample is converted to iron(III) ions. The colorless thiocyanate ion, SCN^-, reacts with iron(III) to form an intensely red ion:

$$Fe^{3+}(aq) \ + \ SCN^-(aq) \longrightarrow Fe(SCN)^{2+}(aq)$$

| Iron(III) ion | Thiocyanate ion | Iron(III) thiocyanate ion (red color) |

The intensity of the resulting red color is related to the actual concentration of iron(III) originally present in the solution. The test is so sensitive that iron concentrations in the part-per-million range produce a noticeable reddish color! You will have color standards available that contain known concentrations of iron(III). Visual estimates of iron(III) concentrations are made by comparing the colors of test solutions with those of the color standards.

To remove organic portions of the foods that would interfere with the tests, the food samples are heated at a high temperature. The organic compounds burn and are driven off as water and carbon dioxide. Minerals present, such as iron, remain in the ash and are dissolved by an acid solution.

Procedure

1. Weigh out in separate porcelain crucibles 2.5 g samples of each of the two foods you have been assigned.
2. Place one food-containing crucible on a clay triangle supported by a ring stand. Heat the crucible (without cover) strongly with a hot Bunsen burner flame.
3. Continue heating until the food sample has turned to ash (preferably grayish white). Be careful that the ash is not blown from the crucible.
4. Remove the Bunsen burner and allow the crucible to remain in the clay triangle while it cools.
5. Begin heating the other food-containing crucible on a second clay triangle-ring stand set up. Continue heating until the sample has turned to ash.
6. Remove the Bunsen burner and allow the second sample to cool in place on the clay triangle.
7. When the first sample has cooled, transfer the entire ash residue to a 50 mL (or larger) beaker. Add 10 mL of 2 M HCl to the beaker and stir vigorously for 1 minute. Then add 5 mL of distilled water.
8. Prepare a filtration apparatus, including a ring stand, funnel support, and funnel. Place a piece of filter paper in the funnel and position a test tube under the funnel to collect the filtrate.
9. Pour the mixture from the beaker into the filtration apparatus and collect 5 mL of the filtrate in a test tube. Discard the residue left on the filter paper and the rest of the solution.
10. Add 5 mL of 0.1 M KSCN to the test tube containing the filtrate. Seal with the stopper. Invert the tube once to mix the solution.

11. Compare the resulting red color to the color standards. It may be helpful to hold white paper behind the tubes in making this comparison. Or try looking down into the tubes from the top on a light table if one is available; the intensities of colors will be greater this way.

12. Record the approximate iron concentration present in your sample, based on your comparison with the color standards.

13. Complete the procedure in steps 7–12 with your other food sample.

14. Obtain the iron results from other laboratory teams, recording the food product name and the estimated iron level in each resulting solution.

Questions

1. The color standards allowed you to estimate the percent iron in the solutions prepared from your food samples. Do these values also apply to the original 2.5-g food samples? Why or why not?

2. Based on this laboratory activity, name the foods that are the best and poorest sources of iron among the food samples tested by your class.

3. What kinds of materials might be found in the solid residues filtered from your solutions? (Can you name some elements that might be found?)

D.5 Food Additives: Necessity or Nuisance?

Vitamins and minerals are essential, naturally occurring substances present in food in small amounts. Some foods, especially processed foods (e.g., packaged cookies or frozen entrees) contain small amounts of **food additives**—substances added during processing to enhance the nutrition, storage life, appeal, or ease of production of foods.

A typical food label might give the following information:

Sugar, bleached flour (enriched with niacin, iron, thiamine, and riboflavin), semi-sweet chocolate, animal and/or vegetable shortening, dextrose, wheat starch, mono-calcium phosphate, baking soda, egg white, modified corn starch, salt, nonfat milk, cellulose gum, soy lecithin, xanthan gum, mono- and diglycerides, BHA, BHT.

Courtesy of The Pillsbury Company

Precise quality control is essential in food manufacturing facilities.

Quite a collection of ingredients! (Can you guess the identity of the food product with this label?) You probably recognize the major ingredients such as sugar, flour, shortening, and baking soda, and some additives such as the vitamins (thiamine, riboflavin) and the minerals (iron and monocalcium phosphate). But you probably do not recognize many of the additives, such as xanthan gum (an emulsifier) or BHT (butylated hydroxytoluene, a preservative).

Many food additives serve valuable purposes, especially in preserving foods or increasing their nutritive value. Others improve the consistency, taste, and appearance of foods. Intentional food additives have been used since ancient times. For example, salt has been used for centuries to preserve foods. As people have moved greater distances from farms, greater reliance has been placed on food preservation additives. Table IV.14 summarizes the major food additive categories. The chemical structures of a few common additives are shown in Figure IV.12.

Jon Jacobson

Why is it not necessarily a good idea to eliminate all additives and preservatives?

Figure IV.12 Common food additives.

Table IV.14 *Food additives*

Additive type	Purpose	Examples
Nutrients	Improve nutritive value	Vitamins and minerals; iodine in iodized salt, B vitamins in enriched flour
Flavoring agents	Add or enhance flavor	Salt, monosodium glutamate (MSG), spices
Preservatives, antimyotic agents (growth inhibitors)	Prevent spoilage, microbial growth	Propionic acid, sorbic acid, benzoic acid, and salt retard mold growth on cheese, bread; sodium nitrite in meats adds to flavor, maintains pink color, and prevents growth of *Clostridium botulinum*
Antioxidants	Prevent fat rancidity	BHA and BHT react with free radicals to prevent oxidation of unsaturated fats
Coloring agents	Increase visual appeal	Carotene—natural yellow color added to butter and margarine, converted to vitamin A in the body; synthetic dyes
Leavening agents	Make foods light in texture	Baking powder and baking soda produce CO_2, which expands food as it cooks
Bleaches	Whiten foods such as flour and cheese; hasten maturing of cheese	SO_2 bleaches, disinfects, and preserves dried foods; seems safe in foods except for persons allergic to it
Emulsifiers	Give texture, smoothness, other desired consistencies; stabilize oil-water mixtures	Cellulose gums, dextrins in whipped cream, cake mixes, mayonnaise
Anticaking agents	Keep foods free flowing	Sodium ferrocyanide added to salt to prevent caking
Humectants	Retain moisture	Glycerin
Sweeteners	Impart sweet taste	Sugar (sucrose), dextrin, fructose, saccharin, aspartame, sorbitol, mannitol

A processed food may also contain contaminants, materials that find their way into foods accidentally. Typical contaminants are trace amounts of pesticides from plants, antibiotics used to treat animals, or even traces of food packaging materials or dirt from the processing plant.

When we buy food at grocery stores or restaurants, we assume it is completely safe to eat. And, for the most part, this is true. Nonetheless, concerns have been raised often in recent years about food additives or contaminants suspected of posing hazards to human health.

Food quality in the United States is protected by law. The basis of the law is the Federal Food, Drug and Cosmetic Act of 1938, which authorizes the Food and Drug Administration (the FDA), as directed by Congress, to monitor the safety, purity, and wholesomeness of food. This act has been amended as concerns arose about various substances in foods, including the Miller Pesticide Amendment (1954; to establish safe levels of pesticide residues), the Color Additives Amendment (1958; to establish the safety of food dyes), and the Food Additives Amendment (1958), which addressed growing concerns over **carcinogens**—cancer-causing agents—in foods. Each amendment requires manufacturers to complete tests and provide extensive information on the safety of proposed products. Only with government approval based on the data provided can a new product be put on the market.

When the Food Additive Amendment was passed, ingredients that had been used for a long time and were known not to be hazardous were exempted. These substances are not legally defined as additives and make up the "Generally Recognized as Safe" (GRAS) list. This list is periodically reviewed in light of new findings. The GRAS list includes items such as salt, sugar, vinegar, vitamins, and some minerals.

The Delaney Clause in the Food Additives Amendment requires the testing of additives with animals. Approval of an additive is prohibited if it causes cancer when eaten in any amounts by animal species. There is concern today that the Delaney Clause went too far. In some cases, for example, amounts comparable to those that cause cancer in animals would be vastly more than could ever be encountered in a human diet. But the law stands, and causes some genuine chemical quandries.

Sodium nitrite ($NaNO_2$) is used as a color stabilizer and spoilage inhibitor in cured meats, such as hot dogs and bologna. Nitrites are particularly effective in inhibiting the growth of the bacterium *Clostridium botulinum,* which produces botulin toxin, cause of the disease known as botulism. Botulin toxin is so potent a poison that only one gram, suitably distributed, could kill the entire population of this planet.

The possibility that sodium nitrite is a cancer-causing agent has arisen. In the stomach, nitrites are converted to nitrous acid.

$$NaNO_2(aq) \quad + \quad HCl(aq) \quad \longrightarrow \quad HNO_2(aq) \quad + \quad NaCl(aq)$$

| Sodium nitrite | Hydrochloric acid | Nitrous acid | Sodium chloride |

Under certain conditions, nitrous acid can react with compounds formed during protein digestion. Some of the products formed are very potent carcinogens.

$$HNO_2 + R-\underset{\underset{R}{|}}{N}-H \longrightarrow R-\underset{\underset{R}{|}}{N}-N=O + H_2O$$

| Nitrous acid | Secondary amine | A nitrosamine | Water |

CHEM*QUANDARY*

The issue of nitrite additives in meats involves a complex balance of opposing risks. Eliminating nitrites from meats might increase the risk of botulin toxin formation—certainly a hazardous situation. But the presence of nitrites creates its own potential hazard, the possibility of formation of carcinogens in the body. Prepare a list of questions you believe should be researched to help resolve this dilemma.

We are a diet-conscious society, and sweeteners have attracted considerable attention. A new sweetener, aspartame (available under the trade name NutraSweet) was approved by the government not long ago, resulting in the release of "improved" diet sodas and other diet foods. The estimated cost of testing a chemical compound like aspartame to permit it to be marketed as a food additive is in the millions and requires three to ten years of research. The protection we desire is expensive; we pay for it in increased food costs.

Aspartame is a chemical combination of two natural amino acids, aspartic acid and phenylalanine. Gram for gram, it contains roughly the same quantity of food energy as table sugar (sucrose). However, it is about two hundred times sweeter. Thus, much smaller quantities of aspartame are needed to sweeten a product, explaining its appeal as a "low-calorie" sweetener. It has good flavor and no unpleasant aftertaste, a property that makes other low-calorie sweeteners (e.g., saccharin) less appealing.

As is possible for any food additive (and also many natural food components), aspartame may pose a hazard to a small number of individuals who are unable to utilize this sweetener in their body chemistry. Scientific evidence continues to be collected, but no serious alarm will be sounded unless evidence is found of grave potential harm. There are many reasons that persons with specific conditions may wish to avoid certain food additives. Diabetics must restrict their intake of sugar. Persons with high blood pressure must avoid salt. Some persons are allergic to certain foods and additives. If such restrictions apply to you, it is essential that you read food labels.

The Fair Packaging and Labeling Act of 1967 was a step in the direction of improved food labeling. Processed foods must be labeled with their contents listed in decreasing order of abundance, the most plentiful first. However, not all labels directly provide complete ingredient information. Also, some food labels are required to provide only the name of the food. The original act of 1938 gave approximately three hundred common foods, such as mayonnaise, what it called standards of identity. The law defined the basic ingredients of these foods; labels of any food with these basic ingredients do not list them, but the list is readily available.

Actually, being aware of what we eat is a wise habit for everyone. In the following activity, you'll investigate food labels and consider the additives listed.

D.6 *You Decide:* Food Additive Survey

1. Read the labels of 15 packaged foods. Select no more than three of the same food type—that is, no more than three breakfast cereals or three canned soups.

2. From the ingredient listings on the packages, select 10 additives that are not naturally found in foods.

3. Complete a summary table with the following format:
   a. List the 10 additives in a vertical column along the left side of the page.
   b. Fill in vertical columns for each additive with the following headings: Food product in which found, purpose of additive (if described on the label), other information regarding additive.

4. Use Table IV.14 to review the purpose of specific food additives. Then answer the following question: Which of the additives that you found do you think should be included in that particular food? Give your reasons.

5. Is it possible to purchase the same food product without some of the additives you found? If so, where? Is there a difference in price? If so, which is more expensive?

6. Are there alternatives to additives used to prevent spoilage?

PART D
SUMMARY *QUESTIONS*

1. Compare water-soluble and fat-soluble vitamins in terms of daily requirements, toxicity concerns with megadoses, and cooking precautions. List two examples of each type of vitamin and their function and dietary sources.

2. Defend or refute this statement: Macrominerals are more important than trace minerals. As part of your answer, cite an example of each including their function and dietary sources.

3. Given the typical serving sizes indicated (in Appendix A), which food group (fruits and vegetables, dairy products, meats, grains) is the best source of
   a. Calcium
   b. Iron
   c. Vitamin C
   d. Vitamin A

4. Calculate the number of cups of orange juice (consult Appendix A) a 17-year-old must drink to meet the RDA for vitamin C. How many cups of milk would be needed to meet this RDA?

5. Defend or refute this statement: All food additives represent unnatural additions of chemicals to our food and should be prohibited.

6. Of the additive types listed in Table IV.14, which do you think are the least essential? Which is (are) the most essential? Why?

7. Why is it wise to consider both risks and benefits when discussing banning certain food additives?

8. State the Delaney Clause and cite one argument in its favor and one argument against.

E PUTTING IT ALL TOGETHER: NUTRITION AROUND THE WORLD

What image do you have of nutrition in the United States? Are we the best-fed nation in the world? Are our farmers the most productive? How does the diet of a typical U.S. resident compare with other diets around the world? You are now ready to analyze your own diet and representative diets from various parts of the world. You will also be challenged in this closing food activity to analyze factors that influence the world's food supply.

E.1 *You Decide:* Your Diet, Part 2—Diet Analysis

Your teacher will redistribute the diet diary you completed in the opening days of studying this unit. You will use the information in Appendix A and previous text material to analyze the adequacy of your own diet. In the next section, you will compare the quality of your own diet with other diets.

Judging the nutritional quality of a diet would be simple if we consumed neatly packaged products labeled "carbohydrate," "protein," "fat," "vitamin C," and so on. Unfortunately for the purposes of our analysis, the foods we eat are generally mixtures of nutrients. A form of bookkeeping is needed to keep track of the nutrients consumed.

Jon Jacobson

Is this meal nutritionally balanced?

Appendix A provides the nutrient content for a variety of common foods. Suppose you have eaten four slices of roast beef and want to know how much iron you have consumed. First, you have to estimate how many ounces of beef you ate. Two ¼-inch slices of meat each about 2 × 4 inches represent 3 oz of meat. Let's assume your slices were twice this big. The table gives an iron content of 7.5 mg for 3 oz of beef (2 slices). You ate four slices that were twice as big, so you consumed 4 × 7.5 mg, or 30 mg of iron.

1. Using Appendix A and your three-day diet diary, find your total intake for the 3 days of each nutrient listed below. Where necessary, estimate portion sizes. Also, if something you ate is not listed, estimate its nutrient content based on values for similar foods.

   Food energy (in Calories)
   Protein (in grams)
   Iron (in milligrams)
   Vitamin B_1 (in milligrams)

2. Divide each nutritional total by 3 to obtain a daily average for each nutrient listed.

U.S. RDA values
Protein   65 g
Iron   18 mg
Vitamin B_1 1.5 mg

3. Listed in the margin are the U.S. Recommended Dietary Allowances for protein, iron, and vitamin B_1 (used to calculate the % RDA values listed on food packages). Calculate the percent of each of these three RDA that your diet provides. Also, calculate the percent of the average caloric intake in your diet (assume that an average daily diet includes 2400 Calories). How does your diet rate in terms of nutritional balance?

4. What suggestions do you have to improve the overall quality of your diet?

5. Would you be willing to make such changes in your diet? Why?

E.2 *You Decide:* Diet Analysis—Diets Around the World

Many factors influence food choices. Some are practical, such as cost and availability. Others are the result of cultural differences and habit. We have seen that protein needs can be met by different combinations of foods. In the United States we look primarily to meat, eggs, and dairy products for protein. In this country most beef cattle are raised in feedlots and eat grain. It takes approximately 16 kg of grain to grow 1 kg of beef. In other countries, cattle may graze on open range, digesting plant cellulose that most other creatures cannot digest. Although it takes considerable land area to produce one cow, the land is often of little value for other human uses.

6 kg of cornmeal would provide 20 people with 100% of the U.S. RDA for protein.

To the Eskimos and the Japanese, protein often means fish; to a Mexican it may be rice and beans combined. For the Tuareg, a tribe of nomads that roams the Sahara, the primary source of protein is a combination of millet and lentils.

The food energy, protein, iron, and vitamin B_1 in typical meals from several cultures are listed in Table IV.15, which also includes a U.S. "fast food" meal and a U.S. regular meal. By answering the following questions, you will compare the nutritional values of these typical meals.

1. Choose two cultures other than the United States from Table IV.15. Using the RDA values given in the margin in Part E.1, calculate the percent of the RDA and the percent caloric intake (based on an average of 2400 Calories daily) for these cultures just as you did in Part E.1 for your own daily average diet.

2. Find the corresponding percent values for the U.S. "fast food" meal and the U.S. regular meal listed in Table IV.15.

3. Choose a single representative main meal from your own diet diary. Find the corresponding values for this meal.

Table IV.15 *Some nutrients in a representative meal around the world*

	Food energy (Cal)	Protein (g)	Iron (mg)	Vitamin B$_1$ (mg)
Chinese	797	36	610.5	0.66
Eskimo	872	94	19.0	0.6
Japanese	766	47	8.8	0.56
Mexican	889	27	11.0	1.14
Tuareg	852	29	13.0	1.2
Ugandan	828	32	6.5	0.8
U.S. citizen				
Quick meal	886	23	4.8	0.08
Regular meal	1212	30	6.9	0.33

Source: Adapted from S. DeVore and T. White, *The Appetites of Man: An Invitation to Better Nutrition from Nine Healthier Societies.* Anchor Books, Anchor/Doubleday, Garden City, N.Y., 1978.

4. Which of the cultures you chose provides the most nutritious representative meal, based on its RDA values? Is this meal more or less nutritious than a U.S. regular meal? A U.S. "fast food" meal? Your own representative meal?

5. Your teacher will provide an opportunity to compare your results with those found for the other cultures. Which cultures (if any) have more nutritious representative meals than the U.S. meals in Table IV.15 and your own meal? Which have less nutritious meals?

6. What factors might determine the protein sources used in each culture? Are the major protein sources in your own diet the same as those in the United States in general?

7. The table below lists a daily diet that might be found in a developing nation. Perform an analysis of this diet by filling in the table.

Data table					
Meal	**Food**	**Calories**	**Proteins**	**Iron**	**Vitamin B$_1$**
Morning	Any fresh fruit				
Noon	Rice, ½ lb				
Snack	Any fresh fruit				
Evening	Rice, ½ lb				
	Fish, 1 serving (if available)				
TOTAL					
% U.S. RDA		—			
% 2400 Calories			—	—	—

8. How does this diet compare with others you have examined? Keep in mind that this diet is for a whole day, while Table IV.15 lists single representative meals.

9. What foods could be added to improve the overall quality of this daily diet? What factors should be kept in mind in choosing foods to supplement this diet if it were found in a developing nation?

The Bettmann Archive

As a result of a flood which wiped out the summer rice harvest, this family from northern Bangladesh is near starvation.

E.3 World Hunger

For most U.S. residents, getting a nutritionally balanced diet should be simply a matter of knowing what foods are needed and eating them. Everything necessary is available. Despite this, 20 million people in the United States are malnourished or undernourished (8% of the population), even though we produce enough to sell food to other countries. Let's explore some of the causes of hunger in this and other countries.

Three factors determine the abundance or scarcity of a resource, whether that item is gasoline, clean water, baseball cards, or food:

- Supply (How much is available?)
- Demand (How much is needed?)
- Distribution (Where is it and how can it be obtained?).

To analyze the complex, ever-changing relationships that govern the abundance of food, make use of Figure IV.13, what you have learned in this unit, and your general knowledge in considering the following questions.

Questions
1. List three factors that have caused food supplies to increase over the years.
2. List two major factors that influence the total demand for food.
3. List three major factors that influence the ways food is distributed either within a country or among countries.
4. Now think of the factors that determine the world's food supply as the "reactants" in a "chemical reaction."
   a. What natural factors serve as limiting reactants on the world's total food supply?
   b. How can modern science and technology overcome problems associated with these limiting reactants?
   c. Are there any "limiting reactants" which affect the food supply that cannot be overcome by science and technology?

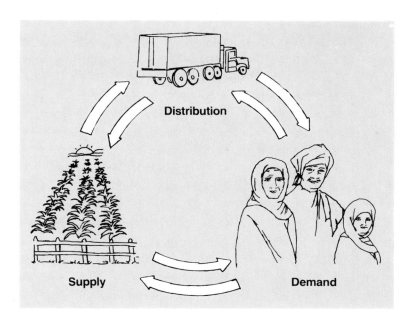

Figure IV.13   Food systems model.

d. Considering what you have already learned in this course about natural resources, propose and defend your choice of one limiting reactant of greatest importance in controlling expansion of the world's food supply through modern agricultural practices.

5. Based on the information given below, decide for yourself whether there is a worldwide food shortage:

- Annual world agriculture production, in Calories: 12,595,000,000,000
- Calories required daily, per person: 2400
- Number of people in the world: 5,200,000,000.

6. Give three reasons why hunger can still exist even when world food supplies are adequate.

7. Between 1966 and 1975 food production increased about 33% in the developed world and about 38% in the developing world—almost the same increase. In the same period, per capita food production increased about 20% in the developed world but remained virtually unchanged in the developing world. How can this be?

8. Estimates are that by the year 2000 the world population will be 6.5 billion. What does this mean for worldwide food production? How should the trend described in question 7 be taken into account in world wide food production?

E.4 Looking Back and Looking Ahead

As we conclude this fourth *ChemCom* unit, we have reached the halfway point in this chemistry course. You have considered many fundamental aspects of chemistry and chemical resources, as well as personal and social issues surrounding them. In the second half of this course, you will extend your understanding of chemical principles by exploring other important resources.

Our dependence on resources such as water, metals, petroleum, and food is quite apparent by now. However, with nuclear science, we will next encounter a topic that is probably more shrouded in misconceptions and justifiable public concern than any other topic we have considered thus far. In addition to introducing important chemical concepts, this topic will expand your understanding of the benefits and burdens of science and technology. One general goal remains to help you enter into enlightened public discussion of science-related social issues. Chemistry and you can make a difference.

Appendix A

Composition of Common Foods

Calories are entered first, along with the percentage of calories derived from protein, carbohydrate, and fat. The percentages may not always add up to 100, due to rounding. NA means not available.

The amounts of protein, vitamin A, vitamin C, thiamin (B_1), riboflavin (B_2), niacin, calcium, and iron are given next. Zero (0) indicates the nutrient is missing. The word "trace" means a nutrient is present in minimal amounts. Dashes (—) indicate the presence of a nutrient but lack of reliable data as to quantity.

Vitamin A in the Comprehensive List and the U.S. RDA is listed in International Units (IU). The 1980 Recommended Daily Dietary Allowances express vitamin A in Retinol Equivalents (R.E.). When the diet is composed of mixed foods, five IU equal one R.E. During the first six months of life, when it is assumed that all the vitamin A is supplied by milk, 1400 IU equal 420 R.E.

The nutrient amounts have been converted to percentages of the U.S. Recommended Daily Allowances (U.S. RDA). The raw percentages are rounded to the nearest whole percent, except for those under two, which are rounded to the nearest tenth of a percent.

Courtesy National Dairy Council

Milk

Milk	Calories	% Cal. from protein	% Cal. from carbohydrate	% Cal. from fat	Protein g	Vitamin A IU	Vitamin C mg	Thiamin (B₁) mg	Riboflavin (B₂) mg	Niacin mg	Calcium mg	Iron mg	% 2000 Calories	% 2500 Calories	% 3000 Calories	Protein %RDA	Vitamin A %RDA	Vitamin C %RDA	Thiamin (B₁) %RDA	Riboflavin (B₂) %RDA	Niacin %RDA	Calcium %RDA	Iron %RDA
Buttermilk, 1 cup (245 g)	99	33	47	20	8.11	81	2.40	.083	.377	.142	285	.12	5	4	3	18	1.6	4	6	22	0.7	29	0.7
Cheese, American, 1 oz (28 g)	106	24	1.7	75	6.28	343	0	.008	.100	.020	174	.11	5	4	4	14	7	0	0.5	6	0.1	17	0.6
Cheese, Cheddar, 1 oz (28 g)	114	25	1.3	74	7.06	300	0	.008	.106	.023	204	.19	6	5	4	16	6	0	0.5	6	0.1	20	1.1
Cheese, Cheddar, 1¼ oz (35 g)	142	25	1.3	74	8.83	375	0	.010	.133	.029	255	.24	7	6	5	20	8	0	0.7	8	0.1	26	1.3
Cheese, Cottage, ½ cup (105 g)	109	48	10	39	13.12	171	Trace	.022	.171	.133	63	.15	5	4	4	29	3	—	1.5	10	0.7	6	0.8
Cheese, Swiss, 1 oz (28 g)	107	30	4	65	8.06	240	0	.006	.103	.026	272	.05	5	4	4	18	5	0	0.4	6	0.1	27	0.3
Cocoa, ¾ cup (188 g)	164	17	47	37	6.83	239	1.80	.077	.326	.274	224	.59	8	7	5	15	5	3	5	19	1.4	22	3
Cream, Sour, 1 tbsp (12 g)	26	6	8	87	.38	95	.10	.004	.018	.008	14	0.1	1.3	1.0	0.9	0.8	1.9	0.2	0.3	1.1	—	1.4	0.1
Cream, Whipped, 1 tbsp (8 g)	26	2	3	96	.16	110	.045	.002	.008	.003	5	Trace	1.3	1.0	0.9	0.4	2	0.1	0.1	0.5	—	0.5	—
Half-and-Half, 1 tbsp (15 g)	20	9	13	77	.44	65	.13	.005	.022	.012	16	.1	1.0	0.8	0.7	1	1.3	0.2	0.3	1.3	0.1	1.6	0.1
Ice Cream, Vanilla, ½ cup, ¼ pint (67 g)	135	7	47	48	2.40	272	.35	.026	.165	.067	88	.06	7	5	5	5	5	0.6	1.7	10	0.3	9	0.3
Milk, 1 cup (244 g)	150	21	30	49	8.03	307	2.29	.093	.395	.205	291	.12	8	6	5	18	6	4	6	23	1.0	29	0.7
Milk, ¾ cup (183 g)	113	21	30	49	6.02	230	1.72	.070	.296	.154	218	.09	6	5	4	13	5	3	5	17	0.8	22	0.5
Milk, ½ cup (122 g)	75	21	30	49	4.02	154	1.15	.047	.198	.103	146	.06	4	3	3	9	3	1.9	3	12	0.5	15	0.3
Milk, Chocolate, 1 cup (250 g)	208	15	50	37	7.92	302	2.28	.092	.405	.313	280	.60	10	8	7	18	6	4	6	24	1.6	28	3
Milk, Lowfat (2%), 1 cup (244 g) fortified with vitamin A	121	27	39	35	8.12	500	2.32	.095	.403	.210	297	.12	6	5	4	18	10	4	6	24	1.1	30	0.7
Milk, Skim, 1 cup (245 g) fortified with vitamin A	86	39	55	5	8.35	500	2.40	.088	.343	.216	302	.10	4	3	3	19	10	4	6	20	1.1	30	0.6
Milkshake, Chocolate, 10.6 oz container (300 g)	356	10	71	20	9.15	258	0	.141	.666	.372	396	.93	18	14	12	20	5	0	9	39	1.9	40	5
Pudding, Chocolate, ½ cup (130 g)	161	11	68	21	4.4	169	Trace	0.03	0.20	0.1	133	0.4	8	6	5	10	3	—	2	12	0.5	13	2
Yogurt, Strawberry, 1 cup (227 g)	225	16	75	10	9.04	111	1.36	.077	.368	.195	314	.14	11	9	8	20	2	2	5	22	1.0	31	0.8

Meat and other protein-rich foods

Food																							
Bacon, ½ oz (15 gm)	92	21	2	76	4.6	0	—	0.08	0.05	0.8	2	0.5	5	4	3	10	0	—	5	3	4	0.2	3
Beans, Refried, ½ cup (150 gm)	142	22	75	5	8.85	—	—	—	—	—	4.5	—	7	6	5	14	—	—	—	—	—	0.5	—
Beef, Roast, 3 oz (85 gm)	182	60	0	40	25.5	17	—	0.04	0.20	3.9	11	3.2	9	7	6	57	0.3	—	3	12	20	1.1	18
Beef Liver, 3 oz (85 gm)	195	49	9	42	22.5	45417	23	0.22	3.56	14.0	9	7.5	10	8	7	50	908	38	15	209	70	0.9	42
Bologna, 1 oz (28 gm)	86	17	1.4	82	3.4	0	—	0.05	0.06	0.7	2	0.5	4	3	3	8	0	—	3	4	4	0.2	3
Chicken, Fried, 3 oz (85 gm)	201	55	3	42	26.0	148	0	0.06	0.38	5.9	12	2.0	10	8	7	58	3	—	4	22	30	1.2	11
Egg, Fried, large (46 g)	83	26	2	70	5.37	286	0	.033	.126	.026	26	.92	4	3	3	12	6	0	2	7	0.1	3	5
Egg, Hard-cooked, large (50 g)	79	31	3	64	6.07	260	0	.037	.143	.030	28	1.04	4	3	3	13	5	0	2	8	0.2	3	6
Egg, Scrambled, large (64 g)	95	25	6	67	5.96	311	.13	.039	.156	.042	47	0.93	5	4	3	13	6	0.2	3	9	0.2	5	5
Frankfurter, 2 oz (57 gm)	172	17	2	81	7.0	—	—	0.09	0.11	1.4	3	0.9	9	7	6	16	—	—	6	6	7	0.3	5
Ham, Baked, 3 oz (85 gm)	179	61	0	39	25.7	0	—	0.56	0.26	4.9	11	3.2	9	7	6	57	0	—	37	15	25	1.1	18
Meat Loaf, 3 oz (85 gm)	230	28	23	48	15.3	106	Trace	0.27	0.24	3.4	68	2.4	12	9	8	34	2	—	18	14	17	7	13
Meat Patty, 3 oz (85 gm)	186	53	0	47	23.3	17	—	0.08	0.20	5.1	10	3.0	9	7	6	52	0.3	—	5	12	26	1.0	17
Peanut Butter, 2 tbsp (32 gm)	186	17	12	71	8.9	—	0	0.04	0.04	5.0	20	0.6	9	7	6	14	—	0	3	2	25	2	3
Peanuts, Salted, ¼ cup (36 gm)	211	15	13	71	9.4	—	0	0.12	0.05	6.2	27	0.8	11	8	7	14	—	0	8	3	31	3	4
Peas, Blackeye (immature), ½ cup (124 gm)	134	26	68	6	10.0	434	21	0.37	0.14	1.7	30	2.6	7	5	4	15	9	35	25	8	9	3	14
Peas, Blackeye (mature), ½ cup (124 gm)	94	23	74	4	6.3	12	—	0.20	0.05	0.5	21	1.6	5	4	3	10	0.2	—	13	3	3	2	9
Perch, Fried, Breaded, 3 oz (85 gm)	193	NA	NA	NA	16.2	—	—	0.09	0.09	1.5	28	1.1	10	8	6	36	—	—	6	5	8	3	6
Pork Chop, 3 oz (85 gm)	308	29	0	71	20.8	0	—	0.82	0.24	4.9	9	2.7	15	12	10	46	0	—	55	14	25	0.9	15
Sausage, 1 oz (28 gm)	135	16	Trace	84	5.1	0	—	0.22	0.10	1.1	2	0.7	7	5	5	11	0	—	15	6	6	0.6	4
T-Bone Steak, 3⅓ oz (95 gm)	212	58	0	42	29.0	19	—	0.08	0.22	5.6	11	3.5	11	8	7	64	0.4	—	5	13	28	1.1	19
Tuna, 3 oz (85 gm)	168	62	0	38	24.5	68	—	0.04	0.10	10.1	7	1.6	8	7	6	54	1.4	—	3	6	51	0.7	9

Fruit-Vegetable	Calories	% Calories from protein	% Calories from carbohydrate	% Calories from fat	Protein g	Vitamin A IU	Vitamin C mg	Thiamin (B_1) mg	Riboflavin (B_2) mg	Niacin mg	Calcium mg	Iron mg	% 2000 Calories	% 2500 Calories	% 3000 Calories	Protein (RDA)	Vitamin A (RDA)	Vitamin C (RDA)	Thiamin (B_1) (RDA)	Riboflavin (B_2) (RDA)	Niacin (RDA)	Calcium (RDA)	Iron (RDA)
Apple, medium (138 gm)	80	1.3	90	8	0.3	124	6	0.04	0.03	0.1	10	0.4	4	3	3	0.5	2	10	3	1.8	0.5	1.0	2
Applesauce, ½ cup (128 gm)	116	0.9	94	0.7	0.3	51	1	0.03	0.01	Trace	5	0.6	6	5	4	0.5	1.0	1.7	2	0.6	—	0.5	3
Apricots, Dried, 4 halves (15 gm)	39	7	92	2	0.8	1635	2	Trace	0.02	0.5	10	0.8	2	1.3	1.3	1.2	33	3	—	1.2	3	1.0	4
Asparagus, 4 spears, ½ cup (60 gm)	12	26	65	7	1.3	540	16	0.10	0.11	0.8	13	0.4	0.6	0.5	0.4	2	11	27	7	6	4	1.3	2
Banana, medium (119 gm)	101	4	94	1.7	1.3	226	12	0.06	0.07	0.8	10	0.8	5	4	3	2	5	20	4	4	4	1.0	4
Beans, Green, ½ cup (63 gm)	16	15	76	5	1.0	338	8	0.04	0.06	0.3	31	0.4	0.8	0.6	0.5	1.5	7	13	3	4	1.5	3	2
Beans, Lima, ½ cup (85 gm)	94	24	73	- 4	6.5	238	14	0.15	0.09	1.1	40	2.1	5	4	3	10	5	23	10	5	6	4	12
Beets, ½ cup (83 gm)	31	7	90	3	0.8	17	2	0.01	0.02	0.1	16	0.6	1.6	1.2	1.0	1.2	0.3	3	0.7	1.2	0.5	1.6	3
Broccoli, stalk, ½ cup (78 gm)	20	29	62	8	2.4	1938	70	0.07	0.16	0.6	68	0.6	1.0	0.8	0.7	4	39	117	5	9	3	7	3
Cabbage, ⅙ head, ½ cup (73 gm)	13	13	80	13	0.7	87	17	0.01	0.01	0.1	30	0.2	0.7	0.5	0.4	1.1	1.7	28	0.7	0.6	0.5	3	1.1
Cantaloupe, ¼ medium (96 gm)	29	8	89	3	0.7	3273	32	0.04	0.03	0.6	13	0.4	1.5	1.0	1.0	1.1	65	53	3	1.8	3	1.3	2
Carrots, ½ cup (73 gm)	22	9	89	4	0.7	7613	4	0.04	0.04	0.4	24	0.4	1.1	0.7	0.7	1.1	152	7	3	2	2	2	2
Carrot Sticks, 5" carrot (50 gm)	21	8	90	4	0.6	5500	4	0.03	0.03	0.3	19	0.4	1.1	0.8	0.7	0.9	110	7	2.0	1.8	1.5	1.9	2
Cauliflower, ½ cup (60 gm)	13	26	69	6	1.4	36	33	0.05	0.05	0.4	13	0.4	0.7	0.5	0.4	2	0.7	55	3	3	2	1.3	2
Celery Sticks, 8" stalk (57 gm)	10	12	79	8	0.5	136	5	0.02	0.02	0.2	22	0.2	0.5	0.4	0.3	0.8	3	8	1.3	1.2	1.0	2	1.1
Coleslaw, ½ cup (57 gm)	82	2	12	85	0.7	91	16	0.03	0.03	0.2	25	0.2	4	3	3	1.1	1.8	27	2	1.8	1.0	3	1.1
Corn, ½ cup (83 gm)	70	8	84	8	2.2	291	3	0.02	0.04	0.8	4	0.4	4	3	2	3	6	5	1.3	2	4	0.4	2
Corn, 5" ear (125 gm)	114	9	82	10	4.1	500	11	0.15	0.13	1.8	4	0.8	6	5	4	6	10	18	10	8	9	0.4	4
Fruit Salad, ½ cup (170 gm) apple, orange, banana, lettuce	99	5	90	4	1.5	530	44	0.11	0.08	0.7	45	0.9	5	3		2	11	73	7	5	4	5	5
Grapefruit, pink, ½ medium (118 gm)	48	4	94	1.7	0.6	94	45	0.05	0.02	0.2	19	0.5	2	1.6	1.6	0.9	10	75	3	1.2	1.0	1.9	3
Grapes, ½ cup (71 gm)	48	3	92	3	0.4	71	3	0.04	0.02	0.2	9	0.3	2	1.6	1.6	0.6	1.4	5	3	1.2	1.0	0.9	1.7

258

Greens, ½ cup (78 gm) mustard greens, kale, turnip greens	17	27	61	10		1.9	5306	36	0.08	0.13	0.4	104	1.4	0.9	0.7	0.6	3	106	60	5	8	2	10	8
Lettuce, ⅙ head, ½ cup (76 gm)	10	17	79	8		0.7	250	5	0.05	0.05	0.2	15	0.4	0.5	0.4	0.3	1.1	5	8	3	3	1.0	1.5	2
Lettuce Leaves, 2 large (50 gm)	9	19	71	19		0.7	950	9	0.03	0.04	0.2	34	0.7	0.5	0.4	0.3	1.1	19	15	2	2	1.0	3	4
Okra, 4 pods, ½ cup (43 gm)	12	18	77	7		0.9	208	9	0.06	0.08	0.4	39	0.2	0.6	0.5	0.4	1.4	4	15	4	5	2	4	1.1
Onions, ½ cup (105 gm)	30	12	87	3		1.3	Trace	7	0.03	0.03	0.2	25	0.4	1.5	1.2	1.0	2	—	12	2	1.8	1.0	3	2
Orange, medium (131 gm)	65	7	89	4		1.3	263	66	0.13	0.05	0.5	54	0.5	3	3	2	2	5	110	9	3	3	5	3
Orange Juice, ½ cup (125 gm)	56	5	93	1.4		0.9	249	56	0.11	0.01	0.4	11	0.1	3	2	1.9	1.4	5	93	7	0.6	2	1.1	0.6
Peaches, ½ cup (128 gm)	100	1.8	97	1.1		0.5	550	4	0.01	0.03	0.8	5	0.4	5	4	3	0.8	11	6	0.9	1.5	4	0.5	2
Pear, medium (166 gm)	101	4	90	6		1.2	33	7	0.03	0.07	0.2	13	0.5	5	4	3	1.9	0.7	12	2	4	1.0	1.3	3
Peas, Blackeye (see meat)																								
Peas, Green, ½ cup (80 gm)	54	26	71	3		4.1	480	10	0.22	0.07	1.4	15	1.5	3	2	1.8	6	10	17	15	4	7	1.5	8
Pineapple, large slice (122 gm)	90	1.5	95	0.9		0.4	61	9	0.10	0.02	0.2	13	0.4	5	4	3	0.6	1.2	15	7	1.2	1.0	1.3	2
Potato, Baked, large (142 gm)	132	8	91	0.6		3.7	Trace	28	0.14	0.06	2.4	13	1.0	7	5	4	6	—	47	9	4	12	1.3	6
Potatoes, Boiled, 2 small (122 gm)	79	8	90	1.1		2.3	Trace	20	0.11	0.04	1.5	7	0.6	4	3	3	4	—	33	7	2	8	0.7	3
Potatoes, French-Fried, 20 pieces (85 gm)	233	4	53	40		3.7	Trace	18	0.11	0.07	2.6	13	1.1	12	9	8	6	—	30	7	4	13	1.3	6
Potatoes, Mashed, ½ cup (98 gm)	63	10	81	10		2.0	20	10	0.08	0.05	1.0	23	0.4	3	3	2	3	0.4	17	5	3	5	2	2
Potato, Sweet, ½ medium (55 gm)	78	4	92	3		1.2	4455	12	0.05	0.04	0.4	22	0.5	4	3	3	1.9	89	20	3	2	2	2	3
Prunes, Stewed, 4 medium, 2 tbsp juice (60 gm)	108	2	94	0.8		0.7	456	1	0.02	0.04	0.4	19	0.9	5	4	4	1.1	9	1.7	1.3	2	2	1.9	5
Raisins, 4½ tbsp (43 gm)	123	3	96	0.7		1.1	9	Trace	0.05	0.03	0.2	26	1.5	6	5	4	1.7	0.2	—	3	1.8	1.0	3	8
Squash, Summer, ½ cup (105 gm)	16	17	74	10		1.1	462	12	0.05	0.08	0.8	26	0.4	0.8	0.6	0.5	1.7	9	20	5	5	4	3	2
Squash, Winter, ½ medium, ½ cup (103 gm)	56	8	92	1.5		1.9	1435	13	0.05	0.13	0.7	40	1.1	3	2	1.8	3	29	22	3	8	4	4	6
Strawberries, ½ cup (75 gm)	28	6	81	12		0.5	45	44	0.02	0.05	0.4	16	0.7	1.4	1.1	0.9	0.8	0.9	73	1.3	3	2	1.6	4
Tomato, ½ medium (100 gm)	22	17	77	8		1.1	900	23	0.06	0.04	0.7	13	0.5	1.1	0.9	0.7	1.7	18	38	4	2	4	1.3	3

Fruit-Vegetable—Continued / **Grain**

Food	Calories	% Calories from protein	% Calories from carbohydrate	% Calories from fat	Protein g	Vitamin A IU	Vitamin C mg	Thiamin (B₁) mg	Riboflavin (B₂) mg	Niacin mg	Calcium mg	Iron mg	% 2000 Calories	% 2500 Calories	% 3000 Calories	Protein % Calories	Vitamin A % RDA	Vitamin C % RDA	Thiamin (B₁) % RDA	Riboflavin (B₂) % RDA	Niacin % RDA	Calcium % RDA	Iron % RDA
Tomato Juice, ½ cup (122 gm)	26	14	78	3	1.1	972	19	0.06	0.04	1.0	9	1.1	1.3	1.0	0.9	1.7	19	32	4	2	5	0.9	6
Tossed Salad, ¾ cup (59 gm) lettuce, green pepper, radish, carrot	13	14	76	6	0.7	1380	26	0.03	0.04	0.3	26	0.6	0.6	0.5	0.4	1.1	28	43	2	2	1.5	3	3
Watermelon, 1 cup (200 gm)	52	6	89	6	1.0	1180	14	0.06	0.06	0.4	14	1.0	2	1.7	1.5	1.5	24	23	4	4	2	1.4	6
Grain																							
Bagel (55 gm)	165	15	70	10	6	30	0	0.14	0.10	1.2	9	1.2	8	7	6	9	0.6	0	9	6	6	0.9	7
Biscuit, Baking Powder, enriched (28 gm)	103	8	51	41	2.1	Trace	Trace	0.08	0.08	0.8	34	0.4	5	4	3	3	—	—	5	5	4	3	2
Bread, White, slice, enriched (23 gm)	61	13	78	10	2.0	Trace	Trace	0.09	0.06	0.8	19	0.6	3	2	2	3	—	—	6	4	4	1.9	3
Bread, Whole Wheat, slice (23 gm)	55	16	74	11	2.4	Trace	Trace	0.06	0.03	0.6	22	0.5	3	2	1.8	4	—	—	4	1.8	3	2	3
Cornbread, 2½" × 3", enriched (85 gm)	191	12	64	24	6.0	264	1	0.14	0.20	0.9	93	1.2	10	8	6	9	5	1.7	9	12	5	9	7
Cornflakes, ¾ cup (19 gm)	72	8	92	1.2	1.5	0	0	0.08	0.02	0.4	3	0.3	4	3	2	2	0	0	5	1.2	2	0.3	1.7
Crackers, Graham, 2 (14 gm)	54	7	72	20	1.1	0	0	0.01	0.03	0.2	6	0.2	3	2	1.8	1.7	0	0	0.7	1.8	1.0	0.6	1.1
Crackers, Saltines, 5 (14 gm)	60	8	67	24	1.2	0	0	Trace	0.01	0.1	3	0.2	3	2	2	1.9	0	0	—	0.6	0.5	0.3	1.1
Hominy Grits, ½ cup, enriched (123 gm)	62	8	91	1.4	1.5	74	0	0.05	0.04	0.5	1	0.4	3	2	2	2	1.5	0	3	2	3	0.1	2
Noodles, Egg, ½ cup, enriched (80 gm)	100	13	77	10	3.3	56	0	0.11	0.06	1.0	8	0.7	5	4	3	5	1.1	0	7	4	5	0.8	4
Oatmeal, ½ cup (120 gm)	66	13	72	15	2.4	0	0	0.10	0.02	0.1	11	0.7	3	3	2	4	0	0	7	1.2	0.5	1.1	4
Pancake, 4" diameter, enriched (27 gm)	61	13	59	29	1.9	68	Trace	0.06	0.08	0.3	58	0.3	3	2	2	3	1.4	Trace	4	5	1.5	6	1.7
Rice, ½ cup (103 gm)	112	7	92	0.7	2.1	0	0	0.11	0.07	1.0	10	0.9	6	4	3	3	0	0	7	4	5	1.0	5
Roll, Frankfurter, enriched (40 gm)	119	11	73	15	3.3	Trace	Trace	0.16	0.10	1.3	30	0.8	6	5	4	5	—	—	11	6	7	0.8	4
Roll, Hamburger, enriched (40 gm)	119	11	73	15	3.3	Trace	Trace	0.16	0.10	1.3	30	0.8	6	5	4	5	—	—	11	6	7	1.0	4
Roll, Hard, enriched (50 gm)	156	13	79	9	4.9	Trace	Trace	0.20	0.12	1.7	24	1.2					—	—	13	7		3	7

Food	1	2	3	4	5	6	7	8	9	10	11	12	13	14	15	16	17	18	19	20	21	22	23
Toast, White, slice (20 gm)	61	13	78	10	2.0	Trace	Trace	0.09	0.06	0.8	19	0.6	3	2	2	3	—	—	6	4	4	1.9	3
Tortilla, Corn, 6″ diameter, enriched (30 gm)	63	NA	NA	NA	1.5	6	0	0.04	0.02	0.3	60	0.9	3	3	2	2	0.1	0	3	1.2	1.5	6	5
Waffles, 2, 3½″ × 5½″, enriched (47 gm)	130	13	54	34	4.2	109	Trace	0.09	0.14	0.6	113	0.6	6	5	4	7	2	—	6	8	3	11	3
Combinations																							
Beans, Baked, Pork and Tomato Sauce, ½ cup (128 gm)	156	17	63	19	7.8	166	3	0.10	0.04	0.8	69	2.3	8	6	5	12	3	5	7	2	4	7	13
Beef and Vegetable Stew, 1 cup (235 gm)	209	29	28	44	15.0	2303	16	0.14	0.16	4.5	28	2.8	10	8	7	23	46	27	9	9	23	3	16
Chili Con Carne with Beans, 1 cup (250 gm)	333	22	37	41	18.8	150	—	0.08	0.18	3.3	80	4.3	17	13	11	29	3	—	5	11	17	8	24
Custard, Baked, ½ cup (133 gm)	152	20	37	43	7.2	464	Trace	0.05	0.25	0.1	148	0.5	8	6	5	16	9	—	3	15	0.5	15	3
Macaroni and Cheese, ½ cup (100 gm)	215	16	38	45	8.4	430	Trace	0.10	0.20	0.9	181	0.9	11	9	7	13	9	—	7	12	5	18	5
Pizza, Cheese, ¼ of 14″ pie, enriched (150 gm)	354	20	49	31	18.0	945	12	0.38	0.49	3.8	332	2.7	18	14	12	28	19	20	25	29	19	33	15
Soup, Chicken Noodle, 1 cup (226 gm)	59	23	52	27	3.2	45	Trace	0.02	0.02	0.7	9	0.5	3	2	1.9	5	0.9	—	1.3	1.2	4	0.9	3
Soup, Cream of Tomato, 1 cup (250 gm)	173	14	50	36	6.5	1200	15	0.10	0.25	1.3	168	0.8	9	7	6	10	24	25	7	15	7	17	4
Spaghetti, Meat Balls and Tomato Sauce, 1 cup (248 gm)	332	22	47	31	18.6	1587	22	0.25	0.30	4.0	124	3.7	17	13	11	29	32	37	17	18	20	12	21
Taco, Beef (108 gm)	216	NA	NA	NA	16.9	352	4	0.10	0.19	3.0	174	2.6	11	9	7	38	7	7	7	11	15	17	14
Others																							
Bar, Milk Chocolate, 1 oz (28 gm)	147	6	40	55	2.2	77	Trace	0.02	0.10	0.1	65	0.3	7	6	5	3	1.5	—	1.3	6	0.5	7	1.7
Beer, 1½ cups (360 gm)	151	3	37	0	1.1	—	—	Trace	0.11	2.2	18	Trace	8	6	5	1.7	—	—	6	6	11	1.8	—
Butter, 1 tsp (5 gm)	36	Trace	Trace	100	0.4	153	0	Trace	0.002	0.002	1	Trace	1.8	1.4	1.2	0.1	3	0	0.1	0.1	—	0.1	—
*Cake, Devil's Food, ¹⁄₁₆ of 9″ cake (69 gm)	234	4	64	32	3.0	104	Trace	0.02	0.06	0.2	41	0.6	12	9	8	5	2	—	1.3	4	1.0	4	3
Cake, Sponge, ½ of 10″ cake (66 gm)	196	11	72	17	5.0	297	Trace	0.03	0.09	0.1	20	0.8	10	8	7	8	6	—	2	5	0.5	2	4
Chocolate Syrup, 2 tbsp (38 gm)	93	1.8	91	7	0.9	Trace	0	0.01	0.03	0.15	6	0.6	5	4	3	1.4	—	0	0.7	1.8	0.8	0.6	3

Others—Continued

Food	Calories	% Cal. from protein	% Cal. from carbohydrate	% Cal. from fat	Protein g	Vitamin A IU	Vitamin C mg	Thiamin (B_1) mg	Riboflavin (B_2) mg	Niacin mg	Calcium mg	Iron mg	% 2000 Cal.	% 2500 Cal.	% 3000 Cal.	Protein % RDA	Vitamin A % RDA	Vitamin C % RDA	Thiamin (B_1) % RDA	Riboflavin (B_2) % RDA	Niacin % RDA	Calcium % RDA	Iron % RDA
Coffee, Black, ¾ cup (170 gm)	2	Trace	Trace	Trace	Trace	0	0	0	Trace	0.5	3	0.2	0.1	0.08	0.06	—	0	0	0	—	3	0.3	1.1
Cookie, Sugar, 3″ diameter, enriched (20 gm)	89	6	60	34	1.2	22	Trace	0.04	0.04	0.4	16	0.3	4	4	3	1.9	0.4	—	3	2	2	1.6	1.7
Doughnut, Cake Type, enriched (32 gm)	125	5	53	42	1.5	26	Trace	0.07	0.07	0.5	13	0.4	6	5	4	2	0.5	—	5	4	3	1.3	2
French Dressing, 1 tbsp (16 gm)	66	0.5	16	83	0.1	—	—	—	—	—	2	0.1	3	3	2	0.2	—	—	—	—	—	—	0.6
Gelatin Dessert, ½ cup (120 gm)	71	10	90	0	1.8	—	—	—	—	—	—	—	4	3	2	3	—	—	—	—	—	0.2	—
Jelly, Current, 1 tbsp (18 gm)	49	0	100	0	0	2	1	Trace	0.01	0	4	0.3	2	2	1.6	0	0	1.7	—	0.6	0	0.4	1.7
Mayonnaise, 1 tbsp (14 gm)	101	0.8	1.0	98	0.2	39	—	Trace	0.01	Trace	3	0.1	5	4	3	0.4	0.8	—	—	0.6	—	0.3	0.6
Pie, Apple, ⅙ of 9″ pie, enriched (158 gm)	403	3	58	38	3.5	47	2	0.15	0.13	1.7	13	1.1	20	16	13	5	0.9	3	10	8	9	1.3	6
Popcorn, Plain, 1 cup (6 gm)	23	9	81	11	0.8	—	0	—	0.01	0.1	1	0.2	1.2	0.9	0.8	1.2	—	0	—	0.6	0.5	0.1	1.1
Potato Chips, 10 chips (20 gm)	114	3	35	62	1.1	Trace	3	0.04	0.01	1.0	8	0.4	6	5	4	1.7	—	5	3	0.6	5	0.8	2
Roll, Danish Pastry (65 gm)	274	7	44	49	4.8	202	Trace	0.05	0.10	0.5	33	0.6	14	11	9	7	4	—	3	6	3	3	3
Sherbet, Orange, ½ cup (97 gm)	135	3	87	13	1.08	93	2	0.02	0.04	0.07	51.5	0.16	7	5	4	2	2	3	1.3	2.4	0.3	5	0.8
Soft Drink, Cola, 1 cup (246 gm)	96	0	99	0	0	0	0	0	0	0	—	—	5	4	3	0	0	0	0	0	0	—	—
Sugar, 1 tsp (4 gm)	14	0	100	0	0	0	0	0	0	0	0	Trace	0.7	0.6	0.5	0	0	0	0	0	0	0	—
Wine, Rosé, 3½ oz (102 gm)	87	0.4	19	—	0.1	—	Trace	Trace	0.01	0.1	9	0.4	4	3	3	0.2	—	0	—	0.6	0.5	0.9	2

Column groups: *Caloric Information* (Calories, % Calories from protein, % Calories from carbohydrate, % Calories from fat); *Nutritive Values* (Protein g … Iron mg); *% Calories* (% 2000 Calories, % 2500 Calories, % 3000 Calories); *% U.S. RDA* (Protein … Iron).

1. Formula for computation of percentages of the National Research Council's Recommended Daily Dietary Allowances (NRC RDA)

$$\left(\frac{\text{Amount of a nutrient (or Calories) in the food}}{\text{NRC RDA for that nutrient}}\right) \times 100\% = \underline{\quad\quad} \%$$

2. Formula for computation of percentages of the Food and Drug Administration's Recommended Daily Allowances (U.S. RDA)

$$\left(\frac{\text{Amount of a nutrient in the food}}{\text{U.S. RDA for that nutrient}}\right) \times 100\% = \underline{\quad\quad} \%$$

Example:

$$\frac{25.5\text{ g (protein in beef, roast)}}{44\text{ g (NRC RDA for protein for girl, 11–14)}} = 0.579 \qquad 0.579 \times 100 = 58\%$$

UNIT *FIVE*

**Nuclear
Chemistry in
Our World**

CONTENTS

INTRODUCTION

Naturally occurring nuclear phenomena have been part of everyday life since time began. Our sun runs on nuclear power, as does every other star. When scientists unlocked the secrets of the atom, they unleashed on Earth the Universe's strongest known force. The nuclear energy liberated from a few grams of nuclear fuel is equivalent to that released by burning thousands of gallons of gasoline. How can we best make use of this energy and how can we deal wisely with the potential dangers associated with it, such as nuclear weapons and nuclear waste?

One goal of this unit is to present some of the most exciting discoveries of the past century—ones that have reshaped not only the world of science, but our everyday world as well. Another goal is to provide you with the scientific understanding needed to consider rationally some social, political, economic, and ethical questions raised by nuclear technology.

Almost every application of nuclear science can have either positive or negative aspects. Nuclear science has made important technological contributions to our energy needs, to industry, to biological research, and especially to medicine. Nuclear radiation, one cause of cancer, can be used also to treat cancer. But producing and using nuclear energy involve some risk of accidents. Any radioactive material must be handled with extreme care. Instruments are the only way to sense the presence of radioactivity. Furthermore, all applications of nuclear technology contribute to a problem that has not yet been resolved: What should be done with the radioactive waste?

All new technologies create new risks. Are the risks of nuclear technology worth the benefits? Some uses of nuclear technology create greater risks than others, and some offer greater benefits than others. With the information provided in this unit you should be better able to decide which uses of nuclear technology are worth the risks they create. As a voting citizen you will help influence the use of nuclear technology in our society.

How much of your information about nuclear science and technology is actually true? How much is false? And how much is a matter of controversy—even among experts? The following activity will allow you to assess your knowledge of nuclear issues.

I.1 *You Decide:* Public Understanding of Nuclear Phenomena

Following is a survey consisting of a set of statements. Take the survey yourself. During the next week, give it to three other individuals: two persons born before 1945, and a third person who is a high school junior or senior not presently taking chemistry. All survey results will be combined and analyzed in the final section of this unit.

Survey on Nuclear Phenomena

First complete these two introductory items:

Birthdate:

_____ Before 1945   _____ After 1945

Major source of your knowledge of nuclear phenomena:
_____ School _____ Television _____ Scientific magazines
_____ Magazines/newspapers _____ Conversations with others

The following statements are designed to survey your understanding of nuclear-related phenomena. Mark the blanks to indicate whether you agree (A), disagree (D), or are unable to answer because of insufficient knowledge (U).

_____ 1. The atom is the smallest particle in nature.

_____ 2. Home smoke detectors may contain radioactive materials.

_____ 3. Radioactive materials and radiation are unnatural. They did not exist on Earth until created by scientists.

_____ 4. All radiation causes cancer.

_____ 5. Most of the space occupied by an atom is "empty."

_____ 6. Electromagnetic radiation should be avoided at all costs.

_____ 7. The human body is capable of detecting radioactivity.

_____ 8. Nuclear wastes are initially both thermally "hot" and radioactive.

_____ 9. All atoms of a given element are alike in all respects.

_____ 10. Radiation can be used to limit the spread of cancer.

_____ 11. Individuals vary widely in their ability to "safely" absorb radiation.

_____ 12. Small amounts of matter are converted into immense quantities of energy in nuclear bombs.

_____ 13. The human body naturally contains a small amount of radioactive material.

_____ 14. Cancer caused by radiation exposure can be distinguished by physicians from cancer having other causes.

_____ 15. Television tubes emit radiation.

_____ 16. The majority of nuclear waste generated to date has come from nuclear power plants.

_____ 17. Radioactive and nonradioactive forms of an element behave the same chemically.

_____ 18. Cells that divide rapidly are more sensitive to radiation than are cells that divide slowly.

_____ 19. Physicians use injections of radioactive elements in the diagnosis and treatment of certain disorders.

_____ 20. Medical X rays carry potential risks as well as benefits.

_____ 21. Nuclear reactors were originally designed to generate electricity.

_____ 22. Nuclear plants are the only electric power plants that create serious hazards to public health and the environment.

_____ 23. To date, no one has died from radiation released by nuclear power plants.

_____ 24. Nuclear power plants do not emit air pollution during normal operation.

_____ 25. Regardless of risks, nuclear power plants are necessary to keep the nation functioning and to free us from dependence on foreign oil.

_____ 26. A nuclear power plant can explode like a nuclear bomb, killing millions of people.

_____ 27. The major difference between a nuclear power plant and a coal-fired power plant is the fuel used to boil the water.

_____ 28. Some nuclear wastes must be stored for hundreds of years to prevent dangerous levels of radioactivity from escaping into the environment.

_____ 29. Nuclear power presently supplies more than 10% of our country's total energy needs and is increasing in importance each year.

_____ 30. If the half-life of a radioactive substance is six hours, all of it will have decayed in 12 hours.

_____ 31. More federal dollars have been spent on nuclear power development than on all other alternative forms of energy combined.

_____ 32. In the United States, the largest source of man-made radiation comes from nuclear power plants.

_____ 33. Some states have banned the construction of new nuclear power plants.

_____ 34. Nuclear wastes can be neutralized or made nonradioactive.

_____ 35. Nuclear power plants produce material that could be converted into nuclear weapons.

_____ 36. Nuclear power plants use much smaller quantities of fuel than coal-fired plants.

_____ 37. Nuclear power plants are less expensive to build than are coal-fired plants.

_____ 38. A national system for the long-term storage of radioactive wastes is now in operation.

_____ 39. The rate of radioactive decay can be slowed down by extreme cooling.

_____ 40. The United States should increase its reliance on nuclear power to generate electricity.

Based on results of your class survey, consider the following questions:

1. Do you feel there is a need for better public education on nuclear issues? Why, or why not?
2. Do you feel there is public fear of radiation? Give reasons for your answer.
3. Do you know what radiation is?

Argonne National Laboratory

This is the only photograph made during construction of the first nuclear reactor. This photograph was taken in November 1942 and shows the laying of a 19th layer made of graphite. Alternate layers of graphite contained uranium metal and uranium oxide were spaced by layers of "dead" graphite. There were 57 layers in all.

A ENERGY AND ATOMS

A.1 Laboratory Activity: How Observable Are Nuclear Phenomena?

Getting Ready

The purpose of this activity is to investigate whether some objects that you might encounter every day emit radiation. The objects will be placed on a piece of sensitive paper, which forms an image on its surface when exposed to radiation. The paper and items will be removed from sunlight, so that only radiation from radioactive materials will expose the paper.

Procedure

1. Using forceps, place the five objects, one near each corner and one in the middle, on a piece of sun-sensitive paper.
2. Place the paper and the objects in a closed laboratory drawer overnight.
3. The next day lift each item and examine the paper as directed by your teacher. Note whether spots are left on the paper. The presence of a spot in the absence of sunlight indicates that the paper has been exposed to radiation. It also suggests that the object which made a spot on the paper is radioactive.

Questions

1. Which materials are radioactive, based on this test?
2. Do you think the radioactivity serves any useful purpose for each particular item, or might it just be incidental?
3. Can you suggest an indicator more sensitive than sun-sensitive paper for the presence of radioactivity?

Although most common items are not radioactive, "nuclear energy" is important in our daily lives as we will see throughout this unit. First, however, we must learn what is meant by radioactivity and radiation—two often misunderstood terms.

A.2 Different Kinds of Radiation

You may have been taught that atoms are generally unchanging—an atom of aluminum always remains aluminum, an iron atom is always iron. However, some atoms do change spontaneously, because they have unstable nuclei. Usually they change to produce an atom of a different element (one with a different nucleus), an additional particle, and energy is released. **Radioactivity** is the result of this process, which is referred to as **radioactive decay.** The emitted particles and energy together make up nuclear radiation. Many benefits and also hazards of nuclear technology are due to nuclear radiation.

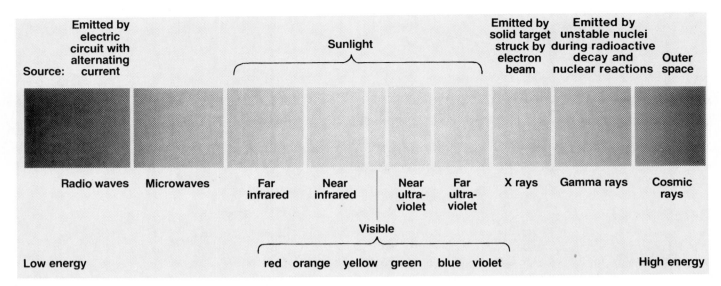

Figure V.1   The electromagnetic spectrum.

The energy emitted during radioactive decay is in the form of high-energy **electromagnetic radiation.** Visible light, microwaves, and radio waves are also electromagnetic radiation, but of lower energy. Figure V.1 shows the major portions of the electromagnetic spectrum and their sources.

Electromagnetic radiation from all regions of the spectrum has several common properties:

- It is a form of energy and has no mass.
- It travels at the speed of light.
- It can travel through a vacuum; its movement does not depend on a medium such as air or water to "carry" it, as sound or ocean waves do.
- It is emitted by atoms as they decay, or when they are energized, such as by heating the tungsten filament in a light bulb or by lighting the fuse that explodes the compounds in fireworks.
- It moves through space as bundles, or packets, of energy called **photons.** Each photon has a characteristic frequency, like the frequencies of the radio waves received by your radio.
- The higher the frequency of electromagnetic radiation, the higher the energy of its photons.

What happens when either nuclear radiation or electromagnetic radiation interacts with living things or other kinds of matter depends upon the energy of the radiation. **Ionizing radiation** has the highest energy and the greatest potential for harm. It may be either high-energy electromagnetic radiation (X rays, γ rays) or high-energy electrons, ions, or other particles emitted during radioactive decay. Energy from such radiation is transferred to the electrons that bind atoms into molecules. This added energy can cause electrons to be ejected from molecules, creating highly reactive molecular fragments often in the form of ions, hence the name "ionizing radiation." These molecular disruptions can cause serious damage to living systems. All nuclear radiation is ionizing radiation.

Nonionizing radiation has lower energy. Electromagnetic radiation in the ultraviolet, visible, and lower energy regions of the spectrum (see Figure V.1) is nonionizing radiation. When this form of radiation transfers its energy to matter it causes excitation; molecules vibrate or electrons move to higher energy levels. Chemical reactions can sometimes occur as a result of the energy transferred to the molecules, such as the reactions that occur when you use a microwave oven to cook food. Excessive exposure to nonionizing radiation can also be harmful.

Jon Jacobson

Ultraviolet radiation from the sun can be very harmful.

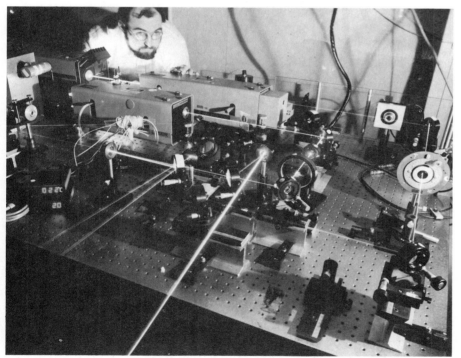

Hughes Aircraft Company

The laser amplifies electromagnetic radiation (**l**ight **a**mplification by **s**timulated **e**mission of **r**adiation).

A sunburn, for example, results from overexposure to nonionizing radiation from the sun. Microwave and infrared radiation can be lethal. Ultraviolet radiation can cause skin cancer.

The difference between the effects of nonionizing and ionizing radiation is something like the difference between being hit with a speeding baseball and being hit with a speeding bullet. The body may absorb more total energy from the baseball, but with less damage, because the impact is spread out over a large area. In the case of the bullet, the smaller force is more focused and is often more damaging.

Scientists have long been interested in light and other types of radiation. However, nuclear radiation was hard to detect. When did scientists first identify it and how did this come about?

CHEM*QUANDARY*

How true is the statement "All radiation is harmful and should be avoided"?

A.3 The Great Discovery

Fluorescent minerals can glow in the dark if illuminated with ultraviolet radiation.

In 1895, the German physicist W. K. Roentgen was studying **fluorescence.** He found that certain minerals glowed or fluoresced when hit by beams of electrons.

Beams of electrons are known as **cathode rays,** because they flow from the cathode when electricity passes through an evacuated glass tube. **Cathode ray tubes** were an experimental curiosity in Roentgen's time. Today these tubes are most commonly used to generate television and computer monitor images. High

Figure V.2 An X-ray tube. The stream of electrons emitted by the hot tungsten cathode is focused on a metal target. The impinging electrons excite atoms in the target. In returning to a lower energy state, these atoms emit X rays.

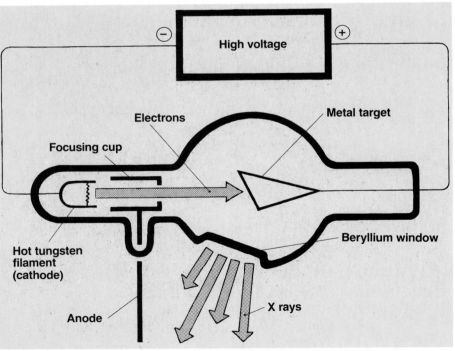

Source: Kieffer, W. F. *Chemistry: A Cultural Approach,* Harper & Row, 1971, p. 34.

electrical potential (voltage) causes the electron beam to travel through the tube and strike fluorescent substances on the inside of the screen. This generates the visual image.

Roentgen was working with a cathode ray tube covered with a black paper shield. A glow of light from a piece of paper across the room caught his eye. The paper, coated with a fluorescent material, would be expected to glow when exposed to radiation. Roentgen quickly investigated and discovered a new form of radiation that could pass unseen through the black paper. He named the rays **X rays,** X being a symbol for the unknown.

Further experiments showed that the penetrating ability of X rays depends on the thickness and identity of the material they strike. X rays cannot pass through dense materials such as lead and bone. X rays are now known to be high-energy electromagnetic radiation (see Figure V.1). They are formed in an X-ray tube (Figure V.2) when the cathode beam strikes heavy metal atoms such as silver.

Scientists soon realized that X rays could be useful in medicine. The first X-ray photograph ever taken was of a human hand. Figures V.3 and V.4 show modern X-ray pictures.

Roentgen's discovery excited his fellow physicists. Soon hundreds of researchers, including the Frenchman Henri Becquerel, were studying these new rays. Becquerel, who was especially interested in fluorescence, wondered if fluorescent minerals might emit X rays.

In 1896, he placed a fluorescent mineral, which just happened to contain uranium, in sunlight. He then wrapped a photographic plate in black paper, and placed it next to the mineral. If the mineral gave off X rays as it fluoresced, the film would be exposed even though it had been shielded from sunlight. To Becquerel's delight, he found that after he developed the plate it had darkened.

The days following Becquerel's initial success were cloudy, preventing him from continuing his experiments. Becquerel had stored the covered photographic plates and the mineral in a drawer. He decided to develop the plates on the chance that the mineral fluorescence might have persisted, causing some fogging of the plates. What he found astounded him. Instead of a faint exposure, the plates had been strongly exposed.

Such a high level of exposure could not have been caused by a fluorescent mineral in a desk drawer. In fact, there was no easy explanation for Becquerel's observations. He interrupted his work on fluorescence and X rays to study the mysterious rays apparently given off by the uranium compound. These rays proved to be more energetic and possess much greater penetrating power than did X rays. Radioactivity had been discovered.

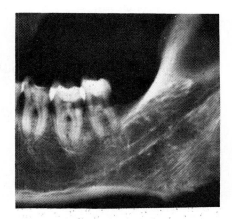

Figure V.3 An X ray of the human jaw. Such X rays are useful for detecting cavities and other dental problems.

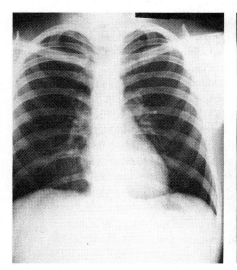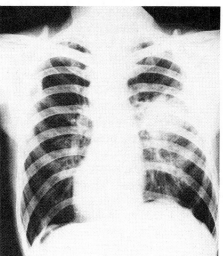

American Cancer Society. Used with permission.

Figure V.4 Chest X rays. Left, normal lungs; right, cancerous lungs.

CHEM*QUANDARY*

What do the following events have in common with Becquerel's discovery of radioactivity?

- Louis Pasteur found that some chickens which had recovered from cholera sickness did not get sick again from another dose of cholera bacteria. He later became famous for inventing vaccination as a prevention for disease.
- Charles Goodyear accidentally let a mixture of sulfur and natural rubber (a sticky material that melts when heated and cracks when cold) touch a hot stovetop; he noted that the rubber did not melt. Vulcanization, the process that makes rubber more widely useful by modifying its properties, resulted from this observation.
- Alexander Fleming noticed a circle of dead bacteria in a dish where a colony of bacteria was growing. He later discovered penicillin.
- Roy Plunkett was using gaseous tetrafluoroethylene ($F_2C = CF_2$) from a storage cylinder, but the flow of gas stopped long before the cylinder was empty. He cut the cylinder open with a hacksaw and discovered a white solid. Today we know this solid as Teflon (polytetrafluoroethylene).

Further research revealed all uranium compounds are radioactive. This led the husband-and-wife team of Pierre and Marie Curie to suggest that radioactivity might be a property of heavy elements. Finding that the radioactivity level of the uranium ore pitchblende was four to five times greater than expected for its known uranium content, the Curies suspected the presence of yet another radioactive element. After processing more than one ton of pitchblende, they isolated tiny amounts of two new radioactive elements, polonium (Po) and radium (Ra).

Interest in the new type of radiation continued to grow among scientists. Some realized that a better understanding of these rays could provide clues to the nature of the atom. One scientist who was particularly successful in penetrating the atom's mysteries was Ernest Rutherford.

A.4   Nuclear Radiation

In 1899, Ernest Rutherford showed that radioactivity consisted of two different types of rays, which he named **alpha rays** and **beta rays.** He placed thin sheets of aluminum in the pathway of radiation from uranium. The beta rays could pass through a thicker stack of aluminum sheets than the alpha rays. (You will do a similar experiment in Part B.1 of this unit.) Shortly afterward, a third type of ray was found to be produced by radioactive elements and was named **gamma rays.**

α, β and γ are the first three letters of the Greek alphabet.

It was known at the time that when charged particles pass through a magnetic field they are deflected. Positively charged particles are deflected in one direction, and negatively charged particles in the opposite direction. Neutral particles and electromagnetic radiation are not deflected by magnetic fields.

Observation of magnetic field deflections showed that alpha rays consist of positively charged particles and beta rays consist of negatively charged particles. Gamma rays are not deflected by a magnetic field and were later identified as high-energy electromagnetic radiation, similar to X rays. An experiment in which all three types of radiation might be observed is shown in Figure V.5.

The nature of radioactivity was thus established. As often happens in science, a new discovery toppled an old theory. Before the discovery of radioactivity,

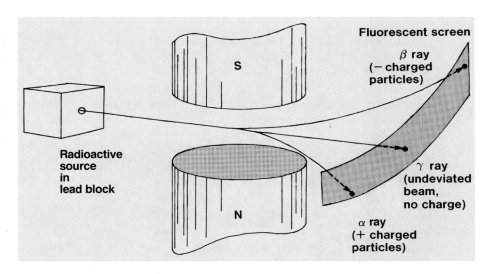

Figure V.5 Lead block experiment, showing behavior of alpha (α) rays, beta (β) rays, and gamma (γ) rays in a magnetic field.

it was believed that the atom was the smallest, most fundamental unit of matter. After alpha, beta, and gamma rays were identified, scientists were convinced that atoms must be composed of still smaller particles.

A.5 Laboratory Activity: Black Box Experiment

Getting Ready

Experiments, like those of Roentgen, Becquerel, and Rutherford, illustrate that indirect evidence is useful in exploring the properties of an object you cannot see or touch. In this activity you will try to identify objects in sealed boxes, which in many ways resembles the work of scientists in determining the nature of the atom—a more fundamental "sealed box."

Procedure

Two sealed boxes, numbered 1 and 2, are at your laboratory bench. Each box contains three different objects.

1. Select one box. Gently shake, rotate, or manipulate the box. From what you observe, try to determine the size of each object, its general shape, and the material from which it is made. Record your observations, designating the three objects a, b, and c.
2. Compare your observations and ideas about the three objects with those of other team members. What conclusions can you and your team reach? Can you identify the objects?
3. Repeat the above steps with the second box.
4. Make your final decisions about the identities of all objects in Boxes 1 and 2. Identify each object by name and a sketch.

Questions

1. Which of your senses did you use to collect data?
2. In what ways does this experiment resemble the efforts of scientists in exploring atomic and molecular structure?
3. Name some theories about the nature of the world based primarily on indirect evidence.

From another experiment, Rutherford proposed the fundamental atomic model that remains useful even today. In doing so he developed an ingenious, indirect way to look at atoms.

Courtesy Rutherford Museum, McGill University, Montreal, Quebec

Rutherford conducted many important experiments on the nature of alpha rays. Here he is seen in his laboratory at McGill University in Montreal.

A.6 The Gold Foil Experiment

Prior to Rutherford's experiment several ideas had been proposed to explain how electrons and positively charged particles might be arranged in atoms. In the most popular model, an atom was viewed as a solid mass of positively charged materials, with negatively charged electrons embedded within, like raisins in pudding.

Hans Geiger and Ernest Marsden, working in Rutherford's laboratory, focused a beam of alpha particles, the more massive of the two types of radioactive particles, at a sheet of gold foil 0.00004 cm (about 2000 atoms) thick. They surrounded the metal sheet with a specially coated screen (Figure V.6). The screen emitted a small flash of light where each alpha particle landed. This permitted the researchers to deduce the paths of the alpha particles interacting with the gold foil.

Rutherford expected that alpha particles passing through the gold foil would scatter as they were deflected by the gold atoms, producing a pattern similar to spray from a nozzle. He was in for quite a surprise.

First of all, most of the alpha particles passed straight through the gold foil as if nothing were there (Figure V.7). This implied that most of the volume taken up by atoms is essentially empty space. But what surprised Rutherford even more was that a few alpha particles, about one in every 20,000, bounced back toward the source. Rutherford described his astonishment by saying, "It was about as incredible as if you had fired a 15-inch shell at a piece of tissue paper and it came back and hit you."

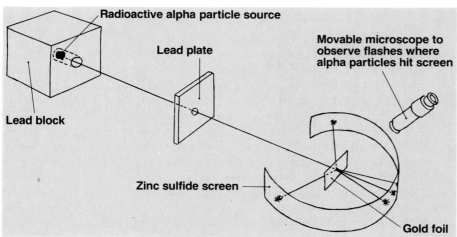

D. D. Ebbing: *General Chemistry*. Copyright © 1987 by Houghton Mifflin Company. Redrawn by permission.

Figure V.6   The alpha particle scattering experiment.

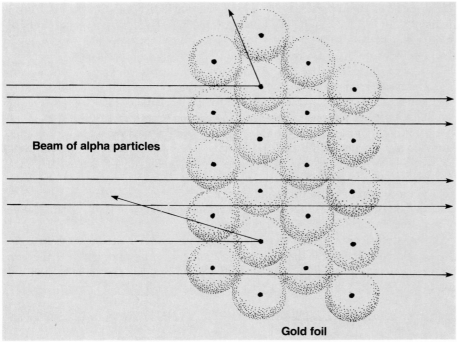

D. D. Ebbing: *General Chemistry*. Copyright © 1987 by Houghton Mifflin Company. Redrawn by permission.

Figure V.7   Result of the alpha particle scattering experiment. Most alpha particles passed through the foil; a few were deflected.

What the few rebounding alpha particles encountered must have been relatively small, because most alpha particles missed it. But whatever they hit must also have been substantial and electrically charged, to scatter some alpha particles as observed.

From these results, Rutherford developed the model of the nuclear atom. He named the tiny, massive, positively charged region at the center of the atom the nucleus. He envisioned electrons as orbiting the nucleus, somewhat as planets orbit the sun.

A.7   The Architecture of Atoms

Since Rutherford's time, our understanding of the structure of atoms has expanded and in some ways changed. We now know from later research that, although useful, the idea of orbiting electrons is too simplified. Each electron is believed to occupy a specific region in which it spends most of its time. We can identify the region, but not the location of the electron at a given instant. Rutherford's image of a central, massive nucleus surrounded mostly by empty space is still accepted.

We can think of the atomic nucleus as composed of two types of particles, neutrons and positively charged protons. Neutrons are electrically neutral. A neutron and a proton have about the same mass, 1.7×10^{-24} g. While this mass is incomprehensibly small, it is much larger than the mass of an electron. As shown in Table V.1, one mole of protons or neutrons has a mass of about 1 g, while the same number of electrons has a mass of only 0.0005 g. Protons and neutrons account for most of the mass of the universe.

The diameter of a typical atom is about 10^{-8} cm. An average nuclear diameter is 10^{-12} cm. In other words, the nucleus has a diameter only one ten-thousandth of the diameter of an atom. The nucleus occupies only about one trillionth (10^{-12}) the volume of an atom. For comparison, imagine that a billiard ball represents the nucleus of an atom. The electrons surrounding this billiard-ball nucleus would occupy space up to a mile away in all directions.

As you learned in the unit on "Conserving Chemical Resources," each atom of the same element has the same number of protons in the nucleus. This number of protons, called the atomic number, identifies the element. For example, carbon atoms contain six protons per nucleus and carbon has an atomic number of six.

However, all atoms of the same element do not necessarily have the same number of neutrons in the nucleus. Atoms of the same element with different numbers of neutrons are called **isotopes** of that element. Carbon atoms, each containing six protons per nucleus may have six, seven, or even eight neutrons. The composition of these three isotopes of carbon is summarized in Table V.2. The carbon isotope with eight neutrons has an unstable nucleus—it is radioactive and is therefore referred to as a **radioisotope.**

Isotopes are distinguished from one another by having different **mass numbers.** The mass number is the approximate mass of an isotope. It also is the sum of the protons and neutrons in an atom of a given isotope. The three carbon isotopes in Table V.2 have mass numbers of 12, 13, and 14.

Particles smaller than atoms are called "subatomic particles."

Isotopes of an element have the same atomic number and different mass numbers.

Table V.1   *Three important subatomic particles*

Particle	Location	Charge	Molar mass (g/mol)
Proton	Nucleus	1+	1
Neutron	Nucleus	0	1
Electron	Outside of nucleus	1−	0.0005

Table V.2   *Three isotopes of carbon*

Name	Number of protons (atomic number)	Number of neutrons	Mass number	Number of electrons outside nucleus
Carbon–12	6	6	12	6
Carbon–13	6	7	13	6
Carbon–14	6	8	14	6

Table V.3 *Some common isotopes*

Symbol	Name	Number of protons (atomic number)	Number of neutrons	Mass number	Number of electrons
^1_1H	Hydrogen-1	1	0	1	1
^7_3Li	Lithium-7	3	4	7	3
$^{19}_9F$	Fluorine-19	9	10	19	9
$^{208}_{82}Pb$	Lead-208	82	126	208	82
$^{208}_{82}Pb^{2+}$	Lead-208, (II) ion	82	126	208	80

To represent a specific isotope, the atomic number and the mass number are added to the symbol for the element, for example,

$$^{90}_{38}Sr$$

The symbol above represents an isotope of strontium with atomic number 38 and mass number 90. To name an isotope in words, add the mass number to the element's name—this is strontium-90. An ion of strontium-90 would be shown as $^{90}_{38}Sr^{2+}$. The symbols, names, and nuclear composition of some isotopes are illustrated in Table V.3.

YOUR*TURN*

V.1 Isotope Notation

Suppose you know that one product of a certain nuclear reaction is an isotope containing 85 protons and 120 neutrons. It therefore has a mass number of 205 (85 protons + 120 neutrons). What is the name of this element?

$$^{205}_{85}?$$

Consulting the periodic table, we see that the element with atomic number 85 is astatine

$$^{205}_{85}At$$

1. Use the periodic table to complete the missing information, and prepare a table like Table V.3 for these isotopes.

$$^{12}_?C \quad ^{14}_7? \quad ^{16}_?O \quad ^{24}_{12}?^{2+} \quad ^{108}_?Ag \quad ^{200}_?Hg \quad ^{238}_{92}?$$

2. What relationship do you observe between the number of protons and the number of neutrons for atoms of lighter elements? For those of heavier elements?

A.8 Laboratory Activity: Isotopic Pennies

Getting Ready

You found earlier (Unit Two, Part A) that pre-1982 and post-1982 pennies have different compositions. As you might suspect, they have different masses also. In this laboratory activity, a mixture of these pennies will represent the naturally occurring mixture of two isotopes of the imaginary element "coinium." With the pennies, you will simulate one way that scientists can determine the relative amounts of different isotopes present in a sample of an element.

You will be given a sealed bag containing a mixture of pre-1982 and post-1982 pennies. Your bag could contain any combination of the two "isotopes." Your task is to determine the isotopic composition of the element coinium without opening the sealed bag.

To illustrate how this can be done, think it through as if you had billiard balls and ping pong balls instead of coins.

Say you have several samples of 10 balls each. Ten billiard balls will weigh much more than 10 ping pong balls. The less a mixture of 10 of these balls weighs, the more ping pong balls you have present. The relationships can be represented mathematically by the following equality:

Total mass of mixture of balls = Number of billiard balls × Mass of one billiard ball + Number of ping pong balls × Mass of one ping pong ball

Now let's get back to our pennies. The total mass of pennies equals the mass of the sealed bag minus the mass of the empty sealed bag.

Let x = the number of pre-1982 pennies in the bag. Then, $10 - x$ = number of post-1982 pennies in the bag.

Also, the mass of all the pre-1982 pennies is equal to the number of pre-1982 pennies (x) multiplied by the mass of one pre-1982 penny. The mass of all post-1982 pennies is equal to the number of post-1982 pennies ($10 - x$) times the mass of one post-1982 penny. We can write the relationship as

$$\text{Total mass of mixture of pennies} = x \times \text{mass of pre-1982 penny} + (10 - x) \times \text{mass of post-1982 penny}$$

This equation can be solved for x after the three masses have been determined.

Procedure

1. Your teacher will give you a pre-1982 penny, a post-1982 penny, a sealed bag of 10 mixed pre- and post-1982 pennies, and the mass of the empty sealed bag. Record the code number of your sealed bag.
2. Find the mass of the pre-1982 penny and the post-1982 penny separately.
3. Find the mass of the sealed bag of pennies.
4. Subtract the mass of the empty bag to find the total mass of the pennies.
5. Calculate the value of x (the number of pre-1982 pennies) and $10 - x$ (the number of post-1982 pennies).
6. Calculate the percent composition of the element "coinium" from your data.

Questions

1. What property of the element "coinium" distinguishes its pre- and post-1982 forms from each other?
2. Why is the element "coinium" a good analogy or model for actual element isotopes? In what ways is the analogy misleading or incorrect?
3. Name at least one other familiar item that could serve as a model for isotopes.

A.9 Isotopes in Nature

Most elements exist naturally as mixtures of isotopes. From a chemical viewpoint, this presents few problems because all isotopes of an element are virtually identical in their chemistry. They differ only slightly in mass. Some isotopes of an element may be radioactive, while others are not.

The composition of the naturally occurring isotope mixture of an element is usually the same everywhere on Earth. The reported atomic and molar masses of an element are the average masses based on the relative abundances of its isotopes. The following *Your Turn* illustrates this and provides some practice in calculating molar masses of elements from isotopic abundances.

Molar mass was introduced in Unit Two, Part C.3.

YOUR *TURN*

V.2 Molar Mass and Isotope Abundance

To calculate the molar mass of an element, you must use the concept of a weighted average. You can do this for the element "coinium" from your laboratory activity. Suppose you found that $x = 4$, that is, your mixture contained 4 pre-1982 pennies and 6 post-1982 pennies. In decimal fractions, the composition of your mixture was 0.4 pre-1982 pennies and 0.6 post-1982 pennies. These fractions together with the masses of the pennies (the two isotopes of "coinium") would be used in the following equation to calculate the weighted average mass.

Avg. mass of a penny = (fraction, pre-1982 pennies) (mass, pre-1982 penny) + (fraction, post-1982 pennies)(mass, post-1982 penny)

Try this calculation for your actual coinium mixture and compare the calculated average mass with the total mass of your pennies divided by 10.

Now let's do an example for an actual isotopic mixture.

Naturally occurring copper consists of 69.1% copper-63 and 30.9% copper-65. The molar masses of the pure isotopes are, for copper-63, 62.93 g/mol and, for copper-65, 64.93 g/mol. Calculate the molar mass of naturally occurring copper.

The general relationship for finding average molar masses is as follows (compare it with the equation you used for "coinium"):

Molar mass = (fraction of isotope 1)(molar mass of isotope 1) + (fraction of isotope 2)(molar mass of isotope 2) + . . .

For copper, the average molar mass is found as follows:

Molar mass of copper = (0.691)(62.93 g/mol) + (0.309)(64.93 g/mol)
= 63.5 g/mol

This is the value given in the periodic table (rounded to the nearest 0.1 unit).

Try the following:

1. Naturally occurring uranium is a mixture of three isotopes: 99.28% is uranium-238 (U-238), which has a molar mass of 238.05 g/mol; 0.7110% is uranium-235 (U-235; used in power plants and weapons), which has a molar mass of 235.04 g/mol; and 0.0054% is uranium-234 (U-234) with a molar mass of 234.04 g/mol. Is the molar mass of naturally occurring uranium closer to 238, 235, or 234? Why? Calculate its molar mass.

2. Using the equation given above as a model, create the equation you would use to calculate the percent of two isotopes in a sample of an element. Assume you are given the molar mass of the element and the molar mass of each of the two isotopes. Your fraction of one isotope can be x and the fraction of the other can be $1 - x$.

3. Hydrogen is composed of three naturally occurring isotopes: hydrogen-1 (H-1), 1.0078 g/mol; hydrogen-2 (H-2, known as deuterium), 2.0141 g/mol; and hydrogen-3 (H-3, known as tritium), 3.016 g/mol. Deuterium, though rare, is extracted from seawater as heavy water (D_2O) for use in some nuclear reactors. Tritium is synthetically produced in nuclear reactors and is used in weapons and tracer studies. Discounting the negligible percent of tritium, use the equation you wrote in Question 2 to calculate the percent of each of the other two naturally occurring isotopes of hydrogen, given that the molar mass of hydrogen is 1.0079 g/mol.

Table V.4 *Some naturally occurring radioisotopes and their abundances*

Isotope	Relative isotopic abundance (%)
$^{3}_{1}H$	0.00013
$^{14}_{6}C$	Trace
$^{40}_{19}K$	0.0012
$^{87}_{37}Rb$	27.8
$^{115}_{49}In$	95.8
$^{138}_{57}La$	0.089
$^{144}_{60}Nd$	23.9
$^{147}_{62}Sm$	15.1
$^{176}_{71}Lu$	2.60
$^{187}_{75}Re$	62.9
$^{190}_{78}Pt$	0.012
$^{232}_{90}Th$	100
$^{235}_{92}U$	0.72
$^{238}_{92}U$	99.28

Jon Jacobson

The age of excavated artifacts can be determined by measuring the extent of decay of particular radioactive isotopes in the artifacts.

Marie Curie originally thought that radioactivity was a characteristic only of heavy elements. It is true that naturally occurring radioisotopes are more common among heavy elements. For example, isotopes of elements with an atomic number greater than 83 (bismuth) are radioactive. However, many lighter radioactive isotopes also occur naturally, and it is possible to make a radioactive isotope of any element. Table V.4 lists some naturally occurring radioisotopes and their isotopic abundances.

The history of science is full of discoveries that build upon earlier discoveries. The discovery of radioactivity was an event in itself. But as you have seen, it also made possible investigation of the structure of the atom.

In the next part of this unit, you'll learn more about the process of radioactive decay and how the forms of radiation emitted are described and detected.

PART A
SUMMARY *QUESTIONS*

1. List two identifying characteristics and two examples of electromagnetic radiation.
2. The discovery of X rays led to investigations of the nucleus. Describe the historical events that connect these two areas of research.
3. Describe how Becquerel distinguished among the phenomena of fluorescence, X rays, and natural radioactivity.
4. Describe the experimental results supporting the contention that radioactive sources emit charged particles as well as electromagnetic radiation (gamma rays).

5. Describe experimental evidence in support of each contention:
   a. An atom is mainly empty space.
   b. An atom contains a tiny, yet relatively massive, positively charged center.
6. Approximately how many times heavier is a proton than an electron?
7. Complete the following table:

Data table					
Symbol	**Name**	**Atomic number**	**Number of protons**	**Mass number**	**Number of neutrons**
?	?	6	?	12	?
$^{60}_{27}?$	?	?	?	?	?
$^{207}_{?}Pb$	?	?	?	?	?

8. The element potassium, present in your body, occurs as a mixture of three isotopes with these molar masses: 38.964 g/mol, 39.964 g/mol, and 40.962 g/mol. If the molar mass for the element potassium is 39.098 g/mol, which isotope is the most abundant? (Give the element name and mass number.) Explain your answer.
9. The element neon is found in the Earth's atmosphere, at concentrations of about 1 part in 65,000. All three naturally occurring isotopes are equally useful in neon signs and other chemical applications. The vital statistics for the isotopes are in Table V.5. Do you expect the molar mass of neon to be closer to 20, 21, or 22? Why? Calculate the molar mass of neon.

Table V.5   *Neon isotopes*

Isotope	Mass	% Natural abundance
Ne-20	19.992	90.51
Ne-21	20.994	0.27
Ne-22	21.991	9.22
		100.00

10. The element boron exists essentially in two isotopic forms: B-10 and B-11. While both isotopes behave chemically alike and are equally useful in fireworks (green color), antiseptic boric acid, and heat-resistant glass, only B-10 is useful as a control material in nuclear reactors, as a radiation shield, and in instruments used for detecting neutrons. If the molar mass of boron is 10.81 g/mol, which of these two isotopes is more abundant in nature?
11. What is the minimum amount of information needed to identify a particular isotope?

EXTENDING *YOUR KNOWLEDGE (OPTIONAL)*

Choose one of the following subatomic particles and investigate how scientists determined its existence and properties: proton, neutron, electron, neutrino, quark, pi meson, positron, or gluon. What (if any) are the practical results of such scientific studies?

B RADIOACTIVE DECAY

Some 350 isotopes of 90 elements are found in our solar system. About 70 of these isotopes are radioactive. (Almost 1600 more isotopes have been made in the laboratory.) For elements with atomic numbers of 83 or less, the natural abundance of radioisotopes is quite low relative to that of stable isotopes.

Radioactive isotopes decay spontaneously, giving off alpha or beta particles and gamma radiation. There are many medical and industrial uses for radioisotopes. How each is used depends on the kind of radiation emitted. In addition, the three types of radiation present different hazards to human health. Because nuclear radiation cannot be detected by human senses, various devices have been developed to detect it and measure its intensity.

B.1 Laboratory Activity: Distinguishing Alpha, Beta, and Gamma Rays

Getting Ready

One of the first devices developed to detect radioactivity was the **Geiger counter,** which produces an electrical signal when particles emitted from a radioactive source come in contact with it. In this activity or teacher demonstration you will use a modern-day counter to compare alpha, beta, and gamma radiation in terms of their penetrating ability through cardboard, glass, and lead.

When ionizing radiation enters the counter's detecting tube, or probe, ions are formed and enhance the electric current flowing in the tube. Most radiation counters register the current flow as both audible clicks and a meter reading. The unit of measure on the meter, counts per minute (cpm), indicates the **intensity** of the radiation.

A constant quantity of natural radioactivity is always present in the environment. This is known as **background radiation.** Because of its presence, before readings are taken from a known radioactive source, an initial reading of the background radiation must be taken. This background count must then be subtracted from each reading taken from a radioactive source.

The radioactive materials in this activity pose no danger to you. Nuclear materials are strictly regulated by state and federal laws. Sources used emit only very small quantities of radiation and their use requires no special license. Nevertheless, all radioactive samples will be treated with the same care required for licensed materials. You will wear rubber or plastic gloves. Do not allow the radiation counter to come in direct contact with the radioactive material. Check your hands with a radiation monitor before you leave the laboratory.

First Day

Prepare a data table like the one below.

Data table					
	Counts per minute (cpm)				First material to reduce intensity
Radiation	No shielding	Cardboard	Glass	Lead	
Alpha Beta Gamma					

Procedure

Part 1: The Penetrating Ability of Alpha, Beta, and Gamma Radiation

1. Set up the apparatus as shown in Figure V.8.
2. Turn on the counter; allow it to warm for at least three minutes. Determine the intensity of the background radiation by counting clicks for one minute in the absence of any sources. Record this background radiation in counts per minute (cpm).
3. Put on your gloves. Using forceps, place an alpha source on the ruler at a point where it produces a nearly full-scale reading on the meter (Figure V.8). Watch the meter for 30 seconds; estimate the average cpm detected during this period. Subtract the background reading from this value and record the result.

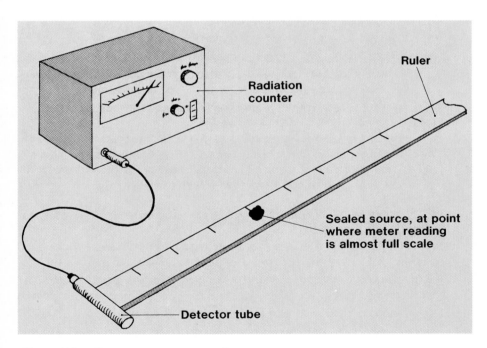

Figure V.8   The apparatus setup for Part 1.

Figure V.9   Place the shield between the probe and the radiation source.

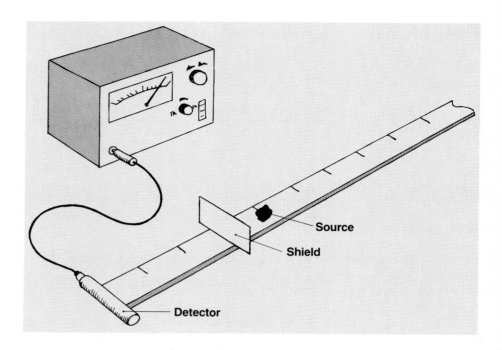

4. Without moving the source, place a piece of cardboard between the probe and the source, as shown in Figure V.9.

5. Again watch the meter for 30 seconds. Correct the average reading for background radiation and record the result.

6. Repeat Steps 4 and 5 using a glass plate.

7. Repeat Steps 4 and 5 using a lead plate.

8. Repeat Steps 3 through 7 using a beta particle source.

9. Repeat Steps 3 through 7 using a gamma ray source.

10. Analyze the results you obtained from Steps 4 through 8. Which shielding materials most reduced the intensity for each type of radiation?

11. Now answer the following questions about the procedure you have just completed.
    a. How do the three types of radiation tested compare in penetrating power?
    b. Of the shielding materials tested, which do you conclude is the most effective in blocking radiation? The least? What properties of a material do you think determine its radiation-shielding ability?

Part 2: Determining Radiation Types and the Effect of Distance on Radiation Intensity

1. Prepare a data table containing two columns: one in which to list distance from the probe, and the other to list radiation intensity (cpm) values.

2. As directed by your teacher, place the Minigenerator at a point on the ruler that produces nearly a full-scale reading (usually a distance of about 5 cm).

3. Record the corrected average reading for a 30-second period.

4. Place a piece of cardboard between the Minigenerator and the probe. Record a corrected average reading for a 30-second period.

5. Repeat Step 4 using a glass plate.

6. Repeat Step 4 using a lead plate.

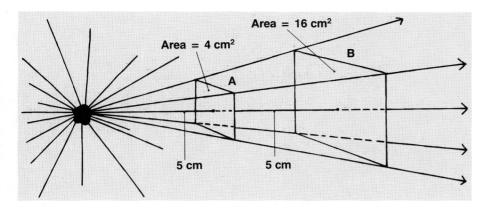

Area = 16 cm²

Area = 4 cm²

A

B

5 cm   5 cm

Figure V.10   The relationship between the distance from source and the intensity of radiation. Intensity is counts per minute in a given area. Note how the same amount of radiation spreads over a larger area as the distance from the source increases.

7. Analyze the results from Steps 3 through 6 and decide what types of radiation were emitted by the Minigenerator. Record this information.

8. Remove the lead plate, and move the source so that the initial distance from the probe is doubled.

9. Record a corrected average reading over 30 seconds.

10. Move the source twice more, so the original distance is first tripled, then quadrupled, recording a corrected reading after each move. For example, if you started at a distance of 5 cm, you would take readings at 5, 10, 15, and 20 cm.

11. Prepare a graph, plotting the corrected cpm on the y axis, and the distance of the source from the probe (in cm) on the x axis.

12. Now answer the following questions about the procedure you have just completed.
    a. Based on your experimental results, what type or types of radiation does the Minigenerator emit?
    b. Analyze the graph you prepared in Step 11. By what whole-number factor did the intensity of radiation (measured in counts per minute) decrease when the initial distance was doubled? Did this same whole-number factor apply when the distance was doubled again? Try stating the mathematical relationship between distance and intensity using this factor and Figure V.10.

Second Day

Part 3: Lead vs. Glass Shielding

1. Prepare a one-page data table with three columns: number of lead sheets, number of glass plates, and cpm.

2. Using the forceps, place the Minigenerator at the point on the ruler that produces nearly a full-scale reading.

3. Take an average reading over 15 seconds and correct for background.

4. Place one lead sheet between the source and probe. Take an average reading over 15 seconds, correcting for background.

5. Add one more sheet of lead. Record your average reading over 15 seconds, correcting for background.

6. Repeat Step 5 until the shield consists of 10 lead sheets.

Radioactive materials are handled safely in this Hot Fuel Examination Facility at Argonne National Laboratory–West in Idaho.

7. Find the thickness of one piece of lead. Put 10 sheets in a pile. Press the sheets together tightly and measure the thickness of the pile. Divide the measured value by 10.

8. Calculate the thickness of lead shielding at which each reading was made.

9. Prepare a graph, plotting corrected cpm on the y axis and thickness of lead shielding (in cm) on the x axis.

10. From your graph determine the thickness of lead needed to reduce the intensity of radiation by half. Record this value.

11. Repeat Steps 2 through 5, using glass plates instead of lead sheets.

12. Add glass plates and take additional readings until the average corrected reading is less than half the original value.

13. Calculate and record the thickness of glass shielding needed to reduce the intensity of radiation by half.

14. Discuss and compare your results with those of your classmates. Your discussion should focus on the following questions.

Questions

1. How does the ability of a material to block radiation vary with its thickness?

2. Compare the thicknesses of glass and lead needed to reduce the radiation intensity by half. How many times greater is the glass thickness than the lead thickness?

3. In the 1950s, concern over the possibility of nuclear war prompted some individuals and communities to build fallout shelters. In addition to offering some hope of protection against the direct effects of blast and heat, why were such shelters built underground?

4. When receiving medical or dental X rays, adjacent parts of the body should be shielded with a blanket. What material would make a good choice for this blanket? Why?

5. Assuming that a source of radiation is outside the body, which type of radiation is likely to be the most dangerous to living organisms? Why?

You have found that the penetrating ability of different kinds of radiation differs greatly. Why is this so? What are alpha and beta particles? And how do we explain their origin? We'll answer these questions in the following section.

B.2 Natural Radioactive Decay

An alpha particle is composed of two protons and two neutrons. It is the nucleus of a helium-4 atom: $^4_2\text{He}^{2+}$. Alpha radiation is emitted by radioactive isotopes of some elements with atomic numbers higher than 83. An alpha particle is nearly 8,000 times more massive than a beta particle, but has very poor penetrating power. Alpha particles are stopped by a few centimeters of air. An alpha-emitter can be held safely for a short time in your hand, since alpha particles cannot penetrate skin.

The alpha particle's large mass can cause great damage, however, over very short distances. Inside the body, in blood or critical organs (for example, if inhaled into the lungs), alpha particles are very powerful tissue-damaging agents.

Figure V.11 illustrates a radium-226 nucleus emitting an alpha particle. The radium nucleus loses two protons, so its atomic number drops from 88 to 86. It also loses two neutrons, so the mass number drops by four to 222, leaving an isotope of a different element, radon-222. The decay process can be represented by this equation:

$$^{226}_{88}\text{Ra} \quad \longrightarrow \quad ^4_2\text{He} \quad + \quad ^{222}_{86}\text{Rn}$$

Radium-226 $\qquad$ Alpha particle $\qquad$ Radon-222

(The charge is usually left off of nuclear symbols.)

Note that atoms are not necessarily conserved in nuclear reactions, as they are in chemical reactions. Atoms of different elements can appear on each side of a nuclear equation.

However, mass numbers and atomic numbers are conserved in nuclear reactions. In the equation above, the sum of the mass numbers of the reactants equals that of the products (226 = 4 + 222). Also, the sum of the atomic numbers of the reactants equals that of the products (88 = 2 + 86). Both of these relations hold true for all nuclear reactions.

Beta particles are fast-moving electrons emitted from the nucleus during the decay process. Because they are much less massive than alpha particles and travel at very high velocities, beta particles have much greater penetrating power than do alpha particles, but they are not as damaging to living tissue.

During beta decay, a neutron is transformed into a proton and an electron. The proton remains in the nucleus, and the electron is ejected at high speed. A third particle, an antineutrino, is also released. The following equation describes the process

$$^1_0\text{n} \quad \longrightarrow \quad ^1_1\text{p} \quad + \quad ^{0}_{-1}\text{e} \quad + \text{ Antineutrino}$$

Neutron $\qquad$ Proton $\qquad$ Beta particle
$\qquad\qquad\qquad\qquad\qquad$ (electron)

Note that a beta particle is assigned an "atomic number," that is, a nuclear charge, of -1, and a mass number of 0.

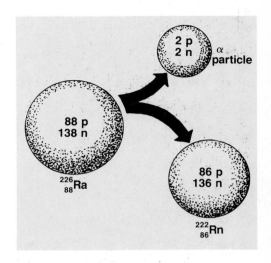

Figure V.11   Alpha particle emission from radium-226. The mass number decreases by 4 (2p + 2n) and the atomic number decreases by 2 (2p) in alpha particle emission.

β decay is always accompanied by emission of an antineutrino.

Figure V.12   Beta decay of lead-210.

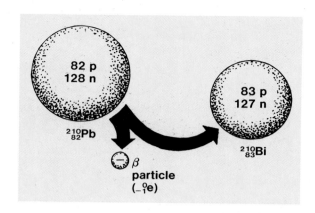

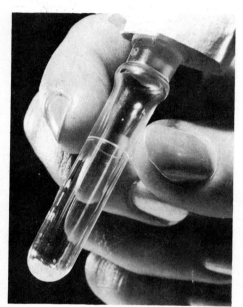

Lawrence Livermore National Laboratory

This test tube contains 4 mg of uranium that will decay to lead.

Figure V.12 shows beta decay in the nucleus of lead-210. The net result is that the lead nucleus loses one neutron, but gains one proton. Thus the mass number remains unchanged at 210, but the atomic number increases to 83. The new nucleus is that of bismuth-210.

$$^{210}_{82}\text{Pb} \longrightarrow \quad ^{210}_{83}\text{Bi} \quad + \quad ^{0}_{-1}\text{e}$$

Lead-210   Bismuth-210   Beta particle

Once again, note that the sum of all mass numbers remains constant during this nuclear reaction. The sum of atomic numbers (the nuclear charge) remains constant, as well.

Alpha and beta decay often leave nuclei in an excited state. This type of excited state is described as metastable. It is designated by the symbol m, as in ^{99m}Tc, which represents a technetium isotope in a metastable excited state. Energy released from isotopes in such excited states is given off as gamma rays, high-energy electromagnetic radiation, with equal or greater energy per photon than X rays. (Examine Figure V.1 which shows the electromagnetic spectrum.) Gamma rays are the most penetrating, and under some circumstances the least tissue-damaging per distance traversed, of the three forms of radiation. Tissue damage is related to the extent of ionization created by the radiation, expressed as the number of ionizations per unit of tissue. Alpha particles cause considerable damage over short range, but are easily shielded. Beta and gamma radiation do less damage over longer range but are more difficult to shield.

Since gamma rays have no mass or charge, their emission does not change the mass or charge balance in a nuclear equation.

The new isotopes produced in radioactive decay are often radioactive and therefore will decay further. The elements uranium and thorium are the parents of three natural decay series, which begin with U-238, U-235, and Th-232. Each series ends with the formation of a stable isotope of lead. The decay series starting with uranium-238 contains 13 steps as shown in Figure V.13.

Table V.6 summarizes general information regarding natural radioactive decay. Use the table to complete the following exercise.

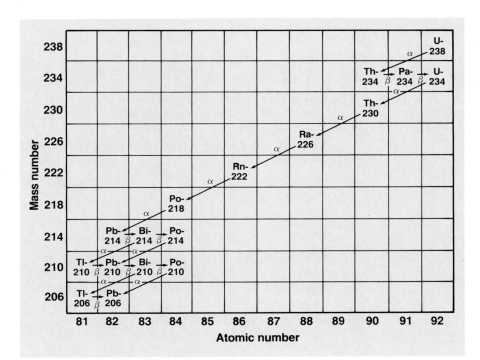

Figure V.13 The uranium-238 decay series. Diagonal lines show alpha decay, horizontal lines show beta decay.

Table V.6 *Changes resulting from nuclear decay*

Decay type	Particle symbol	Change in number of protons in nucleus (atomic number)	Change in number of neutrons in nucleus	Change in mass number
Alpha	^4_2He	Decreased by 2	Decreased by 2	Decreased by 4
Beta	$^0_{-1}e$	Increased by 1	Decreased by 1	No change
Gamma	$^0_0\gamma$	No change	No change	No change

YOUR*TURN*

V.3 Nuclear Balancing Act

The key to balancing nuclear equations is to recognize that both atomic numbers and mass numbers are conserved.

Consider the following question:

Cobalt-60 is a common source of ionizing radiation for medical therapy. Complete the following equation for the beta decay of cobalt-60:

$$^{60}_{27}Co \longrightarrow {}^0_{-1}e + ?$$

Beta emission causes no change in mass number; therefore the new isotope will also have mass number 60, $^{60}?$. Because the atomic number increases by 1 during beta emission, the new isotope will have atomic number 28.

The periodic table shows that nickel has this atomic number. The completed equation is

$$^{60}_{27}\text{Co} \longrightarrow \,^{0}_{-1}\text{e} + \,^{60}_{28}\text{Ni}$$

1. Write the appropriate symbol for the type of radiation given off in each reaction:

   a. $^{14}_{6}\text{C} \longrightarrow \,^{14}_{7}\text{N} + ?$

   This decay process allows archaeologists to date the remains of ancient biological materials. Living organisms take in carbon-14 and maintain a relatively constant amount of it. After death no more is taken in, so the amount gradually decreases due to decay.

   b. $^{241}_{95}\text{Am} \longrightarrow \,^{237}_{93}\text{Np} + ?$

   This decay process takes place in some types of household smoke detectors.

2. Thorium (Th) occurs in nature as three isotopes: Th-232, Th-230, and Th-228. The first of these is more abundant than the others. Thorium's radiation level is quite low; its compounds can be used without great danger if kept outside the body. In fact, thorium oxide (ThO_2) was widely used in gas mantles in Europe and America during the gas-lighting era to speed combustion of the gas. This is the source of the radioactivity you detected in the lantern mantle you tested in Part A.1.

   Th-232 is the parent isotope of the third natural decay series; this series and the U-238 series are believed responsible for much of the heat generated inside the Earth (The U-235 series contribution is negligible since the abundance of U-235 is quite low.) Complete the following equations, representing the first steps in this series, by identifying the missing species:

   a. $^{232}_{90}\text{Th} \longrightarrow ? + \,^{228}_{88}\text{Ra}$ d. $^{228}_{90}\text{Th} \longrightarrow \,^{4}_{2}\text{He} + ?$

   b. $^{228}_{88}\text{Ra} \longrightarrow \,^{0}_{-1}\text{e} + ?$ e. $? \longrightarrow \,^{4}_{2}\text{He} + \,^{220}_{86}\text{Rn}$

   c. $? \longrightarrow \,^{0}_{-1}\text{e} + ?$

   The series continues through Po-216, Pb-212, Bi-212, and Po-212, and finally stops with the formation of stable Pb-208.

Different radioactive isotopes have different lifetimes, just as do biological species, such as bacteria, dogs, and Galapagos turtles. Scientists have identified the rate of decay for each isotope. In the next section, you will learn about rates of radioactive decay, an important factor in determining how useful or hazardous a radioisotope may be.

B.3 Half-Life: A Radioactive Clock

How long does it take for a sample of radioactive material to decay? Knowing the answer to this question allows scientists to determine the length of time a radioisotope used in medical diagnosis will remain active within the body, to determine the length of time nuclear wastes must be stored, and to estimate the ages of ancient civilizations and of the Earth itself.

The rate of decay of radioisotopes is measured in **half-lives.** One half-life is the time it takes for one-half the atoms in a sample of radioactive material to decay. For example, consider carbon-14. This isotope has a half-life of 5730 years. If we start with 2 mol of carbon-14, in 5730 years 1 mol will have decayed to nitrogen-14, leaving 1 mol of the original carbon-14. In another 5730 years, one-half of the remaining mole will have decayed, leaving only half a mole of carbon-14.

Table V.7 *Half-lives of some common radioisotopes*

Isotope	Decay process				Half-life
Radon-222	$^{222}_{86}Ra$	$\rightarrow$	$^{218}_{84}Po$	$+$	$^{4}_{2}He$	3.82 d
Hydrogen-3	$^{3}_{1}H$	$\rightarrow$	$^{3}_{2}He$	$+$	$^{0}_{-1}e$	12.3 y
Potassium-40	$^{40}_{19}K$	$\rightarrow$	$^{40}_{20}Ca$	$+$	$^{0}_{-1}e$	1.28×10^9 y

Half-lives vary greatly for different radioisotopes. For example, the half-life of polonium-212 is 3×10^{-7} seconds, while that of uranium-238 is 4.5 billion years. Table V.7 lists half-lives for some common radioisotopes.

After 10 half-lives the activity of a radioisotope is about 1/1000th or 0.1% of its initial activity. (Can you verify this statement with your own calculations?) In many cases this is considered a safe level; in many cases it is not. Since there is no way to speed up the rate of radioactive decay, radioactive waste disposal is a very difficult problem. We will look into this in a later section.

The concept of half-life is examined in the following activity.

B.4 Laboratory Activity: Half-life Simulation

The goal of this activity is to simulate radioactive decay with pennies. The pennies can be used to discover the relationship between the passage of time and the number of radioactive nuclei that decay. As with real nuclei, the passage of time will be measured in half-lives.

Suppose that a heads-up penny represents an atom of a radioactive isotope of the element coinium—let's call it headsium. The product of this isotope's decay is a tails-up penny that represents the isotope tailsium.

You will be given 80 pennies and a container. Placing all the pennies in the container heads up and shaking the container will represent one half-life period. During this period a certain number of headsium nuclei will decay to give tailsium (some pennies will flip over).

Construct a data table like that below in your notebook. The first data entry has been made for you.

Data table

Number of half-lives	Number of decayed "atoms"	Number of nondecayed "atoms"
0	0	80

Procedure

1. Place the 80 pennies heads up in the box. Close the box and shake it vigorously.

2. Open the box and count the atoms of decayed headsium (coins that have turned over). Record the number of decayed and undecayed atoms of headsium at the end of this first half-life.

3. Remove the atoms of tailsium (the turned over coins). Close the box.

4. Repeat Steps 2 and 3 three more times. At this point you will have simulated four half-lives. You should have five numbers in your final column, representing the number of atoms remaining after zero, one, two, three, and four half-lives.

5. Following your teacher's instructions, pool the class data by finding the total number of atoms decayed for the whole class after the first half-life, the second half-life, and so on.

6. Using the pooled data, prepare a graph by plotting the number of half-lives on the x axis and the number of undecayed atoms remaining for each half life on the y axis.

Questions

1. Describe the appearance of your graph line. Is it straight or curved? Based on the characteristics of your graph, why do you think radioactive decay is measured in half-lives?

2. How many undecayed headsium nuclei would remain in a sample of 600 nuclei after three half-lives?

3. If 175 headsium nuclei remain from a sample of 2800 nuclei, how many half-lives have passed?

4. Name at least one similarity and one difference between this simulation and the actual process of radioactive decay. (*Hint:* Why was it advisable to pool the class data?)

5. How could you modify this simulation to demonstrate that different isotopes have different half-lives?

6. How many half-lives would it take for a 1-mol sample of radioactive atoms (6.02×10^{23} atoms) to decay to 6.25% (0.376×10^{23} atoms) of the original number of atoms? After 10 half-lives, would any of the original radioactive atoms still remain? After 100 half-lives?

7. In this simulation is there any way to predict when a specific penny will "decay"? If you could follow the fate of an individual atom in a sample of radioactive material, could you predict when it would decay? Why or why not? How could you modify your experiment to test your prediction?

8. Can you think of any other processes that could be described in terms of "half-life"? Can you think of another way to model this concept?

The curve that you constructed in this activity applies to the decay of every radioactive isotope. The only difference is that the half-life is a different time period for each isotope. A half-life can be a very long period measured in years, or a very short period measured in seconds. Your curve also shows the rate of decay expressed not only in numbers of nuclei, but in masses. The following exercises will give you more practice in using the half-life concept.

YOUR *TURN*

V.4 Half-lives

1. Suppose you were given $1000 and told that you could spend one-half of it in the first year, one-half of the balance in the second year, and so on. One year thus corresponds to the half-life of the $1000.
   a. If you spent the maximum allowed each year, at the end of what year would you have $31.25 left?
   b. How much would be left after 10 half-lives (i.e., 10 years)?

2. Cobalt-60 is a radioisotope used as a source of ionizing radiation in cancer treatment; the radiation it emits is effective in killing rapidly dividing cancer cells. Cobalt-60 has a half-life of five years.
   a. If a hospital starts with a 1000-mg supply, how many milligrams of Co-60 would it need to purchase after 10 years to replenish the original supply? Does your answer depend on whether or not the cobalt isotope is used to treat patients? Why or why not?

b. How many half-lives would it take for this supply to dwindle to less than 10% of the original? To less than 1% of the original? To less than 0.1% of the original?

3. Even though the activity of a sample is only 0.1% of its original value after 10 half-lives, theoretically it would take forever for a sample of radioactive material to decay completely. To help you understand this concept, consider the following analogy:

A person is attempting to reach a telephone booth which is 512 m away. Assume that the person covers half this distance (256 m) in the first minute, half the remaining distance (128 m) in the second minute, half the remainder (64 m) in the third minute, and so on. In other words, the "half-life" for this moving process is one minute. If the individual never covers more than half the remaining distance in each one-minute interval, theoretically how long will it take the person to reach the phone booth? Calculate the number of half-lives it will take to get within 25 cm of the booth.

4. Strontium-90 is a radioactive by-product of nuclear explosions. If it gets into the food supply from fallout from above-ground nuclear testing, it is especially dangerous since it behaves chemically like calcium (the two elements are in the same chemical family). Thus instead of passing through the body, it is incorporated into the bone structure. Responding to this and other dangers of fallout, in 1963 the United States, the Soviet Union, and several other countries signed a nuclear test ban treaty, which ended most above-ground weapons testing. The strontium-90 released in previous explosions remains in the environment, however.

Graph the decay of the strontium-90 present in the atmosphere in 1963 in the following way: Given the Sr-90 half-life of 27.6 years, calculate the years that would represent one, two, three, etc., half-lives, using 1963 as year zero, when 100% of the strontium-90 released was present. Plot the percent of original radioactivity, from 0% to 100%, on the y axis, and the years 1963 to 2100 on the x axis. Connect the data points with a smooth curve. What percent of the Sr-90 present in 1963 remains today? What percent will remain in the year 2100?

Since we cannot see, hear, feel, taste, or smell radioactivity, we must use special detection devices to indicate its presence. You have already used a radiation counter. This and some other radiation detectors are explained in the next section.

B.5   Radiation Detectors: Extrasensory Protectors

To detect radioactive decay we must observe the results of the interaction of radiation with matter. In the radiation counter you used earlier (Part B.1), for example, argon gas is ionized by entering radiation. The ionized gas conducts electric current, and an electric signal is generated as the ions and the components of radiation pass through the probe, as shown in Figure V.14.

Devices called **scintillation counters** detect entering radiation as light emitted by the excited atoms of a solid. The scintillation counter probe pictured in Figure V.15 is lined with sodium iodide (NaI), which emits light when ionizing radiation strikes it. **Solid-state detectors,** which monitor the movement of electrons through silicon and other semiconductors, are the primary detectors used today for detecting and measuring radioactivity.

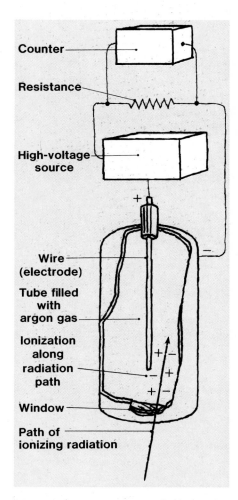

Counter

Resistance

High-voltage source

Wire (electrode)

Tube filled with argon gas

Ionization along radiation path

Window

Path of ionizing radiation

Figure V.14   Diagram of a radiation counter showing how radiation entering the probe causes ionization of gaseous atoms or molecules.

You learned earlier in this unit that radioactivity will expose photographic film. Workers who handle radioisotopes wear film badges or other detection devices to measure their exposure. If they get a dose in excess of federal limits, they are temporarily reassigned to jobs that minimize exposure to radiation.

Ionizing radiation can also be detected in a cloud chamber. You will try out this method of detection in the following activity.

B.6 Laboratory Activity: A Simple Cloud Chamber

Getting Ready

A **cloud chamber** is a glass container filled with air which is saturated with water or other vapor, like the air on a humid day. If cooled, the air inside will become supersaturated. (Recall from Unit One, Part C that this is an unstable condition.) If a radioactive source is placed near a cloud chamber filled with supersaturated air, the radiation will ionize the air inside as the radiation passes through the chamber. Vapor condenses on the ions formed, leaving a white trail behind each passing radiation. The trail resembles that from a high-flying aircraft and reveals the path of the particle or ray. Figure V.16 is a picture taken in a cloud chamber.

The cloud chamber you will use consists of a small plastic container and a felt band moistened with isopropyl alcohol. This alcohol evaporates more rapidly than water and saturates air more readily. The cloud chamber will be chilled with dry ice to facilitate supersaturation and cloud formation.

Procedure

1. Fully moisten the felt band on the inside of the cloud chamber with the isopropyl alcohol. Place a small quantity of alcohol on the container bottom.
2. Using gloves and forceps, quickly place the radioactive source on the bottom of the chamber and replace the lid.
3. To cool the chamber, place it on top of a flat piece of dry ice or embed it in crushed dry ice. Make sure the chamber remains level.
4. Let the chamber sit on the dry ice for three to five minutes.

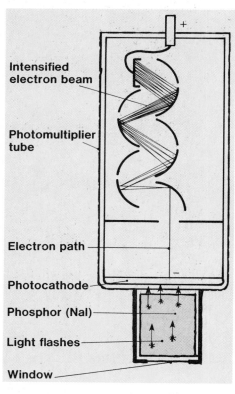

Figure V.15   A scintillation counter probe. Ionizing radiation causes flashes of light (scintillations) in the phosphor. At the photocathode each light flash is converted into an electron pulse that is increased manyfold as it moves through the photomultiplier tube.

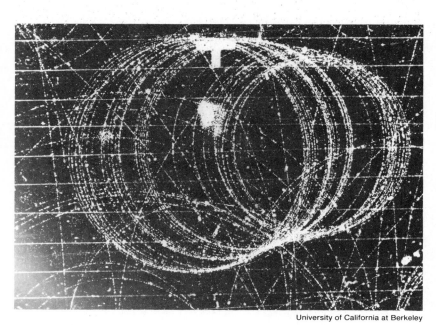

University of California at Berkeley

Figure V.16   A photograph of vapor trails in a cloud chamber.

5. Dim or turn off the room lights. Focus the light source through the lid at an oblique angle (not straight down) so that it illuminates the base of the chamber.

6. Observe the air in the chamber near the radioactive source. Record your observations.

Questions

1. What differences did you observe in the tracks?
2. Which type of radiation do you think made the more visible track and why?
3. What is the purpose of the dry ice?

Recall that the radiation observed in a cloud chamber is emitted from an unstable, radioactive isotope which is eventually converted into a stable, non-radioactive isotope. Do you think it would be possible to reverse the process, converting a stable isotope into an unstable isotope? You'll find the answer to this question in the next section.

B.7   Artificial Radioactivity

To find out whether radioactive elements could be made in the laboratory, Ernest Rutherford in 1919 enclosed nitrogen gas in a glass tube and bombarded it with alpha particles from a radioactive source. After analyzing the gas remaining, he found that some of the nitrogen had been converted to an isotope of oxygen, according to the following equation:

$$\underset{\text{Helium-4}}{{}^{4}_{2}\text{He}} \quad + \quad \underset{\text{Nitrogen-14}}{{}^{14}_{7}\text{N}} \quad \longrightarrow \quad \underset{\text{Oxygen-17}}{{}^{17}_{8}\text{O}} \quad + \quad \underset{\text{Hydrogen-1}}{{}^{1}_{1}\text{H}}$$

Rutherford had made the first synthetic or artificial nucleus. However, it was not radioactive. Although he continued his work, Rutherford was limited by the moderate energies of the alpha particles he used. But **transmutation** of the elements—the conversion of one element to another—was a reality.

By 1930, particle accelerators had been developed that could produce the highly energetic particles needed for additional bombardment reactions. The first radioactive artificial isotope was produced in 1934 by Frederic and Irene Joliot-Curie. They bombarded aluminum with alpha particles, producing radioactive phosphorus-30:

$$_{2}^{4}\text{He} + _{13}^{27}\text{Al} \longrightarrow _{15}^{30}\text{P} + _{0}^{1}\text{n}$$

Since then many transformations of one element to another element have been completed. In addition, a number of new elements have been synthesized in nuclear reactions.

YOUR*TURN*

V.5   Bombardment Reactions

Each of the following reactions involves four particles:

- The target nucleus is the stable isotope that is bombarded in the experiment.
- The projectile (bullet) is the particle fired at the target nucleus.
- The product is the heavy nucleus produced in the reaction.
- The ejected particle is the light nucleus or particle emitted from the reaction.

For example, in the production of the first artificially radioactive isotope described above, the particles involved can be identified as shown below:

Target nucleus		Projectile		Product nucleus		Ejected particle
$^{27}_{13}\text{Al}$	$+$	$^{4}_{2}\text{He}$	$\rightarrow$	$^{30}_{15}\text{P}$	$+$	$^{1}_{0}\text{n}$
Aluminum-27		Alpha particle		Phosphorus-30		Neutron

As you learned earlier, completing nuclear equations involves balancing atomic and mass numbers.

Nobelium, No, was produced by bombarding curium, Cm, a manmade element, with nuclei of a light element. Identify this element by completing the following equation.

$$^{246}_{96}\text{Cm} + ? \rightarrow ^{254}_{102}\text{No} + 4\,^{1}_{0}\text{n}$$

The total of the atomic numbers of the products is 102. Therefore the projectile must have the atomic number 6 ($96 + 6 = 102$), which means it was a carbon atom. The total mass number of the products is 258, indicating that the projectile must have been carbon-12 ($246 + 12 = 258$). The completed equation is

$^{246}_{96}\text{Cm}$	$+$	$^{12}_{6}\text{C}$	$\rightarrow$	$^{254}_{102}\text{No}$	$+$	$4\,^{1}_{0}\text{n}$
Target nucleus		Projectile		Product nucleus		Ejected particles

For the following questions, complete the equations by supplying the missing numbers or symbols. Name each particle. Then identify the target nucleus, the projectile, the product nucleus, and the ejected particle.

1. $^{59}_{27}? + ^{?}_{?}\text{n} \rightarrow ^{60}_{?}?$

    In this reaction, a naturally occurring nonradioactive isotope is converted into a medically useful, radioactive form of the same element.

2. $^{96}_{42}? + ^{?}_{?}\text{H} \rightarrow ^{97}_{43}? + ^{1}_{0}?$

    Until its synthesis in 1937, technetium (Tc) existed only as a "hole" in the periodic table; its isotopes are all radioactive. Any technetium originally on Earth has disintegrated. The first new element produced artificially, technetium, is now used extensively for commercial and medical applications. Each year, millions of bone scans are obtained using technetium.

3. $^{209}_{83}? + ^{4}_{2}? \rightarrow ^{211}_{85}? + ?\,^{1}_{0}\text{n}$

    With the synthesis of astatine (At) in 1940, another gap in the preuranium periodic table was filled. Since its creation in the laboratory, it has been detected on Earth. However, at any one time, less than 30 g of the element is present on the entire planet!

Not only does the ability to transform one element into another give us greater technological capabilities, it also has changed the way we view elements. Within the last 50 years, 17 **transuranium** elements (those with atomic numbers greater than uranium [atomic number 92]), have been added to the periodic table. With their creation, the periodic table has expanded to include a new series of elements, the **actinide series.** (See the periodic table inside the cover of this book.)

CHEM*QUANDARY*

Ancient alchemists searched in vain for a way to transform lead or iron into gold (transmutation of the elements). Has transmutation become a reality? From what you know about nuclear changes, how probable is it that lead or iron could be changed into gold?

Figure V.17 Sculptor Henry Moore was commissioned by the Trustees of the Art Institute of Chicago to create a work to commemorate the birth of the nuclear age. The sculpture was unveiled at the University of Chicago on the twenty-fifth anniversary of the construction of the first nuclear reactor.

In the late 1930s a bombardment reaction involving uranium-238 unlocked a new source of energy on Earth. It led to development of both nuclear power and nuclear weapons. This was the beginning of the nuclear age (see Figure V.17). A force capable of great evil and great good was now ours to command. It will be the topic of Part C.

PART B
SUMMARY*QUESTIONS*

1. Name the type of radioactive radiation released in each of the following:
   a. An isotope of iodine undergoes radioactive decay to form an isotope of xenon that has a higher atomic number but the same mass number as the iodine.
   b. Technetium-99m undergoes radioactive decay but both its atomic number and mass number remain constant.
   c. An isotope of thorium undergoes radioactive decay to form an isotope of radium that has a lower atomic number and mass number.

2. Use the periodic table and your knowledge of nuclear equations to complete the following:

   a. $^{60}_{27}\text{Co} \longrightarrow ? + _{-1}^{0}\text{e}$

   This reaction represents the decay mode of the medically important, synthetic radioisotope, Co-60.

   b. $? \longrightarrow ^{40}_{20}\text{Ca} + _{-1}^{0}\text{e}$

   Some 0.0117% of the naturally occurring quantity of this element is radioactive. It is one of the main radioisotopes in your body. It has a half-life of 1.28×10^9 years and decays by the above process.

   c. $^{241}_{95}? \longrightarrow ^{?}_{?}? + ^{4}_{2}\text{He}$

   This artificially produced radioisotope (half-life = 450 years) finds practical use in household ionization smoke detectors. Why would an alpha emitter with a relatively long half-life be suitable for such an application?

3. Define the term half-life. Then answer the following:
   a. Suppose you have a sample containing 800 nuclei of a radioactive isotope. If after one hour only 50 of the original nuclei remain, what is the half-life of this isotope?
   b. You have 400 μg (micrograms) of a radioisotope with a half-life of five minutes. How much will be left after 30 minutes?

4. Gold exists primarily as one natural isotope, Au-197. A variety of synthetic radioisotopes of gold, varying in mass number from 177 to 203, have been produced in the laboratory. Suppose you have a 100-μg sample of pure Au-191, which has a half-life of 3.4 h. Make a graph of its decay curve. Estimate how much will remain after 10, 24, and 34 h. List two reasons why the synthetic gold would not be a good substitute for natural gold in jewelry.

5. List three ways that ionizing radiation can be detected.

6. Using the appropriate symbol notation, list the three types of radiation given off by radioactive sources, in order of increasing penetration power.

7. Beginning in 1940, Glenn Seaborg and associates at the University of California-Berkeley began a series of nuclear bombardment reactions that resulted in the production of a variety of **transuranium** elements (having higher atomic numbers than uranium). Although not found naturally on our planet, several of these elements have found practical use as miniature power generators in weather satellites and space probes. In each case, the heat generated by the radioactive decay is converted directly into electricity.

   Complete the following equations, representing the synthesis of some transuranium radioisotopes. For each, name the projectile, the element formed, and the ejected particle(s).

   a. $^{239}_{?}Pu + ? \rightarrow ^{242}_{?}Cm + ^{1}_{0}n$

   Half-life = 24,400 years to form Cm-242 which has a half-life of 163 days

   b. $^{239}_{92}U + ? \rightarrow ^{238}_{93}? + 2\,^{1}_{0}n$

   Half-life = 2.1 days to form Pu-238, which has a half-life of 89 years

   c. Which of these radioisotopes would be most useful for powering a space probe? Why? Which would be the least useful for any practical application? Why?

EXTENDING *YOUR KNOWLEDGE (OPTIONAL)*

- **Neutrinos** are fundamental particles that have very little mass (much less than the electron), and no charge. Look into the discovery of the neutrino. It is a story of great scientific conviction and persistence. Would you expect an instrument such as a cloud chamber to show neutrino trails? Explain your answer.

- A variety of charged particles (such as alpha and beta particles), uncharged particles (neutrons), and gamma rays have been used as projectiles in nuclear bombardment studies. What are the advantages and disadvantages of each? How are the velocities of these nuclear projectiles controlled? How are they "aimed"? Topics you may wish to explore include electrostatic generators, cyclotrons, and linear accelerators. Also of interest is the role played by nuclear reactors in synthesizing radioisotopes.

- U-235 is the parent isotope for the decay series ending with Pb-207. The entire series can be represented as:

$$^{235}_{92}U \rightarrow \ldots \rightarrow ^{207}_{82}Pb + ?\,^{4}_{2}He + ?\,^{0}_{-1}e$$

Based on the observed changes in atomic numbers and mass numbers between the parent isotope and the final stable product, how many alpha and beta particles are emitted in this decay series per atom of U-235?

- Look into the use of radioactive isotopes for the dating of artifacts and rocks, and for the analysis of the authenticity of paintings.

C NUCLEAR ENERGY: POWER OF THE UNIVERSE

How did scientists first unleash the enormous energy of the atom, and how was it harnessed to generate electricity to power homes? These topics are our focus in the following sections.

C.1 Splitting the Atom

In 1938, two German scientists, Otto Hahn and Fritz Strassman, bombarded uranium with neutrons. Unexpectedly, they found that one reaction product was the element barium, atomic number 56. Austrian physicist Lise Meitner, working in Denmark, first understood what had happened. She suggested that the neutron bombardment had split the uranium atom into two nearly equal parts. Other scientists immediately verified Meitner's explanation. The world had seen its first **nuclear fission reaction.** Hahn and Strassman had observed a complex reaction that represented simply is:

$$\underset{\text{Uranium-}235}{^{235}_{92}\text{U}} + \underset{\text{Neutron}}{^{1}_{0}\text{n}} \rightarrow \underset{\text{Barium-}140}{^{140}_{56}\text{Ba}} + \underset{\text{Krypton-}93}{^{93}_{36}\text{Kr}} + \underset{\text{Neutrons}}{3\,^{1}_{0}\text{n}} + \underset{\text{Energy}}{\text{Gamma rays}}$$

Scientists soon found that the uranium-235 nucleus can split into numerous combinations of fission products. Uranium-235 is the only naturally occurring isotope that undergoes fission. Many synthetic nuclei, in particular uranium-233, plutonium-239, and californium-252 also split under neutron bombardment.

C.2 The Strong Force

Fission induced by the neutron bombardment of uranium-235 and other fissionable isotopes releases at least a million times as much energy as that produced in any chemical reaction. This energy is what makes nuclear explosions so devastating and nuclear energy so powerful.

The source of nuclear energy lies in the force that holds the protons and neutrons together in the nucleus. This force, called the **strong force,** is fundamentally different from, and a thousand times stronger than, the electrical force that holds atoms and ions together in chemical compounds. The range of the strong force is exceedingly short. It does not extend beyond the diameter of the atomic nucleus.

U.S. Information Service

Austrian physicist Lise Meitner.

How is the strong force related to the energy released in nuclear reactions? Recall what you learned about the energy from petroleum and food. In chemical reactions when chemical bonds are stronger in products than in reactants energy is released, often as heat. In nuclear reactions the strong force can be stronger in product nuclei than in those of the reactants. This also results in a release of energy. However, energy from nuclear reactions is so much greater than that from chemical reactions that something more must be involved.

In ordinary chemical and physical changes energy may be converted from one form to another, but we observe no net energy gain or loss (the law of conservation of energy). Mass also is observed to neither increase nor decrease in ordinary chemical reactions (the law of conservation of mass).

Energy = (mass) (speed of light)^2

In nuclear reactions, it is not just mass, or just energy, that is conserved, but the two together. Mass and energy are related according to Einstein's famous equation, $E = mc^2$. The energy released is equal to mass lost times the speed of light squared. The complete conversion of one gram of matter to energy would release an amount of energy equivalent to that of burning 700,000 gallons of octane fuel.

When changes take place in atomic nuclei, energy and mass are interconverted as predicted by the Einstein equation. In nuclear fission, the mass of the fission products is slightly less than the mass of the atom that split. The mass lost is so small that it does not affect the mass numbers of the reactants and products. But the conversion of this mass into energy accounts for the vast power of nuclear energy.

C.3   Chain Reactions

Another unique result of fission is the emission of two or three neutrons from the fragments of each nucleus. Since neutrons start the fission reaction, their production can keep it going by splitting other nuclei. The result is a **chain reaction.**

Recall, however, that most of an atom is empty space. The probability that a neutron formed in a fission reaction will split another nucleus depends on the amount of fissionable material available. A certain minimum volume is needed to assure that the neutrons will encounter enough nuclei to sustain the chain reaction. Otherwise neutrons are lost to the surrounding nonfissionable material. When the **critical mass** of fissionable material is present, a chain reaction results. Figure V.18 illustrates a nuclear chain reaction. Recognition that such reactions were possible and could be utilized in bombs came shortly after the first fission reaction was observed. Germany and the United States soon initiated projects to build "atomic bombs." In 1945, United States aircraft dropped atomic bombs on Hiroshima and Nagasaki in Japan.

The following activity will give you a clearer picture of the dynamic nature of a chain reaction.

C.4   *You Decide:* The Domino Effect

1. Obtain a set of dominoes or equivalently shaped objects. Set them up as shown in Figure V.19. Arrange the dominoes so that each one that falls will knock over two others. The more dominoes you use, the more dramatic the effect will be.

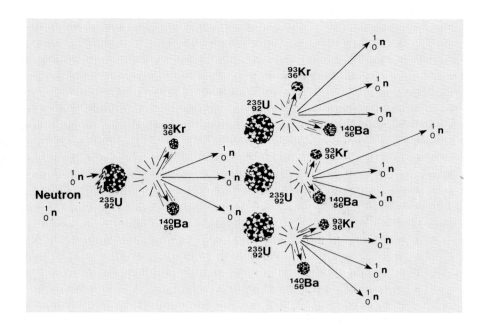

Figure V.18   A nuclear chain reaction. The reaction is initiated by a neutron colliding with a uranium-235 atom. It continues, in chain-like fashion, as long as the emitted neutrons encounter other fissionable atoms. The products of each individual fission can vary.

Knock over the lead domino. Observe the effect on the other dominoes. Would you call this an example of an expanding ("out of control") or limited ("controlled") chain reaction? Why?

2. Set up the dominoes again. This time arrange them so that most, when they fall, will knock over only one other domino or none at all. Set up a very few dominoes so that they will knock over two dominoes (as in the first arrangement). Make a sketch of your design. Knock over the lead domino. Observe the reaction. Is it an expanding or a limited chain reaction? Why?

3. Of these two cases, which do you think models what happens when a nuclear bomb explodes? Which models a reaction in a nuclear power plant? Explain.

4. Imagine that you had the dominoes arranged as in Step 2. What might you do to stop the reaction once it began? Do you think it would be as practical to attempt to stop the reaction you observed in Step 1? Why or why not?

5. In what way is this simulation like a nuclear chain reaction? How is it different? Can you design a different way of modeling this process?

By controlling the rate of fission in the chain reaction, scientists make it possible to use the heat released to generate electricity. In the following section we will discuss how this is done.

C.5   Nuclear Power Plants

The first nuclear reactors were designed during World War II solely to produce plutonium-239 for use in atomic bombs. Today in the United States, about 80 commercial nuclear reactors (like that in Figure V.20) produce electricity (see Figure V.21). In 1984, nuclear power met 4.85% of our total energy needs, and 13.56% of our electrical energy needs.

Figure V.19   A "domino" chain reaction. Dominos arranged to simulate a chain reaction.

Nuclear fission is carried out under controlled conditions in nuclear reactors.

Figure V.20   The Trojan nuclear power plant in Prescott, Oregon.

Portland General Electric Company

Figure V.21   Nuclear power reactors in the United States.

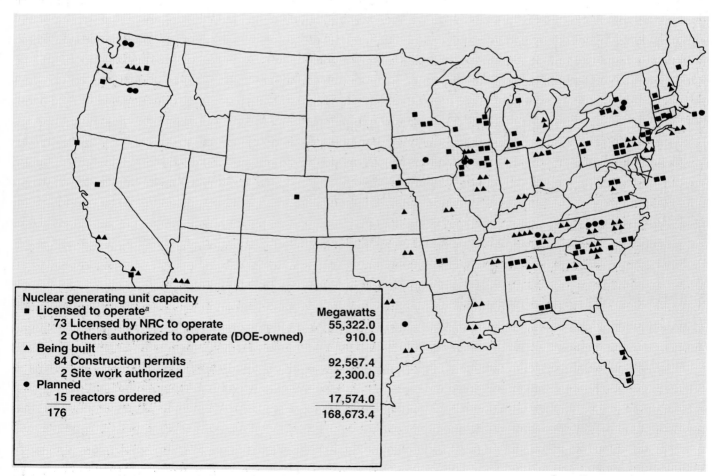

Nuclear generating unit capacity	
■ **Licensed to operate**[a]	**Megawatts**
73 **Licensed by NRC to operate**	55,322.0
2 **Others authorized to operate (DOE-owned)**	910.0
▲ **Being built**	
84 **Construction permits**	92,567.4
2 **Site work authorized**	2,300.0
● **Planned**	
15 **reactors ordered**	17,574.0
176	168,673.4

Source: Department of Energy, 1981 Data.

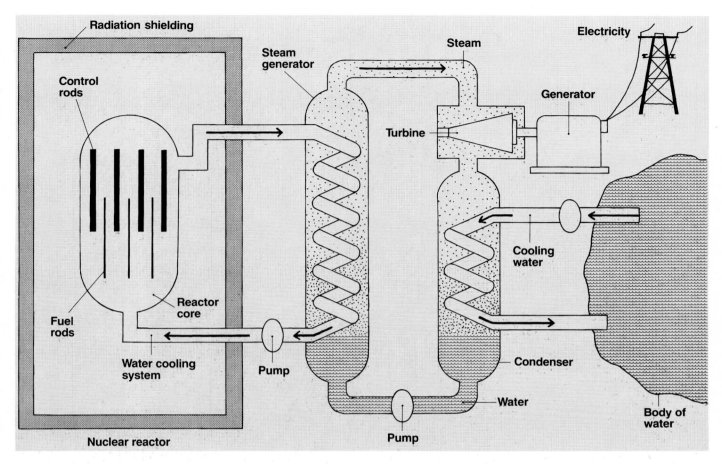

Figure V.22 Diagram of a nuclear power plant.

Most electrical power plants generate electricity by producing heat that is used to boil water. The resulting steam spins the turbines of giant electrical generators. A nuclear power plant is no exception. But, whereas coal, oil, and natural gas-powered generators use the heat of combustion of fossil fuels to boil the water, nuclear power plants use the heat of the nuclear fission reactions.

The essential parts of a nuclear reactor, shown on the left in Figure V.22, are the fuel rods, the control rods, and the cooling system.

The Fuel Rods

While coal-fired power plants require tons of coal on a daily basis, the fuel for a nuclear reactor occupies a relatively small volume and is loaded in only about once a year. The fuel for the reactor is in the form of pellets about the size and shape of a short piece of chalk. There may be as many as 10 million fuel pellets per reactor. These pellets are arranged in steel cylinders several feet long called fuel rods. The fission chain reaction takes place inside these fuel rods.

The fuel pellets contain uranium dioxide, UO_2. Most of the uranium is nonfissionable uranium-238 isotope. Only a fraction, about 3%, is fissionable uranium-235. This is enough to sustain a chain reaction but not enough to permit a nuclear explosion. (Uranium for weapons is enriched to greater than 3% uranium-235.)

Figure V.23 Control rod drive shafts (Point Beach nuclear plant).

Wisconsin Electric Power Company

The Control Rods

The control rods are made of a material, such as boron or cadmium, that absorbs neutrons very efficiently. Recall that neutrons are the particles that trigger nuclear fission. Their absorption in nonfissionable materials reduces the number that can cause fission. The rate of the chain reaction is controlled by moving the control rods up and down between the fuel rods (see Figure V.23).

The Cooling System

In all commercial nuclear reactors, the fuel and control rods are surrounded by a system of circulating water. In the simpler reactors, the fuel rods boil this water, and the resulting steam spins the turbines of the generator. In another type of reactor, this water is superheated under pressure, and does not boil. Instead, it circulates through a heat exchanger, where it boils the water in a second cooling loop. This is the type of reactor shown in Figure V.22.

The core of the nuclear reactor is surrounded by concrete walls 2–4 m thick, in order to prevent the escape of radioactive material, should some malfunction release radioactive material, including the cooling water. In addition, the reactor is housed in a building made with walls of steel-reinforced concrete, 1 m thick, designed to withstand the force of a chemical explosion or of an earthquake.

Is nuclear fission the only source of nuclear energy? In the next section you'll read about the nuclear reaction that fuels the stars, and explore the frontier of nuclear power research.

Sandia National Laboratories

Figure V.24   This giant accelerator, located at Sandia National Laboratories, Albuquerque, New Mexico, is the world's most powerful particle beam fusion accelerator. It is believed to be the first machine with the potential of igniting a controlled laboratory fusion reaction.

C.6   Nuclear Fusion

In addition to harvesting energy by splitting heavy nuclei, it is also possible to release nuclear energy by fusing light nuclei together. When two light nuclei are forced together, they may form a new, heavier atom. As with fission, the energy released by **nuclear fusion** can be enormous, due, again, to the conversion of mass into energy.

Nuclear fusion powers the sun and the stars. Scientists believe that the sun formed when a huge quantity of interstellar gas, mostly hydrogen, condensed under the force of gravity. When the gravitational pressure became great enough to heat the gas to 15 million degrees Celsius, hydrogen atoms began fusing into helium, and the sun began to shine, releasing the energy which drives our solar system. Scientists estimate that the sun, which is about 4.5 billion years old, is about halfway through its life cycle.

The following nuclear equation has been suggested to describe the sum of several nuclear fusion reactions that occur in the sun. The ejected particles are **positrons,** primary particles with the mass of an electron, carrying a positive charge.

$$4\,{}^{1}_{1}\text{H} \longrightarrow {}^{4}_{2}\text{He} + 2\,{}^{0}_{+1}\text{e}$$

Exactly how much energy does a nuclear fusion reaction produce? By adding the masses of the products in the above equation and subtracting the masses of the reactants, we find that 0.0069005 g of mass is lost when 1 mol of hydrogen undergoes fusion to produce helium.

Then, using Einstein's equation, $E = mc^2$, we find that the energy released by the fusion of 1 mol of hydrogen is 6.2×10^8 kJ. This means that the nuclear energy released from the fusion of 1 mol (1 g) of hydrogen-1 atoms is equivalent to the thermal energy released from burning nearly 5,000 gallons of gasoline.

Try the following energy calculations for yourself.

YOUR*TURN*

V.6   Energy from Fusion

1. Use the following information to calculate the mass lost when 3 mol of helium fuse into 1 mol of carbon in the sun and the stars.

   Molar mass of He-4 $=$ 4.002600 g/mol
   Molar mass of C-12 $=$ 12.000000 g/mol

   The reaction is $3 \, {}^{4}_{2}\text{He} \longrightarrow {}^{12}_{6}\text{C} + ?\text{kJ}$

   (See next to last paragraph above.)

2. Conversion of one gram of mass yields 9×10^{10} kJ of energy. How much energy is produced when 1 mol of carbon is formed in the reaction described in Question 1?

3. Calculate the number of gallons of octane (gasoline) that must be burned to produce the same quantity of energy that you found in Question 2.

4. Is the term "combustion" appropriate to describe a nuclear fusion reaction? Why?

Nuclear fusion reactions have been used in the design of weapons. The hydrogen bomb is a fusion bomb that is ignited with a small atomic (fission) bomb.

Can we harness the energy of nuclear fusion to produce electricity on Earth? Scientists have spent more than 30 years pursuing this possibility (Figure V.24).

Presently, the difficulties of maintaining the incredibly high temperatures needed to sustain controlled nuclear fusion have not yet been overcome. If scientists should succeed in controlling nuclear fusion in the laboratory, there is still no guarantee that it will become a practical source of energy. Even though the low-mass isotopes that would fuel the reactors are plentiful and inexpensive, confinement of the reaction would be very expensive. Furthermore, while the fusion reaction itself would produce much less radioactive waste than nuclear fission, capturing the heat of the reaction and shielding it could generate as great a volume of radioactive waste as is produced by fission power plants.

We have split the atom and unleashed the energy that fuels the universe. Much good has come of it. But we have also raised scientific, social, and ethical questions that have not been answered. Along with great benefits, there are also great risks. How much risk is worth how much benefit? We'll explore this issue next.

PART C
SUMMARY *QUESTIONS*

1. Name three isotopes that undergo neutron-induced fission. How is fission different from the radioactive decay that Ernest Rutherford explained?

2. Complete the following equation for a nuclear fission reaction:

$$_?^?n + _{92}^{235}U \rightarrow _?^{87}Br + _{57}^{146}? + ?$$

3. What is a nuclear chain reaction? Under what conditions will a chain reaction occur? What is the difference between an expanding and a controlled chain reaction?

4. Why is it impossible for a nuclear power plant to become a nuclear bomb?

5. How is a nuclear power plant like a fossil-fuel-fired power plant? How is it different? Name one advantage and one disadvantage of each.

6. How does the system that controls the chain reaction in a nuclear power plant work?

7. Describe the difference between nuclear fission and nuclear fusion.

8. One kilojoule of heat energy raises the temperature of one liter of water by 0.24 °C. How many liters of water can be increased in temperature by 5 °C by the 6.2×10^8 kJ of energy released when one mole of hydrogen atoms undergo fusion in the sun and stars?

9. Explain how both of the following statements can be true:
   a. Nuclear fusion has not been useful as an energy source on Earth.
   b. Nuclear fusion is the number one energy source for Earth.

EXTENDING *YOUR KNOWLEDGE*
(OPTIONAL)

• Although nuclear power plants are designed to be incapable of having a nuclear bomb type explosion, accidents such as that at Three Mile Island and Chernobyl do raise the possibility of chemical explosions spreading radioactive isotopes over an area. Investigate these accidents to find out about this concern.

• Investigate the breeder reactor, a nuclear reactor that produces more nuclear fuel than it uses.

• How and where do you think the elements that make up our bodies, our planet, and our universe might have been formed? Investigate possible answers to this question.

D LIVING WITH BENEFITS AND RISKS

Since the dawn of civilization, people have accepted the risks of new technologies in order to reap the benefits. Fire, one of the earliest tools of civilization, gave people the ability to cook, to keep warm in winter, and to forge tools from metals. However, fire, when out of control, can be destructive of property and life threatening. Every subsequent technology has offered its benefits at a price.

Improvements in water systems, nutrition, and health care have given human beings in the developed nations the longest average life span in history. Still, people often oppose the introduction of new technologies on the grounds that the benefits are not worth the risks. Many opposed the introduction of both trains and automobiles. Nuclear power has generated more continuing opposition than most technologies.

In the following sections, we will examine how to balance for ourselves the benefits and risks of any new technology. One must weigh the benefits of the technology against the number of people who might be seriously harmed or killed by it. Statistics and logic would define as acceptable those new technologies in which the probability of risk is low or the benefits outweigh the risks.

Unfortunately, risk-benefit analysis is not an exact science. For example, some technologies present immediate high risks, and others may present chronic, low-level risks for years, or even for decades into the future. Some risks are impossible to measure with certainty. Some can be controlled by the individual, while others must be controlled by government. It is very difficult to compare different risks. Still, decisions must be made.

You have already made several risk-benefit analyses in earlier *ChemCom* units. In the chemical resources and petroleum units you weighed our rapid use of nonrenewable resources against the possibility of running out. In the fourth unit, "Understanding Foods," you considered the use of food additives.

Jon Jacobson

Every form of transportation has its risks!

Before reading the discussion on nuclear benefits and risks, take a few minutes to weigh the benefits and risks of different modes of transportation for a proposed journey. This will help clarify your thinking about benefits and risks.

D.1 *You Decide:* The Safest Journey

Suppose you wish to visit a friend who lives 500 miles (800 km) away using the safest means of transportation. Insurance companies publish reliable statistics to help you determine the safety of different methods of travel. Using Table V.8, answer the following questions:

1. Assume that there is a simple, linear relationship between distance traveled and chance of accidental death. What is the numerical value of your risk factor for traveling 500 miles by each mode of transportation? For example, Table V.8 shows that the risk factor (chance of accidental death) for biking increases by 0.000001 for each 10 miles. Therefore, the risk factor in visiting your friend is

$$(500 \text{ mi}) \left(\frac{0.000001 \text{ risk factor}}{10 \text{ mi}} \right) = 0.00005$$

   Which is the safest mode (the one with the smallest risk factor)? Which is the least safe?
2. The results obtained in Question 1 might surprise many persons. Why?
3. List the benefits of each mode of transportation. Do the benefits of the modes that are less safe outweigh their increased risks? Explain your reasoning.
4. Do you think these same statistics will be true 25 years from now? Why or why not?
5. What other factor(s) besides the risk to personal safety would you want to consider in this risk-benefit analysis before making the journey?
6. Which mode of transportation would you choose and why? Would such a risk-benefit analysis yield the same results for all individuals? In other words, all factors considered, is there a single "best" method of transportation? Explain your answer.

Table V.8 *Risk involved in some methods of travel*

Mode of travel	Distance at which one person in a million will suffer accidental death[a]
Bicycle	10 miles
Auto	100 miles
Scheduled airline	1000 miles
Train	1200 miles
Bus	2800 miles

[a]On average, chance of death is increased by 0.000001.

CHEM*QUANDARY*

Is there any way of visiting your friend that is risk-free? Would it be safer not to visit your friend?

Some uses of nuclear energy and radioactivity are unquestionably worth the risk they create. These include compact power sources, radioisotopes for diagnosing and treating disease, smoke detectors, and many applications for research and development. Others, like the continued stockpiling of nuclear weapons, are controversial.

Our purpose here is to provide you with a basic understanding that will help you evaluate the benefits and risks of nuclear technology as you encounter it through media reports and personal experience. We will begin with an in-depth look at some of the benefits of radioisotopes.

D.2 Benefits of Radioisotopes

You have already seen how the energy from the uranium atom can be used to supply electricity. Most other nuclear technologies use the ionizing radiation given off by the decay of specific radioisotopes in tracer studies, where the object is to detect the presence of the isotope, or in irradiation, where the radiation is used as an energy source. Tracer applications are important in medicine, industry and fundamental research.

Radioisotopes are used in medicine to trace abnormalities in body function, to locate damaged areas, and in therapy. Doctors place radioisotopes having short half-lives into the body, to find out what is happening. These radioisotopes are called **tracers.** They have several properties that make them ideally suited for this task. First, radioisotopes behave chemically and biologically like stable isotopes of the same element. Doctors know that certain elements collect in specific parts of the body; thus, to investigate that part of the body, they send the appropriate radioisotope.

Lawrence Berkeley Laboratory

The element 104 hunters. From left to right, Matti J. Nurmia, James A. Harris, Kari A. Y. Eskola, Glenn T. Seaborg, Pirkko Eskola, and Albert Ghiorso.

The radioisotopes are detectable with a nuclear radiation detection system, which allows a doctor to determine whether that element is being properly distributed in the body. Tracer compounds can be supplied to the body in solution, or biologically active compounds can be synthesized to contain a radioactive atom, then fed to or injected into the patient (see Figure V.25).

For example, a radioisotope tracer is used to diagnose thyroid problems. At one time, if a doctor suspected that a person's thyroid was not functioning properly, diagnosis was done by surgery. Today, radioactive isotopes offer a much less drastic option. The patient simply drinks a solution containing radioiodine (I-131). The doctor then follows movement of the I-131 tracer in the thyroid with a radiation detection system, measuring the rate at which it disappears.

A healthy thyroid will incorporate a known amount of iodine. An overactive or underactive thyroid will take up more or less iodine. The doctor then compares the measured rate to a normal rate for a person of that age, sex, and weight, and takes appropriate action.

Technetium-99m, a synthetic radioisotope, has replaced exploratory surgery as a way of locating brain tumors. Tumors are areas of runaway cell growth. The element concentrates where cell growth is fastest. A bank of radiation detectors around the patient's head can pinpoint the precise location of the tumor. Phosphorus-32 can be used in a similar way to detect bone cancers.

In some types of cancer therapy, the diseased area is exposed to ionizing radiation with the goal of killing cancer cells. For thyroid cancer, the patient receives a highly concentrated internal dose of radioiodine. In treatment of many other cancers, cobalt-60 is used to beam ionizing radiation from an external source at the cancerous spot. Such treatments must be administered very carefully because the higher doses of radiation can kill or damage normal cells as well.

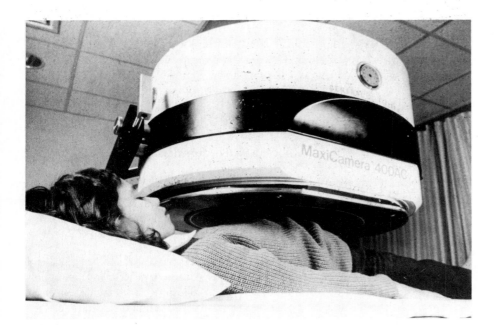

Figure V.25   Injection of a radioisotope makes it possible to produce a non-invasive image of the abdomen.

Table V.9 *Selected medical applications of radioisotopes*

Radioisotope	Use
Used as tracers	
Cobalt-58	Determine the intake of vitamin B_{12} (which contains nonradioactive cobalt)
Iron-59	Determine the rate of red blood cell formation (these contain Fe)
Chromium-51	Determine blood volume and the lifespan of red blood cells
Hydrogen-3 (tritium)	Determine the volume of water in a person's body; determine the use of (labeled) vitamin D in the body; research in cellular chemistry of many kinds
Strontium-85	Bone scans
Gold-198	Liver scans
Used for irradiation therapy	
Cesium-137 (external source)	Treatment of shallow tumors
Phosphorus-32 (external source)	Treatment of skin cancers
Strontium-90 (external source)	Treatment of eye disease
Iridium-192	Treatment of tumors with imbedded wire
Yttrium-90	Internal treatment of pituitary gland cancer with ceramic beads
Gold-198	Treatment of body cavity cancers with a radiocolloid that coats the body cavity

U.S. Atomic Energy Commission

Figure V.26 The bottom potato was preserved with gamma radiation; the top one was not treated. Both were stored for 16 months; these photos were then taken. The irradiated potato was still firm, fresh-looking, and edible, and it had no sprouts.

Both the tracing and cell-killing properties of many radioisotopes are used to diagnose and treat other cancers. Radiosodium (Na-24) can be used to look for abnormalities in the circulatory system, and radioxenon (Xe-133) can be used to search for embolisms (blood clots), and abnormalities of the lung. Table V.9 outlines still other medical applications of radioisotopes.

Irradiation is used in industrial processes, including sterilization of medical disposables such as injection needles, surgical masks and gowns, and for destroying microorganisms in food. Is also is used for sealing plastic containers. There are over 35 **irradiators** operating in the United States, and well over 100 worldwide.

Irradiators are very simple. They have an irradiation chamber that contains pellets of a radioisotope, usually cobalt-60. The material to be irradiated is placed upon a conveyer belt that slides past the radioisotope. Irradiation is one way to preserve food, because it can destroy bacteria that cause food to spoil (see Figure V.26).

High doses of irradiation are used to sterilize meat, so that it can be kept vacuum packed for years at room temperature. Although several foreign countries have small food irradiation industries, U.S. food processors have been slow to adopt the method. The U.S. Food and Drug Administration approved the sterilization of pork by irradiation in 1985.

Since the 1950s, radioisotopes have been used in many fields. To give you a clearer sense of the value of this technology, complete the following activity.

D.3 *You Decide:* Putting the Atom to Work

Each problem listed below has already been solved in real life through the use of radioisotopes. See if you can design your own solution to each problem, making use of radioisotopes. Your teacher will assign you to a team to work on these items.

For each problem prepare a brief, one-paragraph description of your proposed solution. Each team member should also be prepared to make a brief oral presentation on one of your solutions.

You may wish to consider these points:

- What type of radioisotope should be used? Consider half-life, the specific type of radiation, and the physical and chemical state of the radioactive material.
- How should the system be designed? You may construct a diagram.
- What, if any, safety and health precautions are necessary?
- Does the problem require continuous use of radioisotopes or a one-shot approach?
- Could a non-nuclear technology solve the problem just as easily?

Problems

1. Many oil companies share the same pipelines to ship oil and gas from Texas to midwestern states. How can radioisotopes be used to inform operators in Michigan which particular company's oil or gas is arriving at any given time?

2. An automobile manufacturer exploring ways to extend the life and efficiency of automobile engines wants to know how fast the piston rings will wear.

3. Applying more fertilizer than crops can use harms the environment through runoff into streams. It's also a waste of money. An agricultural chemist wants to know what application method will result in the highest ratio of fertilizer uptake to runoff.

4. A doctor treating a patient with inoperable lung cancer wishes to kill the maximum number of cancer cells while causing the least damage to healthy tissues.

We have looked at what nuclear technology can and does do for us. It is now time to turn to the dangers of radiation. To begin, we will introduce you to the units used to measure biological effects of radiation.

D.4 Measuring Ionizing Radiation

Radiation is measured in several ways. When you investigated the differences between alpha, beta, and gamma radiation you measured radiation directly in counts per minute (cpm). Radiation also is measured by the quantity absorbed by the body or by the damage it does to body tissue.

The **rad** (radiation absorbed dose) is the absorbed dose of any type of ionizing radiation. (The SI metric unit is the **gray.**) The **rem** (roentgen equivalent man) measures the power of radiation to cause ionization in human tissue. This unit takes into account the levels of tissue damage caused by different types of ionizing radiation. It is calculated by multiplying rads by a unit of biological damage. (The SI unit is the **sievert.**)

Remember that each type of radiation can cause harm in different ways. X rays and gamma rays, ionizing forms of electromagnetic radiation, can penetrate deeply into the body, but they are less damaging per amount of tissue traversed, compared to alpha and beta particles. Alpha particles are easily stopped, but if they reach the lungs or the bloodstream, they cause extensive damage over a very short path length (about 0.0025 cm) because of their relatively large mass and slower velocities. The primary factors that determine tissue damage are the density of ionization (the number of ionizations per unit area) and the dose (the quantity of radiation received).

D.5   Radiation Damage: Now and Later

Ionizing radiation breaks bonds and therefore tears molecules apart. At low levels of radiation, only a very small number of molecules are harmed, and the body systems can usually repair the damage.

However, the greater the dose (or quantity of radiation) received, the more molecules are affected. Damage to proteins and nucleic acids is of greatest concern. Proteins form much of the body's soft tissue structure and make up the enzymes, molecules that control bodily functions. When a large number of these molecules are torn apart in close proximity to one another, the body may not have enough functioning molecules to heal itself within a suitable period.

The nucleic acids that make up DNA (the molecules that control cell reproduction and the synthesis of bodily proteins) can be damaged in two ways. Minor damage causes mutations, changes in the structure of the DNA, which can result in the synthesis of new proteins. Most mutations kill the cell. If the cell is a sperm or ovum cell, the change might show up as a birth defect. Some mutations may lead to cancer—a disease of cell growth and metabolism out of control. If, on the other hand, the DNA in many body cells is severely damaged, the immediate effect is that bodily proteins can no longer be synthesized to replace damaged ones, and death follows. Table V.10 gives a list of the factors determining the extent of biological damage from radiation. Table V.11 shows the biological effects of increasing dosages of radiation.

The effects of large doses of radiation are drastic. Conclusive evidence that high doses of radiation cause cancer have come from uranium miners, accident victims, and bomb victims in Hiroshima and Nagasaki. Some of the best case studies were made on workers who painted the numbers on radium watch dials. Unknowingly, they touched the paintbrushes to their tongues to sharpen the tips, and thus took radium into their bodies.

Table V.10   *Factors affecting biological damage from radiation*

Factor	Effect
Dose	Most scientists assume that increase in radiation dose produces a proportionate increase in risk
Length of time of exposure	The more a given dose is spread out over time, the less harm it does. The same is true for drugs and alcohol
Area of body exposed	The larger the area exposed to a given number of rems, the greater the damage
Type of tissue exposed	Rapidly dividing cells, such as blood cells and sex cells, are more susceptible to radiation damage than slowly dividing or non-dividing cells such as nerve cells. Fetuses and children are more susceptible to radiation damage than are adults

Table V.11 *Biological effects of different dose levels*

Dose (rems)	Effect
0–25	No immediate observable effects
25–50	Small decrease in white blood cell count causes lowered resistance to infections
50–100	Marked decrease in white blood cell count Development of lesions
100–200	Radiation sickness: Nausea, vomiting, loss of hair. Blood cells die
200–300	Hemorrhaging, ulcers, deaths
300–500	Acute radiation sickness. Fifty percent die in a few weeks
> 700	One hundred percent die

Leukemia, cancer of the white blood cells, is the most rapidly appearing and the most common cancer associated with radiation. Other forms of cancer may also occur, as well as anemia, heart related problems, and cataracts (opaque spots on the lens inside the eye).

There is considerable controversy over whether very low doses of radiation can cause cancer. Most data concerning cancer have come from human exposure at high doses, with mathematical projection back to lower doses. Few studies have reported direct observation of cancer resulting from low radiation doses. Although most scientists will agree that natural levels of radiation (about 150 millirem [mrem]) are safe for most people, a report released in 1981 by the National Academy of Sciences and the Nuclear Regulatory Commission argues that any increased quantity of radiation increases the probability for cancer. This approach to the problem is similar to that of the food additives regulations for chemical carcinogens (Unit Four, Part D.5).

How much radiation do we experience each year? What are the sources? Do we have any choice in the matter? We'll deal with these questions in the next section.

D.6 Exposure to Radiation

We all receive background radiation at low levels from natural and human sources. Among natural sources are the following:

- Cosmic rays—exceedingly high energy particles that bombard Earth from outer space
- Radioisotopes in rocks, soil, and groundwater—uranium (U-238, U-235), thorium (Th-232) and their decay products; other natural radioisotopes
- Radioisotopes in the atmosphere— radon (Rn-222) and its decay products, including polonium (Po-210)

The human sources of background radiation include

- Fallout from nuclear weapons testing
- Increased exposure to cosmic radiation during air travel
- Medical X rays
- Radioisotopes released into the environment during generation of nuclear power and other uses of nuclear technology

Harry R. Black

These climbers on the Matterhorn are exposed to a higher radiation dosage than they would be at sea level.

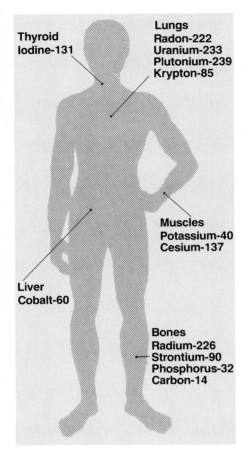

Figure V.27   All living things contain some radioactive isotopes, including these, which are found in specific parts of the human body.

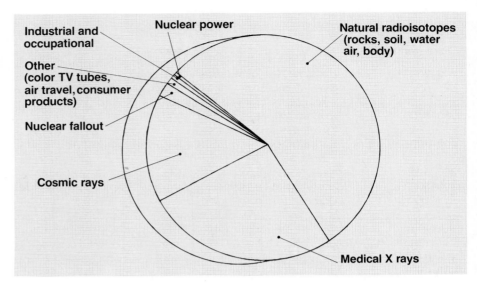

Figure V.28   Sources of background radiation.

Some radiation to which we are naturally exposed comes from sources within our bodies (see Figure V.27). The total background exposure is estimated at 135 mrem per year at sea level. Figure V.28 shows the relative quantities of background radiation we receive from each source.

What level of radiation is considered safe for the average person? The current radiation standard, set in 1977 by the Nuclear Regulatory Commission for the general public, allows the population to receive an average annual dose of 170 mrem. An individual may receive 500 mrem (0.5 rem) a year, or about three times the natural background. For those occupationally exposed, the annual limit is 5 rem per year. This level of radiation increases the risk of cancer by 1–3%, according to the National Institutes of Health.

CHEM*QUANDARY*

Why would standards for exposure levels for some individuals be different from standards for the general public? Why are they different for occupationally exposed persons?

Although we cannot avoid some radiation sources, such as those in the ground and atmosphere, we do have a choice about other sources of radiation. We can choose whether or not to have a diagnostic X ray. We can decide whether or not we will undergo medical tests that use radioactive isotopes. We can choose whether to fly and how often, thereby limiting our exposure to cosmic radiation. We can choose where we live and try to control our home environment, in ways that reduce our risk to radon and other radiation sources. Each of these situations, of course, involves benefit-risk analysis.

D.7   Radon in Homes

Radon has been in the Earth's atmosphere from the very beginning. It is a decay product of uranium. In the 1980s the public learned of a high concentration of radioactive radon gas in some U.S. homes.

What is new is the way we build and use our homes. Air conditioning decreases the need to open windows. To conserve energy, many new homes are more air-tight than they used to be. The result is that air inside may have little chance to mix freely with outside air.

Radon is produced as uranium decays in the soil and in building materials. Some radon produced in the soil dissolves in groundwater. Many houses have cracks in the foundation open to soil and moisture below. Radon seeps into the houses, where it stays because there is little chance to escape.

The harmful nature of radon is enhanced by its radioactive decay product, polonium, a solid alpha particle emitter.

Alpha radiation is highly ionizing at short range from within the body. Polonium drawn into the lungs with household dust can be harmful. Possible protective measures include opening windows more often, sealing cracks in floors, and removing radon from ground water.

Radon is but one of many sources of background radiation that each of us is exposed to. Complete the following activity to get an idea of how much radiation you receive.

D.8   *You Decide:* Your Radiation Dosage Per Year

On a separate sheet of paper list the numbers and letters of the exercise below. Then fill in the blanks with the missing numbers. Add the millirem values when you finish, to approximate the dosage of radiation you receive each year.

Source of radiation	Quantity per year
1. Location of your town or city.	
a. Cosmic radiation at sea level (U.S. average). (Cosmic radiation is radiation emitted by stars across the universe. Much of this is deflected by the Earth's atmosphere and ionosphere.)	30 mrem
b. Add an additional millirem value based on your town or city's elevation above sea level: 1000 m (3300 ft) above sea level = 10 mrem; 2000 m (6600 ft) above sea level = 30 mrem; 3000 m (9900 ft) above sea level = 90 mrem. (Estimate the mrem value for any intermediate elevation.)	_____ mrem
2. House construction. Choose the material from which your house is made; enter the correct value. (Building materials contain a very small percentage of radioisotopes.) Brick, 75 mrem; wood, 40 mrem; concrete, 85 mrem.	_____ mrem
3. Ground. Radiation from rocks and soil (U.S. average).	15 mrem
4. Food, water, and air (U.S. average).	25 mrem
5. Fallout from nuclear weapons testing (U.S. average).	4 mrem

Source of radiation	Quantity per year
6. Medical and dental X rays.	
a. Chest X ray (number of visits times 10 mrem per visit).	_____ mrem
b. Gastrointestinal tract X ray (number of visits times 200 mrem per visit.)	_____ mrem
c. Dental X rays (number of visits times 10 mrem per visit).	_____ mrem
7. Jet travel. (Jet travel increases exposure to cosmic radiation.) Number of flights (five-hour flights at 30,000 ft or 9000 m) times 3 mrem per flight.	_____ mrem
8. Nuclear power plants. If your home is adjacent to a plant site add 1 mrem.	_____ mrem
Total	_____ mrem

Questions

1. How does your yearly dosage compare with the standard? How does it compare with the average background per year?

2. How might you change the way you live to reduce the quantity of radiation you are exposed to?

A major unanswered question regarding exposure to radioactivity faces everyone living in countries using nuclear technology. It is the question of how to dispose of nuclear waste. We'll look at this difficult problem in the next section.

D.9 Nuclear Waste: Twentieth Century Pandora's Box

Imagine this situation. You live in a clean, comfortable home. But you have one big problem. You can't throw away your garbage. The city forbids this because it has not decided what to do with it. Your family has compacted and wrapped the garbage the best way possible for more than 30 years. You are running out of room. Some of the bundles are leaking and creating a health hazard. What can be done?

The nuclear power industry, and the nuclear weapons industry in particular, have a similar problem. Spent (used) nuclear fuel and radioactive waste products have been accumulating for more than 30 years. This material is still highly radioactive.

Let's take a closer look at the problem of spent nuclear fuel. Every year, about one-third of the fuel rods in a nuclear reactor must be replaced. This is necessary for two reasons. First, a fraction of the uranium-235 fuel has been fissioned. Second, the accumulating fission products interfere with the fission process itself.

The spent fuel rods are highly radioactive, and remain dangerous for hundreds of years. Table V.12 lists the half-lives of just a few of the isotopes resulting from nuclear fission, and found in spent fuel rods.

E. I. du Pont de Nemours and Company

Figure V.29 High-level waste storage tanks.

Table V.12 *Some isotopes in spent fuel rods*

Isotope	Half-life
Plutonium-239	24,000 y
Strontium-90	25 y
Barium-140	12.8 d
Krypton-94	1.4 s

By federal law, the waste must be stored at each reactor site. Figure V.29 shows typical nuclear waste storage tanks. Available storage space, however, is limited. Final disposal of radioactive waste is the responsibility of the federal government. The U.S. government has not yet provided an alternative permanent disposal system.

The amount of military waste is greater than the amount of commercial waste. It is in liquid form, for it is a by-product of extracting plutonium from spent fuel rods of military reactors. Plutonium could be extracted from the spent fuel rods of commercial reactors. However, it is illegal in the United States to use the by-products of civilian reactors for military purposes. As the isotopes in the liquid waste decay, they emit radiation and thermal energy. In fact, without cooling, such wastes can become hot enough to boil. This makes military waste containment extremely difficult.

Why hasn't the government acted? The Nuclear Regulatory Commission announced in 1980 that the technology for waste disposal is available. The problem is a political and social one—acceptable sites must be found.

The method for disposing of radioactive waste favored by the U.S. Department of Energy is mined geologic disposal, shown in Figure V.30. The radioactive waste would be buried over 1000 m below the Earth's surface.

To prepare the waste for burial, it is first allowed to cool for 7–10 years. This is already occurring at each nuclear reactor site. Spent fuel rods are placed in large pools of water. As time passes, the isotopes decay, lowering the level of radioactivity to a point at which the materials can be handled. They become thermally cooler as well. This storage is only a temporary measure, since the tanks require too much maintenance to be safe for longer periods of time.

Figure V.30   The mined geologic disposal plan.

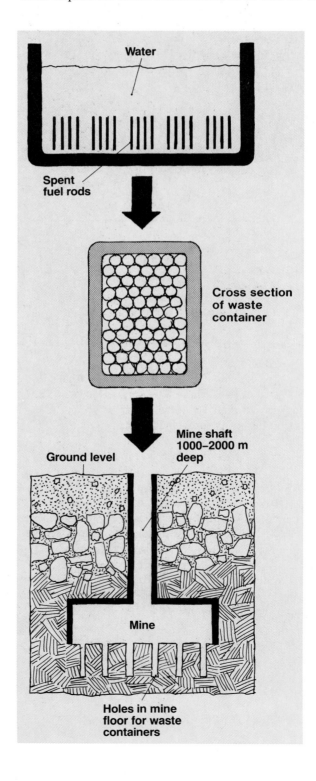

Next, cooled radioactive wastes would be locked inside leak-proof packages. Several methods have been proposed to "package" military wastes. They can be solidified—that is, transformed into a type of glass or rock. This is called **vitrification.** The glassy or rocky material would still be highly radioactive, but would be much less likely to leak into the environment. The vitrified wastes would be packed into special containers made of glass, stainless steel, or concrete, that provide a protective shield. Solid wastes from commercial reactors would be easier to dispose of, but they still would be packed in special containers.

Sites thought safe from earthquakes and other geological disturbances have been selected to test mined geologic disposal.

The vitrification process has been demonstrated only on a laboratory scale in the United States. Vitrification is currently used in France, where 60% of its electric power comes from nuclear reactors. Nowhere in the world, however, has the waste been buried. The problem is, again, finding politically and socially acceptable sites. In small countries using nuclear power, such as Japan, where land mass is at a premium, deep ocean burial is being considered.

Some geological sites formerly assumed to be stable enough for radioactive waste disposal have been found unsafe. For example, some plutonium was buried as Maxey Flats, Ky., in ground that geologists believed would remain stable for thousands of years. Within 10 years, some of the buried plutonium had moved dozens of meters away. In a natural underground reactor in the African nation of Gabon, however, no movement appears to have occurred in billions of years. Tanks designed to serve as temporary storage for military reactor wastes for 50 years in the state of Washington developed leaks after only 14 years.

How much high-level radioactive waste is there? A commercial nuclear reactor produces 30 tons of spent fuel each year. This means that roughly 2400 tons of waste are being generated each year by the commercial reactors operating in the United States. The nuclear weapons program has contributed about 20 million liters of stored liquid waste.

In addition to these high-level wastes, millions of tons of less radioactive waste exist in this country. Much has been produced by the mining and processing of uranium for fuel. Hospitals and other users of radioactive substances also make small contributions to this total. Eventually, nuclear reactors themselves will become nuclear waste.

Department of Energy

Checking and securing low-level radioactive waste shipments at the disposal facility in Richland, Washington.

What are the plans to resolve these problems? By U.S. law, the President must select two sites for permanent radioactive waste disposal from several options chosen by the Department of Energy. The Nuclear Regulatory Commission must either issue a permit for the first of these or reject it by 1989. The Department of Energy must begin burying wastes in the first repository by Jan. 31, 1998. Any state or Indian tribe whose land is chosen as a site for a repository may veto that selection. Such a veto can be overridden by joint action from both Houses of Congress. If a waste disposal site is rejected, the search for permanent storage must continue.

CHEM*QUANDARY*

Why do you think other countries are currently using nuclear power to a much greater extent than we are in the United States?

Nuclear waste disposal is a pressing issue. There is another possibly hazardous situation related to the use of nuclear technology that we must consider in a risk-benefit analysis.

D.10 Catastrophic Risk: A Nuclear Power Plant Accident

Although a nuclear power plant cannot become an atomic bomb, other accidents could occur, either through malfunction, earthquake, or human error, that could release large amounts of radioactive matter into the environment. We have seen major accidents at Three Mile Island in the United States and Chernobyl in the Soviet Union. Ongoing studies of the results of these accidents will add to our knowledge of the risks of nuclear power.

It is very difficult, however, to define the precise risk of personal injury from a catastrophe at a nuclear plant. In 1985, the Nuclear Regulatory Commission told a Congressional Committee that there was a 45% chance, over the next 20 years, of a "severe" **meltdown** at a nuclear plant. In this situation, the fuel within the rods would become hot enough to melt. (This is roughly equal to the chance that a major earthquake will occur in California over the same period.) If a meltdown were to occur, the chance of a "major release" of radioactivity would range from 10–50%, depending on the plant involved, according to the NRC. The NRC made no attempt to define the risk to individuals.

Some estimates of risk to individuals from the generation of nuclear power have been made. In 1975, a study by MIT scientists for the Energy Research and Development Agency suggested that the chance of dying from a nuclear power plant accident, either from high doses of radiation at the time of the accident, or from lower doses suffered from the resulting fallout, would be a little greater than the chance of dying in a plane crash. (Keep in mind that airplane travel is very safe.)

However, risk assessment calculations for airplane travel are quite certain, while risk assessment calculations for nuclear accidents are so uncertain that the MIT study results may mean that nuclear plants are either much safer, or much more dangerous than air travel. The reason for the great uncertainty is that scientists must attempt a much more complicated calculation based on limited experience.

It is impossible to be certain that all possible accident sequences have been considered. To complicate matters, the potential accident scenarios are different for each kind of nuclear plant, and even for individual nuclear plants of the same general type.

What does this mean for determining the risk of nuclear accidents? The Nuclear Regulatory Commission has concluded that because of the wide range of uncertainty, it is impossible to use such studies as a basis for policy.

In the 1950s, utility companies refused to develop nuclear power until Congress passed the Price-Anderson Act in 1957. This law limits the liability of a utility or the federal government, should a nuclear accident occur, to $560 million. Insurance companies refuse to provide insurance against damage from nuclear radiation.

Is nuclear power worth the risk? It is our responsibility to decide what we want for ourselves and for our nation, and to make our wishes known to those who govern. What are your impressions at this time? Do you feel better able to approach these difficult issues? We hope so. In the next part of this unit you will have an opportunity to review the highlights of your study of nuclear phenomena, and to see how other class members respond to these questions.

PART D
SUMMARY *QUESTIONS*

1. Define the term "tracer" as it applies to the medical applications of radioisotopes. Briefly discuss one example of a medical tracer.
2. Discuss one industrial and one agricultural application of radioisotopes. Include a brief discussion on the risk-benefit ratio of these applications.
3. From a human health standpoint, what is the difference between ionizing radiation and nonionizing radiation? Provide two examples of each.
4. Name the common unit for measuring the biological effects of radiation.
5. Explain why alpha emitters are fairly harmless if outside the human body, but quite dangerous if inside it.
6. List four factors that determine the extent of biological damage caused by radiation.
7. Radiation is more destructive to rapidly dividing cells than it is to those reproducing more slowly. In what sense can this be both a benefit (i.e., put to positive use) and a risk?
8. Briefly discuss three problems encountered in assessing the risks of radiation exposure at low dose levels. In the absence of better data, how do you think we should regulate allowable exposures at the low dose levels?
9. Compare the minimum radiation dose at which immediate, observable effects have been detected, the maximum annual allowable dose for radiation workers, and the radiation standards for the average person. Explain why these values are different.
10. Explain the basic problem of nuclear waste "disposal" in terms of the concepts of radioactive decay, half-life, and radiation shielding.
11. Briefly discuss the benefits and risks of reprocessing nuclear wastes.
12. Even if nuclear power generators were phased out, we would need to deal with the wastes that have already been generated, plus the much greater wastes associated with continuing production of nuclear weapons. Briefly discuss one possible solution to this problem. In your discussion include at least one technological and one practical (political) problem associated with this solution.

E PUTTING IT ALL TOGETHER: SEPARATING FACT FROM FICTION

At the start of this unit you took, and administered, a survey dealing with the public's understanding of nuclear phenomena. Undoubtedly you discovered a range of responses. You probably noted that different people relied upon different sources of information.

The survey results probably raised as many questions as they answered. This is often the case in science—attempts to answer one question raise a series of new questions. In working through the activities and readings of this unit, you have found answers to many of them. Others—those that do not necessarily have a single "right" answer—may still be troublesome. In this final activity you will reexamine the survey to begin to separate fact from fiction and clarify your own views on some important nuclear issues.

E.1 Processing the Survey Information

Part 1

Your teacher will provide you with a copy of the survey you took at the start of this unit. As a homework assignment, retake the survey, answering the questions in light of what you've learned. This is not a test (at least in the sense of earning a grade), so don't attempt to use your text to find the "right" answers—just answer the items based on your knowledge and values.

Part 2

Your teacher will return your original survey form. Compare your pre- and post-unit responses. Note the items for which your responses changed. Circle or otherwise clearly mark these items for later discussion.

Jon Jacobson

Jon Jacobson

We receive information from many varied sources, not just from the classroom.

Your teacher will then assign you to a group of four to six students. By group consensus, place each of the survey items into one or more of the following categories. You may wish to mark the designated symbols S, P, V, and NA (defined below) on the survey form.

Scientific reality (S). The item is either scientifically correct or incorrect as stated. It reflects a principle that can be verified or disproved via observations in a clear-cut experiment.

Political reality (P). Data published in reputable journals, magazines, or newspapers would support the notion that the item reflects (either positively or negatively) the public opinion or current situation.

Value-laden statement (V). The item contains emotionally charged words and reflects a definite pro- or anti-nuclear stance. Note it is possible for such an item to be either based on, or in contradiction to, some scientific principle.

Not addressed in this unit (NA). The item may be either correct or incorrect, value-laden or not, but was not discussed in the unit.

During the last part of the class period you will bring the results of your individual group analysis to a full class discussion. The class will decide which items (approximately 10) are worthy of further discussion for the next day's class. Such items should fit one or more of the following criteria:

- Pre- and post-unit responses that varied considerably.
- Post-unit responses that are still highly debatable—some of your fellow students strongly agree while others strongly disagree.
- Post-unit responses that still reflect high uncertainty.

Each group will be assigned two items to discuss in further detail in class.

Part 3

In the first half of the period, return to your previous groups and discuss your two assigned items. Use the following questions to guide your discussion. Each item on the survey may fit more than one category.

Scientific Reality (S)

1. Is the statement correct or incorrect as stated?
2. If false as stated, how should the item be reworded to read correctly?
3. Within your group, was there much discrepancy between the first and second surveys on this particular item? If so, why do you think this is the case? If the item was answered incorrectly, does the same misconception appear in the responses of other teenagers and adults?
4. How would the individuals' misconceptions of this item affect their opinions about nuclear phenomena? Would it tend to make them anti- or pro-nuclear?

Political Reality (P)

5. Do you agree or disagree with the majority's position on the item? Why?
6. Is the political reality likely to change in the near future? If so, what factors might lead to this change?

Value-Laden Statement (V)

7. What word(s) suggest that the statement is value-laden?
8. Is the statement more likely to reflect the view of a pro- or anti-nuclear activist?
9. Does the item simultaneously reflect a scientific reality and a value position?

Not Addressed in This Unit (NA)
10. Where might you seek reliable information pertaining to this item?

In the second half of the class period, two members of each group will give a brief (1–2 minute) oral report on the initial group discussion regarding each item. Following these brief presentations, the full class will have an opportunity to raise any questions or issues of concern.

E.2 Looking Back and Looking Ahead

As we stated earlier, the purpose of this unit has not been to teach you everything known about nuclear chemistry or to provide the "right" answer on any particular nuclear issue. Our aim has been to provide you a basis for further exploration of this important area, which falls between scientific principles and social policies.

Except for nuclear weapons, the most controversial nuclear technology undoubtedly is electric power generation. As discussed in this unit, it is a technology with real benefits and definite risks. As you learned in earlier units, energy conversions typically involve some form of pollution. One of the chief benefits of nuclear power is its relative cleanliness in terms of air pollution.

In the next unit we will explore air and air pollution. But beyond this, we will examine the Earth's atmosphere as a resource, which like the hydrosphere and lithosphere, is both a source of essential substances used by communities and a depository for unwanted by-products.

Argonne National Laboratory

This wall of the power-plant building of the Atomic Energy Commission's National Reactor Testing Station in Idaho records the first known production of useful electric power from atomic energy. The future of the industry will depend on decisions made by an informed citizenry.

UNIT *SIX*

Chemistry, Air, and Climate

CONTENTS

INTRODUCTION

Although we live *on* the Earth's surface, we live *in* its atmosphere. Air surrounds us just like water surrounds aquatic life. And like the Earth's crust and its bodies of water, the atmosphere is both a mine for obtaining chemical resources and a sink for discarding waste products. We use specific gases from the atmosphere when we breathe, burn fuels, and carry out various industrial processes. Humans, other living organisms, and natural events also add gases, liquid droplets, and solid particles to the atmosphere. These added materials may have no effect, or they may disrupt the environment locally—or globally.

Since human activities can sometimes lower the quality of air, the problem of air pollution leads to important social questions: Should air be considered a free resource? How clean should air be? How much will it cost to maintain clean air? What financial and environmental costs are associated with polluted air? Who should be responsible for pollution control? Citizens will continue to debate these and other questions at local, state, and national levels in the years ahead.

Acceptable answers to such difficult questions depend at least in part on understanding the basic chemistry of the atmosphere and the gases in it. We need to know about the atmosphere's composition and structure, general properties of gases, processes influencing climate, and natural recycling, which renews the atmosphere.

This unit explores the basic chemistry related to these topics, and examines current pollution control efforts. It offers another opportunity to sharpen your chemical knowledge and your decision-making skills. Take a deep breath and exhale slowly. The air you just moved so easily in and out of your lungs is our topic of study.

National Center for Air Pollution Control

This photo shows the Cincinnati City Hall (1963) half-way through a cleaning process to remove 34 years of dirt.

A LIFE IN A SEA OF AIR

It's said that we don't appreciate the value of things until we have to do without them or pay for them. This is certainly true of the Earth's atmosphere. Unless we are astronauts, long-distance runners, patients with diseased lungs, or scuba divers, we seldom think about the sea of colorless, odorless gases surrounding us. You are probably no more aware of the 14 kg or so of air you breathe daily than a fish is of the water passing over its gills. As long as air is present and not too polluted, we tend to take it for granted. We shall see that this has not proved wise.

How much do you know about the atmosphere and problems involving air quality? Test your knowledge by completing the following exercise.

A.1 *You Decide:* Air, the Mysterious Fluid in Which We Live

On a separate sheet of paper indicate whether you believe each numbered statement below is true (T) or false (F), or whether you are too unfamiliar with it to judge (U). Then, for each statement you believe is true, write a sentence describing a practical consequence or application of the fact. Reword each false statement to make it true.

Don't worry about your score. You won't be graded on this exercise; its purpose is to start you thinking about the mixture of gases in which you live.

1. You could live nearly a month without food, and a few days without water, but deprived of air, you would survive for only a few minutes.
2. The volume of a given sample of air (or any gas) depends on its pressure and temperature.
3. Air and other gases are weightless.
4. The atmosphere exerts a force of nearly 15 pounds on each square inch of your body.
5. The composition of the atmosphere varies widely at different locations on Earth.
6. The atmosphere acts as a filter to prevent harmful radiation from reaching the Earth's surface.
7. In the lower atmosphere, air temperature usually increases as altitude increases.
8. Minor components of air such as water and carbon dioxide play major roles in the atmosphere.
9. Two of the top 10 industrial chemicals are "mined" from the atmosphere.
10. Ozone is a pollutant in the lower atmosphere, but an essential component of the upper atmosphere.
11. Clean, unpolluted air is a pure substance.
12. Air pollution first occurred during the Industrial Revolution.
13. No human deaths have ever been directly attributed to air pollution.

14. Natural events, such as volcanic eruptions and forest fires, can lead to significant air pollution.

15. Destruction of materials and crops by air pollution represents a significant economic loss for our nation.

16. Industrial activity is the main source of air pollution.

17. The "greenhouse effect" is a natural warming effect that may become harmful through excessive burning of fuels.

18. In recent years, rain in industrialized nations has become less acidic.

19. Most air pollution caused by human activity originates with combustion.

20. Pollution control has not improved overall air quality.

When you are finished, your teacher will give you answers to these items, but won't elaborate on them. However, each item will be discussed at some point in this unit. The next section includes some demonstrations and at-home activities that illustrate the nature of the air you breathe.

A.2 Laboratory Demonstration: Gases— Much Ado about Nothing?

Since the gases in the atmosphere are colorless, odorless, and tasteless, you might be tempted to think they are "nothing." But gases, like solids and liquids, have definite physical and chemical properties. You and your classmates will observe several demonstrations that illustrate some of these properties. The twelve demonstrations answer four major questions about air.

- Is air really matter?   Demonstrations 1–3
- What is air pressure all about?   Demonstrations 4–8
- Why does air sometimes carry odors?   Demonstrations 9–10
- Is air heavy? Will it burn?   Demonstrations 11–12

To get the most out of the demonstrations, follow these steps:

1. Try to predict the outcome of the demonstration.

2. Carefully observe the demonstration and, if necessary, account for differences between your prediction and the actual outcome.

3. Try to identify the specific property of gases being demonstrated. Try to decide why gases exhibit this property.

4. Think of practical consequences on Earth that result from each property as exhibited by atmospheric gases.

Try the following additional activities at home, and record both the results and your explanation of them in your notebook.

1. Place two straws in your mouth. Place the free end of one in a glass of water and the other outside the glass. Try to drink the water through the straw. Account for your observations.

2. In the screw-on lid of a jar, punch a hole into which a straw will fit. Insert a straw and seal the connection with clay, putty, or wax. Fill the jar to the brim with water. Screw the top on and try to drink the water through the straw. Account for your observations. Explain how it is possible to drink through a straw.

The properties of the elusive stuff called air make it vitally important in our lives. Let's examine one facet of air's importance.

A.3   Air: The Breath of Life

Seen from the moon's surface, Earth's atmosphere blends with its waters and land masses, presenting a picture of considerable beauty. Other planets possess exotic beauty as well, but as far as unmanned explorations have determined, their beauty is not accompanied by support of life. Earth supports millions of species of living organisms, from one-celled amoebas to redwood trees and elephants.

In the first unit, on water, you considered the key role of water in supporting life on Earth. Although the present atmosphere was formed much later than the waters of the Earth, it also helps sustain plants and animals.

A major role of the atmosphere is to provide oxygen gas needed for respiration. The following activity will help you understand that role.

YOUR*TURN*

VI.1   Breath Composition and Glucose Burning

Below are questions about oxygen in inhaled and exhaled air, and in burning glucose in the body. All can be answered by using concepts you have already studied (moles and the molar relationships shown by chemical equations). To illustrate, consider how the following questions are answered.

In a certain sample of air, 0.80% of the molecules are those of carbon dioxide (CO_2). Assume there are 125×10^{20} molecules in each breath you take. How many carbon dioxide molecules pass into your lungs with each breath of this air?

It is convenient to express percent as number of molecules per 100 molecules. The air sample is 0.80% CO_2, so there would be 0.80 CO_2 molecule per 100 air molecules. A breath contains

$$\left(\frac{125 \times 10^{20} \text{ air molecules}}{1 \text{ breath}}\right) \times \left(\frac{0.80 \text{ } CO_2 \text{ molecule}}{100 \text{ air molecules}}\right)$$

$$= 1.0 \times 10^{20} \text{ } CO_2 \text{ molecules/breath}$$

How many moles of carbon dioxide are present in each breath? How many grams? There are 6.02×10^{23} molecules per mole of any substance and the molar mass of CO_2 is 44.0 g/mol.

First, we can find the moles of CO_2 from the molecules of CO_2 in each breath.

$$\left(\frac{1.0 \times 10^{20} \text{ } CO_2 \text{ molecules}}{1 \text{ breath}}\right) \times \left(\frac{1 \text{ mol } CO_2}{6.02 \times 10^{23} \text{ } CO_2 \text{ molecules}}\right)$$

$$= 1.7 \times 10^{-4} \text{ mol } CO_2/\text{breath}$$

Then, we can find the quantity in grams:

$$\left(\frac{1.7 \times 10^{-4} \text{ mol } CO_2}{1 \text{ breath}}\right) \times \left(\frac{44.0 \text{ g } CO_2}{1 \text{ mol } CO_2}\right) = 7.5 \times 10^{-3} \text{ g } CO_2/\text{breath}$$

Each breath contains 7.5×10^{-3} g, or 7.5 mg of carbon dioxide.

The following exercise will help you solve problems such as how much oxygen or glucose you need each day, each hour, or each minute.

How many grams of oxygen will be consumed in completely burning 650 g of methane (CH_4), the principal component of natural gas? The equation is

$$CH_4(g) + 2 \text{ } O_2(g) \longrightarrow CO_2(g) + 2 \text{ } H_2O(g)$$

Mole and molar mass were introduced in Unit Two, Part C.3.

The equation shows relative numbers of moles. Therefore, the mass given must be converted into moles. Taking 16.0 g/mol as the molar mass of methane gives

$$650 \text{ g CH}_4 \times \left(\frac{1 \text{ mol CH}_4}{16.0 \text{ g CH}_4}\right) = 40.6 \text{ mol CH}_4$$

The chemical equation shows that for every mole of methane that burns, two moles of oxygen gas are required, so we need 2 × 40.6 mol of O_2, or

$$40.6 \text{ mol CH}_4 \times \left(\frac{2 \text{ mol O}_2}{1 \text{ mol CH}_4}\right) = 81.2 \text{ mol O}_2$$

which is equivalent to

$$81.2 \text{ mol O}_2 \times \left(\frac{32.0 \text{ g O}_2}{1 \text{ mol O}_2}\right) = 2.60 \times 10^3 \text{ g O}_2$$

In burning 650 g of methane, 2.60×10^3 g of oxygen will be consumed. This answer could have been found with a single math setup as follows:

$$650 \text{ g CH}_4 \times \left(\frac{1 \text{ mol CH}_4}{16.0 \text{ g CH}_4}\right) \times \left(\frac{2 \text{ mol O}_2}{1 \text{ mol CH}_4}\right) \times \left(\frac{32.0 \text{ g O}_2}{1 \text{ mol O}_2}\right)$$
$$= 2.60 \times 10^3 \text{ g O}_2$$

Burning 1 g of methane releases 54 kJ of heat energy. How much heat energy is released by burning 650 g of methane?

$$650 \text{ g CH}_4 \times \left(\frac{54 \text{ kJ}}{1 \text{ g CH}_4}\right) = 3.5 \times 10^4 \text{ kJ}$$

Burning 650 g of methane releases 3.5×10^4 kJ of heat energy.

1. Consider Figure VI.1 which compares the composition of the gases we breathe in with that of the gases we breathe out.
   a. Summarize the changes in the composition of air that result from its entering and then being exhaled from the lungs. How do you account for these changes?

Compare the energy from burning 650 g of CH_4 with that from burning a similar mass of glucose. See Question 2c.

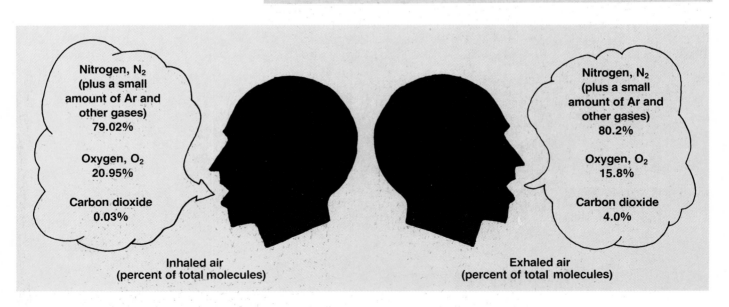

Figure VI.1   The composition of inhaled and exhaled air.

    b. Assuming an average of 14 breaths per minute, how many breaths do you take per day? What factors could result in different answers? Why?

    c. Say the volume of air inhaled with each breath is 500 mL. How many liters of air would you inhale each minute? Each day?

    d. According to Figure VI.1, your lungs extract only a small fraction of the inhaled oxygen gas. What do you think determines the amount of oxygen used?

    e. Assume that there are 250×10^{20} molecules in a 1-L sample of air. Using your answer to Question 1c, calculate how many oxygen molecules are present in the air you inhale each day? In the air you exhale each day? How many oxygen molecules do you use per day?

    f. Use the result of your final calculation in Question 1e plus the number of molecules per mole (6.02×10^{23}) and the molar mass of oxygen gas to calculate the mass of oxygen you use per day.

2. Write the chemical equation for the "burning" (combustion) of 1 mol of glucose ($C_6H_{12}O_6$) to give carbon dioxide (CO_2) and water (H_2O). This will represent what occurs in the body.

    a. Given an equal number of moles of oxygen gas and glucose, which would be the limiting reactant in this combustion reaction? Why? (Refer to Unit Four, Part C.2 if you wish to review limiting reactants.)

    b. Given equal masses of oxygen gas and glucose, which would be the limiting reactant? Why?

    c. Using the equation you wrote, the mass of oxygen gas used each day found in the answer to Question 1f, and the molar masses of oxygen and glucose, calculate the mass of glucose burned each day. If glucose produces approximately 17 kJ for every gram burned, how much heat energy would be generated each day?

    d. What substance produced in your body's "burning" of glucose does not appear in Figure VI.1? How could you confirm that this substance is present in exhaled breath?

Plant life needs a continual supply of carbon dioxide—a waste product of animal respiration. Through photosynthesis in green plants (discussed in the food unit), carbon dioxide combines with water, ultimately forming more glucose and oxygen gas. Photosynthesis and respiration thus balance each other—and the concentration of oxygen gas in the atmosphere remains constant (see Figure VI.2).

The atmosphere can restore and cleanse itself if natural systems are not burdened by excessive pollution. Environmental problems arise when human activities overwhelm the natural recycling and cleansing systems. Air pollution will be explored in Parts C and D of this unit, but as a prelude, you will begin to consider this important problem in the next activity.

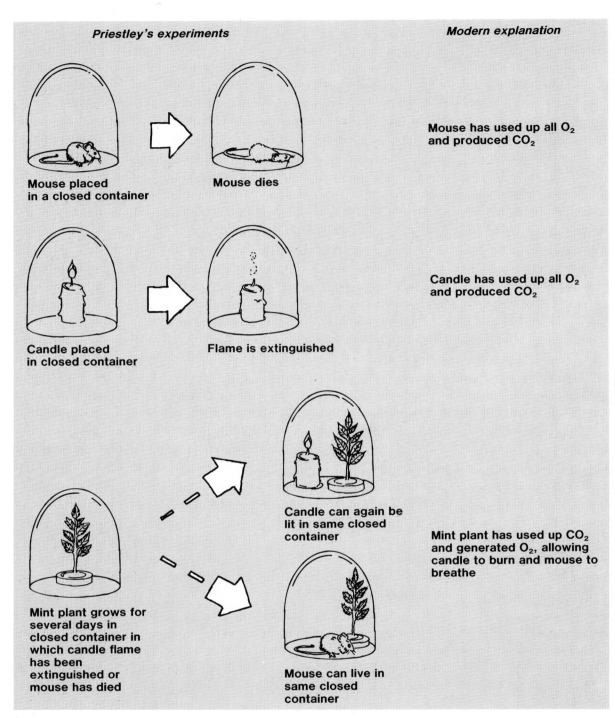

Priestley's experiments

Modern explanation

Mouse placed in a closed container

Mouse dies

Mouse has used up all O_2 and produced CO_2

Candle placed in closed container

Flame is extinguished

Candle has used up all O_2 and produced CO_2

Mint plant grows for several days in closed container in which candle flame has been extinguished or mouse has died

Candle can again be lit in same closed container

Mouse can live in same closed container

Mint plant has used up CO_2 and generated O_2, allowing candle to burn and mouse to breathe

Figure VI.2 Joseph Priestley's experiments in photosynthesis and respiration. In the late 1700s, Priestley performed experiments in which he observed the effects on air of plants, animals, and combustion in various combinations. Although it was not understood until many years later, Priestley had demonstrated that plants use carbon dioxide and give off oxygen, but animals use oxygen and give off carbon dioxide.

A.4 *You Decide:* Air—Just Another Resource?

Consider these two points of view:

View A: Access to air is a fundamental human right; therefore to tax or fine individuals or industries that extract materials from or add pollutants to air is unjust.

View B: Access to air is a fundamental human right; therefore air cleanliness should be ensured by government regulations, which provide taxes or fines upon individuals or industries that lessen air quality.

Identify at least five scientific, practical, or social questions you would like answered before choosing between these positions. As you proceed through this unit, try to seek answers to the questions you have listed.

Given the potentially damaging effects of human activities on air quality, we must learn how to use the atmosphere wisely. As a first step, we must understand its chemical composition and some properties of gases. This is the focus of the next part of our study.

PART A
SUMMARY *QUESTIONS*

1. Describe at least two ways air is similar to and two ways it is different from other resources (such as water, minerals, and petroleum) that you have already studied.

2. Defend or refute each of these statements about gas behavior, based on the gas properties you saw demonstrated earlier in this unit.
   a. An empty bottle is not really empty.
   b. Atmospheric pressure acts only in a downward direction.
   c. Gases naturally "mix" or diffuse by moving from regions of low concentration to regions of high concentration.
   d. All colorless gases have the same physical and chemical properties.

3. As we have noted, you inhale about 14 breaths of air per minute, or about 14 kg of air per day. Based on these data, what is the mass (in grams) of a typical breath of air? If we are concerned with the chemistry involved in breathing, suggest another way the "size" of a breath of air might be expressed. Why would this be useful?

B INVESTIGATING THE ATMOSPHERE

Concern with air quality began with the discovery of fire. Fires for heating, cooking, and metalworking created air pollution problems in ancient cities. In 61 A.D., the philosopher Seneca described "the heavy air" of Rome and "the stink of the smoky chimneys thereof." The Industrial Revolution, beginning in the early 1700s, triggered increased air pollution in and around cities. These developments were accompanied by increased interest in the chemistry and physics of the atmosphere.

In the following sections you'll extend your understanding of the atmosphere, based in part on the results of the demonstrations you observed in Part A.2. This knowledge will be useful in predicting the general behavior of gases. It will help you understand how the sun's radiant energy interacts with atmospheric gases to create weather and climate. Also, this discussion sets the stage for a later discussion of air pollution. We will begin by preparing and investigating some atmospheric gases.

B.1 Laboratory Activity: Chemical Composition of the Atmosphere

Getting Ready

Air, as was shown in Figure VI.1, is composed primarily of nitrogen (N_2) and oxygen (O_2) gases together with much smaller amounts of carbon dioxide and several other gases. Each component of air has distinct physical and chemical properties. In this activity your class will generate two gases present in the atmosphere—oxygen and carbon dioxide—and examine some of their chemical properties.

Oxygen will be generated by the following reaction

$$2\ H_2O_2(aq) \xrightarrow{MnO_2} 2\ H_2O(l) + O_2(g)$$

Hydrogen peroxide   Water   Oxygen gas

Carbon dioxide will be generated by adding antacid tablets to water. These tablets contain a mixture of sodium bicarbonate and potassium bicarbonate ($NaHCO_3$ and $KHCO_3$) and citric acid (an organic acid present in lemons and oranges). When dissolved in water, the bicarbonate ions (HCO_3^-) react with hydrogen ions (H^+) from the citric acid to generate carbon dioxide (the "fizz"):

$$H^+(aq) + HCO_3^-(aq) \rightarrow H_2O(l) + CO_2(g)$$

Oxygen gas extracted from air is a valuable resource.

The behavior of oxygen and carbon dioxide in the presence of burning magnesium, hot steel wool, and burning wood will be investigated. Do oxygen and carbon dioxide support the combustion of these materials?

Next, you will observe whether these gases react with limewater (a solution of calcium hydroxide, $Ca(OH)_2$). Finally, the acid-base properties of oxygen and carbon dioxide will be investigated. Acidic substances produce H^+ ions in aqueous solution, basic substances produce OH^- in aqueous solution, and neutral substances produce neither. In Unit One, Part C.6, you learned that the pH scale can be used to express the acidity or basicity of a solution. Universal indicator contains various compounds; each changes color at a different pH. (In Parts D.13 and D.14 of this unit, acids and bases are discussed further.)

If a tank of compressed nitrogen gas is available, your class also will investigate the properties listed above for nitrogen.

Read the procedures below and set up a data table in your notebook for the results of the tests on nitrogen, oxygen, and carbon dioxide. If nitrogen is not available to be tested, your teacher will give you the information needed to fill in the blanks.

Procedure

Part 1: Gas Preparation
All Groups
Label two gas-collecting bottles "Sample 1" and "Sample 2." Label three test tubes "Sample 3," "Sample 4," and "Sample 5."

Figure VI.3   Gas-generating setup.

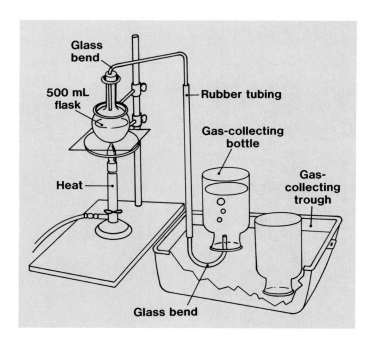

Oxygen Group

1. Set up the apparatus illustrated in Figure VI.3 for generating oxygen gas.

2. Fill the gas-collecting trough with enough tap water to cover the small shelf to a depth of about 3 cm. Fill the two gas-collecting bottles with water. Position them in the trough as your teacher directs.

3. Add 200 mL of 3% hydrogen peroxide (H_2O_2) to a 250-mL graduated cylinder. Weigh 1 g of manganese dioxide (MnO_2) on a clean paper square. (*Caution:* Avoid inhaling any MnO_2 dust.)

4. Pour the hydrogen peroxide into a 500-mL flask and carefully add the manganese dioxide to the flask.

5. Quickly place the stopper with attached glass and rubber tubing in the flask. Place the other end of the tubing under the surface of the water in the trough, but not yet under the mouth of the gas collection bottle. If the reaction is not occurring fast enough to generate a steady stream of gas bubbles, heat the mixture *gently* (but do not allow it to boil) until it reaches a constant rate of gas evolution, and then continue to heat gently as you collect the gas in Step 6.

6. Once the reaction is smoothly under way, allow gas to bubble into the water for one minute. Then position the tube under the collecting bottle mouth.

7. Collect two bottles and three test tubes of the prepared gas as follows: When the first jar is filled you'll observe bubbles rising to the surface of the trough water. Hold a glass plate tightly to the mouth of the inverted jar. Remove the sealed jar from the trough. Set it upright on the table, with the glass plate covering the top. Move the tubing and fill the second bottle.

   To collect a test tube of gas, fill the test tube completely with water. Hold a finger tightly over the opening and invert the tube in the water tray. Direct the stream of gas into the inverted test tube mouth. When gas fills the tube, cover the tube mouth with your finger and remove it from the tray. Immediately close the tube with the stopper.

   If the reaction stops before you have collected the necessary volume of oxygen gas, remove the stopper from the generating flask, remove the burner and allow the flask to cool for five minutes. Then add 20 mL of H_2O_2 solution to the reaction flask.

8. After sufficient gas has been collected, remove the stopper from the generating flask before removing the heat.

Carbon Dioxide Group

1. Set up the apparatus illustrated in Figure VI.3 for generating carbon dioxide gas. The burner is not needed here.

2. Add tap water to the gas-collecting trough to cover the small shelf to a 3-cm depth. Fill two gas-collecting bottles with water. Position them in the trough as your teacher directs.

3. Place 250 mL of water in the 500 mL flask in the generating apparatus. Drop two antacid tablets into the water.

4. Quickly place the stopper with attached glass and rubber tubing in the flask. Place the other end of the tubing under the water surface in the trough, but not under either gas collection bottle.

5. Allow the gas to bubble into the trough for one minute. Then position the tube under the mouth of a collecting bottle.

6. Collect two bottles and three test tubes of the gas as described in Step 7 of the oxygen procedure. If the gas generation slows down before you are finished, add another antacid tablet to the generating flask.

Nitrogen Group

Fill two gas-collecting bottles and three test tubes with nitrogen gas from the nitrogen tank. Follow the procedure described in Steps 1, 2, 5, and 6 for the carbon dioxide group, with any modifications your teacher specifies.

Part 2: Gas Tests

Each group will perform the following on its assigned gas, and share results with the class. Record observations for each gas in your data table.

1. Light a bunsen burner. Using tongs, hold a 10–15 cm-long piece of magnesium ribbon in the flame until it ignites. (*Caution:* Do not look directly at the intense light of the burning magnesium.) Quickly remove the cover plate from Sample 1 and plunge the burning magnesium into the gas in the jar. Hold it there until you and the other class members have observed the result. Record your observations.

2. Pour about 10 mL of water into the bottom of Sample 2, quickly, with the cover pushed aside just a little. Using tongs, hold a piece of steel wool (spread out; not in a tight ball) in the burner flame until it glows red hot. Quickly plunge the steel wool into Sample 2. Hold it there, noting the result.

3. Using tongs, hold a wood splint in the burner flame until it lights. Blow out the flame, then blow on the embers so they glow red. Remove the stopper from Sample 3, and quickly plunge the glowing splint into the collected gas. Turn off the burner.

4. Add about 2 mL of limewater to Sample 4. Close the tube with the stopper and shake carefully. Note any changes in the appearance of the liquid.

5. Add two drops of universal indicator solution to Sample 5. Put the stopper back in the tube and shake carefully. Compare the results with the color chart provided with the indicator. Report the estimated pH to the class.

Questions

1. Why was it important to allow some gas to bubble through the water before you collected a sample?

2. Which gas appears to be the most reactive? The least reactive?

3. Which gas appears to support rusting and burning? This gas makes up (about) what percent of air molecules? (See Figure VI.1.) If our atmosphere contained a higher concentration of this gas, what might be some consequences?

4. Carbon dioxide is used in some types of fire extinguishers. Explain why it works.

5. Figure VI.1 suggests that human lungs expel carbon dioxide. Describe two ways you would verify that your exhaled breath contains CO_2.

What gases in addition to nitrogen, oxygen, and carbon dioxide are present in the atmosphere? Using a variety of sampling and measuring techniques, scientists have pieced together a detailed picture of the atmosphere's chemical composition. This is the subject of the next section.

B.2   A Closer Look at the Atmosphere

Most of the atmosphere's mass, and all of the weather, are located in the 10 to 12 km immediately above the Earth's surface. This region, called the **troposphere** (after the Greek word meaning "to turn over"), is the one in which we live. We will examine it first.

Continuous mixing of gases occurs within the troposphere, making its chemical composition reasonably uniform (Table VI.1). Analysis of glacial ice core samples suggests that the troposphere's composition has remained relatively constant throughout human history.

Table VI.1   *Composition of pollution-free, dry tropospheric air*

Substance	Formula	Percent of gas molecules
Major components		
Nitrogen	N_2	78.08
Oxygen	O_2	20.95
Minor components		
Argon	Ar	0.934
Carbon dioxide	CO_2	0.0314
Trace components		
Neon	Ne	0.00182
Ammonia	NH_3	0.00100
Helium	He	0.000524
Methane	CH_4	0.000200
Krypton	Kr	0.000114

NASA

The only component of the atmosphere visible from space is condensed water vapor.

In addition to the gases listed in Table VI.1, actual air samples may contain up to 5% water vapor. In most locations the normal range for water vapor is 1–3%. Other gases are naturally present in concentrations below 0.0001% (1 ppm). These include hydrogen (H_2), xenon (Xe), ozone (O_3), nitrogen oxides (NO and NO_2), carbon monoxide (CO), and sulfur dioxide (SO_2). Human activity can alter the concentrations of carbon dioxide and some trace components. It can also add new substances that may lower air quality, as we shall see.

If air is cooled under pressure, it condenses to a liquid that boils at about −185 °C. Distilling this liquid produces pure oxygen, nitrogen, and argon.

Liquid air distillation is basically the same as petroleum distillation.

Imagine that we have one mole each of oxygen, nitrogen, and argon gas. Assume we place these identical amounts in three very flexible balloons. Here is what we would observe:

- The three balloons would occupy the same volume, assuming external air pressure and temperature are the same for each.
- The three balloons would shrink to half this volume if the outside air pressure were doubled and the temperature held constant.
- The three balloons would expand to the same extent if the temperature were increased by 10 °C and the external air pressure held constant.
- Each balloon would shrink to half its original volume if half the gas were removed and neither the external air pressure nor the temperature changed.

Study has shown that a balloon filled with one mole of any other gas expands and contracts in exactly the same way, provided the temperature does not drop too low or the external pressure rise too high. All gases share these same expansion and contraction properties.

The four observations described above suggest some important conclusions about gases. One of these is this simple relationship: **Equal volumes of gases at the same temperature and pressure contain the same number of molecules.** This idea was first proposed in 1811 by an Italian chemistry teacher, Amedeo Avogadro (it is called **Avogadro's law**). If you look carefully, you can see the law at work in each observation above.

In the first three cases, each balloon contains 6.02×10^{23} molecules: one mole. In the first observation, all three balloons have the same volume at the same temperature and pressure—just as Avogadro suggested. In the second observation, the external pressure is doubled and the gas volume is half of what it was. Despite this change in conditions, all three balloons are the same size, and all contain the same number of molecules.

Now it's your turn.

YOURTURN

VI.2 Avogadro's Law

Explain how Avogadro's law is illustrated in the third and fourth observations.

An important consequence of Avogadro's law is that all gases have the same **molar volume** if they are at the same temperature and pressure. (The molar volume is the volume occupied by 1 mol of a gas.) Scientists refer to 0 °C and 1 atm (atmosphere) pressure as **standard temperature and pressure,** or **STP.** At STP the molar volume of any gas is 22.4 L.

At STP, gas molar volume = 22.4 L/mol

The fact that all gases have the same molar volume under the same conditions simplifies our thinking about reactions involving only gases. For example, consider these equations:

$$N_2(g) \ + \ O_2(g) \ \longrightarrow \ 2 \ NO(g)$$
$$2 \ H_2(g) \ + \ O_2(g) \ \longrightarrow \ 2 \ H_2O(g)$$
$$3 \ H_2(g) \ + \ N_2(g) \ \longrightarrow \ 2 \ NH_3(g)$$

You've learned that the coefficients in such equations represent the relative numbers of molecules or moles of reactants and products. Using Avogadro's law (equal numbers of moles occupy equal volumes), you can interpret the coefficients in terms of gas volumes:

$$1 \text{ volume } N_2(g) \ + \ 1 \text{ volume } O_2(g) \ \longrightarrow \ 2 \text{ volumes } NO(g)$$
$$2 \text{ volumes } H_2(g) \ + \ 1 \text{ volume } O_2(g) \ \longrightarrow \ 2 \text{ volumes } H_2O(g)$$
$$3 \text{ volumes } H_2(g) \ + \ 1 \text{ volume } N_2(g) \ \longrightarrow \ 2 \text{ volumes } NH_3(g)$$

The actual volumes could have any specific values, such as 1 L, 10 L, or 100 L. In the third equation, for example, we could use 300 L of H_2 and 100 L of N_2, and expect to make 200 L of NH_3 if the conversion is complete.

Rather than determining the masses of reacting gases, chemists can monitor some reactions by measuring the volumes of the gases involved. Unfortunately, similar "short cuts" do not work for reactions involving liquids and solids. There is no simple relation between moles of solids and liquids and their relative volumes.

Complete the following activity to check your understanding of the concepts discussed in this section.

YOUR*TURN*

VI.3 Molar Volume and Reactions of Gases

1. What volume would be occupied at STP by 3 mol of $CO_2(g)$?

2. In a certain reaction, 2 mol of $NO(g)$ reacts with 1 mol of $O_2(g)$. How many liters of $O_2(g)$ would react with 4 L of NO gas?

3. Poisonous carbon monoxide gas forms when fossil fuels such as petroleum burn in the presence of insufficient oxygen gas. The CO is eventually converted into CO_2 in the atmosphere. Automobile catalytic converters are designed to speed up this conversion:

   Carbon monoxide gas + Oxygen gas → Carbon dioxide gas

   Write the equation for this conversion. How many moles of oxygen gas would be needed to convert 50 mol of carbon monoxide to carbon dioxide? How many liters of oxygen gas would be needed to react with 1120 L of carbon monoxide? (Assume both gases are at the same temperature and pressure.)

4. In the third unit on petroleum, you studied the combustion of octane in air:

   $$2 \ C_8H_{18}(l) \ + \ 25 \ O_2(g) \ \longrightarrow \ 16 \ CO_2(g) \ + \ 18 \ H_2O(g) \ + \text{ Energy}$$

   You now know that air is a mixture of about 21% O_2 and 79% N_2 molecules (with small amounts of argon and other gases). How many moles of nitrogen gas pass through the engine with each 25-mol sample of oxygen gas? How many grams of nitrogen? At STP, how many liters of nitrogen gas would this represent?

Now that you have explored the composition and properties of gases at the bottom of the sea of air in which we live, let's continue our study of the atmosphere by swimming up to higher levels.

B.3 *You Decide:* How Do Atmospheric Properties Vary with Altitude?

If you were to dive from the ocean's surface downward you would encounter increasing pressures and decreasing temperatures. Creatures deep in the ocean live in a much different environment than those living near the surface. Similarly, the environment at sea level is quite different from that at higher altitudes. From early explorations of the atmosphere in hot-air and lighter-than-air balloons to current journeys through the atmosphere and beyond, scientists have obtained information regarding conditions in the atmosphere.

Picture yourself in a craft designed to fly from the Earth's surface to the farthest regions of our atmosphere. The instruments in your imaginary craft have been set to record altitude, air temperature, and pressure readings. One-liter gas samples can be taken at specific heights. You'll receive a report on the mass, number of molecules, and composition of each sample.

As the craft rises, the composition of the air remains essentially constant at 78% N_2, 21% O_2, 1% Ar, plus trace elements. At 12 km you notice that you are above the clouds. The tallest mountains are far below. The sky is a light blue color, and the sun shines brilliantly. The craft is now above the region where commercial aircraft fly and weather develops.

Above 12 km, air composition is about the same as at lower altitudes, except there is more ozone (O_3). You also notice that the air is quite calm, unlike the turbulent air you encountered below 12 km.

Air samples taken at 50–85 km contain relatively few particles. Those present are charged species such as O_2^+ and NO^+. Above 200 km, your radar detects various communication satellites in orbit.

Your aircraft now returns to Earth, and you turn to analysis of the data you collected.

Plotting the Data
Table VI.2 presents the data recorded during the flight. The last two columns provide comparisons of equal-volume (1-L) samples of air at different altitudes.

Jon Jacobson

What limits the height to which this type of balloon can rise?

Table VI.2 *Atmospheric Data*

Altitude (km)	Temperature (°C)	Pressure (mmHg)[a]	Mass of 1-L sample (g)	Total molecules (in a 1-L sample)
0	20	760	1.225	250×10^{20}
5	−12.5	407	0.736	153×10^{20}
10	−45	218	0.414	86×10^{20}
12	−60	170	0.377	77×10^{20}
20	−53	62.4	0.089	19×10^{20}
30	−38	17.9	0.018	4×10^{20}
40	−18	5.1	0.004	0.80×10^{20}
50	2	1.5	0.001	0.22×10^{20}
60	−26	0.42	0.0003	0.06×10^{20}
80	−87	0.03	*b*	*b*

[a]Millimeters of mercury (mmHg), a common pressure unit, is discussed in Part B.4.
[b]Values too small to be measured.

Prepare two graphs. One should be a plot of temperature vs. altitude; the other, pressure versus altitude. Arrange your axes to use the full sheet of paper for each graph. The x axis scale (altitude) for each graph should range from 0 to 100 km. The y axis scale (temperature) on the first graph should range from −100 °C to +40 °C. The y axis scale (pressure) in the second graph should run from 0 to 780 mmHg, a common unit for pressure (see Part B.4).

Plot the data collected and connect the points with the smoothest line possible. (Note that a "line" may be straight or curved.) Use these graphs and the knowledge gained from your flight to answer the following questions.

Questions

1. Compare the ways air temperature and pressure change with increasing altitude. Which follows a more consistent pattern? Try to explain this behavior.

2. Would you expect barometric pressure to rise or fall if you traveled from sea level to
   a. Pike's Peak (4270 m above sea level)?
   b. Death Valley (85 m below sea level)? Explain your answers.

3. When two rubber plungers (like those plumbers use) are pressed together, it is difficult to separate them (you may wish to try this). Why? Would it be easier or harder to separate them at the top of a mountain? Explain your answer.

4. How do your values of mass and molecules per liter of air change with increasing altitude? If you plotted these values, what would be the appearance of the lines on the graph?

5. Scientists often consider the atmosphere in terms of layers: **troposphere** (nearest earth), **stratosphere, mesosphere,** and **thermosphere** (outermost layer). What flight data evidence supports the idea of such a "layered" atmosphere? Mark the graphs with horizontal lines to indicate where you think various layer boundaries are.

In previous sections we have used the term "air pressure." In the next section we'll clarify what a scientist means by pressure.

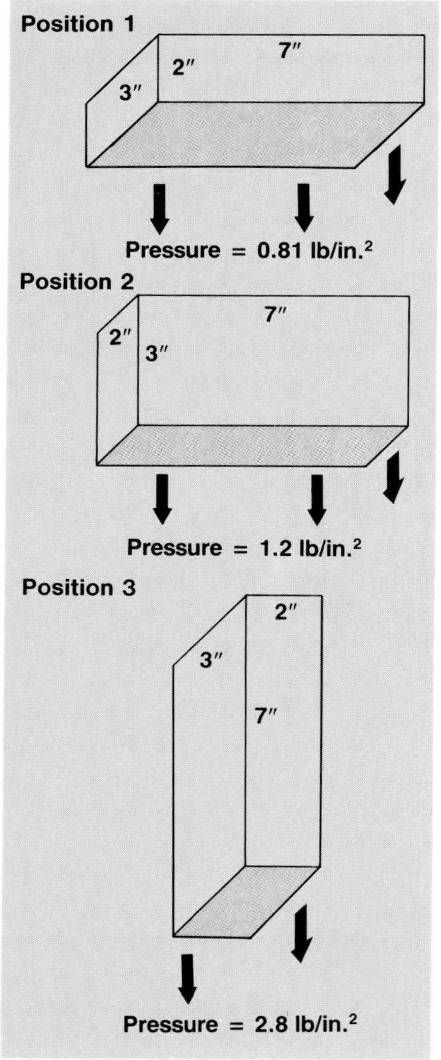

B.4 Air Pressure

In everyday language, we speak of being pressured, meaning we feel forced into behaving in certain ways. The greater the pressure, the less "space" we feel we have. To a scientist, "pressure" also refers to force and space, but in a physical way.

Pressure represents the force applied to one unit of surface area:

$$\text{Pressure} = \frac{\text{Force}}{\text{Area}}$$

To get a better idea of this, consider a lead block with a 7.0-in. length, 3.0-in. width, and 2.0-in. height. Such a block would have a weight (exert a force downward) of 17 lb. Although the block's weight remains constant, the pressure it exerts depends upon which side the block is resting on (see Figure VI.4). The calculations of the pressure exerted in each position are

Position 1: $\dfrac{17\text{ lb}}{7.0\text{ in.} \times 3.0\text{ in.}} =$ 0.81 lb/in.²

Position 2: $\dfrac{17\text{ lb}}{7.0\text{ in.} \times 2.0\text{ in.}} =$ 1.2 lb/in.²

Position 3: $\dfrac{17\text{ lb}}{2.0\text{ in.} \times 3.0\text{ in.}} =$ 2.8 lb/in.²

Let's consider some practical applications of a scientific view of pressure.

Position 1
Pressure = 0.81 lb/in.²
Position 2
Pressure = 1.2 lb/in.²
Position 3
Pressure = 2.8 lb/in.²

Figure VI.4 The pressure exerted by the lead block depends upon which side is down. For the same block, the pressure is greatest for the side with the smallest area, in this case, the 3 in. × 2 in. side.

CHEM*QUANDARY*

1. During the 1950s, stiletto-heeled shoes were quite popular. Floors across the nation became scarred with tiny dents. When tennis shoes or shoes with broader heels were worn, no such problem developed. Why? (See Figure VI.5.)
2. To avoid excessive record wear, the tone arm on a turntable should be adjusted so that the stylus (needle) has a very light tracking weight. Why does this help extend the life of records (and of the stylus)?

Figure VI.5 The pressure a shoe heel exerts depends upon its area.

1 atm = 14.7 lb/in.² = 760 mmHg

How do lead blocks, high-heeled shoes, and record styluses relate to the atmosphere? As this unit's opening demonstrations showed, the atmosphere exerts a force on every object within it. On a typical day, at sea level, air exerts a pressure of about 14.7 lb on every square inch of your body. This pressure is equal to one atmosphere. But there is yet another way in which pressure is expressed. The pressure data on the imaginary flight were given in **mmHg (millimeters of mercury)**. A weather report may include "the barometric pressure is 30 inches of mercury." Air pressure can also be expressed as the height of a mercury column. Why? A simple demonstration will clarify matters.

Fill a graduated cylinder (or soft drink bottle) completely with water. Cover it with your hand and invert it into a container of water. What happens to the water level inside the cylinder? What force supports the weight of the column of water in the cylinder?

Now imagine repeating this with a taller cylinder, and again with an even taller cylinder. If the cylinder were made taller and taller, at a certain height water would no longer fill the cylinder to the top when it is inverted into a container of water. Why?

This experiment was first performed in the mid-1600s. The researchers discovered that one atmosphere of pressure could support a column of water no taller than 33.9 ft (10.3 m). If one tries the experiment with even taller cylinders, the water drops to the 10.3-m level, leaving a partial vacuum above the liquid. Obviously, such a tall device would be rather awkward to handle. Scientists decided to replace the water with mercury, which is 13.6 times more dense. The resulting mercury barometer (see Figure VI.6) is shorter than the water barometer by a factor of 13.6.

In the following sections we will study the effects of pressure and temperature changes on gas volume. This knowledge will help us understand the gases in our bodies, those trapped in rocks on Earth, and those in the atmosphere through which jetliners and spacecraft travel. We'll consider the effect of changes in pressure first.

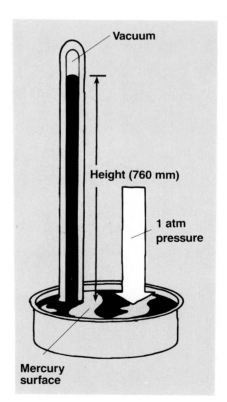

Figure VI.6 A mercury barometer. The atmosphere at sea level will support a column of mercury 760 mm high. The pressure unit "atmospheres" is thus related to pressure in millimeters of mercury, 1 atm = 760 mmHg.

B.5 Boyle's Law: How to Put the Squeeze on a Gas

Unlike the volume of a solid or a liquid, the volume of a gas can easily be changed. Applying pressure to a sample of gas decreases its volume—it is "compressed." By compressing a gas, a greater mass of the gas can be stored in a given container. Tanks of compressed gas are quite common. For example, propane tanks are used by campers, mobile home owners, and people whose homes are in rural areas; welders buy tanks of oxygen and acetylene gas; and hospitals use tanks of pure oxygen gas for patients with breathing problems. Tanks of gas are often used in chemistry laboratories.

Try the following Chem Quandary.

CHEM*QUANDARY*

A chemistry teacher notices a large difference in the price of hydrogen gas sold by two companies. Company A offers a 1-L cylinder of hydrogen gas for $8; Company B offers a 1-L cylinder of the gas for $15. The teacher discovers that Company B offers a better bargain. Explain how this could be.

Atmospheric air undergoes compression and expansion, changing with altitude (as you observed in your imaginary journey) and with weather conditions. Pressure tends to fall before a storm, and to rise as the weather clears.

How much does gas volume decrease with a given increase in pressure? You already know the answer to this. In Part B.2 it was the second of the four observations on the behavior of gases in balloons. When the pressure on the balloons was doubled, their volume decreased to half the original value.

This change in volume illustrates a relationship common to all gases. It is called **Boyle's law,** after the 17th-century English scientist who first proposed it. One way to state Boyle's law is the following: at a constant temperature, the product of the pressure and the volume of a given gas sample is a constant. Suppose we have 12 L of gas under 2 atm pressure (2 atm $\times$ 12 L = 24 L atm). Doubling the pressure to 4 atm will halve the volume to 6 L (4 atm $\times$ 6 L = 24 L atm). Note that 2 atm $\times$ 12 L = 4 atm $\times$ 6 L. Such relationships hold for any change in either the volume or pressure. If the volume is decreased to 4 L, the pressure will increase to 6 atm (2 atm $\times$ 12 L = 6 atm $\times$ 4 L).

Boyle's Law: at constant T, P·V = constant for a fixed amount of gas.

The general mathematical statement of Boyle's law is

$$P_1V_1 = P_2V_2$$

where P_1 and V_1 are the original pressure and volume of a gas, and P_2 and V_2 are the new pressure and volume at the same temperature. Plotting a series of pressure and volume values for any gas sample gives a curve similar to that in Figure VI.7.

Boyle's law allows predictions to be made of changes in the pressure or volume of a gas sample at constant temperature when any three of the values P_1, V_1, P_2, or V_2 are known. Consider the following example:

A tank of gas used in a chemistry laboratory may have a volume of 1.0 L and contain gas at a pressure of 56 atm. What volume would the gas from such a tank occupy at 1.0 atm (and the same temperature)?

We use Boyle's law to solve the problem in the following way:

1. Identify the starting and final conditions:

$$P_1 = 56 \text{ atm} \qquad P_2 = 1.0 \text{ atm}$$
$$V_1 = 1.0 \text{ L} \qquad V_2 = ?$$

2. Rearrange the equation $P_1V_1 = P_2V_2$ to solve for the unknown, in this case, V_2 (the volume after the pressure decrease):

$$V_2 = \frac{P_1V_1}{P_2}$$

Investigating the Atmosphere 351

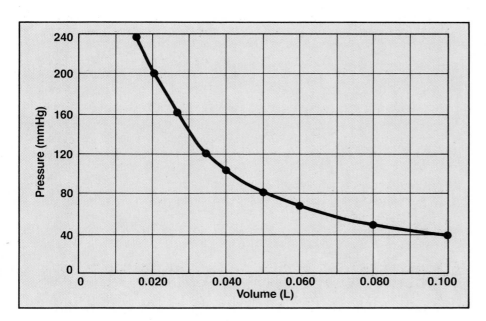

Figure VI.7 Boyle's law: The volume of a gas sample, maintained at constant temperature, is inversely proportional to its pressure. Hence the product of P × V is constant. A plot of pressure vs. volume for any gas sample at constant temperature will be similar to this one.

3. Substitute the values into the equation and solve for the unknown:

$$V_2 = \frac{(56 \text{ atm})(1.0 \text{ L})}{1.0 \text{ atm}} = 56 \text{ L}$$

A reasoning method can be used to solve the same problem:

If the pressure decreases from 56 to 1.0 atm, the volume will increase by a proportional amount. Therefore, to find the new, larger volume, the known volume must be multiplied by a pressure ratio larger than one:

$$1.0 \text{ L} \times \frac{56 \text{ atm}}{1 \text{ atm}} = 56 \text{ L}$$

If the gas pressure increases, then the volume must decrease. (This assumes that the temperature remains constant.) In this case the pressure ratio used must be less than one. Similar reasoning applies to problems in which the initial and final volume are known and the final pressure is to be found.

Work the following problems, which show some common applications of Boyle's law.

YOUR*TURN*

VI.4 Pressure-Volume Relationships

1. Explain each of these statements:
   a. Even when provided ample oxygen gas to breathe, aircraft passengers become uncomfortable if the cabin loses its pressure. (*Hint:* What will gases in the human body do if the body is exposed to a sudden drop in air pressure?)
   b. Bottles of carbonated soft drink "pop" when opened.
   c. Tennis balls are sold in pressurized cans. (*Hint:* Each tennis ball contains gases at elevated pressure to give it good bounce.)
   d. When climbing a mountain or ascending a tall building in an elevator, your ears may "pop."

National Severe Storms Laboratory

Dramatic changes in air pressure are associated with the passage of a tornado.

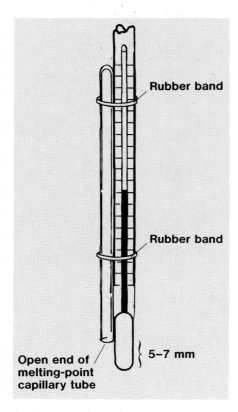

Figure VI.8 Apparatus to study variation of gas volume with temperature.

2. You can buy helium in small aerosol cans to inflate party balloons. The label on such a can states that it contains "about 0.25 cubic feet (or 7080 mL) of helium." Assume that this volume refers to the volume of helium at 1 atm pressure (760 mmHg). If the volume of the can is 492 mL, what is the gas pressure inside the can (at the same temperature)?

3. Suppose that on a hot, sticky spring afternoon, a tornado passes near your high school. The air pressure inside and outside your classroom (volume = 430 L) is 760 mmHg before the storm. At the peak of the storm, pressure outside the classroom drops to 596 mmHg. To what volume would the air in the room try to change to equalize the pressure difference between the inside and the outside? (Assume no change in air temperature.) Why is it a good idea to open the windows slightly as such a storm approaches?

4. Automobile tire pressure is usually measured with a gauge that reports the difference in pressure between the air in the tire and atmospheric pressure. Thus, if the tire gauge reads 30 lb/in.^{2} on a day when the atmospheric pressure is 14 lb/in.^{2}, the total tire pressure is 44 lb/in.^{2}. What volume of air from the atmosphere (at 14 lb/in.^{2}) would be needed to fill a 40.0-L tire to a gauge reading of 30 lb/in.^{2}? Why does pumping up an automobile tire by hand take such a long time?

In all these problems, we assumed that gas temperature remained constant. How does temperature influence gas volume if the pressure remains constant? The answer to this question is important because many reactions in laboratory work, in chemical processing, and all those in cooking are done at roughly constant atmospheric pressure. Did you ever wonder why cakes and bread rise as they bake? Read on and you'll find out.

B.6 Laboratory Activity: Temperature-Volume Relationship for Gases

Getting Ready

Most forms of matter expand when heated and contract when cooled. As you know, gases expand and contract to a much greater extent than do either solids or liquids.

In this activity you will investigate how the temperature of a gas influences its volume when pressure remains unchanged. To do this, you will raise the temperature of a thin glass tube containing a trapped air sample, and then record volume changes as the air sample cools.

Procedure

1. Tie a capillary tube to the lower end of a thermometer using two rubber bands (Figure VI.8). The open end of the tube should be placed closest to the thermometer bulb and 5–7 mm from the bulb's tip.

2. Immerse the tube and thermometer in a hot oil bath that has been prepared by your teacher. Be sure the entire capillary is immersed in the oil. Wait for your tube and thermometer to reach the temperature of the oil (approximately 130 °C). Record the temperature of the bath.

3. After your tube and thermometer have reached constant temperature, lift them so that about three-quarters of the capillary tube is elevated out of the oil bath. Pause here for about three seconds to allow some oil to rise into the tube. Then quickly carry the tube and thermometer (on a paper towel to avoid dripping) back to your desk.

4. Lay the tube and thermometer on a paper towel on the desk. Make a reference line on the paper at the sealed end of the melting-point tube. Also mark the upper end of the oil plug (Figure VI.9). Alongside this mark write the temperature at which the air column had this length.

5. As the temperature of the gas sample drops, make at least six marks representing the length of the air column trapped above the oil plug; write the corresponding temperature next to each mark. Allow enough time so that the temperature drops by 80 to 100 degrees. Since the tube has a uniform diameter, length serves as a relative measure of the gas volume.

6. When the thermometer shows a steady temperature (near room temperature), make a final length and temperature observation. Discard the tube and the rubber bands according to your teacher's instructions. Wipe the thermometer dry.

7. Measure and record (in centimeters) the marked lengths of the gas sample.

8. Prepare a sheet of graph paper for plotting your volume (length) and temperature data. The vertical scale should range from 0 to 10 cm; the horizontal scale should include values from -350 °C to 150 °C. Label your axes and arrange the scales so the graph fills nearly the entire sheet. Plot the temperature-length data. Draw the best straight line through the plotted points. Using a dashed line, extend this straight graph line so it intersects the x axis. Turn in one copy of your data; keep another copy for the questions that follow.

Questions

1. What was the total change in the length of your sample of gas from the first reading to the last? What was the corresponding overall change in temperature?

2. Use your Question 1 answers to find the change in length for each degree of temperature change. For instance, if the length decreased by 5.0 cm while the temperature dropped 100 °C, the ratio would be

$$\frac{5.0 \text{ cm}}{100 \text{ °C}} = 0.050 \text{ cm per °C}$$

3. Use the value calculated in Question 2 to find the gas temperature that would correspond to a sample length of 0 cm.

4. Compare the temperature found in Question 3 with the temperature noted at the point where your extended graph line intersected the horizontal axis. Both values represent estimates of the gas temperature required to shrink its volume to "zero." (This assumes, of course, that the temperature-volume trend continues to low temperatures.) Which is the better estimate of this "zero gas volume" temperature? Why?

5. If you were to continue cooling the trapped gas sample, do you think the gas would finally reach "zero volume"? Why?

Experiments similar to the one you just performed were first completed in the late 1700s. They resulted in some new ideas, including a more useful temperature scale.

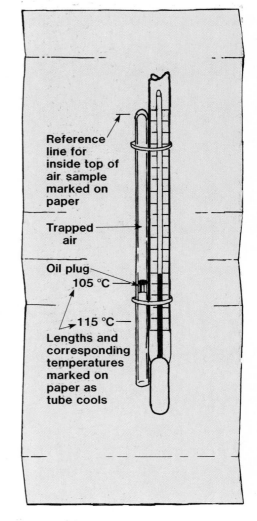

Figure VI.9 Marking the length and temperature of the air sample. The air trapped in this tube has cooled from 115 °C to 105 °C and shrunk as shown.

B.7 *You Decide:* A New Temperature Scale

Studies of changes in gas volume caused by temperature changes at constant pressure were conducted in the 1780s by French chemists (and hot-air ballooning enthusiasts) Jacques Charles and Joseph Gay-Lussac. Some data illustrating their observations are shown in Figure VI.10. The plots for different gases and different sample sizes begin at different points, but if extended to the *x* axis (an extrapolation), all meet at the same temperature.

Clearly, there is a simple relationship between gas volume and temperature (at constant pressure). However, expressing this mathematically proved difficult because of the need to deal with temperatures that are negative numbers on the Celsius scale. Lord Kelvin (William Thomson, an English scientist), solved the problem by proposing a new temperature scale.

Let's see if the pooled data found by your class in the just-completed lab activity will reveal what Kelvin discovered. Answer the following questions:

1. At what temperature does your extended graph line intersect the *x* axis?

2. What would be the volume of your gas sample at this temperature?

3. Why is this volume only theoretical?

The kelvin is the SI unit for temperature.

Now renumber the temperature scale on your graph, assigning the temperature at which the graph intersects the *x* axis the value zero. The new scale expresses temperature in kelvin units (K), and is sometimes referred to as the kelvin temperature scale. One kelvin is the same size as one degree Celsius, but the zero point of the scale has been changed so that kelvin temperatures are all positive numbers. Zero kelvins is the lowest temperature theoretically possible: absolute zero.

4. Based on your graph, what temperature in kelvins would correspond to 0 °C, the freezing point of water? What temperature would correspond to 100 °C, the boiling point of water at one atmosphere pressure?

5. How do you convert a temperature in degrees Celsius units to its corresponding temperature in kelvins? How would you convert a temperature in kelvins to its corresponding value in degrees Celsius?

Figure VI.10 Temperature–volume measurements of various gas samples at 1 atm pressure. Extrapolation has been made for temperatures below liquefaction (O_2 is −183 °C, N_2 is −196 °C).

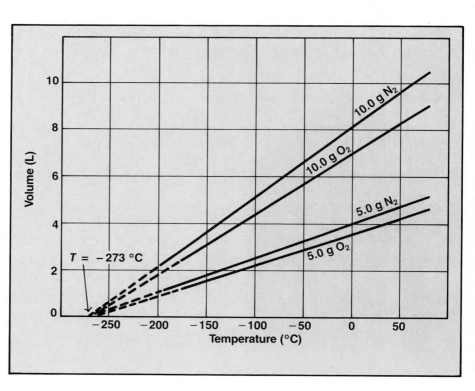

The kelvin temperature scale led to a simple temperature-volume relationship for gases. Doubling the kelvin temperature of a gas sample causes its volume to double, provided external pressure remains constant. Halving the kelvin temperature causes the gas volume to decrease by half, and so on. Such relationships are summarized in **Charles' law:** At constant pressure, the kelvin temperature divided by the volume of a given gas sample is a constant.

Charles' law: At constant P, $\dfrac{T}{V} = constant$ for a fixed amount of gas.

CHEM*QUANDARY*

Knowing how gases behave when temperature increases at constant pressure, answer the following questions:

a. Why does bread rise when baked? (*Hint:* $CO_2(g)$ is produced by yeast action.)

b. Is hot air more dense or less dense than cold air?

c. Why do hot air balloons rise?

d. If you can install only one thermostat in a two-story house, should it be placed on the first or second floor?

Try the following gas behavior problems using the approach you prefer. In each problem identify the variable (pressure or volume) that is assumed to be constant.

YOUR*TURN*

VI.5 Temperature-Volume-Pressure Relationships

1. If the kelvin temperature of a fixed volume of gas increases to three times its original value, what will happen to the pressure of the gas? Give an example of such a situation.

2. If a sample of gas is cooled and contracts at a constant pressure to one-fourth of its initial volume, what change in its kelvin temperature must have occurred? Give an example of such a situation.

3. Explain why car owners in severe northern climates often add air to their tires in winter and release air from the tires when summer arrives.

4. When the volume of a gas sample is reported, the pressure and the temperature must also be given. Why? This is not necessary for liquids and solids. Why?

5. Use gas laws to explain each of the following situations:
    a. A rising weather balloon encounters decreasing pressure and decreasing temperature. It expands as it rises.
    b. Thunderheads towering high into the sky form where warm, moist air and cold air masses meet.
    c. The Earth's weather is most changeable in the middle lattitudes in the northern and southern hemispheres.

Why do all common gases at normal atmospheric conditions behave in accord with Boyle's law and Charles' law? In the next section an explanation will be developed.

B.8 In Ideal Cases, Nature Behaves Simply

By the early 1800s, scientists had discovered the gas laws you have just explored. Balloon flights also provided valuable information on the composition and structure of the atmosphere. However, explanations for why gases behave so consistently and similarly were somewhat sketchy.

Since the 17th century, scientists have pictured gases as composed of tiny particles separated by great distances. But not until the early 19th century did the atomic theory lay the groundwork for understanding gas behavior. Bit by bit, scientists pieced together the **kinetic molecular theory** of gases.

To understand the theory, you must first understand the concept of **kinetic energy.** Kinetic energy is simply energy possessed by a moving object. It is related to both the mass and the velocity of that object. At a given velocity, a more massive object has greater kinetic energy than a less massive object. And a given object has greater kinetic energy as its velocity increases.

The kinetic molecular theory of gases is based on the following postulates:

A postulate is an accepted principle used as the basis for reasoning or study.

- Gases consist of tiny particles (atoms or molecules) that have negligible size compared with the great distances separating them.
- Gas molecules are in constant, random motion. They often collide with each other and with the walls of their container. Gas pressure is the result of molecular collisions with the container walls.
- Molecular collisions are elastic. This means that although individual molecules may gain or lose kinetic energy, there is no net (or overall) gain or loss of kinetic energy from these collisions.
- At a given temperature, molecules in a gas sample have a range of kinetic energies. However, the average kinetic energy of the molecules is constant and depends only on the kelvin temperature of the sample. In samples of different gases at the same temperature, the average kinetic energy of the molecules is the same. As the temperature increases, so do the average velocities and kinetic energies of the molecules.

An analogy may be helpful in understanding the molecular picture presented by the kinetic molecular theory.

YOUR*TURN*

VI.6 Kinetic Molecular Theory: An Analogy

1. Imagine that people dancing in an enclosed space are a two-dimensional representation of gas molecules bouncing around a container (that is, they move across the floor, but not up to the ceiling and down). Identify which variable (volume, temperature, pressure, or number of molecules) is most like the following:
   a. The number of dancers
   b. The size of the room
   c. The tempo of the music
   d. The number and force of collisions between dancers.
2. Which law (Boyle's, Charles', Avogadro's or other) best applies to each of these situations?
   a. The tempo of the music and the number of dancers remain constant, but a partition is closed, leaving less space for dancing. (What will this do to the number and force of collisions?)

Jon Jacobson

A ballroom model for molecules in motion.

b. The size of the room and number of dancers are kept constant, but the tempo of the music is increased. (What will this do to the number and force of collisions?)

c. The room size and the tempo of music are kept constant, but the number of dancers is increased. (How will this affect the number and force of collisions?)

Other analogies sometimes used to help picture gases at the molecular level include a room swarming with tiny gnats, or one full of bouncing superballs. Although helpful in understanding molecular behavior, such models fail to represent these characteristics:

- The extremely small size of the molecules relative to the total volume of a sample of gas. Less than one ten-thousandth of the volume of nitrogen gas is taken up by particles. The rest of the space is empty.
- The extremely high velocities of the molecules. Under normal conditions of pressure and temperature, most molecules move at speeds greater than 1700 km/h (1100 mph).
- The extremely high frequency of collisions.

Because of these differences, the actual behavior of gases can be represented precisely only through mathematical expressions.

Complete the following exercises to check your understanding of the kinetic molecular theory of gases.

YOUR*TURN*

VI.7   Gas Molecules in Motion

Use the kinetic molecular theory to explain the following observations regarding gases. Where appropriate, discuss such factors as the kinetic energies, spaces between molecules, and collisions of molecules. A sketch of molecules in motion may also be helpful for some items. An example is provided for you.

> Increasing the volume of a gas sample will decrease its pressure if the temperature is constant.

> Increasing the volume of a sample of gas molecules gives the molecules more room to move. Thus molecules must travel farther (on average) before colliding with the container walls. Fewer molecular collisions with the walls in a given period of time means that the pressure will decrease.

1. Decreasing the volume of a gas sample held at constant temperature causes the gas pressure to increase.
2. At constant pressure, the volume of a gas changes when the temperature changes.
3. At constant volume, the pressure of a gas changes when the temperature changes.
4. The atmosphere exerts a pressure on our bodies, yet this pressure doesn't crush us.
5. a. Filled balloons eventually leak even if they are tightly sealed.
   b. Helium balloons leak faster than those inflated with human breath.
6. Gases spread out from regions of greater concentration (or higher pressure) to regions of lesser concentration (or lower pressure) until they become uniformly mixed. This process is called **diffusion.** Explain these examples of gaseous diffusion:
   a. Smelly gaseous pollutants can be detected several kilometers from their source even on days with no noticeable breeze.
   b. The percentage of different gases in the troposphere is essentially constant (except for H_2O) at all geographic locations and altitudes.

Gases that behave as the kinetic molecular theory predicts are referred to as **ideal gases.** At very high pressures or very low temperatures, gases do not behave ideally. Boyle's law and Charles' law no longer accurately describe gas behavior under such conditions. At low temperatures the molecules move more slowly and the weak attractions between them may become so important that the gas will condense into a liquid. At high enough pressures, if the temperature is not too high, the molecules are forced so close together that these forces of attraction may again cause a gas to condense. However, under conditions normally encountered in our atmosphere, most gases behave close to ideally and their behavior is well explained by the kinetic molecular theory.

Now that you understand how chemists account for some of the properties of gases, you are ready to explore further how the gases in our atmosphere interact with the sun's radiant energy to create weather and climate.

PART B
SUMMARY *QUESTIONS*

1. Oxygen gas is essential to life as we know it. Our atmosphere contains approximately 21% oxygen. Would a higher percentage of atmospheric oxygen be desirable? Explain.

2. Explain the following reaction using a molecular picture, a chemical equation, and words:

    1 L Hydrogen gas + 1 L Chlorine gas → 2 L Hydrogen chloride gas

3. Does Avogadro's law apply to liquids and solids? Explain your answer.

4. In terms of the pressure exerted at various depths, how is our atmosphere similar to the oceans?

5. Explain why a suction cup hook can support the weight of a small object.

6. Explain why life does not naturally exist above the troposphere.

7. Solve these problems. As part of each answer, identify which gas variable was assumed constant and which gas law applied:
    a. A small quantity of the inert gas argon (Ar) is added to light bulbs to reduce the vaporization of tungsten atoms from the filament. What volume of argon at 760 mmHg of pressure is needed to fill a 0.210-L light bulb at 1.30 mmHg pressure?
    b. A tank at 300 K contains 0.285 L of gas at 1.92 atm pressure. The maximum pressure the container is capable of withstanding is 5.76 atm. Assuming that doubling the kelvin temperature causes the pressure to double, at what temperature will the tank burst? Would it explode in a 1275 K fire?

8. Convection, the process whereby warm air rises and cold air falls, is important to the natural circulation and cleansing of the troposphere. Explain from a molecular point of view why convection occurs.

9. How does the kinetic molecular theory explain the fact that you can smell your mother's cooking the moment you enter your home?

EXTENDING *YOUR KNOWLEDGE*
(OPTIONAL)

- In what ways is an "ocean of gases" analogy useful in thinking about the atmosphere? How does the atmosphere differ from the hydrosphere? (You may wish to compare a dive down into the ocean with a flight up through the atmosphere.)
- Boyle's law is illustrated each time you breathe in or breathe out. Explain.
- Boyle's law is a matter of life and death to scuba divers. On the surface of the water, the diver's lungs, tank, and body are under 1 atm pressure. However, under water the diver's body is under the combined pressure of atmosphere and water.
    a. When the diver is 34 ft below the surface of the ocean, how much pressure does his or her body experience?
    b. Why are pressurized tanks needed when diving to great depths?
    c. What would happen to the volume of the tank if it were not made strong enough to withstand such pressure?
    d. Why is it necessary to exhale and rise slowly when ascending from the ocean depths?
    e. How do the problems of a diver compare with those of a pilot climbing to a high altitude in an unpressurized plane?

- If air at 25 °C has a density of 1.28 g/L, and your classroom has a volume of 2×10^5 L,
  a. What is the mass of air in your classroom?
  b. If the temperature increased, how would this affect the mass of air in the room? Assume the room is not completely sealed.
- The kelvin temperature scale has played an important role in theoretical and applied chemistry.
  a. Find out whether zero kelvins (0 K) has been reached in the laboratory. If not, how close have scientists come to this temperature?
  b. At 0 K, how would matter behave?
  c. Research from the field of **cryogenics** (low-temperature chemistry and physics) has many possible applications. Do research in the library to learn about activities in this field.

Environment Canada

The sulfur and nitrogen oxides generated here will probably be carried many miles across country to do their damage.

C ATMOSPHERE AND CLIMATE

Imagine a place where noonday sunshine on a rock makes it hot enough to fry an egg, where the night is cold enough to freeze carbon dioxide gas to dry ice, where the sun's ultraviolet rays are strong enough to burn your exposed skin in minutes. That place is the moon. Its extreme conditions are due to the absence of an atmosphere.

Together, the sun's radiant energy and the Earth's atmosphere help maintain a hospitable climate for life on our planet. The atmosphere delivers the oxygen gas we breathe and makes exhaled carbon dioxide available to plants for photosynthesis. It also serves as a sink for airborne wastes from people, industry, and technology—a role which causes increasing concern. And the atmosphere protects our skin from the sun's ultraviolet rays.

To understand the basis for our hospitable climate, it's important to know how solar energy interacts with the Earth's atmosphere. The sun warms the surface of the Earth. The Earth's warm surface, in turn, warms the air above it. Since warm air expands, its density decreases and it rises. Colder, more dense air falls. This gaseous movement creates continual air currents that drive the weather.

Let's look more closely at the sun's energy. What makes it so useful?

C.1 The Sunshine Story

As noted in the previous unit on nuclear energy, the enormous quantity of solar energy is generated by the fusion of hydrogen nuclei into helium. Most of this energy escapes from the sun as electromagnetic radiation. About 9% of solar radiation is in the **ultraviolet (UV)** region of the electromagnetic spectrum, 46% is in the **visible,** and 45% is in the **infrared (IR)** region of the spectrum. The complete solar spectrum is shown in Figure VI.11.

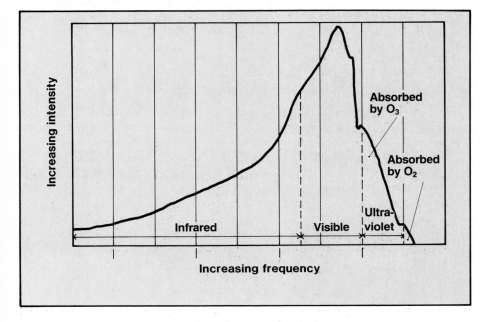

Figure VI.11 The solar spectrum. The higher the frequency, the higher the photon energy of the radiation. Intensity, plotted on the y axis, is a measure of the quantity of radiation at a given frequency.

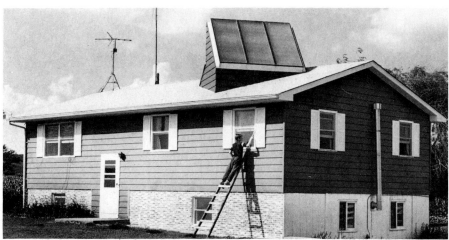

Jon Jacobson

Utilizing the energy of the sun.

Electromagnetic radiation, as you learned in the previous unit, is composed of photons, each possessing a characteristic frequency and quantity of energy. The higher the frequency, the higher the energy of the photon. Photon energy determines the effect of radiation on matter.

Infrared radiation, with frequencies between 10^{12} and 10^{14} Hz (cycles/s), causes molecules to vibrate faster. As we have seen in our study of the kinetic molecular theory (Part B.8), this raises the temperature.

Visible light is of higher energy (frequency about 10^{14} Hz) and can energize electrons in some chemical bonds. One photon delivers its energy to the electrons in one bond. Such photon-electron interactions are taking place right now in double bonds of molecules in your eyes, making it possible for you to see this printed page. Visible light also interacts with electrons in chlorophyll molecules in green plants, providing the energy needed for the reactions of photosynthesis.

The still higher energy carried by photons of ultraviolet radiation, with frequencies ranging from 10^{14} to 10^{16} Hz, can break single covalent bonds. As a result, chemical changes can take place in materials exposed to ultraviolet radiation, including damage to tissues in living organisms.

As solar radiation passes through the Earth's atmosphere, it interacts with molecules and other particles in the atmosphere. Once it reaches the Earth's surface it is absorbed or used in other ways. To better appreciate the effects of solar radiation, let's briefly consider some factors that affect the average temperature of the Earth.

C.2 The Earth's Energy Balance

The mild 15 °C (59 °F) average temperature at Earth's surface is determined partly by the inward flow of photons from the sun. However, certain properties of the Earth determine how much thermal energy it can hold near its surface—where you can feel it—and how much energy it radiates back into space.

Figure VI.12 shows the fate of solar radiation as it enters the Earth's atmosphere. Some incoming solar radiation never reaches the Earth's surface. It is reflected directly back into space by clouds and particles in the atmosphere. A small amount of the radiation is also reflected when it strikes such materials as snow, sand, or concrete on the Earth's surface. Visible light reflected in this way allows the Earth's illuminated surface to be seen from space.

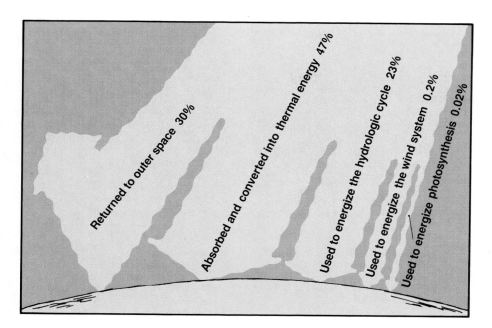

Figure VI.12   The fate of incoming solar radiation.

About one-fourth of the incoming solar energy fuels the hydrologic cycle, which you learned in Unit One is the continuous cycling of water into and out of the atmosphere by evaporation and condensation.

Almost half of the solar energy is absorbed, warming the atmosphere, oceans, and continents. All objects above zero kelvins radiate energy, the quantity being directly related to the object's temperature. The Earth's surface re-radiates most of the absorbed radiation, not at the original frequencies, but at lower frequencies in the infrared region of the spectrum. This returning radiation plays an extremely important role in the Earth's energy balance. Its lower energy photons are absorbed by molecules in the air more easily than the original solar radiation, thus warming the atmosphere.

Carbon dioxide (CO_2) and water (H_2O) are good absorbers of infrared radiation. So are methane (CH_4) and halogenated hydrocarbons such as CF_3Cl. Clouds (concentrated droplets of water or ice) also absorb infrared radiation. The energy absorbed by these molecules in the atmosphere is once again re-radiated. Energy can pass back and forth between the Earth's surface and the molecules in the atmosphere many times before it escapes once again into outer space. This trapped energy keeps us warm.

Without water and carbon dioxide molecules in the atmosphere to absorb and re-radiate thermal energy to Earth, our planet would reach thermal balance at the lower temperature of $-25\ °C$ ($-13\ °F$), quite close to the average temperature on Mars.

The trapping and returning of radiation by carbon dioxide and other substances in the atmosphere is referred to as the **greenhouse effect,** because it reminds people of the way heat is held in a greenhouse on a sunny day. The planet Venus provides an example of a runaway greenhouse effect. There the atmosphere is composed mainly of carbon dioxide and prevents the escape of most infrared radiation. Thermal balance is maintained at a much higher temperature than on Earth.

Check your understanding of the interaction of radiation with matter and the role of radiation in the Earth's energy balance by answering the following questions.

CO_2, H_2O, CH_4, CF_3Cl (and others) are "greenhouse gases."

YOURTURN

VI.8 Earth's Energy Balance

1. Why is ultraviolet radiation potentially more harmful than infrared radiation?
2. Describe two essential roles played by visible radiation from the sun.
3. What might occur if human activities increase the concentration of carbon dioxide or other greenhouse gases in the troposphere?
4. Suppose Earth had a thinner atmosphere than it does at present.
   a. How would average daytime temperatures be affected? Why?
   b. How would average nighttime temperatures be affected? Why?

CHEMQUANDARY

Why does it cool off faster on a clear night than on a cloudy night?

Climate is also influenced by factors other than the interaction of solar radiation with the atmosphere. These factors include Earth's rotation on its axis (causing day and night and influencing wind patterns), its revolution around the sun (causing seasons), the uneven distribution of solar radiation across the Earth's surface (influencing wind patterns), and the different thermal properties of materials on the Earth's surface. In the next section we will examine the last of these factors.

C.3 Thermal Properties at the Earth's Surface

If you have visited states in the South or Southwest (or if you live there), you may have noticed that many trucks and cars are light colored. A property of materials called **reflectivity** helps keep the vehicles cool. When light photons strike a surface some are absorbed, increasing the temperature of the surface, and some are reflected. The reflected radiation does not contribute to raising the temperature of the object.

The color of an object is determined by the frequencies of the radiation it reflects. If all frequencies of the visible spectrum are reflected, it appears white. If all visible frequencies are absorbed (and none are reflected), the object appears black. Because light-colored surfaces reflect more radiation, they remain cooler than dark-colored surfaces.

Variations in the reflectivity of materials at the Earth's surface help to determine the surface temperature. On a hot day it is much more comfortable to walk barefoot across a plowed field than across an asphalt parking lot. The plowed field reflects almost 30% of the sun's rays, while the asphalt reflects very little. Clean snow reflects almost 95% of solar radiation, while forests are not very reflective.

CHEMQUANDARY

What might happen if large quantities of dust were to settle out on snow fields at the North and South Poles? What might happen if large quantities of dust of high reflectivity were to enter the atmosphere?

Each kind of material at the Earth's surface has a characteristic reflectivity and also a characteristic heat capacity, properties which together determine how fast the material warms up. The **heat capacity** is the quantity of thermal energy (heat) needed to raise the temperature of a given mass of a material by 1 °C. In effect, heat capacity is a measure of a material's thermal energy storage capability. The lower the heat capacity of a material, the greater will be its temperature increase for a given quantity of added energy. The higher the heat capacity, the smaller will be the temperature increase for a given quantity of added energy. Thus, a material with a higher heat capacity can store more thermal energy.

Heat capacity is often given in units of joules per gram per °C (J/g °C).

Water is uniquely suited for its important role in the Earth's climate. One way is through its high heat capacity. Bodies of water are slow to heat up, to cool down, and can store large quantities of thermal energy. By contrast, land surfaces cool off much more rapidly and reach lower temperatures in the absence of sunlight. Oceans, lakes, and rivers, therefore, have a moderating effect on the temperature. For example, on a warm day breezes blow from the ocean toward the land, for the temperature over the land is higher. The warmer, less dense air rises, allowing cooler and more dense air from the ocean to move in. Then in the evening the land cools off more rapidly and the breezes shift direction, blowing from the now-cooler land toward the ocean. In general, temperatures fluctuate less near the ocean than in regions far from the coast.

YOUR*TURN*

VI.9 Thermal Properties of Materials

1. Which of the following would you expect to be cooler to the touch on a hot day in the sun:
   a. a concrete sidewalk or an asphalt sidewalk?
   b. a black plastic bicycle seat or a tan fur bicycle seat?
2. Would you expect the average temperature to be lower in a winter with large quantities of snow or with very little snow?
3. Why is water (heat capacity 4.2 J/g °C) a better fluid for a hot-water bottle than alcohol (heat capacity 2.6 J/g °C)?
4. Beach sand feels hotter than grass on a hot day. Which is more responsible for this observation—heat capacity or reflectivity?
5. Why does the temperature drop further on a clear, cool night than on a cloudy, cool night?
6. Which of the two cities listed, at the same latitude and longitude, would you expect to be hotter in the summer? Why?
   a. A medium-sized city with many asphalt roads and concrete buildings.
   b. The same city, but located near a large body of water.

Could the thermal balance of our planet be upset? Is human activity affecting climate? We'll examine these questions in the next section.

C.4 Drastic Changes on the Face of the Earth?

More than 100 years ago it was suggested that the rapidly increasing use of fossil fuels might release enough carbon dioxide into the atmosphere to change the climate. You read in Part C.2 that water and carbon dioxide in the atmosphere act as one-way screens. They let in sunlight, and then limit the escape of re-radiated infrared photons, producing the greenhouse effect, which keeps Earth at a comfortable average temperature.

Natural disasters such as the eruption of Mt. St. Helens can adversely affect atmospheric conditions.

The greenhouse effect is constant as long as the water vapor and carbon dioxide in the atmosphere remain at their normal concentrations and no significant amounts of other greenhouse gases are added. Both the hydrologic cycle (studied in Unit One) and the carbon cycle (Figure VI.13) maintain constant concentrations of water and carbon dioxide. However, human activity must be taken into consideration. In the case of water no problem is apparent. The atmosphere contains about 12 trillion metric tons of water vapor, a quantity so large that we cannot significantly affect it. There is much less carbon dioxide, however. Human activity has already increased its concentration by about 15% over the past century.

We increase CO_2 levels in several ways. In clearing forests we remove vegetation, which consumes CO_2 through photosynthesis (Figure VI.14). When limestone, a form of calcium carbonate, $CaCO_3$, is converted to concrete, some CO_2 is released. Most significantly, burning fossil fuels releases CO_2 into the air, as these equations illustrate:

$$\text{Burning coal: } C(s) + O_2(g) \rightarrow CO_2(g)$$
$$\text{Burning natural gas: } CH_4(g) + 2\,O_2(g) \rightarrow CO_2(g) + 2\,H_2O(g)$$
$$\text{Burning gasoline: } 2\,C_8H_{18}(l) + 25\,O_2(g) \rightarrow 16\,CO_2(g) + 18\,H_2O(g)$$

If more CO_2 is added to the atmosphere than can be removed by natural processes, its concentration can increase significantly. This could result in the atmosphere retaining enough additional infrared radiation to cause a rise in the Earth's surface temperature.

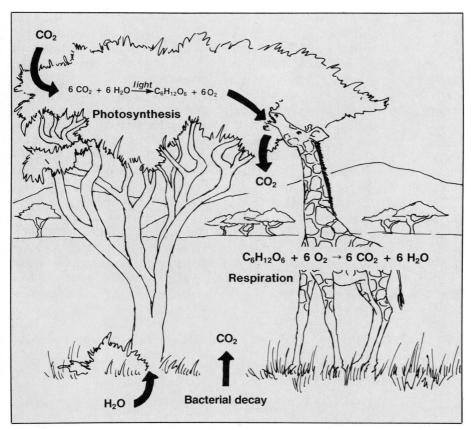

Source: Adapted from D. D. Ebbing: *General Chemistry*. Copyright © 1987 by Houghton Mifflin Company. Redrawn by permission.

Figure VI.13 The carbon cycle. How does this figure illustrate the cycling of carbon throughout the biosphere?

The equations shown in the figure:

$$6\,CO_2 + 6\,H_2O \xrightarrow{light} C_6H_{12}O_6 + 6\,O_2$$

Photosynthesis

$$C_6H_{12}O_6 + 6\,O_2 \rightarrow 6\,CO_2 + 6\,H_2O$$

Respiration

Bacterial decay

Figure VI.14 Deforestation accounts for increases in atmospheric CO_2.

Will this occur? And if so, will the warming be enough to melt the polar caps, flood coastal cities, and change the Earth's climate? Perhaps the greatest impact in such a changing climate would be destruction of major food-growing areas. Some countries could lose all their arable land, while in other countries, the best grain-growing regions could change locations.

Scientists predict that doubling the preindustrial level of CO_2 in the atmosphere would increase average global temperatures by 2.8 °C. The greatest temperature increases would occur in the Northern Hemisphere above 40° latitude, where the burning of fossil fuels and seasonal changes in plant growth are greatest. Predictions are that above a line which runs through Northern California, Denver, Indianapolis, and Philadelphia, droughts would be common, and many fertile food-producing areas would turn to dust bowls.

Although increasing carbon dioxide will have a warming influence on the globe, no one can yet predict exactly what the climate will do. Too many factors affect climate, and most of these affect each other, often in ways not well understood. Human settlements warm the Earth by lowering its reflectivity—darkening it with cities and farms that replace forests and plains. Automobiles and air pollution affect local temperatures. Smog particles can both warm and cool the climate. On top of all this, the Earth's climate runs in cycles of alternating ice ages and warm periods.

Some scientists predict we are nearing another ice age. In that case, an increase in CO_2 might be just what the world needs to counteract that trend. But don't count on it.

C.5 *You Decide:* Examining Trends in CO_2 Levels

The CO_2 level data given in Table VI.3 show average measurements taken at the Mauna Loa Observatory in Hawaii and at the South Pole, where the air is well mixed, far from local CO_2 sources.

Part 1

1. Plot the data in Table VI.3. Prepare your horizontal axis to include the years 1870 to 2050. The vertical axis will represent CO_2 levels from 280 ppm to 600 ppm. Plot the appropriate points, and draw a smooth curve representing the trend of the plotted points. (Do not draw a straight line or attempt to connect every point. A smooth curve shows general trends.)
2. Assuming that the trend in your smooth curve continues from 1985 to 2050, extend your curve with a dashed line to the year 2050. This extrapolation is a prediction for the future based on past trends.

Part 2

You will now make some predictions using the graph you have just completed and evaluate these predictions. Keep in mind that extrapolations of this type are always tentative. Completely unforeseen factors may arise in the future.

1. What does your graph indicate about the general change in CO_2 levels since 1870?
2. Predict CO_2 levels today, in the year 2000, and in 2050, based on your extrapolation.
3. Does your graph predict a doubling of the 1870 CO_2 level?
4. Which predictions from Question 2 are the most accurate? Why?
5. What assumption do you make in extrapolating known data?
6. Describe factors that might cause these extrapolations to be incorrect.

Table VI.3 *Global air CO_2 levels*

Year	Approx. CO_2 level (ppm)
1870	291
1900	287
1920	303
1930	310
1960	317
1965	320
1970	325
1974	328
1976	330
1978	333
1980	337
1982	340
1983	342
1985	345

C.6 Laboratory Activity: Measuring CO_2 Levels

Getting Ready

The air we normally breathe has a very low CO_2 level. However, the CO_2 concentration in an area can be dramatically increased by burning coal or petroleum, decomposing organic matter, or accumulating a crowd of people or animals.

In this activity you will compare the amount of CO_2 in several air samples. To do this, the air will be bubbled through water that contains an indicator, bromthymol blue. Carbon dioxide reacts with water to form carbonic acid:

$$CO_2(g) + H_2O(l) \rightarrow H_2CO_3(aq)$$

As the concentration of carbonic acid in solution increases, bromthymol blue changes in color from blue to green to yellow.

Procedure

Part 1: CO_2 in Normal Air

1. Pour 125 mL of distilled or deionized water into a filter flask and add 10 drops of bromthymol blue. The solution should be blue. If it is not, ask your teacher for assistance in adjusting the acid content of the water.

2. Pour 10 mL of the solution prepared in Step 1 into a test tube. Put this aside; it is your control (to be used for comparison).

3. Assemble the apparatus illustrated in Figure VI.15 (without the candle).

4. Turn on the water tap so that the aspirator pulls air through the flask. Note the position of the faucet handle so you can run the aspirator at this same flow rate each time.

5. Let the aspirator run for 10 min. Turn off the water. Remove the stopper from the flask.

6. Pour 10 mL of the used indicator solution from the flask into a second test tube. Compare the color of this sample with the control. Save this test tube.

Figure VI.15   Apparatus for collecting air. Part 1 is done without candle.

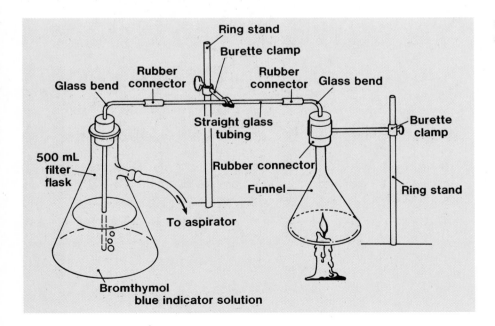

Part 2: CO₂ from Combustion

1. Empty the filter flask and rinse it thoroughly with distilled or deionized water.
2. Refill the flask with indicator solution according to Step 1 in Part 1. Reassemble the apparatus as in Step 3 in Part 1.
3. Light a candle and position it and the funnel so that the tip of the flame is level with the funnel base.
4. Turn on the water tap to the preset mark. Note the starting time. Run the aspirator until the indicator solution turns yellow. Record the time this takes in minutes.
5. Pour 10 mL of the indicator solution into a clean test tube. Compare the color with that of the other two solutions. Record your observations.

Part 3: CO₂ in Exhaled Air

1. Pour 125 mL of distilled or deionized water into an Erlenmeyer flask and add 10 drops of bromthymol blue. As before, consult with your teacher if the color is not blue.
2. Note the time, then exhale into the solution through a clean straw, until the indicator color changes to yellow. Record the time this takes.
3. Pour 10 mL of the indicator solution into a clean test tube. Compare the color with that of your other three solutions. Record your observations.

Questions

1. Compare the colors of the indicator solutions from each test. Which sample contained more CO_2?
2. Compare the times and color changes with plain air and air from above the candle. Explain the differences.
3. Which contained more CO_2, air in the absence of the burning candle or exhaled air?
4. Indicate what effect the following would have on the color of the indicator solution:
   a. Plants were growing in the room.
   b. Fifty more people enter and remain in the room.
   c. The room has better ventilation.
   d. Half the people in the room begin smoking.

C.7 *You Decide:* Reversing the Trend

Scientists believe they will have a clear picture of the influence of CO_2 on world climate within 10–15 years. This picture may show a well-documented global warming trend. In this case concerted action may be needed to reverse the warming trend.

Answer the following questions. Be prepared to discuss your opinions in class.

1. Describe possible actions the world community and individuals might take to halt an increase in CO_2 in the atmosphere.
2. Do you think the public would seriously consider taking action to halt such a global warming trend? If so, which action in your answer to Question 1 do you believe would gain strongest support?

C.8 Off in the Ozone

Although a small dose of ultraviolet radiation is necessary for health, too much is dangerous. In fact, if all of the ultraviolet radiation in sunlight were to reach the Earth's surface, serious damage to life on Earth would occur. Ultraviolet photons, we have seen, have enough energy to break covalent bonds. The resulting chemical changes cause sunburn and cancer in humans and damage to many biological systems.

Fortunately, Earth has an ultraviolet shield high in the stratosphere. The shield consists of a layer of ozone, $O_3(g)$, which absorbs ultraviolet radiation.

As sunlight penetrates the stratosphere, the highest-energy ultraviolet photons react with oxygen molecules, splitting them into oxygen atoms. Individual oxygen atoms are very reactive. They immediately react further, most with oxygen molecules to produce ozone. A third molecule (typically N_2 or O_2, represented by M in the equation below) carries away excess energy but is unchanged.

Each ozone molecule formed can absorb a medium-energy ultraviolet photon in the stratosphere. Decomposition results, producing an oxygen molecule and an oxygen atom, which can then carry on the cycle by undergoing the second reaction to produce more ozone:

$$O_2 + \text{Ultraviolet photon} \rightarrow O + O$$
$$O_2 + O + M \rightarrow O_3 + M$$
$$O_3 + \text{Ultraviolet photon} \rightarrow O_2 + O$$

The concentration of ozone in the stratosphere is so small that if the molecules were located on the surface of the Earth at atmospheric pressure, they would surround the Earth in a layer only 3 mm thick (about the thickness of a hardback book cover).

Human activities may have endangered this fragile ozone layer. The major culprit may be chlorine atoms from chlorinated hydrocarbon molecules such as the Freons (e.g., CCl_3F). These substances have been used as propellants in aerosol cans and as cooling fluids in the sealed cooling systems of air conditioners and refrigerators.

Other gases that may deplete ozone: methane (CH_4) and other hydrocarbons; nitrogen monoxide (NO).

Although Freons are highly stable molecules, at an altitude of 30 km ultraviolet photons of suitable energy split chlorine atoms from them. The freed chlorine atoms can then participate in a series of reactions that destroy ozone:

$$Cl + O_3 \rightarrow ClO + O_2$$
$$ClO + O \rightarrow Cl + O_2$$

Notice that the chlorine atom consumed in the first reaction is regenerated in the second reaction. Thus, each chlorine atom can participate in a large number of these ozone-destroying reactions. The sum of these two reactions is

Chlorine atoms serve as catalysts here.

$$O + O_3 \rightarrow 2\,O_2$$

Jon Jacobson

Freons are used in sealed refrigerator cooling systems.

Other uses of Freons:
Production of foam for insulation and packaging; sterilizing medical supplies.

The net effect of the reactions is the conversion of ozone molecules into oxygen molecules, triggered by free chlorine atoms released from molecules such as those of Freons.

Because of concern for the ozone layer, use of Freons in aerosol cans in the United States was banned in 1978. However, these substances are still widely used in this and other countries. In 1985 growing concern over depletion of the ozone layer, combined with the obvious need for international cooperation on this global problem, led 20 nations to sign an agreement to study means of protecting the ozone layer, possibly by limiting production and/or emissions.

We have seen that human activity may modify Earth's average temperature and its exposure to ultraviolet radiation by altering natural quantities of carbon dioxide and ozone. The chemistry of the atmosphere is very complex and difficult to study, and a complete picture of what is happening has not yet been developed. However, there is clear evidence of human alteration of the atmosphere in other ways. We'll look at this subject in the next few sections.

PART C
SUMMARY *QUESTIONS*

1. Compare infrared, visible, and ultraviolet radiation in terms of the relative energies of their photons. Cite one useful role each plays in a life process or a process important to life.
2. Explain why the Earth's atmosphere can be considered a one-way screen. How does this make Earth more hospitable to life?
3. List and briefly describe two functions of the stratosphere.
4. From a scientific viewpoint, why do tennis players and desert-dwellers wear white or light-colored clothing?
5. Compare ocean water and beach sand in terms of how quickly they heat up in the sun and how quickly they cool at night. What property of these two materials accounts for these differences?
6. Describe how atmospheric concentrations of CO_2 and water help to maintain moderate temperatures at the Earth's surface.
7. List the two ways humans increase the amount of CO_2 in the atmosphere. Which way involves greater contribution of CO_2?
8. What changes in atmospheric composition could result in:
   a. An increase in the average surface temperature of Earth.
   b. A decrease in the average surface temperature of Earth.
9. Describe an important role of the Earth's ozone shield.

EXTENDING *YOUR KNOWLEDGE (OPTIONAL)*

A satellite carrying instruments that monitor worldwide ozone concentration was launched in 1978. In 1986 many newspaper and magazine stories reported evidence from this satellite that an "ozone hole" was growing over Antarctica. The "hole" is a region where ozone depletion might be as high as 50%. Investigate the various theories proposed to explain the ozone hole.

D HUMAN IMPACT ON THE AIR WE BREATHE

Dirty air is so common in the United States that weather reports for some major cities now include indexes of certain air pollutants. Depending on where you live, cars, power plants, or industry may be the major polluter. However, air pollution is not only an outdoor problem. Indoor air is often highly polluted by people smoking or by fumes that spontaneously evaporate from certain products, such as from polymeric materials in furniture.

Air pollution smells bad, looks ugly, and blocks the view of the stars at night. But beyond being unpleasant, air pollution causes billions of dollars of damage every year. It corrodes buildings and machines. It stunts the growth of agricultural crops and weakens livestock. It causes or aggravates diseases such as bronchitis, asthma, emphysema, and lung cancer and so adds to the world's hospital bills. By some estimates, air pollution costs the United States $16 billion per year.

D.1 To Exist Is to Pollute

To threaten human health or damage property, the concentration of a pollutant must reach a harmful level in a specific location. Many natural processes emit substances that could become pollutants, but in most cases emission occurs over such a wide area that we do not notice it. Furthermore, the environment may dilute or transform substances before they can accumulate to harmful levels.

By contrast, pollution from human activities is usually generated in a small area. When the quantity of a pollutant overwhelms the ability of nature to dispose of it or disperse it, air pollution becomes a serious problem. Many large cities are prone to high concentrations of pollutants. If smog from Los Angeles were spread out over the entire West Coast, it would be much less noticeable.

Table VI.4 lists the major air pollutants and the quantities emitted worldwide from human and natural sources. These substances are all **primary air pollutants**—they enter the atmosphere in the chemical form listed. For example, methane (CH_4, the simplest hydrocarbon) is a by-product of fossil fuel use and a component of natural gas that leaks into the atmosphere. It is also produced by anaerobic bacteria and termites as they break down organic matter.

In addition to those listed in Table VI.4, there are several other important categories of air pollutants:

- *Secondary air pollutants.* These are substances formed in the atmosphere by chemical reactions between primary air pollutants and/or natural components of air. For example, sulfur dioxide (SO_2) reacts with oxygen in the air to form sulfur trioxide (SO_3), and the two oxides are always present together. Further reactions with water in the atmosphere can convert the sulfur oxides to sulfates (SO_4^{2-}) or sulfuric acid (H_2SO_4), a secondary pollutant partly responsible for acid rain (discussed in Part D.11).

$SO_2 + SO_3$ are referred to as SO_x ("socks").

Table VI.4   *Annual worldwide emissions of air pollutants (10^{12} g/yr or 10^6 metric tons/yr)*

Pollutant	Human source	Quantity	Natural source	Quantity
CO_2	Combustion of wood and fossil fuels	22,000	Biological decay; release from oceans, forest fires, and respiration	1,000,000
CO	Incomplete combustion (especially automotive)	700	Forest fires and photochemical reactions	2100
SO_2	Combustion of coal and oil; smelting of ores	212	Volcanoes and biological processes	20
CH_4	Combustion; natural gas leakage	160	Anaerobic biological decay and termites	1050
NO_x	High-temperature combustion (NO_x = NO and NO_2)	75	Lightning; bacterial action in soil	180
NMHC[a]	Incomplete combustion (especially automotive)	40	Biological processes	20,000
NH_3	Sewage treatment and fertilizers	6	Anaerobic biological decay	260
H_2S	Petroleum refining and sewage treatment	3	Volcanoes and anaerobic biological decay in soil and water	84

[a]NMHC = Nonmethane hydrocarbons.
Source: Adapted from Stern et al. *Fundamentals of Air Pollution,* 2nd ed.; Academic Press, Inc.: Orlando, FL, 1984; pp. 30–31. Table adapted by permission of Elmer Robinson, Mauna Loa Observatory.
Data based on conditions prior to 1980.

- *Particulates*. This major category of pollutants includes all solid particles that get into the air, either from human activities (e.g., power plants, waste burning, road building, mining) or natural processes (e.g., forest fires, wind erosion, volcanic eruptions). Particulates include visible emissions from smoke stacks or automobile tail pipes.
- *Manmade substances*. Some pollutants, such as the Freons, are produced only by human activity and would not otherwise be present at all.

© 1985 Ernie Leyba PHOTOSTAFF INC.

© 1986 Ernie Leyba PHOTOSTAFF INC.

Automobile emissions are a principal cause of air-quality problems in Denver.

D.2 *You Decide:* What Is Air Pollution? Where Does It Come from?

Use the information in Table VI.4 to answer the following questions.

1. What pattern was used to organize the data in Table VI.4? For what reason might this pattern have been chosen? Should the relative quantities of pollutants from human sources determine which pollutants should be reduced or controlled? If not, what other factors should be considered?

2. For all cases except one, natural contributions of these potentially polluting substances greatly exceed contributions from human activities.
   a. Does this imply that human contributions of these substances can be ignored? Why?
   b. For which substance does the contribution from human activity exceed that from natural sources? What does this suggest about modern society?

3. Refer to Table VI.1 in Part B.2. Which of the pollutants listed in Table VI.4 also occurs naturally in the atmosphere at concentrations of 0.0001% or more?

4. What is the major source of human contributions to air pollutants listed in Table VI.4?

5. Considering the large quantities of potential air pollutants from natural sources, why might adding small quantities of substances that do not exist naturally in the atmosphere pose a problem?

D.3 *You Decide:* Identifying Major Pollutants

Air pollution is a by-product of manufacturing, transportation, and energy production. Table VI.5 gives a detailed picture of the sources of some of the major air pollutants in the United States. Use this information to answer the following questions.

1. Overall, is industry the main source of air pollution? If not, what is the main source?

2. For which pollutants is one-third or more contributed by industry?

Table VI.5 *U.S. pollutant emissions by source, 1983 (in 10^6 metric tons/yr)*

Source	TSP	SO$_x$	NO$_x$	HC	CO	Total
Transportation (petroleum burning)	1.3	0.9	8.8	7.2	47.7	65.9
Fuel burning for space heating and electricity	2.0	16.8	9.7	—	—	28.5
Industrial processes	2.3	3.1	—	7.5	4.6	17.5
Solid waste disposal and miscellaneous	1.3	—	0.9[a]	5.2[b]	15.3	22.7
Totals	6.9	20.8	19.4	19.9	67.6	134.6

Symbols used:
TSP = Total suspended particulates.
SO$_x$ = Sulfur oxides (SO$_2$ and SO$_3$).
NO$_x$ = Nitrogen oxides (NO and NO$_2$).
HC = Volatile organic compounds (methane and nonmethane hydrocarbons).
CO = Carbon monoxide.
[a]This value is a composite of industrial processes and the solid waste, miscellaneous category.
[b]This value includes a small contribution from fuel consumption and nonindustrial solvent use.

---

3. For which pollutants is one-third or more contributed by transportation?

4. For which pollutants is one-third or more contributed by burning fuel for space heating and electricity (usually referred to as "stationary fuel burning")?

How much pollution do *you* produce? If you drive, you are a major polluter—automobiles contribute about half the total mass of air pollutants. When you spend time in heated buildings, use electricity, or buy food and other products, air has been polluted for your benefit. As a comic strip character once said, "We have met the enemy, and he is us."

D.4 Smog: Spoiler of Our Cities

When weather forecasters give the air quality index along with humidity and temperature, to what are they referring? The U.S. Environmental Protection Agency has devised an index based on concentrations of pollutants that are major contributors to smog over cities. You can see in Table VI.6 that the combined health effects of these pollutants can become quite serious. Smog can kill. During one of the deadliest smogs, in London in 1952, the death rate among residents was more than double the normal rate. Similar although less severe episodes have occurred in other cities before and since.

The composition of smog depends on the type of industrial activity and power generation in an area and also on climate and geography. Over large cities containing many coal- and oil-burning industries, power-generating stations, and homes, the principal components of smog are sulfur oxides and particulates.

Coal and petroleum both contain varying quantities of sulfur, from which sulfur oxides are formed during combustion. One successful approach to improving air quality sets limits on the quantity of sulfur that may be present in the fuels burned.

Table VI.6 *U.S. Pollutant Standards Index (PSI)*[a]

Air quality index value	Air quality description	Air pollutant levels (micrograms per cubic meter)					Effects and suggested actions
		Total suspended particulate matter (24 hours)	Sulfur dioxide (24 hours)	Carbon monoxide (8 hours)	Ozone (1 hour)	Nitrogen dioxide (1 hour)	
500	Hazardous	1,000	2,620	57,500	1,200	3,750	Healthy people experience symptoms that affect normal activity. All should remain indoors with windows and doors closed, minimize physical exertion and avoid vehicular traffic. Premature death of some in high risk group.[a]
400	Hazardous	875	2,100	46,000	1,000	3,000	High risk individuals should stay indoors and *avoid* physical activity. Decreased exercise tolerance in healthy persons. General population should avoid outdoor activity.
300	Very unhealthful	625	1,600	34,000	800	2,260	High risk group has significant aggravation of symptoms and decreased exercise tolerance and should stay indoors and *reduce* physical activity. Widespread irritation symptoms in the healthy population.
200	Unhealthful	375	800	17,000	400	1,130	Those with lung or heart disease should reduce physical exertion and outdoor activity. Healthy individuals notice irritations.
100	Moderate	260	365	10,000	235	Not reported	Some damage to materials and vegetation but human health not affected unless levels continue for many days.
50	Good	75	80	5,000	118	Not reported	No significant effects.
0		0	0	0	0	0	

[a]High risk group includes elderly people and those with heart or lung diseases.
Source: U.S. Environmental Protection Agency.

A synergistic interaction results when a total effect is greater than the sum of the individual contributing factors.

Particulates from burning fossil fuels consist of unburned carbon or solid hydrocarbon fragments and trace minerals. Some particles contain toxic compounds of metals such as cadmium, chromium, lead, or mercury.

The fatality rate in severe smogs has been higher than predicted from known hazards of sulfur oxides or particulates alone. According to some researchers, this may be due to **synergistic interactions** in which the combined effect of the two pollutants is greater than the sum of the effects of either one alone. One way this can happen is that smaller particles have more surface area per unit mass than do larger particles, allowing them to absorb and concentrate greater amounts of gaseous pollutants. Also, the smaller the particles, the more likely they are to be carried into the lungs and bloodstream.

Before discussing smog resulting from automobile emissions, we will look at what can be done to decrease pollution, and what industry is doing to clean up its smoke.

D.5 Pollution Control

There are several basic ways to control air pollution:

- Energy technologies that cause air pollution can be replaced with technologies that don't require combustion, such as solar power, wind power, and nuclear power.
- Pollution from combustion can be reduced by energy conservation measures, such as getting more from what we burn and therefore burning less.
- Pollution-causing substances can be removed from fuel before burning. For example, most sulfur can be removed from coal.
- The combustion process can be modified so that fuel is more completely oxidized.
- Pollutants can be trapped after combustion.

All pollution control options cost money. When deciding upon a pollution control strategy, two key questions must be answered: What will the pollution control cost? What benefits will the pollution control offer?

CHEM*QUANDARY*

Consider this pollution control option: "Clean the atmosphere after the pollution is emitted." Is this a reasonable or practical strategy? Explain your answer. Would cloud-seeding to cause rain, or issuing filtering devices such as gas masks to individuals be reasonable alternatives? Explain.

D.6 Controlling Industrial Emission of Particulates

Power plants and smelters generate more than 60% of the particulate matter emitted in the United States. Several cost-effective methods for controlling particle emissions are being used; in recent years great progress has been made in cleaning up this type of pollution.

Electrostatic precipitation. This is currently the most important technique for controlling pollution by particulates. Combustion by-products pass through a strong electrical field, where they become charged. The charged particles collect on plates of opposite charge. This technique removes up to 99% of the total particulates, leaving only particles smaller than one-tenth of a micrometer (0.1 μm, where 1 μm = 10^{-6} m). Dust and pollen collectors installed in home ventilation systems are often based on this technique.

Mechanical filtering. This works like the bag in a vacuum cleaner. Combustion by-products pass through a cleaning room (bag house) where huge filters trap up to 99% of the particles.

Cyclone collection. Combustion by-products pass rapidly through a tight circular spiral chamber. Particles thrown outward to the walls drop to the base of the chamber where they are removed. This technique removes 50–90% of larger, visible particles but relatively few of the more harmful particles (those smaller than 1 μm).

Scrubbing. This method controls particles and the sulfur oxides accompanying them. Substances that react with the pollutants are added to the stream of combustion by-products.

In dry scrubbing (on the left in Figure VI.16) powdered limestone (calcium carbonate, $CaCO_3$) is blown into the combustion chamber where it decomposes:

$$CaCO_3(s) + \text{Heat} \rightarrow CaO(s) + CO_2(g)$$

The lime (CaO) then reacts with sulfur oxides to form calcium sulfite ($CaSO_3$) and calcium sulfate ($CaSO_4$):

$$CaO(s) + SO_2(g) \rightarrow CaSO_3(s)$$
$$CaO(s) + SO_3(g) \rightarrow CaSO_4(s)$$

These products are washed away as a slurry (a mixture of solids and water).

Wet scrubbing (on the right in Figure VI.16) removes sulfur dioxide using an aqueous solution of calcium hydroxide, $Ca(OH)_2(aq)$ produced by the reaction of lime (CaO) with water. The reactions are as follows:

$$CaO(s) + H_2O(l) \rightarrow Ca(OH)_2(aq)$$
$$Ca(OH)_2(aq) + SO_2(g) \rightarrow CaSO_3(s) + H_2O(l)$$

Scrubbers can remove up to 95% of sulfur oxides. They are required for all new coal-burning plants in the United States. Their use adds significantly to the cost of electrical power.

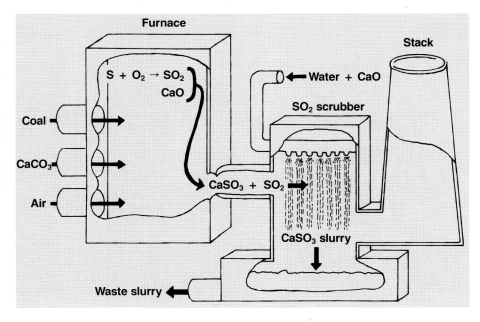

Figure VI.16 A scrubber for removing sulfur dioxide and particulate matter from products of industrial combustion processes. Dry scrubbing occurs in the furnace and wet scrubbing in the SO_2 scrubber.

D.7 Laboratory Demonstration: How Industry Cleans Its Air

Your teacher will demonstrate two pollution control methods.

Part 1: The Electrostatic Precipitator
1. Observe what happens to the smoke. Record your observations.
2. Observe the chemical reaction that occurs on the copper rod. Record your observations.

Part 2: Wet Scrubbing
1. Observe the color of the liquid and pH paper in each flask as the reaction proceeds. Record your observations.

Questions
1. Write an equation for the reaction that occurs between HCl and the NH_3 in Part 1.
2. What information does the universal indicator provide in each flask in Part 2?
3. What information does the pH paper at the neck of each flask provide?
4. What is the overall effect of the scrubbing, as shown by the indicators?
5. List the two ways the quality of the air in the reaction vessel was changed by wet scrubbing.
6. What advantages do precipitators have over wet scrubbers? What are their disadvantages?

CHEM*QUANDARY*

Explain why treating smoke before it is released from power plants is an important goal, but why, at the same time, it may mislead the general public concerning what is required to obtain clean air.

YOUR*TURN*

VI.10 Pollutants by the Ton

Large coal- or oil-fired power plants and large smelters can produce tons of pollutants or tons of scrubbing products in each hour of operation. You can estimate the amount produced from such operations using what you learned earlier about mass and molar mass relationships (Your Turn VI.1).

Assume that a coal-fired power plant burns 1.0×10^6 kg (or 1000 metric tons) of coal each hour. The coal contains 3.0% sulfur by mass. If the sulfur were converted to $SO_2(g)$ during combustion, how many moles of $SO_2(g)$ would be released to the atmosphere each hour? How many tons of $SO_2(g)$ is this?

First, we can find the mass in kilograms of sulfur in the coal burned each hour:

1 metric ton = 1000 kg = 1 × 10⁶ g

$$\left(\frac{1.0 \times 10^6 \text{ kg coal}}{1 \text{ h}}\right) \times \left(\frac{3.0 \text{ kg S}}{100 \text{ kg coal}}\right) = 3.0 \times 10^4 \text{ kg S/h}$$

From this we can calculate the moles of sulfur produced each hour:

$$\left(\frac{3.0 \times 10^4 \text{ kg S}}{1 \text{ h}}\right) \times \left(\frac{1000 \text{ g S}}{1 \text{ kg S}}\right) \times \left(\frac{1 \text{ mol S}}{32 \text{ g S}}\right) = 9.4 \times 10^5 \text{ mol S/h}$$

Knowing that sulfur burns to form SO_2 according to the equation

$$S(s) + O_2(g) \rightarrow SO_2(g)$$

and observing that each mole of sulfur produces one mole of SO_2, we recognize that 9.4×10^5 mol of SO_2 will be released each hour. The mass in metric tons of this quantity of SO_2 is

$$\frac{9.4 \times 10^5 \text{ mol SO}_2}{1 \text{ h}} \times \left(\frac{64 \text{ g SO}_2}{1 \text{ mol SO}_2}\right) \times \left(\frac{1 \text{ metric ton}}{1 \times 10^6 \text{ g SO}_2}\right)$$

$$= 60 \text{ metric tons SO}_2/\text{h}$$

Now it's your turn.

1. If the exhaust gases in the sample problem above are dry-scrubbed with lime (CaO) according to the reaction shown in Part D.6, what mass of calcium sulfite, $CaSO_3(s)$, would be formed each hour?

2. A coal-producing company is considering removing sulfur from their coal and using the sulfur to produce sulfuric acid (H_2SO_4). The sulfuric acid can be sold at a small profit. The coal contains 7.5% sulfur (by mass). Forty percent of the sulfur can be removed by a known method. (a) How many moles of sulfur can be removed from each 5.0 kg of coal? (b) How many kilograms of sulfuric acid can be produced from this sulfur? (The molar mass of sulfuric acid is 98 g/mol.)

Furnaces and power plants are not the only sources of smog. Automobiles contribute many air pollutants.

D.8 Photochemical Smog

The ill effects of pollution from automobiles were first noted in the Los Angeles area in the 1940s. A brownish haze that irritated the eyes, nose, and throat and damaged crops appeared in the air. It puzzled researchers for some time. Los Angeles has no significant industrial or heating activities. The city has an abundance of automobiles and sunshine. Also, mountains rise on three sides of it. These geographic conditions produce temperature inversions about 320 days each year.

Normally, air at the Earth's surface is warmed by solar radiation and by re-radiation from surface materials. This warmer, less dense air rises, carrying pollutants with it. Cooler, less polluted air then moves in. In a temperature inversion, a cool air mass is trapped beneath a less dense warm air mass, often in a valley or over a city. Pollutants cannot escape and their concentration may rise to dangerous levels. Los Angeles is smog-prone, primarily because of its location. But there is more to the story for Los Angeles smog was much worse than seemed reasonable.

As so often happens in science, a serendipitous discovery provided a piece of the puzzle of smog. In 1952, chemist Arie J. Haagen-Smit was attempting to isolate the main ingredient of pineapple odor. Working on a smoggy day, he detected a greater concentration of ozone (O_3) in his experiment than is normally found in clean, tropospheric air. He delayed his research to identify its source. Within a year, he published a ground-breaking paper, "The Chemistry and Physics of Los Angeles Smog," in which he described the importance of sunlight in smog chemistry, and coined the term **photochemical smog.**

Any reaction initiated by light is a photochemical reaction.

Nitrogen oxides are essential ingredients of such smog. At the high temperature and pressure of automotive combustion (2800 °C and about 10 atm), nitrogen and oxygen react to produce the pollutant nitrogen monoxide (NO).

$$N_2(g) + O_2(g) + \text{Energy} \longrightarrow 2\,NO(g)$$

In the atmosphere, nitrogen monoxide is oxidized to orange-brown nitrogen dioxide (NO_2).

$$2\,NO(g) + O_2(g) \longrightarrow 2\,NO_2(g)$$

Carbon monoxide from automobile exhaust is also present.

The photochemical smog cycle begins as photons from sunlight initiate dissociation of NO_2 into NO and oxygen atoms (O). The atomic oxygen then reacts with oxygen molecules to produce ozone in the same way that it does in the stratosphere.

$$NO_2(g) + \text{Energy} \longrightarrow NO(g) + O(g)$$
$$O_2(g) + O(g) \longrightarrow O_3(g)$$

We have now accounted for two of the harmful and unpleasant ingredients of photochemical smog: Nitrogen dioxide has a pungent, irritating odor. Ozone is a very powerful oxidant. At concentrations as low as 0.1 ppm ozone can crack rubber, corrode metals, and damage plant and animal tissues.

The highly reactive ozone undergoes a complex series of reactions with the third essential ingredient of photochemical smog—hydrocarbons that escape from gasoline tanks or are emitted during incomplete combustion of gasoline. The products of these reactions cause burning eyes, are harmful to individuals with respiratory or heart disease, and can injure plants and damage materials such as rubber and paint.

For our purposes, the following equation represents the key ingredients and products of photochemical smog:

$$
\begin{array}{c}
\text{Auto exhaust} \quad + \quad \text{Sunlight} + O_2(g) \longrightarrow \\
\text{(Hydrocarbons} + CO + NO_x) \\[4pt]
O_3(g) + NO_x(g) + \quad \text{Organic compounds} \quad + CO_2(g) + H_2O(g) \\
\text{(oxidants and irritants)}
\end{array}
$$

NO + NO$_2$ are referred to as NO$_x$ ("nocks").

Table VI.7 shows how the concentrations of some important components of photochemical smog can vary from a relatively clear day to a smoggy day. Complete the following activity to discover how some of the key reactions in photochemical smog were pieced together.

Table VI.7   *Varying concentrations of smog components[a]*

Pollutant	Concentration (ppm)		
	Clear day	**Smoggy day**	**Increase**
Carbon monoxide	3.5	23.0	×6.5
Hydrocarbons	0.2	1.1	×5.5
Peroxides	0.1	0.5	×5.0
Oxides of nitrogen	0.08	0.4	×5.0
Lower aldehydes	0.07	0.4	×6.0
Ozone	0.06	0.3	×5.0
Sulfur dioxide	0.05	0.3	×6.0

[a]Clear day visibility is 7 mi; smoggy day visibility is 1 mi.

Source: From *Chemistry, Man and Society,* 4th ed. by Jones, M. M.; Johnston, D. O.; Netterville, J. T.; Wood, J. L. © 1983 by CBS College Publishing. © 1984, by Saunders College—Holt, Rinehart, & Winston. Copyright 1972 and 1976 by W. B. Saunders Co. Reprinted by permission of Holt, Rinehart, & Winston, Inc.

D.9 *You Decide:* Automobile Contributions to Smog

Use the data in Figure VI.17 to answer these questions.

1. Between what hours do the concentrations of nitrogen oxides and hydrocarbons peak? Account for this fact in terms of traffic patterns.

2. Give two reasons why a given pollutant may be observed to decrease in concentration over several hours.

3. The concentration maximum for NO_2 occurs at the same time as the concentration minimum of NO. Explain this phenomenon.

4. Although ozone is necessary in the stratosphere to protect us from ultraviolet light, on the surface of the Earth it is a major component of photochemical smog. Determine from Figure VI.17 which chemicals, or species, are at minimum concentrations when $O_3(g)$ is at maximum concentration. What does this suggest about the production of $O_3(g)$ in polluted tropospheric air?

Smog is being produced faster than the atmosphere can dispose of it. However, the nation has made considerable progress in smog control. Many cities have cleaner air than they did 30 years ago. The following section will explore the control of pollution from automobiles.

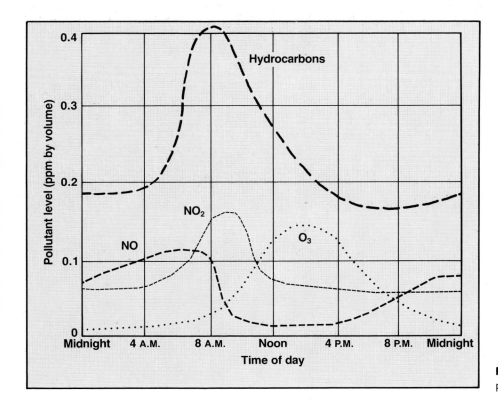

Figure VI.17 Species involved in photochemical smog formation.

Exhaust emissions from slow-moving traffic on crowded freeways is a major source of the Los Angeles photochemical smog shown in this 1970 photo.

D.10 Controlling Automobile Emission of Pollutants

In 1970 an amendment to the Federal Clean Air Act authorized the Environmental Protection Agency (EPA) to set emissions standards for new automobiles. Maximum limits were set for hydrocarbon, nitrogen oxide, and carbon monoxide emissions. These values were to be achieved in gradual steps by 1975. Improvements in automobile engines were made between 1970 and 1975 by modifying the air-fuel ratio, adjusting the spark timing, adding carbon canisters to absorb gasoline that would normally evaporate before combustion, and installing exhaust gas recirculation systems.

To decrease emissions enough to meet the standards completely, however, required further measures. The result was development of the **catalytic converter.** The converter is a reaction chamber attached to the exhaust pipe. The exhaust gases and outside air pass over several catalysts which help convert nitrogen oxides to molecular nitrogen and hydrocarbons to carbon dioxide and water. The

Jon Jacobson

Emissions testing has become an essential component of tuning an automobile.

carburetor air-fuel ratio is set to produce exhaust gases with relatively high concentrations of carbon monoxide and hydrogen. These gases enter the first half of the catalytic converter where nitrogen oxides are reduced, for example,

$$2\ NO(g)\ +\ 2\ CO(g) \xrightarrow{\text{Catalyst}} N_2(g)\ +\ 2\ CO_2(g)$$

$$2\ NO(g)\ +\ 2\ H_2(g) \xrightarrow{\text{Catalyst}} N_2(g)\ +\ 2\ H_2O(g)$$

The second half of the converter then further oxidizes carbon monoxide and hydrocarbons to carbon dioxide and water.

What exactly is a catalyst? You have encountered catalysts several times now. Enzymes that aid in digesting food and in other body functions are biochemical catalysts. The manganese dioxide added in generating oxygen in the laboratory activity in Part B.1 was a catalyst. In every case, the catalyst increases the rate of a chemical reaction which, without the catalyst, would proceed too slowly to be useful. A catalyst is not considered a reactant because it remains unchanged after the reaction is over.

How can a catalyst speed up a reaction and escape unchanged? Reactions between two or more species can occur only if their molecules collide with sufficient energy and the correct orientation to disrupt bonds. The minimum energy required for such effective collisions is called the **activation energy.** You can think of the activation energy as an energy barrier that stands between the reactants and products. Reactants must have enough energy to mount the barrier before reaction can occur. The higher the barrier, the fewer the molecules that have the energy to mount it, and the slower the reaction proceeds.

A catalyst increases the rate of a chemical reaction by providing a different reaction pathway, one with a lower activation energy. The result is that more molecules have sufficient energy to react within a given period of time. Thus, more product is formed. In automotive catalytic converters, 1−3 g of such metals as platinum, palladium, and rhodium act as catalysts.

Table VI.8 *Passenger car regulatory exhaust emission control requirements in the United States (emissions are expressed in grams per mile [g/mi])*

Model year	HC	CO	NO$_x$
1975–76	1.5	15	3.1
1977–79	1.5	15	2.0
1980	0.41	7.0	2.0
1981–82	0.41	3.4[a]	1.0[b]
1983	0.41	3.4	1.0
Pre-1968 (uncontrolled) values	8.6	87.5	3.5

[a]Possible two-year waiver to 7 g/mi.
[b]Possible waiver to 1.5 g/mi for diesel or innovative technology through 1984.

Source: Taylor, K. C. "Automobile Catalytic Converters," in *Catalysis Science and Technology;* Anderson, J. R., Boudart, M., Eds.; Springer-Verlag: New York, 1984; V. 5, Ch. 2, pp. 120–70.

Table VI.8 shows the gradually decreasing emission limits over the years called for by legislation. While catalytic converters have contributed to cleaning up automobile exhaust, the legislated goals have not yet been met. In particular, it has proved difficult to meet the nitrogen oxides standards.

CHEM*QUANDARY*

From a practical point of view, why might controlling air pollution from our nation's 140 million automobiles be more difficult than controlling air pollution from our power plants and industries?

D.11 Acid Rain

It started in Scandinavia. Then, it appeared in the northeastern United States. Now, the problem seems to exist in much of the industrialized world. Fish disappear from major lakes. The surfaces of limestone and concrete buildings and marble statues crumble. Crops grow more slowly and forests begin to die out. Although New England and Scandinavia are among the regions hardest hit by acid rain, it is widespread in the industrialized world. Even the Grand Canyon suffers from acid rain due to air pollution from coal-fired power plants miles away.

Although the cause of German forest die-outs is subject to debate, the rest of these problems have been traced definitively to acid rain. Naturally occurring substances, chiefly carbon dioxide, have always caused rainwater to be slightly acidic. Normally, rainwater's pH is about 5.6. Carbon dioxide reacts with rainwater to form carbonic acid:

$$CO_2(g) + H_2O(l) \rightarrow H_2CO_3(aq)$$

Field Museum of Natural History (neg. #PP-173-a), Chicago

Air pollutants are responsible for the partial disintegration of this classic Greek sculpture.

Oxides of sulfur and nitrogen emitted from power plants, various industries, and automobiles react with rainwater to form acids that have lowered the pH of rainwater to 4–4.5 in the northeastern United States. The key reactions are

$$H_2O(l) + SO_2(g) \rightarrow H_2SO_3(aq)$$
Sulfurous acid

$$H_2O(l) + SO_3(g) \rightarrow H_2SO_4(aq)$$
Sulfuric acid

$$H_2O(l) + 2\ NO_2(g) \rightarrow HNO_3(aq) + HNO_2(aq)$$
Nitric acid   Nitrous acid

Occasionally the levels of these oxides in air produce enough acid to lower the pH to 3. (A pH of 4–4.5 is about the acidity of orange juice; a pH of 3 is about that of vinegar.)

The lower the pH, the more acidic the solution.

Sulfuric acid contributes close to two-thirds of the acidity of rain in New England; acids of nitrogen contribute most of the other third.

This more acidic rain lowers the pH of lakes, killing fish eggs and other aquatic life; some species are more sensitive than others. Statues and monuments, such as the Parthenon in Greece, which have stood uneroded for centuries, suddenly began corroding because of acid rain and sulfates. The acid attacks calcium carbonate in limestone, marble, and concrete:

$$H_2SO_4(aq) + CaCO_3(s) \rightarrow CaSO_4(s) + H_2O(l) + CO_2(g)$$

Calcium sulfate is more soluble than calcium carbonate. Therefore, the stonework decays as the calcium sulfate is washed away to uncover fresh calcium carbonate that can react further with the acid rain.

Salts of sulfuric acid, which contain the sulfate ion (SO_4^{2-}), are also present in acid rain and atmospheric moisture. In the air they scatter light, causing haze. And they are potentially harmful to human health if they are deposited in large enough amounts in the lungs.

Many different and interrelated reactions are involved in producing acid rain. Studies aimed at a more complete understanding of the causes are under way. One puzzle is how sulfur dioxide is oxidized to sulfur trioxide. Oxygen dissolved in water oxidizes sulfur dioxide very slowly. The reaction may be accelerated in the atmosphere by sunlight or by catalysts such as iron, manganese, or vanadium in soot particles.

The control of acid rain is made difficult because air pollution knows no political boundaries. Acid rain often appears hundreds of kilometers from the sources of pollutants. For example, much of the acid that rains on Scandinavia is thought to come from Germany and the United Kingdom. The rain that falls on New England may come largely from the industrial Ohio Valley, in the Midwest.

Next, you will have an opportunity to work directly with solutions having acidity approximately equal to that of acid rain.

D.12 Laboratory Activity: Acid Rain

Getting Ready

In this activity you will create a mixture similar to that in acid rain by burning sulfur in air and then adding water. You will observe the effects of acid rain chemistry on plant material (represented by an apple peel), living creatures (represented by a culture of microorganisms), an active metal, and marble.

Procedure

1. Cut a piece of skin from an apple, and place it in an empty 500-mL glass bottle.

2. Fill a combustion spoon half full of powdered sulfur.

3. *In a fume hood:* Turn on a tap water spigot so that it drips slowly. (If there is no spigot in the hood, adjust the one at your laboratory bench, and return to the fume hood to perform the following procedures.) Light the Bunsen burner. Ignite the sulfur by holding the combustion spoon over the burner flame until you observe a blue flame. Quickly insert the spoon into the bottle and cover as much of the bottle opening as possible with a glass plate.

4. When smoke fills the bottle, remove the spoon. Quickly cover the bottle opening with the glass plate. Extinguish the sulfur fire by holding the spoon under the dripping tap water. Turn off the spigot.

5. Observe the contents of the bottle for approximately three minutes. Record your observations.

6. Add 10 mL of distilled water to the smoke-filled bottle. Quickly replace the lid. Take the bottle to your laboratory bench. Swirl the contents of the bottle carefully for one minute.

7. Place a drop of *Paramecium* (or mixed) culture on a microscope slide. Examine it under the microscope. Look for the living organisms. Record your observations.

8. Add three drops of solution from the bottle to the slide. Be sure that the drops fall evenly over the original *Paramecium* drop. Observe the events happening under the microscope for three minutes. Record your observations.

9. Remove the apple skin from the bottle and note any changes in its appearance.

10. Using a stirring rod, place a drop of distilled water on pieces of red and blue litmus paper and on a piece of pH paper. Record your observations.

11. Pour about 2 mL of the liquid from the glass bottle into a test tube. Use a stirring rod to test the solution with each color of litmus paper and with pH paper. Record your observations. Acid rain has a pH of 4–4.5. Is your solution more or less acidic than this?

12. Drop a 1-cm length of magnesium ribbon into the test tube. Observe it for at least three minutes. Record your observations.

13. Add two marble chips to the solution in your bottle. Observe for at least three minutes. Record your observations.

Questions

1. Write an equation for the burning of sulfur in air.

2. When the gas produced by burning sulfur dissolved what effect did it have on the acidity of the distilled water?

3. Describe what happened to the *Paramecium* culture when the solution from the glass bottle was added. If this solution were steadily added to a small lake over a long period of time, might it affect organisms living there? Explain.

4. If liquid similar to the solution in the glass bottle were allowed to stand on a marble statue or on steel girders supporting a bridge, what effect might it have?

5. What information would you need to make you more confident of your answers to the second question in item 3 and to item 4 above?

D.13   Acids and Bases: Structure Determines Function

In 1883 the Swedish chemist Svante Arrhenius defined an acid as any substance which, when dissolved in water, generates hydrogen ion (H^+). He defined a base as a substance that generates hydroxide ion (OH^-) in water solutions. It is the hydrogen ion in solution ($H^+(aq)$) that makes a solution acidic and reactive enough to cause damage. The equations for formation of solutions of some common acids are:

$$HCl(g) \xrightarrow{\text{water}} H^+(aq) + Cl^-(aq)$$

$$HNO_3(l) \xrightarrow{\text{water}} H^+(aq) + NO_3^-(aq)$$

$$H_2SO_4(l) \xrightarrow{\text{water}} H^+(aq) + HSO_4^-(aq)$$

Most common acids are molecular compounds that contain covalently bonded hydrogen atoms. At least one hydrogen atom in each molecule is bonded in a way that the hydrogen atom can be attracted away in water solution. The hydrogen atom leaves behind an electron and is transferred to a water molecule as a hydrogen ion (H^+). As shown above, the remainder of the acid molecule becomes an anion.

Many common bases, unlike acids, are ionic compounds—they contain ions to begin with. As with all soluble ionic compounds, when such a base dissolves in water, the ions separate from each other and disperse uniformly in the solution. The hydroxide ion (OH^-) in solution imparts the properties we associate with basic solutions. Equations for dissolving some bases are as follows:

$$NaOH(s) \xrightarrow{\text{water}} Na^+(aq) + OH^-(aq)$$

$$KOH(s) \xrightarrow{\text{water}} K^+(aq) + OH^-(aq)$$

$$Ba(OH)_2(s) \xrightarrow{\text{water}} Ba^{2+}(aq) + 2\,OH^-(aq)$$

The reaction between equal amounts of $H^+(aq)$ and $OH^-(aq)$ to produce water results in disappearance of both the acidic and basic properties. This **neutralization** reaction can be represented by a total ionic equation. For the neutralization of hydrochloric acid ($HCl(aq)$) by sodium hydroxide ($NaOH(aq)$), the total ionic equation is:

$$H^+(aq) + Cl^-(aq) + Na^+(aq) + OH^-(aq) \rightarrow H_2O(l) + Cl^-(aq) + Na^+(aq)$$

Note that Na^+ and Cl^- ions appear on both sides of the equation. They are sometimes called **spectator ions** because they do not take part in the reaction. Omitting them from the equation leaves a **net ionic equation,** which shows only the reaction that takes place. The net ionic equation for this reaction is:

$$H^+(aq) + OH^-(aq) \rightarrow H_2O(l)$$

You can see why the acidic and basic properties of the solutions disappear. After a neutralization reaction, only water, a neutral substance, remains.

Some of the acids in acid rain, such as sulfurous acid (H_2SO_3), nitrous acid (HNO_2), and carbonic acid (H_2CO_3), are weak. Others, such as sulfuric acid (H_2SO_4) and nitric acid (HNO_3), are strong. A common base in the environment, ammonia (NH_3), is a weak base. The next section explains why some acids and bases are stronger than others.

D.14   Acid and Base Strength

Acids and bases are classified as weak or strong according to how readily they produce hydrogen ions ($H^+(aq)$) or hydroxide ions ($OH^-(aq)$) in water. Note that we are not referring here to the amounts of acid or base in solution, but to the nature of the individual acids or bases themselves.

The more readily an acid produces hydrogen ions in water solution, the stronger an acid it is. When a "strong acid" dissolves in water, almost every molecule splits into a hydrogen ion and an anion. Nitric acid, for example, is a strong acid; formation of a nitric acid solution is represented by the following equation:

$$HNO_3(l) \xrightarrow{\text{water}} H^+(aq) + NO_3^-(aq)$$

In a nitric acid solution there are very few HNO_3 molecules and large numbers of hydrogen and nitrate ions.

In a "weak acid" only a few acid molecules split into hydrogen ions and anions; most acid molecules remain as molecules in solution. Nitrous acid is a weak acid. The equation for formation of a nitrous acid solution is written:

$$\underset{\text{molecular form}}{HNO_2(l)} \underset{}{\overset{\text{water}}{\rightleftharpoons}} \underset{\text{ionized form}}{H^+(aq) + NO_2^-(aq)}$$

A solution of nitrous acid always contains many more HNO_2 molecules than $H^+(aq)$ and $NO_2^-(aq)$ ions. Note the double arrow written in the equation above. One meaning of a double arrow is that the reactants are not completely consumed, but that the solution contains both reactants and products. (Most often a double arrow means the reaction is in chemical equilibrium. In a chemical reaction at equilibrium both the forward reaction and its reverse occur at the same rate. The result is unchanging concentrations of all reactants and products.)

Ionic bases, such as sodium hydroxide (NaOH) and potassium hydroxide (KOH), are strong bases—their solutions contain only cations and OH^- ions. However, the concentration of OH^- ions in solution sometimes is limited by the low solubility of the base. Magnesium hydroxide ($Mg(OH)_2$) is such a base.

A common weak base is ammonia, which forms OH^- ions in solution by the following reaction:

$$NH_3(g) + H_2O(l) \rightleftharpoons NH_4^+(aq) + OH^-(aq)$$

YOUR*TURN*

VI.11   Acids and Bases

1. The following strong acids are found in acid rain. For each, give the name and write an equation for the formation of ions in aqueous solution.
    a. HNO_3. The nitrate ions from its ionization can be used to fertilize plants.
    b. H_2SO_4. One of its ionization products is responsible for damaging buildings and monuments.
2. The following weak acids are found in acid rain. For each, give the name and write an equation for the formation of ions in aqueous solution.
    a. H_2CO_3. Decomposition of this acid gives the fizz to carbonated soft drinks.
    b. H_2SO_3. A component of acid rain that damages plants and man-made structures.

3. Each of the following strong bases has importance in commercial and industrial applications. Give the name of each and write an equation showing the ions formed in aqueous solution.
   a. $Mg(OH)_2$. This is one of the compounds in the mineral magnesite. It is also the active ingredient in milk of magnesia, an antacid for upset stomachs.
   b. $Al(OH)_3$. This compound is used to affix dyes to fabrics.

4. The following equation represents the formation of an aqueous solution of methylamine (CH_3NH_2), a weak organic base used in the chemical industry. Which species shown are present in an aqueous solution of methylamine?

$$CH_3NH_2(g) + H_2O(l) \rightarrow CH_3NH_3^+(aq) + OH^-(aq)$$

5. Write the total ionic equation for the reaction between $HNO_3(aq)$ and $Mg(OH)_2(s)$. This is one reaction that occurs when acid rain falls on the mineral magnesite. Then write the net ionic equation.

D.15 pH

Water and all its solutions contain both hydrogen and hydroxide ions. In pure water and neutral solutions, the concentrations of these ions are very small but equal. In acid solutions, the hydrogen ion concentration is high and the hydroxide concentration is extremely low. In basic solutions, the hydroxide ion concentration is high and the hydrogen ion concentration is extremely low. The pH concept is built on the relationship between hydrogen ions and hydroxide ions in water. The term pH stands for the "power of hydrogen ion"—a solution in which the hydrogen ion concentration is 10^{-3} M has a pH of 3. (The concept of pH was introduced in the water unit, in Part C.6.)

A pH value of 7 in a water solution at 25 °C represents a neutral solution, one where the concentrations of $H^+(aq)$ and $OH^-(aq)$ are both equal to 10^{-7} M. The pH of pure water is 7.

Values of pH lower than 7 represent acidic solutions. The lower the pH value, the greater the acidity of the solution. In an acidic solution, the concentration of H^+ ion is greater than that of OH^- ion. An acidic solution with a pH of 1 has a hydrogen ion concentration of 10^{-1} M. This is more acidic than a solution of pH 2, where the hydrogen ion concentration is 10^{-2} M.

In contrast, values above pH 7 represent basic solutions. A solution with a pH of 14 has the very low H^+ concentration of 10^{-14} M and an OH^- concentration of 1 M. It is considerably more basic than a solution of pH 8, which has an H^+ concentration of 10^{-8} M and an OH^- concentration of 10^{-6} M.

As you see, with each step up or down the pH scale the acidity changes by a factor of 10. Thus, lemon juice, pH 2, is 10 times more acidic than a soft drink, at pH 3, which is 10,000 times more acidic than pure water. (Figure I.24 in the water unit gives typical pH values for some common materials.)

YOUR *TURN*

VI.12 pH

1. Following are listed some common aqueous solutions with their typical pH values. Classify each as either acidic, basic, or neutral. Arrange them in order of increasing hydrogen ion concentration.
   a. Stomach fluid, 1
   b. A solution of baking soda, 9
   c. A cola drink, 3
   d. A solution of household lye, 13
   e. Milk, drinking water, 6
   f. Sugar dissolved in pure water, 7
   g. Household ammonia, 11

2. How many more times acidic is a cola drink than milk?

PART D
SUMMARY *QUESTIONS*

1. Identify the major types of air pollutants.
2. In what sense is "pollution free" combustion an impossibility?
3. Identify the major components of smog and their sources.
4. Define the term "synergism" and explain its relevance to air pollution.
5. In which region of the United States is acid rain most prevalent? Why?
6. Name the major substances responsible for acid rain. What are their sources?
7. How might efforts to control air pollution result in other kinds of pollution?
8. Pollution has sometimes been defined as "a resource out of place." Name a substance that is a resource in one part of the atmosphere and a pollutant when found in another part.
9. Write the ionic equation for the reaction of NO_2 with rainwater.
10. Which of the following compounds do you recognize as acids? as bases?
    a. NaOH
    b. HNO_3
    c. CH_4
    d. $C_{12}H_{22}O_{11}$ (table sugar)
    e. H_2SO_3
11. Which of the following solutions has the lowest pH? the highest pH?
    a. lemon juice
    b. stomach fluid
    c. drain cleaner (NaOH)
12. Technology to prevent acid rain is available. Why, then, is acid rain still a problem?

EXTENDING *YOUR KNOWLEDGE (OPTIONAL)*

- Carbon monoxide can interfere with the body's O_2 transport and exchange system. Investigate the health effects of CO and its relationship to traffic accidents.
- Investigate the advantages and disadvantages of various alternatives to the standard internal combustion engine. Options include the electric engine, gas turbine, Rankine engine, stratified charge engines, Wankel engine, Stirling engine, diesel engine, and expanded mass transportation systems.
- Make an acid-base indicator at home with red cabbage juice. (Consult your teacher for instructions.)
- Find out how acidic rainwater is in your locality. Wash a plastic (not glass) container with 6 M HCl, and rinse it thoroughly with deionized water. Test the rinse water with pH paper to be sure all the HCl has been rinsed out. Then collect some rainwater. Filter the rainwater through clean filter paper and determine its acidity with pH paper or with a pH meter. If you cannot analyze it immediately, refrigerate it in a sealed container to prevent a change in pH. (What might cause such a change?)

Argonne National Laboratory

An environmental scientist at the Department of Energy's Argonne National Laboratory uses sophisticated instrumentation to measure the effect of legally permissable levels of atmospheric sulfur dioxide on soybean growth and yield.

E PUTTING IT ALL TOGETHER: IS AIR A FREE RESOURCE?

Thus far we have investigated the general properties of gases, the structure and functions of the atmosphere, and how human activity may alter the atmosphere. We have also surveyed ways to control air pollution. However, we have not considered the overall success of such efforts. In fact, how clean should the air be? At what cost? These concerns will also be considered in this final activity.

E.1 Air Pollution Control: A Chemical Success Story?

In Section D.3 you were introduced to the main culprits of air pollution. You examined the relative amounts of total suspended particles (TSP), sulfur oxides (SO_x), nitrogen oxides (NO_x), hydrocarbons (HC), and carbon monoxide (CO) emitted by various sectors of our economy. Later several ways of controlling these emissions were described. Most of these control technologies were instituted since the early 1970s. How successful have they been?

Figure VI.18 presents information summarizing U.S. pollutant additions to the atmosphere from 1975–1983, estimated by the Environmental Protection Agency. Refer to the figures to answer these questions.

1. Estimate the overall percent change in total emissions for each of the four pollutants using the following formula:

$$\text{Percent change} = \frac{1983 \text{ value} - 1975 \text{ value}}{1975 \text{ value}} \times 100$$

   a. Do the overall trends represent an improvement or a worsening of air quality since 1975?
   b. From 1975 to 1983 an increase in overall economic activity led to increased demand for energy and products. For example, during this period the total distance traveled by U.S. vehicles increased by about 20%. Why is it difficult to improve air quality when energy consumption is increasing?

2. On a separate sheet of paper, complete a table similar to the one below. Compare 1975 emissions data with those from 1983 by indicating how specific sources contributed to the overall emissions of each pollutant. The first category has been completed for you.

Data table: Shift in emission patterns, 1975 to 1983			
Pollutant	**Increased**	**Unchanged**	**Decreased**
SO_x	Transportation	None	Fuel combustion; industrial processes
TSP			
NO_x			
HC			

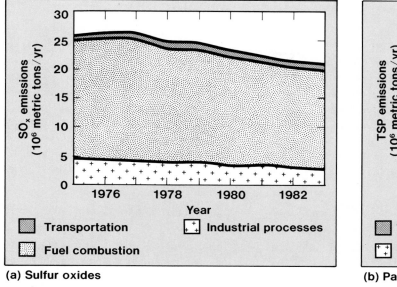

(a) Sulfur oxides

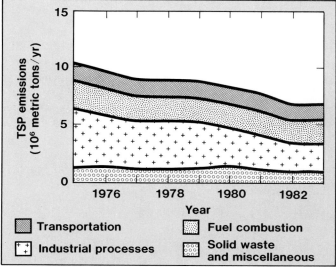

(b) Particulates

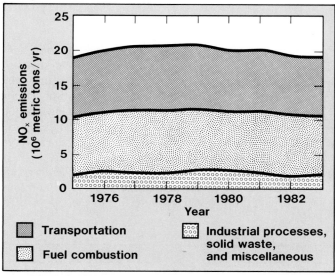

(c) Nitrogen oxides

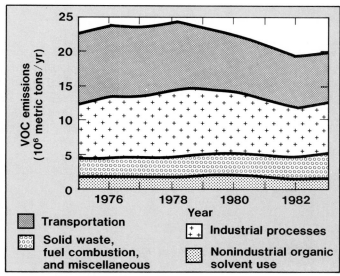

(d) Volatile organic compounds

U.S. Environmental Protection Agency, Washington, 1985

Figure VI.18 National trends in the emission of four air pollutants from 1975–1983; (a) sulfur oxides (SO_x); (b) particulates (TSP, total suspended particulates); (c) nitrogen oxides (NO_x); (d) volatile organic compounds (VOC; primarily hydrocarbons).

    a. What factors could account for a decrease in the total emissions of each pollutant from 1975 to 1983?

    b. What factors could account for an increase in emissions of a given pollutant from any particular source?

    c. Note that some sources emitted the same quantity of a given pollutant in 1983 as in 1975. Does this necessarily indicate that no new pollution control methods were used? Why or why not?

3. Do you agree or disagree with the following statement? "Great strides have been made in improving the quality of the air we breathe." Explain your answer. In addition to emissions data, what evidence would be useful in judging the effects of pollution control technologies?

4. What information would you want to consider before you decided to agree or disagree with the following statement? "Stricter laws and better methods are needed to control air pollution."

E.2 Paying the Price

Earlier in this unit we noted that air pollution costs the United States an estimated $16 billion per year. This financial loss shows up in destroyed crops, weak-
ened livestock, corrosion of buildings and machines, and higher workmen's
compensation and hospital costs for those with air-pollution-related diseases.
However, this does *not* include less visible, but potentially disastrous long-term
costs associated with altering nature's cycles.

Of course, pollution control has its own costs. Whether one considers catalytic converters in automobiles or scrubbers in power plants, pollution control
technologies increase the costs of material goods and energy. In other words, using
the atmosphere as a "free" resource and repository actually involves real expense. With or without pollution control, citizens in industrialized nations pay a
price for the quality of air they breathe.

Economists deal with pollution control policy issues (as they do many issues) in terms of cost-benefit analyses. Each consequence of a given policy is
reduced to a common denominator: dollars. The total cost of any air pollution
control policy is the sum of two elements. One is **damage costs:** tangible losses,
such as those discussed above, and intangible costs, such as reduced visibility and
respiratory irritation. The other element consists of **control costs**—the direct costs
of pollution control methods along with any indirect costs, such as unemployment
created by a plant shutdown or relocation.

The overall result of the costs and benefits of pollution control are combined
in plots like those in Figure VI.19. The plots start at the left with pollution levels
reduced practically to zero (high air quality). As you might expect, at this point
the cost of the control measures is the highest. Also, at the highest air quality
on the left, the cost of pollution damage is very low. Note the changes as air
quality is allowed decrease, represented by moving from left to right on the figure.
Control costs decrease as the level of pollution is allowed to increase. However,
simultaneously, damage costs increase with increasing pollution levels.

The top curve represents the total cost to society of pollution controls and
pollution damage. Look at the vertical line marked on the plot. At the pollution
level shown by point *a,* the damage costs are given by the distance *ab,* the control

Figure VI.19   The cost of air pollution.

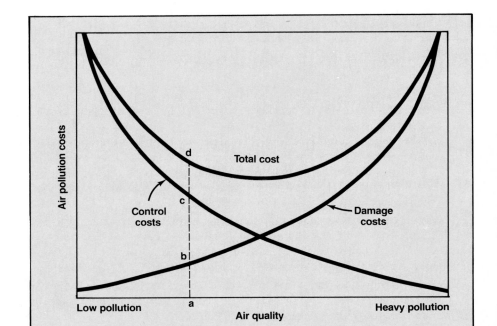

costs are given by the distance *ac,* and the total costs to society are given by *ad,* equal to the sum of *ab* plus *ac.* At this point the cost to society for control is greater than the cost due to damage.

Theoretically, the best balance of control costs and damage costs is where the total cost curve reaches a minimum. This point, will, of course, be different for different pollution and control combinations. Such a cost-benefit analysis is most straightforward for a single business that will bear both the costs of control and damage. Often pollution control analyses are more complicated because the costs of control and damage do not apply to the same group.

Based on what you have learned in this unit and the relationships illustrated in Figure VI.19, answer the following questions:

1. At low pollution levels (high air quality) which costs are highest? Which are lowest? Explain your answers.

2. At high pollution levels (low air quality), which costs are highest? Which are lowest? Explain your answers.

3. Is it possible, technologically or economically, to eliminate all pollution or damage costs? Why?

4. How would the development of new control technologies (such as catalytic converters which use cheaper, more readily available metals) affect the control costs curve?

5. Which costs (damage costs or control costs) do you think can be estimated with greater certainty? Why? What are some difficulties in estimating the other kind of cost?

6. For each point on the graph, the total cost equals the sum of control costs and damage costs. Many economists would say the objective of pollution control is to minimize the total cost. What assumptions are built into such a cost-benefit analysis? Do you think these assumptions are valid? Why?

7. Counting only direct costs that can be measured easily in dollars, the damage costs of U.S. air pollution are currently calculated as $68.38 per year for each individual. Do you think this figure is a fair total cost figure? Why?

8. Automobile emissions of CO, HC, and NO_x have been reduced (respectively) by 96%, 95%, and 71% compared to pre-1968, uncontrolled levels. Assuming you favor stricter pollution control, how much would you be willing to pay (on the price of a new car or for modifying an old one) to decrease the NO_x emissions an additional 25%? When considered on a personal level, control costs seem much higher than damage costs. Why?

9. Are the benefits of cleaner air shared equally by all? Are the control costs of cleaner air shared equally? Why?

10. How much (in dollars) is it worth to you to see a clear blue sky? How much is it worth to you to smell fresh, clean air? Are these questions fair? Are they important?

E.3 Looking Back and Looking Ahead

At this point, you have explored the chemistry of matter and energy interactions in the Earth's atmosphere, land, and water. You have also considered some social issues surrounding our use of these portions of our world as resources and repositories.

The previous units also have been concerned with a fourth "sphere"—the **biosphere**—supported by vital interactions with the other three. In the next unit you will explore the chemistry within the marvelously intricate "ecosystem" of the human body. You will see how individual and social decisions can affect our well-being. As you might suspect, chemistry continues to help us make wiser decisions and define questions for further research. You'll enter the world of "personal chemistry" in the next unit.

FMC Corporation: Air Quality Control Operation

The crane is setting the seven-ton top section on a 105-foot-tall absorber—part of the air pollution control system for Northern Indiana Public Service Company's Rollin M. Schahfer Station, units 17 and 18, near Wheatfield, Indiana. Each unit has four absorbers which use a sodium-based scrubbing solution to absorb up to 12 tons of sulfur dioxide per unit per hour. In a separate section of the plant lime will regenerate the sodium solution for reuse and convert the collected sulfur dioxide into a solid for landfill disposal with fly ash.

UNIT SEVEN

Chemistry and Health

CONTENTS

INTRODUCTION

To a degree unparalleled in history, we have gained control over the causes of illness. Diseases we rarely hear of today—tuberculosis, diphtheria, polio, and stomach inflammation—were once feared as much as we fear cancer. If people still perished from these diseases at the rate they did in 1900, more than three-quarters of a million U.S. citizens would die from them each year. But their yearly toll is fewer than 10,000 lives. These and other diseases have been conquered by a combination of sanitation and mass immunization. That three-quarters of today's deaths result from degenerative diseases such as cancer, heart disease, and stroke—primarily diseases of aging—is evidence of our success.

Many U.S. adults die prematurely by today's standards. (The average life-span in the United States is in the low seventies for men and in the high seventies for women.) However, more than half of these premature deaths can be prevented by changes in behavior, according to the U.S. Centers for Disease Control. In fact, health has increasingly become a matter of personal choice for people in this country. Decisions you make every day influence your health now and in the future.

You Decide: Health Style Survey

Complete the survey on the following two pages to learn your own health style score. Record your responses on the form provided by your teacher. Do not write in this book.

American Cyanamid Company

The development of antibiotics, from cultures such as these species of *Streptomyces* organisms, has made a tremendous contribution to our control over infectious diseases.

healthstyle a self-test

All of us want good health. But many of us do not know how to be as healthy as possible. Health experts now describe *lifestyle* as one of the most important factors affecting health. In fact, it is estimated that as many as seven of the ten leading causes of death could be reduced through common-sense changes in lifestyle. That's what this brief test, developed by the Public Health Service, is all about. Its purpose is simply to tell you how well you are doing to stay healthy. The behaviors covered in the test are recommended for most Americans. Some of them may not apply to persons with certain chronic diseases or handicaps, or to pregnant women. Such persons may require special instructions from their physicians.

Cigarette Smoking

If you <u>never smoke</u>, enter a score of 10 for this section and go to the next section on *Alcohol and Drugs*.

	Almost Always	Sometimes	Almost Never
1. I avoid smoking cigarettes.	2	1	0
2. I smoke only low tar and nicotine cigarettes *or* I smoke a pipe or cigars.	2	1	0

Smoking Score:_____

Alcohol and Drugs

	Almost Always	Sometimes	Almost Never
1. I avoid drinking alcoholic beverages *or* I drink no more than 1 or 2 drinks a day.	4	1	0
2. I avoid using alcohol or other drugs (especially illegal drugs) as a way of handling stressful situations or the problems in my life.	2	1	0
3. I am careful not to drink alcohol when taking certain medicines (for example, medicine for sleeping, pain, colds, and allergies), or when pregnant.	2	1	0
4. I read and follow the label directions when using prescribed and over-the-counter drugs.	2	1	0

Alcohol and Drugs Score:_____

Eating Habits

	Almost Always	Sometimes	Almost Never
1. I eat a variety of foods each day, such as fruits and vegetables, whole grain breads and cereals, lean meats, dairy products, dry peas and beans, and nuts and seeds.	4	1	0
2. I limit the amount of fat, saturated fat, and cholesterol I eat (including fat on meats, eggs, butter, cream, shortenings, and organ meats such as liver).	2	1	0
3. I limit the amount of salt I eat by cooking with only small amounts, not adding salt at the table, and avoiding salty snacks.	2	1	0
4. I avoid eating too much sugar (especially frequent snacks of sticky candy or soft drinks).	2	1	0

Eating Habits Score:_____

Exercise/Fitness

	Almost Always	Sometimes	Almost Never
1. I maintain a desired weight, avoiding overweight and underweight.	3	1	0
2. I do vigorous exercises for 15-30 minutes at least 3 times a week (examples include running, swimming, brisk walking).	3	1	0
3. I do exercises that enhance my muscle tone for 15-30 minutes at least 3 times a week (examples include yoga and calisthenics).	2	1	0
4. I use part of my leisure time participating in individual, family, or team activities that increase my level of fitness (such as gardening, bowling, golf, and baseball).	2	1	0

Exercise/Fitness Score:_____

Stress Control

	Almost Always	Sometimes	Almost Never
1. I have a job or do other work that I enjoy.	2	1	0
2. I find it easy to relax and express my feelings freely.	2	1	0
3. I recognize early, and prepare for, events or situations likely to be stressful for me.	2	1	0
4. I have close friends, relatives, or others whom I can talk to about personal matters and call on for help when needed.	2	1	0
5. I participate in group activities (such as church and community organizations) or hobbies that I enjoy.	2	1	0

Stress Control Score:_____

Safety

	Almost Always	Sometimes	Almost Never
1. I wear a seat belt while riding in a car.	2	1	0
2. I avoid driving while under the influence of alcohol and other drugs.	2	1	0
3. I obey traffic rules and the speed limit when driving.	2	1	0
4. I am careful when using potentially harmful products or substances (such as household cleaners, poisons, and electrical devices).	2	1	0
5. I avoid smoking in bed.	2	1	0

Safety Score:_____

What Your Scores Mean to YOU

Scores of 9 and 10

Excellent! Your answers show that you are aware of the importance of this area to your health. More important, you are putting your knowledge to work for you by practicing good health habits. As long as you continue to do so, this area should not pose a serious health risk. It's likely that you are setting an example for your family and friends to follow. Since you got a very high test score on this part of the test, you may want to consider other areas where your scores indicate room for improvement.

Scores of 6 to 8

Your health practices in this area are good, but there is room for improvement. Look again at the items you answered with a "Sometimes" or "Almost Never." What changes can you make to improve your score? Even a small change can often help you achieve better health.

Scores of 3 to 5

Your health risks are showing! Would you like more information about the risks you are facing and about why it is important for you to change these behaviors. Perhaps you need help in deciding how to successfully make the changes you desire. In either case, help is available.

Scores of 0 to 2

Obviously, you were concerned enough about your health to take the test, but your answers show that you may be taking serious and unnecessary risks with your health. Perhaps you are not aware of the risks and what to do about them. You can easily get the information and help you need to improve, if you wish. The next step is up to you.

YOU Can Start Right Now!

In the test you just completed were numerous suggestions to help you reduce your risk of disease and premature death. Here are some of the most significant:

 Avoid cigarettes. Cigarette smoking is the single most important preventable cause of illness and early death. It is especially risky for pregnant women and their unborn babies. Persons who stop smoking reduce their risk of getting heart disease and cancer. So if you're a cigarette smoker, think twice about lighting that next cigarette. If you choose to continue smoking, try decreasing the number of cigarettes you smoke and switching to a low tar and nicotine brand.

 Follow sensible drinking habits. Alcohol produces changes in mood and behavior. Most people who drink are able to control their intake of alcohol and to avoid undesired, and often harmful, effects. Heavy, regular use of alcohol can lead to cirrhosis of the liver, a leading cause of death. Also, statistics clearly show that mixing drinking and driving is often the cause of fatal or crippling accidents. So if you drink, do it wisely and in moderation. *Use care in taking drugs.* Today's greater use of drugs—both legal and illegal—is one of our most serious health risks. Even some drugs prescribed by your doctor can be dangerous if taken when drinking alcohol or before driving. Excessive or continued use of tranquilizers (or

"pep pills") can cause physical and mental problems. Using or experimenting with illicit drugs such as marijuana, heroin, cocaine, and PCP may lead to a number of damaging effects or even death.

 Eat sensibly. Overweight individuals are at greater risk for diabetes, gall bladder disease, and high blood pressure. So it makes good sense to maintain proper weight. But good eating habits also mean holding down the amount of fat (especially saturated fat), cholesterol, sugar and salt in your diet. If you must snack, try nibbling on fresh fruits and vegetables. You'll feel better—and look better, too.

 Exercise regularly. Almost everyone can benefit from exercise—and there's some form of exercise almost everyone can do. (If you have any doubt, check first with your doctor.) Usually, as little as 15-30 minutes of vigorous exercise three times a week will help you have a healthier heart, eliminate excess weight, tone up sagging muscles, and sleep better. Think how much difference all these improvements could make in the way you feel!

 Learn to handle stress. Stress is a normal part of living; everyone faces it to some degree. The causes of stress can be good or bad, desirable or undesirable (such as a promotion on the job or the loss of a spouse). Properly handled, stress need not be a problem. But unhealthy responses to stress—such as driving too fast or erratically, drinking too much, or prolonged anger or grief—can cause a variety of physical and mental problems. Even on a very busy day, find a few minutes to slow down and relax. Talking over a problem with someone you trust can often help you find a satisfactory solution. Learn to distinguish between things that are "worth fighting about" and things that are less important.

 Be safety conscious. Think "safety first" at home, at work, at school, at play, and on the highway. Buckle seat belts and obey traffic rules. Keep poisons and weapons out of the reach of children, and keep emergency numbers by your telephone. When the unexpected happens, you'll be prepared.

Where Do You Go From Here:

Start by asking yourself a few frank questions: *Am I really doing all I can to be as healthy as possible? What steps can I take to feel better? Am I willing to begin now?* If you scored low in one or more *sections* of the test, decide what changes you want to make for improvement. You might pick that aspect of your lifestyle where you feel you have the best chance for success and tackle that one first. Once you have improved your score there, go on to other areas.

If you already have tried to change your health habits (to stop smoking or exercise regularly, for example),don't be discouraged if you haven't yet succeeded. The difficulty you have encountered may be due to influences you've never really thought about—such as advertising—or to a lack

of support and encouragement. Understanding these influences is an important step toward changing the way they affect you.

There's Help Available. In addition to personal actions you can take on your own, there are community programs and groups (such as the YMCA or the local chapter of the American Heart Association) that can assist you and your family to make the changes you want to make. If you want to know more about these groups or about health risks, contact your local health department or the National Health Information Clearinghouse. There's a lot you can do to stay healthy or to improve your health—and there are organizations that can help you. Start a new HEALTHSTYLE today!

For assistance in locating specific information on these and other health topics; write to the National Health Information Clearinghouse.

National Health Information Clearinghouse
P.O. Box 1133
Washington, D.C. 20013

A CHEMISTRY INSIDE YOUR BODY

A.1 Balance and Order: Keys to Life

Some items in the health survey you just took involve common sense. It doesn't take any specialized knowledge of body chemistry to know that you should wear seat belts and obey the speed limit. But other items involve maintaining your body properly, and this is easier to do if you understand how your body works.

Whether you plunge into icy water or play ball in the hot sun, your body temperature rarely deviates more than two degrees from 37 °C. If it does, you are probably ill. Likewise, the pH of your blood remains virtually constant, as do the concentrations of many substances in your blood and cells. Your body would quickly fail if its chemistry fell out of balance.

To do their jobs, cells must be supplied with necessary chemical substances, waste products must be removed promptly, and proper temperature and pH must be maintained. Blood serves as a conduit for supplies and wastes. Also, it insulates the cells from harmful changes in physical and chemical conditions.

Maintenance of balance in all body systems is called **homeostasis.** Failure of homeostasis leads to illness, and if not corrected, eventually leads to death.

The most impressive and important feature of body chemistry is its controlled complexity. Every minute your cells make hundreds of different compounds, and they do so more quickly and more accurately than any chemical factory. These compounds take part continuously in the multitude of reactions that occur simultaneously in each cell.

The best way to stay healthy is to help your body chemistry stay in balance. For example, as you read in the fourth unit, "Understanding Foods," eating a balanced diet provides your body with all the building-block molecules and ions it needs to make new tissues.

Exercise is important because it keeps the cardiovascular system (heart, lungs, veins, and arteries) fit. This system supplies food and fuel to your tissues, and the oxygen to burn that fuel.

Under normal conditions, both your body and the external environment contain well-balanced ecosystems of many kinds of bacteria. Although harmful bacteria are all around us, they generally fail to cause disease, in large part because they must compete with the harmless bacteria in the body and in the environment. Sickness often results from a population explosion of harmful bacteria in the body.

This is where the external environment comes in. Harmful bacteria proliferate in a dirty environment. Before the time of municipal sewage treatment, water supplies often were contaminated and provided ideal environments for harmful bacteria. Drinking water risked invasion by armies of these bacteria. Municipal sewage treatment has been a major contributor to public health.

Despite the best of modern medicine and sanitation, occasionally we become sick. Fortunately, the body is very good at regaining its balance. Given a healthful environment, proper care, and a good diet, most of us can recover from most diseases by ourselves. But in some cases the body needs assistance to overcome an illness. Chemists have developed many drugs that promote recovery and relieve pain caused by illness.

An ecosystem consists of organisms and their environment.

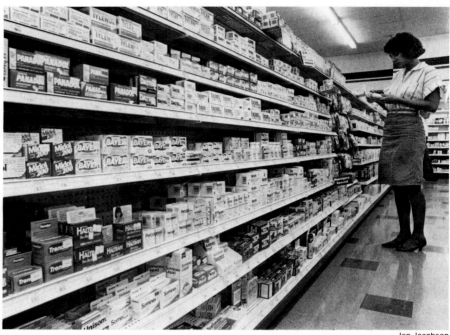

Jon Jacobson

Informed decision making is an important part of personal health care.

However, body chemistry is so delicately balanced that a drug that helps one system regain equilibrium may throw other systems out of balance. This is what doctors mean by side effects. Sometimes we must decide which creates greater problems—the disease or the cure.

A.2 *You Decide:* Burdens and Benefits of Aspirin

Aspirin is discussed further in Part C.2.

Aspirin is a drug with many beneficial uses. In most cases it is regarded as quite safe. However, it has a few side effects. Aspirin is an acidic compound, and some persons get an upset stomach if they take it. Prolonged use of this drug also creates a risk of some hearing loss.

Doctors often prescribe from four to eight aspirin tablets each day for individuals suffering from arthritis. Imagine that your joints ached constantly, limiting your activity. Aspirin could relieve the pain.

Would you take the aspirin? In other words, would you prefer to live with the pain, or with the side effects of the treatment? If you decide to take aspirin, what option(s) might be available to counteract the long-term side effects? Why should you take medications only when they are really needed?

In the following sections, we will look at the composition and chemistry of the body, and explore some of the built-in mechanisms that maintain homeostasis.

A.3 Elements in the Human Body

Table VII.1 lists twenty-seven elements your body requires and the quantities of each element normally found in a healthy adult. These elements are present in the body in biomolecules or as ions in solution in body fluids.

Oxygen, carbon, hydrogen, and nitrogen are the most abundant. Together, they make up more than 99% of body mass. Sixty-three percent of all atoms in the body are hydrogen, 25% are oxygen. Nearly 10% are carbon, and 1.4% are

---

Table VII.1 *Elemental composition of a 70-kg human adult*

| Elements | Abundance in body | |
	ppm	Percent of body mass
Hydrogen, oxygen, carbon, nitrogen, calcium	10,000 to 630,000	99
Phosphorus, chlorine, potassium, sodium, sulfur, magnesium	400 to 7,000	1
Iron, zinc	25 to 50	0.01
Copper, tin, manganese, iodine, bromine	1 to 10	Trace[a]
Fluorine, molybdenum	0.2 to 0.5	Trace[a]
Arsenic, cobalt, chromium, lithium, nickel	0.02 to 0.04	Trace[a]
Cadmium, selenium	Less than 0.02	Trace[a]

[a]Less than 0.001%

---

nitrogen. Most of these atoms are present in organic compounds such as the carbohydrates, proteins, and fats described in the food unit. (For a review, see Unit Four, Parts B.3, B.4, and C.3, and Figures IV.3–IV.9.)

Elements such as iodine, selenium, copper, and fluorine are essential to health, even though they normally are present in less than 10 parts per million (ppm) of body mass (10 pennies in $10,000, all in pennies, also is 10 ppm). Table IV.12 in the food unit describes the functions of some trace elements in the body.

YOUR*TURN*

VII.1 Elements in the Body

1. Select five elements found in the body. Using Table VII.1, Table IV.12, and what you learned in the food unit, answer the following questions:
   a. Where in the body or in what type of biomolecule is each element found?
   b. What role does each element play in maintaining health?
2. Is it reasonable to say that elements highly abundant in the body, such as calcium and phosphorus, are more essential than trace elements such as iron and iodine? Why? (*Hint:* Consider the concept of a limiting reactant.)
3. Why might a change in diet more likely cause a deficiency of trace elements than of highly abundant elements? Why are cases of overdose poisoning more common with trace elements? (*Hint:* Consider percent change and chemical balance.)

Consuming more of a trace element than is needed can sometimes interfere with body chemistry. However, the body will excrete some trace elements before they accumulate to toxic levels.

To understand how cellular chemistry contributes to health and well-being, and what you can do to assist it, we will next consider some of the important principles involved.

A.4 Cellular Chemistry: Fast, Efficient, Precise

How quickly can you pull back your hand from a hot stove? How quickly can you move your foot from the accelerator to brake your car to a stop? Many cellular chemical reactions must take place very rapidly to allow you to do these things.

A human cell makes hundreds of different substances, each at exactly the right moment and in precisely the amount required. And it generates its own energy and chemical machinery to do so.

The cell is the scene of action in your body. Cellular chemistry is fast, efficient, and precise. You have learned that food is "burned" to supply the body's continuous energy needs. This occurs in the cell, where energy is released and used with great speed and efficiency. The building function of the body also occurs with incredible efficiency in the cells. Each healthy cell synthesizes exactly the molecules it needs—no more and no less, and precisely at the moment the need arises.

The secret behind these features lies with the enzymes present in all cells. Enzymes are biological catalysts; they speed up reactions without undergoing a net change themselves. The speed of an enzyme-catalyzed reaction is hard to comprehend. In one second, a single enzyme molecule in your blood can catalyze the decomposition of 600,000 H_2CO_3 molecules:

$$H_2CO_3(aq) \rightarrow H_2O(l) + CO_2(g)$$

In that second, 600,000 molecules of carbon dioxide are liberated into your lungs as you exhale. Also in one second an enzyme in saliva can free 18,000 glucose molecules from starch chains:

-glucose-glucose-glucose $+$ $H_2O(l)$ $\xrightarrow{\text{Enzyme}}$ -glucose-glucose $+$ glucose
        (portion of starch   (remaining portion
            molecule)   of starch molecule)

Before looking further at how enzymes do their jobs, your teacher will conduct a demonstration so you can see for yourself the speed of an enzyme-catalyzed reaction.

A.5 Laboratory Demonstration: Decomposing Hydrogen Peroxide with an Enzyme

The reaction to be investigated is the decomposition of hydrogen peroxide to water and oxygen:

$$2\ H_2O_2(aq) \rightarrow 2\ H_2O(l) + O_2(g)$$

You used this reaction to generate oxygen in your study of atmospheric gases (Unit Six, Part B.1). The manganese dioxide (MnO_2) added in that experiment was a catalyst. This demonstration will show the action of a biological catalyst—an enzyme—on this reaction.

Answer the following questions at the conclusion of the demonstration.

Questions
1. What did the foam in the test with the fresh liver indicate?
2. Why was there little observable reaction when boiled liver was used?
3. Why does commercial hydrogen peroxide contain preservatives?

4. An old belief is that when hydrogen peroxide is added to a cut, foaming shows that infection is present. What is the real reason?

5. What two important features of hydrogen peroxide help in treating wounds? Explain their benefits.

   In the following section you will see why enzymes are so effective.

A.6 How Enzymes Work

Enzymes speed up reactions by making it easier for molecules to react. Enzymes and many of the molecules they help to react are very large. If such large molecules are to interact with each other at specific sites or functional groups, they must approach so that these functional groups are in close proximity.

In general, enzymes function in the following manner:

- Reactant molecules, known as **substrates,** and enzymes are brought together. The substrate molecule is fitted into the enzyme at an **active site** where its key functional groups are held in the necessary position (Figure VII.1).
- In this enzyme-substrate complex, the enzyme interacts with the substrate molecule(s), weakening key bonds and lowering the reaction's activation energy. Our discussion of automobile catalytic mufflers described how catalysts function—the reaction is speeded up because the activation energy barrier is lowered (Unit Six, Part D.10).
- The reaction occurs and the products depart from the enzyme surface, freeing the enzyme to interact with other substrate molecules.

   Some enzymes require the presence of coenzymes. For example, B vitamins are coenzymes in the release of energy from food molecules (see Table IV.9 in Unit Four). How some coenzymes function is shown in Figure VII.2.

   Enzymes are as selective as they are fast. How does the cell carry out only the necessary reactions when substrates for many unnecessary reactions are present? Why do your cells oxidize glucose to CO_2 and water instead of reducing it to CH_4 and water? Why do stomach cells digest protein rather than starch or fat? The answer to all these questions is that normally an enzyme can catalyze only one specific type of reaction, and a cell can carry out only those reactions for which it has enzymes. So the cell has precise control over which reactions take place.

   Nearly all body cells have the enzymes they need to produce energy, make essential compounds, and replace damaged parts. What distinguishes, say, skin cells from muscle cells is that some of the substances they make are different.

Figure VII.1 Model of the interactions of enzyme and substrate molecules.

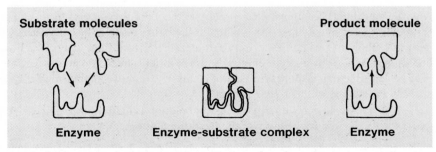

Substrate molecules   Product molecule

Enzyme   Enzyme-substrate complex   Enzyme

Figure VII.2   Schematic view of a vitamin serving as a coenzyme.

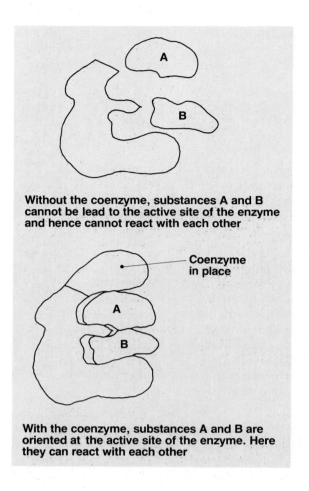

Without the coenzyme, substances A and B cannot be lead to the active site of the enzyme and hence cannot react with each other

Coenzyme
in place

With the coenzyme, substances A and B are oriented at the active site of the enzyme. Here they can react with each other

Genetic engineering is the relatively new technology that allows genes to be modified.

Every cell (except blood cells) has an identical set of instruction molecules composed of chains of DNA (deoxyribonucleic acid) molecules. **Genes**—small segments of DNA molecules—store the instructions for specific traits such as hair color, height, and other individual characteristics. Various chemical regulators "turn on" only those genes appropriate to the cell type. Exactly how these regulators choose the appropriate genes is still a mystery.

A.7   How Energy Is Released and Stored

Body chemistry is not only fast and selective, but extremely energy efficient. Here's why: Some cellular reactions release energy; others require energy. Just as longer-term storage for money reserves is often in the bank, reserves of body energy are kept in carbohydrates and fats. Between its release from these energy-rich molecules and its use in the cell, energy is stored briefly in biomolecules known as ATP (adenosine triphosphate). Think of it this way—between obtaining cash and spending it, you store it in your pocket.

The body's primary energy-releasing reaction is oxidation of glucose (Unit Four, Part C.1), for which we use the overall equation:

$$C_6H_{12}O_6(aq) + 6\ O_2(g) \rightarrow 6\ CO_2(g) + 6\ H_2O(l) + 2.87 \times 10^3\ kJ/mol\ glucose$$

As we noted before, this equation summarizes what happens in a sequence of more than 20 chemical reactions. More than 22 enzymes are involved in these reactions. One molecule at a time, glucose passes through this sequence in cells throughout your body. Energy contained in glucose is set free bit by bit in individual reactions and immediately is placed in short-term storage in ATP molecules.

Photo courtesy of The Des Moines Register

ATP provides the energy needed for all human activity.

In the energy storage reaction, ADP (adenosine diphosphate) adds a phosphate group to form ATP and water:

$$\text{Energy} + \text{ADP}(aq) + \text{HPO}_4{}^{2-}(aq) \longrightarrow \text{H}_2\text{O}(l) + \text{ATP}(aq)$$

(31 kJ/mol ADP)   Hydrogen
                        phosphate ion

Oxidation of one mole of glucose produces enough energy to add 38 mol of ATP to the cell's short-term energy storage.

Each ATP molecule contains a conveniently small quantity of energy that can be used as needed to power individual steps in cellular reactions. An ATP molecule is much like a dollar bill—a convenient denomination that the cell uses to pay for its minute by minute biochemical work. Some steps in reactions require less energy than is stored in a single ATP molecule, while others must use the energy from several ATP molecules.

As energy is needed, it is released in the reverse of the energy storage reaction shown above

$$\text{ATP}(aq) + \text{H}_2\text{O}(l) \longrightarrow \text{ADP}(aq) + \text{HPO}_4{}^{2-}(aq) + \text{Energy (31 kJ/mol ADP)}$$

The structures of ATP and ADP are pictured in the margin. In the body's solutions, they exist as ions. Every day your body stores and later releases energy from at least 100 mol (6.0×10^{25} molecules) of ATP.

The extraordinary efficiency with which energy is released, stored, and released again as needed is the result of enzyme speed and specificity. Besides using glucose, your body can obtain energy from the fatty acids stored in fats or from protein. To oxidize these substances, cells use many of the same enzymes that oxidize glucose.

ATP

ADP

YOUR*TURN*

VII.2 Enzymes and Energy in Action

Consider this sample problem: Table IV.2 stated that sitting burns 100 kcal/h. (a) If all this energy were obtained from ATP and each mole of ATP yields 7.3 kcal (31 kJ), how many moles of ATP would be needed to provide the energy to sit for one hour? (b) If each mole of glucose burned produces 38 mol of ATP, how many grams of glucose would have to be burned to provide this energy?

First, we find the moles of ATP needed for one hour of sitting:

$$100 \, \frac{\text{kcal}}{\text{h}} \times \left(\frac{1 \text{ mol ATP}}{7.3 \text{ kcal}} \right) = 14 \text{ mol ATP/h}$$

The moles of glucose and then the grams of glucose can be found in a single setup as follows (the molar mass of glucose, $C_6H_{12}O_6$, is 180 g/mol):

$$\frac{14 \text{ mol ATP}}{1 \text{ h}} \times \left(\frac{1 \text{ mol glucose}}{38 \text{ mol ATP}} \right) \times \left(\frac{180 \text{ g glucose}}{1 \text{ mol glucose}} \right) = 66 \text{ g glucose/h}$$

Now try these items:

1. One minute of muscle activity requires about 10^{-3} mol of ATP per gram of muscle. How many moles of glucose must be oxidized per pound (454 g) of muscle to dribble a basketball for three minutes? How many grams of glucose is this?

2. If your body produces approximately 100 mol of ATP per day, how many moles of glucose must be consumed to produce this much ATP? How many grams of glucose is this?

3. **Amylase,** an enzyme present in saliva, catalyzes the release of glucose from starch. Under optimum conditions of temperature and pH, one molecule of amylase can generate as many as 18,000 molecules of glucose each second (as noted in Part A.4). See if you can detect a change in the taste of a soda cracker (all contain starch) as you chew one for a minute or more before swallowing it. Describe any taste change you detect. Explain what caused the change.

Besides controlling release and storage of energy, enzymes catalyze reactions that break down food molecules to building blocks your cells can use. The following is an investigation of this role of enzymes.

A.8 Laboratory Activity: Studying Enzyme Action

Getting Ready

You will observe the activity of two enzymes that aid in digestion by detecting the products of digestion.

The major protein in egg white—albumin—is digested in the small intestine by the enzyme **pepsin.** When albumin is decomposed in the laboratory, the extent of reaction can be judged by the amount of cloudiness (insoluble product) that appears as time passes. The greater the turbidity, the larger the amount of protein decomposed. You will test the action of pepsin on the form of albumin that you usually consume—the white of a cooked egg.

Some detergent formulations include enzymes that attack proteins.

An enzyme in saliva, amylase, breaks down starch molecules into individual glucose units (see Part A.4 and *Your Turn* VII.2). The glucose is detected by Benedict's reagent, with which it forms a yellow-to-orange precipitate. The amount of precipitate increases with the concentration of glucose.

The activity of each enzyme will be observed at two temperatures (room temperature and refrigerator temperature) and at several pH values. You will be assigned to a group of four students. Each group member should carry out tests to check the activity of one of the following:

1: Pepsin enzyme at room temperature.
2: Refrigerated pepsin enzyme.
3: Amylase enzyme at room temperature.
4: Refrigerated amylase enzyme.

Read the procedures below and prepare a data table with appropriately labeled columns for data collected by each group member.

Day 1: Preparing the Systems

Pepsin Tests
1. Label four test tubes near the top with the temperature of your assigned test and a pH value of 2, 4, 7, or 8.
2. Using solutions provided by your teacher, place 5 mL of the pH 2, 4, 7, and 8 solutions in the appropriate test tubes.
3. Place 1.5 g of egg white (the size of a large kidney bean) into each test tube.
4. Add 5 mL of 0.5% pepsin solution to each test tube. Continue with Steps 5–7 below.

Amylase Tests
1. Label five test tubes near the top with the temperature of your assigned test and a pH value of 2, 4, 7, 8, or 10.
2. Using solutions provided by your teacher, place 5 mL of the pH 2, 4, 7, 8, and 10 solutions in the appropriate test tubes.
3. Add 2.5 mL of starch suspension to each test tube.
4. Add 2.5 mL of 0.5% amylase solution to each test tube. Continue with Steps 5–7 below.

All Tests
5. Put a stopper in each test tube and shake well.
6. Leave test tubes that are to remain at room temperature in the laboratory overnight as directed.
7. Give your teacher test tubes that are to be refrigerated.

Day 2: Evaluating the Results
1. Pepsin tests. Observe the test tubes for cloudiness (turbidity). Record your observations.
2. Amylase tests. Follow the steps below.
   a. Prepare a hot-water bath by adding about 100 mL of tap water to a 250-mL beaker. Add a boiling chip and heat the beaker on a ring stand with a Bunsen burner.
   b. Place 5 mL of Benedict's reagent in each test tube. Replace the stoppers, being careful not to mix them up, and shake well.
   c. Make sure that the tubes are clearly labeled. Remove or loosen the stoppers and place the test tubes in the water bath.

d. Heat the water bath until the contents of at least one test tube have turned yellow or orange. Then heat for 2–3 more minutes.

e. Use tongs to remove the test tubes from the water bath. Place the tubes in a test tube rack in order of increasing pH.

f. Observe and record the color of the contents of each tube.

3. Share your data with other members of your group.

Questions

1. At which pH and temperature was each enzyme most effective?

2. Make a general statement about the effect of temperature on an enzyme-catalyzed reaction.

3. Bases that liberate relatively low concentrations of $OH^-(aq)$, such as calcium carbonate ($CaCO_3$), aluminum hydroxide ($Al(OH)_3$), and magnesium hydroxide ($Mg(OH)_2$), are used in stomach antacids. Why must the bases used in such preparations produce only small amounts of hydroxide ion?

A.9 Energy and Exercise

Metabolism is the sum of all body processes for building and burning.

Although your body can burn fat or protein, glucose is the fuel of choice, because it can be metabolized fastest. By comparison, fat metabolism is slow. However, during prolonged exercise, your body rations available glucose, and metabolizes about 50% fat. Why?

The energy contained in body fat is many times greater than the small quantity of energy (about a day's worth) the body can store in glucose and other carbohydrates. Furthermore, some glucose must be saved for the brain, which cannot metabolize fat. (The body cannot store protein, so it burns protein from its own structure when it runs out of other fuels.)

Fat molecules are stored in fat tissues. Glucose molecules are stored in the liver and muscles after they have been strung together into highly branched chains of animal starch called **glycogen.** Once the glycogen stores of the muscle and liver are full, much of the remaining glucose is transformed into fat in the fat cells and liver. Typically, more than half of the carbohydrate you eat is stored as fat.

When the body needs energy, glucose and fat easily come out of storage. During prolonged strenuous exercise, the concentration of fatty acids in the blood quadruples. The reactions of fat that produce ATP are similar to those of glucose.

How your body makes use of different sources of fuel is best illustrated by how different athletic events draw on different stores of energy. Sprinters in 100-m and 200-m events get most of their power from muscle reserves of ATP and a similar molecule called **phosphocreatine.** During strenuous exercise, your muscles run low on stores of these high-energy phosphates after only about half a minute.

In a 400-m dash, the muscular store of glucose (as glycogen) becomes important. However, your muscles need energy more quickly than it can be supplied by oxidizing glucose all the way to carbon dioxide. Instead, energy is obtained by carrying out only a portion of the steps normally required. In this situation, glucose is rapidly divided into two three-carbon molecules of lactic acid, in a process requiring no oxygen. This quick-energy sequence is called **anaerobic glycolysis** (Figure VII.3).

Although anaerobic glycolysis generates energy faster than does aerobic metabolism, it is actually a very inefficient way to use fuel. Furthermore, during glycolysis, lactic acid quickly builds up in the muscles, causing leg pain such as that you may have experienced after running up several flights of stairs. This limits the time your body can run on anaerobic glycolysis to less than a minute.

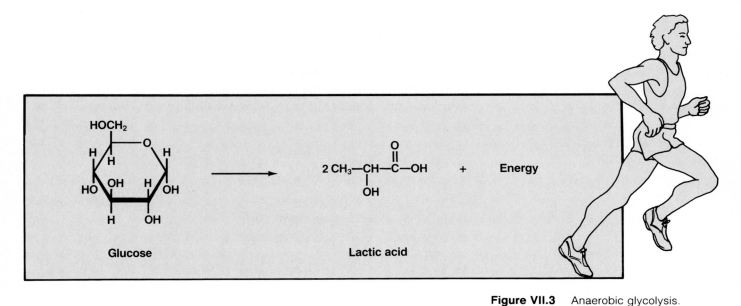

Figure VII.3 Anaerobic glycolysis. Quick energy for short runs or emergency movement is provided in this manner.

During the first hour of strenuous exercise the body burns mainly glucose. In part, this is because it takes about that long for the body's fat metabolism system to get warmed up. The longer you exercise, the greater the proportion of fat you burn.

What should you eat to prepare for several hours of exercise? Protein is a poor source of fuel. Before it can be used, nitrogen atoms of the amino acids must be removed and excreted. This process consumes extra body water, which becomes a precious commodity during heavy exercise, particularly in hot weather.

And despite its billing as a quick energy source, sugar actually saps energy during exercise. Studies show that those who consume quantities of sugars before they exercise produce up to 25% less power during exercise and have high concentrations of lactic acid in their blood.

The recommended fuel for prolonged exercise is complex carbohydrates, in the form of grains, fruits, and vegetables. Filling up on these ensures that your glycogen stores are full. There is no need to eat fat, because whatever carbohydrate the body cannot store will be converted to fat.

YOUR*TURN*

VII.3 Food and Energy

What kinds of foods would you recommend for individuals in each of these situations?

1. A person preparing for a marathon run the next day.
2. A sprinter preparing for a 100-m dash.
3. A sailor, just rescued from a lifeboat, who has not eaten for several days and is very weak.
4. A weightlifter who hopes to increase shoulder muscle size and shape.
5. A tennis player who must play a long match in very hot weather.

A.10 A Closer Look at Proteins

Millions of kinds of proteins exist. They are the most abundant polymers in the body: Much of the machinery and structure of every living cell is protein.

Proteins in all living things are formed from essentially the same 20 or so amino acids.

As you learned in the food module, proteins are polymers (long chains) of amino acid units. About 20 different amino acids are found in the proteins in your body. Amino acids can be represented by this general structural formula

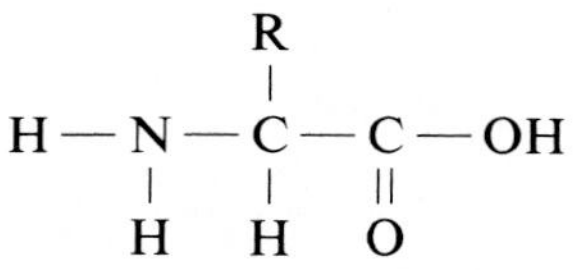

$$H-N-\overset{\overset{\displaystyle R}{|}}{\underset{\underset{\displaystyle H}{|}}{C}}-\overset{\overset{\displaystyle }{}}{\underset{\underset{\displaystyle O}{\|}}{C}}-OH$$

where R can be a hydrogen atom or a group of atoms, such as a hydrocarbon chain. Three common amino acids are:

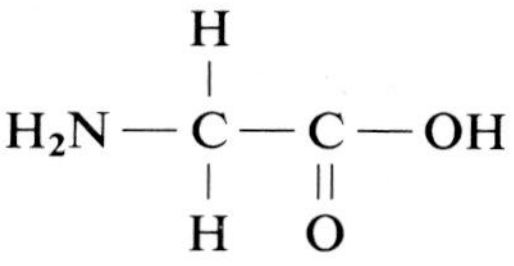

Amino acids and proteins often take an ionic form

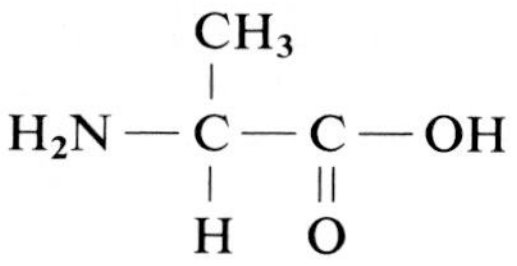

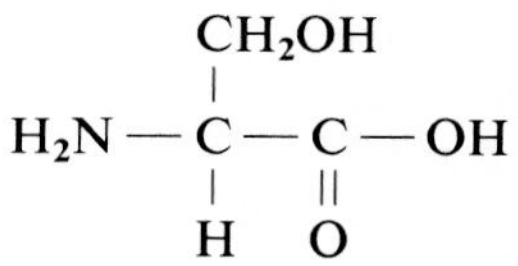

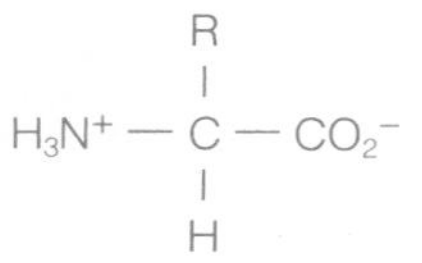

$$H_3N^+ - \overset{\overset{\displaystyle R}{|}}{\underset{\underset{\displaystyle H}{|}}{C}} - CO_2^-$$

in body fluids.

$$H_2N - \overset{\overset{\displaystyle H}{|}}{\underset{\underset{\displaystyle H}{|}}{C}} - \overset{}{\underset{\underset{\displaystyle O}{\|}}{C}} - OH$$
Glycine (Gly)

$$H_2N - \overset{\overset{\displaystyle CH_3}{|}}{\underset{\underset{\displaystyle H}{|}}{C}} - \overset{}{\underset{\underset{\displaystyle O}{\|}}{C}} - OH$$
Alanine (Ala)

$$H_2N - \overset{\overset{\displaystyle CH_2OH}{|}}{\underset{\underset{\displaystyle H}{|}}{C}} - \overset{}{\underset{\underset{\displaystyle O}{\|}}{C}} - OH$$
Serine (Ser)

When two amino acids combine during formation of protein, a water molecule is produced (Figure VII.4). As few as 50 or as many as thousands of amino acids can link to form a protein molecule. The result is a long, stringlike structure (see Figure VII.5).

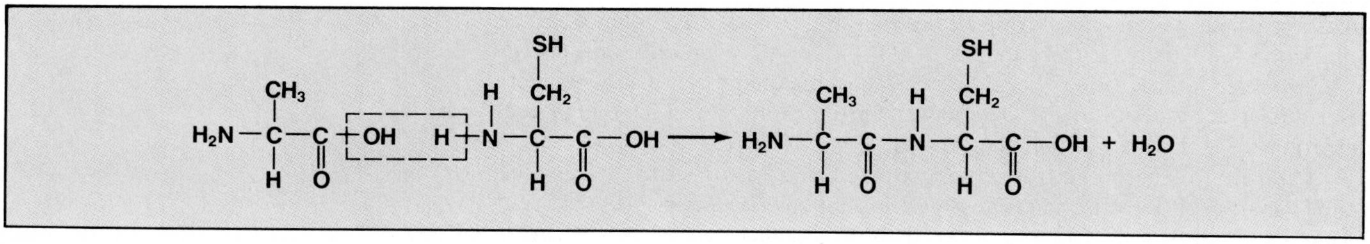

Figure VII.4 The formation of a protein segment.

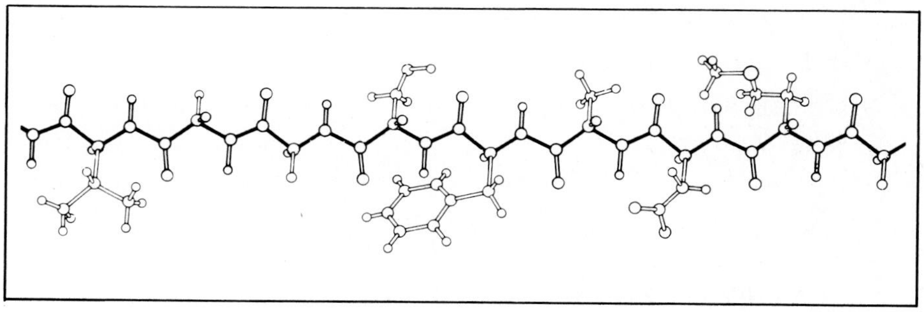

Figure VII.5 A portion of a protein molecule. Covalent bonds (solid black lines) connect carbon and nitrogen atoms in the backbone of the chain (compare with the amino acid structure).

Proteins have many jobs. Some catalyze reactions, as described above. Others serve as **hormones,** special substances formed in certain organs and conveyed by blood to other organs, where they stimulate biochemical activity. For example, a series of hormones switches on the activities that prepare a woman's body for pregnancy. Still other proteins are the trucks of the body, carrying vital molecules from one place to another. Hemoglobin is one such molecule; it carries oxygen from the lungs to the tissues. Proteins also form most of the body's structural material. Hair, muscle, skin, cartilage, and nails are all made of protein. (See also Table IV.6 in Unit Four on food.)

How can strings of amino acids do so many things? Why do enzymes always act like enzymes, and not like hemoglobin or skin proteins, for example?

The answer to these questions lies in two basic concepts. First, proteins differ because each has a distinctive sequence of amino acid units. The twenty or so different amino acids can be arranged in any order, and different amounts of individual amino acids can be used. Thus, an enormous number of unique chains, or different proteins, can be formed. The human body may contain as many as five million different kinds of proteins.

Second, the stringlike protein chains can fold into an almost infinite variety of shapes. The sequence of amino acids in a protein determines its shape, and shape determines the protein's function.

Figure VII.6 illustrates the sequence of amino acids in bovine ribonuclease, an enzyme that catalyzes certain cellular reactions in cows. This particular enzyme was formed from 124 amino acid molecules; each is represented in the drawing by a standard three-letter abbreviation.

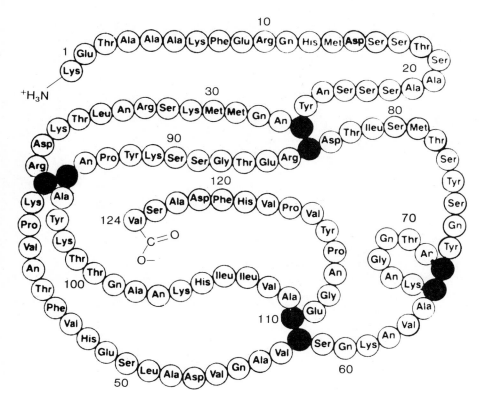

Figure VII.6   The sequence of amino acids in the enzyme bovine ribonuclease.

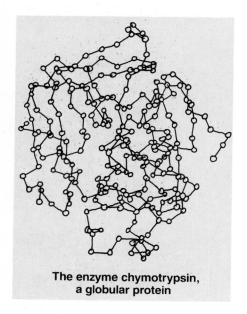

**The enzyme chymotrypsin,
a globular protein**

Figure VII.7   Ball-like structure assumed by the chains of many globular proteins.

Figure VII.8   Interactions between adjacent extended chains characteristic of many fibrous proteins.

The shape assumed by its chain enables a protein to play its role in the cell or in the body. Some protein chains fold themselves into balls. Others remain extended and interact with neighboring chains to form sheet-like or rope-like structures. Figure VII.7 illustrates the ball-like structure characteristic of **globular proteins.** Figure VII.8 illustrates the extended chain interactions characteristic of many **fibrous proteins.**

Globular proteins include hormones, enzymes, and carrier proteins. These are all proteins that move around in the cellular fluid or in the circulatory system. This kind of mobility requires water solubility. The ball-like structure has nonpolar (water-insoluble) chemical groups on the inside, and polar and ionic (water-soluble) groups on the outside.

Fibrous proteins are present in hair, muscles, skin, and fingernails or toenails. They can be remarkably tough. For example, the eyeball can withstand four times the pressure of a high-pressure bicycle tire (approximately 400 lb/in.^{2}).

The interactions that cause proteins to form and retain ball-like or sheet-like structures are illustrated in Figure VII.9, and described below:

Hydrogen bonding (Figure VII.9a) is an unusually strong attraction between a polar (partially positive) hydrogen atom and a strongly electron-attracting atom like nitrogen or oxygen. In protein chains, the hydrogen atom in such a bond usually is covalently bonded to a nitrogen atom and is strongly attracted to an oxygen atom in a neighboring chain or in a folded-back portion of its own chain. All active proteins contain hundreds of hydrogen bonds closely spaced along their chains. The many hydrogen bonds serve to hold the protein chains in their ball-like or sheet-like structures.

In many fibrous proteins, the chains are not fully extended, but are coiled, much like a "curly" telephone cord. Many hydrogen bonds keep the coils in place; others hold the chain to neighboring chains. This occurs in hair protein, as illustrated in Figure VII.10.

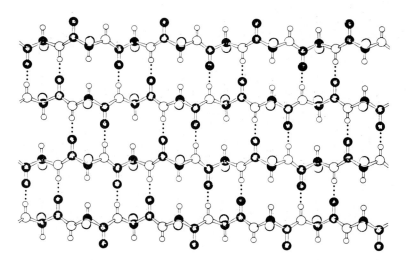

Ionic bonding (Figure VII.9b) is an attraction between an ionic structure in one chain and an oppositely charged ionic structure in a neighboring chain or in a folded-back portion of the same chain. Such bonds are extremely important in hemoglobin, for example.

Nonpolar interaction (Figure VII.9c) is a relatively weak attraction between nonpolar R groups. It often occurs in the interior of ball-like structures of globular proteins. Although weak, many such interactions help keep the structure intact, largely by preventing water molecules from entering.

Many proteins contain a few *covalent bonds* that link together neighboring chains or folded-back portions of the same chain. Most often these are disulfide bonds as illustrated in Figure VII.9d. Disulfide bonds form between two cysteine residues. (The "residue" is the portion of the amino acid molecule present in the protein chain.) The R group in the amino acid cysteine contains an $-S-H$ unit. Two cysteine residues can react at their $-S-H$ units by losing hydrogen and forming a disulfide bond.

$$\sim\sim\sim S-H + H-S \sim\sim\sim \rightarrow \sim\sim\sim S-S\sim\sim\sim + H_2$$

As we shall see, disulfide bonds are important in curling or straightening hair.

Sometimes small changes in environment cause important changes in shape that affect protein function. For example, a slight increase in blood pH loosens the protein chains of hemoglobin structures as they pass through the lung. This exposes oxygen-bonding iron ions, allowing them to bond oxygen molecules more readily. A return to a lower pH environment tightens the chains again, helping hemoglobin release oxygen molecules as it passes cells that need oxygen.

Figure VII.9 Interactions between protein chains. (a) Hydrogen bonding between units in backbone. (b) Ionic bond between R groups. (c) Interactions between nonpolar R groups creating region from which water molecules are excluded; a type of interaction in cell membranes. (d) Disulfide bond formed between S—H groups in cysteine (Cys) units.

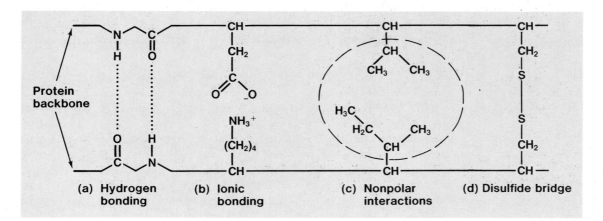

(a) Hydrogen bonding   (b) Ionic bonding   (c) Nonpolar interactions   (d) Disulfide bridge

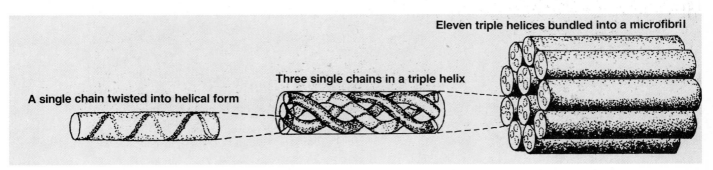

Source: Reprinted with permission by Dickerson and Geis from *The Structure and Action of Proteins.* Benjamin-Cummins, Menlo Park, CA, 1969. Illustration copyright by R. E. Dickerson and I. Geis.

Figure VII.10 Hair keratin, a fibrous protein. The helical chains are twisted into a triple helix, and these helices are bundled into a microfibril. As shown in Figure VII.20, microfibrils form the core of each strand of hair.

Figure VII.11 Denaturing a globular protein. In many cases, return to an environment like that in the cell will restore original shape and reactivity.

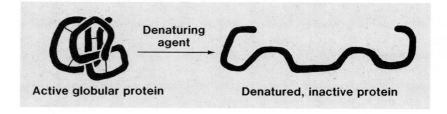

Active globular protein   Denatured, inactive protein

Jon Jacobson

Denaturing the protein in eggs.

Too much of a change in chemical environment, however, can destroy the ability of a protein to work properly by drastically distorting its shape. Heat, alcohol or other solvents, salts of heavy metals, or changes in acidity can alter protein shape by disrupting the bonding between chains (Figure VII.11). In some cases, the change, called **denaturation,** is permanent. You can see such a change when you cook an egg. Albumin, the major protein in egg white, is denatured, as shown by its change in appearance and texture. In other cases, the change is temporary and if the protein is returned to an environment like that in a cell, its original shape and chemical reactivity are restored.

YOUR TURN

VII.4   Protein Structure

1. What would be the result of breaking the carbon-to-nitrogen bonds in the backbone of a protein?
2. The sequence of amino acids in proteins can be modeled by using different colored pop beads to represent different amino acids. Describe three ways you could vary the sequence of beads to make different protein models. How can such a large number of proteins be created to meet specific body needs?

3. An enormous number of proteins can be created from 20 amino acids. Can you think of another situation where a relatively small number of parts combine in a large number of different, useful ways?

4. Fibrous proteins include hair, skin, muscle, and nails, all of which have structural functions. Globular proteins such as enzymes and hormones have specific internal biochemical jobs to do. Compare the shapes and water solubilities of these two classes of proteins. Why is the water solubility of most fibrous proteins so different from that of globular proteins?

Even small changes in body temperature or pH could shut down enzymes. In the following activity you will investigate the effect of these two critical factors on enzyme activity.

A.11 Laboratory Activity: Denaturing Protein

Getting Ready
Earlier (Part A.7), you observed the action of enzymes in digesting hard-boiled egg white protein, which is denatured albumin. Albumin is a globular protein soluble in water and body fluids. On heating in solution it is denatured and precipitates as a white jelly-like substance. You will test the effect on a 2% aqueous albumin solution of the following agents:

- heat
- an acid (hydrochloric acid, HCl)
- a base (sodium hydroxide, NaOH)
- a salt of a heavy metal (silver nitrate, $AgNO_3$)
- a salt containing sodium ion (Na^+), an ion found in body fluids.

You will also determine if denaturation of aqueous albumin caused by changing pH can be reversed.

Read the entire procedure below and prepare a table in your notebook in which to record your results.

Procedure

Part 1: Denaturing a Protein
1. Label: 5 small test tubes a to e.
2. Pour 4 mL of 2% albumin solution into each test tube.
3. Perform the tests listed below. Be sure to rinse the stirring rod well after each use so the next test will not be contaminated. Record the results in your data table.

        Test tube a. Heat the tube for 6–10 seconds (until cloudy) by grasping it with a test tube holder and gently moving it back and forth through a Bunsen burner flame.

        Test tube b. Add 2 mL of 3 M HCl.

        Test tube c. Add 2 mL of 3 M NaOH.

        Test tube d. Add five drops of 0.1 M $AgNO_3$ and stir.

        Test tube e. Add five drops of 0.1 M $NaNO_3$ and stir.

Part 2: Testing for Reversibility in Denaturing a Protein

1. Place 1 mL of 2% albumin solution in a test tube and add a drop of universal indicator. Shake carefully and compare the color of the tube contents with the scale provided with the indicator. Record the estimated pH.

2. Place 1 mL of 2% albumin solution in a test tube. Add 1 mL of 3 M HCl. Record the results. Now add two drops of universal indicator and record the pH.

3. Follow these steps:
   a. Place 10 mL of 2% albumin solution in a 125-mL Erlenmeyer flask. Add 10 mL of 3 M HCl. Observe and record the results. Save the flask.
   b. Fill a clean 50-mL buret with 3 M NaOH.
   c. Place the flask from Step 3a under the buret. Slowly add NaOH solution to the flask, stopping to stir after each addition. Add NaOH more slowly as the contents begin to clear, stirring and pausing after each addition to see if solution will clear. Stop adding solution when the liquid in the flask is clear.
   d. Add five drops of universal indicator to the flask. Observe the color of the flask contents. Compare with the indicator scale and record the estimated pH.

Questions

1. List the agents and conditions that resulted in turbidity of the protein solution (denaturation).
2. Explain your observations in Part 2.
3. Explain why, in food preservation, heat is used to kill bacteria.
4. Spoilage bacteria break down milk sugar (lactose) into glucose and galactose. These sugars are then oxidized to lactic acid to produce energy. What effect would lactic acid have on protein in milk? Explain.
5. Which substance is most likely to precipitate protein: potassium nitrate, (KNO_3) or lead nitrate ($Pb(NO_3)_2$)? (*Hint:* Compare locations of sodium, silver, potassium, and lead in the periodic table.)
6. Very dilute solutions of $AgNO_3$ are placed in the eyes of newborn babies to prevent infection. Why is this solution used?
7. Egg white or milk is given as an antidote when mercury or lead salts are accidentally ingested. This treatment is followed by an emetic (an agent that causes vomiting). Explain why these agents are used.

We have seen that the body's proteins, especially enzymes, are very sensitive to changes in acidity or concentrations of foreign materials (such as heavy metal ions) in their environment. Yet acids and other substances are continuously added to and removed from cells and body fluids. How can the body handle this without denaturing its proteins? This is our next topic.

A.12 Acids, Bases, and Buffers in the Body

Under normal conditions, the pH of your blood rarely exceeds 7.45 or drops below 7.35. Even though large quantities of acid enter the blood daily, the body has a variety of mechanisms that keep blood pH constant.

Much of the acid that invades the blood comes from the carbon dioxide that cells give off as they oxidize glucose. Carbon dioxide reacts with water in the blood to produce carbonic acid (H_2CO_3).

$$CO_2(g) + H_2O(l) \rightarrow H_2CO_3(aq) \rightarrow H^+(aq) + HCO_3^-(aq)$$

The amount of carbon dioxide dissolved in the blood controls the concentration of carbonic acid.

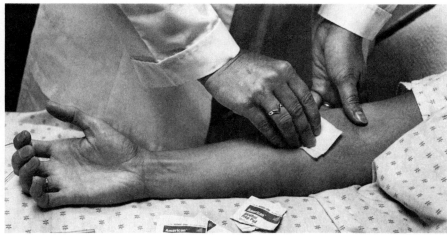

Jon Jacobson

Alcohol is an effective and convenient topical antiseptic.

Your body produces 10–20 mol of carbonic acid daily. Other acids, including phosphoric acid (H_3PO_4) and lactic acid ($CH_3CHOHCOOH$) are produced in the digestion of foods. How does the body maintain a constant pH in spite of this continuous influx of acids?

It uses chemical buffers to control the pH of its fluids. A **buffer solution** contains relatively high concentrations of a weak acid and a salt of that acid. For example, citric acid and sodium citrate form a buffer combination often found in commercial food products.

How does a buffer solution control pH? It contains a weak acid which reacts with bases and a weak base which reacts with acids.

Earlier we saw that salts containing the OH^- ion are bases. The OH^- ion reacts as a base as follows:

$$H^+(aq) + OH^-(aq) \rightarrow H_2O(l)$$

The anions of weak acids act as bases in the same way as shown below for bicarbonate ion (HCO_3^-).

A weak acid and its salt buffer (protect) a solution against a pH change caused by adding small amounts of acid or base in the following manner: If base is added to a buffer solution, the buffer's weak acid neutralizes the base, preventing a large change in pH. If acid is added to the solution, the buffer's weak base—the anion from the salt—neutralizes it, preventing a large change in pH.

The blood's primary buffer system is carbonic acid (H_2CO_3) and sodium bicarbonate ($NaHCO_3$). The addition of acid or base to this system results in the following reactions:

$$\begin{array}{ccccc} H^+(aq) & + & HCO_3^-(aq) & \rightarrow & H_2CO_3(aq) \\ \text{From added} & & \text{Bicarbonate ion} & & \text{Carbonic acid} \\ \text{acid} & & \text{acting as a base} & & \end{array}$$

$$\begin{array}{cccccc} OH^-(aq) & + & H_2CO_3(aq) & \rightarrow & HCO_3^-(aq) & + & H_2O(l) \\ \text{From added} & & \text{Carbonic acid} & & \text{Bicarbonate ion} & & \text{Water} \\ \text{base} & & & & & \end{array}$$

The products become part of the buffer system that keeps the pH constant.

Other buffer systems also help maintain body pH balance. One involves the oxygen-carrying protein, hemoglobin, which is a weak acid. Another is the phosphate buffer system composed of the two anions $H_2PO_4^-$ and HPO_4^{2-}. (Which of these anions reacts as an acid with excess base and which reacts as a base with excess acid?)

In the following laboratory activity you will examine the behavior of the carbonate buffer system.

A.13 Laboratory Activity: Buffers in Action

Getting Ready

In this activity, you will prepare and test a carbonate buffer. Addition of acid and base to water will be compared to addition of acid and base to the buffered solution.

Your teacher will assign you to an "acid" group or a "base" group. Read the procedures below and prepare a data table for your results. The table should contain five columns: original pH, pH after five drops of acid (base), initial volume of acid (base) in buret, final volume of acid (base) in buret, volume of acid (base) added.

Procedure

Acid Groups

Water Plus Acid

1. Fill a clean buret to above the 0 mL mark with 0.50 M HCl. Briefly open the valve, letting solution run into a beaker until no air is left in the buret tip and the liquid surface is at or below the 0 mL mark. Record the volume.

2. Place 40 mL of deionized (or distilled) water in a clean 125-mL Erlenmeyer flask. Add 10 drops of universal indicator. Compare the color of the flask contents to the indicator scale. Record the pH.

3. Place the flask under the buret. Slowly open the buret valve and add five drops of acid to the flask. Swirl the flask. Record the pH of this unbuffered acid solution. Retain this flask as a color standard for comparison with the buffered solution.

Carbonate Buffer Plus Acid

4. Add 40 mL of 0.10 M NaHCO$_3$ solution to a clean 125-mL Erlenmeyer flask. Use a clean straw to blow exhaled breath containing carbon dioxide into the flask for 3 min. The carbonate buffer has now been prepared. Discard the straw.

5. Add 10 drops of universal indicator. Swirl the flask. Record the solution color and pH.

6. Record the initial buret volume.

7. Add five drops of the 0.50 M HCl from the buret to the flask and swirl. Record the color and pH.

8. Continue to add HCl solution until the color and pH are identical to those in the color standard flask from the water plus acid procedure above. Record the final buret volume.

9. Calculate the volume of HCl solution added. Record this value.

10. Drain the HCl solution from the buret. Rinse the buret by pouring deionized or distilled water through it and allowing it to drain into a beaker. Repeat this rinse step.

Base Groups

Water Plus Base

1. Fill a buret with 0.50 M NaOH as described in Step 1 for the acid groups. Record the buret volume.

2. Repeat Steps 2 and 3 given above for the acid groups, using 0.50 M NaOH instead of HCl.

Carbonate Buffer Plus Base

Follow Steps 4–10 above for the acid group, using 0.50 M NaOH instead of the acid.

Questions

1. Did the carbonate buffer solution work for you? What observations led you to this answer?

2. Compare the volumes of 0.50 M HCl needed to reach the same pH when added to water and to the carbonate buffer. Do the same for the 0.50 M NaOH.

3. Write an equation showing how the carbonate buffer would prevent the pH of the blood from rising if a small quantity of base (OH⁻) were added.

4. A buffer is a solution of a weak acid and its salt, or a weak base and its salt. Classify each of the substances below as a strong or weak acid or base, or as the salt of a strong or weak acid or base. (Refer to Part D.14 of Unit Six, "Chemistry, Air, and Climate.") Then determine which one of the following pairs of substances would make the best buffer system:
   a. KCl and HCl
   b. NaOH and H_2O
   c. $NaNO_3$ and HNO_3
   d. $NaC_2H_3O_2$ and $HC_2H_3O_2$

A.14 pH Balance in the Body

Body pH balance is maintained even in many abnormal situations by the combined action of blood buffers, breathing rate, and the kidneys. Changes in breathing rate affect the concentration of dissolved carbon dioxide, which, we have seen, is a major source of acid in the blood.

Large enough concentrations of added acid or base can overwhelm a buffer. In your body, the kidneys help to prevent this and to maintain the body's pH balance on a day-to-day basis. They can excrete excess acidic or basic substances. They also provide a backup neutralization system for abnormal conditions. If the blood is too acidic, the kidneys produce the weak bases $HCO_3^-(aq)$ and $HPO_4^{2-}(aq)$ to neutralize it. If the blood is too basic, the kidneys neutralize it with the weak acids $H_2CO_3(aq)$ and $H_2PO_4^-(aq)$. The reaction products are eliminated in urine.

Should blood pH drop and stay below 7.35, a condition known as **acidosis** develops. Mild acidosis can occur if the lungs temporarily fail to expel CO_2 efficiently, causing a build up of carbonic acid in the blood. The central nervous system is affected by acidosis, in mild cases causing mental confusion and disorientation. In extreme cases shock, coma, and even death can result.

Photo courtesy of The Des Moines Register

Extreme physical exertion can cause bodily systems to become unbalanced temporarily.

When the pH of blood rises and stays above 7.4, **alkalosis** develops. Temporary alkalosis can occur after severe vomiting in which large amounts of hydrochloric acid (HCl) are lost from the stomach. Chronic alkalosis can produce weak, irregular breathing and muscle contractions. Severe alkalosis can lead to convulsions and death.

Apply what you have learned about pH balance in the body by answering the following questions.

YOUR*TURN*

VII.5   Conditions that Affect pH Balance

1. Hyperventilation is a condition of forced, heavy breathing that typically occurs when an individual is frightened. How would this affect the concentration of CO_2 in the blood? How would this affect the pH? Fortunately, the body has an automatic response—fainting—that stops hyperventilation before serious damage is done.

2. If you held your breath, how would this condition affect the concentration of CO_2 in the blood? How would this condition alter pH?

3. Strenuous muscle activity, such as long-distance running, can cause lactic acid to accumulate in the blood, resulting in a wobbly feeling in leg muscles. How would the accumulation of lactic acid affect blood pH?

4. Cardiac arrest occurs when the heart stops and blood circulation is halted, but cellular reactions continue. When this occurs, doctors often inject sodium bicarbonate solution ($NaHCO_3(aq)$) which contains the base HCO_3^-, directly into the heart muscle even before restarting the heart. (In television medical dramas, doctors are frequently heard to order "sodium bicarb STAT.") What effect would cardiac arrest have on blood pH? Why? How would the injection counteract this effect?

5. What condition of acid-base imbalance might be caused by a large overdose of aspirin?

When a physician says "STAT," this means "IMMEDIATELY."

CHEM*QUANDARY*

Chicken eggshells are composed mainly of calcium carbonate ($CaCO_3$). The major source of carbon in the shells is carbon dioxide from the blood.

In summer, eggshells are often so thin that they break easily. Farmers solve this problem by feeding chickens carbonated (soda) water, water saturated with carbon dioxide. What causes the problem? How does soda water eliminate it? (*Hint:* Instead of perspiring, chickens pant to keep cool.)

Having explored the chemical composition of the human body and some mechanisms within it for maintaining chemical balance, we next look at chemistry at the body surface, where we have more control over what happens.

PART A
SUMMARY *QUESTIONS*

1. How can more than half the premature deaths in the U.S. be prevented?

2. What is meant by homeostasis? How is it related to the normal functioning of your body?

3. Identify some factors that contribute to homeostasis in a healthy human body.

4. Name the five most common elements in the human body, in order of decreasing abundance.

5. List three characteristics of chemical reactions in cells. Show how each is important in everyday activities.

6. What class of cellular compounds is primarily responsible for the above characteristics? Briefly describe how these compounds work.

7. How is energy released from the oxidation of food materials stored in the body?

8. The production of 1 g of protein requires about 17 kJ of energy. The molar mass of the protein albumin is 69,000 g/mol. How many ATP (adenosine triphosphate) molecules must react to energize the formation of 1 mol of albumin?

9. Carbohydrates, fats, and proteins can all provide bodily energy. Which class of substances provides energy most rapidly? Which class can be used as a building material in the body? Which is the most efficient as an energy-storage system?

10. What are the structural units in protein? Even though there are fewer than two dozen kinds of these units, there are thousands of different proteins. Why?

11. List the two major types of bodily proteins and their functions.

12. What happens chemically when a protein is denatured? What are some agents that cause denaturing?

13. Describe the composition and function of a buffer system.

14. Name four conditions that can overload the body's buffer systems. In each case describe the chemistry of the overload and its effect on blood pH.

B CHEMISTRY AT THE BODY'S SURFACE

Keeping clean is important, not just for appearances, but for good health. Lack of cleanliness can lead to skin infections, loss of hair or teeth, or disease caused by bacteria picked up from the surroundings.

Considerable chemistry is involved in keeping clean and maintaining a pleasing appearance. Understanding this chemistry will help you make better choices concerning your health. First, let's look at the skin and substances that can keep it clean without damaging it.

B.1 Some Chemistry of Keeping Clean

Have you ever wondered why a frog feels slimy? Its skin has glands that secrete skin-moistening oils. Human beings also have glands to produce oils that keep skin flexible. Chapped lips show how uncomfortable a shortage of these oils can be.

The most obvious skin secretion is perspiration. We perspire to keep body temperatures from rising during hot weather or heavy exercise. Sweat, mostly water, also contains about 1% sodium chloride.

If that was all there were to sweat, there would be less need to bathe with soap. But areas of the body that perspire profusely also secrete oils, producing body odors as unique to individuals as their facial appearances. These odors quickly turn stale as bacteria attack the oils.

Jon Jacobson

Keeping clean may be important, but may not always be possible.

426

So keeping clean involves several related tasks: removing dirt and grease we pick up from outside sources, and removing the waxes and oils from perspiration and excess lubricating oil before bacteria can get to them. Mainly, cleaning skin requires removing oils and greases. But cleaning can be taken too seriously. Too much cleaning can damage the skin by removing natural oils and drying it out.

Cleaners remove oil and dirt by dissolving them. For example, grease is highly soluble in a water solution of ammonia ($NH_3(aq)$). This is why ammonia is an effective kitchen cleaner. However, concentrated ammonia solutions are strong enough to damage human skin.

Water alone will not dissolve oil and grease. If you've ever mixed oil and vinegar (vinegar is a solution of acetic acid in water) to make salad dressing, you know what the problem is. Shake them all you want: When you stop, the oil and vinegar immediately begin to separate. Oil and water also fail to mix if you bathe or shower without soap. This is why water alone fails to clean your skin.

To understand how soap can help clean your skin, it is important to review the molecular basis of solubility.

The polarity of water molecules gives rise to hydrogen bonding between hydrogen atoms of a water molecule and oxygen atoms of adjacent water molecules (Figure VII.12). Hydrogen bonds are weaker than the covalent bonds that hold hydrogen and oxygen atoms together in water molecules. But they are strong enough to pull water molecules into clusters, causing water to "bead" on a flat surface. By contrast, nonpolar oil molecules are less strongly attracted to each other and do not form round droplets. When water and nonpolar substances are mixed, the hydrogen bonds hold the water molecules together so tightly that the nonpolar molecules are forced to form a separate layer.

Still, many substances do dissolve in water. Salt and rubbing alcohol are examples. Their ions or molecules are attracted to water molecules so that they fit comfortably among them.

Earlier (Unit One, Parts C.11 and C.12) you explored the meaning of "like dissolves like" and found that in general polar or ionic substances dissolve in water and nonpolar substances dissolve in nonpolar solvents. Compatible attractive forces are the key to solubility. As you will see, some large molecules can be soluble in polar solvents at one end and in nonpolar solvents at the other end.

Complete the following activity to review the connection between polarity and solubility.

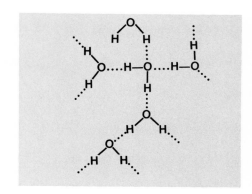

Figure VII.12 Hydrogen bonding in water.

YOUR*TURN*

VII.6 Polarity and Solubility

1. Indicate whether each substance below is nonpolar, polar, or ionic. Then predict whether it is water soluble or soluble in nonpolar solvents. Base your reasoning on bond polarity, charge, and molecular shape.
    a. NaOH, sodium hydroxide; a base used in making soaps
    b. $(CH_3CH_2)_2O$, diethyl ether; an industrial solvent
    c. CH_2OHCH_2OH, ethylene glycol; permanent antifreeze
    d. KNO_3, potassium nitrate; a fertilizer

2. Consider the chemical structures of a fatty oil (a triglyceride) and glucose. Which will dissolve in water and which will dissolve in gasoline? Why? What is different about the two molecules?

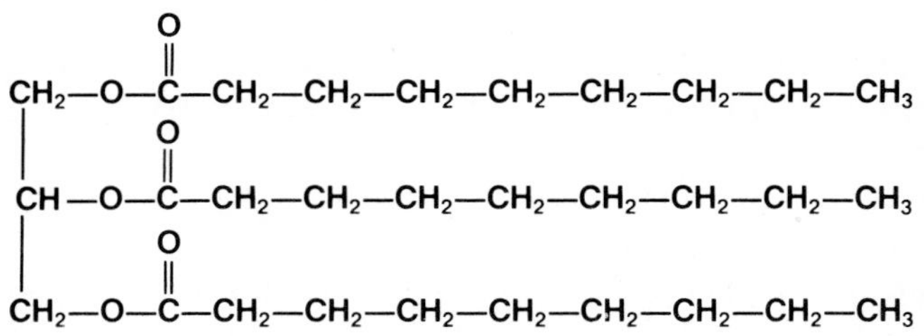

$$CH_2—O—\overset{\displaystyle O}{\overset{\|}{C}}—CH_2—CH_2—CH_2—CH_2—CH_2—CH_2—CH_2—CH_3$$

$$CH—O—\overset{\displaystyle O}{\overset{\|}{C}}—CH_2—CH_2—CH_2—CH_2—CH_2—CH_2—CH_2—CH_3$$

$$CH_2—O—\overset{\displaystyle O}{\overset{\|}{C}}—CH_2—CH_2—CH_2—CH_2—CH_2—CH_2—CH_2—CH_3$$

A triglyceride

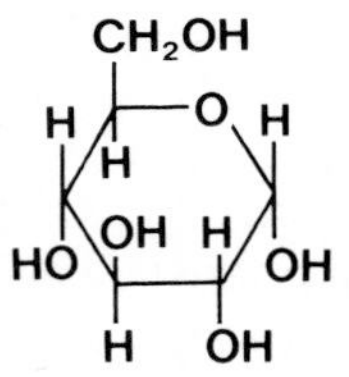

Glucose

3. Ethanol (CH_3CH_2OH) is a water soluble organic molecule. Its solubility in water is due to its small size and polar —OH group, which allow for hydrogen bonding in water. Cholesterol ($C_{27}H_{46}O$), an animal fat associated with heart disease, is not water soluble even though, like ethanol, it contains an —OH group. Why? Would you expect cholesterol to dissolve in nonpolar solvents? Why?

4. Sodium lauryl sulfate, $CH_3(CH_2)_{11}OSO_3^-Na^+$, is a synthetic detergent. Recalling the behavior of detergents, do you think this compound is soluble in water? In oil? Explain your answer in terms of the rule "like dissolves like."

Jon Jacobson

Soap works because it is strongly attracted to both oil and water.

Skin cleaners, soaps, and detergents have structures with split personalities when it comes to solubility. One end of each structure is polar and the other is nonpolar. For example, the long hydrocarbon chain in the soap sodium stearate (Figure VII.13) dissolves in oil but not in water. However, the oxygen atom at the other end of the structure has a negative charge, which is strongly attracted to polar water molecules.

Thus, sodium stearate, and other soaps and detergents like it, are strongly attracted to both water and oil. This enables wash water to remove oil and grease. The long skinny molecules cluster around an oil droplet with the water-insoluble ends pointing inward and the charged ends pointing out into the water (Figure VII.14). The oil-containing droplet enters the wash solution and is rinsed away.

"Soaps" are made from fats. "Detergents" are not made from fats. Most are made from petroleum.

Today, most people buy commercial soaps and detergents. In the nineteenth century, however, people often made their own soap from lye (sodium hydroxide, NaOH) and animal fat: Glyceryltripalmitate (a typical fat molecule) reacts with lye (a base) to form the soap sodium palmitate:

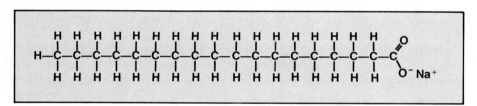

| Glyceryltripalmitate | Sodium palmitate | Glycerol |

Because lye soap contains unreacted lye it can damage skin.

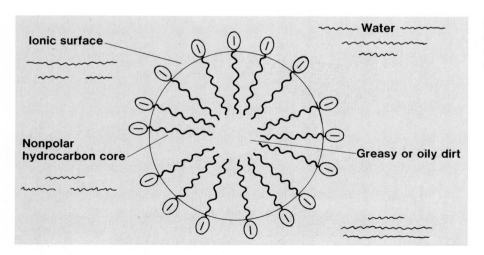

Figure VII.13 Sodium stearate, a soap. Commercial soaps are mixtures of structures such as this.

Figure VII.14 Spherical cluster of soap molecules in water. This is how soaps and detergents remove grease and oil from soiled surfaces.

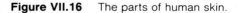

Figure VII.15   Benzoyl peroxide structure. This substance is used in controlling acne.

CHEM*QUANDARY*

Acne pimples are small infections caused by bacteria that eat skin oil. During adolescence, many persons' bodies produce too much skin oil. The key to controlling acne is to keep the skin very clean and the pores open. Abrasive lotions help remove the layer of dead cells, dirt, and oil. Keeping hands and hair away from the face also helps keep dirt and bacteria away.

Preparations containing benzoyl peroxide, a mild oxidizing agent, also are effective in controlling acne (Figure VII.15). How would this kind of substance help?

In severe acne cases, doctors sometimes prescribe antibiotics. Why are they effective?

Most acne remedies offer only temporary relief; the only real cure for acne is to outgrow it.

B.2   Skin: It's Got You Covered

Skin is your body's area of contact with the outside world. It protects you from mechanical damage and from bacteria. It helps keep your body temperature constant by sweating. Through the sense of touch it offers an important source of information about the world. And it plays a role in communicating human emotions.

Human skin, about 3 mm thick, has two major layers (Figure VII.16). The inner layer, the **dermis,** contains two kinds of protein fibers that give the skin strength and flexibility. Sweat and oil glands are located in this lower layer, with tubes (ducts) leading to pores on the surface. All cells of the dermis are alive, and must be supplied with blood. If you bleed when you scrape your skin, you have reached the dermis.

The cells of the dermal layer constantly divide. Some of these new cells get pushed upward to form the **epidermis,** the skin's outer layer. As the cells are pushed upward, their nuclei die and their fluid is replaced by protein fiber. Oil secreted by glands in the dermis forms a protective film on the surface, keeping these dead cells soft, and preventing excessive water loss. This oily layer is slightly acidic, thereby protecting protein fibers that can be disintegrated by bases.

Figure VII.16   The parts of human skin.

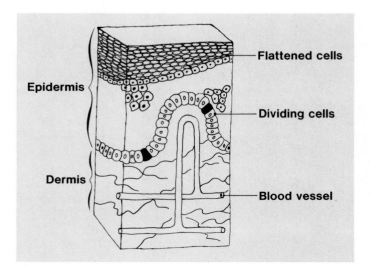

Older cells at the skin's surface continuously flake off as pieces that are generally too small to see. Dandruff is composed of dead epidermal cells that stick together, falling off in relatively large pieces. Some people waste considerable time and money trying to "cure" dandruff with germ-killing shampoos. Dandruff has nothing to do with germs. The best dandruff shampoos contain substances that prevent dead epidermal cells from clustering and slow down the rate at which cells die.

It may seem strange that skin cells should die and be replaced continuously. Can you think of a good reason why this should happen?

Persons with excessive dandruff have a faster than average death rate of skin cells.

Maintaining healthy skin is a simple matter. Eat wisely. Keep clean, but don't overdo it. Too much bathing will remove all of your skin's oils, drying out and possibly damaging your skin. Most of all, avoid getting too much sun.

B.3 Protecting Your Skin from the Sun

The sun's radiation provides energy and light that we need and welcome, but its ultraviolet component can seriously damage exposed skin. Ultraviolet radiation is powerful enough to energize electrons in molecules, occasionally causing the molecules to break. These breaks are most damaging when they occur in the DNA, the genetic instruction molecules. Although the cell has mechanisms to repair these breaks, when they go unrepaired they cause mutations (changes in the instructions).

This kind of damage is greatest in rapidly dividing tissue, because the mutations are quickly passed on to daughter cells. Skin cells are replaced monthly. Mutations are responsible for age spots, wrinkling, and general aging of the skin. Eventually they can lead to cancer.

The most immediate effect of excessive sun is sunburn. Even minimal sunburn injures cells and temporarily swells the dermal blood vessels. It may also increase the rate of cell division. A bad sunburn kills many cells. The skin blisters and the dermal cells divide more rapidly, thickening the epidermis.

Ultimately, tanning and particularly sunburning can lead to skin cancer. Scientists have conclusively linked so-called nonmelanoma cancers to exposure to sunlight. About 300,000 U.S. citizens get nonmelanoma skin cancers yearly. Such cancers are rarely fatal. There also may be a connection between so-called melanoma skin cancers and too much sun; it has not yet been clearly established. Melanoma skin cancers are much rarer, but are very often fatal.

The skin-darkening material that forms during a suntan is **melanin,** the same black pigment responsible for black hair and naturally dark skin.

The formation of melanin takes place in several steps. When an ultraviolet photon of suitable energy strikes a melanin-producing cell, it activates an enzyme that triggers the oxidation of molecules of the amino acid tyrosine. Less energetic ultraviolet photons cause the modified tyrosine to form a polymer. The final melanin structure is a treelike branching of chains of modified tyrosine. Figure VII.17 shows some steps in the melanin-forming process.

Dark-skinned and tan individuals are more resistant than light-skinned people to the damaging effects of the sun's radiation. Melanin in the epidermis absorbs much of the sun's ultraviolet radiation, dispersing the energy and preventing it from damaging the living, dividing cells below.

Good suntan lotions prevent both skin damage and tanning. The active ingredient in many sunscreen lotions is **para-aminobenzoic acid (PABA).** The key to blocking ultraviolet radiation is the benzene ring in PABA.

That benzene ring absorbs ultraviolet photons and spreads their energy among all six chemical bonds in the ring, converting it into harmless heat. In this way, the ultraviolet photons are prevented from reaching the skin.

Jon Jacobson

Zinc oxide provides effective protection against solar radiation.

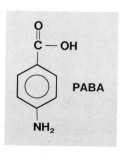

PABA

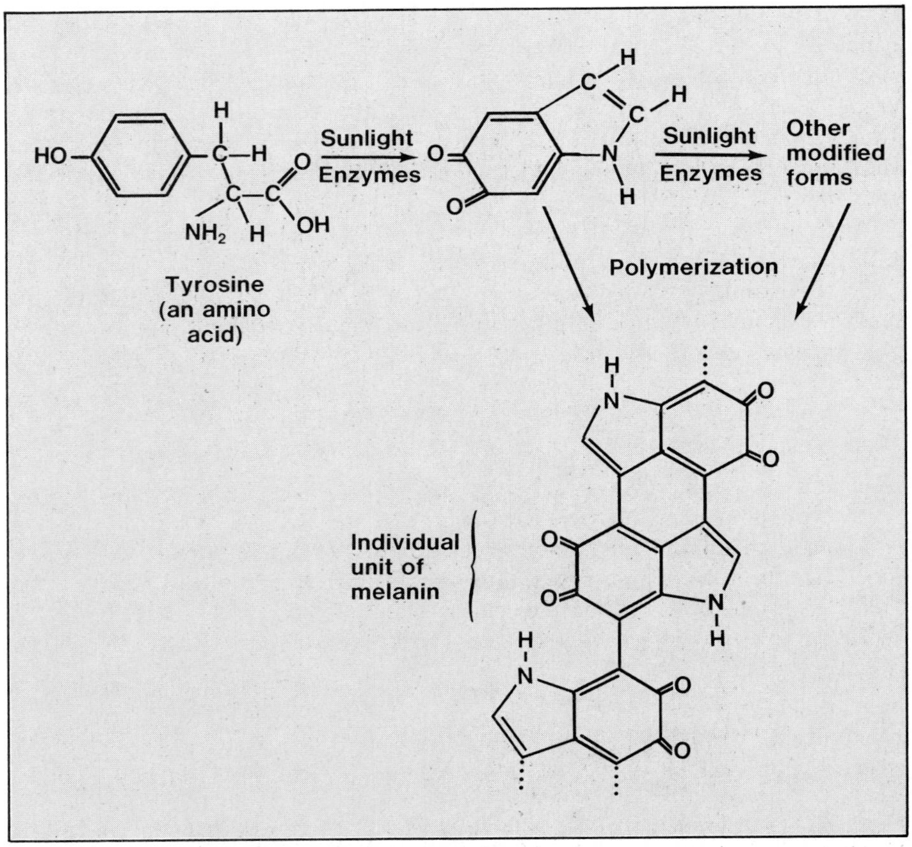

Figure VII.17   Melanin formation, as it might occur during suntanning. Melanin is the dark pigment in skin and hair.

Table VII.2   *Sun protection factors (SPFs)*

Rating of sun protection product	SPF values	Protection
Minimal	2–4	Offers least protection; permits tanning. Recommended for people who rarely burn but tan profusely
Moderate	4–6	Offers moderate protection from sunburning; permits some suntanning. Recommended for people who burn minimally and always tan well
Extra	6–8	Offers extra protection from sunburn; permits limited suntanning. Recommended for people who burn moderately and tan gradually
Maximal	8–15	Offers high protection from sunburn; permits little or no tanning. Recommended for people who always burn easily and tan minimally
Ultra	15 or more	Offers most protection from sunburn, permits no tanning. Recommended for people who always burn easily and never tan

Sunscreens contain various concentrations of PABA, so you can obtain just the level of protection you need. Table VII.2 describes the levels of protection.

You can see the differences in sunscreen protection for yourself in the following activity.

B.4 Laboratory Activity: Comparing Sunscreens

Getting Ready

In this activity you will observe the screening abilities of a series of oils or creams with different sun protection factors (SPFs, Table VII.2). The relative quantities of sunlight each allows to pass will be detected by exposing sun-sensitive paper. The papers exposed by these known screens will be used to determine, by comparison, the sun protection factor of an unknown oil or cream.

The preparations to be tested will be spread on an acrylic sheet that allows solar radiation to pass through. Any sunlight passing through the oil or cream will therefore reach the sun-sensitive paper.

Read the Procedure below and prepare a data table in your notebook for recording your observations.

Procedure

1. Label four pieces of acrylic sheet with the SPF numbers of the four knowns and label a fifth piece with the code number of your unknown.
2. Spread one drop of the appropriate oil or cream as evenly as possible over the acrylic sheet (but not on the labeled end).
3. Place the prepared acrylic sheets and two pieces of covered sun-sensitive paper in a carrying tray. Take the tray outside.
4. Lay the paper on a flat surface, such as a sidewalk, and place the pieces of acrylic on the paper. Write the numbers of the samples on the sun-sensitive paper near each piece of acrylic.
5. Allow the samples to remain in the sunlight until the visible areas of the sun-sensitive paper fade to a very light blue color. This may take up to 15 min depending on the brightness of the sunshine.
6. Remove the slides and quickly replace the cover on the print paper.
7. Return to the classroom, and record the relative shading provided by each slide.

Questions

1. Compare the shading allowed by the unknown lotion with that allowed by the known lotions. Estimate the sun protection number for your unknown.
2. Suntanning is believed to be a major cause of skin cancer. However, most of us spend time in the sun anyway, trading off some probable future harm for the immediate pleasure of being outside, or of having a beautiful tan. Identify other trade-offs we make in everyday life that involve risks and benefits.
3. People with dark skin have a lower incidence of skin cancer. Why?

Ultraviolet radiation has its dangers, but a little ultraviolet light is actually necessary for health.

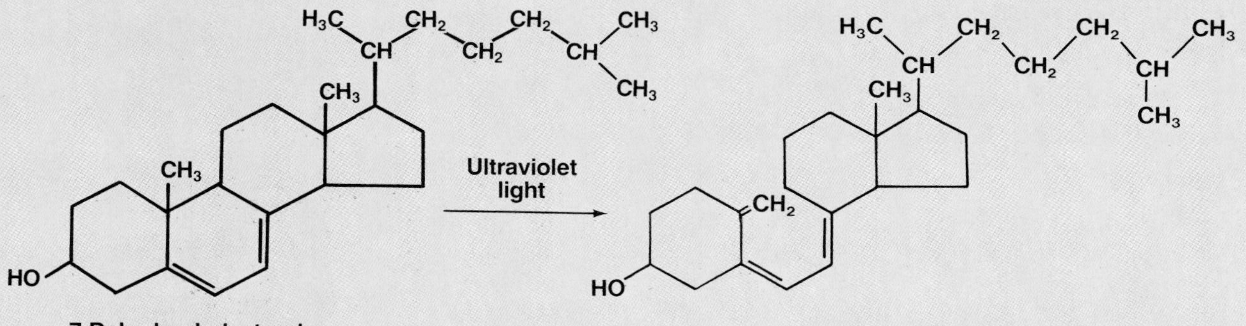

Figure VII.18 Sunlight produces vitamin D. One example of how small differences in molecules cause differences in function.

B.5 Getting a "D" in Photochemistry

During the Industrial Revolution in Europe, many children were forced to work indoors for as long as 12 hours each day. These children had little exposure to the sun. (Child labor laws subsequently ended this abuse.) Many children developed **rickets,** a disease that caused their bones to become soft and easily deformed. Indoor rest only made the disease worse. Surviving victims frequently had bowed legs and other crippling disorders.

Doctors soon realized that children living outside cities rarely got rickets. Children with rickets were quickly cured if they were sent to the country. These clues eventually led to the discovery that sunlight prevented rickets. Scientists learned later that sunlight helps the body produce vitamin D from another compound, 7-dehydrocholesterol, which is present in all body cells (see Figure VII.18).

Bedouin women who always cover all but their eyes often suffer softened bones. Why?

CHEM*QUANDARY*

Without vitamin D, our bodies cannot use the calcium ions (Ca^{2+}) in food. Vitamin D carries calcium ions out of the digestive tract and into the blood. It deposits calcium ions from the blood into the bones. What does this suggest might be a cause of rickets?

Today hardly anyone gets rickets. The quantity of sunlight needed to prevent calcium deficiencies varies with the season and latitude. In Boston during the summer, for example, a daily 15-min exposure on the face alone is all that is necessary to prevent rickets for Caucasians. In northern latitudes Blacks suffer from vitamin D deficiency more often than Caucasians do. Can you explain this?

Another aid to the prevention of vitamin D deficiency is the presence in many foods of additives that the body can convert into vitamin D. For example, some milk cartons list among the ingredients a compound called irradiated ergosterol, which has a chemical structure almost identical to that of 7-dehydrocholesterol. Today, doctors worry that the American diet may actually contain too much vitamin D. In excess it can cause unwanted calcium deposits, such as kidney and gall bladder stones.

CHEM*QUANDARY*

Look back at the structure of vitamin D in Figure VII.18. In which body material, fat or blood, will this molecule tend to dissolve? Why might this be a problem if the body contains too much vitamin D?

B.6   Our Crowning Glory

Among all personal features on which we spend time and money, hair ranks first. We wash, wave, curl, color, cut, and comb it.

Each hair grows out of a small, deep pocket in the scalp called a **follicle** (see Figure VII.19). Although hair is nonliving, fibrous protein, the growth of hair begins in cells that are modified skin cells. These cells emerge from the bottom of the follicle, and move outward towards the surface of the scalp the way dermal cells move outward to become epidermal cells. But before they reach the surface, they die, leaving nothing but amino acid chains they have added to the bottom of the hair.

The same kinds of oil glands that lubricate skin also keep the scalp and hair from drying out. In addition, oil helps protect the scalp from growth of bacteria and fungi. But because hair is essentially nonliving material, it has no way to repair itself.

The structure of hair is quite complex, as shown in Figure VII.19 and Figure VII.20. A protein chain, **alpha keratin,** is the basic structural unit. Three coiled chains of alpha keratin form a supercoiled, three-strand rope, and 11 three-stranded ropes make up a **microfibril.** Each hair is made of many microfibrils surrounded by a tough outer layer, the **cuticle.** This is several layers of tough, flat cells that overlap like shingles on a roof.

Hair flexibility is due to the ability of protein chains in the cuticle layer to separate from one another and shift position slightly. This flexibility makes it possible to style hair, but it can also lead to hair damage. You will test the condition of your hair as part of the following laboratory activity.

Jon Jacobson

A knowledge of protein chemistry helps explain the effects of hair treatment.

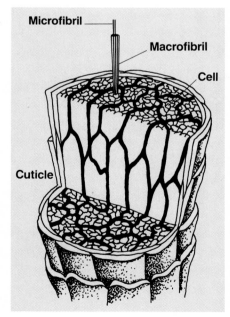

Source: Reprinted with permission by Dickerson and Geis from *The Structure and Action of Proteins.* Benjamin-Cummins, Menlo Park, CA, 1969. Illustration copyright by R. E. Dickerson and I. Geis.

Figure VII.20   The structure of a hair (see Figure VII.10 for more detail on arrangement of protein chain).

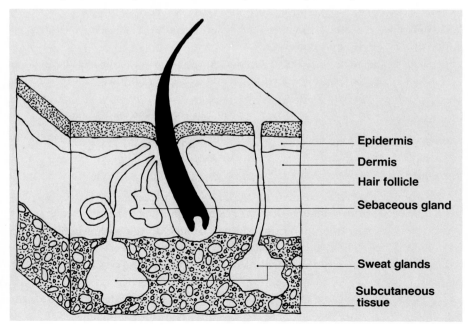

Epidermis
Dermis
Hair follicle
Sebaceous gland

Sweat glands

Subcutaneous tissue

Figure VII.19   Hair growing in a follicle.

B.7 Laboratory Activity: The Chemistry of Hair

Getting Ready

Healthy hair has a well-developed structure. Scalp oils and the natural acid coating protect this structure. However, many agents can remove the oils, destroy the acid coating, and even damage the hair structure itself.

We use some of these agents to satisfy our hair styling needs—to change the structure of our hair and make it curly or straight. In Part 1 you will test the effectiveness of various solutions in altering the structure of hair. In Part 2 you'll test some observable characteristics of your own hair to determne its health.

Read Parts 1 and 2 and prepare two data tables, one for each part.

Procedure

Part 1: Effect of Various Solutions on Hair

For this part of the activity, you will be assigned to a group of four students. Each group member will test hair with one of the following solutions: (1) pH 4 hydrochloric acid, HCl(*aq*); (2) pH 8 sodium hydroxide, NaOH(*aq*); (3) permanent wave solution; (4) permanent wave solution plus permanent wave neutralizer.

1. Obtain a hair bundle. Using a rubber band, securely fasten the hair to the end of a wooden splint as illustrated in Figure VII.21.

2. If you are making tests 1, 2, or 3, place 15 mL of your solution in a test tube and label the test tube. If you are making test 4, place 15 mL of permanent wave solution in one test tube and 15 mL of permanent wave neutralizer in a second test tube; label the test tubes.

3. For tests 1, 2, or 3, place a splint with hair in each solution for 15 minutes. For test 4, place a splint with hair in the permanent wave solution and allow it to remain for 10 minutes. Then rinse the hair under running water and place the splint in the test tube containing the neutralizer for 5 minutes.

4. Begin work on Part 2 while the hair samples remain in the solutions for the time required in Step 3.

5. After the specified times, remove the splints from the test tubes and place them on paper toweling. Dab lightly with a folded paper towel to absorb excess moisture. Label the towel with the name of the solution in which the hair was immersed. Allow the hair to dry partially. (Drying may be hastened with a light bulb or hair dryer.)

6. When the hair is fairly dry, remove the rubber band and carefully unwind the hair bundle from the stick. Be careful not to disrupt the curl. Record the extent of curl you observe for each test.

7. Examine the hair from the other tests and record the extents of curl.

8. Remove about six hairs from your bundle. Grasp each end of one hair and pull gently until the hair breaks. Repeat this test using a bundle of five hairs. Record your observations and share them with other members of your group.

9. Thoroughly moisten your bundle of hair under a gentle stream of tap water.

10. Squeeze out excess water from the hair by gently pressing as you pull the hair between two fingers. Do not squeeze or pull too hard.

11. Allow the hair to dry. (Again, you may hasten drying with a light bulb or hair dryer.)

12. Observe and record the extent of curl now present in your sample and the others.

13. Repeat the stretch test (Step 8) on one hair, and on a group of five hairs from your bundle. Record your observations and share with other members of the group.

Many shampoos are buffered ("pH balanced"). You will see why.

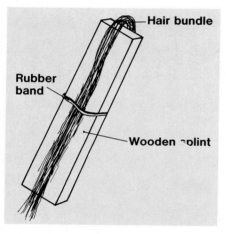

Figure VII.21 Hair bundle attached to wooden splint for use in testing effect of solutions.

Part 2: Testing Your Hair

Structure Test

1. Obtain a single 15-cm strand of hair from your head by clipping it with scissors. If you are courageous, you may elect instead to pull one hair from your head. If the hair is healthy, it won't break off, but will detach with its root, the little bulb at the end. If your hair has been colored, styled, permed, or otherwise treated, take your hair sample from just behind your ear. (This hair is least likely to have been affected by treatment.)

2. Hold one end of your hair sample between your thumb and index finger. With your other hand, hold the thumbnail and index fingernail together with the hair between. Hold tightly as you slide your fingers down the length of the hair, as if you were curling a ribbon to put on a gift.

3. Now hold the strand by each end and gently pull it straight. Stretch it for 15 seconds, then release and observe. If the curl is gone, your hair is structurally weak. The extent to which the curl returns indicates the relative strength of your hair structure. Record your observations.

Stretch Test

1. Obtain a second strand of hair from your head. Hold the ends of the strand between the thumb and index finger of each hand, and stretch the hair gently. Do not jerk it. Healthy hair will stretch up to 30% (at average humidity), somewhat like a rubber band. Unhealthy hair has little or no stretch. A seriously damaged hair will break easily. Record the results.

2. Obtain another hair strand. Wet it with tap water. Repeat Step 1 on this wet hair.

3. If time permits, repeat Steps 1 and 2 with a hair donated by a classmate.

Cuticle Test

1. Hold a small bundle of your hair about 3 cm from your scalp with your thumb and finger.

2. Grasp the bundle near the outer end with the thumb and finger of the other hand, and pull your hand along the bundle toward your head. Record whether the hair strands pile up in front of your finger and thumb, or lie flat as your hand moves toward your head.

Questions

1. It takes more force to stretch coarse hair than fine hair. Why?
2. Explain the results of the cuticle test.
3. Is your hair healthy or damaged?
4. Which solutions were the best curling agents prior to rewetting?
5. Which solutions helped retain the curl after wetting?
6. Which solutions made the hair most brittle?
7. What combination of conditions cause the most damage to hair?
8. Propose a chemical explanation for the difference in the curl produced by water and that produced by permanent wave solutions.
9. Is an acidic or basic solution more damaging to hair? Why?
10. Permanent wave solutions are basic. Compare the results observed from treatment with sodium hydroxide solution and permanent wave solution.
11. How might you protect your hair after swimming and before sunbathing?

B.8 Hair Styling by Rearranging Chemical Bonds

As we have seen (Figures VII.10 and VII.20), hair is made of intertwined protein chains. The individual chains are held in place by hydrogen bonding, ionic bonding between R groups, and disulfide bridges, all of which were illustrated in our discussion of how the shapes of protein molecules are maintained (Figure VII.9, Part A.10).

Hair styling is a matter of breaking bonds between protein chains and forming new ones. (If the protein chains do not form new bonds, the strands separate. This is one cause of split ends.)

Your laboratory work with hair confirmed what you probably already knew: If you wet your hair it becomes easier to style. Here's why: Wetting your hair allows water molecules to break hydrogen and ionic bonds between hair strands. Water forms new hydrogen bonds with the side chains. Thus separated, the side chains no longer hold the strands tightly in their natural position. As you comb your hair, the strands are free to slide into new positions. When the water evaporates, these side branches form new hydrogen or ionic bonds in their new positions, locking the chains in whatever position they happen to be.

Solutions that are too acidic can permanently weaken hair. Even after the hair dries, some excess hydrogen ions may remain bonded to the side chains, preventing them from forming new ionic bonds with each other.

Heat applied with blow-dryers and curling irons helps you style hair quickly, because the higher temperatures speed up interactions between protein strands. But excessive heat can disperse hair oils, and even split protein chains.

The problem with the hair styling methods described so far is that once hair is wet again, their effects are quickly erased. To get a waterproof hairstyle— a permanent—it's necessary to rearrange bonds that are not affected by water. These are the covalent bonds of the disulfide bridges.

The curliness of your hair is determined by the way disulfide linkages between parallel protein chains are joined. In permanents, curls are created or removed in three steps. First, disulfide links between protein chains are chemically broken. Next, a form is used to curl or uncurl the hair. Third, the disulfide links between protein chains, in their new orientation, are chemically reformed. Figure VII.22 illustrates the process.

CHEM*QUANDARY*

Will repeated chemical treatments either to curl or straighten your hair alter it permanently?

As you have learned, chemistry and chemical reactions are responsible for much that happens in your body. In the next part of this unit, you will learn how body chemistry can be altered by drugs and how it responds to toxic substances.

PART B
SUMMARY*QUESTIONS*

1. What substances are removed during proper skin cleansing? Why must they be removed? What problems result from excessive skin cleansing?
2. Predict which of the following materials would be soluble in water and which must be washed away with soap or detergent.
   a. Salt (NaCl), a component of perspiration
   b. Nondiet soft drink (essentially sugar water) spilled on your hands

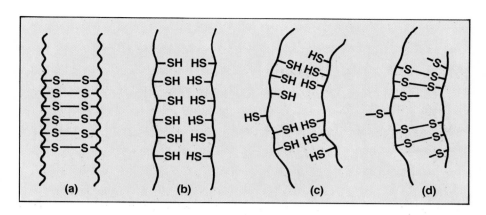

Figure VII.22 (a) Parallel protein chains before treatment, held in place by disulfide bonds; (b) a chemical reaction (reduction) breaks disulfide bonds and adds hydrogen atoms; chains are now free to move relative to each other; (c) the hair is curled or straightened; (d) a chemical reaction (oxidation) reforms disulfide bonds between relocated chains. Lower figure gives expanded view of links between chains.

Expanded view of disulfide bond between chains

    c. Grease on your hands from eating french fries with your fingers
    d. Rubbing alcohol (70% isopropyl alcohol in water).

3. Explain the action of a soap or detergent in washing.

4. What are the functions of your skin?

5. Describe the chemical process of tanning.

6. Briefly describe the link between tanning and skin cancer.

7. Describe how a sunscreen protects the skin.

8. Describe the symptoms of rickets. How is this disease prevented?

9. Why does healthy hair stretch somewhat like a rubber band?

10. Explain the difference in stretch between dry and wet hair.

11. Explain the different effects water and permanent wave solution have on hair structure.

EXTENDING *YOUR KNOWLEDGE* *(OPTIONAL)*

• Why is dark skin an advantage for people living in tropical countries? Why is light skin a disadvantage?

• Investigate the causes and mechanism of formation for malignant melanoma, a serious form of cancer.

C CHEMICAL CONTROL: DRUGS AND TOXINS IN THE HUMAN BODY

With the development of synthetic organic chemistry has come a great variety of drugs. These substances have helped alleviate much illness and suffering. Life for many is much more enjoyable than it might have been. But in addition to relieving suffering, drugs also have contributed to it. Drug addiction is present in every segment of society.

What are drugs? How do they work? Are they totally foreign to the human system? What does the body do to save itself from their negative effects?

C.1 A Glimpse of Drug Function

Drugs alter body or brain chemistry. In this sense, aspirin, amphetamines, LSD, the caffeine in coffee, nicotine from cigarettes, and the powerful painkiller morphine are all drugs. There are drugs for many purposes. Some stimulate or depress the brain. Others relieve pain or stop infection. Still others make up for chemical deficiencies. All function at the molecular level, most often in a specific area of the body.

Jon Jacobson

Most communities provide help and information regarding drug-related problems.

Toxins, by contrast, harm the body. Sodium cyanide (NaCN), carbon monoxide (CO), dioxin, polychlorinated biphenyls (PCBs), and the potent nerve poison strychnine are all toxins. Chemical toxins, like drugs, function at the molecular level in the body. The difference between a drug and a toxin is often a matter of dose. Any substance, even water, can become toxic at too large a dose. An overdose of the painkiller morphine can cause death by shutting down the respiratory system. On the other hand, the poison strychnine is a useful anaesthetic in very small doses.

Once transported to its action site in the body, how does a drug function? Drug specificity, like enzyme specificity, often depends upon molecular shape. Many drugs act at **receptors**—regions on proteins or cell membranes with just the shape and chemical properties needed to interact with the drug molecule and help it initiate the desired biological response (pain relief, fever depression, etc.).

As an example, consider adrenaline. It is both a product of body chemistry and is present in prescription nosedrops and nasal sprays used for the relief of severe allergic symptoms. When you are suddenly frightened, the adrenal gland releases adrenaline. This hormone circulates in the bloodstream, activating the heart and other organs. Settled at its receptor sites, adrenaline initiates a cascade of reactions that prepare the body in various ways for the physical activity of "fight or flight." (It increases heart rate, for example.) A model of an adrenaline molecule at its receptor is shown in Figure VII.23.

To further illustrate drug action, let's look at some drugs that relieve intense pain. Classified as a **narcotic analgesics,** these include morphine, meperidine, and methadone.

To relieve pain, nerve signals from the pain source must be blocked on their path to the brain. Blocking occurs if drugs of the right shape and composition interact with receptors on proteins in the membranes of key brain cells. The drug molecule distorts the shape of the membrane protein enough to block the pain signal.

The receptor sites for narcotic analgesics appear to have the following features:

- a negative ion site that can bind an ammonium ion (NH_4^+) or its equivalent
- a flat surface to which a flat cyclic group of atoms (an aromatic group) can bind
- between these, a cavity into which a chain of atoms connecting the aromatic group and the ammonium ion may fit

All potent analgesics studied thus far either possess or may adopt the shape needed to allow bonding to this receptor.

One might wonder why brain cells have receptors of just the right type for morphine-like drugs that are foreign to the body. It has been found that the brain's own natural painkillers, called **endorphins** and **enkephalins,** act at these same receptors.

Although the structural formulas of morphine and endorphins or enkephalins do not look much alike to the untrained eye (Figure VII.24), in fact several parts of the molecules are identical. It is these parts that are believed to be most important to the action of these painkillers.

Morphine and other narcotic analgesics are used in cases of severe or enduring pain, but for common aches and pains we use another kind of painkiller.

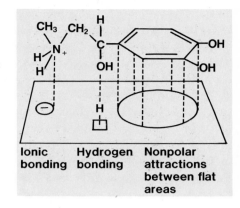

Figure VII.23 An adrenaline molecule at a receptor.

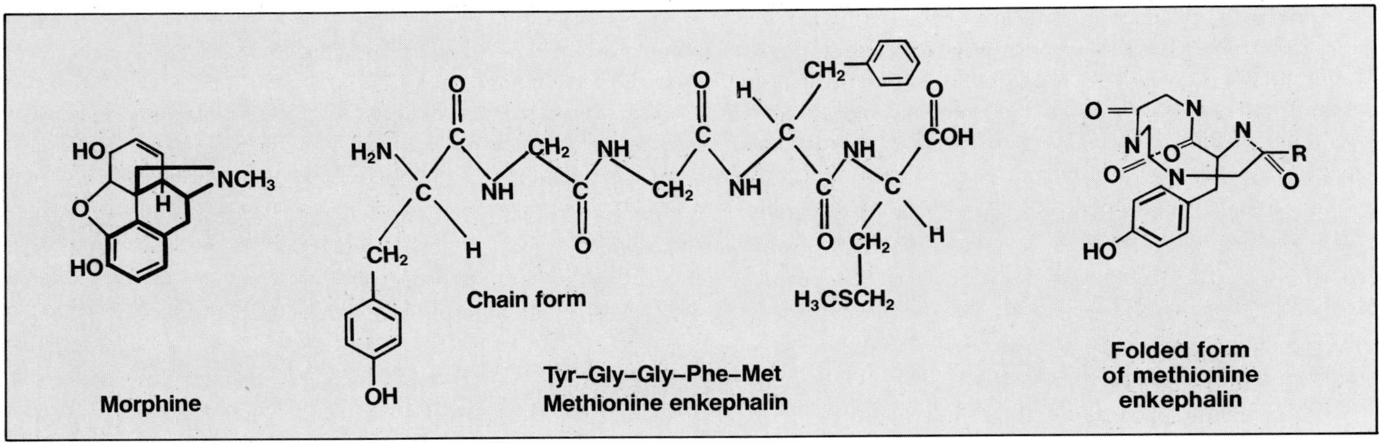

Figure VII.24 Morphine and an enkephalin, both painkillers. The protein chain of the enkephalin folds to give a shape similar to that of morphine, a shape that fits the body's painkilling receptors.

C.2 The Pain Reliever Doctors Recommend Most

The most widely used pain killers belong to the family of **salicylates.** Acetylsalicylic acid, commonly known as aspirin, is the most familiar of these. Aspirin is a versatile drug: It can reduce fever and swelling or inflammation, and it relieves pain.

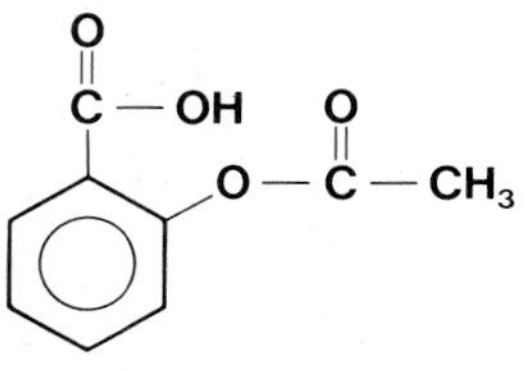

Acetyl salicylic acid

Aspirin is an example of a drug made more useful by chemical modification. Salicylic acid was the original aspirin-type drug, but it produced severe irritation of the mouth and upper digestive tract.

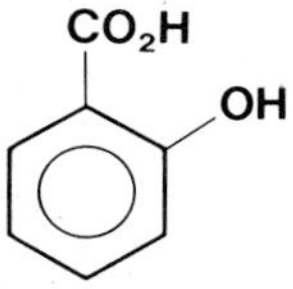

Salicylic acid

To reduce irritation and help the molecule pass more rapidly into the blood and to appropriate target areas, chemists tried changing the chemical structure of salicylic acid. Some changes rendered it useless as a drug. Others created unwanted side effects. When the H of the —OH group was replaced with an acetyl group, —CO—CH₃, chemists found what they wanted. This modification produced a drug that, although not perfect, has been a valued medication for more than 90 years. Many other drugs have similarly been tailored to do specific jobs in the body.

C.3 *You Decide:* The Effects of Alcohol

Not all drugs act at specific receptors as morphine and endorphins do. Alcohol appears to act on all or many **neurons** (nerve cells). It depresses transmission of nerve signals. This can slow down functioning of the entire brain. To understand how this happens, consider how nerve signals are transmitted.

While the neuron is resting, calcium ions are concentrated in packages at the nerve ending. When an impulse passes through a neuron, calcium ions are released and in turn cause release of messenger molecules, which travel to neighboring cells, transmitting the signals to them. Alcohol appears to deplete the number of calcium ions at the nerve endings. This prevents release of messengers and thus prevents transmission of the signal. When this happens on a large scale, the normal function of the entire brain is slowed down or diminished.

The effect of alcohol on behavior varies with the amount consumed, the weight of the individual, and the time passed since consumption. Table VII.3A presents data for estimating the percent alcohol in the blood. The effects on behavior of various blood alcohol levels are listed in Table VII.3B.

In most states, the legal alcohol limit for driving is 0.10% (0.10 g of alcohol per 100 mL of blood). Driving with a lower blood alcohol level is not guaranteed to be safe. A study of 13,000 drivers in Grand Rapids, Michigan, showed that the probability of causing an accident doubled when a driver's blood alcohol was just 0.06%. The National Highway Traffic Safety Administration considers that alcohol is involved in an accident when it is present in any detectable amount.

Table VII.3   *Alcohol in the blood*

Part A gives blood alcohol level (percent) if drinks are consumed rapidly (within 15 min). One drink is a bottle of beer, a glass of wine, or a shot (one ounce) of whiskey or other 86-proof liquor. The shaded portion shows blood alcohol levels above the 0.10 legal limit. To find change in percent with time, subtract 0.015% for each hour.

A. Percent alcohol in the blood according to number of drinks and body weight[a]

No. of drinks	Body weight (lbs)						
	100	125	150	175	200	225	250
1	0.03	0.03	0.02	0.02	0.01	0.01	0.01
2	0.06	0.05	0.04	0.04	0.03	0.03	0.03
3	0.10	0.08	0.06	0.06	0.05	0.04	0.04
4	0.13	0.10	0.09	0.07	0.06	0.06	0.05
5	0.16	0.13	0.11	0.09	0.08	0.07	0.06
6	0.19	0.16	0.13	0.11	0.10	0.09	0.08
7	0.22	0.18	0.15	0.13	0.11	0.10	0.09
8	0.26	0.21	0.17	0.15	0.13	0.11	0.10
9	0.29	0.24	0.19	0.17	0.14	0.13	0.12
10	0.33	0.26	0.22	0.18	0.16	0.14	0.13
11	0.36	0.29	0.24	0.20	0.18	0.16	0.14
12	0.39	0.31	0.26	0.22	0.19	0.17	0.16

B. Effect of blood alcohol level on behavior

Blood alcohol level (%)	Behavior
0.05	Lowered alertness; reduced coordination
0.10	Reaction time slowed 15–25%; visual sensitivity reduced up to 32%; headlight recovery 7–32 seconds longer
0.25	Severe disturbance of coordination; dizziness; staggering; senses impaired
0.35	Surgical anaesthesia; reduced body temperature
0.40	50% of people die of alcohol poisoning

[a]Data in Part A from MADD (Mothers Against Drunk Driving)

Use the information in Table VII.3 to answer the following questions.

1. If a 125-lb person consumes two bottles of beer, what will the blood alcohol level be if it is measured immediately? What will it be after two hours?

2. List two kinds of behavior you might observe if an individual has a blood alcohol level of 0.15%.

3. If a 175-lb person has six drinks in rapid succession and drives an automobile one hour later, will the individual be considered legally intoxicated in most states?

4. If a 100-lb person consumes 10 drinks in rapid succession, will the individual be in any danger of death?

5. How long should a 200-lb person who has consumed three drinks wait before driving an automobile?

C.4   A Note on Cocaine

Like alcohol, cocaine acts on neurons, altering the transmission of nerve signals in several parts of the brain. It functions as an anaesthetic by reducing the sensitivity of nerve membranes to return of messengers. It also prevents destruction of messenger molecules after a signal has passed. The basis for its euphoric effects are only partly understood, but they sometimes are accompanied by brain hemorrhages, dangerous increases in blood pressure, and even death.

C.5   Drugs in Combination

The effect of some combinations of drugs is simply a sum of the action of each (e.g., aspirin for a fever and an antibiotic for an infection). Other drug combinations produce mainly undesirable effects. Some drugs interfere with each other. For example, tetracycline is an antibiotic that kills bacteria by binding free iron and other important ions in your system. This makes these ions unavailable to bacteria. If you take iron tablets to compensate for anemia (iron-poor blood) and your doctor prescribes tetracycline at the same time, you could lose the benefits of both. The tetracycline may bind to the added iron, putting both the drug and the iron out of commission.

Some combinations of drugs are deadly. It is essential to tell a doctor prescribing a medication for you of any other medication or drug you might be taking. Also, it is wise to understand the trouble you can get into by mixing drugs on your own.

One of the deadliest combinations is alcohol and sedatives, which include tranquilizers, sleeping pills, and the addictive street drugs known as "downers." These drugs slow brain activity. They act by retarding communication between nerve cells, just as alcohol does.

Like the interaction of air pollutants in smog (Unit Six, Part D.8), combining alcohol with sedatives or certain other drugs is synergistic—the total effect is greater than that of either drug alone. Sedatives and alcohol can so depress nerve activity that even involuntary functions such as breathing may shut down. The lethal dose of a barbiturate (e.g., phenobarbital) is decreased by 50% when it is combined with alcohol. Diazepam (a common tranquilizer, e.g., the active ingredient of Valium) and alcohol is also a frequently fatal combination. Antihistamines and alcohol can cause excessive drowsiness, and the combination of narcotic analgesics and alcohol can upset control of body movements. Essentially, beware of the combination of alcohol with *any* drug.

Given all the damage that drugs and foreign substances can do within the body, you might wonder how we survive. But the body is not defenseless. We'll take a look at this in the next section.

C.6 How the Body Handles Toxic Substances

Your body has a number of defense mechanisms that help protect you from toxic and disease-causing substances or organisms. For example, the membranes that cover body surfaces, including the lining of the digestive tract and lungs, resist infection by most disease-causing organisms. These membranes also protect you against invasion by many chemicals from the environment. The acid in gastric juice (pH 1–2) also helps destroy many microorganisms in the stomach before they can enter the bloodstream.

These external defenses are backed by internal defenses. Let's look at two of them: how the liver detoxifies the blood, and how the body deals with the presence of foreign proteins.

Detoxification in the Liver

Foods and other swallowed substances are partially digested in the stomach, but are mainly digested in the small intestine. Digested food, other small molecules, and some ions pass through the lining of the small intestine into the blood, where they are carried directly to the liver. Undigested material and molecules or ions that do not pass through the intestinal wall proceed to the large intestine and are eliminated from the body. Some toxic substances that enter the stomach are removed from the body in this way.

The liver further separates useful from harmful or undesirable substances. Useful substances including glucose and other simple carbohydrates, amino acids, and fatty acids are released to the blood for general circulation to cells that need them. Some of these molecules are retained by the liver: glucose, which is stored as glycogen, the body's reserve carbohydrate; and amino acids, which are converted to proteins for use in the blood.

Some harmful or undesirable substances separated by the liver are eliminated from the body directly. Carried in bile to the intestines, they exit through the bowels.

Other harmful substances undergo reactions in the liver to make them less toxic and more soluble in water. In this form they are more easily eliminated by the body. A typical chemical alteration in the liver is the conversion of benzene (not very water soluble) to catechol (water soluble):

Benzene　　　　**Catechol**

Another typical reaction is the conversion of sulfite, a poison, to sulfate.

$$2\,SO_3^{2-}(aq) + O_2(aq) \xrightarrow{\text{Enzyme}} 2\,SO_4^{2-}(aq)$$

The enzyme that catalyzes this reaction contains molybdenum ions. Without tiny amounts of these ions in the liver, many foods would poison us. The liver also chemically alters and eliminates many hormones and drugs that accumulate in the blood.

The liver's ability to detoxify materials is limited. Excessive ingestion of harmful substances can place a heavy burden on it. As a result, liver function may be diminished, which can cause problems in the distribution of essential molecules—glucose and amino acids—and in the synthesis of important proteins. Overburdening the liver also can result in the accumulation of harmful molecules in the body's fat reserves.

The liver is the body's largest internal organ; it is extremely important. In many ways it saves us from our bad eating, drinking, and perhaps even drug-taking habits. But it can take only so much abuse before damage occurs.

Now consider how body chemistry handles the invasion of foreign protein.

Defense Against Foreign Protein

Foreign protein most often enters the body as part of disease-causing agents such as viruses, bacteria, fungi, and parasites. Body chemistry depends so strongly on having exactly the right protein at exactly the right spot at the right time that the presence of any invader protein is a signal to marshal a defense against the potential harm it might do. The body's defense strategy, carried out by its immune system, is to build a protein that surrounds part of the invader molecule. Here again, biochemical interaction is made possible by complementary molecular shapes. Once surrounded, the invader cannot react to cause harm.

Any foreign agent that sets this defense mechanism in motion is called an **antigen,** and the complementary substance created by the body to destroy the effectiveness of the antigen is an **antibody.** Figure VII.25 illustrates the action of antibodies. Formation of an antigen-antibody complex precipitates the invader from solution in the blood or other body fluids and allows it to be destroyed or otherwise removed by the body's waste disposal system.

Building antibodies with exactly the right complementary protein is no easy task. In your body, only certain kinds of white blood cells can do it. Once such cells learn to build a specific antibody, they can easily make more of the same. This is how you develop immunity to certain bacterial and viral infections. Once the blood has been exposed to a certain kind of bacteria, some of its white cells can henceforth rapidly synthesize the antibodies needed to destroy the bacteria. A person then has acquired an immunity to the disease caused by that bacterium.

Unfortunately, the body cannot protect itself against all disease-causing agents. The AIDS virus is one of these. The letters stand for *acquired* (not inherited) *immune deficiency* (a lack of immune response) *syndrome* (symptoms that occur together).

Once inside the body, the AIDS virus avoids the blood cells that could produce antibodies to destroy it. It then invades master cells that coordinate the work of the entire immune system, including the manufacture of antibodies. The virus can remain inactive within the cells for an indeterminate period during which no disease symptoms appear. It has the ability to reproduce itself manyfold, however. When this happens, new virus molecules invade more and more master cells, destroying their effectiveness. Soon, the body's immune system is too depleted of active master cells to fight against invading proteins. A host of diseases normally warded off by the immune system can attack the body.

The number of AIDS cases and of those exposed to AIDS is growing rapidly. The virus is spread in the majority of cases by contact with the blood, or certain other body fluids of someone carrying the virus (not necessarily someone who is sick at the time). Those who are not sexually active and who do not use needles to inject drugs have little risk of being exposed. At present there is no cure for AIDS and no vaccine against it.

C.7 Laboratory Activity: Comparing Cigarette Smoke

Getting Ready

In this experiment you will observe the effects of cigarette smoke on a living organism. *Euglena* is a one-celled organism found in water; it "swims" by moving a thread-like projection (a flagellum).

In Part 1 a procedure is given for creating a smoking apparatus and trapping particles from the smoke. Your teacher may, instead, choose to provide pre-smoked cigarette filters to use in the test with *Euglena*. In this case, you will do only Part 2.

A vaccine contains antigen that induces antibody formation, but does not cause disease.

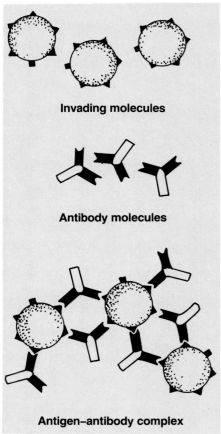

Invading molecules

Antibody molecules

Antigen–antibody complex

Source: From *Biochemistry*, 2nd ed. by Lubert Stryer. Copyright © 1975, 1981. Reprinted with the permission of W. H. Freeman and Company.

Figure VII.25 Antibodies precipitate invading molecules.

Procedure

Part 1: "Smoking" the Cigarettes

In this part you will trap particles from the smoke of a nonfiltered, high tar cigarette and a filtered, lower tar cigarette and note the difference between them.

1. Set up the apparatus shown in Figure VII.26.
2. Turn on both aspirators.
3. Light a cigarette. Adjust the aspirator flow so that smoke is drawn through both chambers and none escapes into the room. Allow the cigarette (but not the filter) to burn completely.
4. Turn the aspirators off when no smoke is visible in either chamber.
5. Wearing disposable gloves, open each chamber and use forceps to remove the cotton. Place each piece of used cotton on a paper towel. Label the towel with the cigarette brand and whether the cotton is from the upper or lower chamber. Do not touch the material deposited on the cotton.
6. Repeat Steps 1–5 with a second cigarette.
7. Observe each cotton sample and record.

Part 2: Euglena Test

1. Wearing gloves, use forceps to pull off a wad (about the diameter of a quarter) of the cotton stained by the smoke coming from the upper chamber during smoking of one of the cigarettes.
2. Place the cotton wad in a 50-mL beaker and add 5 mL of water. With your forceps press the cotton into the water and stir carefully until the water becomes stained brown with the smoke residue.
3. Place a drop of *Euglena* culture on each of two microscope slides and cover with a cover slide. Observe and record the natural swimming movements under the microscope.

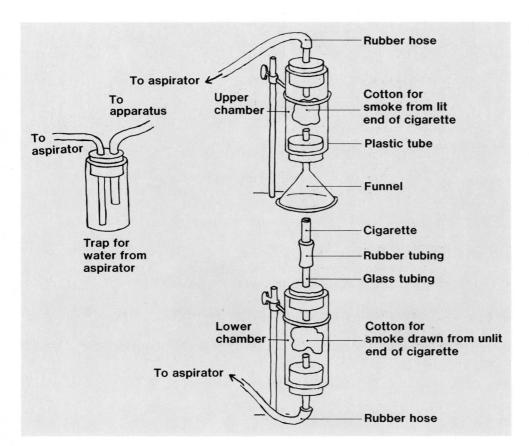

Figure VII.26   Apparatus for smoking experiment.

4. Place two drops of the residue solution on the *Euglena* culture on one of the slides and replace cover slide. Observe and record the movements on this slide under the microscope.

5. Thoroughly rinse your dropper. Repeat Part 2 with a wad of cotton stained from the lower chamber of the cigarette.

Questions

1. Compare the appearance of each piece of cotton from one cigarette. Does it appear that less smoke residue comes from one end than the other?

2. Compare the cotton from the upper chamber during smoking of the two cigarettes. Do the filtered, low-tar cigarettes appear to have less residue, as their makers claim?

3. Compare the movements of the *Euglena* on the treated and untreated slides.

What is the chemistry involved in smoking? How does it harm the body? We'll answer these questions in the next section.

Jon Jacobson

Decision making is a part of everyone's life.

C.8   Where the Smoke Goes

Smoking is like puffing on a smokestack. Inside the glowing tip of a cigarette the temperature soars to 850 °C, setting off chemical reactions that produce more than 3600 substances.

Carbon monoxide in the smoke severely reduces the blood's ability to carry oxygen to the cells. By reacting with hemoglobin 200 times faster than oxygen does, it bonds to hemoglobin's iron ions, preventing them from picking up and carrying oxygen. The body responds to this reduction in oxygen carriers by increasing the number of red blood cells. This thickens blood and puts stress on the heart.

Tars from smoke accumulate in the lungs. In an effort to clear the tars, an enzyme, elastase, is activated. In digesting tars, the enzyme also appears to digest lung membranes, scarring the lungs and reducing their ability to transfer oxygen to blood. Emphysema often results.

Carbon monoxide in the blood of a pregnant woman seems to have a detrimental effect on the fetus. No one knows precisely how smoking damages the fetus, but there is no doubt that the fetus is deprived of necessary oxygen.

Emphysema is a serious, often fatal, condition in which breathing is difficult because lung function is poor.

Numerous compounds in cigarette smoke can cause cancer. Among these are nitrosamines and polycyclic aromatic hydrocarbons (PAHs), examples of which are given in Figure VII.27. The presence in smoke of carcinogenic compounds and other highly reactive materials means heavy smokers run a high risk of getting lung cancer.

To smoke or not to smoke is one of many decisions you must make that will influence your health. Some argue that there is still considerable uncertainty about the dangers of smoking. In many other decisions that affect health there is even more uncertainty. In the final activity, you will learn more about how scientists evaluate risks, and about making risk-related decisions in the face of uncertainty.

Carcinogenic compounds are known to cause cancer.

PART C
SUMMARY *QUESTIONS*

1. Describe how narcotic analgesics, such as morphine, are believed to work in the brain. How are these like the brain's own painkillers?
2. Describe the effect of alcohol on nerve cells. Compare this with the effect of cocaine on nerve cells.
3. Give two reasons why you should be sure your doctor knows about all medications or drugs you are taking.
4. Should the fact that you are taking medication make any difference in your eating and drinking habits? Explain.
5. Describe at least four chemical processes that occur regularly in the liver.
6. List some ways the body deals with toxic substances. Why is it apparently unable to deal with the AIDS virus?
7. List the effects of cigarette smoke on lung tissues and on the circulatory system.

EXTENDING *YOUR KNOWLEDGE*
(OPTIONAL)

- A few folk remedies for illnesses are effective. Chemical studies have shown that there is a molecular basis for their action. One example is the use of willow bark in treating pain. Look into the chemistry of folk remedies, and find why many are successful.
- A newer pain reliever that sometimes is used in place of aspirin is ibuprofen. Look into its chemical structure and how it relieves pain.
- Prepare a library report on some hazardous food-drug interactions.

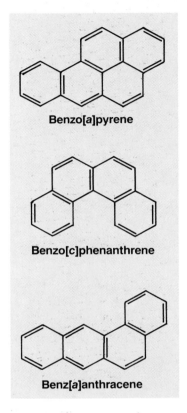

Benzo[a]pyrene

Benzo[c]phenanthrene

Benz[a]anthracene

Figure VII.27 Some carcinogenic compounds found in cigarette smoke. These are all polycyclic aromatic compounds.

United Nations

The opium poppy is the source of morphine and other narcotic drugs. In medicine these drugs are extremely valuable in helping control pain; on the street they bring nothing but pain. Once again we see the benefits and burdens of use of scientific knowledge.

D PUTTING IT ALL TOGETHER: ASSESSING PERSONAL AND PUBLIC HEALTH RISKS

How can you help yourself live out your natural life span? What can society do to help all U.S. citizens live full, healthy lives? First, one must know what causes premature death. Second, one must know the factors that are most responsible for such deaths. These are not necessarily the same as the direct causes. Cancer causes death, but scientists have not all agreed on whether environmental pollution, household pollution, diet, or simple aging is most responsible for cancer. Similar questions surround other causes of premature death and create considerable scientific debate.

Identifying key underlying causes of early death and assessing the risk to you arising from these factors is an important step in improving your chances of living out your natural life span. In the following sections we will illustrate how scientists make judgments about risk. Then you will have a chance to make your own judgments about which risks to avoid and which not to worry about.

D.1 Making Judgments about Risk

Scientists often seek out and investigate events that occur at the same time or in sequence. Events or incidents that happen together are said to be **correlated.** When correlations are found, one scientific goal is to determine whether or how the correlated events are related.

It is easy for advocates of a given position to make the sometimes misleading statement that one event caused another. In fact, other events may cause both. For example, when people start wearing overcoats, home heating bills generally go up. But overcoats do not cause heating bills to rise. The onset of cold weather directly causes both the appearance of overcoats and increased heating bills.

Correlation may also be pure coincidence. For many years skirt lengths and stock market prices increased and decreased together. Do you believe that there is any connection between these two happenings?

YOURTURN

VII.7 Events: Related or Not?

Examine the pairs of events listed below and express the relationship between them by choosing which of the following phrases applies in each case: "correlates with," "directly causes," or "is not related to." (You may find that more than one phrase applies.)

For example, the happenings "Spring" and "hay fever" are correlated for some individuals. After some allergy tests, a cause and effect relationship may be established, and sufferers would know that Spring's renewal of ragweed growth directly causes hay fever for them.

1. Time of day, the tide
2. Position of the moon, the tide
3. Temperature, the seasons
4. Ocean swimming, the tide
5. Atmospheric temperature, the tide
6. Class attendance, grade in chemistry
7. Temperature, rate of evaporation of water
8. Guns, homicides
9. Poverty, lack of food
10. Temperature, amount of dissolved oxygen
11. Length of carbon chain, boiling point
12. Catalyst, rate of reaction
13. Alcoholism, stress
14. Practice, solving chemistry problems
15. Good looks, number of dates
16. Smoking, lung cancer
17. Protein-free diet, hair growth
18. Glucose metabolism, ATP production

CHEM*QUANDARY*

In 1966, the federal government ordered cigarette manufacturers to place this statement on each package of cigarettes and on each advertisement:

> Caution: The Surgeon General Has Determined That Cigarette Smoking May Be Dangerous To Your Health.

In 1970, the federal government changed the label:

> Warning: The Surgeon General Has Determined That Cigarette Smoking Is Dangerous To Your Health.

In 1985, officials decided to have several stronger messages printed on smoking product packages. One of them reads:

> Surgeon General's Warning: Smoking Causes Lung Cancer, Heart Disease, Emphysema, And May Complicate Pregnancy.

What do the changes in the warnings on cigarette packages indicate? In particular, what did the Surgeon General imply by changing the words "caution" to "warning" and "may be" to "is" on cigarette labels?

D.2 Epidemiology: Studying Human Disease and Mortality

In chemical research, it is relatively easy to control most variables. In medical research, it is never easy to do so, partly because it is unacceptable to expose human subjects to potentially damaging agents.

Instead, scientists often conduct experiments with animals. Such experiments have considerable value, but they cannot predict absolutely how human beings will respond to the same agents. The body chemistry of animals is always at least slightly different from that of humans. Furthermore, it is difficult to perform certain kinds of experiments with animals. Scientists have trouble getting laboratory animals to smoke, for example.

Animal studies, therefore, are supplemented by **epidemiological studies.** Scientists study specific populations of people in a search for factors that cause or prevent disease. For example, they study victims of heart attacks, gathering information about their living habits to try to determine what makes some people prone to heart attacks. Or they study groups that have a much lower than average incidence of heart attacks to identify what might protect these individuals.

A problem that arises, however, is that a single epidemiological study usually shows correlations, not strict cause-and-effect relationships, and these can mislead even researchers. For example, one study concluded that coffee drinking causes heart attacks. But the study had ignored smoking among coffee-drinkers as a possible cause of heart disease.

D.3 Risks from Alcohol and Other Drugs

To assess your risk of a heart attack, you can consider your family's medical history, your diet, your weight, and other personal habits such as smoking or exercise. With preventing heart attacks in mind, you might decide to modify your diet, lose weight, or exercise more. However, there is no guarantee that these changes can prevent a heart attack. This is one of many aspects of health that cannot be fully controlled. You can't decide not to have a heart attack.

Some health risks are more completely under your control. You *can* decide whether or not you will drink alcoholic beverages or take mind-altering drugs. As you know, the use of these substances is of grave concern for individuals, families, and society. Following is a sampling of information obtained from reliable studies of alcohol and drug abuse. Use this information in assessing the risk to you and your classmates as you contemplate your future. (In the next section you will use these facts in a risk evaluation exercise.)

Information from studies on the risks of drinking alcoholic beverages:

- Drivers who have been drinking are involved in over 50% of all highway deaths in the United States.
- Alcohol-related accidents are the number one cause of death for teenagers.
- Possible impairment due to alcohol abuse includes high blood pressure; diseases of the liver, pancreas, and intestines; blackout periods (long periods during which there is no memory), severe vitamin deficiencies, cardiovascular damage, neuroses.
- The life expectancy of heavy drinkers is estimated to be 10–12 years shorter than that of the general public.
- Children of alcoholics are 3–4 times more likely to become alcoholics.
- 36 million U.S. citizens suffer unhappiness, desertion, divorce, impoverishment, or child displacement due to alcoholism.

Information from studies on the risks of taking mind-altering drugs: Note that many such drugs are illegal, adding the threat of criminal prosecution to their physical and emotional risks.

- Possible impairment due to marijuana use includes decreased visual perception, loss of fine muscle control, headaches, dizziness, vomiting, and hallucinations. Evidence indicates genetic damage, lung damage, and lowered immune response, but cause-effect links have not been firmly established.
- Marijuana smoke may contain a larger concentration of cancer-causing substances than tobacco smoke.
- Possible impairment due to cocaine use includes nasal ulcers; mental confusion, paranoia, and hallucinations; severe depression between doses (contributing to need for more); brain hemorrhaging and permanent changes in brain chemistry; lowered immune response; overdose death.
- Experts have stated that post-euphoric effects of cocaine activate brain depression centers, thereby creating a desperate need to continue its use. This makes cocaine use addictive like heroin.
- The suicide rate among users of heroin, barbiturates, and related drugs is five times more than normal.

D.4 Personal Control of Risk

How much can you reduce the risk of dying prematurely? How much can society help reduce your risk of premature death? To decide, it's necessary to know what causes a fatal illness or condition, and what, if anything, can be done to control those causes. In this activity you will focus on evaluation of the factors involved in risk control.

1. Divide a piece of graph paper into four quadrants. As illustrated in the sketch in the margin, label the left-hand end of the horizontal axis "can be controlled by individual" and the right-hand end "cannot be controlled by individual." Label the top of the vertical axis "risk unknown" and the bottom of the vertical axis "risk known."

   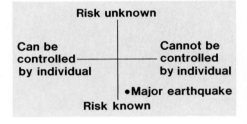

   Using common sense and your own knowledge, select a position for each cause of death listed in the table in the margin. For example, suppose "major earthquake" were on the list. It might be somewhat controllable (you could avoid living in earthquake-prone areas), but if your work and family ties are sufficiently binding, you may be forced to stay in an area. In this case, the point should be somewhat removed from the vertical line on the uncontrollable side. On the other dimension, the risk is more known than unknown—if a major earthquake occurs there is definitely a chance that you might be killed or injured. Therefore, the point should be on the risk known side, but not all the way to the bottom, for there is some uncertainty.

2. Form a group of about five students. Compare your chart with those of the other members of your group. Reach agreement regarding where each cause of death should be located. Then make a consensus graph, representing your group's combined ideas. Write down reasons for the placement of each cause of death.

3. Read over the information on the health risks associated with drinking alcoholic beverages and taking mind-altering drugs given in the preceding section. Assess the risk to you of death or of a severely diminished quality of life caused by each of these two substances. Assign each a position on your grid. Compare your placement with that of other group members. If possible, reach agreement regarding the placements. Add the data to the consensus graph prepared above. Write down reasons for the placement in each case.

**Selected causes of death
in the United States**

Appendicitis	Motor vehicle
Cancer	accidents
Electrocution	Smallpox
Emphysema	vaccination
Heart disease	Stroke
Homicide	Tornado
Lightning	Tuberculosis
	Poison
	Smallpox

4. Are any quadrants of your graph empty? Think of five other causes of death in our society that would belong in each of the empty quadrants. (You may want to think back to causes of death discussed in previous units.)

5. If your task were to decrease the number of fatalities in the United States in the coming year, in which quadrants would you be able to make the greatest reductions?

6. Examine the causes of death placed in the half of the grid labeled "risks unknown." How can science help reduce fatalities from these causes of death? Examine the causes of death in the half of the grid labeled "cannot be controlled by individual." How might society control fatalities from these causes?

7. What additional information would help you complete this exercise?

D.5   Coping with the Risks of Smoking

Smokers often say they derive pleasure from their habit. But evidence indicates that smoking is dangerous, too. How much risk would you be willing to assume, to gain whatever feeling of well-being smoking might offer? Here is some of the evidence:

- Smokers are 10 times more likely to die from lung cancer as are nonsmokers. Lung cancer kills more than 100,000 persons in the United States every year.
- Coronary heart disease kills 565,000 persons in the United States every year. Smokers have a 70% greater risk of coronary heart disease than do nonsmokers.
- Chronic obstructive lung diseases (including emphysema) kill nearly 60,000 persons annually. Smokers are about eight times more likely to die of these diseases than are nonsmokers.
- Smoking during pregnancy exerts direct growth-retarding effects on fetuses. Babies born to women who smoke during pregnancy have (on average) 200 g less mass than do babies born to nonsmoking women.
- The health of smokers can be greatly improved by quitting. On the average, the risk of heart attack in long-term smokers drops 50% within several months of quitting.

Centers for Disease Control, Atlanta, GA

Centers for Disease Control in Atlanta, Georgia conduct many studies to explore the cause of various diseases.

Even in light of this evidence, some claim that there is still no proof that cigarettes cause problems. All these correlations may be due to coincidence, they say.

It's up to you to decide who you are going to believe, and act accordingly. Scientists often have to make decisions in the face of uncertainty. In such cases, the strategy is to minimize error or minimize the consequences of making a wrong decision. They ask themselves what the consequences are of each choice, if it turns out to be incorrect. You can do this yourself.

Think through the risks and benefits of each of the following decisions:
Possibility 1: You decide not to smoke.
Possibility 2: You decide to smoke.

Analyze all factors that would influence either decision. Be prepared to discuss your choice with the class.

D.6 Looking Back and Looking Ahead

In taking control of your personal health, you face many clear-cut decisions, as well as many decisions that involve uncertainty. But the choice is yours. There is much you can do individually to control your health and lifespan.

The last unit of the *Chemistry in the Community* series is titled "The Chemical Industry: Promise and Challenge." In previous units we have dealt with products of the chemical industry. In this final unit we will look more closely at the people, processes, and products associated with this industry—without which our 20th-century lifestyles would not be possible.

UNIT *EIGHT*

The Chemical Industry: Promise and Challenge

CONTENTS

INTRODUCTION

An industrial firm is seeking permission from the Riverwood Town Council to build a chemical manufacturing plant on the edge of town. The plant would make ammonia (NH_3) to be sold as fertilizer and to be used as a reactant in producing other substances. The prospect of jobs for Riverwood citizens has aroused favorable comment among some townspeople, but others are concerned that a chemical manufacturing plant may reduce the quality of life in Riverwood.

The town's Industrial Development Authority has met with officials of the EKS Nitrogen Products Company for several months. Both groups realize that community acceptance of the firm is an important factor in determining the success of this project. The company has arranged public information meetings at Town Hall to talk about the new plant and how it will affect the community.

Chemical Plant Proposed for Community

Riverwood officials have been meeting with representatives of the EKS Nitrogen Products Company for several months to discuss the proposed construction of a chemical plant in the city. This is the first time a major industry has proposed to locate in Riverwood. Six months from now, Riverwood will hold a referendum on whether to allow the company to build the plant. Last night, the plan was unveiled to townspeople at a special meeting at Town Hall.

The Delaware-based company is the nation's third-largest producer of nitrogenous chemicals. EKS's primary products are ammonia and nitric acid. EKS uses these as starting materials for a wide variety of other products, most notably nitrogen fertilizer and explosives. It also sells ammonia and nitric acid to other chemical companies. The proposed plant would produce ammonia and fertilizer.

Mayor Edward Cisko welcomed the plant as a potential boost to the town's economy, and said that on recommendation of the town council he personally had invited the company to consider building a plant in Riverwood. EKS Public Affairs Director Jill Mulligan said that the plant would provide at least 200 new jobs. Recent layoffs at the sawmill have raised Riverwood's unemployment to 7%.

Members of the Riverwood Environmental League questioned the wisdom of locating a chemical plant nearby. Spokesperson Aaron Fosa raised concerns about air quality, possible chemical spills, and waste disposal problems. He suggested that jobs could be created by other industries that might offer fewer potential problems.

Mulligan acknowledged that some chemical companies have previously contributed to such problems. But she said that many companies, including EKS, maintain well-controlled, clean operations. "EKS's Environmental Division continuously monitors processes and equipment to ensure the safest and most pollution-free operation possible. No industry is without risks. Knowing how to handle possible problems is an important part of any operation," Mulligan said.

Citizen reaction to the proposed plant was mixed. "I've got car payments and house payments to make," said Carson Cressey, an unemployed millworker. "Our savings won't last much longer. I hope I can get a job at that chemical plant."

"The unemployment has really cut into my business," said Cynthia Shapiro, owner of the sporting goods store. "I had to lay off my assistant. A new employer in town would help get things going again."

"If it's going to smell like the kitchen when my parents wash the floor, I don't want the plant," said nine-year-old Jimmy Hendricks. "I hate the smell of ammonia!"

See page 6 for a schedule of meetings with EKS representatives at which information about the proposed plant will be presented.

A A NEW INDUSTRY FOR RIVERWOOD

The business of the chemical industry is to change natural materials in ways that make them more useful. Few people have observed such changes as they take place, or even consider what is involved in making a useful product. This creates an air of mystery about how chemical industries operate, how products are manufactured, and what to expect from a chemical plant. But the industry is an important social partner in modern society.

A.1 Industry as a Social Partner

In recent years, both industry and citizens in the United States have begun to recognize a joint responsibility to see that chemical products are manufactured with a net benefit and minimum hazard to society. The U.S. Environmental Protection Agency (EPA), as a representative of the public's interests, has contributed toward this cooperative arrangement.

The chemical industry has the responsibility to make products in ways that are as free from hazard as possible, in workplaces that are as safe as possible. Industry is obliged to deal honestly with the public to ensure that the risks and benefits of chemical operations are clearly known.

Responsible chemical companies are committed to reducing chronic risks—risks that arise from long-term exposure to chemical substances. Industrial scientists—mostly chemists—have developed sensitive instruments and methods for testing the environment as well as human and animal tissues for chemical contamination.

Most data about the effects of chemical substances on health and the environment come from industrial laboratories. Toxicology research on the long-term effects of chemical compounds on human health has been accelerated in recent years.

No activity of the chemical industry or the government can completely eliminate the risks involved in manufacturing chemical substances, any more than the risks of riding in a car can be eliminated. Knowing the risks, continuing to explore them, and dealing prudently with them are essential.

These concerns are not solely the responsibility of the chemical industry. As users of the industry's products, we share this responsibility. We must learn some basic concepts about the manufacture of chemical products. These include how materials are processed, what the energy needs are and how they are to be met, what raw materials will be used and how they will be obtained, what risks are inherent in the operation, and what potential for environmental harm exists. With this knowledge we can take an active part in decisions involving risks and benefits to us and the environment.

To help prepare Riverwood citizens for meetings with EKS representatives, chemistry teacher Richard Knowland invited townspeople to his high school classroom to learn about the chemical industry and some of the processes it carries out. Knowland asked some students to assist him in the presentation.

A.2 Class Activity: A Perspective on the Chemical Industry

In this activity you will serve on a three-member team that will either present a demonstration of a chemical process typical of one carried out by industry or prepare a brief poster talk highlighting background information to help Riverwood citizens gain useful perspective on the chemical industry. In your presentation, you will use knowledge gained from earlier units or from resource materials.

Earlier units, for example, contain laboratory activities representative of industrial processes, including

- Distilling a liquid
- Testing sunscreen preparations
- Preparing copper from copper ore.

Poster topics might cover specific information about the chemical industry such as

- The size and scope of the chemical industry
- Ways an industry can affect a community
- How industry views its responsibilities
- Problems with waste, public safety, and various risks.

Teams making poster presentations should plan their talks and prepare one or two posters to illustrate or highlight major points. Your teacher can direct you to helpful background materials.

A.3 *You Decide:* Products of the Chemical Industry

To prepare yourself for your role in a social partnership with the chemical industry, recall Unit Three, Part A.1, in which you examined familiar products derived from petroleum (see Figure III.1). Petroleum is, of course, a basic raw material for the chemical industry. But so are metals, gases from the atmosphere, and many substances dug from the Earth or gathered from its surface. Almost everything illustrated in Figure III.1 would disappear if all the materials changed by chemical manufacturing or processing were removed.

To get an idea of how pervasive chemical processing is in your life, try to list five items or materials around you that have *not* been produced or altered by the chemical industry. Start by looking around you—at clothes, household items, means of transportation, books and writing instruments, sports and recreation equipment—whatever is nearby.

Write answers to the following questions. Come to class prepared to discuss your answers.

1. Were any items on your list packaged in materials produced by the chemical industry? How important was the packaging material?
2. In what ways are items or materials on your list better or worse than manufactured or synthetic alternatives? Consider factors such as cost, availability and quality.
3. Is a "100% natural" product necessarily one that has not been processed by the chemical industry? Why? Support your answer with at least one example.

A.4 *You Decide:* Asset or Liability

Riverwood citizens will decide by referendum whether they want EKS to build an ammonia production plant near their town. If you were a citizen of Riverwood, how would you make such a decision? Let's consider this in detail:

Discuss in class some of the benefits and risks of building such a chemical plant in Riverwood. Here are things you may wish to consider:

Positive Aspects

The plant will employ 200 local people, working in four shifts. This will add $4 million to the economy of Riverwood each year. Each person employed at the plant will indirectly provide jobs for another four people in local businesses. Currently, 7% of Riverwood's labor force of 21,000 is unemployed.

Fertilizer for farms near Riverwood is now trucked from a fertilizer plant 200 miles away. The transportation costs increase farmers' costs by $14/ton for ammonia-based fertilizer. Each year 700 tons of fertilizer is spread on Riverwood area farms. Thus, local farmers stand to save about $9,800 a year in transportation costs.

A natural gas transmission company will build a line to deliver natural gas (methane, CH_4) to the Riverwood ammonia plant. Town residents, who have always burned fuel oil in their home furnaces, could convert to natural gas. If each of the 11,000 homes in Riverwood burned natural gas rather than oil, emissions of sulfur dioxide and particulate matter would decrease slightly.

The ammonia plant will be taxed at the current commercial rate in Riverwood. This would provide a large increase in revenues for the community.

Negative Aspects

Ammonia is manufactured at high pressure and high temperature. An accident at the plant could kill or injure nearby workers. In 1983 there were 6.2 cases of work-related injury or illness per 100 employees in U.S. fertilizer manufacturing plants. There was one death in a manufacturing plant. Total U.S. ammonia production was about 13 million metric tons.

Ammonia, a gas at ordinary temperature and pressure, is extremely toxic at high concentrations. It is often shipped in tanker trucks. An accident on the roadway or at the plant releasing large amounts of ammonia could create a health hazard. In 1976, a tanker crashed in Houston, rupturing an ammonia tank. The ammonia persisted for 2½ hours. Five persons were killed and 178 were injured. However, such accidents are rare. In 1983 in the United States 156 injuries and illnesses (in the process of storing and shipping ammonia) and one death were reported. The overall accident rate has declined since the early 1980s.

During its production, small amounts of ammonia dissolve in water and enter waterways. If the plant were to malfunction, excessive releases of this waste could kill some aquatic life in the Snake River. The EPA allows a daily average release of 0.025 kg of nitrogenous waste per 1,000 kg of product. The pH of effluent must be between 6 and 9.

One of the largest consumers of ammonia is the fertilizer industry. Current use of large amounts of fertilizer in agriculture has created controversy. Yields have declined despite application of increased amounts of fertilizer. Many farmers have elected to use less synthetic fertilizer; ammonia demand may decline in the coming years. Ultimately this could hurt Riverwood's economy, even though in the near future the industry would help it.

When making decisions regarding complex issues, it's often possible to analyze the factors involved as in solving math problems—by manipulating numbers. For example, when evaluating the use of the pesticide DDT in the tropics, one can compare the number of lives saved (because deaths from malaria spread by mosquitos declined) with the number of lives lost (because of toxic effects of DDT on human life). Or one can compare the money that is saved when new technology is implemented with the cost of that technology, as you did with air pollution control in the unit "Chemistry, Air, and Climate" (see Unit Six, Part E.2). Can the positive and negative effects of the Riverwood chemical plant be evaluated in such a systematic way?

The citizens of Riverwood were given six months to weigh their decision prior to voting on the proposed plant. During this period, many tried to become acquainted with the chemical industry and the workings of an ammonia plant.

Based on the referendum results, EKS was given approval to build the plant. In the next part of this unit, you will see what Riverwood citizens learned about the chemical industry and how the presence of a major chemical manufacturing operation might influence their lives.

PART A
SUMMARY *QUESTIONS*

1. Describe the nature of the partnership between industry and society. In what ways does each partner need the other? What benefits does each receive from the other?
2. Explain the statement, "The chemical industry plays a pervasive though often hidden role in our lives."
3. List and briefly describe some difficulties in analyzing complex issues (such as whether to build a chemical plant) in purely numerical or financial terms.

B AN OVERVIEW OF THE CHEMICAL INDUSTRY

The Riverwood Rotary Club invited Susanna Sobinski, the proposed plant manager of the Riverwood ammonia facility, to speak at a luncheon meeting. After Mayor Cisko introduced her, she showed some slides of what the plant would look like and discussed how the plant's operations fit into the entire chemical industry.

The chemical industry, loosely defined, is the nation's largest industry, said Sobinski. What John Winthrop, a *Mayflower* passenger, began in Massachusetts in 1635 with the production of alum (potassium aluminum sulfate, $KAl(SO_4)_2 \cdot 12H_2O$) and saltpeter (potassium nitrate, KNO_3) has become a colossus that includes 30 of today's leading industries. Petroleum, pharmaceuticals, tires, clothing, paint, and even processed foods are just a few of the products for which the chemical industry is wholly or partly responsible. Even if the large petroleum and food industries are excluded, the remaining chemical industries make roughly $1 of every $10 earned in manufacturing and employ more than one million U.S. citizens.

Two of EKS's most important products, nitrogen and ammonia, are among the top 10 chemicals in terms of quantity produced, said Sobinski. Each year the chemical industry produces about 100 kg of nitrogen and 56 kg of ammonia for every U.S. citizen. Other chemicals in the top 25 and their recent production levels are given in Table VIII.1.

In the United States in 1986 1.02 million workers were employed in producing chemicals and allied products.

YOUR TURN

VIII.1 The Materials Around You

Some of the materials produced by the chemical industry are purified forms of natural resources or combinations of such materials. For example, sodium chloride, which is not only table salt, but an important chemical raw material, is mined as a solid from rock salt deposits or extracted from brine produced by forcing water into underground salt deposits.

Other products are totally new forms of matter that did not exist before being synthesized by chemists. Many of the petrochemicals discussed in Unit Three are such synthetic materials, which often replace natural materials. Synthetic detergents have replaced soap in many uses.

1. List five examples of materials that are purified forms of natural resources, such as petroleum jelly (Vaseline) and table sugar, and five examples of synthesized materials that represent new forms of matter, such as nylon and synthetic dyes. To start, consider food, clothing, housing, transportation, and health care products.

2. In the case of the five synthetic materials, what are the sources of raw materials used in their manufacture? What are the sources of the original materials in the five natural products?

3. Which of the synthetic materials you listed serve as substitutes for natural products? For each of these materials, compare the advantages and disadvantages of the substitute with those of the original material.

4. Identify any of the synthetic materials on your list that represent a totally new product or process not previously available from natural products.

5. Do your answers to Questions 1–4 support or refute such slogans as "Better living through chemistry," or "Today, something we do will touch your life"? Explain.

Table VIII.1 *Top 25 chemicals produced in the United States in 1986*

Rank		Billions of pounds
1	Sulfuric acid	73.6
2	Nitrogen	48.6
3	Oxygen	33.0
4	Ethylene	32.8
5	Lime	30.3
6	Ammonia	28.0
7	Sodium hydroxide	22.0
8	Chlorine	21.0
9	Phosphoric acid	18.4
10	Propylene	17.3
11	Sodium carbonate	17.2
12	Ethylene dichloride	14.5
13	Nitric acid	13.1
14	Urea	12.1
15	Ammonium nitrate	11.1
16	Benzene	10.2
17	Ethylbenzene	8.9
18	Carbon dioxide	8.5
19	Vinyl chloride	8.4
20	Styrene	7.8
21	Terephthalic acid	7.7
22	Methanol	7.3
23	Hydrochloric acid	6.0
24	Ethylene oxide	5.9
25	Formaldehyde	5.9
	Total organic chemicals	139
	Total inorganic chemicals	331
	Grand total	470

Source: Chemical & Engineering News 1987, June 8, p. 27.

B.1 From Raw Materials to Finished Products

The raw materials of the chemical industry are taken from the Earth's crust, from the oceans, and from the atmosphere. For example, more than half the free world's molybdenum, an important metal in alloys used in such diverse products as jet engines and bicycle frames, comes from a single mine on Climax Mountain in Colorado.

YOUR*TURN*

VIII.2 Metals from Ores

A molybdenum ore contains about 0.40% molybdenum. How many metric tons must be mined and processed to yield 1 metric ton of molybdenum?

The percent given indicates that every 100 metric tons of ore contain 0.40 metric ton of molybdenum. The problem is solved as follows:

$$(1 \text{ metric ton Mo}) \left(\frac{100 \text{ metric tons ore}}{0.4 \text{ metric ton Mo}} \right) = 250 \text{ metric tons ore}$$

To obtain 1 metric ton of molybdenum, 250 metric tons of ore must be processed.

1. How many metric tons of taconite, an ore containing about 25% iron, must be mined to produce 1 metric ton of iron?
2. What mass of rock would be left if you removed all the iron from 1 metric ton of taconite? (One metric ton $= 10^3$ kg.)
3. If the powdered rock from 10^6 metric tons of taconite were used to create a road foundation 40 m wide and 25 cm thick, how long could the road be? Assume the density of the rock is 3.0 g/cm^3.

The Climax Mountain Molybdenum Mine, Climax, Colorado.

Monsanto Chemical Company

The Magna Copper Company sulfuric acid plant in San Manuel, Arizona.

Figure VIII.1 Inorganic resources are combined to produce inorganic intermediates.

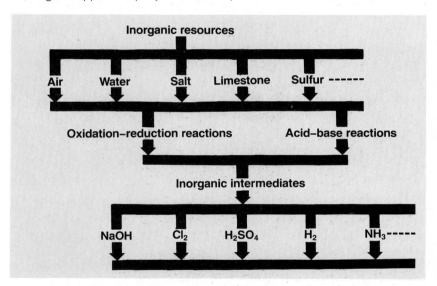

Adapted from *General Chemistry* by Gordon Barrow © 1972 by Wadsworth Publishing Company, Inc. Reprinted by permission of the publisher.

Chemicals, including plastics
Pharmaceuticals
Food
Agriculture
Textiles
Rubber
Paints, dyes, pigments
Petroleum
Pulp and paper
Glass and ceramics
Ferrous metallurgy
Nonferrous metallurgy
Water and sewage
Cleaning and refrigeration
Explosives

Figure VIII.2 Uses of sulfuric acid.

Not all the chemical industry's raw materials are dug from the Earth. Chlorine gas, eighth in terms of total quantity produced in the United States in 1986 (Table VIII.1) is obtained by passing an electric current through salt in aqueous solution ($NaCl(aq)$). Chlorine is used widely in chemical manufacturing processes, in plastics (notably polyvinyl chloride, common in automobile upholstery and plumbing), and in solvents.

Nitrogen gas, second in terms of quantity produced, and oxygen gas, third, are separated from air by low-temperature distillation. Nitrogen gas is a major raw material for EKS.

Once the desired raw materials are obtained and purified, some, such as sodium carbonate (Na_2CO_3), are used directly (for example, sodium carbonate is used for water softening). But many of the inorganic raw materials are converted into **intermediates**—substances used to synthesize consumer products or other chemicals. Figure VIII.1 shows how inorganic resources are combined to produce inorganic intermediates.

Sulfuric acid, the chemical produced in the United States in largest quantity, is a very important intermediate. It is used in fertilizer production, steel processing, petroleum refining, and elsewhere in the chemical industry. Figure VIII.2 lists some of the many products and processes that use sulfuric acid.

The Berkeley open pit copper mine in Butte, Montana.

Anaconda Minerals Company

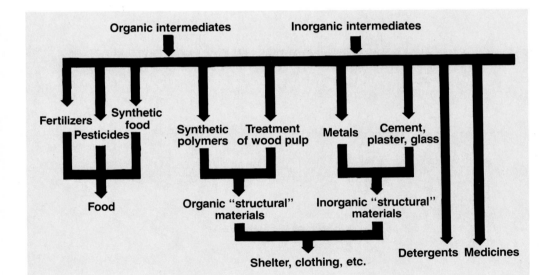

Adapted from *General Chemistry* by Gordon Barrow © 1972 by Wadsworth Publishing Company, Inc. Reprinted by permission of the publisher.

Figure VIII.3 Many products are produced by combining inorganic intermediates and petroleum-based intermediates.

Ammonia is another important intermediate. Although the EKS Company makes fertilizer with the ammonia it manufactures, it also sells ammonia to other chemical companies, where it is used in the manufacture of plastics, resins, fibers, and explosives. Similarly, EKS purchases chemicals from other chemical companies to use in its fertilizers.

Inorganic intermediates are combined with petroleum-based intermediates to synthesize many consumer products (Figure VIII.3). Petroleum-based intermediates, as you learned in the petroleum unit, are obtained by distillation.

The demand for products of the chemical industry is steadily increasing. As more and more natural resources are needed to produce them, a number of problems arise. How do we remove huge quantities of raw materials from the Earth's crust without destroying its beauty and natural balance? How do we dispose of massive amounts of waste, much of which contains toxic materials? How do we control pollution of air and water? How do we prevent and reduce the hazards of chemical spills, and safeguard plant workers and the general public from chemical hazards? Many of these problems have proven harder to solve than the problems of creating new and useful materials.

CHEM*QUANDARY*

Is the desire for a pollution-free and chemically safe environment in direct conflict with the desire for material comfort and convenience?

B.2 From Test Tubes to Tank Cars

Many chemical reactions you have observed in *ChemCom* laboratory experiments are the same reactions used in industry to synthesize intermediates and consumer products. Chemical reactions must be scaled up to produce large quantities of high-quality products at low cost. Three factors become crucial in the scale up: engineering, profitability, and waste.

Chemical engineers face many challenges in designing manufacturing systems for industry. In your laboratory, the small quantity of heat generated by a reaction in a test tube may seem unimportant. But when thousands of liters react in huge tanks, that heat must be planned for and managed. Otherwise, the reaction temperature can rise, creating a potentially dangerous and costly situation.

One way engineers reduce the cost of chemical manufacturing is to run reactions as continuous processes. Like tributaries entering a river and flowing to the ocean, the reactants flow steadily into reaction chambers and product flows out. Figure VIII.4 is a schematic diagram of a continuous-flow process. Rate of flow, time, temperature, and catalyst composition must all be carefully controlled.

Figure VIII.4 A continuous flow process for the production of nitric acid (HNO_3) by the oxidation of ammonia. The reaction takes place in three steps:
$4NH_3(g) + 5O_2(g) \rightarrow 4NO(g) + 6H_2O(g)$
$2NO(g) + O_2(g) \rightarrow 2NO_2(g)$
$3NO_2(g) + H_2O(g) \rightarrow 2HNO_3(aq) + NO(g)$
The first reaction occurs between preheated air and ammonia in the converter (left end of drawing). The second reaction takes place in chambers along the center of the diagram and the third reaction takes place as the gas stream is absorbed in water in the absorber (right end of drawing).

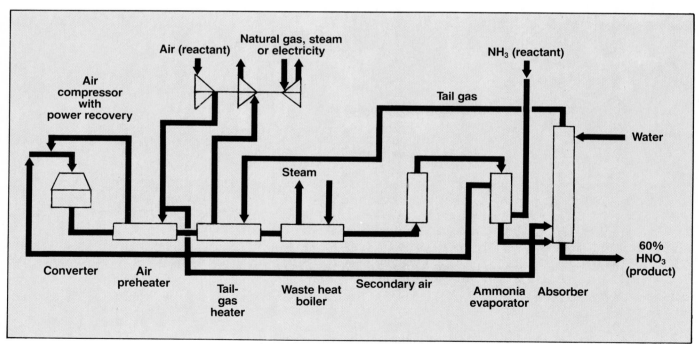

The need to make profits heightens the challenge for chemical engineers. For some products, one penny per liter in production costs can make the difference between profit and loss.

Another problem industry faces is disposing of waste. Waste chemicals quickly accumulate when reactions occur on an industrial scale. A major problem for the EPA is managing the cleanup of hundreds of chemical waste dumps. These dumps are legacies of an earlier time when there were fewer people and the United States appeared larger than it does now. In those days wastes released into the air, rivers, and the ground seemed to disappear.

When EPA put an end to such waste releases many chemical industries discovered that their wastes—sometimes with a little bit of processing—could become some other company's valuable intermediates. Instead of polluting the environment, these wastes-turned-resources provided a new source of profit.

Many products of the chemical industry are shipped from manufacturer to user in railroad tank cars.

B.3 Close-up: The EKS Company

The EKS Company is a good example of how a modern chemical corporation is organized. The company is divided into product and service divisions. Each of the four product divisions concentrates on producing a different class of chemicals, as shown in Figure VIII.5.

Within the service divisions, Analytical Division chemists test the purity of the chemicals EKS produces and the intermediates it purchases from other companies. This division also performs services related to quality control. The Environmental Division monitors the plant's wastes and their effects on the environment. The Research Division invents new products and improves old ones. The Public Relations Division deals with the press, the public, and the government. Riverwood citizens will contact this division when they have a concern about EKS's operations. The Administrative Division oversees the work of all other divisions and handles personnel, company policy, and finances.

Figure VIII.5   The EKS Company.

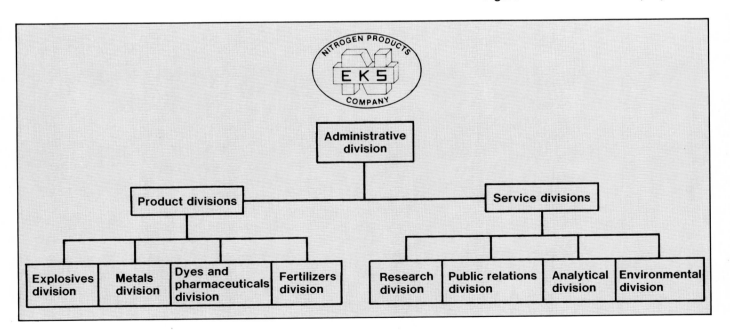

The company is owned by stockholders. Many EKS employees own shares in the company. Riverwood citizens can also buy EKS stock.

Next we will examine two major product areas of this company: fertilizers and explosives. Although these are clearly different categories, both are based on a common raw material—nitrogen gas.

PART B
SUMMARY *QUESTIONS*

1. Provide evidence to support the claim that chemical industry plays a major role in our economy.
2. Identify the top three chemicals (in terms of quantity produced) in the United States, and list two uses of each.
3. What does the term "intermediate" mean in the chemical industry? Give two examples of chemical intermediates.
4. List and briefly describe three factors that must be considered when a reaction is scaled up from a laboratory level to an industrial level.
5. Briefly describe the role played by each of the following divisions within a chemical company:
   a. Analytical division
   b. Environmental division
   c. Public relations division
   d. Administrative division
   e. Research division.

C NITROGEN PRODUCTS AND THEIR CHEMISTRY

EKS Nitrogen Products Company is committed to producing high-quality fertilizer at a reasonable cost, using the best technology available. The company manufactures complete fertilizers, which provide the major nutrients needed by growing plants. The list of nutrients is slightly different for each fertilizer, because different soils require different mineral supplements.

C.1 Laboratory Activity: What Is in Fertilizer?

Getting Ready

In this laboratory activity you will play the role of a technician in the Analytical Division of the EKS company. You will be asked to identify some anions and cations in a fertilizer solution. First, you will examine and perform tests on known solutions of three anions and three cations which might be present in the fertilizer. By performing the same tests on the fertilizer solution and comparing the results with those on the known ions, you should be able to identify the ions present.

Prepare the data table below in your notebook. The six known ions are listed across the top. The tests and reagents are listed in the left-hand column. The Xs indicate tests that need not be carried out.

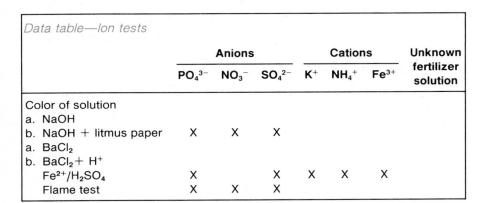

Data table—Ion tests	Anions			Cations			Unknown fertilizer solution
	PO_4^{3-}	NO_3^-	SO_4^{2-}	K^+	NH_4^+	Fe^{3+}	
Color of solution							
a. NaOH							
b. NaOH + litmus paper	X	X	X				
a. $BaCl_2$							
b. $BaCl_2$ + H^+							
Fe^{2+}/H_2SO_4	X		X	X	X	X	
Flame test	X	X	X				

Procedure

Part 1: Tests on Known Ions

1. Obtain about 5 mL of solutions of each of the six known ions. Examine the colors of the solutions and record them in your data table.

2. NaOH test.
   a. Place 2–3 drops of each test solution in a depression in a spot plate using a medicine dropper or micropipet. One by one, test each solution by adding 1–2 drops of 3 *M* sodium hydroxide (NaOH) solution. Record your observations. Clean and rinse the spot plate.

b. Place 1–2 drops of each cation test solution in separate clean small test tubes. Moisten three pieces of red litmus paper and place them on a watch glass. Using a micropipet, add 1 mL of 3 M NaOH to the solution in one test tube. Take care to get no NaOH on the test tube walls or lip. Immediately after adding the NaOH, place a piece of the moistened red litmus paper into the test tube, being sure to keep the paper well above the solution. Heat the test tube gently for one minute, but do not boil the contents. Note your observations after waiting about 30 seconds. Repeat this procedure for each remaining test tube.

3. $BaCl_2$ test.
   a. Repeat Step 2a, testing all six ions with barium chloride instead of with sodium hydroxide, but do not yet clean the spot plate. Record the results.
   b. To the six test solutions in the spot plate to which you have added barium chloride, next add 3 drops of 6 M HCl. Record your observations. Clean the spot plate.

4. Brown ring test (Fe^{2+}/H_2SO_4). The combination of Fe^{2+} and sulfuric acid gives a characteristic reaction with nitrate ion (NO_3^-) only. Place 8 drops of the nitrate ion solution into a small, clean test tube. Carefully add 1 mL of concentrated sulfuric acid (H_2SO_4) and mix well. *Caution:* Conc. H_2SO_4 is a very corrosive strong acid. Add the $FeSO_4$ reagent slowly and gently, pouring it along the inside of the tilted test tube so that it flows along the walls and appears to form a second layer above the existing layer. Allow the test tube to stand for 1–2 minutes. Observe any change that occurs at the interface between the two layers. Record your observations.

5. Flame test.
   a. Obtain a platinum or nichrome wire fastened into glass tubing or a cork stopper, which will serve as a handle.
   b. Set up and light a Bunsen burner. Adjust it so that there is a steady inner light blue cone, and a more luminous outer pale blue cone.
   c. Place 2 mL of 12 M HCl in a test tube. Dip the wire into the HCl, and then insert it into the flame. Position the wire in the outer "luminous" part of the flame, and not in the center cone.

      As the wire heats to a bright red, the flame may become colored. The color of the flame is due to cations on the wire. Continue to dip the wire into the HCl, and insert it into the flame, until there is little or no color in the flame when the wire is bright red. The wire is now clean.
   d. Dip the clean wire into one of the cation test solutions. Then insert it into the flame as before. Note the color of the flame, the intensity of the color, and the duration of the flame (How many seconds does it last?).
   e. Clean the wire with HCl until there is no flame color produced.
   f. Repeat Steps 5d and 5e for the other two cations.
   g. After you have observed the flame colors for all of the cations, observe the K^+ flame through a cobalt-blue glass (or a didimium glass). Again, note the color, the intensity, and the duration of the flame. Your partner can hold the wire in the flame while you observe. Then, change places.
   h. Record all flame test observations in your data table.

Part 2: Tests on Fertilizer Solution

1. Obtain about 20 mL of an unknown fertilizer solution from your teacher. The solution will contain one or more anions and one or more cations tested for in Part 1. Observe and record the color of the solution.

2. By following the appropriate instructions above, carry out each of the tests listed in your table on the fertilizer solution. Be sure to use clean equipment for each test. Record your observations. (Repeat a test if you wish to confirm your observations.)

3. Compare your results with those on the unknowns. Identify the ions in the table that are present in your fertilizer solution.

Questions

1. Name two compounds that could have provided the ions present in your unknown.
2. Describe a test you could perform to determine whether a fertilizer sample contains phosphate ions.
3. If a sample of a fertilizer solution tested basic with litmus, which of the six ions in this experiment is/are likely to be absent?
4. Would a candle flame be suitable for conducting a flame test? Explain.
5. Would the information provided in this activity be sufficient to judge the suitability of a fertilizer for a particular use? Explain.

C.2 The Chemical Role of Fertilizer

Each year EKS manufactures more than 3 million tons of ammonia and more than 1.5 million tons of nitric acid. Most of these products are used in various fertilizer formulations that are then sold to farmers and gardeners.

Farmers add fertilizer to the soil because they want to increase the growth rate and yield of their crops. Recall the concept of a limiting reactant (Unit Four, "Understanding Food," Part C.2). The purpose of any fertilizer is to add enough nutrients to the soil so that plants have all they need of each one.

The raw materials used by growing crops are mainly carbon dioxide from the atmosphere and mineral nutrients from the soil. Tiny openings in leaves called **stomata** take in carbon dioxide. The plants then photosynthesize sugar molecules, which are assembled into starches and cellulose (Unit Four, Part B.3).

Photosynthesis requires chlorophyll and an elaborate system of enzymes, other proteins, and nucleic acids. These compounds are made mainly from nutrients obtained from the soil.

Mineral nutrients such as nitrate (NO_3^-), phosphate (PO_4^{3-}), magnesium (Mg^{2+}), and potassium (K^+) ions are absorbed from the soil by the roots. Phosphate becomes part of the energy storage molecule ATP (adenosine triphosphate; Unit Seven, Part A.7) and the nucleic acids RNA and DNA (Unit Seven, Part A.6), and other phosphate-containing compounds. Magnesium ions are a key component of chlorophyll, which is essential for the photosynthesis reaction in plants.

Potassium ions are present in the fluids and cells of most living things. Without adequate potassium ions, a plant's ability to convert carbohydrates from one form to another and to synthesize proteins is hindered.

Nitrogen is critically important in plant growth, because plant cells are largely protein, and about 16% of the mass of protein molecules is nitrogen. There is abundant molecular nitrogen (N_2) in the atmosphere, but it is so unreactive that plants cannot make use of it.

Jon Jacobson

Applying nitrogen-containing fertilizer to the soil has resulted in a healthy corn crop.

National Severe Storms Laboratory

Lightning storms contribute to a series of reactions that "fix" atmospheric nitrogen as a dilute solution of nitric and nitrous acids, directly available for plant use.

Ammonia (NH_3) or ammonium ion (NH_4^+) added to soil is oxidized to nitrate ions (NO_3^-) by soil bacteria. In building amino acids, plants first reduce the nitrate to nitrite ions (NO_2^-) and then to ammonia. They then use ammonia directly in amino acid synthesis. Unlike animals, higher plants can synthesize all the amino acids they need, starting with ammonia or nitrate ions.

Lightning and combustion can "fix" nitrogen from the atmosphere—that is, they cause nitrogen gas to combine with other elements so that plants can use it. In addition, certain plants called **legumes** (clover and alfalfa are examples) harbor nitrogen-fixing bacteria in their roots.

Science and industry are exploring biological approaches to make atmospheric nitrogen more available to plants. These include incorporating genes that produce nitrogen-fixing enzymes into microorganisms and even into higher plants. Both approaches would make it possible for plants or their bacteria to produce their own nitrogen fertilizer, as legumes do.

When organic matter decays, much of the nitrogen that is produced is recycled among plants and animals, but some returns to the atmosphere. Thus some of the nitrogen gas removed from the atmosphere through nitrogen fixation eventually cycles back to its origin. Figure VIII.6 shows the nitrogen cycle.

*Conversion of N_2 to nitrogen compounds usable by plants is called **nitrogen fixation**.*

YOUR *TURN*
VIII.3   Plant Nutrients

1. Some farmers rotate plantings of legumes between harvests of grain crops. Why?
2. Why is it wise to return nonharvested parts of plant crops to the soil?
3. How might research on new ways to fix nitrogen help to lower farmers' operating costs?
4. Briefly describe the effects at plants' cellular level of an insufficient supply of
   a. Nitrate ions
   b. Phosphate ions
   c. Potassium ions.

In laboratory activity C.1 you identified some major ions present in fertilizer. In the next activity you will complete a quantitative study of one of these ions.

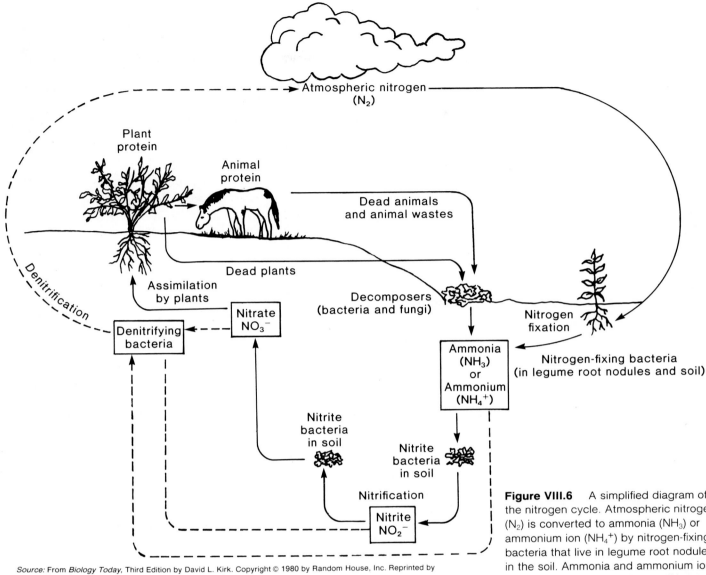

Atmospheric nitrogen
(N₂)

Plant protein

Animal protein

Dead animals and animal wastes

Denitrification

Dead plants

Assimilation by plants

Decomposers (bacteria and fungi)

Nitrogen fixation

Denitrifying bacteria

Nitrate NO₃⁻

Ammonia (NH₃) or Ammonium (NH₄⁺)

Nitrogen-fixing bacteria (in legume root nodules and soil)

Nitrite bacteria in soil

Nitrite bacteria in soil

Nitrification

Nitrite NO₂⁻

Source: From *Biology Today,* Third Edition by David L. Kirk. Copyright © 1980 by Random House, Inc. Reprinted by permission of Random House, Inc.

Figure VIII.6 A simplified diagram of the nitrogen cycle. Atmospheric nitrogen (N_2) is converted to ammonia (NH_3) or ammonium ion (NH_4^+) by nitrogen-fixing bacteria that live in legume root nodules or in the soil. Ammonia and ammonium ion, in turn, are oxidized by various soil bacteria, first into nitrite (NO_2^-) ion and then into nitrate (NO_3^-) ion. It is in the form of nitrate that most nitrogen is taken up by the roots of higher plants. The nitrogen can then be passed along the food chain to animals, which feed on plants, and to animals, which feed on other animals. When these organisms die, their proteins and other nitrogen-containing molecules are broken down by decomposers (mostly bacteria and fungi), and nitrogen not assimilated by the decomposers is released as ammonia or ammonium ion. Thus much nitrogen recycles through the living world without returning to the atmosphere. Some nitrogen, however, is "lost" to the atmosphere when certain bacteria, called denitrifying bacteria, convert ammonia, nitrite, or nitrate to gaseous nitrogen.

C.3 Laboratory Activity: Phosphate Content of Commercial Fertilizer

Getting Ready

Most fertilizer packages give the percent by mass of the essential nutrients contained in the fertilizer. In this activity you will use a **colorimetric method** to determine the mass and percent of phosphate ion in solution. In this method, the intensity of the solution's color indicates the phosphate ion concentration. You will carry out a chemical reaction that converts colorless phosphate ions (PO_4^{3-}) to colored ions. The color of the unknown solution will be compared with the colors of standard solutions to determine the percent of phosphate ion present.

To prepare the unknown fertilizer solution, you will carry out a 50-fold dilution of a solution of 0.5 g of fertilizer in 250 mL of water. This procedure yields a solution sufficiently dilute for comparison with color standards.

Procedure

1. Label five test tubes as follows: 10 ppm, 7.5 ppm, 5 ppm, 2.5 ppm, and unknown.

2. Complete the following steps to prepare the unknown fertilizer solution:
   a. Place 0.50 g of fertilizer in a 400-mL beaker.
   b. Add 250 mL of distilled water. Stir until the fertilizer is completely dissolved. Label the beaker "original."
   c. Pour 5 mL of the solution prepared in Step 2b into a clean 400-mL beaker. Discard the remaining 245 mL of original solution.
   d. Add 245 mL of distilled water to the 5 mL of original solution in the beaker. Stir to mix. Label this beaker "dilute."

3. Place 20 mL of the dilute solution prepared in Step 2d in the test tube labeled "unknown." Discard the remaining dilute solution.

4. In the tube labeled 10 ppm, place 20 mL of standard 10 ppm phosphate ion solution provided by your teacher. Fill the other three test tubes with the dilutions described below:

Concentration (ppm)	Standard 10 ppm phosphate solution (mL)	Distilled water (mL)
7.5	15	5
5	10	10
2.5	5	15

5. Add 2 mL of ammonium molybdate-sulfuric acid reagent to each of the four prepared standards and to the unknown.

6. Add a few crystals of ascorbic acid to each tube. Stir to dissolve.

7. Prepare a water bath by adding about 200 mL of tap water to a 400-mL beaker. Place the beaker on a ring stand above a Bunsen burner. Place the five test tubes in the water bath.

8. Heat the water bath containing the test tubes until a blue color develops in the 2.5-ppm solution. Turn off the burner.

9. Allow the test tubes to cool briefly. Then, using tongs, remove the test tubes from the water bath and place them numerically in the test tube rack.

10. Compare the color of the unknown solution with those of the standard solutions. Place the unknown between those with the closest-matching colors.

11. Estimate the concentration (ppm) of the unknown solution from the known color standards. (For example, if the unknown solution color falls between the 7.5-ppm and 5-ppm color standards, you might decide to call it 6 ppm.) Record the estimated value.

12. Calculate the mass of phosphate ion in the fertilizer using the following equation.

$$\text{g PO}_4^{3-} = 50 \times \underline{\hspace{1cm}} \text{ ppm} \times 250 \text{ g solution} \times \frac{10^{-6} \cdot \text{g PO}_4^{3-}}{1 \text{ ppm} \cdot \text{g solution}}$$

The factor 50 in the calculation compensates for the 50-fold dilution of the fertilizer solution. Record the calculated mass of phosphate ion.

13. Calculate the percent phosphate ion (by mass) in the fertilizer sample:

$$\% \text{ PO}_4^{3-} = \frac{\text{Mass of phosphate ion (from Step 12)}}{\text{Mass of fertilizer sample (0.50 g)}} \times 100$$

Record this value.

Questions

1. Name two household products or beverages for which you can estimate relative concentration by noting their color intensities.

2. Instruments have been designed to determine solute concentration by measuring the quantity of light that passes through an unknown sample as compared with the light that passes through a known standard solution. What advantage might such instruments have over the human eye?

3. Explain this statement: The accuracy of colorimetric analysis depends on the care taken in preparing the standards.

4. How might a reaction producing a precipitate be used to determine the concentration of an ion?

5. Why is it important for farmers to know the accurate percentage composition of the fertilizers they use? What risks (or costs) are associated with applying more of a given nutrient than is needed?

C.4 Fixing Nitrogen: An Oxidation–Reduction Challenge

In searching for ways to fix nitrogen artificially, scientists in 1780 first used an electric spark to cause atmospheric nitrogen and oxygen to combine. However, the cost of electricity makes this process too expensive for commercial use. A less expensive method, the **Haber process,** has replaced it. This is the process the EKS Riverwood plant will use to produce ammonia. Here is some of the chemistry behind it.

When atoms give up electrons to form ions, the process is called **oxidation.** The opposite process, of receiving electrons, is called **reduction.** (For review, see Unit Two, Part D.3.) Electrons can be transferred to or from atoms, molecules, or ions. As a result, all elements and compounds can be oxidized or reduced, and products of oxidation–reduction reactions can be atoms, molecules, or ions.

Oxidation-reduction reactions are sometimes called "redox" reactions.

Consider the key reaction in the Haber process, which is written below using electron-dot formulas:

$$\text{:N:::N: } + \text{ 3 H:H} \rightarrow \text{ 2 } :\overset{\displaystyle H}{\underset{\displaystyle H}{\text{N}}}:\text{H}$$

Note that each nitrogen atom originally shares electrons with another nitrogen atom. Each nitrogen atom has an equal attraction for the shared electrons. In the course of the chemical reaction, each nitrogen atom becomes covalently bonded to three hydrogen atoms. The bonded atoms each share a pair of electrons, but the electrons are not shared equally. Nitrogen atoms have a greater attraction for the shared electrons than do hydrogen atoms. Therefore, the nitrogen atoms in NH_3 molecules have gained more control over the electrons than they had in the N_2 molecules. The nitrogen atoms have been *reduced* in their reaction with hydrogen.

Reduction is electron gain.

Similarly, hydrogen atoms have lost some control of their electrons in the reaction. They have been *oxidized.*

Oxidation is electron loss.

Once nitrogen is chemically combined with another element, it is easily converted to other nitrogen-containing compounds. Thus the great value of the Haber process is that it converts difficult-to-use nitrogen molecules from the air to easy-to-use ammonia molecules (Figure VIII.7). For example, under proper conditions, ammonia reacts readily with oxygen gas to form nitrogen dioxide:

$$4 \text{ NH}_3(g) + 7 \text{ O}_2(g) \rightarrow 4 \text{ NO}_2(g) + 6 \text{ H}_2\text{O}(g)$$

Figure VIII.7   Nitrogen gas and
hydrogen gas react to form ammonia.

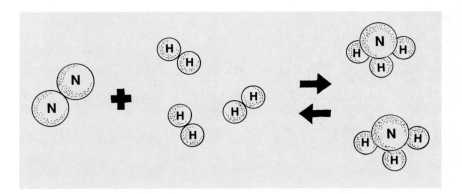

This is also an oxidation–reduction reaction. In forming NO_2, the nitrogen atoms
have been oxidized (in the reaction they have lost some control of electrons because oxygen attracts electrons more strongly than hydrogen), and the oxygen
atoms have been reduced (in the reaction they have gained more control of electrons than they had in O_2).

Because the nitrogen atom in ammonia has more control of its electrons
than it has in elemental nitrogen, it is said to have a **negative oxidation state.** In
nitrogen dioxide, where the nitrogen atom has less control of its electrons than
in elemental nitrogen, it has a **positive oxidation state.** In elemental nitrogen or
elemental oxygen, each atom has a **zero oxidation state.** Oxidation state is a useful
concept in understanding oxidation–reduction reactions.

All uncombined elements are assigned zero oxidation state.

The tendency of atoms to attract electrons to themselves in covalent compounds is called **electronegativity,** and numerical values have been assigned to
this tendency. The electronegativity values for some important elements are shown
in Table VIII.2.

Table VIII.2   *Electronegativity values for selected elements*

Name	Symbol	Electronegativity
Potassium	K	0.8
Sodium	Na	0.9
Magnesium	Mg	1.2
Manganese	Mn	1.5
Aluminum	Al	1.5
Zinc	Zn	1.6
Iron	Fe	1.8
Lead	Pb	1.8
Nickel	Ni	1.8
Tin	Sn	1.8
Copper	Cu	1.9
Silver	Ag	1.9
Hydrogen	H	2.1
Gold	Au	2.4
Carbon	C	2.5
Iodine	I	2.5
Sulfur	S	2.5
Bromine	Br	2.8
Chlorine	Cl	3.0
Nitrogen	N	3.0
Oxygen	O	3.5
Fluorine	F	4.0

YOUR TURN

VIII.4   Electronegativity and Oxidation State

Oxidation state is a convenient way of expressing the degree of oxidation or reduction of atoms in chemical substances. Each atom in an element or compound can be assigned a numerical oxidation state. The higher the oxidation state, the more the atom has been oxidized. The lower the oxidation state, the more it has been reduced. In assigning oxidation states, in binary compounds (compounds between two elements) for example, atoms of more electronegative elements are given negative oxidation state values—corresponding to gain of electrons or a reduced state. Similarly atoms of lower electronegativity are assigned positive oxidation states—corresponding to loss of electrons or an oxidized state.

"Oxidation state" is sometimes referred to as "oxidation number."

> In aluminum oxide (Al_2O_3), which element has the positive oxidation state and which the negative oxidation state?

Checking the values in Table VIII.2 shows that aluminum has an electronegativity of 1.5 and oxygen has 3.5. This indicates that oxygen has greater electron-attracting ability than does aluminum. Therefore, in aluminum oxide, aluminum is assigned a positive oxidation state and oxygen a negative oxidation state.

The combination of aluminum and oxygen

$$4\,Al(s) + 3\,O_2(g) \rightarrow 2\,Al_2O_3(s)$$

is an oxidation–reduction reaction in which aluminum is described as oxidized, because its oxidation state changes from zero in the free element to a positive value, and oxygen is described as reduced, because its oxidation state changes from zero to a negative value.

1. Using the electronegativity scale, determine which element is assigned a positive oxidation state and which is assigned a negative oxidation state in each of these compounds.

   a. SO_3
   b. N_2H_4
   c. H_2O
   d. HCl
   e. $NaCl$
   f. CO
   g. IF_3
   h. MnO_2

2. Which element has the negative and which the positive oxidation state in each of these compounds formed from a metal and a nonmetal?

   a. PbF_2
   b. NaI
   c. K_2O
   d. NiO
   e. $FeCl_3$
   f. PbS

   What conclusion can you draw about the oxidation states of metals and nonmetals in binary compounds?

3. In the following redox reaction, which element is oxidized and which is reduced?

$$Ni(s) + S(s) \rightarrow NiS(s)$$

The relative ease of conversion of one nitrogen compound to another is used in the chemical industry to make a large number of compounds from ammonia. Table VIII.3 gives examples of nitrogen compounds manufactured in this way.

Table VIII.3   *Industrial nitrogen compounds*

Compound	Structure	Use
Ammonia, NH_3	NH_3	Fertilizer, explosives, fibers, plastics
Nitric acid, HNO_3	$HO-NO_2$	Fertilizer and explosive synthesis, organic chemicals manufacture
Hydrazine, N_2H_4	H_2N-NH_2	Rocket fuel, plastics production
Amines, R-NH_2[a] e.g., propylamine	$CH_3CH_2CH_2NH_2$	Intermediate
Nitrates, MNO_3[b] e.g., sodium nitrate	$Na^+NO_3^-$	Fertilizer, explosives, food preservative
Nitrites, MNO_2[b] e.g., sodium nitrite	$Na^+NO_2^-$	Rubber chemical, metal treating, food preservative
Hydroxylamine, NH_2OH	$H-\overset{\displaystyle ..}{\underset{\displaystyle \mid}{N}}-OH$ $\mid$ H	Reducing agent
Phenylhydrazine, $C_6H_5N_2H_3$	⬡—$NHNH_2$	Dye intermediate
Urea	$H_2N\overset{\displaystyle \mid\mid}{\underset{\displaystyle O}{C}}NH_2$	Fertilizer, plastics

[a]R = Hydrocarbon group.
[b]M = Metal ion.

C.5   Nitrogen Fixation at the Riverwood Plant

The synthesis of ammonia from nitrogen and hydrogen is a difficult chemical reaction for several reasons. For one, the synthesis does not consume all the available nitrogen and hydrogen to produce ammonia. As soon as the first ammonia molecules form in the reactor, they begin to decompose to form nitrogen and hydrogen molecules. This kind of reaction is called a **reversible reaction.** The reversibility limits the amount of ammonia that can be obtained. Chemists represent reversible reactions with double arrows linking the products and reactants.

$$N_2(g) + 3\ H_2(g) \rightleftharpoons 2\ NH_3(g)$$

The reaction reaches a state of dynamic equilibrium when the rate at which ammonia forms is equal to the rate at which it decomposes.

All reversible reactions in closed containers reach equilibrium if conditions such as temperature and pressure remain constant.

One way to increase the yield of ammonia is to remove the ammonia as fast as it is formed. Ammonia decomposes in the reactor because of the high temperature, but is stable once it is out of the reactor. Removing ammonia prevents the reaction from reaching equilibrium. Meanwhile ammonia continues to form. Removing ammonia in this way would be very expensive.

Because ammonia is unstable at high temperatures, it might at first seem that a solution would be to run the reactor at a low temperature so the ammonia would not decompose. This doesn't work, however. Simply mixing three volumes of hydrogen with one volume of nitrogen at ordinary temperatures doesn't produce noticeable quantities of ammonia, regardless of how long the gases remain together.

Finding a suitable catalyst was the breakthrough that led to a workable ammonia process. With a catalyst, it became possible to produce ammonia at a lower temperature, at which it is more stable. Modern ammonia plants give a 20%–30% yield, depending on the temperature and pressure used.

Commercial ammonia production involves more than simply allowing nitrogen and hydrogen to react in the presence of a catalyst. First, the reactants must be obtained. Nitrogen gas is taken from the air. Hydrogen is obtained from natural gas (mainly methane, CH_4). This is why Riverwood's ammonia plant requires the construction of a natural gas pipeline.

Sulfur-containing compounds are removed from the natural gas by passing it through absorptive beds. Next, methane reacts with steam to produce hydrogen gas.

$$CH_4(g) + H_2O(g) \rightleftharpoons 3 H_2(g) + CO(g)$$

In modern ammonia plants, this endothermic reaction takes place at 200–600 °C, at pressures of 200–900 atm. The ratio of methane (CH_4) to steam must be carefully controlled to prevent the formation of a variety of carbon compounds.

Carbon monoxide is converted to carbon dioxide, a marketable product, and removed from the hydrogen. Then the hydrogen gas is purified of all other compounds.

Steam turbines compress the hydrogen and nitrogen to high pressures. Ammonia forms as the gases flow over a catalyst of reduced iron oxide (Fe_3O_4):

$$N_2(g) + 3 H_2(g) \rightleftharpoons 2 NH_3(g)$$

C.6 The Other Face of Nitrogen

The first use of synthetic ammonia was to make explosives during World War I. Almost all chemical explosives contain nitrogen compounds. Until the war, fixed nitrogen was available in large quantities only from nitrate deposits in the deserts of Chile. Fixed nitrogen in the form of ammonia made it possible for Germany to continue fighting the war after the British Navy cut off its link to Chilean supplies.

World ammonia production has increased dramatically since 1950, as farmers around the world have increased their use of fertilizer. The chemical industry's capacity to produce ammonia increased about 11-fold in the past decade. Eighty percent of this is now used in fertilizer, and 5% is used in explosives.

Monsanto ammonia plant, Muscatine, Iowa.

Monsanto Chemical Company

C.7 Explosives: Business Is Booming

Explosives have uses other than in weapons. Most road-cuts you see along interstate highways were carved by chemical forces unleashed by explosives. To cut through the stone faces of hills and mountains, road crews drill holes, drop in explosive cannisters, and detonate them.

The explosion is generally caused by rapid formation of gaseous products from liquid or solid reactants. A gas takes up more than a thousand times the volume of the same molar quantity of solid or liquid.

To be useful, an explosive must react readily, but not too readily. This caused a lot of trouble in the 1880s. It also made and lost fortunes several times for a family named Nobel. The father and his four sons were all interested in explosives, but Alfred, one of the sons, was the most persistent experimenter.

In 1846, nitroglycerin, a powerful explosive, was invented. It was too sensitive to be useful. One never knew when it was going to explode. The Nobels built a laboratory in Stockholm to try to find a way to control this unstable substance. Carelessness and ignorance of the properties of nitroglycerin resulted in many terrible explosions. Alfred's brother, Oscar, was killed in one of them. Finally, the city of Stockholm insisted that Alfred go elsewhere to do his experimenting. Grimly determined to make nitroglycerin less dangerous, Alfred rented a barge and continued his experiments in the middle of a lake. He finally discovered that if the oily nitroglycerin was adsorbed on finely divided sand (diatomaceous earth), it became stable enough to transport and store, but would still explode with the help of a blasting cap. This new form of the explosive was called dynamite.

A new era had begun. At first, dynamite served only peaceful uses in mining and in road and tunnel construction. But in the latter part of the century, it was used in war.

Explosives were used to cut through this hillside to make way for a Maryland highway.

Maryland Department of Transportation

This caused Alfred Nobel considerable anguish and motivated him to use his fortune for the benefit of humanity. His will authorized awarding annual prizes in physics, chemistry, physiology and medicine, literature, and peace. Later, the Swedish parliament added another area: economics. The first Nobel prizes were awarded in 1901. To this day, the Nobel prize is considered the highest honor a scientist can receive. Some recent Nobel laureates in chemistry are listed in Table VIII.4, along with their contributions to chemical science.

Table VIII.4 *Nobel laureates in chemistry, 1979–86*

Year	Winners	Contribution
1986	Dudley Herschbach, United States, Harvard University Yuan T. Lee, Taiwan, University of California John A. Polyanyi, Canada, University of Toronto	Development of methods for tracking individual molecules in chemical reactions
1985	Herbert A. Hauptman, United States, Medical Foundation of Buffalo Jerome Karle, United States, Naval Research Laboratory	Development of direct mathematical methods used to determine crystal structures of molecules from X-ray data
1984	R. Bruce Merrifield, United States, Rockefeller University	Development of a method for solid-phase synthesis of peptides and other biopolymers
1983	Henry Taube, United States, Stanford University	Determination of mechanisms for electron-transfer reactions, especially in metal complex ions. The research has applications in industry and biology
1982	Aaron Klug, South Africa, Cambridge University	Development of technique to determine detailed structures of viruses and genetic components within cells
1981	Kenichi Fukui, Japan, Kyoto University Roald Hoffmann, United States, Cornell University	Application of mathematical description of atoms (quantum mechanics) to predict the outcomes of chemical reactions
1980	Paul Berg, United States, Stanford University	Completion of fundamental studies of the biochemistry of nucleic acids, with particular regard to recombinant DNA
	Walter Gilbert, United States, Harvard University Frederick Sanger, United Kingdom, Cambridge University	Development of methods for determining the base sequences in nucleic acids (recognition shared by Gilbert and Sanger)
1979	Herbert C. Brown, United States, Purdue University Georg Wittig, West Germany, Heidelberg University	Development of ways to induce chemical reactions leading to the production of important pharmaceutical and industrial chemicals. Brown developed organoboranes, while Wittig worked with phosphorus-containing compounds

Chemical & Engineering News

The Nobel medallion.

Figure VIII.8   Some explosives EKS
produces.

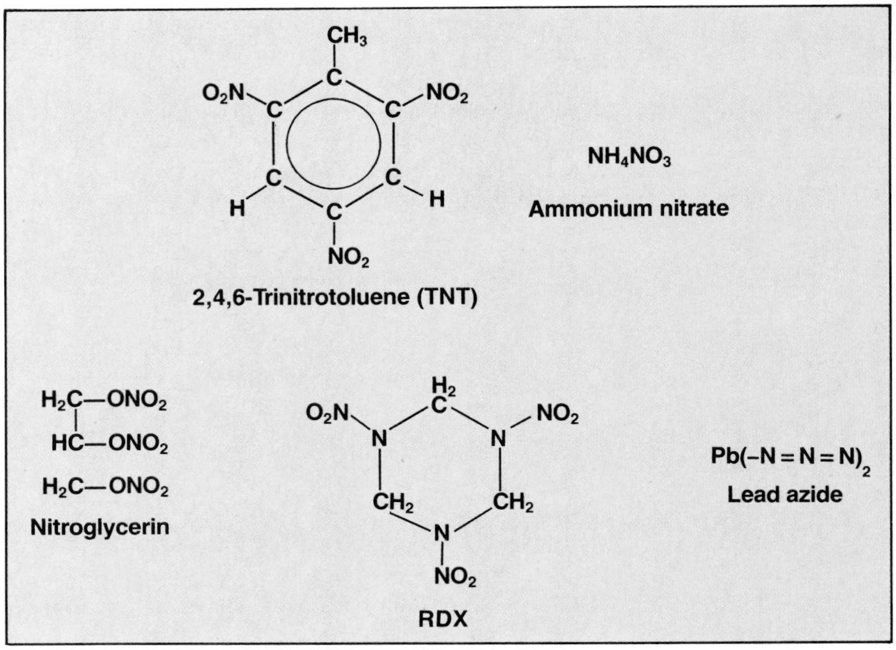

2,4,6-Trinitrotoluene (TNT)

NH_4NO_3

Ammonium nitrate

Nitroglycerin

RDX

$Pb(-N=N=N)_2$

Lead azide

Explosive reactions are rapid exothermic redox reactions that release large amounts of gas.

EKS produces several chemicals in its Explosives Division. Names and formulas of some of these are shown in Figure VIII.8. The formulas are very different, but one thing they have in common is nitrogen atoms. Most have nitrogen in a positive oxidation state and carbon in a negative oxidation state in the same molecule. This creates conditions for a very rapid transfer of electrons from carbon to nitrogen, with the release of vast quantities of energy. The reactions of explosives are not reversible; they go to completion. Many different products are possible. Below are two examples of explosive reactions.

Nitroglycerin:
$$4\ C_3H_5(NO_3)_3(l) \longrightarrow 12\ CO_2(g) + 6\ N_2(g) + 10\ H_2O(g) + O_2(g)$$
TNT:
$$4\ C_7H_5N_3O_6(s) + 21\ O_2(g) \longrightarrow 28\ CO_2(g) + 10\ H_2O(g) + 6\ N_2(g)$$

Refer to these equations in answering the questions in the next exercise.

YOUR*TURN*

VIII.5   Chemistry of Explosives

1. How many moles of gas are formed in the explosion of 1 mol of TNT?

2. Assume that gases at a given temperature occupy 1000 times more space than do the same number of moles of a solid at that temperature. Assume that 1 mol of TNT occupies one volume of space. Using the value you found in answering Question 1, calculate the number of volumes of gas that would be present after explosion of 1 mol of TNT, if the temperature remained constant. By what factor would the volume increase?

3. In fact, when TNT explodes the temperature rise causes the volume to increase by an additional factor of eight. By what combined factor, then, does the volume increase in an actual TNT explosion?

4. Which equations might represent possible explosive reactions?

    a. $C_5H_{12}(l) + 8\ O_2(g) \longrightarrow 5\ CO_2(g) + 6\ H_2O(g) + Energy$

    b. $CaCO_3(s) + Energy \longrightarrow CaO(s) + CO_2(g)$

    c. $C_3H_6N_6O_6(s) \longrightarrow 3\ CO(g) + 3\ H_2O(g) + 3\ N_2(g) + Energy$

C.8 *You Decide:* Food or Armaments

Chemicals necessary for war and peace alike are synthesized from ammonia. This nitrogen-containing compound is the starting material for both explosives and fertilizers. One issue that scientists have long debated is whether they are responsible for the social consequences of their discoveries: Should they try to control the use of these discoveries? Do scientists have a greater responsibility than other citizens in making such decisions?

1. It is 1917. A group seeking to ban production of ammonia asks you to join. What is your decision? Give reasons for your choice.

2. If after World War I the artificial fixation of nitrogen had been banned, what would some consequences have been? How might the world be different?

3. Compare the two faces of nitrogen with the two faces of nuclear energy. Answer Questions 1 and 2, substituting nuclear power for ammonia and nitrogen, and the present for the early 1900s.

4. You are the Minister of Food Supplies for a nation with a population of 5 million (5×10^6). Each person requires 20 kg of protein a year.
   a. How much protein is required to feed the nation for one year?
   b. If $\frac{1}{16}$ as much fertilizer as food is needed, how much fertilizer must your nation produce each year?

5. The Minister of Armaments has announced that he will need 10% of the available fixed nitrogen for explosives. This year he used only 5%, so the increase must come from the fertilizer allotment. How would you, as Minister of Food Supplies, respond?

Like many other chemical companies, EKS has diversified chemical interests and activities. We'll learn in the next part of this unit that EKS is also active in electrochemical processes—chemical changes that produce or are caused by electrical energy.

PART C
SUMMARY *QUESTIONS*

1. How does the concept of limiting reactants relate to the use of fertilizers?

2. Molecular nitrogen represents 78% of all the molecules in the atmosphere, yet nitrogen can be a limiting reactant for plants. Explain.

3. Answer the following questions based on this equation:

$$N_2(g) + 3 H_2(g) \rightleftarrows 2 NH_3(g) + Energy$$

   a. What are the sources of the raw materials for this reaction?
   b. Is the forward reaction endothermic or exothermic? Given your answer, would you expect the forward reaction to be favored at high or low temperatures? What is the disadvantage of running the reaction at these temperatures?
   c. What role does a catalyst play in this reaction?

4. What is meant by oxidation state? How is oxidation state related to oxidation and to reduction? Illustrate how this concept applies to this equation:

$$4 NH_3(g) + 7 O_2(g) \rightarrow 4 NO_2(g) + 6 H_2O(g)$$

EXTENDING *YOUR KNOWLEDGE*
(OPTIONAL)

Visit a garden store and read the labels on various fertilizer preparations. What materials are commonly sold?

D CHEMICAL ENERGY ↔ ELECTRICAL ENERGY

The people of Riverwood have found that EKS Nitrogen Products Company is a positive contributor to life in the town. The company is now considering diversifying into the production of aluminum.

Aluminum is obtained from its ore, bauxite, by electrolysis. The process requires so much electricity that electrical costs are extremely important. The hydroelectric plant located at the Snake River Dam produces much more electric power than is needed to serve Riverwood and surrounding communities. Power company officials have offered EKS large quantities of electrical power at very competitive rates.

The following laboratory activities and discussions provide information on electrochemistry that will help you understand what the proposed new plant will do.

D.1 Laboratory Activity: Voltaic Cells

Getting Ready

In the unit on resources you learned that some metals release electrons (become oxidized) more readily than others—they are more active (Unit Two, Part D.3). The relative tendencies for metals in contact with water to release electrons can be summarized in an activity series of the metals (see Table VIII.5). A metal that is higher in the activity series will give up electrons more readily than one that is lower.

Table VIII.5 *Activity series of common metals*

Metal		Products of metal reactivity		
$Li(s)$	$\rightarrow$	$Li^+(aq)$	$+$	e^-
$Na(s)$	$\rightarrow$	$Na^+(aq)$	$+$	e^-
$Mg(s)$	$\rightarrow$	$Mg^{2+}(aq)$	$+$	$2\,e^-$
$Al(s)$	$\rightarrow$	$Al^{3+}(aq)$	$+$	$3\,e^-$
$Mn(s)$	$\rightarrow$	$Mn^{2+}(aq)$	$+$	$2\,e^-$
$Zn(s)$	$\rightarrow$	$Zn^{2+}(aq)$	$+$	$2\,e^-$
$Cr(s)$	$\rightarrow$	$Cr^{3+}(aq)$	$+$	$3\,e^-$
$Fe(s)$	$\rightarrow$	$Fe^{2+}(aq)$	$+$	$2\,e^-$
$Ni(s)$	$\rightarrow$	$Ni^{2+}(aq)$	$+$	$2\,e^-$
$Sn(s)$	$\rightarrow$	$Sn^{2+}(aq)$	$+$	$2\,e^-$
$Pb(s)$	$\rightarrow$	$Pb^{2+}(aq)$	$+$	$2\,e^-$
$Cu(s)$	$\rightarrow$	$Cu^{2+}(aq)$	$+$	$2\,e^-$
$Ag(s)$	$\rightarrow$	$Ag^+(aq)$	$+$	e^-
$Au(s)$	$\rightarrow$	$Au^{3+}(aq)$	$+$	$3\,e^-$

We use the differing tendencies of metals to lose electrons to obtain electrical energy from a chemical reaction. We do this by making an electrochemical cell, also called a **voltaic cell,** in which electrons flow spontaneously through a wire connecting the two metals. The flow of electrons is called **current.** In this laboratory activity you will study several voltaic cells.

When two metals of differing electron-releasing tendencies are connected in a voltaic cell, an **electrical potential** is created between the metals. This electrical potential, measured in volts, is like the pressure in a water pipe. It is the "push" that drives electrons through the wire connecting the two metals. The greater the difference in activity of the metals, the greater the "electron pressure," or electrical potential, of the cell. To provide both electrical conduction inside the cell and receptors for electrons leaving the wire or external circuit, a voltaic cell is prepared by immersing each of the two metals in a solution of its ions.

Procedure

Prepare an appropriate data table for the following procedures.

Zinc–copper Electrochemical Cell

1. Pour 70 mL of 0.5 M $CuCl_2$ into a 75-mL porous cup.
2. Pour 200 mL of 0.5 M $ZnSO_4$ into a 400-mL beaker.
3. Place a copper strip in the porous cup.
4. Place a zinc strip in the beaker.
5. Place the porous cup in the beaker. Be sure the top of the cup remains above the liquid level in the beaker. (See Figure VIII.9.)
6. Attach wire leads to the metal strips. Then attach one wire lead to the voltmeter. Very quickly and lightly touch the second wire lead to the other terminal of the voltmeter. If the needle is deflected in the positive direction, secure the wire to the terminal. If the needle is deflected in the negative direction, detach the first wire lead, reverse the positions of the leads, and attach them to the terminals.
7. Record the reading on the voltmeter dial.
8. Disconnect the wire leads, remove the metal strips, and dispose of the liquids as your teacher directs.

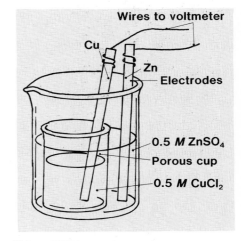

Figure VIII.9   A zinc-copper electrochemical cell.

Jon Jacobson

If a car battery is deficient in electrical energy, the energy must be "borrowed" from another source.

Magnesium–copper Electrochemical Cell

1. Refer to the activity series of metals and predict the change in your results with a magnesium–copper cell.
2. Repeat Steps 1–8 above, this time using a 15-cm length of magnesium ribbon and 200 mL of 0.5 M $MgCl_2$ in place of the zinc and its solution in the beaker.

Iron–copper Electrochemical Cell

1. Refer to the activity series of metals and predict the change in your results with an iron–copper cell.
2. Repeat Steps 1–8 in the procedure for the zinc–copper electrochemical cell, using an iron strip and 200 mL of 0.5 M $FeCl_3$ in place of the zinc and its solution in the beaker.

Studying Electrode Size

1. Dry the zinc and copper strips and cut them in half lengthwise.
2. Repeat Steps 1–7 in the zinc–copper electrochemical cell procedure.
3. Disconnect the wire leads. Remove the pieces of metal from the solutions, dry them, and cut them in half lengthwise again.
4. Repeat Steps 1–8 in the zinc–copper procedure.

Questions

1. List the three voltaic cells that you prepared in order of decreasing electrical potential. Explain the observed order in terms of the activity series.
2. Predict whether the electrical potential would be higher or lower than that of the Zn-Cu cell for cells with the following metal combinations:
   a. Zn and Cr
   b. Zn and Ag
   c. Sn and Cu
3. How did a decrease in the size (surface area) of the electrodes affect the measured electrical potential?
4. Would a Ag-Au cell be practical? Why or why not?

D.2 Principles of Electrochemistry

In the voltaic cells you made in the laboratory activity, each metal and the solution of its ions was a **half-cell.** In the zinc-copper cell, oxidation (electron loss) occurred in the half-cell with zinc metal immersed in zinc nitrate solution. Reduction (electron gain) took place in the half-cell composed of copper metal in copper(II) chloride solution. The activity series helps us predict that zinc is more likely to be oxidized (lose electrons) than copper. The **half-reactions** (individual electron-transfer steps) for this cell are:

$$\text{Oxidation: } Zn(s) \rightarrow Zn^{2+}(aq) + 2\text{ e}^-$$
$$\text{Reduction: } Cu^{2+}(aq) + 2\text{ e}^- \rightarrow Cu(s)$$

The electrode at which oxidation takes place is the **anode.** Reduction occurs at the **cathode.**

The overall reaction in the zinc-copper voltaic cell is

$$Zn(s) + Cu^{2+}(aq) \rightarrow Zn^{2+}(aq) + Cu(s).$$

Because a barrier separates the reactants (Zn and Cu^{2+}), electrons released by zinc in the zinc-copper voltaic cell must go through the wire to reach the copper ions. The greater the difference in reactivity of the two metals, the greater the tendency to transfer electrons and the greater the cell potential. A cell containing zinc and gold and their ions generates a larger potential than does the zinc-copper cell, for example.

Voltaic cells are a simple way to convert chemical energy to electrical energy in small portable containers. Chemists have packaged various combinations of metals and ions to make useful commercial cells. Ordinary dry cells (Figure VIII.10)—often called batteries—use zinc as the anode and manganese dioxide (MnO_2) as the cathode. The solution of ions contains ammonium and zinc chlorides in the most common dry cells. In alkaline batteries, the solution contains potassium hydroxide (KOH).

The battery of a car, a lead storage battery, is a series of electrochemical cells, consisting of lead plates that act as one electrode and lead dioxide plates (PbO_2) that act as the other electrode. All plates are immersed in sulfuric acid. See Figure VIII.11.

When you turn the key in the ignition, an electrical circuit is completed, and the chemical energy of the lead storage battery is converted to electrical energy to run the starter motor. The lead electrode is oxidized (it loses electrons). These electrons travel through the circuitry to the lead dioxide electrode, reducing it (it gains electrons). As the electrons travel between the electrodes, they energize the car's electrical systems.

The half-reactions for the oxidation and reduction are

Oxidation: $Pb(s) + SO_4^{2-}(aq) \rightarrow PbSO_4(s) + 2\ e^-$
Reduction:

$PbO_2(s) + SO_4^{2-}(aq) + 4\ H^+(aq) + 2\ e^- \rightarrow PbSO_4(s) + 2\ H_2O(l)$

The overall reaction is

$PbO_2(s) + Pb(s) + 4\ H^+(aq) + 2\ SO_4^{2-}(aq) \rightarrow 2\ PbSO_4(s) + 2\ H_2O(l)$

If an automobile battery is used too long without recharging, it runs down because the lead sulfate formed eventually coats both electrodes and reduces their ability to produce current. To maintain the battery's charge, the generator or alternator converts some mechanical energy of the car's running engine to electrical energy, which is used to recharge the battery. Recharging causes electrons

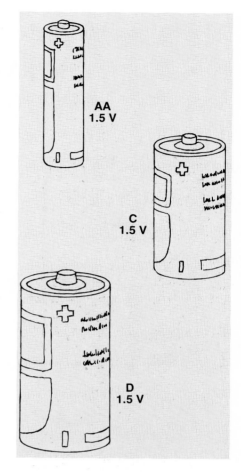

Figure VIII.10 Despite the differences in size, all these dry cells generate 1.5 V, since they are based on the same chemistry.

Figure VIII.11 One cell of a lead storage battery.

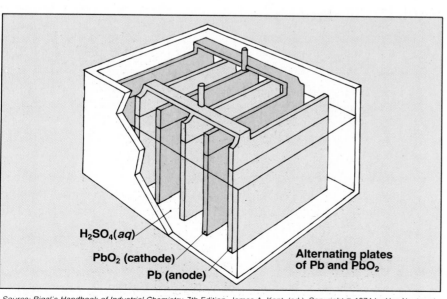

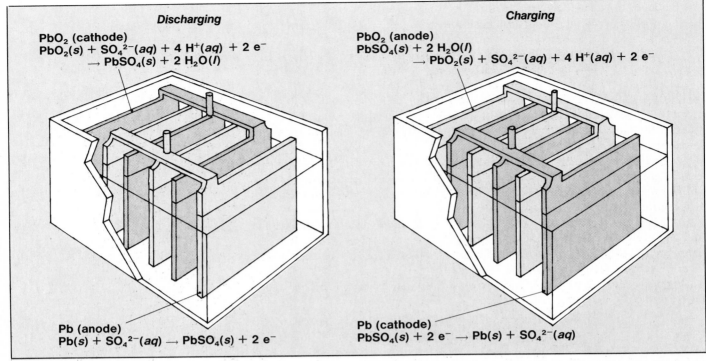

Figure VIII.12   Charging and discharging a car battery.

to move in the opposite direction through the battery. This reverses the chemical reaction of the battery. Reversing the reaction charges the battery (Figure VIII.12).

Lead storage batteries can be quite dangerous when they are being rapidly charged from an outside voltage source. Hydrogen gas can be produced at the lead electrode. A spark or flame can ignite the hydrogen, causing an explosion.

YOUR *TURN*

VIII.6   Electrochemistry

Consider the following questions about a voltaic cell in which lead (Pb), silver (Ag) and solutions of lead nitrate ($PbNO_3$) and silver nitrate ($AgNO_3$) are appropriately arranged:

  a. Predict the direction of electron flow in the wire connecting the two metals.
  b. Write equations for the two half-reactions.
  c. Which metal is the anode and which the cathode?

a. Table VIII.5 shows that lead is the more active metal. Therefore, electrons should flow from lead to silver.

b. The half-reactions are the formation of Pb^{2+} ions from Pb as shown in Table VIII.5 and the formation of Ag from Ag^+, by the reverse of the reaction shown in the table.

$$Pb \rightarrow Pb^{2+} + 2\ e^-$$
$$Ag^+ + e^- \rightarrow Ag$$

c. In the cell reaction, each lead atom loses two electrons. Lead metal is therefore oxidized. By definition, then, lead metal is the anode. Each silver ion gains one electron. This is a reduction reaction. Since reduction takes place at the cathode, silver metal must be the cathode.

Now try these questions on your own:

1. Predict the direction of electron flow if a voltaic cell is made from each combination of metals in solutions of their ions.
   a. Al and Sn
   b. Pb and Mg
   c. Cu and Fe

2. The overall equation for the reaction in a voltaic cell using the metals tin and cadmium is:

$$Sn^{2+}(aq) + Cd(s) \rightarrow Cd^{2+}(aq) + Sn(s)$$

   a. Write the half-reactions.
   b. Which metal, Sn or Cd, loses electrons more easily?

3. Sketch a voltaic cell whose half-cells are composed of Ni-Ni(NO$_3$)$_2$ and Cu-Cu(NO$_3$)$_2$.

4. In each of the following cells, identify the anode and the cathode.
   a. Cu-Zn cell with appropriate ionic solutions
   b. Al-Zn cell with appropriate solutions
   c. Mg-Mn cell with appropriate ionic solutions
   d. Au-Ni cell with appropriate ionic solutions.

D.3 Laboratory Activity: Electroplating

Getting Ready

All the reactions observed in Part D.1 were spontaneous. Materials were arranged so that electrons would spontaneously move through wires. Voltaic cells involving such reactions generate electrical energy that can run engines and do other useful work.

One type of useful work often done by electricity is that of causing non-spontaneous or difficult chemical reactions to proceed. The charging of the lead storage battery in an automobile is an example.

In electroplating, the electrical energy from a battery or other source provides electrons to convert metal ions to atoms. Electroplating produces a thin layer of metal deposited on another surface to protect the surface or to make it more beautiful. Coating inexpensive jewelry with a very thin layer of gold makes it more attractive. Chromium plated on a car bumper protects it and improves its appearance. An electroplating cell, used to accomplish these chemical changes, consists of two electrodes (anode and cathode), a solution of ions, and a source of electricity. Electroplating is one form of electrolysis, a technique you used in Unit Two, Part D.4.

In this laboratory activity you will electroplate an object of your choice. The object will become one of the electrodes; a piece of copper will serve as the other electrode.

Procedure

Part 1: Preliminary Electroplating Test

1. Place 250 mL of 0.5 M CuSO$_4$ in a 400-mL beaker.

2. Attach the alligator clips of two wire leads to the terminals of a 6-V battery.

3. Attach the other ends of the leads to two carbon (graphite) sticks, which will serve as electrodes.

4. Dip the carbon electrodes into the solution in the beaker. Do not allow the electrodes to touch each other. See Figure VIII.13.

Figure VIII.13   Electrolysis cell setup.

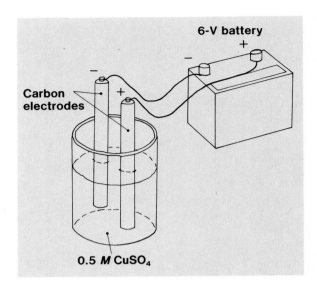

Figure VIII.14   Electroplating cell setup.

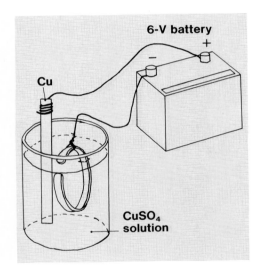

5. Allow the current to flow until you observe a change in one of the electrodes. Record your observations.

6. Disconnect the leads from the battery. Remove the carbon electrodes, and rinse them with running tap water.

Part 2: Electroplating an Object

1. Place 250 mL of 0.5 *M* CuSO₄ in a 400-mL beaker.

2. Clean the object to be plated with the steel wool pad. Decide which wire lead should be attached to the copper strip and which to the object, based on your observations from Part 1. Complete the wire connections to the copper and to the object.

3. Immerse the object and the copper strip in the plating solution. Do not let the electrodes touch each other. Attach the alligator clips of the wire leads to the appropriate terminals of the battery.

4. Allow the current to flow until copper plating is observed. See Figure VIII.14.

5. Record your observations.

6. Disconnect the leads from the battery. Remove the object from the plating solution with tongs. Rinse the object under running tap water. Dry it with a paper towel.

7. Examine the object and record your observations.

Questions

1. Which electrode was the anode? Which was the cathode?

2. In which direction did electrons flow during the reaction?

3. Write the half-reaction for the oxidation and for the reduction.

4. Diagram an electroplating cell for plating a ring with gold.

5. Diagram an electroplating cell that could plate silver onto spoons. Label all the parts.

6. Diagram an electroplating cell that could purify copper metal. Label all the parts.

D.4   Industrial Electrochemistry

The industrial production of aluminum is only one of many processes that use electrical energy to produce chemical change. Electrolysis is involved in manufacturing many products in the chemical industry.

Electrolysis is use of electricity to cause chemical change.

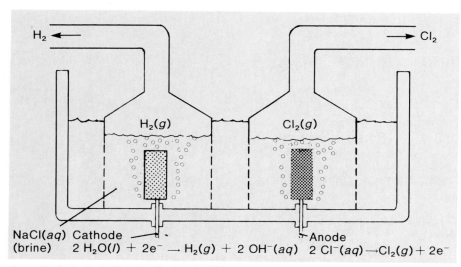

Figure VIII.15   Electrolysis of NaCl(*aq*).

ALCOA

The aluminum cap on the Washington Monument. The cap is about four inches high.

When a solution of sodium chloride in water (brine) is electrolyzed, chlorine gas, Cl_2, is produced at the anode and hydrogen gas, H_2, at the cathode (Figure VIII.15). Sodium ions remain in solution, but electrolysis leaves hydroxide as the negative ion in solution replacing the chloride ion:

$$2\,Na^+(aq) + 2\,Cl^-(aq) + 2\,H_2O(l) \longrightarrow$$
$$2\,Na^+(aq) + 2\,OH^-(aq) + H_2(g) + Cl_2(g)$$

This single electrolysis reaction produces three important, high-volume industrial chemicals: hydrogen gas, chlorine gas, and sodium hydroxide. The hydrogen and chlorine gases can be used essentially without additional purification, because no other gases are released at the anode and cathode. The sodium hydroxide, on the other hand, must be purified, since it remains in solution with unreacted sodium chloride.

In the nineteenth century, aluminum was a semiprecious metal, despite the fact that it is the most plentiful metal ion in the Earth's crust. The 6-lb aluminum pyramidal cap on the Washington Monument in Washington, D.C., cost considerably more than the same mass of silver would have cost when the cap was installed in 1884. Aluminum was so expensive at that time because it was very difficult to reduce to the metallic state.

Aluminum ion, Al^{3+}, is very stable. No common substances give up electrons easily enough to transfer them to aluminum ions to produce aluminum metal from aluminum compounds. For example, carbon, which is an excellent reducing agent for metal compounds such as iron oxide or copper sulfide, simply doesn't work with aluminum compounds.

A reactant that causes another reactant to be reduced is called a reducing agent.

In 1886, 22-year-old Charles Martin Hall, one year after graduation from Oberlin College in Ohio, devised a method for reducing aluminum using electricity (see Figure VIII.16). Hall's method is still used worldwide to produce aluminum. Aluminum oxide (bauxite) is dissolved in molten cryolite (Na_3AlF_6) at a temperature of 950 °C in a large steel tank lined with carbon. The carbon tank lining is made the negative electrode by a source of direct current. This carbon cathode transfers electrons to aluminum ions, reducing them to molten metal. Molten aluminum sinks to the bottom, where it is drawn off periodically. The aluminum is then formed into shapes and used to manufacture everything from stepladders to airplane parts.

Figure VIII.16   The Hall process for aluminum manufacture.

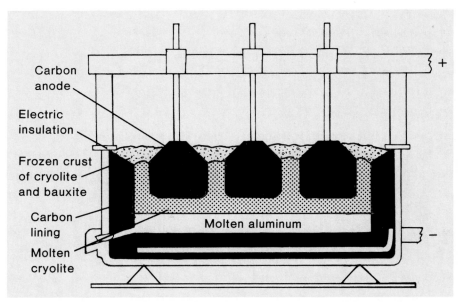

The positive electrode (anode) is also made of carbon, and is oxidized during the reaction. As the carbon rod anodes slowly burn away, they are lowered farther into the molten cryolite bath. The half-reactions for making aluminum are:

$$4\ Al^{3+}(melt) + 12\ e^- \rightarrow 4\ Al(l)$$
$$3\ C(s) + 6\ O^{2-}(melt) \rightarrow 3\ CO_2(g) + 12\ e^-$$

Ions from cryolite carry the electric current in the molten mixture.

Because they use large quantities of electricity, aluminum plants are often located near sources of hydroelectric power; many are in the Pacific Northwest. Electricity from hydropower is generally considerably cheaper than electricity from thermal power plants (those that produce steam to spin the generator turbines).

YOUR*TURN*

VIII.7 Aluminum Electrochemistry

Write the overall equation for making aluminum using the Hall process. How many moles of electrons are needed to reduce Al^{3+} ions in the production of 1.0 kg of aluminum?

D.5 *You Decide:* Planning for Riverwood's Aluminum Plant

To help the citizens of Riverwood understand the building and operation of the EKS aluminum plant, your class will be divided into groups of three. Each group will look into one component of the plant operation and make a brief report regarding what citizens should know about that component. The following are suggested components:

1. Where the starting materials (bauxite, carbon, etc.) will come from and how they will be delivered to Riverwood.

2. Aspects of electric power consumption and how these may affect individual citizens and the town.

3. Products produced and how these will be stored and distributed.
4. Waste disposal and environmental changes expected as a result of the plant.

Your teacher will provide suggested sources of material for this research activity.

PART D
SUMMARY *QUESTIONS*

1. Does the electrical potential produced in a voltaic cell depend on the size of the cell (how much metal is used), the specific metals used, or both? Explain.

2. To maximize electrical potential, should a voltaic cell be designed with two metals that are close together or far apart on the activity series? Explain.

3. The following questions refer to this equation:

$$PbO_2(s) + Pb(s) + 4 H^+(aq) + 2 SO_4^{2-}(aq) \rightarrow 2 PbSO_4(s) + 2 H_2O(l)$$

   a. Does this reaction represent the charging or discharging of a lead storage battery?
   b. Electrical energy or work can be extracted from the reaction shown above. What does this imply about the reverse reaction?
   c. Would the reverse reaction be endothermic or exothermic? Would it represent battery charging or discharging?
   d. Why can the condition of a lead storage battery be tested with a device that measures liquid density (a hygrometer)? In a fully charged condition, will the liquid density be greater or less than in a discharged state? Why? (*Hint:* Sulfuric acid solutions have a greater density than liquid water.)
   e. Identify the species being oxidized and the species being reduced.
   f. Under what conditions will a lead storage battery produce hydrogen gas? Why does this pose a hazard?

4. Magnesium and aluminum are active metals. Would a voltaic cell using these two metals produce high electrical potential? Why or why not?

5. Predict the direction of electron flow in voltaic cells composed of the following pairs of metals and their ions:
   a. Al and Cr
   b. Mn and Cu
   c. Fe and Ni

6. Compare the chemical reactions that occur in voltaic cells with those that occur in electroplating cells. Consider such factors as energy released or absorbed, spontaneity vs. nonspontaneity, and the direction of electron flow.

7. Iron and copper were available as free metals long before aluminum was, even though aluminum is far more abundant in the Earth's crust. Why? Why is the reduction of aluminum oxide a more difficult task than the reduction of iron oxide? How is this reduction carried out?

EXTENDING *YOUR KNOWLEDGE (OPTIONAL)*

Prepare a brief report on an electrolysis reaction or electroplating process that is used to produce some item you encounter daily.

E PUTTING IT ALL TOGETHER: THE ROLE OF CHEMICAL INDUSTRY PAST, PRESENT, AND FUTURE

Throughout the earlier *ChemCom* units you discovered that chemistry is concerned with the composition and properties of matter, the changes in matter, and the energy involved in these changes. This unit has presented examples of how chemical industries apply basic chemical principles to produce material goods and services.

In this final activity you will have an opportunity to plan, with industry, for the future. You will begin by reviewing how the chemical industry is helping to provide for some basic human needs today and where it is heading in coming years.

E.1 Basic Individual and Societal Needs Met by Chemical Industries

Since the early days of civilization, chemistry has been used to help meet basic needs. In colonial Massachusetts, as in other coastal colonies, seawater was evaporated to obtain salt that was used to preserve fish and cure hides. Ashes from fireplaces were washed to obtain potash (KOH), which was then used to make soap and candles from animal fats. In general, the chemical technologies used then were rather simple. They were used on a small scale and primarily to satisfy basic survival needs.

As chemical knowledge increased, we made better use of natural resources. New products and processes were created to meet basic survival requirements and to provide additional comfort and convenience. This is especially evident in chemical technologies developed during the past 50 years. During this period the chemical industry has grown from a few small companies producing a very limited range of basic products to hundreds of companies that produce thousands of different products, forming the fifth largest manufacturing industry in the United States. In fact, if food and petroleum are included, the chemical industry is the world's largest.

It is important to recognize that an industry exists to supply needed products or services. It must do so in a way that enables the companies to pay employees and debts, and to deliver products to consumers at a profit.

Following is a brief overview of areas served by the chemical industry, emphasizing the contributions being made today and some plans and expectations for the future. A more complete discussion can be found in the National Research Council's report, "Opportunities in Chemistry" (see the magazine *Chemical & Engineering News*, 1985, Oct. 14, p. 9).

A small magnet floats in the air above a superconductor surface.

ChemTech

Ceramic materials, such as these parts for a gas turbine, may replace metals in many uses.

New processes. As of late 1985, the U.S. chemical industry had a $12-billion positive balance of trade (that is, more is exported than is imported). Continued competitiveness depends on constant improvement of existing processes and introduction of new ones. Advances in chemical catalysis and synthesis will give us such things as tougher ceramics, which will be able to withstand mechanical shock, high temperatures, and corrosive atmospheres. They will replace metals in many materials. Also on the horizon are superplastic, lightweight building materials that will make cars, homes, and appliances more energy efficient and affordable.

More energy. Ninety-two percent of our current energy consumption is based on chemical technology; this will remain true well into the twenty-first century. However, new chemistry-based energy sources will have to be tapped. These new sources will give us low-grade fuels; better control of their chemical reactivity will be needed to protect the environment while providing energy at reasonable cost.

Availability of food. To make food more available to all, we need improvements in its production and preservation, in soil conservation, and the use of photosynthesis. In collaboration with those working in related scientific disciplines, chemists will play a central role in clarifying the chemistry of biological life cycles. Once these are understood, the industry will use the knowledge to provide products and services that can minimize hunger and malnutrition.

Better health. Since the 1930s, but more dramatically since 1950, the pharmaceutical industry has used the chemist's skill in manipulating molecules, the biochemist's understanding of cellular chemistry, and the chemical engineer's expertise in designing technologies to produce drugs that have helped make us healthier and more comfortable over a longer lifespan.

All life processes—birth, growth, reproduction, aging, and death, as well as mutation—involve chemical change. Chemistry and the chemical industry will continue to make important contributions to physiology and medicine through rational drug design and then through synthesis of new compounds that promote health and alleviate ailments such as atherosclerosis, hypertension, cancer, and disorders of the central nervous or immune systems.

Biotechnology. Remarkable progress has been made in recent years by molecular biologists and biochemists in understanding the basic chemical principles that determine the structures of biomolecules and the functioning of molecules and supermolecules (proteins, DNA) within biological systems. The industry is planning now for uses of the projected new biotechnologies that result from genetic engineering—the ability to control chemistry at the cellular level in living things.

New materials. For 50 years, the industry has provided new materials for building, clothing, and household uses of many kinds. Synthetic fibers are one example. They provide cheaper, easier to care for, and more versatile clothing, carpets, and wall coverings. The next two decades will bring many changes in the materials we use, as new substances are tailored to replace and outperform traditional or scarce materials.

Better environment. Public concern has made the industry sensitive to the need for environmental protection. In the face of increasing world population, urbanization, and rising standards of living, the environment must be protected. Effective strategies for safeguarding our surroundings require that we know what chemicals are there, where they came from, and what we can do about them. Chemistry lies at the heart of the answers to each of these questions. The industry can provide services and methods, such as analytical techniques, that give early warning of emerging problems, help us determine their origins, and provide access to alternative products and processes to help avoid environmental damage.

With this broad overview in mind, the following activity will give you a chance to do a little forecasting of developments in chemical industries.

E.2 Future Developments

Chemists and those who manage chemical companies continually pursue ideas for new products or processes. Figure VIII.17 summarizes the major factors that can influence the evolution of new chemical technology. To illustrate how some of these factors exercise their influence, let's look back to the rubber industry 50 years ago.

Figure VIII.17 The evolution of chemical technology.

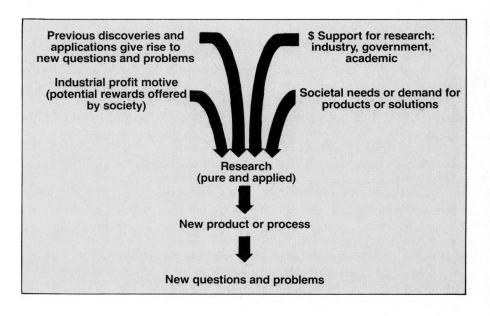

The state of chemistry in the United States in 1927 was summarized in a book meant to create ". . . a more adequate appreciation of what chemistry means to the economic and political future of the nation" (*The Story of Chemistry,* by F. I. Darrow, Bobbs-Merrill, 1927). Below, we have used quotations from the chapter on the rubber industry to illustrate some factors which, at that time, were influencing the evolution of rubber technology. Read through the quotations and decide how and where the factors described in each quotation might fit into the scheme in Figure VIII.17.

Some uses of rubber in 1927:
Hose
Shoeheels
Boots
Water bottles
Golfballs
Tires
Rubber bands
Covering on insulated wire
Bulbs

- The consumption of rubber in the United States rose from approximately 100,000 tons in 1913 to about 500,000 tons in 1925, and in the same time the manufacture of automobiles increased from a few hundred thousand a year to three and a half million. During the same period, too, the dealer's cost of a tire dropped from $21.30 to $9.90, and the quality of the tire was twice as good. Confronted with a tremendous world demand for a new commodity, capital and science entered into a partnership to meet it.
- Rubber touches life at innumerable points. . . . New uses are constantly being discovered. What it means to be without adequate supplies of rubber was keenly brought home to the German nation during the war, when it was cut off from the outside world. Rubber independence has become a factor of vast significance in international politics and in the maintenance of world peace. Without ample supplies of rubber, a nation's place in the sun is insecure.
- Goodyear soon learned that the process of vulcanization could be greatly hastened by mixing with the rubber and sulfur chemicals such as lime, magnesium, white lead. . . . However, it was not until 1906 that real chemical work was begun on the influence of these "accelerators" of vulcanization. . . . The time of vulcanization has been reduced by two-thirds. . . . An expert of the rubber industry says, "I assume that this discovery alone has been the means of saving to investors clearly $200,000,000."
- An evil property of rubber has been the ease and rapidity with which it would age. . . . Within the memories of many now active in the fire departments of our cities, fire hose was a source of peril. In time of direst need, it might unceremoniously burst. Millions of dollars have been lost from aging and decaying hose lines. The chemist has changed all this. Fire hose is as dependable as the water supply and often more so.
- I know that it is synthetic rubber about which you have been waiting to hear. What are the prospects of being able to duplicate or possibly outstrip the handiwork of Mother Nature? . . . It has long been known that isoprene, the fundamental hydrocarbon in the composition of rubber, may be obtained from turpentine, petroleum, starch, and coal tar. . . . It is only a matter of time till the rubber molecules yield their secrets.
- Three great research funds have been recently initiated. The first of these is a fund of a half-million dollars, contributed in equal proportions by John D. Rockefeller and the Universal Oil Products Company for pure research in the chemistry of petroleum.

Using the model given in Figure VIII.17 as a starting point, work in a group to develop the idea for a new chemical product or process. It might be something as general as synthetic rubber, or something highly specific, such as a new kind of pencil eraser. As part of your initial brainstorming for a suitable idea, consider the issue of need. That is, does a need for your product or process exist? If so, describe the nature of the need. If not, what kind of public campaign might be used to create a need? After using this question to focus your group's attention on a single product or process, outline your idea by using the questions below as a guide.

Prepare a presentation to the class explaining your idea and the factors that might influence its development. The entire class will be given the chance to vote on the best idea.

1. Assuming a need exists, how will your product or process fill the need? If your product or process will serve as an alternative to a current product or process, what are the advantages of the new development over the old?
2. What financial and human resources will be needed to develop your idea? Will multidisciplinary teams be needed? Describe the nature of the development task.
3. What matter and energy resources will be needed? Are adequate supplies of these resources available in the United States or must they be imported? If the latter is the case, where might we obtain them? Are there any political issues involved?
4. What safety tests must be run? What are some of the potential negative environmental effects of widespread use of your product or process? Will people have reason to object to the location of the facilities that produce the product or use the process? Why? Will people be motivated to argue in favor of your facility?
5. What, if any, ethical considerations are involved in the development and use of your product or process?
6. How long might it take to develop your idea into a marketable product or process?

E.3 Looking Back and Looking Ahead

In these eight *ChemCom* units you have discovered how basic chemical principles are involved in all the matter and energy changes that occur on our planet. Beyond this, you have explored the roles of chemistry and chemical technology in contributing to the growth and well-being of human communities, as well as some problems their activity has created.

You have also seen that to maximize the benefits and minimize the costs (and risks) of chemical technology, individuals such as yourself must combine an understanding of chemistry with their own values to make intelligent personal and societal decisions.

Whether you choose to take additional chemistry courses or not, reading popular science magazines, viewing educational television programs, visiting science museums, attending public forums on environmental issues, and many other options are available to further your "chemical common sense." It is our hope that this course is merely the beginning of a lifelong exploration of science-related issues for you.

Chemistry will contribute to improving modern life as long as citizens continue to ask questions, consider options in light of the best available information, and make intelligent decisions. The real challenge is for you to look ahead to your future and decide what kind of world you want—and how you, science, technology, and other components of society can contribute to achieving it. The challenge is great, as we have suggested in these *ChemCom* units, but so are the potential rewards.

GLOSSARY

a

acid
molecular substance or other chemical species that yields $H^+(aq)$ ions in aqueous solution

acidosis
harmful condition in which blood pH stays below 7.35

activation energy
minimum energy required for successful collision of reactant particles in a chemical reaction

active site
in biochemistry, the site on an enzyme where the substrate molecule(s) is made ready for reaction

activity series
ranking of elements in order of chemical reactivity

addition polymer
polymer formed by addition reactions at double bonds, e.g., polyethylene

addition reaction
in organic chemistry, a reaction at the double (or triple) bond in an organic molecule which results in adding or bonding atoms or groups of atoms to each atom of the double (or triple) bond; one type of polymerization reaction

aeration
mixing of air (or more particularly oxygen gas) into a liquid, e.g., as in water flowing over a dam

aerobic bacteria
oxygen-consuming bacteria

alcohol
nonaromatic organic compound whose molecules contain one or more $-OH$ groups

alkalosis
harmful condition in which blood pH stays above 7.4

alkane
hydrocarbon having a general formula C_nH_{2n+2} whose molecules contain only single covalent bonds

alkene
hydrocarbon whose molecules contain a double covalent bond

alkyne
hydrocarbon whose molecules contain a triple covalent bond

alloy
solid mixture consisting of atoms of different metals

alpha keratin
key protein structural unit of hair

alpha particle (ray)
helium nucleus emitted during radioactive decay

amino acid
organic compound whose molecules contain an amino ($-NH_2$) and a carboxyl ($-COOH$) group; proteins are polymers of amino acids

amylase
enzyme in saliva that catalyzes breakdown of starch to glucose

anaerobic bacteria
bacteria that do not require oxygen

anaerobic glycolysis
cellular process for quick release of energy from glucose by non-oxygen-consuming reactions; lactic acid is produced

anion
ion possessing a negative charge

anode
electrode at which oxidation occurs in electrochemical cell

antibody
complementary protein created by body to inactivate specific foreign protein molecules (antigens)

antigen
foreign protein that triggers body's defense mechanisms to produce antibodies

aquifer
porous rock structure beneath the Earth's surface that holds water

aromatic compound
compound like benzene whose molecules are cyclic and can be represented as having alternating double and single bonds between carbon atoms

atomic mass
mass of an atom

atomic number
number of protons in an atom; distinguishes atoms of different elements

atoms
smallest particles possessing the properties of an element; all matter is composed of atoms

Avogadro's law
equal volumes of gases at the same temperature and pressure contain the same number of molecules

b

background radiation
radiation from naturally radioactive sources present in the environment

base
chemical species that yields $OH^-(aq)$ ions in aqueous solution

beta particle (ray)
electron emitted during radioactive decay

biodegradable
able to be broken down into simpler substances by bacteria

biomolecules
large molecules found only in living systems

biosphere
a combination of portions of Earth's waters, land, and atmosphere that supports living things

Boyle's law
at constant temperature, the product of the pressure and volume of a given gas sample is a constant

branched-chain alkane
alkane that consists of molecules in which one or more carbon atoms are bonded to three or four other carbon atoms; e.g.,

$$CH_3 - CH - CH - CH_3$$
$$\quad\quad | \quad\quad |$$
$$\quad\quad CH_3 \quad CH_3$$

buffer solution
solution that resists changes in pH; contains a weak acid and a salt of that acid, or a weak base and its salt

C

Calorie
1000 cal, or 1 kcal; the dieticians' energy unit

calorimetry
technique for determining heat of reaction or other thermal properties, and for finding caloric value of foods

carbohydrate
energy-rich compound composed of carbon, hydrogen and oxygen; e.g., starch and sugar

carbon chain
carbon atoms linked to one another, forming a string-like sequence in a molecule

carboxylic acids
organic compounds whose molecules contain the $-COOH$ group

carcinogen
substance that causes cancer

catalyst
substance that speeds up a chemical reaction but is itself unchanged

catalytic converter
reaction chamber in auto exhaust system designed to reduce harmful emissions

cathode ray
beam of electrons emitted from cathode when electricity passes through evacuated tube

cathode
electrode at which reduction occurs in electrochemical cell

cation
ion possessing a positive charge

cellular respiration
oxidation of glucose or other energy-rich substances in living cells to produce CO_2, H_2O, and energy

cellulose
polysaccharide composed of chains of glucose molecules; makes up fibrous and woody parts of plants

ceramics
materials made by heating or "firing" clay or components of certain rocks; include bricks, glass, and porcelain ware

chain reaction
in nuclear fission, reaction that produces enough neutrons to allow the reaction to continue

Charles' law
at constant pressure, the volume of a given gas sample is directly proportional to the kelvin temperature

chemical bond
force that holds atoms or ions together in chemical compounds

chemical change
change in matter resulting in a change in the identity of one or more substances

chemical compound
substance composed of two or more elements that cannot be separated by physical means

chemical equation
combination of chemical formulas that represent what occurs in a chemical reaction, e.g., $2H_2(g) + O_2(g) \rightarrow 2H_2O(g)$

chemical equilibrium
condition when forward and reverse reactions occur at same rate, and concentrations of all reactants and products remain unchanged

chemical formula
combination of symbols that represents the elements present in a substance with subscripts showing the number of atoms of each element, e.g., the formula for ammonia is NH_3

chemical property
property of a substance related to a chemical change that the substance undergoes

chemical reaction
change in matter in which one or more chemical species are transformed into new or different species

coefficient
number preceding a formula in a chemical equation; specifies the relative number of units of a species participating in the reaction

coenzyme
molecule or ion that assists an enzyme in performing its function

colloid
mixture containing macro-size particles that are small enough to remain suspended

colorimetric method
method for determining concentration of a solution by observing color intensity

complementary proteins
combinations of proteins that include all essential amino acids

compound
substance composed of two or more elements that cannot be separated by physical means

concentration
quantity of solute dissolved in a specific quantity of solvent or solution

condensation polymer
polymer formed by condensation reactions, e.g., polyester

condensation reaction
chemical combination of two molecules, accompanied by loss of water or another small molecule, e.g., $CH_3OH + HOCCH_3$
$$\quad\quad\quad\quad\quad\quad || $$
$$\quad\quad\quad\quad\quad\quad O$$
$$\rightarrow CH_3OCCH_3 + H_2O; \text{ one type of}$$
$$\quad\quad || $$
$$\quad\quad O$$
polymerization reaction

condensation
conversion of a substance from a gaseous to the liquid or solid state

condensed formula
formula such as $CH_3CH_2CH_3$ in which symbols are written on same line and subscripts are used; in contrast to structural formula

conductor
material that allows electricity to flow through it

control cost
in cost-benefit analysis, total cost of controlling a potentially damaging effect, e.g., air pollution

correlated
happening together; scientists often identify and seek explanation for correlated events

corrosion
deterioration or "eating away" of a material

covalent bond
a force that holds two atoms tightly to each other, found when the two atoms share one or more electron pairs

cracking
process in which hydrocarbon molecules from petroleum are converted to smaller molecules

critical mass
mass of fissionable material needed to sustain a nuclear chain reaction

crude oil
petroleum as it is pumped from underground

cryogenics
studies of the chemistry and physics of materials and systems at very low temperatures

cuticle
tough outer layer in, e.g., hair

cycloalkane
saturated hydrocarbon whose molecules contain carbon atoms joined in a ring

d

damage cost
in cost-benefit analysis, total cost of tangible and intangible damage

data
objective pieces of information, often the information gathered in experiments

denaturation
alteration of protein shape and function by disruption of folding and coiling in molecules

density
the mass per unit volume of a given material

dermis
inner layer of the skin

developed world
fully industrialized nations

developing world
nations not fully industrialized

diffusion
intermixing of molecules or other particles when two or more materials are placed in contact, e.g., the spread of cooking or perfume odors in air, the dispersion of color when a drop of ink is placed in water

dipeptide
compound made from two amino acids

disaccharide
compound made from two simple sugars, e.g., maltose (two glucose units)

distillate
condensed products of distillation

distillation
method of separating substances due to differences in their boiling points

double covalent bond
bond in which four electrons are shared by two bonded atoms

e

electrical potential
potential for moving or pumping electric charge in electrical circuit or by an electrochemical cell; measured in volts

electrochemical cell
device to carry out an electrolysis, or to produce electricity from a chemical reaction

electrodes
two strips of metal or other conductors serving as contacts between the solution or molten salt and the external circuit in an electrochemical cell; reaction occurs at each electrode

electrolysis
use of electrical energy to cause a non-spontaneous oxidation-reduction reaction to occur

electromagnetic radiation
radiation moving at the speed of light, ranging from low-energy radio waves to high-energy cosmic and gamma rays; includes visible light

electrometallurgy
use of electrical energy to process metals or their ores

electron dot formula
formula for a substance in which dots represent the outer electrons in each atom, and show the sharing of electron pairs between atoms

electron
negatively charged particle present in all atoms

electroplating
deposition of a thin layer of metal on a surface by electrolysis

elements
fundamental chemical substances from which all other substances are made

endorphins
natural painkillers produced in the brain

endothermic
a process requiring energy

endpoint
point during a titration at which the reaction is complete

enkephalins
natural painkillers produced in the brain

enzyme
catalyst for a biochemical reaction

epidermis
outer layer of the skin

essential amino acid
one of eight amino acids that the human body cannot synthesize and which must be included in the diet

esters
organic compounds containing the —COOR group, where R represents any stable arrangement of carbon and hydrogen atoms

evaporation
conversion of a substance from the liquid to the gaseous state

exothermic
an energy-releasing process

f

family (periodic table)
vertical column of elements in the periodic table; also called a group; members of a family share similar properties

fat
lipid resulting from reaction of glycerol and fatty acids; storage form for food energy in animals

fatty acid
organic compound whose molecules consist of a long hydrocarbon chain and a —COOH group; combined with glycerol in fats

fibrous protein
protein whose molecules form rope-like or sheet-like structures in, e.g., hair, muscles, skin

filtrate
liquid collected after filtration

filtration
separation of solid particles from a liquid by passing the mixture through a material that retains the solid particles

fluorescence
emission of visible light following exposure to ultraviolet radiation

formula unit
group of atoms or ions represented by chemical formula of a compound; simplest unit of an ionic compound

fossil fuel
petroleum, natural gas, or coal

fraction (petroleum)
mixture of petroleum-derived substances of similar boiling points and other properties

functional group
atom or group of atoms that imparts characteristic properties to an organic compound, e.g., — Cl, — OH, — COOH

g

gamma ray
high-energy electromagnetic radiation emitted during radioactive decay

gaseous state
state of matter with no fixed volume or shape

Geiger counter (radiation counter)
device that produces an electrical signal in the presence of ionizing radiation

gene
segment of DNA molecule that stores instructions for a specific trait, e.g., hair color

globular protein
protein whose molecules assume ball shapes and are water soluble because of polar and ionic groups on surface; may function as hormone, enzyme, carrier protein

glycogen
polymer made of repeating glucose units; synthesized in liver and muscles as reserve source of glucose

gram
SI unit of mass commonly used in chemistry (kg is the SI base unit)

gray
SI unit for absorbed dose of ionizing radiation

greenhouse effect
retention of energy at or near Earth's surface as carbon dioxide and other atmospheric gases capture escaping radiation and return it to Earth's surface; result is surface warming

groundwater
water which collects underground

group (periodic table)
See family

h

Haber process
industrial process for catalyzed synthesis of ammonia from nitrogen and hydrogen

half-cell
metal (or other electrode material) and its surrounding solution of ions in a voltaic cell

half-life
time needed for decay of one-half the atoms in a sample of radioactive material

half-reaction
half of oxidation-reduction reaction in which electrons are either lost or gained; e.g., the process that occurs in one half-cell of a voltaic cell

hard water
water containing relatively high concentrations of calcium (Ca^{2+}), magnesium (Mg^{2+}), or iron(III) (Fe^{3+}) ions

heat capacity
quantity of heat required to raise the temperature of a given sample of matter by 1 °C

heat of combustion
quantity of thermal energy released when a specific amount of a substance burns

heat of fusion
quantity of heat required to convert a specific amount of a solid to a liquid at its melting point

heat of vaporization
quantity of heat required to convert a specific amount of a liquid to a gas at its boiling point

heavy metals
metals of high atomic mass, generally from fifth or sixth row of the periodic table

heterogeneous
not uniform throughout as in a heterogeneous mixture

homeostasis
maintenance of balance in all body systems

homogeneous
uniform throughout, as in a homogeneous mixture

hormone
biomolecule that serves as a specific messenger to stimulate biochemical activity at specific sites in the body

hydrocarbons
molecular compounds composed solely of carbon and hydrogen

hydrogen bonding
attraction between molecules or between parts of the same molecule involving hydrogen atoms and strongly electron-attracting atoms such as nitrogen or oxygen

hydrologic cycle
circulation of water between Earth's atmosphere and surface layer

hydrometallurgy
methods of processing metals or their ores using water

i

ideal gas
gas that behaves as predicted by kinetic molecular theory

infant mortality rate
number of infants less than one year old that die for every 1000 live births

infrared radiation
electromagnetic radiation of slightly lower energy than visible light; raises temperature of objects that absorb it

intensity (radiation)
measure of quantity of radiation per unit time

intermediate (chemical)
product of chemical industry used to synthesize consumer products or other chemicals, e.g., sulfuric acid is an intermediate in the manufacture of certain detergents

ionic bond
attraction between oppositely charged ions in an ionic compound

ionic compounds
substances composed of ions

ionizing radiation
electromagnetic radiation or high-speed particles, possessing enough energy to ionize atoms and molecules; emitted during radioactive decay

ion
an atom or group of atoms that has become electrically charged by gaining or losing electrons

isomer
compound having the same molecular formula but different structural formula (arrangement of atoms in molecule) than another compound

isotopes
atoms of the same element with different numbers of neutrons

k

kinetic energy
energy associated with the motion of an object

kinetic molecular theory of gases
theory that accounts for properties of gases based on kinetic energy and constant random motion of molecules in mostly empty space

l

legumes
plants that harbor nitrogen-fixing bacteria in their roots

length
linear distance; the SI base unit of length is the meter (m)

limiting reactant
the starting substance used up first as a chemical reaction occurs

lipid
member of a class of biomolecules not soluble in water, e.g., a fat

liquid state
state of matter with fixed volume but no fixed shape

liter
unit of volume (L) equal to 1 dm³, 1000 cm³ or 1000 mL

m

macromineral
essential mineral present in amount of 5 g or more in adult human body

malleable
a property that permits a material to be flattened without shattering

malnourishment
receiving inadequate amounts of essential nutrients such as protein, vitamins, minerals

mass number
sum of the number of protons and neutrons in an atom of a given isotope

melanin
body pigment responsible for dark skin, dark hair, and sun tanning

mesosphere
region of atmosphere above stratosphere

metalloid
element with properties intermediate between those of metals and nonmetals

meter
SI base unit of length (m)

microfibril
bundle of coiled protein chains, e.g., component of hair

milliliter
unit of volume (mL) equal to 1 cm³

millimeters of mercury (mmHg)
a pressure unit; 1 atm = 760 mmHg

mixture
combination of two or more substances in which each substance retains its separate identity

molar concentration
concentration of a solution expressed in moles of solute per liter of solution

molar mass
mass (usually in grams) of one mole of a substance

molar volume
volume occupied by one mole of a substance; at STP, molar volume of a gas is 22.4 L

molarity
concentration of a solution expressed as moles of solute per liter of solution

mole
an amount of substance or chemical species equal to 6.02×10^{23} units, where the units may be atoms, molecules, formula units, electrons or other specified entities; chemist's "counting" unit

molecular structure
arrangement and bonding of atoms in a molecule

molecule
smallest particle of a substance retaining the properties of the substance; a particle composed of two or more atoms joined by covalent bonds

monomer
compound whose molecules react to form a polymer

monosaccharide
simple sugar, e.g., glucose

n

narcotic analgesic
drug that relieves intense pain

negative oxidation state
negative number assigned to atom in a compound when that atom has greater control of its electrons than as free element

net ionic equation
equation showing only those species that participate in a reaction involving ions in aqueous solution

neutralization
reaction of an acid with a base in which the characteristic properties of both are destroyed

neuron
nerve cell

neutron
neutral particle present in nuclei of most atoms

nitrogen fixation
conversion of nitrogen gas (N_2) to nitrogen compounds usable by plants

nonconductor
material that does not allow electricity to flow through it

nonionizing radiation
electromagnetic radiation possessing insufficient energy to ionize atoms or molecules; e.g., visible light

nonpolar
having no electrical dissymmetry or polarity, as in a nonpolar molecule

nonrenewable resource
resource that will not be replenished by natural processes during the time frame of human experience

nuclear fission
splitting of one atom into two smaller atoms; undergone by uranium-235 when bombarded with neutrons

nuclear fusion
combining of two atomic nuclei to form a single more massive nucleus

nucleus, atomic
dense central region in an atom; contains all protons and neutrons

nutrients
components of food needed in the diet

o

octane number
rating indicating combustion quality of gasoline

ore
rock or mineral from which it is profitable to recover a metal or other useful substance

organic compound
compound composed mainly of carbon and hydrogen atoms; a hydrocarbon or a compound derived from a hydrocarbon

oxidation-reduction, or redox, reactions
reactions in which oxidation and reduction occur

oxidation
any process in which electrons are lost or the extent of electron control decreases

p

para-aminobenzoic acid (PABA)
active ingredient in many sunscreen lotions

patina
a surface film or coating, e.g., the stable green coating on copper exposed to the atmosphere

pepsin
enzyme that aids in digesting protein

peptide linkage
—CONH— linkage formed by reaction of the —NH_2 group of one amino acid and the —COOH group of another amino acid; linkage between amino acid residues in proteins

periodic law
when elements are arranged in order of increasing atomic number, elements with similar properties occur at regular intervals

periodic table
table in which elements, arranged in order of increasing atomic number, are placed so that those with similar properties are near each other

periods (periodic table)
horizontal rows of elements in the periodic table

petrochemical
substance produced from petroleum or natural gas

petroleum
liquid fossil fuel composed mainly of hydrocarbons, but also containing compounds of nitrogen, sulfur and oxygen along with small amounts of metal-containing compounds

pH
number representing acidity of an aqueous solution; at 25 °C, solution with pH 7 is neutral, pH < 7 is acidic, pH > 7 is basic

phosphocreatine
substance whose molecules are an energy source during short-term strenuous muscle activity

photochemical smog
smog produced when sunlight interacts with nitrogen oxides and hydrocarbons in atmosphere

photon
packet of energy present in electromagnetic radiation

photosynthesis
process by which green plants and plankton make sugars from carbon dioxide and water in the presence of sunlight

physical change
change in matter in which the identity of the substance involved is not changed; e.g., melting of ice

physical property
property that can be observed or measured without changing the identity of a sample of matter; e.g., color, boiling point

polar
having electrical poles, or regions of positive and negative charge, as in a polar molecule

polyatomic ion
ion containing two or more atoms, e.g., SO_4^{2-}

polymer
substance whose large molecules are composed of many identical repeating units

polysaccharide
polymer made from simple sugar molecules, e.g., starch

positive oxidation state
positive number assigned to atom in a compound when that atom has less control of its electrons than as free element

positron
particle with mass of electron but possessing a positive charge

precipitate
insoluble solid substance that has separated from a solution

primary air pollutant
pollutant in the form originally emitted to the atmosphere

product
substance formed in a chemical reaction

protease
enzyme that aids digestion of proteins

proteins
polymers made from amino acids; important compounds in body including, e.g., hair, nails, muscle, enzymes, hormones

proton
positively charged particle present in nuclei of all atoms

pyrometallurgy
use of heat (or thermal energy) to process metals or their ores

r

rad
unit for indicating absorbed dose of ionizing radiation (radiation absorbed dose)

radioactive decay
emission of alpha, beta, or gamma rays by unstable isotopes

radioactivity
spontaneous decay of unstable atomic nuclei accompanied by emission of ionizing radiation

radioisotope
a radioactive isotope

reactant
starting substance or ingredient in a chemical reaction

receptors
proteins in membranes of key body cells, shaped to receive the molecule of a hormone, drug or other activator, and having done so, to activate chemical processes within the cell

recycling
reprocessing materials in manufactured items so they can be reused as raw materials in manufacturing new items

reduction
any process in which electrons are gained or the extent of electron control increases

reflectivity
property of a surface of returning radiation that strikes it

rem
unit indicating power of ionizing radiation to cause damage to human tissue (roentgen equivalent man)

renewable resource
resource that is replenished by natural processes in the time frame of human experience

reversible reaction
chemical reaction in which reverse reaction can occur simultaneously with forward reaction

rickets
disease caused by lack of vitamin D; occurs in absence of exposure to sunlight, which helps body to produce vitamin D

s

salicylates
family of painkillers that includes aspirin (acetylsalicylic acid)

saturated fat
fat whose molecules contain no carbon-carbon double bonds

saturated hydrocarbon
hydrocarbon consisting of molecules in which each carbon atom is bonded to four other atoms

saturated solution
solution in which the solvent has dissolved as much solute as it can stably retain at a given temperature

science
a group of disciplines that gather, analyze and organize knowledge about natural phenomena and natural objects

scintillation counter
sensitive radiation-measuring device; produces flashes of light in the presence of ionizing radiation

sewage treatment plant
installation built for post-use cleaning of municipal water

sievert
SI unit for damage to human tissue caused by ionizing radiation

single covalent bond
bond in which two electrons are shared by the two bonded atoms

solubility
quantity of a substance that will dissolve in a given quantity of solvent to form a saturated solution

solute
the dissolved substance in a solution, usually the component present in the smaller amount

solution concentration
quantity of solute dissolved in a specific quantity of solvent or solution

solution
homogeneous mixture of two or more substances

solvent
component of a solution present in the largest amount

specific heat
quantity of heat needed to raise the temperature of 1 g of a material by 1 °C

spectator ions
ions present that do not participate in a reaction in solution

STP
standard temperature and pressure; 0 °C and 1 atm

starch
polysaccharide made by plants to store glucose

stomata
openings in plant leaves that take in carbon dioxide

straight-chain alkane
alkane consisting of molecules in which each carbon atom is linked to no more than two other carbon atoms, e.g., $CH_3CH_2CH_2CH_3$

stratosphere
region of atmosphere above troposphere

strong force
force of attraction between particles in atomic nucleus

structural formula
chemical formula showing the arrangement of atoms and covalent bonds in a molecule

substrate
reactant molecule or ion, e.g., that in an enzyme-catalyzed biochemical reaction

supersaturated solution
solution containing a higher concentration of solute than a saturated solution at the given temperature

surface water
water which flows on the surface of the ground

suspension
mixture containing such large, dispersed particles that it appears cloudy; e.g., muddy water

symbol
a one or two letter expression that represents an element, e.g., Na represents sodium

synergistic interaction
combination of interactions that produces a total effect greater than the sum of the individual interactions, e.g., combined effect of air pollutants

t

technology
application of science to create useful goods and services

tetrahedron
a regular triangular pyramid; the four bonds of each carbon atom in molecules of alkanes point to the corners of a tetrahedron

thermosphere
outermost region of Earth's atmosphere

titration
laboratory technique used to determine solution concentrations or the amount of a substance in a sample

toxin
substance harmful to the body

trace mineral
essential mineral present in amounts of less than 5 g in adult human body

tracer, radioactive
radioactive isotope used to follow movement of material, e.g., used in medicine to detect abnormal functioning in body

transmutation
conversion of one element to another; unknown before discovery of radioactivity

triglyceride
an ester whose molecules were formed by combination of glycerol with three fatty acid molecules; a fat

tripeptide
compound made from three amino acids

troposphere
region of atmosphere from surface to 10 km above Earth's surface

Tyndall effect
pattern caused by reflection of light from suspended particles in a colloid

U

ultraviolet radiation
electromagnetic radiation of slightly higher energy than visible light; can cause tissue damage

undernourishment
receiving less food than needed to supply bodily energy needs

unsaturated fat
fat whose molecules contain carbon-carbon double bonds

unsaturated hydrocarbon
hydrocarbon whose molecules contain double or triple bonds, e.g., alkenes, alkynes

unsaturated solution
solution containing a lower concentration of solute than a saturated solution at the given temperature

V

viscosity
measure of a fluid's resistance to flow

visible radiation
electromagnetic radiation visible by human eye

vitamins
biomolecules needed in small amounts for body function; must be provided in food or as food supplement

voltaic cell
electrochemical cell in which a spontaneous chemical reaction is used to produce electricity

W

water softening
removal from water of ions that cause its hardness (see hard water)

X

X rays
high-energy electromagnetic radiation; normally unable to penetrate bone or lead, but can penetrate less dense materials

Periodic Chart of the Elements

1 **H** 1.008																	2 **He** 4.003
3 **Li** 6.941	4 **Be** 9.012											5 **B** 10.81	6 **C** 12.01	7 **N** 14.01	8 **O** 16.00	9 **F** 19.00	10 **Ne** 20.18
11 **Na** 22.99	12 **Mg** 24.31											13 **Al** 26.98	14 **Si** 28.09	15 **P** 30.97	16 **S** 32.07	17 **Cl** 35.45	18 **Ar** 39.95
19 **K** 39.10	20 **Ca** 40.08	21 **Sc** 44.96	22 **Ti** 47.88	23 **V** 50.94	24 **Cr** 52.00	25 **Mn** 54.94	26 **Fe** 55.85	27 **Co** 58.93	28 **Ni** 58.69	29 **Cu** 63.55	30 **Zn** 65.39	31 **Ga** 69.72	32 **Ge** 72.59	33 **As** 74.92	34 **Se** 78.96	35 **Br** 79.90	36 **Kr** 83.80
37 **Rb** 85.47	38 **Sr** 87.62	39 **Y** 88.91	40 **Zr** 91.22	41 **Nb** 92.21	42 **Mo** 95.94	43 **Tc** 98.91	44 **Ru** 101.1	45 **Rh** 102.9	46 **Pd** 106.4	47 **Ag** 107.9	48 **Cd** 112.4	49 **In** 114.8	50 **Sn** 118.7	51 **Sb** 121.8	52 **Te** 127.6	53 **I** 126.9	54 **Xe** 131.3
55 **Cs** 132.9	56 **Ba** 137.3	57 **La**★ 138.9	72 **Hf** 178.5	73 **Ta** 180.9	74 **W** 183.9	75 **Re** 186.2	76 **Os** 190.2	77 **Ir** 192.2	78 **Pt** 195.1	79 **Au** 197.0	80 **Hg** 200.6	81 **Tl** 204.4	82 **Pb** 207.2	83 **Bi** 209.0	84 **Po** (210.0)	85 **At** (210.0)	86 **Rn** (222.0)
87 **Fr** (223.0)	88 **Ra** 226.0	89 **Ac**• 227.0	104 (261)	105 (262)	106 (263)	107 (262)											

★ Lanthanoid series

58 **Ce** 140.1	59 **Pr** 140.9	60 **Nd** 144.2	61 **Pm** 144.9	62 **Sm** 150.4	63 **Eu** 152.0	64 **Gd** 157.3	65 **Tb** 158.9	66 **Dy** 162.5	67 **Ho** 164.9	68 **Er** 167.3	69 **Tm** 168.9	70 **Yb** 173.0	71 **Lu** 175.0

• Actinoid series

90 **Th** 232.0	91 **Pa** 231.0	92 **U** 238.0	93 **Np** 237.0	94 **Pu** 239.1	95 **Am** 243.1	96 **Cm** 247.1	97 **Bk** 247.1	98 **Cf** 252.1	99 **Es** 252.1	100 **Fm** 257.1	101 **Md** 256.1	102 **No** 259.1	103 **Lr** 260.1

INDEX